GROLIER

ENCYCLOPEDIA
OF KNOWLEDGE

Grolier Incorporated
Danbury, Connecticut

ISBN 0-7172-5300-7 (complete set)
ISBN 0-7172-5307-4 (volume 7)

Printed and manufactured in the United States of America.

This publication is an abridged version of the *Academic American Encyclopedia*.

10 9 8 7 6 5 4 3

elf see FAIRY

Elgar, Sir Edward [el'-gahr] Sir Edward Elgar, b. near Worcester, June 2, 1857, d. Feb. 23, 1934, is generally considered England's greatest native-born composer since Henry Purcell.

As a composer Elgar was self-taught. He succeeded (1885) his father as a church organist in Worcester and pursued a minor, local career—teaching, conducting, and composing. Gradually, Elgar's oratorios, other choral music, and orchestral works won him growing success and prestige. He was knighted in 1904 and made a baronet in 1931. Identified with the Edwardian era and the British Empire, he became, despite his Roman Catholicism, a symbol of English national pride. His later years, after his wife's death in 1920, were lonely and unproductive.

Besides his ever-popular *Pomp and Circumstance March No. 1*, Elgar wrote magnificent orchestral scores in the late romantic tradition: concertos for violin (1910) and cello (1919), two symphonies (1908, 1911) and the celebrated *Enigma Variations* (1899). He also wrote chamber music, piano pieces, songs, church music, and incidental music for the stage. His oratorio *The Dream of Gerontius* (1900) is often considered Elgar's masterpiece.

Sir Edward Elgar is widely regarded as the first internationally prominent English composer since the 17th century. Admired for their brilliant orchestration, Elgar's works include symphonies, concertos, overtures, marches, and oratorios.

Elgin, James Bruce, 8th Earl of James Bruce, 8th earl of Elgin, b. July 20, 1811, d. Nov. 20, 1863, was a British colonial administrator. After serving (1842–46) as governor of Jamaica, Bruce became governor-general of Canada (1847–54), where he oversaw the granting and implementation of responsible government. Sent (1857) as a special envoy to China after armed British intervention in Guangzhou, he negotiated (1858) the Treaty of Tianjin (1858); when the Chinese refused to honor it, he returned with an Anglo-French force in 1860 and captured Beijing. He served as viceroy of India from 1861 until his death.

Elgin Marbles [el'-gin] The Elgin Marbles, an important group of ancient Greek sculptures from the ACROPOLIS, include portions of the frieze, pediments, and metopes from the Parthenon and a caryatid from the Erechtheum. They were collected (1801–03) and taken to England by Thomas Bruce, 7th Earl of Elgin, then Britain's ambassador to Turkey. Purchased by the British government in 1816, they are now exhibited in the British Museum, although the Greek government has requested their return.

Elgon, Mount [el'-gahn] Mount Elgon is a large extinct volcano on the Kenya-Uganda border. At its base the mountain is about 80 km (50 mi) in diameter. Its crater is about 8 km (5 mi) across and nearly 610 m (2,000 ft) deep. The crater contains several peaks, the highest reaching 4,321 m (14,178 ft). Its lower slopes are densely populated and planted with coffee and grains.

Eliade, Mircea [ay-lee-ah'-day] Mircea Eliade, b. Romania, Mar. 9, 1907, d. Apr. 22, 1986, was a historian of religions known for his study of myth and symbolic language. He found in primordial myth a pure form of religious expression that provides a universal foundation underlying all religious phenomena. Eliade taught at Bucharest and Paris before joining (1957) the University of Chicago as a professor of the history of religions. His many writings include *The Myth of the Eternal Return* (1949; Eng. trans., 1954).

Elijah Elijah was a 9th-century BC Hebrew prophet, active in the northern kingdom of Israel principally during the reign of King AHAB. The biblical accounts about Elijah are contained in 1 Kings 17–19, 21:17–29, and 2 Kings 1–2.

At a time when the Israelites were threatened by foreign cults, Elijah upheld monotheism. In a famous contest of faith between Elijah and the priests of BAAL on Mount Carmel, Elijah emerged victorious, and the priests were slain. Elijah also came into conflict with Ahab's queen, JEZEBEL, who supported Baalism. According to tradition he did not die but was taken up to heaven in a whirlwind. The incident was witnessed by his disciple ELISHA.

Later generations, remembering Elijah's departure, expected his return as a herald of the Messiah. It is thus significant that in the New Testament account of Jesus' transfiguration Elijah and Moses appear as witnesses of the event.

Elijah ben Solomon Elijah ben Solomon (Zalman), b. Apr. 23, 1720, d. Oct. 9, 1797, was a Lithuanian Jewish scholar. Often referred to as Elijah Gaon, or the Vilna Gaon, he opposed the spread of Hasidism, a pietistic movement in Judaism. A child prodigy, he mastered the Jewish religious tradition at an early age. Later he advocated the study of astronomy, mathematics, and geography for a heightened understanding of the ancient Jewish documents.

Eliot, Charles William   Charles William Eliot, b. Boston, Mar. 20, 1834, d. Aug. 22, 1926, was a reforming president of Harvard University and editor of the Harvard Classics. Appointed president of Harvard in 1869, he introduced the sciences to the curriculum and replaced rigidly required courses with an elective system. By the time of his retirement in 1909, Harvard had increased its faculty and student body, added professional schools and Radcliffe College (for women), and improved the standards in its law and medical schools, gaining a prominent place among the world's universities.

By raising Harvard entrance requirements, Eliot spurred a rise in secondary-school standards. As chairman of the National Education Association's committee to reform the school curriculum, he advocated introducing foreign languages and mathematics into the seventh-grade curriculum and opposed separating children into different educational tracks.

Eliot, George   George Eliot, pseudonym of Mary Ann Evans, b. Chilvers Cotton, Warwickshire, England, Nov. 22, 1819, d. Dec. 22, 1880, one of the great realists of Victorian fiction and the author of MIDDLEMARCH (1871–72), possibly the era's most impressive NOVEL, was a woman of remarkable intellectual range and daring. Her rejection of traditional Christianity in favor of materialist, philosophical humanism, together with her decision (1854) to live with the unhappily married writer George Henry LEWES, isolated her from more conventional society. Yet she lived to see herself revered as a sage.

Eliot was a precociously intelligent and solemnly evangelical child. It was her vast reading and her acquaintance with independent thinkers in Coventry that later led her to reject Christianity. Devoted to Christian ideals but convinced that Christian dogma was a myth, she translated the key text of German higher criticism of the Bible, D. F. Strauss's *The Life of Jesus* (1846), and Ludwig Feuerbach's humanist reading of the Christian myth, *The Essence of Christianity* (1854). It was only after her father's death in 1849, however, that she moved to London, the center of the avant-garde intellectual developments that interested her.

In London she became editor of *The Westminster Review*, restoring to the quarterly the respectability it had once earned under the editorship of John Stuart Mill. Involved in a painful emotional relationship with the review's owner, John Chapman, his wife, and his mistress, she was rescued by her relationship with Lewes. It was Lewes who encouraged her to write fiction and to adopt her pseudonym.

In 1855 she began writing the three short novels that appeared as *Scenes of Clerical Life* (1858). It was with *Adam Bede* (1859), however, that she made her reputation as a great moral realist, announcing her commitment

The British novelist George Eliot, pseudonym of Mary Ann, or Marian, Evans, illuminated 19th-century literature with such novels of compassion and moral insight as Adam Bede *(1859),* Silas Marner *(1861), and her masterpiece,* Middlemarch *(1871–72).*

to make her readers see freshly and with compassion the weaknesses and strengths of ordinary people and working out movingly the complex relationship between individual egos and a larger, traditional community. The semiautobiographical *The Mill on the Floss* (1860), set in a provincial society being transformed by modern commerce, pushed this mode of fiction to a tragic conclusion.

The Wordsworthian yet very modern evocation of childhood in *The Mill on the Floss* reflected Eliot's attempt to imagine her novels in the context of a past, as well as of a living, community. Even in so successful a moral fable as SILAS MARNER (1861) these social and historical elements are present. The story of the miser redeemed by love into the community makes a paradigm of George Eliot's concerns, visible in more strenuous and complicated ways in her historical novel *Romola* (1863) and her political novel *Felix Holt* (1866).

Middlemarch constitutes the apex both of Eliot's art and of Victorian REALISM. Making use of at least four major plots, it traces the intertwined fates of many characters within a provincial community at the time of the First Reform Bill (1832). Here, social-historical precision blends with psychological analysis and the exploration of marriage, vocation, death, and the power of circumstance to compromise individuals.

Eliot's last novel, *Daniel Deronda* (1876), marks a new development in her art. Seriously disenchanted with the possibilities of English society, she here reaches beyond realism toward the visionary. The realistically drawn egoistic heroine is cut off from the young hero, who must find a messianic vocation outside England in his efforts to help establish a Jewish state in Palestine.

After Lewes died in 1878, Eliot turned to a young admirer, John Cross, whom she married in 1880. Her death came seven months later, after her completion of Lewes's last manuscript, *Problems of Life and Mind* (1873–79).

Buried in Highgate Cemetery, she was enshrined in Westminster Abbey in 1980.

Eliot, Sir John (English parliamentarian)   Sir John Eliot, b. Apr. 11, 1592, d. Nov. 28, 1632, was a leader of the parliamentary opposition to King CHARLES I of England. He started (1626) impeachment proceedings against the king's favorite, the duke of Buckingham, and helped to formulate the Petition of Right, a statement of civil liberties presented to Charles in 1628. In 1629, Eliot presented a further protest against the king's practices; as he did so, the speaker of the House of Commons was held down in his seat to prevent his adjourning Parliament. Eliot was subsequently imprisoned and died in the Tower of London.

Eliot, John (missionary)   John Eliot, b. 1604, d. May 20, 1690, was an English Puritan minister and New England's chief missionary to the Indians. Immigrating to New England in 1631, he persuaded the Massachusetts government to establish special towns for the Indians. Eliot prepared an Indian catechism (1653); translated the Bible into the Algonquian tongue (1661–63), the first Bible to be published in North America; and wrote an Indian grammar (1666) and primer (1669). But the havoc caused by KING PHILIP'S WAR (1675–76) destroyed the missionary effort.

Eliot also helped prepare the *Bay Psalm Book* (1640), served as an overseer at Harvard (1642–85), and contributed to the formulation of Puritan doctrine. However, his vision of an ideal theocracy governed exclusively by the Bible, described in *The Christian Commonwealth...* (1659), was too radical for Massachusetts, and was banned.

Eliot, T. S.   An Anglo-American poet, critic, dramatist, and editor, Thomas Stearns Eliot, b. St. Louis, Mo., Sept. 26, 1888, d. Jan. 4, 1965, was a major innovator in modern English poetry, famous above all for his revolutionary poem The WASTE LAND (1922). His seminal critical essays, such as those published in *The Sacred Wood* (1920), helped to usher in literary MODERNISM by stressing tradition, continuity, and objective discipline over indulgent romanticism and subjective egoism. In rejecting the poetic values of the English romantics and Victorians, Eliot, along with William Butler Yeats and Ezra Pound, set new poetic standards equal to those established by James Joyce and Marcel Proust in fiction. In 1948 he was awarded the Nobel Prize for literature.

Eliot was descended from a distinguished New England family. Between 1906 and 1914 he attended Harvard, studying widely in literature and philosophy. As a graduate student in philosophy, Eliot went abroad to study principally at the Sorbonne and Oxford. With the outbreak of World War I in 1914, he decided to take up permanent residence in England and became a British subject in 1927. In 1915 he married Vivien Haigh-Wood,

T.S. Eliot, an American-born English poet, critic, playwright, and editor, was influential in the modernist movement in poetry. He received wide recognition after publication of The Waste Land *(1922).*

whose mental instability led to her confinement in institutions from 1930 until her death, in 1947. The emotional difficulties produced by the marriage evidently prompted some intense passages in Eliot's poetry. Living in London, he worked as a teacher and bank clerk and helped edit the imagist magazine *The Egoist* (1917–19). In London he also met his countryman Ezra Pound, who read Eliot's poems and responded enthusiastically. From 1920 to 1939, Eliot edited *The Criterion* and in 1925 joined the publishers Faber and Gwyer as an editor; he subsequently became a director of the firm, later renamed Faber and Faber. In 1927 he joined the Church of England. Eliot was awarded the British Order of Merit in 1948 and the American Medal of Freedom in 1964.

As a young poet Eliot found inspiration in French Symbolist poetry, particularly the ironic, self-deprecating verse of Jules LAFORGUE, and in the flexible, colloquial blank verse of 17th-century METAPHYSICAL POETRY and Jacobean drama (see JACOBEAN LITERATURE). These influences are apparent in his first important poems, "The Love Song of J. Alfred Prufrock" (1909–11) and "Portrait of a Lady" (1915), both published in *Prufrock and Other Observations* (1917). Equally influential were his readings of Dante, Shakespeare, ancient literature, modern philosophy, and Eastern mysticism, all of which influenced other early poems, such as "Mr. Apollinax" (1916), "Sweeney among the Nightingales" (1918), and "Gerontion" (1920), a poem that anticipates the power of *The Waste Land*.

Eliot was not a prolific poet, but his small output soon gained respectful attention from readers of modern poetry on both sides of the Atlantic. During the postwar years his prevailing sense of despair and sour irony, and his conviction that contemporary civilization falls short of past grandeur, struck a responsive chord in many readers. The appearance of *The Waste Land* in 1922 aroused both notoriety and genuine admiration. It was notorious because it appeared bafflingly obscure, and at the same time slangy and iconoclastic, a gesture of defiance toward traditional literary ideals; it seemed a poetic expression of the Jazz Age. More discerning readers responded to the deeper aspects of the poem: its juxtaposition of disparate, clashing images; its superimposition of past and present, ancient myths being reenacted in a modern urban setting, Dante and Shakespeare counterpointed against blues and ragtime. In a 1971 published facsimile of the original manuscript, it became evident how much the final form of the poem owed to the extensive revisions made, at Eliot's request, by Ezra Pound, whose help and encouragement benefited Eliot greatly.

Two years before *The Waste Land* appeared, Eliot's collection of essays on poetry and criticism, *The Sacred Wood*, was published (1920). His best-known essay, "Tradition and the Individual Talent," advanced the key points of all his later criticism: the importance of literary history and tradition and the belief that poetry lies not in an unbridled expression of emotion but in an escape from emotion. In "Hamlet and His Problems," he called Shakespeare's play an "artistic failure" because of Hamlet's inexpressible emotional attachment to Gertrude and coined the term objective correlative, meaning an image or metaphor that arouses emotional response in the reader. Other essays on Dryden, Donne, and the metaphysical poets generated new interest in these writers.

Following his conversion to Anglo-Catholicism, Eliot's poetry took on new spiritual dimensions. The six-part poem *Ash Wednesday* (1930) traces a pattern of spiritual progress. Based on Dante's *Purgatorio*, it draws on a narrower range of associations than *The Waste Land*. The emphasis is on the struggle toward belief rather than the triumphant assertion of it. Eliot's last major poetic sequence, FOUR QUARTETS (1943), written in four sections from 1935 to 1942 and that he believed to be his finest achievement, is religious in a very broad sense. It deals with ideas of incarnation, the intersection of time and eternity, and the discovery of spiritual insight in sudden and unexpected moments of revelation.

With his best-known play, *Murder in the Cathedral* (1935; film, 1952), based on the murder of Thomas Becket, Eliot hoped to revive poetic drama. His other plays—*The Family Reunion* (1939), *The Cocktail Party* (1949), *The Confidential Clerk* (1953), and *The Elder Statesman* (1959)—are contemporary secular dramas that draw on a variety of literary sources. Eliot commented at length on the subject of drama in "Rhetoric and Dramatic Poetry" (1919) and "Dialogue on Dramatic Poetry" (1928).

Elisabethville   see LUBUMBASHI

Elisha [ee-ly'-shuh]   Elisha was the disciple and successor of the biblical prophet ELIJAH. His activities in the northern kingdom of Israel from 850 to 800 BC are narrated in 2 Kings 1–13. Elisha's use of his master's mantle illustrates that he carried on Elijah's attempt to shape the national destiny by announcing God's will.

elites   *Elite* is a term applied to those individuals or groups in any society who exercise power, possess superior wealth, or enjoy elevated status and prestige. The modern sociological theory of elites is associated with the writings of the late-19th-century social thinkers Vilfredo PARETO and Gaetano Mosca. They attempted to explain the great changes then occurring in European societies, namely the rise of the bureaucratic state, the spread of market economies, and the process of industrialization. Pareto and Mosca located the source of change in the activity of elite ruling groups, who directed the government and economy. Pareto and Mosca were interested in how the various elites—military, religious, political, and intellectual—were internally organized and related; how they perpetuated their power, wealth, and status; and how they replaced each other over time, alternating between innovative and conservative factions.

The central debate that dominated research on elites in the United States from the 1950s to the mid-1970s was between those, such as C. Wright MILLS, who asserted that there was a power elite—a close-knit, integrated organization of elites at the highest levels of political, economic, and cultural institutions—and those, such as Robert Dahl, who asserted that the organization of elites in American society was pluralistic. According to the latter view, elites were not one coordinated organization dominating society but rather many groups of diverse origin competing for positions of power and prestige. Current research has focused on the culture, ideologies, lifestyles, and outlooks of elites. It thus points to the more subtle, indirect ways in which elites affect society through their involvement in routine affairs of state and the making of policy. While retaining some of the ideas of Pareto and Mosca, current studies owe more to Marxist theory.

Elizabeth   A seaport on Newark Bay in northeastern New Jersey and a suburb of Newark and New York City, Elizabeth is the seat of Union County and has a population of 110,002 (1990). The city is highly industrialized, with shipyards, oil refineries, steel mills, and diverse manufactures. Its port has berthing facilities for ocean vessels and has some of the world's largest containerized shipping docks. The Goethals Bridge (1928) over Arthur Kill connects Elizabeth with Staten Island, N.Y.

Elizabeth was settled in 1664 on land purchased from the Indians. The city served (1668–82) as the first colonial capital of New Jersey and was the original seat of what became Princeton University, founded there in 1746. By the time of the American Revolution, Elizabeth was a busy seaport with tanning, brewing, and shipbuilding industries. Four Revolutionary War battles were fought there, and the city was partially destroyed. Industrialization began in the late 1800s.

Elizabeth, Saint   Elizabeth, the mother of Saint JOHN THE BAPTIST, was the wife of Zechariah and a relative of Mary, mother of Jesus Christ. According to Luke 1:5–66, she gave birth to John when she was old and thought to be barren. Feast day: Nov. 5 (Western); Nov. 8 (Eastern).

Elizabeth I, Queen of England

Elizabeth I, queen of England from 1558 to 1603, is famous for the glamour of her court, the success of her policies, and her long-preserved virginity.

She was born on Sept. 7, 1533, the daughter of HENRY VIII and his second wife, Anne BOLEYN. Henry, who married Anne in the hope of begetting a male heir, was initially disappointed at Elizabeth's birth. He soon convinced himself, however, that Anne would eventually produce a son. When she failed to do so and when suspicion of infidelity was cast upon her, she was executed in 1536. Henry's last wife, Catherine Parr, was for a time an affectionate stepmother to Elizabeth.

During the reign of her half brother EDWARD VI, Elizabeth was involved in an amorous episode with Thomas Seymour, whose brother was the Protector, Edward Seymour, duke of Somerset. For this and for a suspected attempt to gain improper influence over Edward VI, Thomas was executed (1549). While her half sister MARY I was queen (1553–58), Elizabeth lived quietly, awaiting her opportunity to succeed.

Religious Settlement and Foreign Affairs. Her reign began on Nov. 17, 1558, when Mary died. Elizabeth immediately named Sir William Cecil (later Lord BURGHLEY) her chief minister, and with his help she concluded the famous Elizabethan Settlement for the Church of England (see ENGLAND, CHURCH OF). Moderate Protestantism had been practiced under Henry VIII, and more radical Protestant programs were implemented under Edward VI; but Mary had restored the Roman Catholic faith and papal jurisdiction to England. Elizabeth herself was a moderate Protestant. Her settlement again excluded papal authority, and it brought back the BOOK OF COMMON PRAYER, an English-language liturgy, but it did not recognize the demands of the more extreme Puritans (see PURITANISM).

Foreign affairs, always linked with religion, presented an ongoing threat to Elizabeth's security. The great fear was that an alliance of Catholic powers might force her from the throne and reintroduce a Catholic monarch. In the end no such Catholic league was formed, but Elizabeth did send English forces to fight on the Protestant side in two European conflicts, the Wars of Religion in France and the revolt of the Dutch against Spanish rule.

Rival Claimants. The position of MARY, QUEEN OF SCOTS, threatened Elizabeth's safety as well. Mary was the granddaughter of Henry VIII's sister Margaret Tudor by King James IV of Scotland. After the death of her first husband, Francis II of France, Mary returned to Scotland, but her subjects rebelled against her, and in 1568 she fled to England. Since she was a Roman Catholic she immediately became the focus for a number of Catholic conspiracies; these included the Northern Rebellion (1569), the Ridolfi Plot (1571), the Throckmorton Plot (1583), and the Babington Conspiracy (1586). For many years Elizabeth resisted demands that Mary be executed, but she reluctantly signed Mary's death warrant in 1587.

Perhaps the gravest threat to Elizabeth came in 1588 from the SPANISH ARMADA. PHILIP II of Spain intended this

Queen Elizabeth I of England is shown here in one of the few portraits of her painted from life (c.1575). Under Elizabeth's leadership, England became a major European power with prospering commerce and a great navy.

fleet to secure the deposition of Elizabeth in favor of himself, thus restoring Catholicism. The Spanish flotilla was devastated in 1588 in the famous English naval victory.

Essex and Ireland. During the last years of her life Elizabeth was confronted with rebellion in Ireland led by Hugh O'Neill, 2d earl of TYRONE. She first sent (1599) her young favorite, Robert Devereux, 2d earl of ESSEX, to put down the insurrection, but he returned to England without permission, and Lord Mountjoy was responsible for the final English victory. Essex then attempted to lead a rebellion against the queen's advisors in 1601 but failed and was beheaded. Elizabeth mourned his death and was increasingly alone following his execution.

Marriage Question. Elizabeth had many suitors, including Robert Dudley, earl of LEICESTER, to whom she was greatly attracted. She rejected an offer of marriage from the Spanish king, Philip II, but she did allow lengthy courtships by two members of the French royal family—the duc d'Anjou, who became King HENRY III, and his brother François, duc d'Alençon (1554–84). She prided herself on the fact that she lived and died a virgin—the colony Virginia was named for her—and she turned her single state to diplomatic advantage, keeping foreign suitors dangling for years.

Personal Qualities. Elizabeth was unusually intelligent and well educated. She knew a number of modern languages as well as classical Latin and was able to surprise foreign ambassadors by replying in their own tongues. She also loved music and played the virginal. Elizabeth had a nearly unfailing understanding of human character and chose her chief advisors, especially William Cecil and Sir Francis WALSINGHAM, wisely. She was an adroit manipulator of Parliament and grew to be loved deeply by its members, despite increasing conflict with the Commons toward the end of her reign.

Since Elizabeth had no children and there were no other descendants of Henry VIII, the TUDOR line was extinguished upon her death. When Elizabeth died on Mar. 24, 1603, James, the son of Mary, Queen of Scots, but a Protestant, succeeded without incident as JAMES I of England.

Elizabeth II, Queen of England, Scotland, and Northern Ireland

Elizabeth II, Queen of the United Kingdom of Great Britain and Northern Ireland and of Her other Realms and Territories and Head of the Commonwealth, as her proper title puts it, acceded to the throne in 1952. Her ancestry dates back to William I, the Norman who seized the throne of England in 1066.

Born on Apr. 21, 1926, Elizabeth became heir to the throne when her father became king as GEORGE VI upon the abdication of his brother EDWARD VIII in December 1936. On Nov. 20, 1947, she married Philip Mountbatten, duke of EDINBURGH. When George died on Feb. 6, 1952, Elizabeth came to the throne at the age of 25.

Queen Elizabeth was educated in the role of constitutional monarch by her father and her grandmother Queen Mary, wife of GEORGE V. She was also trained by her mother, Queen Elizabeth, the Queen Mother. The public duties of the British monarch are now entirely ceremonial, but Queen Elizabeth sees state papers daily, and the prime minister visits her regularly. Her constitutional role obliges her to keep opinions to herself.

Queen Elizabeth is the wealthiest woman in Britain, having inherited the extensive royal family estates. Her private interests are those of a rich landowner. Horse rac-

Queen Elizabeth II of the United Kingdom was crowned on June 2, 1953.

The Queen appears with the Queen Mother, Elizabeth; the Princess of Wales; Anne, the Princess Royal; and other members of the royal family at the 1986 wedding of the Queen's second son, Andrew, Duke of York, to Sarah Ferguson.

ing, traditionally "the sport of kings," and show jumping are her favorite sports. She has four children: CHARLES, PRINCE OF WALES (b. 1948), the heir to the throne, who married Lady Diana Spencer in 1981; Anne, the Princess Royal (b. 1950), who is separated from her husband, Capt. Mark Phillips; Andrew, duke of York (b. 1960), who married Sarah Ferguson in 1986; and Prince Edward (b. 1964). Of Queen Elizabeth's six grandchildren, Prince William (b. 1982) is second in line to the throne.

Elizabeth of Hungary, Saint

Saint Elizabeth, b. 1207, d. Nov. 17, 1231, was the daughter of King ANDREW II of Hungary. After the death (1227) of her husband, Landgrave Louis IV of Thuringia, she entered the Franciscan third order. She lived in extreme austerity, devoting herself to charity. She was canonized in 1235. Feast day: Nov. 17 (formerly Nov. 19).

Elizabeth, Empress of Russia

Elizabeth Petrovna, b. Dec. 18 (N.S.), 1709, d. Dec. 25 (N.S.), 1761, empress of Russia (1741–61) and daughter of PETER I and CATHERINE I, provided a period of stability that cemented her father's reforms.

During Elizabeth's reign the aristocracy increased its hold over the government and the peasantry, while French cultural influence grew steadily in Russian society. Russian armies penetrated Europe in two major wars, the War of the AUSTRIAN SUCCESSION, 1740–48, and SEVEN YEARS' WAR, 1756–63. Elizabeth brought her nephew, later Emperor PETER III, to Russia and arranged his marriage (1744) to the German princess Sophia of Anhalt-Zerbst (later CATHERINE II).

Elizabethan Age

When ELIZABETH I acceded to the English throne in 1558 following the death of her half-sister, MARY I, England was at its lowest ebb since Tudor rule began in 1485. Elizabeth's immediate and lasting aim was to reunite the country, reestablish the Anglican church (see ENGLAND, CHURCH OF), fend off foreign threats, and bring her people as much peace and prosperity as possible. If she was largely, though not entirely, successful during her reign (1558–1603), a part of her success is reflected in the rise of literature and the arts, especially during the final decade of this period known as the Elizabethan Renaissance.

Politics, Religion, Socioeconomics. The years preceding Elizabeth's accession were marked by severe conflicts in religion and politics, which were closely aligned. Elizabeth's father, HENRY VIII, had brought the REFORMATION to England. During the reign of his adolescent son and successor, EDWARD VI, the king's advisors drove the cause of Protestantism too hard. Queen Mary, however, brought back Roman Catholicism and martyred many of her Protestant subjects, as John FOXE recorded in his *Acts and Monuments* (1563). She further complicated matters by marrying PHILIP II of Spain, casting the shadow of foreign influence, if not domination, over England. Factionalism was intense. Elizabeth therefore had to tread a very careful line to unite her people under a common cause of English nationalism. She did so largely through her political acumen and wit and the advice of her councilors. She effected a religious settlement, embodied in the THIRTY-NINE ARTICLES (1563), broad enough to inspire the loyalties of the great majority of her subjects.

England under Elizabeth experienced a period of economic growth, overseas exploration, and social mobility. Sir John HAWKINS and Sir Francis DRAKE crossed the oceans and fought with Spanish merchant ships and men o' war, bringing home rich spoils of conquest. The Spanish threat was real, and internal threats also caused concern. MARY, QUEEN OF SCOTS, a Catholic, claimed the English throne until Elizabeth reluctantly had her beheaded in 1587. The following year the English defeated Philip II's invasion force, the SPANISH ARMADA. Meanwhile, however, constantly rising prices forced many artisans and farmers into bankruptcy. Repressive POOR LAWS were passed against the resultant vagabondage; begging and thievery increased, even as the rich became richer.

The social historian William Harrison (1534–93), author of *Description of England* (1577), delineated the social structure of the country as consisting of four sorts: gentlemen, citizens or burgesses, yeomen, and artificers or laborers. The lowest class was by far the largest, and within each class were further divisions. While most of the populace lived in the country, London continued to grow in both size and importance. It was to London that the so-called University Wits—among them Christopher MARLOWE, Robert GREENE, Thomas KYD, and George Peele (1558–98)—flocked to make their fortunes, along with those who, dispossessed of land or livelihood, also sought new opportunities.

Literature and the Arts. The heightened activity of this period, uneven though it was, produced a most extraordinary outpouring of great art. The idealism of the age is represented in the living examples of such men as Sir Walter RALEIGH and Sir Philip SIDNEY, who, like Hamlet,

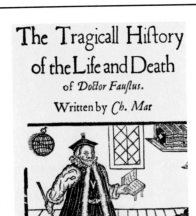

The Tragicall History of the Life and Death of Doctor Faustus.

Written by Ch. Mar

LONDON,
Printed for *Iohn Wright*, and are to be fold at his fhop Without Newgate, at the f   .   he
Bi   1616

In Christopher Marlowe's Doctor Faustus *(c. 1588), the use of allegory echoes the medieval morality play, yet the beauty of the play's language and the compass of its plot—a man's search for forbidden power and knowledge—transcend its antecedents and reflect Renaissance preoccupations.*

embodied the "courtier's, soldier's, scholar's, eye, tongue, sword." Admired by all who knew him, Sidney wrote his spirited *Defence of Poesie* (1579–81; publ. 1595) as well as a long, complex prose pastoral, the *Arcadia* (1590). His contemporary Edmund SPENSER, after composing *The Shepheards Calendar* (1579), a book of pastoral eclogues dedicated to Sidney, embarked on an epic romance, The FAERIE QUEENE (1590–96). This great allegorical poem was intended to demonstrate the virtues of a Christian prince, Arthur, serving England and its sovereign, Elizabeth. The epic owed much to ARIOSTO's *Orlando Furioso* (1516), and many English writers drew heavily on Continental literatures; they also infused their work with native traditions and originality, however, and were unencumbered by principles of classicism, so that their writings were far from merely imitative. Thus, while William SHAKESPEARE borrowed freely from Boccaccio and Montaigne, his plays and poems are not copies but transformations into something "rich and strange."

The language itself experienced an immense expansion and increased flexibility. New words and new uses of existing ones together with borrowings from other languages combined to make English rich and versatile. Only the most pedantic of writers suffered constraints. In drama multiple plots and frank violations of the unities of time and place were the rule, although such "classical" playwrights as Ben JONSON composed excellent comedies like *Every Man in His Humour* (1598) and VOLPONE (1606) within the unities. Translations became popular and influential. Sir Thomas Hoby's translation (1561) of Castiglione's *The Courtier* and Sir Thomas North's translation (1579) of Plutarch's *Lives* in their different ways promoted the ideals of courtly or heroic behavior. Marlowe, George CHAPMAN, and others rendered classical poets into English. Although the novel remained in still ru-

William Shakespeare transformed the English language into a vehicle of amazing fluidity and depth; his plays are still considered among the finest evocations of the human condition. The first folio edition (1623) of his works was prefaced by Ben Jonson's dedicatory verse and Martin Droeshout's engraving. (National Portrait Gallery, London.)

To the Reader.

This Figure, that thou here seest put,
It was for gentle Shakespeare cut;
Wherein the Grauer had a strife
with Nature, to out-doo the life:
O, could he but haue drawne his wit
As well in braße, as he hath hit
Hisface; the Print would then surpaße
All, that was euer writ in braße.
But, since he cannot, Reader, looke
Not on his Picture, but his Booke.
B. I.

dimentary form, Thomas NASHE and Thomas LODGE (also University Wits) were but two of many who wrote prose fiction. John LYLY's novels and plays show an elegant if artificial style that directly influenced other writers and, it is said, even Elizabeth. The first true English-language essayist, Francis BACON, published his *Essays, Civil and Moral* in 1597; Richard HAKLUYT's descriptive geographical works, based on actual voyages, were the most comprehensive of the time; and Raphael HOLINSHED's *Chronicles* (1577) reflected the Elizabethans' interest in history.

The decade of the 1590s evinced a remarkable outburst of lyrical poetry. The SONNETS OF SHAKESPEARE were only one of many sonnet sequences, written by such poets as Michael DRAYTON, Samuel DANIEL, Sidney, and Spenser—all influenced by Petrarch's sonnets. Other lyric forms were popular, too, as well as ballads and broadsides. John DONNE's *Songs and Sonnets* belong to this decade, although they were not published (1633) until after his death. Thus, conventional lyric poetry and the new metaphysical verse coexisted, each in its own way showing wit, imagination, and metrical virtuosity.

A similar, perhaps greater, richness and diversity characterize Elizabethan drama. Plays were performed in any suitable location: innyards, the halls of great manor houses, university towns, the Inns of Court, as well as in public and private theaters (see ELIZABETHAN PLAYHOUSE). Many companies performed plays—including Shakespeare's company, the Lord Chamberlain's Men—and children's companies were also widely admired, competing with other professional troupes. The romantic comedies of Lyly, Greene, and Peele, surpassed only by the joyous comedies of Shakespeare, flourished simultaneously with satirical "humours" comedies by Jonson and Chapman. It was in tragedy, however, that the age realized its most powerful literary achievement. From the earlier, almost primitive plays—such as *Gorboduc* (1561), the first English drama in blank verse—to the

greater accomplishments of Kyd (*The Spanish Tragedy*, c.1586), Marlowe (*Doctor Faustus*, c.1588; *Tamburlaine the Great*, c.1590; *The Jew of Malta*, c.1590; *Edward II*, 1594), and Shakespeare, Elizabethan dramatists continued to develop their art, mixing comic elements with tragic, introducing subplots, and adapting freely from classical or other original sources.

Throughout the Renaissance, whether in Ulysses' speech on "degree" in *Troilus and Cressida*, or Sir John DAVIES's poem *Orchestra* (1596), ideas of order, part and parcel of Elizabethan life, are mirrored in the literature. These ideas are formally organized in one of the great prose tracts of the time, Richard HOOKER's *Treatise on the Laws of Ecclesiastical Polity* (1593).

If literature was its magnificent achievement, the Elizabethan Renaissance also excelled in music. The composers William BYRD, Orlando GIBBONS, and Thomas Morley adapted the madrigal from Italian models to suit English tastes. Thomas TALLIS left a legacy of superb motets, as well as hymn verses and antiphons that give testimony to his virtuosity as an organist. Songs for solo voice, such as those by John DOWLAND, rivaled any composed in Europe. Instrumental music was not ignored, John BULL, Giles Farnaby (c.1565–1640), and Francis Cutting (fl. 1583–c.1603) all contributing scores for various ensembles. In architecture, the Tudor half-timbered house has become almost emblematic of the age, a number of examples surviving to the present day (see ELIZABETHAN STYLE). In painting, however, only the art of the miniature is noteworthy, the work of Nicholas HILLIARD being outstanding.

By the death of Elizabeth in 1603 and the accession to the throne of her cousin, James VI of Scotland, who became James I of England, the exuberance had begun to fade, and a more somber note colored Jacobean life and art. The triumphs of the Virgin Queen were at an end, and the new century brought to the surface problems that eventually led to civil war in 1642 and the temporary overthrow of the monarchy.

Elizabethan playhouse   The Elizabethan "playehowses" of London were historically the first permanent, commercial theaters ever built for the purpose of staging dramatic productions. The first, named simply The Theatre, was erected by the actor James Burbage in 1576 in Shoreditch, a northern suburb of the city. It was followed by The Curtain, built nearby in 1577, and soon afterward by others in the southern suburbs across the Thames. By 1600 no less than eight playhouses were operating in London, not including those inns whose courtyards were also occasionally used for stage productions.

Most playhouses were of the "public" type; that is, they had open yards surrounded by galleries, and performances were held by daylight before audiences estimated to have numbered as many as 3,000. A few so-called private playhouses, such as Blackfriars, constructed within existing buildings held fewer, though usually more select, spectators, and could on occasion house performances by candlelight.

This rendering of an Elizabethan playhouse incorporates most of the features found in the theaters of the time. The circular wooden building featured an open yard into which the stage protruded. "Groundlings" stood on three sides of this raised stage in the area known as the "pit." Covered seating was available for a higher price around the walls at ground level and in two upper galleries. Trapdoors in the stage floor allowed for sudden ascents and descents. A small inner stage, or discovery room, located at the rear of the main acting area, presumably was used as the setting for such confined scenes as those in a cave (The Tempest) or in a bedroom (Othello). The attic stories over the stage contained dressing rooms and machines for moving scenery. This space, known as the "heavens," was illuminated by light from the lantern, which stood between twin peaks of the roof.

In addition to The Theatre and The Curtain, the public playhouses opened during William Shakespeare's lifetime were Newington Butts (c.1579); the Rose (1592; remnants of the theater were uncovered during building excavations in 1989); the Swan Theatre (1596); the Boar's Head (a converted innyard, 1598); the Globe Theatre (1599); the Fortune Theatre (1600); the Red Bull (c.1605–06); and the Hope (c.1613–14). Private playhouses built during the same period were the Blackfriars (1576, remodeled c.1596); St. Paul's (for choirboy players; closed c.1606); and the Whitefriars (c.1606). The Theatre was dismantled in 1599, and its timbers were used to construct the Globe.

Performances at the public playhouses were in the afternoon year-round except during Lent, times of plague, or bad weather. A flag was hoisted over the playhouse on days when performances were to be given. The start of a performance was signaled by three successive trumpet soundings.

On entering the playhouse yard, spectators paid one penny each to a "gatherer" and more money at different gallery entrances, according to the facilities provided. Privileged spectators might even be seated on the stage. "Groundling" spectators in the yard had to stand throughout the performance.

The stage adjoined the encircling galleries only on one

side, where a screen wall stood, with openings for access between the stage and the backstage, or "tiring-house," area. This facade also contained an upper gallery and windows that were available for dramatic uses. Although plays were presented without pictorial scenery, stages were often furnished with elaborate properties, rich costumes, and a variety of special effects including "flying" descents from a "Heavens" overhanging the stage and the use of traps from the "Hell" beneath.

Elizabethan style *Elizabethan style* is a term used to describe the architecture of England in the reign of Queen ELIZABETH I (1558–1603). It is a style that was to some extent influenced by GOTHIC ART AND ARCHITECTURE, although it is completely secular—consisting of large manor houses and great country houses often built by wealthy merchants, courtiers, or ministers of state.

The style of these houses is visibly Renaissance. The plans are deliberately symmetrical (an Italian characteristic); the forms and decorative details come from France—false niches, strapwork, grotesques, broken columns, highly decorated chimneys. The windows tend to be large, square-mullioned forms. Occasionally the plan is based on the letter H. Often a courtyard plan was used, allowing for long sequences of rooms, necessary for courtiers and visitors. The exterior forms are rich and complex. Although the houses are sometimes a little ungainly with too much decoration, they have a force rarely matched in later English architecture. Only two architects are known

Longleat Hall, Wiltshire, built (c.1572) for Sir John Thynne, is the most classical in style of the great Elizabethan houses. It incorporates all three classical orders—Doric on the first floor, Ionic on the second, and Corinthian on the third.

with certainty: Robert Smythson (1535–1614), designer of Hardwick Hall, Wollaton Hall, Worksop Manor, Nottinghamshire (1585; destroyed 1761), and probably Longleat Hall, Wiltshire (1572); and John Thorpe (1568–1620), many of whose drawings have survived.

The male American elk, also known as the wapiti, is recognized by its distinctive call. It bears large, spreading antlers during late summer and throughout the autumn.

elk The American elk, or wapiti, *Cervus canadensis*, is a member of the deer family, Cervidae, order Artiodactyla. It is considered by many authorities to be the same species as the European red deer, *C. elaphus*. Elk weigh up to 350 kg (770 lb), stand 1.5 m (5 ft) high at the shoulder, and may be 2.4 m (8 ft) long. Males have antlers that may span more than 1.5 m (5 ft). The coat is grayish brown, with a white patch on the rump. Overhunted, elk are now found only in southern Canada, the Rockies, and the Central Valley of California, the last being the home of the small tule elk. In Europe, *elk* refers solely to the moose.

Elko Elko, a city on the Humboldt River in northeastern Nevada, is the seat of Elko County and lies at an elevation of more than 1,500 m (5,000 ft). Elko has a population of 14,736 (1990), and the city is a commercial, shipping, and tourist center for a large ranching and mining area. The settlement, established in 1868 as a construction camp for the Central Pacific Railroad, was also a station for the Overland Stage and Overland Telegraph Company and the Pony Express. The National Basque Festival is held in Elko every July.

Ellesmere Island [elz'-meer] Ellesmere Island, with an area of 196,236 km^2 (75,767 mi^2), is the largest of the Queen Elizabeth Islands, which form a part of Canada's Northwest Territories. It is generally mountainous and ice covered. Its Cape Columbia is Canada's northernmost point. Part of the island was made a national park in 1986.

Ellice Islands see TUVALU

Ellington, Duke Edward Kennedy "Duke" Ellington, b. Washington, D.C., Apr. 29, 1899, d. May 24, 1974, was a pianist and an orchestra leader and the most prolific composer in JAZZ history. From 1927 to 1931, Ellington's broadcasts from the Cotton Club in Harlem made him a national celebrity. His first European tour (1933) brought him international fame as well. His orchestra featured many of the greatest jazz artists of the time. Their unique sound and precision won them a reputation as the finest orchestra in jazz.

Ellington wrote more than 1,000 short pieces—"Mood Indigo" (1930) was his first important hit; concertos for orchestra and jazz soloist, including "Clarinet Lament" and "Concerto for Cootie" (both 1935); long concert pieces in the jazz idiom, such as *Black, Brown and Beige* (1943); three large religious works; and several movie scores.

Duke Ellington, composer, pianist, and orchestra leader, is considered by many the most important figure in the history and evolution of jazz. A prolific composer and arranger, Ellington was a superb innovator in every jazz style he adopted, including bebop, stride, and swing.

Elliott, Herb Herbert James Elliott, b. Feb. 25, 1938, is an Australian runner who has been ranked by many authorities as the greatest miler ever. A poll of experts by *Track & Field News* in 1978 accorded him that honor. Elliott set a world record in the mile in 1958 when he ran 3:54.5. He reached his peak at the 1960 Olympic Games, when he established a world record of 3:35.6 in the 1,500 meters, winning the race by the widest margin up to that time. Elliott broke the 4-minute barrier to the mile 17 times—4 times within one month after the Olympics. He retired undefeated at age 22.

---

ellipse An ellipse is a curve formed by a plane that intersects the axis of a circular cone and is not parallel to an element of the cone (see CONIC SECTIONS). An ellipse may also be defined as the locus, or set, of points for which the sum of the distances to two fixed points is constant. Each fixed point is called a focus. This second definition makes it possible to construct an ellipse, as shown in Figure 1. A piece of string of length $2a$ is fastened by its ends at two fixed points F_1 and F_2 (the foci). A pencil that is placed at point P and moved while the string is kept taut will describe an ellipse.

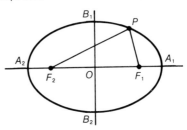

The length $2a = F_1P + F_2P$ is the constant required by the definition. The ellipse is symmetric with respect to its major axis, A_1A_2, and also with respect to its minor axis, B_1B_2, which is the perpendicular bisector of the segment joining the foci. Point O, a point of symmetry for the ellipse, is called the center; points A_1 and A_2 are called the vertices. The area is πab, where a and b (the semimajor and semiminor axes) are the lengths of half the major and minor axes.

The equation for an ellipse with center at the origin O, vertices at $(a, 0)$ and $(-a, 0)$, and semiminor axis of length b (see Figure 2) is $(x^2/a^2) + (y^2/b^2) = 1$.

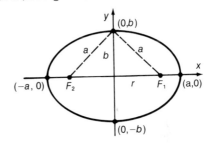

The ECCENTRICITY e of an ellipse is c/a, where c is the distance from the center to a focus. The inequality $0 < e < 1$ holds. An ellipse is thus a conic section with eccentricity less than 1.

Planets travel around the Sun in elliptical orbits (see KEPLER'S LAWS). The focal property of an ellipse gives it special optical and acoustical properties. A light beam or sound beam emanating from one focal point in any direction will always pass through the other focus after being reflected from the ellipse.

Ellis, Havelock Havelock Ellis, b. Feb. 2, 1859, d. July 8, 1939, was a British physician and essayist noted for his investigations of human sexual behavior published in the seven-volume *Studies in the Psychology of Sex*

(1897–1928). Banned on obscenity charges in England, the series was available in the United States only to medical professionals until 1935. He described the ubiquitousness of masturbation, introduced the concept that homosexuality and heterosexuality are both present to varying degrees in everyone, and stressed the role of psychological factors in certain sexual disturbances. Ellis's work was influential in opening up discussion of sexual problems and forwarding the causes of women's rights and sex education.

The American writer Ralph Ellison received international literary recognition with his first and most important novel, Invisible Man (1952).

Photo Jill Krementz © 1974

Ellis Island   Ellis Island is a small island in Upper New York Bay, lying about 1.6 km (1 mi) southwest of the Battery, on Manhattan, and about 396 m (1,300 ft) east of Jersey City, N.J. Although in New Jersey waters, it is under the political jurisdiction of New York. The 11-ha (27-acre) island was a major immigration station for the United States from 1892 to 1943 and an immigrant detention station until 1954. It has been part of the Statue of Liberty National Monument since 1965.

Once a picnic ground for the early Dutch settlers, the island was named for Samuel Ellis, who owned the island in the 1770s. It was purchased by the federal government from New York State in 1808 for use as a government arsenal and fort. After the creation of the Immigration Bureau (1891), the immigration station was moved from Castle Garden (at Battery Park, Manhattan) to Ellis Island. There immigrants were examined and either admitted or deported; at the height of its activity, the Ellis Island station could process 1 million people a year. Twelve million immigrants came through Ellis Island from 1895 to 1924. The Great Hall, where immigrants were processed, was renovated as part of the 1986 Statue of Liberty centennial celebration. The entire Main Building, which includes the Great Hall, has been restored; the Ellis Island Immigration Museum there opened to the public in 1990.

Ellison, Ralph   The American writer Ralph Waldo Ellison, b. Oklahoma City, Okla., Mar. 1, 1914, achieved international fame with his first novel, *Invisible Man* (1952). He was influenced early by the myth of the frontier, viewing the United States as a land of "infinite possibilities." The close-knit black community in which he grew up supplied him with images of courage and endurance and an interest in music.

From 1933 to 1936, Ellison attended Tuskegee Institute, intent upon pursuing a career in music; his readings in modern literature, however, interested him in writing. In 1936 he moved to New York City, met the novelist Richard Wright, and became associated with the Federal Writers' Project, publishing short stories and articles in such magazines as *New Challenge* and *New Masses*.

These early details of his life, set down in *Shadow and Act* (1964) and *Going to the Territory* (1986)—collections of essays and other nonfiction pieces—enhance an understanding of *Invisible Man*. The influences of the frontier tradition, the black community, and Ellison's interest in music combined to create the richly symbolic, metaphorical language of the novel. Its theme is a black man's search for identity in a society where black individuality is "invisible," and blacks are recognized only in the roles they have been assigned by whites. *Invisible Man* won the National Book Award in 1953.

Ellora [el-ohr'-uh]   Ellora, a village in east central Maharashtra state, India, about 435 km (270 mi) northeast of Bombay, is noted for its 34 rock-cut shrines and cave-temples. The sanctuaries—mostly Hindu or Buddhist, with some Jain—were excavated in the scarp of a lava plateau between the mid-4th and late 9th centuries AD. In most of the caves an entrance space leads to a shrine cut in the form of a pillared hall or cluster of halls. The interior effects of structural buildings are imitated in the layout and in the profuse carving of the rock surfaces.

Ellsworth, Lincoln   Lincoln Ellsworth, b. Chicago, May 12, 1880, d. May 26, 1951, was an American polar explorer who led the first aerial crossings of both the Arctic (1926) and Antarctica (1935). A millionaire, he provided financing and accompanied Roald AMUNDSEN on the Polar Flying Expedition of 1925, and in 1926 he completed the first transpolar flight in a dirigible with Amundsen and Umberto Nobile in the latter's airship, *Norge*. Ellsworth planned a trans-Antarctic flight to determine if the Weddell Sea–Ross Sea depressions separated the Antarctic region into two great divisions. His successful flight (1935) over Antarctica was followed by an aerial photographing expedition (1939), which furnished information that led to the first mapping of that part of the world.

Ellsworth, Oliver   With fellow delegate Roger SHERMAN of Connecticut, Oliver Ellsworth, b. Windsor, Conn.,

Apr. 29, 1745, d. Nov. 26, 1807, proposed the Connecticut Compromise, which broke the deadlock between the large and small states at the CONSTITUTIONAL CONVENTION in 1787. Educated at Yale and Princeton, he became a politician and a judge. He helped to swing Connecticut toward ratification of the Constitution and was one of the state's first two U.S. senators (1789–96). He served as chief justice of the U.S. Supreme Court from 1796 to 1800.

elm   Elms, genus *Ulmus*, are deciduous hardwood trees that belong to the elm family, Ulmaceae. About 45 species are distributed worldwide in northern temperate regions. Many elm species are commercially valued as lumber trees and as ornamentals.

Elms generally have spreading crowns and deeply furrowed, gray bark. The twigs are slightly zigzag and, in some species, form corky wings. The short-stalked leaves are commonly pointed at the tip and somewhat rounded at the base. The leaf edges usually have a double saw-toothed pattern. The fruit, known as a samara or key, is thin, flat, and usually bordered with a papery wing. Each fruit contains one flat, brown seed. The seed matures in late spring and is shed promptly.

During the mid-20th century Dutch elm disease, caused by the fungus *Ceratocystis ulmi*, destroyed populations of various elm species in North America and Europe. All native American elms are susceptible, particularly the American elm, *U. americana*. These elms, many of which had been planted in large numbers along streets of cities, have been virtually eliminated by this disease. The English elm, *U. campestris*, has also been affected in epidemic proportions by Dutch elm disease. One solution to the problem has been to breed new varieties of elms that are resistant to the fungus. The Siberian elm, *U. pumila*, is a species that is naturally resistant.

The American elm, a stately shade tree, produces red flowers that have no petals and seeds that provide food for birds and squirrels.

The American elm, *U. americana*, a stately shade tree, produces red flowers that have no petals, and seeds that provide food for birds and squirrels. Most American elms have died of Dutch elm disease.

Elman, Mischa   Mischa Elman, b. Jan. 20 (N.S.), 1891, d. Apr. 5, 1967, was a distinguished Russian-American violinist. He began to study the violin at the age of 4, and in 1902, Leopold Auer accepted him into his class at the Saint Petersburg Conservatory, where he also studied harmony with César Cui. Elman made a sensational debut in Saint Petersburg in 1904 and then toured Germany and England. At the age of 17 he made his American debut in New York City and became a U.S. citizen in 1923. He performed with every important U.S. symphony orchestra and toured the world in recitals.

Elmira   Situated in the Finger Lakes region of south central New York on the Chemung River, Elmira is the county seat of Chemung County. It has a population of 33,724 (1990). Elmira is a manufacturing center, producing fabricated metals, glass containers, tools, and valves. Dairy and poultry farming are important in the region, for which the city acts as a distribution center. Elmira also manufactures sailplanes and gliders. The National Soaring Museum is there, and a national glider meet is held each summer at nearby Harris Hill. Elmira College, established in 1855, was one of the first women's colleges in the United States; it is now coeducational. Settled in 1788, Elmira was the site of a Civil War prison camp where nearly 3,000 Confederate prisoners died; they are buried in nearby Woodlawn National Cemetery. The author Mark Twain spent his later years in the town and is also buried there.

Elsheimer, Adam   [els'-hy-mur]   Adam Elsheimer, 1578–1601, was a German painter noted for his small oil paintings, mostly on copper, which are among the most delicate and sensitive productions of the baroque age. The small house altar *Scenes of the Life of the Virgin* (*c.*1597–98; Staatliche Museum, Berlin-Dahlem), his first masterpiece, shows his assimilation of Albrecht DÜRER's style. The influence of Venetian masters and Paolo VERONESE inspired his *Holy Family* (*c.*1599; Staatliche Museum), in which his skillfully rendered effects of light fuse the landscape and the figures together. In Elsheimer's famous *Tobias and the Angel* ("small" version, *c.*1607–08; Historisches Museum, Frankfurt), nature plays as important a role as the figures; this style ultimately inspired the early work of Claude Lorrain.

Elssler, Fanny   [els'-lur]   Fanny Elssler (originally Franziska Elssler), b. June 23, 1810, d. Nov. 27, 1884, was, along with Marie Taglioni, the greatest of ballerinas in the romantic era, Taglioni being notable for her spirituality, Elssler for her passion and dramatic flair. Elssler, the daughter of Joseph Haydn's copyist and valet K. L. F. Elssler, made her stage debut at the age of eight. In 1834 she danced in Paris with great success and studied further with Auguste Vestris. Elssler's interpretation of *Giselle*, with its emphasis on the tragic events of Act 1, became a model for subsequent ballerinas. She retired from the stage in 1851.

Éluard, Paul [ay-loo-ar'] Paul Éluard, b. Eugène Grindel, Dec. 14, 1895, d. Nov. 18, 1952, was a leading poet of French surrealism. His early work used language experimentally to explore heightened states of consciousness. In the 1930s he wrote some of the finest love poetry in French. Increasingly concerned with politics, he joined the Communist party in 1942 and was one of the outstanding writers of the resistance movement during World War II. Some of his best works include *La Rose publique* (The Public Rose, 1934) and *Les Yeux fertiles* (The Fertile Eyes, 1936).

Elysian Fields [i-lizh'-uhn] In Greek mythology the Elysian Fields, also known as Elysium or the Isles of the Blessed, were the dwelling place after death of virtuous mortals or those given immortality by divine favor. The poets Homer, Hesiod, and Pindar variously describe this happy land as being on the banks of the river Oceanus at the edge of the Earth. In the works of Vergil, Elysium was part of HADES.

Elytis, Odysseus Odysseus Elytis is the pseudonym of the Greek poet Odysseus Alepoudelis, b. Nov. 2, 1911, who first came to prominence with poems characterized by their bright Aegean setting, their affirmation of life and joy, and their debt to surrealism. World War II gave his outlook an added depth, which is apparent in his later collections. His masterpiece, *Seemly It Is* (1959; Eng. trans., 1974), is a vast and complex spiritual autobiography that makes full use of the resources of the Greek language and Greek history. Elytis received the 1979 Nobel Prize for literature. His *The Little Mariner* was published in 1985 (Eng. trans., 1988).

emanationism Emanationism is a philosophical theory that explains the origin of the world by postulating a perfect source from which everything flows. For PLOTINUS, who gave the first full presentation of the theory, mind and idea are generated by emanation from the One, which is the apex of the system. In turn, the world soul (within which individual souls are contained) is generated from mind. Matter is the lowest order of reality, a shadow lying below soul. The analogy of light is often used to illustrate emanation; so is that of overflow, as though the world were a fountain with higher levels spilling over into those below them. Strong traces of emanationism are found in NEOPLATONISM, Jewish philosophy of the Middle Ages, and GNOSTICISM.

In this painting, Abraham Lincoln reads a draft of the Emancipation Proclamation to his cabinet on July 22, 1862. This document, which took effect on Jan. 1, 1863, provided for abolition of slavery in the Confederate states.

Emancipation Proclamation On Jan. 1, 1863, U.S. president Abraham LINCOLN declared free all slaves residing in territory in rebellion against the federal government. This Emancipation Proclamation actually freed few people. It did not apply to slaves in border states fighting on the Union side; nor did it affect slaves in southern areas already under Union control. Naturally, the states in rebellion did not act on Lincoln's order. But the proclamation did show Americans—and the world—that the CIVIL WAR was now being fought to end slavery.

Lincoln had been reluctant to come to this position. A believer in white supremacy, he initially viewed the war only in terms of preserving the Union. As pressure for abolition mounted in Congress and the country, however, Lincoln became more sympathetic to the idea. On Sept. 22, 1862, he issued a preliminary proclamation announcing that emancipation would become effective on Jan. 1, 1863, in those states still in rebellion. Although the Emancipation Proclamation did not end slavery in America—this was achieved by the passage of the 13th Amendment to the Constitution on Dec. 18, 1865—it did make that accomplishment a basic war goal and a virtual certainty.

embalming The contemporary practice of embalming consists of chemically disinfecting and temporarily preserving the dead human body. The primary objectives are to remove the body fluids, to replace them with disinfecting chemicals that reduce the growth of microorganisms, and to introduce preserving chemicals that delay the decomposition of cellular structures. The purpose of the process is to temporarily preserve the body for the funeral rite, to provide for convenient handling of the body, and to reduce the danger of infection or contagion to the public.

The earliest record of embalming was made by the Greek historian Herodotus in about the 5th century BC. Many references are made to embalming in the Book of the Dead, an ancient Egyptian guide for embalmers, and embalming is mentioned in the Book of Genesis. The Egyptians completely eviscerated the cadaver, immersed it in a natron (salt) solution, then filled the body cavities with spices and arabic gums, and finally wrapped the body in copious quantities of linen and similar cloth before placing it in a coffin.

Embalming today is done by a specially trained and licensed practitioner. The disinfecting and preserving chemicals, primarily aldehydes, are injected into various blood vessels.

See also: CEMETERY; EGYPT, ANCIENT; FUNERAL INDUSTRY.

embargo   An embargo, in international law, is a ban on the movement of goods or means of transport of goods to a foreign country by land, sea, or air. There are two types of embargoes: civil and hostile. Civil embargoes restrain goods belonging to the state that imposes the embargo from being transported to foreign territory. Hostile embargoes detain the property of a foreign state. The effect of a hostile embargo is that the property is returned to the foreign state if no war occurs, but it is forfeited to the embargoing state if there is war.

Embargo Act   The Embargo Act passed by the U.S. Congress in 1807 was a response to British and French interference with American ships. It prohibited all exports to Europe and restricted imports from Great Britain. The British were blockading Napoleonic France and its allies and hence interfering with the right of the neutral United States to trade with a belligerent in noncontraband goods. In addition the British had pressed American seamen into service on their ships. President Thomas Jefferson believed that the British needed American food and raw materials so badly that an embargo would force them to respect American neutrality. The embargo provoked strong opposition from American farmers and commercial interests, however. In 1809 it was replaced by the Non-Intercourse Act, permitting trade with some European countries.

embezzlement   Embezzlement, in criminal law, is the fraudulent and usually permanent appropriation of property, generally money, by one to whom it has been entrusted. Embezzlement, a statutory crime, is to be distinguished from common-law LARCENY, which requires that there be an initial taking of property directly from the rightful owner without the owner's consent. Under most state statutes in the United States the embezzler must be a person in a relation of trust toward the owner.

embolism [em'-buh-lizm]   An embolism is an obstruction of a blood vessel by an embolus, which is any foreign substance—a blood clot, a fat globule (from a broken bone), an air bubble, a clump of dislodged tumor cells—that is swept along in the bloodstream until it lodges in a vessel and blocks the flow of blood beyond that point. A thrombus, by contrast, is a blood clot that obstructs a blood vessel by forming at a site because of injury, stagnation of blood flow, or arteriosclerosis. A dislodged thrombus in the blood is called a thromboembolism.

The effects of an embolism depend on the part of the body deprived of blood and may be fatal. Especially critical are cerebrovascular thromboembolisms, blood clots in an artery that serves the brain; and PULMONARY EMBOLISMS, clots in the artery that feeds blood to the lungs. The latter are a leading cause of death among hospital patients, particularly in patients who have had surgery or suffered heart attacks.

Air embolisms may occur in deep-sea divers who ascend too quickly, causing nitrogen bubbles in the blood to lodge in tiny arteries (see BENDS). Fat embolisms are a rare complication of fracture of the long bones.

See also: HEART DISEASE.

embroidery   Embroidery is a textile art that encompasses a wide range of technical procedures that share a common purpose: decorating a foundation material—usually a fabric—with ornamental needlework. The materials most commonly embroidered include linen, silk, satin, wool, velvet, cotton, and cotton canvas. The threads most often used for needlework include silk, linen, cotton, wool, gold, and silver.

Embroidery may be among the world's oldest crafts. Sewing two pieces of fabric (or two skins) together edge-to-edge, using even the simplest stitches, creates a regular pattern along the seam. The devising of more intricate and thus more decorative stitches along the seams of clothing probably occurred from prehistoric times. The art of applied textile decoration, as embroidery is sometimes called, was practiced in numerous ancient cultures. The Chinese were skillful embroiderers, possibly as early as 3000 BC. In the New World the Inca of Peru decorated with embroidery.

In Europe embroidery developed into an important art form in the Middle Ages. The famous BAYEUX TAPESTRY, in fact an embroidery on linen, dates from the late 11th century AD. By the 14th century needle painting, which copied in needlework paintings of religious and secular themes, became popular. In the 16th and 17th centuries, few articles of clothing escaped the embroiderer's needle. Coats, shirts, dresses, hats, gloves, nightcaps, shoes, fans, and handkerchiefs were embroidered, with precious stones often incorporated in the work. Elaborate needlework also covered chair cushions, screens, fabric-covered boxes, draperies, and bed curtains.

Numerous embroidery styles and techniques have been developed. Among the more distinctive are stump work (a padded type worked on satin), tambour work (a chain-stitch technique worked on fabric stretched on a drumlike frame and from which evolved CROCHET and rug hooking), cutwork (a kind of openwork that developed into

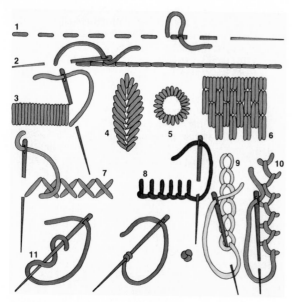

Embroidery, an ancient needlecraft, is used worldwide to decorate fabrics. Basic stitches include the running stitch (1) and the backstitch (2), used for outlining designs, and the satin stitch worked both vertically (3) and diagonally (4). A satin-stitched eyelet (5) can be worked around a hole. Satin stitches laid in a stepped pattern (6) provide the basis for Florentine work, or bargello. The cross stitch (7) is popular in samplers. In the blanket, or buttonhole, stitch (8), which is used for edging borders, circles, and scallops, and in the chain stitch (9) and the feather stitch (10), the needle catches up a loop of thread. To make a French knot (11), the thread is wound around the needle.

needle lace), crewel work (using wool thread), and Spanish blackwork (worked with black thread on linen). Needlework samplers evolved for the purpose of recording and practicing stitches. Important stitches include tent stitch (petit point), feather, chain, cross-stitch, satin, herringbone, *tête de boeuf*, ladder or buttonhole, blanket, and Gobelin.

The use of embroidery declined during the 19th century, and most commercial embroideries today are machine made; however, exceptional peasant embroideries are still produced in many parts of the world.

---

embryo [em'-bree-oh] In biology, the term *embryo* is applied to a multicellular organism in its early stages of DEVELOPMENT and GROWTH from a single egg to maturity. Both animals and plants go through an embryonic stage, but the study of embryos, which is called embryology, is usually grouped among the zoological sciences. (For a discussion of plant embryos, see PLANT.) The term is usually applied to higher animals from the time when they first start to develop to the time of their birth. Specifically, in mammals, embryonic development is the period from gamete, or sex-cell, formation and union to the point when all the organ systems have been formed—eight weeks, in humans. After this point the term *fetus* is commonly used.

The study of embryos can be divided into phases that are recognizable in the development of nearly all animals. Thus, the formation of gametes is divided into oogenesis, or the formation of eggs, and spermatogenesis, or the formation of the male's SPERM. These processes include meiosis, or the reduction of chromosome number (see GENETICS) and gamete differentiation. Oogenesis involves an extensive growth phase, especially in life forms with large, yolky eggs.

Complex processes bring sperm to the immediate area of the egg (see REPRODUCTION). A single sperm will penetrate the egg's membrane, and the sperm nucleus will enter the egg interior and fuse with the egg nucleus. The result is a fertilized egg, or ZYGOTE. Some animals can reproduce asexually, by parthenogenesis, but the processes of embryo development thereafter are like those in other animals.

The first period of actual development is characterized by rapid sequential division of the egg into many small cells, or blastomeres. Growth usually does not occur during cleavage. The cleavage process ends with the formation of the blastula stage. A blastula is a ball of cells with a cavity, the blastocoel, in the center. The structure of the blastula varies depending on the amount of yolk present, which significantly alters the pattern of cleavage.

Following the blastula stage, the embryo enters a critical period when extensive cell rearrangements occur. The blastula is transformed in shape into what is called a gastrula. This consists of two cell layers, and the cavity at the center is now called the archenteron, or primitive gut.

In higher animals, at the end of gastrulation the two-layered gastrula is converted into a three-layered embryo with the establishment of the three germ layers: the ectoderm, mesoderm, and endoderm. All organs of the body are derived from these three germ layers. Therefore, they can be categorized with respect to germ-layer origin. The ectoderm gives rise to the nervous system, skin, sense organs, mouth cavity, and parts of the ears. The mesoderm gives rise to muscles, bone, connective tissues, and the circulatory, excretory, and reproductive systems. The endoderm gives rise to the digestive and respiratory systems.

After the organ rudiments are formed, they increase in size and their cells differentiate. Cell differentiation involves the synthesis of specific molecules that are characteristic of the functioning adult organ, such as, for example, the production of thyroxin by thyroid cells. By the time of birth or hatching, the embryo is ready to become an independent organism.

---

embryology [em-bree-ahl'-uh-jee] Embryology is the study of the DEVELOPMENT and GROWTH of a multicellular life-form during the period in which an EGG is transformed into an independent organism. Embryology is usually considered a zoological science, although plants in their early stages of development are called embryos as well (see PLANT). From a broad point of view, embryology includes all processes of development from egg to adulthood. Commonly, however, it is taken to include only those events leading to birth, hatching, or the onset of METAMORPHOSIS.

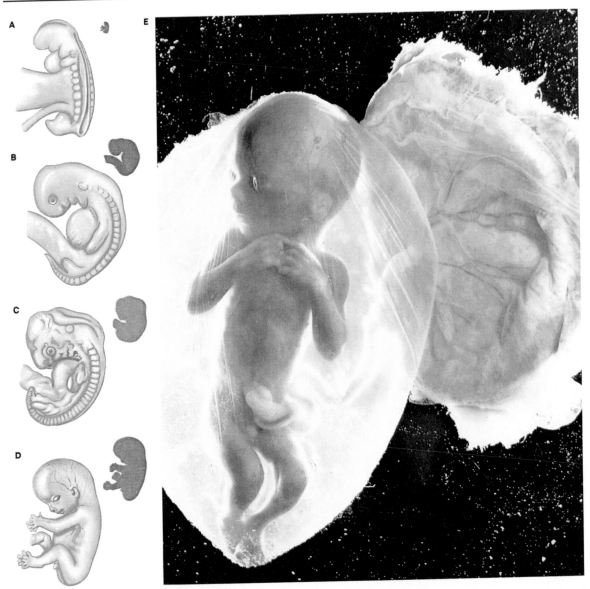

After three weeks of growth (A) the human embryo has a primitive heart and neural tube. Limb buds and rudimentary eyes form by the end of week five (B) and become more developed in week six (C). By the end of eight weeks, the embryo is called a fetus (D). The gray figures beside each drawing indicate actual sizes of embryos. After four months (E) the fetus has grown to about 20 cm (8 in) in length and appears more "human." The skin has become thicker and the first hairs appear on the eyebrows and scalp. The umbilical cord, visible in this picture, attaches the fetus to the placenta (right), which connects with the mother's circulatory system.

Embryology began as an observational science in the 17th century. The field of descriptive embryology dealt with the chronology of changes in the tissues (histology) and the general form (morphology) of the embryo. As such information accumulated, embryologists also began to compare embryos of various species with one another. This field of comparative embryology came to be of great interest in the 19th century, because of the evolutionary theory of Charles Darwin and in particular because of the notion of naturalist Ernst Haeckel that the evolutionary history of an organism can be observed in its developing embryo. This idea, that "ontology recapitulates phylogeny," has since been discredited and in fact proved a hindrance to the growth of embryological science.

Experimental embryology arose in the 20th century, when researchers began to interfere with the normal processes of development in order to understand them better. It has since largely been replaced by embryological studies at the molecular level. Most research today deals with the ontology of molecular diversity and with how different biochemical substances direct and control development. The origin of cellular diversity in an individual composed of genetically identical cells is one of the central themes of embryological research. Cancer research is another field of great relevance, because malignant cells possess many of the characteristics of the more primitive, or embryonic, state.

Embury, Philip   Philip Embury, b. Ireland, c.1728, d. August 1773, was a founder of METHODISM in the United States. Converted by John WESLEY's preaching, he immigrated to America in 1760. He settled in New York City, where, encouraged by his cousin Barbara Hick, "the mother of American Methodism," he began preaching in 1766. By 1770 he had moved to a farm up the Hudson Valley, where he preached and organized Wesleyan societies until his death.

emerald   Emerald, the most valuable of GEMS, is a transparent variety of BERYL that owes its bright green color to small amounts of chromic oxide. Large flawless stones are very rare. Softer and lacking the fire and brilliance of DIAMOND, emerald is usually step cut, with elongated narrow facets and an oblong table, to enhance its color. The finest stones come from Colombia, where they are mined from a dark, bituminous limestone at Muzo, near Bogotá; these deposits were discovered by the CONQUISTADORS in the late 1500s, during the Spanish conquest. Emeralds were discovered in the 19th century near Sverdlovsk in Siberia and in the Blue Ridge Mountains of western North Carolina. They are now synthesized using a process developed by Carroll F. Chatham in the 1930s.

The emerald (Greek: *smaragdos*) of the ancients probably referred to a number of distinct species of green stones; that mentioned in the Old Testament probably was carbuncle garnet. Superstitions concerning the em-

Emeralds occur in nature as transparent to semitransparent, grass-green hexagonal crystals (left). The crystals are usually cut into oblong gems shaped in a traditional step cut (right).

erald, BIRTHSTONE for May, are that it soothes the eyes, preserves chastity, cures dysentery, prevents epilepsy, and drives away evil spirits.

Emerson, Ralph Waldo   The American lecturer, essayist, and poet, Ralph Waldo Emerson, b. Boston, May 25, 1803, d. Apr. 27, 1882, is considered the leading exponent of American TRANSCENDENTALISM. The son of a Boston Unitarian minister, Emerson followed in his father's footsteps by attending the Boston Latin School (1812–17) and Harvard College (1817–21). After running a school for young women, Emerson returned (1825) to Harvard to study divinity and was licensed to preach the next year. Suffering from tuberculosis, he sailed to Charleston, S.C., and St. Augustine, Fla., in late 1826. When he returned to Boston he preached from various pulpits before being ordained (1829) pastor of the Second Unitarian Church in Boston. In September 1829 he married Ellen Louisa Tucker. After Ellen's death in February 1831, Emerson underwent a religious and personal crisis, and the next year he resigned his pulpit and sailed for Europe. There he met William Wordsworth and Thomas Carlyle, forming a lifelong friendship with the latter.

After his return to the United States in 1833, Emerson moved (1834) to Concord, Mass. In 1835 he married Lydia Jackson and began a career as a lecturer. He soon became one of the leaders of the transcendental movement, questioning the established views of literature, philosophy, and religion. He helped to start the Transcendental Club in 1836 and published *Nature* (1836), showing the organicism of all life and the function of nature as a manifestation of invisible spiritual truths. In 1837 he delivered his address "The American Scholar," often called America's literary declaration of independence, before Harvard's Phi Beta Kappa Society; in 1838 his address before the Harvard Divinity School challenged the foundations of conservative UNITARIANISM. He cofounded (1840) the transcendentalists' periodical, the *Dial*, and edited it from 1842 until its collapse in 1844. Emerson established himself during the next decade with the publication of *Essays* (2 vols., 1841, 1844), *Poems* (1847), *Nature: Addresses and Lectures* (1849), and *Representative Men* (1850). By 1850 he was becoming known as the "sage of Concord." *English Traits* (1856) analyzed English society and compared it with American society, and *The Conduct of Life* (1860) showed his growing conservatism, as he balanced his earlier belief in freedom against the "beautiful necessity" of fate.

Essays. Emerson's essays contain his most famous writing. In "Self-Reliance" he tells man to trust himself against a society that "everywhere is in conspiracy against the manhood of every one of its members." He holds that "nothing can bring you peace but yourself." In "Compensation" Emerson asserts that in the nature of the soul is "the compensation for the inequalities of condition." In "Friendship" he recommends truth and tenderness as the basis of genuine friendship.

Emerson shows the interconnectedness of all life in an

Ralph Waldo Emerson, an American essayist, lecturer, and poet, began his literary career espousing and promoting transcendentalist thought. His work influenced such individualistic writers as Thoreau and Whitman.

almost pantheistic view of god-in-matter in "The Over-Soul." "The Poet" lists Emerson's qualifications for the artist who is "the sayer, the namer, and represents beauty." "Experience" describes the "lords of Life" that form man's existence: illusion, temperament, succession, surface, surprise, reality, and subjectiveness. These optimistic early essays are balanced by conservatism in later work, best illustrated in "Fate" (1860). Here, Emerson warns of a "pistareen-Providence" that keeps man from seeing and facing "the terror of life." He also balances his earlier belief in absolute freedom by tempering it with fate or necessity, holding that the natural order of things, which once served merely to guide man, now limits him.

Influence. A seminal figure in American literary history, and central to the so-called American Renaissance, Emerson exerted great influence on his contemporaries, both by his financial support of them, as of A. Bronson Alcott, and by his intellectual companionship, as with his Concord neighbor, Henry David THOREAU. Emerson's discussions of organic form (everything proceeds from a natural order that is followed but not imposed by man), self-reliance, optimism (evil does not exist as an actual force, being merely the absence of good), compensation, universal unity (or the Over-Soul), and the importance of individual moral insight were also all influential in forming the literature and philosophy of 19th-century America. In poetry, too, Emerson was an important force. His organic theory of poetry ("it is not meters, but a meter-making argument that makes a poem") and his view of poets as "liberating gods" or prophets did much to counteract poetic conservatism and led to the experimental verse of Walt Whitman.

emery Emery is a mineral assemblage, an intimate mixture of 60–75% CORUNDUM and 10–35% MAGNETITE that since ancient times has been used as an ABRASIVE because of its hardness (7–9). Sometimes including HEMATITE and SPINEL, emery is a black, fine-grained mineral deposit that resembles an iron ore.

Emigrant Aid Company In April 1854, a month before the KANSAS-NEBRASKA ACT became law, Eli Thayer, a Massachusetts free-soiler, organized the Massachusetts Emigrant Aid Company to assist emigrants in settling the West. The organization soon expanded into the New England Emigrant Aid Company. Though ostensibly established as a profit-making enterprise, the real purpose of the company was to raise funds to send abolitionists to Kansas.

Between 1854 and 1855 the society sent about 1,240 settlers to Kansas. Many of them went equipped with Sharps rifles, called Beecher's Bibles after the well-known antislavery minister Henry Ward Beecher (see BEECHER family). Although they did not represent a large portion of Kansas settlers, their influence was great. The presence of these New England–sponsored antislavery settlers provoked large numbers of proslavery Missourians to cross into Kansas. By 1857 the New England Emigrant Aid Company had disappeared, but conflict between the two groups had turned the territory into "bleeding Kansas."

Emilia-Romagna [ay-meel'-ee-ah-roh-mahn'-yah] Emilia-Romagna is a region of north central Italy. It has an area of 22,123 km^2 (8,542 mi^2) and a population of 3,924,199 (1988 est.). The region is bordered by the Adriatic Sea in the east, the Po River in the north, and the Ligurian and Tuscan Apennines in the west and south. Emilia-Romagna consists of eight provinces, and BOLOGNA is the regional capital. Topographically, the region is divided into an extensive fertile plain in the north and east and the Apennines in the south and west. Emilia-Romagna is one of the most important agricultural regions of Italy. The region takes its name from a Roman road, the Aemilian Way, which ran from Rimini to Piacenza. After the Romans the region came under Lombard, Byzantine, and papal rule. Independent medieval cities gave way to duchies during the Renaissance. Subsequent French and Austrian rule ended with the region's absorption into united Italy in 1860.

eminent domain Eminent domain is the right of the government to take private property for public use (for example, to build a highway), or to authorize the taking of property by private companies when doing so is beneficial to the public (for example, to build a railroad). The process of acquiring the property is called condemnation; although consent is not required, under DUE PROCESS the owner must receive a fair hearing and just compensation for the property.

As late as 1848 the doctrine of eminent domain was contested in the United States as a novel and dangerous exercise of state power. In that year, however, the U.S. Supreme Court, in *West River Bridge* v. *Dix*, held that Vermont could exercise its right of eminent domain to condemn the 100-year franchise of a toll-bridge company and convert the bridge into a free public highway. The

Supreme Court, in 1876, upheld the right of the federal government to take land by eminent domain within a state, and in 1896 it upheld the federal government's right to take Gettysburg battlefield for a national cemetery.

See also: CONSERVATION; ZONING.

---

emir [e-meer'] In Muslim countries, emir (or amir, an Arabic word meaning "commander") is a title conferred on high military officials and provincial governors who exercise administrative or financial control. The term also designates a descendant of Muhammad the Prophet.

Emmet, Robert Robert Emmet, b. 1778, d. Sept. 20, 1803, led an unsuccessful insurrection in Dublin and was later celebrated as a martyr for the cause of Irish nationalism. After a sojourn (1800–02) on the Continent with leaders of the Society of UNITED IRISHMEN as they planned a French-assisted revolt against British rule, Emmet returned to Ireland. The uprising, on the night of July 23, 1803, ended in a debacle. Emmet fled but was soon captured. Found guilty of treason, he made a dramatic speech about his revolutionary ideals. He was then hanged.

Emmy Awards Presented annually by the National Academy of Television Arts and Sciences (NATAS), the Emmy Awards recognize excellence in television performance and production. They have been presented each spring since 1949; since 1955 the awards ceremony has been televised regularly. The "Emmy" trophy is a statuette designed by Louis McManus. Suggested by former NATAS president Harry Lubcke, the name is a play on "Immy," a common nickname for the image orthicon tube.

Emory University Established in 1836, Emory University is a private institution just outside Atlanta, Ga. It is associated with the United Methodist Church. The university has schools of law, theology, nursing, medicine, and dentistry, and its library houses the Joel Chandler Harris manuscripts.

---

emotion Emotions are biopsychological reactions of an individual to important events in his or her life. These reactions involve special kinds of feelings, widespread physiological changes, impulses to action, and, sometimes, overt behavior.

Theories. Experimental researchers have identified emotions in lower animals as well as in humans. Harry HARLOW, for example, has demonstrated that rhesus monkeys who are isolated from all human or animal contact for the first six months of their lives show signs of severe depression. Charles DARWIN, in *The Expression of the Emotions in Man and Animals* (1872), said that it is possible to recognize emotions in animals by observing their naturally occurring expressive behavior and by knowing the circumstances under which they occur. The

expression of anger signals the likelihood of attack; the expression of fear, the likelihood of retreat. This information usually decreases the chances of a deadly fight and thus increases an organism's chances for survival.

Sigmund FREUD, the founder of psychoanalysis, believed that memories were often not reported because they were repressed. Some patients could remember neither the disturbing incident nor the emotion connected with it. Although the emotion was not conscious, it nevertheless continued to influence the patient's behavior. For example, if someone constantly frowns, or grinds his or her teeth, has dreams in which people are being murdered, that person is most likely angry, regardless of what he or she says.

A third major figure in the history of emotion theories was the American philosopher William JAMES. He believed that the perception of a situation led to behavior (for instance, running away) that created physiological changes and that a person's recognition of these internal changes was the actual feeling of emotion.

Although there are some differences among emotions in the pattern of changes in the autonomic nervous system, however, the differences are not large.

In the past few decades a number of theories have been advanced as to which part of the brain controls emotion. The hypothalamus, the limbic system, and the amygdala have all been proposed as centers of emotional expression. Other researchers have approached the issue in behavioral terms, emphasizing interpretations and appraisals as determiners of emotions. Work in delineating the basic emotions, such as joy, sadness, anger, and fear, was undertaken during this time and has become a standard way to talk about emotions. Cross-cultural studies have been completed that demonstrate that people all over the world make the same facial expressions when experiencing a basic emotion.

Primary and Secondary Emotions. It has often been assumed that some emotions are primary and others secondary. Although the names given to the primary emotions differ slightly, most of the following are agreed upon: *anger, fear, joy, sorrow, acceptance, disgust*, and *surprise*. Rarely, if ever, does a person experience one emotion alone. Secondary emotions are formed by the mixing of primary emotions, like the mixing of primary colors to form others.

Empedocles [em-ped'-uh-kleez] Empedocles, c.484–c.424 BC, was a Greek doctor, poet, and philosopher. To account for real change, he assumed that there must be more than one kind of matter, and he postulated four roots as elements: earth, air, fire, and water. Love and hate were considered principles of attraction and repulsion that alternately dominated the universe in a recurring cycle. Empedocles presented a kind of biological theory of natural selection in an imaginative poem, *On Nature*. He also played an important role in the development of the Western or Sicilian school of Greek medicine. He cured a plague at the Sicilian city of Selinus and claimed he was a god. One legend, which forms the basis of Matthew Arnold's poem *Empedocles on Etna*, held that Empedocles, tired of life and wanting people to believe that the gods had taken him with them, committed suicide by leaping into the crater of Mount Etna.

emphysema

emphysema [em-phuh-zee'-muh]   Emphysema is a disease of the LUNGS characterized by structural changes in the small air sacs (alveoli) where exchange of oxygen and carbon dioxide takes place with the blood. The alveoli become dilated, and the alveolar walls undergo dissolution, causing the formation of larger and larger air spaces within the lungs. As alveolar walls are destroyed, they no longer act to hold the small airways, or bronchial tubes, open. These changes result in a reduction of the total functioning surface for gas (O_2 and CO_2) exchange. There is also obstruction to the flow of air out of the lungs, as the bronchioles tend to collapse during the act of expiration.

Because BRONCHITIS often coexists with emphysema, obstruction to airflow may be further compounded by a swelling of the membrane lining the airways, which causes a further narrowing of the bronchial lumen. In addition, the process results in the unequal involvement of tissue, and hence maldistribution of air within the lungs. Generally there is diminished oxygen supply to vital organs and the retention of excessive carbon dioxide in the blood.

Airway obstruction, the predominant feature of emphysema, results in the trapping of too much air within the enlarged air spaces, and overinflation of the lungs occurs until the patient's chest takes on a barrel-shaped appearance. Shortness of breath is the outstanding symptom, and the disease often progresses until the patient is incapable of the slightest exertion. Death may eventually result from accompanying infections, respiratory failure, or cardiac complications.

The exact cause of emphysema is unknown. Cigarette smoking is associated with the disease, and industrial pollution may play a role. In some cases a genetic link is suspected.

Progression of emphysema can be retarded by abstinence from smoking, and symptomatic relief can in some cases be provided by drugs that dilate the bronchi. Prompt treatment of infections is vital. Certain types of emphysema may be localized to a portion of one or both lungs and can be treated by surgical removal.

empire

empire   An empire is a political entity that usually comprises a large area and diverse ethnic groups, epitomized by the Roman Empire, which from the 1st to the 4th centuries AD encompassed western and southern Europe, North Africa, and the Near East. The word *empire* is derived from the Latin *imperium*, which originally meant "supreme administrative power," and was later applied to the territory over which the power was exercised. In medieval and modern European history, the name was used for the BYZANTINE EMPIRE, the HOLY ROMAN EMPIRE, and other states that regarded themselves as heirs of Rome. In French history *empire* refers to the regimes of Napoleon I (the First Empire) and Napoleon III (the Second Empire).

The word was also used to describe the colonial possessions of the European powers in Asia, Africa, and the Americas, especially during the 19th century (see BRITISH EMPIRE; FRENCH COLONIAL EMPIRE); by extension the acquisition of such colonies is called IMPERIALISM. The ruler of an empire is usually called an emperor (from the Latin *imperator*), again in imitation of the rulers of ancient Rome.

See also: COLONIALISM; ROME, ANCIENT.

Empire State Building

Empire State Building   The Empire State Building, built in 1930–31 and situated on Fifth Avenue in New York City, was the tallest building in the world until 1971, when the first tower of the World Trade Center in New York City was completed. Originally 381 m (1,250 ft) in height, the Empire State Building was increased to 448.7 m (1,472 ft) by the addition of television antennas in 1950. The building was opened during the Depression, and much of its 200,485 m^2 (2,158,000 ft^2) of rentable space remained vacant for some time; as a result, the owners depended on sightseers (more than 4 million people by April 1940), who paid to visit the observation decks, to pay the building's taxes. Designed by the firm of Shreve, Lamb, and Harmon and built at a cost of $41 million, the limestone-and-steel building was not structurally innovative. Its most distinctive architectural characteristics are its shimmering facade, partially composed of a chrome-nickel-steel alloy, and the monumental foyer.

Empire style

Empire style   The Empire style of decorative arts flourished in France during the Consulate (1799–1804) and Empire (1804–15) of NAPOLEON I; it was widely copied throughout the Bonaparte kingdoms of Italy, the Two Sicilies, Spain, and Holland, in the Confederation of the Rhine, and elsewhere in Europe. The style was modeled on the forms and decorative motifs of classical antiquity and reflected Napoleon's personal admiration for the arts of imperial Rome, whose grandeur, majesty, and formal purity expressed the artistic aspirations of his own re-

Jacques Louis David's Madame Récamier *(1800) illustrates the Empire style that prevailed in Napoleonic France. David's austere style and such fashions as the sleigh couch and high-waisted gown recalled the grandeur of Rome. (Louvre, Paris.)*

gime. The leading designers of the period were Charles Percier and Pierre François Léonard Fontaine, whose *Recueil de décorations intérieures* (Collections of Interior Design, 1801 and 1812) defined the basic principles and designs of the Empire style as a mixture of antique forms with Napoleonic symbols (bees, giant *N*s in laurel wreaths, and eagles) and Egyptian devices (sphinxes, scarabs, lotus flowers, caryatids, and pyramids), the latter coming into fashion after Napoleon's Egyptian campaign of 1798. Among the most important exponents of the Empire style were the ornamentalist Pierre de La Mésangère, the furniture maker Georges JACOB (who was employed by Napoleon in refurnishing imperial palaces, such as the Tuileries and Fontainebleau), the bronze workers Pierre Philippe Thomire and Delafontaine, the silversmiths Martin Guillaume Biennais and Jean Baptiste Claude Odiot, and the wallpaper manufacturers Jacquemart and Bénard, Jean Zuber, and Joseph Dulfour.

empiricism   Empiricism is the name of a broad tradition in Western philosophy. The term comes from the Greek *empeiria*, meaning "experience"; the basic thesis of empiricism is that legitimate human knowledge arises from what is provided to the mind by the senses or by introspective awareness through experience. Most empiricists do not consider knowledge gained through the imagination, authority, tradition, or logical intuition legitimate.

Empiricism is contrasted with the philosophical tradition of RATIONALISM, which holds that human reason apart from experience is a basis for some kinds of knowledge. Knowledge attainable by reason alone, prior to experience, is called *a priori* knowledge; knowledge based upon experience is called *a posteriori* knowledge. Rationalists claim that knowledge can be derived from certain a priori truths by DEDUCTION. Empiricists claim that for human beings there is no pure reason and that all knowledge is a posteriori and derived from sense experience by INDUCTION. Rationalists focus particular attention on mathematics and related disciplines as providing examples of a priori truths. John Stuart MILL, however, was the first to suggest that even these are merely confirmed generalizations from experience.

The history of empiricism in the West includes thinkers whose views are highly diverse. ARISTOTLE is sometimes said to be the founder of the empiricist tradition, although there are important rationalistic elements in his philosophy. In the Middle Ages, Thomas AQUINAS held the doctrine that "there is nothing in the intellect that is not first in the senses." In the modern period, empiricism was articulated by a series of thinkers who became known as the British Empiricists. John LOCKE, George BERKELEY, and David HUME were the leading figures of this group. Because of its affinity with natural science, empiricism remains an important philosophical point of view. The POSITIVISM and PRAGMATISM of the 20th century represent versions of empiricism.

See also: EPISTEMOLOGY.

employment and unemployment   Employment is the state of having a job for which one receives money or other compensation; unemployment is the lack of such a job. Employment and unemployment also refer to the numbers or percentages of people in the labor force who have or do not have jobs. Because most people must work in order to support themselves and their dependents, governments strive to keep levels of unemployment low and usually measure unemployment rates carefully.

Official U.S. statistics on employment and unemployment are derived from a monthly sample survey of households. The unemployment rate is the percentage of unemployed persons in the total labor force, which is composed of all persons over the age of 16 who either have or are seeking jobs. (United States military personnel were included as part of the total labor force beginning in 1983.) Persons who are not looking for work (including "discouraged" job seekers) are not counted as part of the labor force. Another measurement, the employment ratio, is the percentage of the total working-age population who have jobs.

The Occupational Structure

The types of activities that occupy most workers vary, sometimes dramatically, from one country to another and from one time to another. In most developing countries (and in all countries prior to the 19th century) the vast majority of the labor force work in the agricultural, or primary, sector. Work is almost entirely manual, and most of the country's labor power is devoted to the basic task of feeding the population. Fully developed countries are able to divert far more of their productive resources into other pursuits. In the United States and Canada, for example, only 4 and 7 percent, respectively, of all employed persons work in agriculture, fishing, and mining, compared with more than 70 percent in India.

The manufacturing, or secondary, sector is the traditional backbone of a developed industrial economy. In the United States and Western Europe, employment in this sector grew quickly with the rise of the factory system during the 19th century, before leveling off in the mid-20th century and declining gradually thereafter. In 1990 about one-fourth of all U.S. and Canadian jobs were in manufacturing, construction, and mining. With the advent of new technologies, employment in manufacturing has demanded greater technical skills. This has reduced unskilled labor's share of total employment.

The most striking change in employment in the developed countries during recent years, however, has been the rapid expansion of the service, or tertiary, sector. This sector includes the service trades, teaching, much clerical work, research, medicine, and all other occupations not directly involved in the production of goods. About two-thirds of all employed persons in the United States, Canada, and other developed countries work in the tertiary sector. Work in the service sector, on the average, demands greater literacy and is more likely to be white collar than work in the other two sectors. The rapid expansion of this part of the economy has not, however, altered the character of employment as much as was once expected; the clerical work that forms a large part of this sector can be as repetitive and tedious as work in agriculture or manufacturing (see SERVICE INDUSTRIES).

Changes in the structure of employment in industrial countries have been accompanied by changes in the composition of the labor force. During the 20th century the percentage of women, especially of married women, in the total labor force has increased as the numbers of younger and older workers have declined.

Unemployment and Underemployment

Although unemployment occurs among all social and occupational groups, it is especially concentrated among the young, some racial and ethnic minorities, women, and those who live in declining urban areas. The lack of jobs for the young is a worldwide phenomenon, with unemployment rates for youths in some developing countries exceeding 20 percent.

Some unemployment is cyclical; that is, it varies with business conditions. Workers are laid off when business is bad and rehired when conditions improve. Seasonal unemployment occurs in agriculture, construction, and other industries that are more active at some times of the year than at others. A third type of unemployment is known as frictional. It arises from the normal process of turnover in the labor market as new workers enter the market and search for work and existing workers quit one job to look for a better one.

Structural unemployment, caused by imperfect labor-market adjustment, is the most intractable of the main types. Workers and resources do not move freely to places where they are needed, and long-term structural unemployment is often the result. Many workers who lost their jobs in the Appalachian coal industry during the 1950s and '60s, for example, or in the midwestern steel industry in the 1970s and '80s, lacked skills useful for other local industries. They did not migrate from the region, nor did new industries arrive that could employ them.

A person whose productive capacities are not fully used is underemployed. A part-time worker seeking a full-time job or a skilled worker doing unskilled work for lack of a job in his or her own trade, for example, is underemployed. Underemployment occurs for the same reasons as unemployment, although it is more difficult to measure.

Prior to the 1980s the level of unemployment in European countries was generally lower than in the United States. Between 1980 and 1989, however, the American economy generated 16 million additional jobs, while the combined figure for comparable European economies was less than 2 million.

Policies Toward Unemployment

Governments adopt various policies to restrain rates of unemployment and to train workers for more productive employment. FISCAL POLICY and MONETARY POLICY affect unemployment by stimulating or depressing business activity. Such policies, however, guide the economy as a whole; they are too broad to be aimed at specific industries or population groups that need special help. Programs to create new jobs, to upgrade workers' skills, or to retrain workers for new types of jobs are often adopted to fill these needs.

Governments often set a minimum wage allowable by law to ensure that employees receive at least a subsistence income, although it is sometimes claimed that this increases unemployment among the young by raising the cost of hiring unskilled workers. Governments may also provide subsidies to workers or industries to relocate, and they may direct resources into selected industries or sectors through ECONOMIC PLANNING. The U.S. government combats DISCRIMINATION in hiring and promotion through EQUAL OPPORTUNITY and affirmative-action laws and policies. Finally, many governments seek to ameliorate the often devastating effects of long-term unemployment through UNEMPLOYMENT INSURANCE and social-welfare programs.

---

emu [ee'-mue]   The flightless emu, *Dromaius novaehollandiae*, family Dromiceidae, order Casuariiformes, is widespread over Australia's open country. The largest bird except for the ostrich, the adult emu stands about 1.5 m (5 ft) high and weighs about 55 kg (120 lb). Emus run at speeds of up to 50 km/h (30 mph), defend themselves by kicking, and swim well. The hairlike plumage of both sexes is brownish gray. The slightly smaller male incubates a clutch of 8 to 10 dark green eggs for about 60 days, each egg weighing about 0.7 kg (1.5 lb).

The emu has served as a source of food, and it appears on the Australian coat of arms. Farmers often consider it a pest, however, because it may break fences and feed on crops (while also eating many insects). Smaller

The swift-running emu is exceeded in size only by the ostrich. It is most closely related to the cassowaries and other flightless ratite birds.

species were exterminated by settlers on nearby islands, but Australian emus survived even a brief "emu war" in 1932—an attempt at their mass destruction by using machine guns.

emulsion [ee-muhl'-shuhn]

An emulsion is a colloidal system consisting of one liquid dispersed in another liquid. The roles of dispersed phase and dispersing medium may be reversed, depending on which component predominates in amount; accordingly, both oil-in-water and water-in-oil emulsions exist. Because the droplets of the dispersed component rapidly coalesce to form a separate layer, a third component, called the emulsifying agent, must be present to stabilize the emulsion. A familiar and important example is the emulsifying action of SOAPS AND DETERGENTS, which stabilize oil-in-water emulsions and make possible the removal of oil and grease by water.

See also: COLLOIDAL STATE.

enamel

The use of enamel in art can be traced back to the ancient civilizations of Egypt, Mesopotamia, and Greece. Enamel, in the broadest sense of the word, refers to any hard coating, either decorative or protective, that is applied to another material; its use in art is more precisely defined. There are four basic types of enameling used for artistic purposes: CLOISONNÉ, champlevé, *basse-taille*,

Enameling fuses powdered glass to a metallic base through firing. Enamel consists of 50% silica (A), 35% red lead (B), and 15% potash (C) which, when fused, yield a neutrally colored flux (D). The addition of metallic oxide (E) creates colored enamel (F). Transparent enamel (G) is produced by adding tin oxide (H); lead oxide (I) creates opaque enamel (J). Five enameling methods are shown below: champlevé (K), cloisonné (L), plique-à-jour (M), which is a backless, translucent form of cloisonné, basse taille (N), and painted enamel (O).

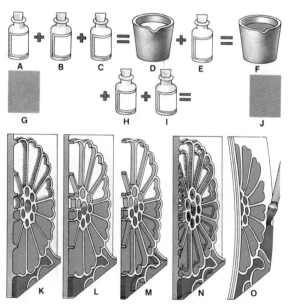

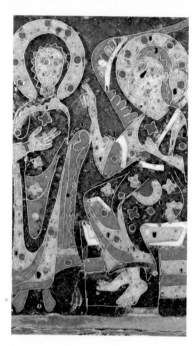

This 11th century cloisonné enamel, Mary Magdalen with Angel at the Grave of Christ, ornamented the Evangelarium of Ariberto da Antimiano, archbishop of Milan (1018–c.1037). Cloisonné technique is the application of enamel to a design described by metal strips; this surface is then fused, filed, and polished. Cloisonné art in Western Europe attained its highest degree of perfection in the 11th and 12th centuries.

and painted enamel, all on metal bases. In addition, enamel colors may be painted on and fused to both glass and ceramics.

Cloisonné is made by soldering thin strips or wires of gold, silver, or copper onto a base plate of the same metal. These cloisons, or compartments, are then filled with powdered glass, which consists of silica or flint mixed with soda or potash and colored with metallic salts. This is baked in a kiln to fuse the glass to the metal. Small amounts of enameling have been found on some artifacts from Mycenae dating from the 13th century BC. The finest cloisonné enameling was created in Europe as early as the 6th century AD, during the Byzantine era (see BYZANTINE ART AND ARCHITECTURE). Most Byzantine cloisonné was done on gold to achieve the opulence and brilliance so important to that civilization.

In the 12th century the technique of champlevé appeared, in which the design is engraved into the base plate. In earlier champlevé this INTAGLIO design is filled with powdered translucent glass colors and fired; it is then polished so that it is flush with the surface of the metal. The technique appeared first in the lands conquered by the Romans, including Britain, and later in Irish Celtic art. As the Byzantine use of gold declined, champlevé was often done on copper or even bronze. Because neither copper nor bronze shows translucent enamel to its best advantage, and because copper discolors when heated, opaque rather than translucent enamels were used to fill the engraved designs that were cut into wrought or cast pieces. Champlevé was an economical way to imitate cloisonné. The chief centers for Romanesque champlevé were the Rhine and Meuse river region of Germany (Mosan work), Limoges in France, and

Spain. Throughout the early 13th century, Mosan work, undoubtedly the finest type of champlevé, often used illuminated manuscripts of the period as models.

Basse-taille, literally bas-relief, enameling results when a design is engraved deeply into the base plate with many variations in depth. Translucent enamels are laid into the intaglio design, which produces shading from light to dark depending on the depth of the glass layer. This technique probably began in Italy in the 13th century, and then spread in the following century to Northern Europe and Scandinavia.

The technique of enameling *en rond bosse*, or in the round, evolved in the 15th century from the earlier techniques, permitting enamel to be applied to 3-dimensional forms. The metal, usually gold, was first roughened to prevent the color from scaling off. Enamel *en rond bosse* was often combined with cloisonné and champlevé, as well as set gems, to produce large objects of great splendor and elegance.

The last technique, painted enamel, came into use in the 15th century in Italy, France, and the Netherlands. Two variations were popular: grisaille, a monochrome work usually in shades of brown, gray, and white; and *camaïeu*, or CAMEO, in which the design is built up in white enamel on a dark ground and then carved back, as in cameo glass.

◼

encaustic painting [en-kaws'-tik] Encaustic painting involves the use of pigments mixed with molten wax in what is called a "burning-in" process (from the Greek word *enkaustikos*); that is, after the colors have been applied, heat is passed over the surface to fuse them into a homogeneous layer. Colors are made by mixing pigments with hot beeswax and resin. The wax protects the paints, enabling them to retain their brilliance. Encaustic paints have been applied successfully to stone, plaster, wood, and canvas. A brush, spatula, or palette knife may be used.

The technique was invented by the ancient Greeks; some of the earliest existing examples are Egyptian mummy portraits dating from the 1st to the 3d century AD. A contemporary practitioner of encaustic painting is Jasper Johns.

◼

encephalitis [en-sef-uh-ly'-tuhs] Encephalitis is an acute inflammation of the brain. The majority of cases are caused by infection, usually viral, although encephalitis may occasionally occur in a case of poisoning by certain chemicals. Among the most common types of encephalitis are Saint Louis encephalitis and herpes simplex type. The herpes virus can be contracted in the birth canal, with encephalitis occurring with primary infections of major organ systems in the newborn. Some causal viruses are carried by various species of tick. Encephalitis may also occur following infectious diseases such as measles or after vaccination. The causative infection may enter the brain via the bloodstream. Many other infections involve only the surface membranes (see MENINGITIS), whereas others affect both meninges and brain and cause meningoencephalitis.

The symptoms of encephalitis progress from headache, fever, and quickened pulse to confusion, stupor, and coma, ultimately leading to death. Some success in treatment has been achieved with antiviral agents. The later therapy is begun, the more severe the aftereffects may be; these aftereffects can include retardation, epilepsy, hydrocephalus (enlargement of the head caused by an accumulation of fluid), and deafness. Encephalitis can be fatal within hours. When it is concurrent with a flu epidemic, the correct diagnosis is often delayed or missed.

◼

Enchi Fumiko [en'-chee foo'-mee-koh] Enchi Fumiko, b. Oct. 2, 1905, d. Nov. 14, 1986, was a Japanese novelist whose fiction is noted for its poetic richness and psychological depth. Her works offer a complex portrait of the Japanese woman, drawn with the studied objectivity of a mature artist. Her masterpiece is probably *The Waiting Years* (1957; Eng. trans., 1971), which describes the humiliations experienced by a woman who is forced to find her husband a mistress.

◼

Encina, Juan del [ayn-see'-nah] Juan del Encina, b. July 12, 1468, d. *c.*1530, was a Spanish poet and composer. Known as the founder of Spanish Renaissance drama, he wrote a series of dramatic eclogues that were published in his *Cancionero* (1496) and that, until the end of the 16th century, were an important source of style and subject matter for Spanish playwrights. Encina created a style of comic peasant speech that was much imitated by later dramatists. His eclogues, or pastoral plays, contain rustic songs for which he also composed the music.

◼

enclosure In European history, enclosure was the process whereby land formerly held in common was divided into fenced (thus enclosed) fields. Under MANORIALISM, the system of landholding that prevailed during the Middle Ages, land was farmed under the open-field system. The arable land of each estate was usually divided into three large tracts; one lay fallow each year (in rotation), and the others were divided into strips, some of which were allotted to the peasants for cultivation. Meadow and wasteland were used in common for grazing and other purposes.

Beginning in the 13th century in England, individual lords were legally permitted to break these large areas into smaller, enclosed fields, of which they enjoyed sole use. Although agricultural efficiency was eventually increased, great hardship ensued for the dispossessed peasants. The main periods of enclosure in England were the 16th century and from about 1750 to 1845, when the process was more or less completed. Elsewhere in Europe enclosure was largely a 19th- and 20th-century development effected by government decree.

◼

encomienda [en-kohm-yen'-dah] *Encomienda* was a form of slavery practiced in the Spanish colonies in

America between the 16th and 18th centuries. In 1503 the Spanish crown began to grant or deed (*encomendar*) loyal colonists a certain number of Indians to use as laborers for a specific number of days a year. The colonist (*encomendero*) pledged to look after his Indians' health, pay them wages, and encourage their conversion to Christianity. However, the settlers very often badly mistreated their charges, exacting more work for less than the stipulated pay. The Spanish crown, pressed by reformers such as Bartolomé de LAS CASAS, attempted to control and then abolish the system through the New Laws of 1542. Although the laws were resisted, *encomienda* died out gradually to be replaced by *repartimiento*, a very similar but more closely regulated system of forced labor. By the end of the 18th century, *repartimiento* had largely given way to debt peonage.

encounter groups see GROUP THERAPY

---

encumbrance An encumbrance is a burden, charge, or LIEN on real or personal PROPERTY amounting to a legal right or interest in favor of a person other than the owner. Encumbrances include such rights and burdens as EASEMENTS, LEASES, MORTGAGES, real-estate taxes and other assessments, restrictive COVENANTS, and rights of way. Encumbrances generally apply to real property, tending to restrict total use or ownership of the piece of land and consequently reduce the market value. The contract of sale and the deed between the buyer and seller of real estate will specify what encumbrances, if any, apply to the property.

---

encyclical [en-sik'-lik-ul] An encyclical is a letter circulated by a bishop to all of the churches in his care. In modern times, the best-known encyclicals have been issued in the Roman Catholic church by popes and in the Anglican Communion by the bishops who assemble at Lambeth every ten years. Papal encyclicals are not an exercise of the pope's INFALLIBILITY, but rather of his ordinary teaching authority. As such, they can be rejected for good reasons without disrupting one's communion with the church.

---

encyclopedia [en-sy'-kloh-pee'-dee-uh] Derived from the Greek *enkyklios paideia* for a "circle of learning," the term *encyclopedia* refers to any work of one or more volumes with articles on all branches of knowledge, or on all aspects of one subject.

History

The modern encyclopedia has evolved from works vastly different from those which are now called encyclopedias, and it has gone through many modifications.

Early Developments. Plato's nephew and disciple, Speusippus, devised an encyclopedialike work (*c*.370 BC) to record permanently the master's lectures on natural history, mathematics, and philosophy. Cato's *Praecepta*

ad filium (*c*.183 BC), reflecting Roman pragmatism, was a self-tutorial work, conceived to develop skills and knowledge in practical fields. The earliest truly encyclopedic work was PLINY THE ELDER's prodigious *Historia naturalis* (AD 77), a series of anthologies concerned with topics such as botany, metallurgy, and cosmography.

Learned and monumental compilations in increasingly elaborate classificatory frameworks dominated the field from ancient times to the invention of movable type in the 15th century. These works were written in Latin and were limited to a scholarly audience. They range from Marcus Terentius VARRO's *Disciplinarium libri IX* (*c*.50 BC) to the works of BOETHIUS, Cassiodorus, and ISIDORE OF SEVILLE (with parallel efforts in Arabia and China). They culminate in Vincent of Beauvais's *Speculum majus* (The Greater Mirror), completed in 1244. Brunetto Latini's *Li livres dou trésor* (*c*.1266), however, represented a significant breakthrough because it was written in French and directed to the Italian upper class.

16th to 18th Century. In the mid-16th century, encyclopedic dictionaries edited by Charles Estienne (1504–64) became popular, proving that readers generally preferred the alphabetic arrangement. Had it not been for the German writer Paul Scalich, the term *encyclopedia* might never have been firmly established. Scalich's *Encyclopaedia, seu Orbis disciplinarum* (Encyclopedia, or Knowledge of the World of Disciplines, 1559) brought the term back into prominence. Among 17th-century dictionaries that were akin to modern encyclopedias was Louis Moréri's *Le Grand Dictionnaire historique* (1674), which went through 20 editions and expanded from a single volume to a ten-volume edition by 1759.

Other encyclopedists in England, Germany, and elsewhere used Moréri's encyclopedia as a model. John Harris (*c*.1666–1719) compiled the first comparable work in the English language. His *Lexicon Technicum, or an Universal English Dictionary of Arts and Sciences* (1704) eliminated biographical entries and downgraded lexicographical elements. Mathematics, physics, and technology were given much attention; bibliographies, engraved plates, and practical advice were incorporated in the text.

A second and even more influential English encyclopedia was Ephraim Chambers's *Cyclopaedia; or an Universal Dictionary of Arts and Sciences* (1728), based on a Baconian classification that covered 47 arts and sciences. With its cross-references and headings, this was the first encyclopedia to closely resemble the modern form. Chambers's effort inspired foreign imitators, among them the significant and justly celebrated *Encyclopédie*.

During this period, precursors of the one-volume encyclopedia appeared in Germany. These included Johann Hübner's *Reales Staats- und Zeitungs-Lexikon* (1704), J. Mencke's *Compendiöses Gelehrten-Lexikon* (1715), and C. G. Jöcher's *Allgemeines Gelehrtenlexikon* (1750–51). French contributions were of a different nature. Pierre BAYLE's *Dictionnaire historique et critique* (1697) offered no new structural features; its importance lay in its skeptical tone.

The Encyclopédie. This nonconformist attitude pervaded the Encyclopédie, which, in its earliest version, was a

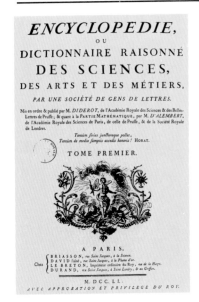

(Left) *The title page of Volume I of the* Encyclopédie *(1751), published in Paris under the supervision of Denis Diderot and Jean d'Alembert, is shown. As a product of the French Enlightenment, it had an incalculable influence on intellectual thought.* (Right) *The project's collaborators were painted by the Swiss artist Jean Huber at a meeting in Voltaire's home.*

translation of the Chambers *Cyclopaedia* into French (1743–45). At first André Le Breton, the Parisian publisher, acquired the necessary royal privilege and issued a prospectus for a five-volume edition. Disagreements with translators led to a cancellation of the original plan, and the privilege to publish a lengthier and more ambitious work was obtained. Finally, the first volume of the *Encyclopédie* appeared in 1751 under the coeditorship of Denis DIDEROT and Jean d'ALEMBERT.

The *Encyclopédie*'s structure was based on Francis BACON's classification of universal knowledge, the most complete and systematic inventory of areas of knowledge and human achievement at that time. Articles were written, not by unknowns, but by leading figures of the French Enlightenment such as Rousseau, Turgot, Montesquieu, and Voltaire. Applied sciences and arts were included, reversing the earlier practice of rejecting utilitarian subjects.

The Britannica. The other major encyclopedia of the 18th century was the *Encyclopaedia Britannica* (1768–71), which has the longest history of any current encyclopedia. It was begun by three Scots, Andrew BELL, Colin MacFarquhar, and William Smellie, who combined the traditional classificatory and dictionary arrangements. Up to that time the alphabetical sequence of subjects in dictionaries had fragmented knowledge and had resulted in overly brief coverage of important topics. On the other hand, the subject arrangement had intimidated nonspecialists, and the sequence of topics had been dictated by compilers' preferences. For example, the Arabic encyclopedias placed food and women at the end, the German gave prime space to science and technology, and the French favored philosophy and mathematics.

The *Britannica*'s solution was to include 45 major subjects but to apportion their treatment within a single alphabetical sequence of main and subordinate articles. The second edition included such improvements as living biographies, maps, and bibliographies for major articles. The ninth (1875–89) and eleventh (1910–11) editions achieved a pinnacle of style and substance.

19th Century to the Present. In the 19th century, the encyclopedia took firm hold as a popular form of publication. The Industrial Revolution, the rise of the middle class, and the revolution in human expectations had joined with advances in printing technology to transform the making of encyclopedias into a potentially profitable business. Among successors to the *Britannica* in England were two very ambitious enterprises, the *Encyclopaedia Metropolitana* (1817–45) and *Penny Cyclopaedia* (1833–43).

The *Metropolitana* was conceived by the poet Samuel Taylor Coleridge. Beautifully illustrated, supported by authoritative writers, and based on a well-thought-out and comprehensive classification scheme, the project failed, in part, because it abandoned alphabetical arrangement and took 28 years to produce, by which time much of its material had become obsolete.

The *Penny Cyclopaedia* was intended to "impart useful information to all classes of the community, particularly to such as are unable to avail themselves of experienced teachers, or may prefer learning by themselves." This effort also failed. The English could not count on translation of their work into other languages because French, not English, was the language read by most cultured Europeans. Also, the belief that factory laborers would be eager to educate themselves was too optimistic.

In 19th-century Germany, three encyclopedias rose to prominence. In 1808, Friedrich Arnold Brockhaus (1772–1823) acquired the rights to the *Frauenzimmer-*

Lexikon, a women's encyclopedia. The resultant Brockhaus *Konversations-Lexikon* set a pattern with its simple, popular, brief articles and its reliability, currency, and generous scope of coverage. Brockhaus was deficient only in science and technology. In these areas, Joseph Meyer's *Der Grosse Konversations-Lexikon* (1840–52) excelled. Finally, the Herder *Konversations-Lexikon* (1853–57) was published to serve the special requirements of Roman Catholic Germans.

In France, Pierre LAROUSSE and Augustin Boyer founded the Librairie Larousse & Boyer in 1852 and published the *Grand dictionnaire universel du XIXe siècle* (1865–76), a composite dictionary-encyclopedia that, in one version or another, is still published today. Ferdinand Camille Dreyfus launched *La grande encyclopédie* between 1886 and 1902.

The *Encyclopedia Americana* was begun as an English-language adaptation of the seventh edition of Brockhaus, produced by Francis Lieber between 1829 and 1833. It was the first general encyclopedia to bear an American imprint. *Chambers's Encyclopedia* (1860–68) also used the Brockhaus *Konversations-Lexikon* as a model.

Similar activity occurred in Eastern Europe with the issuance of the Polish *Encyklopedia Powszechna* (1858–68) and the Russian *Entsiklopedichesky Slovar* (1895). The *Great Soviet Encyclopedia* (*Bolshaya Sovetskaya Entsiklopedya*), modeled after the Meyer *Grosse Konversations-Lexikon*, appeared (1926–47) in 65 volumes. Its second edition was translated into English (31 vols., 1973–82).

Two European encyclopedias, both compiled under totalitarian regimes, have been universally acclaimed: the Spanish "Espasa" or *Enciclopedia universal ilustrada europeo-americana* (1905–70) for its elegance, superior graphics, and thorough treatment of the arts; and the Italian *Enciclopedia italiana di scienze, lettere ed arti* (1929–39) for its authoritative articles, especially its biographies and coverage of art.

Types of Encyclopedias

Three types of encyclopedia exist: the encyclopedia in name only, the special encyclopedia, and the general encyclopedia. Publications such as the *Encyclopedia of Associations* (a directory) or the *Modern Plastics Encyclopedia* (a catalog) are in the first category. Special encyclopedias include collections of specially commissioned essays on a specialized subject (*The Encyclopedia of American Foreign Policy*, for example) or alphabetically arranged articles on a general subject. These latter include such works as the *Encyclopedia of the Social Sciences, McGraw-Hill Encyclopedia of Science and Technology*, and *The Encyclopedia of Religions*. In contrast, the general adult encyclopedia attempts to present the entire realm of knowledge, from the arts and sciences to current critical issues, to data on significant places and persons.

Although several encyclopedia works for children had been published, the first major encyclopedia of this type was *The Children's Encyclopedia*, prepared under the editorship of English writer Arthur Mees in 1908. In 1910 a

U.S. version of the Mees work, *The Book of Knowledge*, appeared; a totally reworked edition, *The New Book of Knowledge*, was first produced in 1966. American encyclopedias for older children include *World Book* (1917), *Compton's* (1922), and *Merit Students Encyclopedia* (1967).

Perhaps the encyclopedia has endured because, despite its flaws and limitations, it provides a more satisfactory solution to its special challenge—the synthesis and summary of useful knowledge—than do competing forms. As Blaise Pascal observed, "Since we cannot know all that is to be known of everything, we ought to know a little about everything."

---

endangered species Endangered species are those whose populations have been so reduced that they are threatened with extinction. Thousands of species are included in this category. The International Union for the Conservation of Nature and Natural Resources (headquartered in Morges, Switzerland) publishes a list of threatened mammals, birds, reptiles, and amphibians. This list is growing at an alarming rate, as is the number of endangered species of fish, invertebrates, and plants.

Causes of Extinction

During the millions of years that preceded the appearance of human life, extinction of organisms was linked to large-

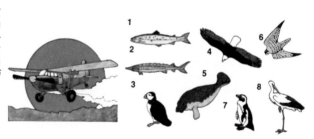

(Above) *Pesticide pollution endangers the bald eagle (4), peregrine falcon (6), and Japanese white stork (8). Oil spills threaten the puffin (3). Water pollution has also led to the decline of the North Atlantic salmon (1), Atlantic sturgeon (2), manatee (5), and black-footed, or jackass, penguin (7) of South Africa.*

(Below) *Animals threatened by introduced predators include the Galápagos giant tortoise (9); kakapo (10), a New Zealand ground parrot; the shrewlike Cuban solenodon (11); kagu (12) of New Caledonia; and Indian wild ass (13). Cattle plague affects the western giant eland (14) of Africa.*

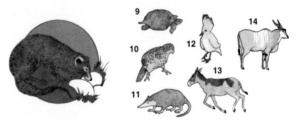

Superstitions endanger such animals as the aye-aye (15), which some Madagascans regard as an evil spirit. Horns of the black rhinoceros (16) and sika deer (19) are thought to have aphrodisiac properties. The Japanese giant salamander (17) and Formosan serow (18) are used for healing.

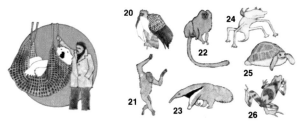

The capture and collection of animals for zoos, pets, or research threatens populations of the Philippine monkey-eating eagle (20); orangutan (21) of Borneo and Sumatra; golden marmoset (22); giant anteater (23); Texas blind salamander (24); Mediterranean spur-thighed tortoise (25); and golden frog (26) of Panama.

scale geologic and climatic changes, the effects of which were translated into major alteration of the environment. Environmental change is still the primary cause of the extinction of animals, but now the changes are greatly accelerated by human activity. Clearing land for farms and towns, lumbering, mining, building dams, and draining wetlands all alter the environment so extensively that ecosystems may be completely destroyed. With a burgeoning human population requiring food, shelter, and clothing and constantly demanding more energy-using devices, the temptation to exploit land for human use without regard for consequences is great.

Frequently, several forms of environmental change are responsible for the disappearance of species. For example, as tropical forests are cut down, primates have progressively smaller feeding and living spaces. They also become more accessible to hunters, who kill monkeys for food and trap many primates for sale as pets, research animals, and zoo specimens. Some animal species may move into human communities when their own are destroyed. Extermination of marauding monkeys, roaming tigers, or foraging deer is easy to justify by people whose livelihood is threatened.

POLLUTION is another form of environmental change. Many species of birds lay thin-shelled or shell-less eggs as a result of ingesting degradation products of DDT and other chemicals that enter the food chain. Species of salamanders in New England are dying out because their habitats are watered by ACID RAIN. Industrial wastes dumped

(Above) *Species whose numbers have been seriously reduced by hunting and over-exploitation include the dugong (27); Bengal and Siberian tigers (28) and (29); several subspecies of leopard (30); the arrau (31), a South American river turtle; Atlantic walrus (32); blue whale (33); European beaver (34); Nile crocodile (35); green turtle (36) of tropical seas; American alligator (37), which is no longer in danger of extinction; wild yak (38) of Tibet; chinchilla (39) of the Chilean Andes; and snow leopard (40) of central Asia.*

(Below) *Shooting for "sport" has endangered many species. The giant sable antelope (41) of Angola has been killed for trophies. Motorized hunting parties are responsible for massive slaughters of the Arabian ostrich (45), which may be extinct, and the Arabian oryx (43). In the 1940s whooping cranes (42) numbered fewer than two dozen, but much-publicized conservation efforts have kept this North American bird from extinction. Other animals threatened by shooting include the trumpeter swan (44) of North America; Aleutian Canada goose (46); California condor (47); and polar bear (48), which was shot for bearskin rugs.*

Many native species are considered pests or predators of introduced species in the new habitats created by human settlement. Animals persecuted for this reason include the Tasmanian wolf, or thylacine (49); wolf (50); black-footed ferret (51) of western North America; Spanish imperial eagle (52); Mexican grizzly bear (53), once believed extinct and still in serious danger; Hawaiian hawk (54); Spanish lynx (55); sea otter (56); northern kit fox (57); Florida cougar (58); and Asiatic lion (59), which exists only in the Gir Forest of western India.

Deforestation, wetland drainage, and other forms of habitat destruction have contributed to the decline of the white-throated wallaby (60); mountain gorilla (61) of central Africa; indri (62), a lemurlike primate of Madagascar; several subspecies of cutthroat trout (63) in the western United States; Komodo dragon (64) on a few Indonesian islands; chimpanzee (65); Everglade kite (66); Hawaiian gallinule (67); Indian elephant (68); woolly spider monkey (69) of Brazil; Comanche Springs pupfish (70) of Texas; and British swallowtail butterfly (71)

in the Mediterranean have so depleted the oxygen supply that some species of bacteria that decompose sewage have been wiped out and the nutrient cycles disturbed.

Many species have been exterminated or endangered because people have killed the animals for food, fur, hides, or feathers. As a result of WHALING, some whale species are close to extinction. Clams and fish are endangered by varying combinations of naturally changing environments, pollution, and overharvesting.

Protective Measures

Many endangered species received a measure of relief in 1973, when the 80 nations that originally participated in the Convention on International Trade in Endangered Species of Wild Flora and Fauna agreed to halt imports of endangered species. In the same year, the U.S. Congress enacted the Endangered Species Act, ensuring protection of the vital habitat of any endangered species. The International Whaling Commission forbids the hunting of blue, bowhead, humpback, gray, and right whales; it set a moratorium on all commercial whaling, effective in 1986, but Japan, Iceland, and Norway continued to hunt and kill certain species.

National parks throughout the world are often havens for threatened organisms. Research stations have been set up to replenish breeding stock and to discover more about the environment and its interrelationships. Several ZOOLOGICAL GARDENS serve similar functions, and in many countries groups of concerned citizens have banded together to bring about change and to distribute information.

Endara, Guillermo [en-dah'-rah,gee-yer'-moh] Guillermo Endara, b. May 12, 1936, was sworn in as president of Panama on Dec. 20, 1989, during the U.S. invasion of that country. Endara, an attorney, headed the opposition coalition said to have won the May 1989 presidential election, which was annuled by a government tribunal controlled by strongman Manuel NORIEGA. Endara advocated national reconciliation and sought U.S. aid in rebuilding the economy.

Endecott, John   John Endecott, b. c.1588, d. Mar. 15, 1655, came to Massachusetts with 60 English colonists in 1628 and joined an already existing settlement at Salem. When the Massachusetts Bay Colony was formed in 1630, he became its chief of militia; his expedition against the Pequot Indians in 1636 helped provoke the PEQUOT WAR of 1637. Between 1644 and his death, he served several terms as the colony's governor.

Enders, John F.   American virologist John Franklin Enders, b. West Hartford, Conn., Feb. 10, 1897, d. Sept. 8, 1985, helped to perfect the techniques by which disease viruses are grown in quantity for the production of vaccines. Enders obtained his doctorate at Harvard University in 1930 and joined the faculty there. In 1946 he established a laboratory at Boston's Children's Hospital, where he and coworkers perfected the growing of viruses in test tubes and found how to identify them by their effects on culture cells. For this work Enders was awarded the 1954 Nobel Prize for physiology or medicine along with former students Fred C. Robbins and Thomas Weller.

---

endive [en'-dive]   Endive, or escarole, *Cichorium endivia*, is a frost-hardy annual or biennial leafy vegetable in the family Compositae. Closely related to chicory, it is cultivated much like lettuce, although it is sometimes blanched before harvest to remove its bitter flavor.

Endive, or escarole, is a frost-hardy, lettucelike plant. Mildly bitter in flavor, it is eaten raw in salads or cooked as a green vegetable. There are two major types, the broad-leaved illustrated here, and a very curly-leaved variety.

---

endocrine system [en'-doh-krin]   The endocrine system consists of specialized glands located in different parts of the body. These glands secrete chemical substances called HORMONES, which transfer information from one set of cells to another. This enables the organism to adjust various activities of the body to the changing demands of the external and internal environment. The endocrine glands have no ducts connecting them to their target organs or tissues (they are hence often called the ductless glands), and so they liberate hormones directly into the bloodstream.

Mammalian endocrine glands include the hypothalamus, pituitary, thyroid, parathyroid, thymus, pancreas, adrenal, testis, and ovary. Invertebrates possess few glands, and many of these are simply clusters of nerve cells. Arthropods have neurosecretory structures in the eyestalks, brain, and ganglia that regulate reproduction, molting, development, pigmentation, water balance, blood-sugar level, and heart rate. The conventional ductless glands of arthropods include the following: Y organs, or prothoracic glands (molting hormones); corpora allata (juvenile hormones); nongonadal androgenic glands (male hormones); ovaries; and intestinal glands that secrete a developmental factor.

Relation to Nervous System

The hormonal system of the body is to a great extent subject to control by the NERVOUS SYSTEM. Both systems share control of the body's activities; they differ, however, in two key features. Hormones act slowly and their effects are long lasting, whereas the nervous system acts quickly and produces almost instantaneous responses. The endocrine system also relies on the circulatory system to deliver hormones to target tissues, whereas the nervous system has a series of interconnected neurons to communicate directly with tissues under their control. The systems resemble each other in that they both require chemical mediators to convey information.

Hormone Relations

Adjustments in endocrine, or hormonal, activity are triggered by the requirements of body tissues for changes in various physiologic processes. The adjustments of many endocrine glands are regulated by the anterior part of the PITUITARY GLAND, or hypophysis. The anterior pituitary is connected with the central nervous system by neurohormonal pathways via the hypothalamus; for this reason the hormonal system is ultimately under nervous control. The anterior pituitary exerts its influence on other glands by tropic hormones, which cause target glands to produce tissue-affecting hormones.

Hypothalamus. The hypothalamus (see BRAIN) is con-

The endocrine glands secrete hormones that affect behavior and body functions such as growth and metabolism. The pituitary (1) is situated in the brain. The thyroid (2) is in front of the larynx, and four parathyroid glands (3) lie on the surface of the thyroid. The thymus (4) is located near the heart. The adrenal glands (5) on top of each kidney are composed of two layers, each of which functions as a separate gland. The pancreas (6) and the sex glands, consisting of ovaries (7) in a female and testes (8) in a male, not only function as endocrine glands but have other roles.

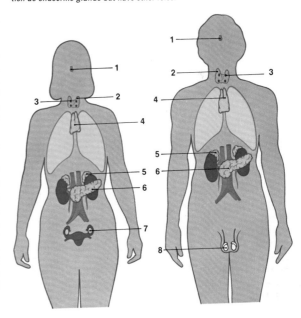

nected to the pituitary gland (hypophysis) by way of the infundibular stalk, and it secretes several factors that stimulate or inhibit various pituitary secretor cells. In some fishes the neurosecretory factors reach their target cells by diffusion. In other animals the neurons release their products into blood vessels that transport the secretions to the pituitary.

Hypothalamic neurons also send processes into a pituitary region where the antidiuretic hormone vasopressin and oxytocin or other chemically related substances are stored for release into general circulation. These substances stimulate kidney water retention, vascular and uterine smooth-muscle contraction, and milk let-down. Hypothalamic neurosecretory factors may function as neurotransmitter substances in other parts of the brain and the nervous system.

Pituitary. The pituitary gland produces several hormones. Growth hormone promotes muscle and bone growth and affects general metabolism. Prolactin's effects range from hydromineral metabolism in fish to milk production in mammals. Thyroid-stimulating hormone (TSH) stimulates thyroid tissue growth and the production of thyroid hormones. Adrenocorticotropic hormone (ACTH) has a similar effect on the adrenal cortex and also influences metabolism in adipose tissues. Gonadotropins stimulate the production of male and female SEX HORMONES, spermatogenesis, and ovarian development. Intermedin, melanophore-stimulating hormone, influences skin pigmentation.

Thyroid. The THYROID, ultimobranchial, and PARATHYROID glands are closely associated in their location and development. Thyroid glands extract iodine from the blood and concentrate it for synthesis of the hormones thyroxine and triiodothyronine, which play a major role in general metabolism, including growth and maturation of the individual.

Parafollicular cells, which form ultimobranchial glands in nonmammalian vertebrates, secrete calcitonin in response to excess blood calcium. Parathyroid hormone (PTH), secreted by glands found only in terrestrial vertebrates, elevates blood-calcium levels. Calcitonin and PTH influence bone integrity, calcium absorption, and renal electrolyte excretion.

Adrenal Gland. The mammalian ADRENAL GLAND is composed of two endocrine tissues, a medullary region and a surrounding cortex. In other vertebrates the tissues may be separated. The adrenal medulla secretes epinephrine and norepinephrine in emergency or emotional situations, stimulating the heart and the vascular system. Epinephrine also stimulates various metabolic activities and elevates blood-glucose levels.

Cortical tissue produces numerous steroid hormones of two general types, whose properties overlap and whose distribution varies among different animals. Glucocorticoids are principally metabolic hormones and are secreted in response to ACTH. Elevated levels of glucocorticoids exert a negative feedback on ACTH secretion, play a role in adjustment to stress, and raise blood-sugar levels. They also have anti-inflammatory properties in pharmacologic dose levels. Mineralocorticoid secretion, princi-

pally aldosterone, is stimulated by the renin-angiotensin system; aldosterone increases the retention of body salt by reducing renal sodium excretion.

Gonads. Under the complex control of gonadotropins, the gonads produce steroid sex hormones that stimulate reproductive processes, maintain secondary sex characteristics, and influence growth, development, and behavior. Testes produce androgens. Ovaries produce estrogens, progesterone, and relaxin. Relaxin conditions the reproductive tract and birth canal during pregnancy and parturition. The placenta, as a temporary endocrine organ, secretes a lactogenic hormone, gonadotropins, estrogens, progesterone, and relaxin.

---

endocrine system, diseases of the   Diseases of the endocrine system often result from excess release (hypersecretion) or insufficient release (hyposecretion) of HORMONES by one or more glands. Hypersecretion of hormones, usually associated with either tumors or abnormal cell proliferation (hyperplasia), occurs because of overstimulation of endocrine glands by factors such as tropic hormones from the pituitary gland. Hyposecretion results from several causes, including surgical or radiation destruction of glands, glandular atrophy, congenital defects in the enzymes involved in hormone synthesis, and dietary conditions.

Hypothalamus and Pituitary Gland

The hypothalamus modulates pituitary activity through release or release-inhibitor hormones, which regulate the release of such hormones as growth hormone (GH), adrenocorticotropin (ACTH), follicle-stimulating hormone (FSH), prolactin (PRL), luteinizing hormone (LH), and thyroid-stimulating hormone (TSH). Secretion from the hypothalamus is affected by such mechanisms as stress, plasma levels of corticosteroid, time of day, and estrogen levels, as well as by tumors, encephalitis, or inflammatory lesions.

GH oversecretion is usually caused by a pituitary tumor. If oversecretion occurs before closure of the epiphyses of the long bones (maturity), the person may grow to 2.1 to 2.4 m (7 to 8 ft), a condition termed pituitary gigantism. If oversecretion occurs after closure of the epiphyses (in adults), the resulting condition, called acromegaly, is marked by overgrowth of the mandible, causing protrusion of the jaw; bone overgrowth and thickening of soft tissue, resulting in coarsening of facial features; wide hands and broad fingers; and, often, soreness of joints. GH excess may also induce deficiency of other hormones.

Cushing's disease is caused by an ACTH-secreting tumor that leads to excess secretion of steroid hormone. The syndrome is characterized by a "moon" face, thin skin, muscle wasting and weakness, and high blood pressure.

Hypersecretion of prolactin due to a pituitary tumor or secondary hypopituitarism (removal of hypothalamic influence) is associated with galactorrhea, amenorrhea, and infertility.

Decreased production of all pituitary hormones simultaneously is termed panhypopituitarism. GH deficiency leads to growth retardation, or dwarfism, most often appearing in childhood. Loss of TSH results in hypothyroidism, evidenced by intolerance to cold, slow speech, and anemia. ACTH loss leads to secondary hypoadrenocorticism—in particular, the loss of cortisol secretion. Symptoms include weakness, circulatory insufficiency, and low blood pressure. Loss of FSH and LH leads to amenorrhea, atrophy of the genitals, absence of libido, absence of sperm and ova production, and infertility. The absence of prolactin inhibits lactation. Treatment of panhypopituitarism consists of replacing the lost hormones; fertility cannot, however, be restored in this manner.

The hypothalamus makes antidiuretic hormone (ADH, vasopressin) and oxytocin, which are released in response to stress and suckling. A deficiency in ADH, called diabetes insipidus, causes large volumes of water to be lost in urine. This state results from either tumors or disease in the hypothalamus or unresponsiveness of the kidney tubules to ADH. If the cause centers in the hypothalamus, the disease can be corrected with animal or synthetic ADH.

Thyroid

A deficiency of the hormones thyroxine and triiodothyronine (hypothyroidism) originates either in the thyroid (primary) or in the controlling pituitary or hypothalamus (secondary). Undersecretion of these hormones in fetal or infant life results in cretinism. Symptoms include dry, wrinkled skin, an enlarged tongue, a drooling mouth, and a broad face. Infants are apathetic and have a slow heart rate and subnormal temperature. As children, they are small for their age; as adults, they are dwarfs. Children are minimally to severely mentally retarded unless the condition is recognized and treated early.

The reaction to the deficiency of thyroid hormone in adults is called myxedema. Symptoms include severe edema, gradual personality changes, hoarse speech, yellowish skin, mental apathy, and slowed brain waves. Treatment consists of administration of thyroid hormone. Myxedema can affect other endocrine glands, and it interferes with reproduction.

Hyperthyroidism is marked by nervousness, rapid heart rate, atrial arrhythmias, hypermetabolism, heat intolerance, and weight loss. The most common form is Graves' disease (exophthalmic GOITER), with protrusion of the eyeballs and an enlarged thyroid. Circulating thyroxine and triiodothyronine are elevated, due to abnormal antibodies that bind to TSH receptors in thyroid cells. Endemic goiter results from a dietary iodide deficiency. TSH is secreted in increasing amounts, stimulating thyroid growth in an attempt to increase synthesis of iodide-containing thyroid hormones.

Adrenal Gland

Adrenocortical insufficiency (ADDISON'S DISEASE) is the result of adrenal atrophy due to AUTOIMMUNE DISEASE or partial destruction by diseases such as tuberculosis or cancer. A progressive loss of aldosterone (mineralocorticoid) and cortisol (glucocorticoid) production leads to muscle weakness and fatigue, hyperpigmentation of the skin, low blood pressure, and weight loss, often with nausea and diarrhea.

The adrenal normally secretes sex hormones that exert minor effects on reproductive function; some congenital enzyme deficiencies, however, lead to a marked overproduction of adrenal androgens. The resulting adrenogenital syndrome is characterized by virilization in the female.

Cortisol excess caused by the administration of large amounts of exogenous hormones, or by a glucocorticoid-secreting tumor, or by the excess secretion of ACTH causes Cushing's syndrome. Severe protein wasting results in thin skin that is easily bruised and rupture of the subdermal tissue that produces purple streaks. Also observed are pronounced muscle weakness and a redistribution of body fat.

Excess mineralocorticoid secretion leads to a marked potassium depletion and to retention of excess body sodium. Symptoms include muscle weakness, hypertension, excess urine volume, and alkalosis due to the potassium loss. This is the clinical picture of Conn's syndrome, which is usually caused by an aldosterone-producing adrenal tumor.

The hypersecretion of epinephrine or norepinephrine from adrenal medullary tumors often results in severe hypertension. Patients may have headaches, palpitations, chest pains, extreme anxiety, skin pallor, and blurred vision.

Parathyroid

Deficiency of parathyroid hormone (PTH) results in hypocalcemia and neuromuscular hyperexcitability. This is caused either by accidental removal or damage during removal of the thyroid gland, or by a form of autoimmune disease.

Hyperparathyroidism increases the rate of bone resorption, resulting in hypercalcemia. Chronic PTH excess may cause some osteolytic changes in the skeleton, and the hypercalcemia may lead to deposition of calcium salts in soft tissue such as the kidney, which may cause irreversible damage.

Gonads

Premature development of the ovaries and testes through early but normal hypothalamus-pituitary maturation, without apparent cause, accelerates body growth but ultimately results in stunting due to premature fusing of the growing ends of bones. This condition is called true sexual precocity; reproduction is possible as early as age 6. Brain tumors and encephalitis can also result from premature development of the ovaries and testes.

The development and functioning of the male reproductive organs and related structures and characteristics depend on the pituitary gonadotropins. LH stimulates the cells of the testes to produce androgen. FSH stimulates the sperm-producing cells of the sex glands. Primary male hypogonadism consists of a failure to synthesize androgens (testosterone) due to defective enzymes. Secondary male hypogonadism is caused by a lack either of LH, which inhibits androgen production, or of FSH, which leads to a failure of spermatogenesis. A deficiency of FSH and LH prior to or during puberty delays the development of genitalia and secondary sex characteristics. Dwarfism occurs if GH is also deficient.

Primary amenorrhea, the failure of a woman to begin menstruation, may be due to pituitary dysfunction (such as tumors) or to other endocrine disorders (such as hypothyroidism). Secondary amenorrhea halts the menstrual cycle.

Pancreas

Juvenile DIABETES mellitus (Type 1) results from both hereditary and environmental factors and is characterized by insulin deficiency and a high blood-sugar level. Without insulin treatment, the disease rapidly causes dehydration, ketoacidosis, low blood volume, hypotension, coma, and death.

endogamy [en-dahg'-uh-mee] Endogamy (Greek: "within marriage") is the social custom or expectation that a person will marry within a culturally defined social group or groups of which he or she is a member. Unlike the converse case of exogamy, universal endogamy is not characteristic of any particular kind of social group. Endogamous groups can include an ethnic group, a village population, a social class, a caste, or a nationality group.

endometriosis [en-doh-mee-tree-oh'-suhs] Endometriosis is a common disease in women of reproductive age. It involves tissues of the endometrium, the inner lining of the uterus (see REPRODUCTIVE SYSTEM, HUMAN). During the menstrual cycle, built-up endometrial tissues normally are shed if pregnancy does not occur. In as many as one out of every 15 women, however, some endometrial cells escape from the womb into the pelvic cavity, where they attach themselves and continue their hormone-stimulated growth cycle. They may also migrate to remote parts of the body.

Mild endometriosis sometimes clears up by itself or as a result of pregnancy. Frequently, however, the disease leads to painful inflammation, soreness, and infertility. Life-threatening complications can also arise, depending on the site of tissue growth. Surgical removal of the ovaries is often required. Nonsurgical treatment centers on using medication to suppress secretion of the female hormone estrogen.

endoplasmic reticulum   see CELL

endorphin   see OPIATE RECEPTOR

endoscope [en'-doh-skohp] An endoscope is a tubular instrument equipped with optical viewing and lighting systems. It is used for examining the inside of certain cavities or hollow organs of the body, or to perform sur-

gery. An endoscope often uses a fiber-optic telescope that provides excellent visibility of minute internal structures. Either suction or pumping methods are used to clear the visual pathway to the target organ. An endoscope can also be equipped with a laser that can vaporize, coagulate, or cut structures, often with more ease and flexibility than a more rigid cutting knife. Endoscopy is visual examination of the interior of the body by inserting an endoscope through a natural body opening, such as the throat, or through a small incision into the body cavity. It is a less invasive method that causes less scarring and a quicker recovery time than other surgical techniques. Several million endoscopic procedures are performed in the United States each year. Common types of endoscopes are the cytoscope to view the bladder, the bronchoscope to view the lungs, the otoscope to view the ear, the arthroscope to view the knee and other joints, and the laparascope to view the female reproductive structures. The most common surgery performed through endoscopy is biopsy, the removal of tissue for microscopic study to detect a malignancy.

endothermic and exothermic reactions   see THERMOCHEMISTRY

endowment   see FOUNDATIONS AND ENDOWMENTS

Endymion [en-dim'-ee-uhn] In Greek mythology Endymion was a handsome young shepherd. As he lay sleeping on Mount Latmos, SELENE, the moon goddess, fell in love with him. When the Olympian gods guessed her secret, Zeus offered Endymion perpetual youth on the condition that he remain asleep forever. Eternally young, and beloved by the moon, Endymion sleeps on.

energy   Energy, from the Greek *energia*, meaning "in-work," is the capacity for doing work. Energy can be measured in terms of mechanical work, but because not all forms of energy can be converted into useful work, it is more precise to say that the energy of a system changes by an amount equal to the net work done on the system.

In classical physics, energy, like work, is considered a scalar quantity; the units of energy are the same as those of work. These units may be ergs, joules, watt-hours, foot-pounds, or foot-poundals, depending on the system of units being used. In modern science, energy and the three components of linear momentum are thought of as different aspects of a single four-dimensional vector quantity, much as time is considered to be one aspect of the four-dimensional spacetime continuum.

Forms of Energy

Energy exists in many different forms. The form that bodies in motion possess is called kinetic energy. Energy may be stored in the form of potential energy, as it is in a compressed spring. Chemical systems possess internal energy, which can be converted by various devices into useful work; for example, a fuel such as gasoline can be

Four hundred hectares (1,000 acres) of mirrored solar collectors stretch across the Mojave Desert, producing electricity for Southern California. This type of solar technology has proved highly efficient in desert regions, where there is an abundance of sunlight and available land.

burned in an engine to propel a vehicle. Heat energy may be absorbed or released when the internal energy of a system changes while work is done on or by the system.

Mass and Energy. Einstein first established that mass itself is one form of energy; this is indicated by the well-known relation $E = mc^2$, which may be interpreted to mean that if a mass m can be converted into energy, the amount of energy produced is given by the product of the mass and the square of the speed of light, c. Because the speed of light is a large number ($c = 3 \times 10^{10}$ cm/sec), an enormous amount of energy is contained in ordinary matter; but it is generally impractical to convert this mass into useful energy.

Kinetic Energy. Masses in motion possess kinetic energy. For example, an object of mass m moving with speed v possesses kinetic energy $\frac{1}{2}mv^2$. A wheel with a MOMENT OF INERTIA I, spinning about its center of mass with an angular speed ω, has a kinetic energy $\frac{1}{2}I\omega^2$. If either of these objects could be brought to rest by appropriate means, useful work could be done; for example, a pulley and rope attached to the wheel could be made to lift a weight. When the speed of an object becomes comparable to the speed of light, such expressions for kinetic energy are no longer valid and must be modified according to the theory of RELATIVITY.

Potential Energy. A compressed spring possesses energy that can be converted to work by allowing the spring to exert a force against an external device and to move until the spring assumes its original length. When a mass of weight W is lifted to a height h, the mass possesses gravitational potential energy Wh, which can be regained by lowering the mass. Electrical charges possess electrostatic potential energy, which can be converted to work by allowing the charges to move toward or away from each other.

Internal Energy. Energy contained in a system by virtue of the motions of, and forces between, the individual atoms and molecules of the system is called internal energy. When the internal energy of a body changes, heat energy is sometimes generated or absorbed. For example, if a piece of metal is placed in a flame, the temperature of the metal will rise: heat has been absorbed by the metal and its internal energy has been increased; the atoms of the metal are vibrating more rapidly and may be at different distances from one another.

Mechanical Equivalent of Heat. The relationship between heat and work was established when it was noticed that when a fixed amount of work is done on a fluid—stirring it, for example—a fixed amount of heat is always generated (see THERMODYNAMICS). The relationship between heat energy, which is usually measured by observing temperature changes in an object, and mechanical work is called the mechanical equivalent of heat. The relationship is expressed as follows: 1 calorie = 4.186 joules, where 1 calorie is the heat required to raise the temperature of 1 gm of water 1° C.

Energy in Other Forms. Numerous other forms of energy exist. Radiant energy is energy contained in the form of electromagnetic oscillations, such as light and radio waves. Currents in the coils of an electromagnet generate magnetic fields, which can be thought of as storing energy in the form of magnetic field energy. Processes of BETA DECAY, such as the radioactive decay of the neutron into a proton, electron, and antineutrino, result in the transport of energy by the antineutrino away from the location of the decay with the speed of light; this energy is the result of weak forces of interaction (see FUNDAMENTAL INTERACTIONS).

Energy Conversion

Certain fundamental laws limit in various ways the conversion of energy from one form to another. Foremost is the law of conservation of energy (see CONSERVATION, LAWS OF), according to which the sum total of all forms of energy of an isolated system remains constant; that is, energy can neither be created nor destroyed, although it can be converted from one form to another. In all conversion processes, however, there is always some waste heat that prevents complete conversion to useful work. A precise expression of the limiting conversion efficiency in cyclic processes, such as those which occur in many engines, is given by the second law of thermodynamics.

ENERGY CONSUMPTION (% OF WORLD TOTAL): PAST, PRESENT, AND PROJECTED

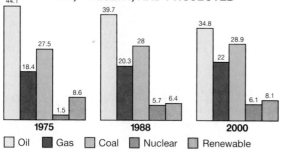

☐ Oil   ◼ Gas   ▨ Coal   ◼ Nuclear   ▨ Renewable

Source: U.S. Energy Information, International Energy Outlook, 1990.

Many notable conversion processes take place in the everyday world. Radiant energy from the Sun is converted into heat when absorbed, or it can be converted directly into electrical energy to solar cells. PHOTOSYNTHESIS converts radiation into chemical energy; the energy contained in fossil fuels can ultimately be traced to this process, since such fuels were once photosynthesizing plants. The most spectacular energy conversion processes are to be found in stars. An ordinary star such as the Sun obtains its energy by converting hydrogen to helium and other heavier elements.

Energy Transport

Energy can be transported from one place to another by several different processes. Electromagnetic energy in the form of radiation propagates with speed c. This is the principal manner in which energy from the Sun is transported to Earth. Mechanical transport of heated fluids, such as air or water, provides the principal transport mechanism of most central heating systems. Heat energy may be conducted through solid objects if there is a temperature difference between opposite sides of the object. Electrical energy is transported along metallic cables from generating plants to user sites.

Energy and Entropy

Thermodynamic systems, or those which are defined by definite temperature, pressure, and volume, have another property, distinct from energy, and related to the amount of useful work that can be obtained from the system. This property is called ENTROPY, from the Greek word meaning "evolution." When energy is used with the necessary generation of waste heat, the system becomes more disordered—it approaches a more probable state—and the entropy of the system increases. Systems having low entropy possess relatively more energy capable of being converted to useful work. In most natural processes the net entropy change is positive, meaning that less energy is available for conversion to useful work; thus, the net entropy of the universe is always increasing. This means that at least one aspect of the ultimate development of the universe will be to reduce temperature differences to zero. When this occurs, there will be no available energy

convertible to useful work. The result will be the so-called heat death of the universe.

energy, binding   see BINDING ENERGY

Energy, U.S. Department of   The U.S. Department of Energy (DOE) was established in October 1977. It consolidated the activities of the Energy Research and Development Administration, the Federal Power Commission, the Federal Energy Administration, and elements of other agencies. The new department was assigned wide-ranging powers to set energy prices, enforce conservation measures, and allocate fuel; it was also empowered to engage in research on new sources of energy. In addition, the department directs nuclear-weapons research and development.

Under authority assumed from the Federal Power Commission, the department issues permits and licenses for hydroelectric-power projects; regulates interstate prices of electric power and natural gas; and administers a number of rules and regulations affecting electric utilities and natural-gas pipeline companies. From the Energy Research and Development Administration the department inherited responsibility for the country's nuclear-energy program, as well as research into solar, geothermal, and other energy sources.

The department acquired the Federal Energy Administration's concern with conservation and fuel efficiency. It establishes standards for gas and oil consumption in factories and on the highways. The DOE also compiles information on the country's energy resources and on the profits of oil companies. Its regulations are enforced by an inspector general.

energy level   see ELECTRON CONFIGURATION; QUANTUM MECHANICS

---

energy sources   Whether the energy needs of a society depend on wood to provide the basic cooking and heating requirements of village life, or on the immensely varied fuel mix of the industrialized nations with their highly complex production and distribution systems, civilization is impossible without an adequate energy supply. In industrialized societies the situation is further complicated by the competition between the use of fossil fuels as an energy source, and their vital role as raw materials for the petrochemical industries, which produce plastics, fertilizers, animal feedstocks, pharmaceuticals, and industrial gases. Thus the so-called energy problem has implications for the whole structure of modern society.

Dimensions of the Energy Problem

Strictly speaking, the "energy problem" is really a FUEL problem because energy is conserved (changing from one form to another or into matter), while fuel when burned in chemical or nuclear reactions cannot be regenerated.

Several factors combine to make the energy problem in these terms an urgent one. World population is steadily increasing, which implies that the demand for energy will also increase, although not necessarily in proportion. Social, economic, and political pressure for economic expansion continues in industrialized countries. This implies an increased energy input. The developing countries are becoming aware that their economic position could be improved by increased energy consumption, and they feel entitled to a larger share of the world's energy resources than they now receive. These pressures require that the world energy supply be increased.

It is now recognized that the supply of the conventional fuels—coal, oil (petroleum), natural gas, uranium, and fuel wood—is limited and insufficient to sustain rapid rates of development. Although there may be debate about the exact length of time available before the effects of a worldwide shortage become apparent, there is agreement that such a shortage will occur. It is only a matter of time; in the case of oil, for example, the debate is not about whether, but about when oil production will peak.

Renewable Resources

Renewable energy resources are those which will replenish themselves naturally in a relatively short time and will therefore always be available. They include geothermal energy, hydroelectric power, peat, ocean thermal energy, solar energy, tidal energy, wind power, and fuel wood.

SOLAR RADIATION is a renewable energy source that can be used to produce electricity, by means of SOLAR CELLS, and heat, by means of solar collectors. SOLAR ENERGY is also indirectly responsible for many other renewable energy sources. The OCEAN CURRENTS and winds (see WINDMILLS AND WIND POWER) are results of the uneven distribution of solar radiation over the Earth's surface, and the winds in turn produce waves whose energy can be utilized. Solar heating of the upper layers of the ocean produces temperature gradients that can be harnessed to generate electricity (see OCEAN THERMAL ENERGY). The Sun also powers the HYDROLOGIC CYCLE, in which ocean water is evaporated, transported over the continents, and precipitated as rain or snow to form rivers, whose flow energy produces HYDROELECTRIC POWER. Finally, the energy locked in such renewable fuel sources as wood and PEAT is derived from the Sun by the process of photosynthesis. Another renewable energy source is GEOTHERMAL ENERGY, which arises through the leakage of heat from the Earth's interior to the surface. One or the other of two criteria is essential for the most efficient use of renewable resources: either they must be used at a rate less than their natural rate of renewal or they must periodically be allowed time to build up again.

Nonrenewable Resources

Nonrenewable resources originated from two processes: (1) photosynthesis, which occurred many millions of years ago, followed by the fossilization of the plant and animal life that resulted, and (2) the formation of the Earth itself. The first gave rise to the fossil fuels—coal, oil (see PETROLEUM), and NATURAL GAS; the second produced the fuels for nuclear energy, such as uranium for fission and lighter elements for fusion. These irreplaceable fuels represent an energy capital that must be invested wisely.

Availability and demand are by no means the only questions associated with nonrenewable energy sources. The case of oil offers an excellent example of the pervasiveness and complexity of energy-supply problems. Oil currently provides between 40 and 50 percent of the world's energy. Complications arise because the nations that consume oil in large amounts do not necessarily produce it in comparable amounts. This situation came forcibly to public attention in the United States during the "oil shocks" of the 1970s, because the nation had passed rapidly from a state of self-sufficiency to one where more than half its oil supplies were imported. The oil shocks of the 1970s were caused by the establishment of the ORGANIZATION OF PETROLEUM EXPORTING COUNTRIES (OPEC), which raised prices on crude oil to levels that had severe economic effects on all oil-importing countries. By 1990 over half the oil consumed in the United States came from imports, and the issue of oil price was perceived as a potential economic threat, a threat that played a role in the onset of the GULF WAR.

The case of coal (see COAL AND COAL MINING) presents a different set of problems. Because coal reserves are much larger and more widely distributed than petroleum reserves, it seems unlikely that any nation or group of nations could control coal production as OPEC controls the oil supply. Coal is thus clearly capable of furnishing a basic energy supply for far longer than oil or natural gas. In addition, it can supply petrochemical feedstocks, although at greater expense than oil. Proposals currently under large-scale investigation for coal gasification and liquefaction (see SYNTHETIC FUELS) would also tend to improve coal's range of usefulness.

With nuclear fuels (see NUCLEAR ENERGY; FISSION, NUCLEAR) the demand possibilities are complicated by the possibilities of BREEDER REACTORS. Without the breeder reactor, uranium is comparable to oil as a fuel reserve; with it, the situation is eased. The other nuclear option is fusion (see FUSION ENERGY). This possibility shows enormous promise, and if present experiments are successful, energy problems could be solved for hundreds or even thousands of years. Unfortunately, no fusion reactor has yet produced useful power output; all estimates of fusion power must therefore be viewed with a certain amount of caution.

Conversion to New Sources

The world's long, nearly total dependence on fossil fuels and hydroelectricity ensures that efforts to solve energy problems by switching to alternative sources will have to overcome a great deal of inertia, both economic and psychological. Such sources as solar power, wind power, and synthetic fuels suffer from the serious drawback that few major installations now exist. A large network of plants would have to be constructed, at great cost, before these sources could begin to supply a significant share of the world's energy needs. In addition, these alternatives are handicapped by the engineering problems of converting the energy to a form useful to human beings.

Geothermal energy is widely exploited, but the proposals for expanding its utility by drilling into hot rocks have yet to materialize. Extraction of oil from shale (see SHALE, OIL) and TAR SANDS is at present limited to a few commercial sites; programs to convert coal and biomass to liquid fuels on a large scale have so far proved uneconomic. In addition, all power sources, including such supposedly clean ones as solar and wind power, have adverse effects on the environment that must be either accepted or overcome by engineering, generally at a high price. Finally, the inefficiencies of conventional energy converters, such as BATTERIES, ENGINES, and TURBINES, make even more essential the search for new ways of harnessing old and new primary energy sources (see POWER, GENERATION AND TRANSMISSION OF).

Friedrich Engels, a 19th-century German socialist, was a lifelong friend and collaborator of Karl Marx. In 1848 they wrote the Communist Manifesto, *which Marx later elaborated in* Das Kapital. *Engels's ideological and financial support of Marx was instrumental in the spread of Marxist doctrine.*

Enesco, Georges [en-es'-koh, zhorzh]   The violin virtuoso Georges Enesco (Enescu), b. Aug. 19, 1881, d. May 4, 1955, is considered Romania's greatest composer. Trained in Vienna and Paris, Enesco was also a skilled pianist and conductor and an influential teacher; among his pupils was Yehudi Menuhin. Included in his works are an opera, *Oedipus* (1932), three symphonies, and other orchestral works, the best known being two *Rumanian Rhapsodies* (1901–02). His style was influenced by the vivid harmonies and dance rhythms of Romanian folk music.

Enfantin, Barthélémy Prosper [ahn-fahn-tan', bar-tay-lay-mee' prohs-pair']   Barthélémy Prosper Enfantin, b. Feb. 8, 1796, d. Sept. 1, 1864, was a French social theorist and leader of Saint-Simonianism. He met the comte de SAINT-SIMON shortly before the latter's death and, with St. Amand Bazard (1791–1832), founded the religious and political movement based on his thought. Saint-Simonianism advocated a highly centralized, planned society, ruled for the good of all by a natural aristocracy of the most talented.

Advocating a moral and social revolution, Enfantin defended free love and feminism. He was briefly imprisoned (1832) for holding secret meetings and for sexual immorality. Shortly afterward he went to Egypt, where he was involved in a futile canal project and a search for the Woman Messiah. After his return to France in 1837, Enfantin became director of a major railway company and also helped develop significant economic innovations in France.

Engels, Friedrich [eng'-els, freed'-rik]   Friedrich Engels, b. Nov. 28, 1820, d. Aug. 5, 1895, was a German socialist who collaborated with Karl MARX in developing the revolutionary social philosophy known as MARXISM. In 1842, Engels went to Manchester, England, to serve as an apprentice in his father's textile factory there. By that time, however, he had already shed the fundamentalist Protestant faith of his youth and passed through Hegelianism to radicalism. In Manchester, Engels wrote on social topics for Robert OWEN's *New Moral World* and Karl Marx's *Rheinische Zeitung*. In 1845 he published *The Condition of the Working Class in England*, a searing criticism of social misery among the factory workers of the industrial cities.

Engels and Marx met in 1844 in Paris; a close relationship began that was to last until Marx's death 40 years later. Marx contributed his considerable analytical skills, while Engels supplied erudition and quick intelligence. Their first joint work was *The German Ideology*, not published during their lifetimes, in which they criticized the ideas of nonrevolutionary German socialists. In 1848, Engels collaborated with Marx on the COMMUNIST MANIFESTO, a stirring call for revolution that summarized their views on history and the class struggle.

During the REVOLUTIONS OF 1848 in Germany, Engels helped Marx edit the liberal *Neue Rheinische Zeitung*. Returning to England after the failure of the revolutions, Engels continued his literary and political activities, propagating both the Marxist view of society and the workers' movement. His most influential work was *Herr Eugen Dühring's Revolution in Science* (1873; Eng. trans., 1934), popularly known as Anti-Dühring. After Marx's death in 1883, Engels edited the complete second and third volumes of Marx's Das KAPITAL.

engine   An engine is a device that converts one of several forms of energy into mechanical energy, which may then be used to perform work. Most modern engines use heat energy, derived from the combustion of fuels such as oil, coal, or gas. Other types of engines convert air or water pressure into mechanical energy. Engine types are described in separate articles: DIESEL ENGINE; HEAT ENGINE; INTERNAL-COMBUSTION ENGINE; JET PROPULSION; MOTOR; STIRLING ENGINE; TURBINE; WANKEL ENGINE. Older forms of energy conversion are the WATERWHEEL and windmill (see WINDMILLS AND WINDPOWER). New methods of energy conversion that bypass the mechanical stage are discussed in POWER, GENERATION AND TRANSMISSION OF.

engine, aircraft see AIRCRAFT

---

engineering Engineering is the profession that deals with the design and building of machines, devices, and structures. It is among the oldest of professions, although until perhaps the 18th century it was rarely distinguished from that of the scientist, the inventor, or the builder. In fact the histories of technology, science, and engineering were intertwined for many centuries—technology being in a sense the product of engineering, and science (the development of theories to explain natural phenomena) often being based on the empirical evidence supplied by the builders of machines and structures (see INVENTION; TECHNOLOGY, HISTORY OF).

Engineering in the Ancient World

The invention of efficient tools and basic processes was the necessary first step in the development of engineering. By the time of the Egyptian empires, early machine tools such as the lathe were already in use; metal smelting, metalworking, and casting processes had been developed; and such basic devices as the windlass, endless chain, and bellows were widely employed. The pyramids and other early monumental structures attest to a highly developed knowledge of quarrying and construction techniques.

The Greeks were talented inventors of mechanical devices, and many of their designs prefigure machines developed centuries later. HERO OF ALEXANDRIA devised two types of heat engines—one for opening the doors of a temple, the other simply a mechanical toy. Hero was the first to study and classify the types of mechanical force, and his categories of simple machines—the lever, wedge, pulley, wheel, and axle—formed the basis of MECHANICAL ENGINEERING.

The waterwheel appeared in the 4th century BC. A machine whose power was not provided by men or animals, it may be called the first true prime mover. Two centuries later, the Greek mathematician and inventor ARCHIMEDES studied the mechanics of solid bodies immersed in fluids, one of the first scientific studies of natural phenomena.

The Romans, while not so inventive as the Greeks, nevertheless adopted and improved on Greek devices, using them in the construction of the great works—roads, aqueducts, edifices—that marked their empire. VITRUVIUS's 10-volume De architectura (1st century AD) was a compendium of Roman engineering practice.

In its inventive abilities ancient China was easily the equal of Greece, but many centuries were to pass before such Oriental devices as the windmill (see WINDMILLS AND WINDPOWER), the double-piston bellows, and the wheelbarrow reached the Western world.

Medieval and Renaissance Engineering

The talents of the engineer in medieval Europe were largely confined to the design and building of military machines and FORTIFICATIONS and to the construction of large buildings. At the same time, however, a fascination with the functions of machinery and with the details of engineering processes began to expand engineering knowledge. Beginning with the spread of the printed word in the 15th century, illustrated books of machines and manuals of technical processes were published by many artist-technologists. The notebooks of LEONARDO DA VINCI, filled with sketches of possible and impossible machines, were by no means unique. Notebooks of this kind were kept by builders, architects, and machinists, and were circulated among their colleagues. The German scientist Georgius AGRICOLA (1494–1555) wrote his famous De re metallica (publ. 1556) as an illustrated compilation of contemporary mining (see MINING AND QUARRYING) and metallurgical processes (see METALLURGY). The Italian Agostino Ramelli (c.1531–1600) published his Le Diverse et Artificiose Machine in 1588; the volume contained illustrations depicting the workings of water-powered machines of every variety.

The tradition of the publication of engineering knowledge and theory established by these writers continued for several centuries.

The Beginnings of Industrialization

Starting with the Renaissance, engineering knowledge was increasingly based on scientific law in addition to the accumulation of empirical experience. The great scientific theorists of the Renaissance and the early modern era created a body of new knowledge that provided engineer-inventors with enormous impetus. In addition, the notion of mechanical invention as the principal means toward industrial progress led many governments to offer rewards to inventive genius and to establish learned societies in which news of the latest discoveries and inventions could be shared.

During the 17th and 18th centuries improvements in basic materials also contributed to engineering progress. Metal—especially cast iron, which could be used in machine construction—gradually replaced wood as a building material, and relatively cheap coal and coke began to be used as fuel in place of wood. The rapidly expanding use of coal required an improvement in mining methods and in TRANSPORTATION; eventually the coal economy inspired the invention and rapid modernization of rail transport (see RAILROAD).

Perhaps the single most important result of the increase in coal mining, though, was the concomitant improvement in PUMP technology. The necessity for pumping water from mine tunnels had occupied the energies of engineers for centuries. In 1698, Thomas Savery invented a steam-powered pump. This machine was followed 14 years later by the first efficient STEAM ENGINE, the Newcomen engine (see NEWCOMEN, THOMAS), which can be said to mark the beginning of the modern age of engineering. (For a more detailed discussion of the inventions that marked Newcomen's time, see MACHINE.)

The Industrial Revolution

The École Nationale des Ponts et Chaussées (the National School of Bridges and Highways) was established in France in 1747. The first formal school of engineering, it represented the notion that builders of public structures—BRIDGES, highways (see ROADS AND HIGHWAYS), CANALS, docks, harbors (see HARBOR AND PORT), sanitation and WATER SUPPLY systems—were a specialized professional group. The designation "civil engineer" was first used by John Smeaton (1724–92), and the first professional engineering society, the Institution of Civil Engineers (known also as "The Smeatonians"; see CIVIL ENGINEERING), was founded in England in 1818. The specialization of mechanical engineering followed shortly. The skills of these engineers derived from the prodigious inventions of such men as James WATT, and paralleled the development of powered MACHINE TOOLS.

The growing dependence of engineering on scientific achievement was reflected in the curriculum of the École Polytechnique (founded in Paris, 1795). Students there studied mathematics, physics, chemistry, and mechanics.

Between 1750 and 1850, civil and mechanical engineers were major participants in the rapid industrialization of western Europe and the United States. A summary of their accomplishments was presented at the Great Exhibition (London) of 1851, where working models of steam engines, and the profusion of machines such as engines were by then powering, were displayed. The exhibition was held in the CRYSTAL PALACE, a splendid cast-iron and glass structure.

The Modern Era

After the mid-19th century, as new inventions, materials, and scientific advances created new problems and possibilities, engineering became more and more specialized. ELECTRICAL AND ELECTRONIC ENGINEERING grew from developments in the field of electricity. The field of chemical engineering emerged as an outgrowth of the study of the chemical reactions involved in manufacturing, and in response to the need to mass-produce chemicals for industrial use. Other specialized engineering fields that developed in the late 19th and early 20th centuries included aeronautical and aerospace engineering (see ASTRONAUTICS); metallurgical, agricultural, and INDUSTRIAL ENGINEERING; and MATERIALS TECHNOLOGY. Present-day engineering is fragmented even further, and almost every major industrial area (including petroleum, ceramics, nuclear energy, waste disposal, and computers) requires engineers trained to meet its specific needs. Public-service fields such as sanitation, transportation, and URBAN PLANNING have also developed their own engineering specialties.

Engineers, Corps of   The U.S. Army Corps of Engineers is charged with building both military and civilian facilities and is the largest engineering and construction organization in the world. Dating from 1775, when military engineers were attached to the Continental Army, the corps in its present form was established by Congress in 1802, when it was also given responsibility for founding and operating the United States Military Academy at West Point, N.Y. (In 1866 the corps established a separate engineering school, now located at Fort Belvoir, Va., and the War Department began to administer West Point.)

Placed in charge of U.S. seaports and inland waterways in 1824, the corps has since built dams, reservoirs, harbors, and lighthouses and is the agency primarily responsible for planning and constructing major flood control projects. During the 19th century it explored, surveyed, and mapped large portions of the American West. Projects during the 20th century included the Panama Canal (1907–14), the St. Lawrence Seaway, and the management of the Manhattan Project during World War II.

England   England is the largest of the constituent parts of the UNITED KINGDOM. It occupies the southern and southeastern part of the island of Great Britain and is bordered on the west by Wales and on the north by Scotland. It covers an area of 130,439 km² (50,363 mi²) and has a population of 47,254,500 (1986 est.). Its capital is LONDON, with a metropolitan area population of 6,775,200 (1986 est.). England derives its name from that of the Angles, a Germanic people who, together with the Saxons, invaded the island in the 5th century.

Land. England can be divided into a lowland zone, which occupies the center, south, and east, and a highland zone in the north and west. The lowlands are generally composed of limestone and chalk. They give rise to low hills that are separated by lowlands floored with clay. The greatest heights in the lowlands scarcely exceed 305 m (1,000 ft). The highland zone includes the southwestern peninsula, the hills along the Welsh border, and the Pennine and Cumbrian mountains in the north. These are composed of ancient crystalline rock. Granite is widespread in the southwest, but an overlaying of Carboniferous deposits, frequently limestone, is common in the north. The PENNINES rise to over 610 m (2,000 ft), and mountains in the LAKE DISTRICT rise to over 915 m (3,000 ft).

England has a moderate marine climate that is characterized by mild winters and cool summers. January

Salisbury Cathedral (1220–60), located in Wiltshire, a county of southern England, is one of the nation's most cherished architectural landmarks. This ornate Gothic structure boasts the tallest church spire (123 m/404 ft) in Great Britain.

THE COUNTIES OF
ENGLAND

—— County boundary

—— National boundary

Exeter County seat

Lond National capital

City type size indicates
relative importance.

0 _____ 100 km
0 _____ 60 mi

Cartographic Production by Lothar Roth & Associates

temperatures range from 3° to 7° C (37° to 45° F), and July averages range from 15° to 18° C (59° to 64° F). Rainfall varies from 510 mm (20 in) near some parts of the east coast to 1,015 mm (40 in) in the hills of the west and north. The highest rainfall occurs in the Lake District of Cumbria, where it averages 3,290 mm (130 in) at Seathwaite. Snow occurs widely in winter but rarely remains on the ground for more than a few days, except in the hills. Humidity is generally high, and fogs are common, especially in industrial areas where they may be compounded by air pollution.

England is drained by many short rivers. The most extensive systems are those of the SEVERN, THAMES, and TRENT. The natural vegetation has almost everywhere been modified by close human regulation.

People. The population of England is ethnically diverse. On the original Celtic population were superimposed the Romans; the Germanic Angles, Saxons, and Jutes; the Scandinavians; the Norman-French; and countless smaller groups. Many Scots, Welsh, and Irish have also settled in England. The most recent arrivals are the Commonwealth immigrants from India and Pakistan and the West Indies.

In Europe only the Netherlands is more densely peopled than England. About 90% of the population are urban, of which about a third live in seven large conurbations; there are 89 cities with a population over 100,000.

English is the prevailing language, although there are strong dialect variations. The Church of England is the state church, but only a minority of its large membership is active. The next largest groups are the Roman Catholics, Methodists, and Baptists.

Economic Activities. England has important industrial resources, including abundant coal and offshore deposits of oil and natural gas. Nuclear energy accounts for 12% of energy production. Coal, now produced at a rate of about 125 million metric tons (138 million U.S. tons) a

White chalk cliffs extend along the shores of the English Channel. The channel, separating England from continental Europe, is less than 34 km (21 mi) across between the English port of Dover and the French port of Calais.

year, is the basis of England's industrial development and is found chiefly in the MIDLANDS and the north. These areas have in consequence become the most highly industrialized. Among the traditional industries are iron and steel in Teeside, woolens in West YORKSHIRE, cottons in LANCASHIRE, and light metals and engineering in BIRMING-

Queen Elizabeth II (mounted, center), the reigning monarch of Great Britain, rides past the Queen Victoria Memorial during the "trooping of the colour," an annual military ceremony during which various regimental banners are displayed.

HAM and the Midlands. About 30% of the employed population is in manufacturing.

Agriculture employs less than 3% but is carried on very efficiently. Its object is to supply milk and dairy produce, vegetables, and some meat for the population. Fishing is important, especially off the east coast.

Transportation is highly developed. A dense railroad network focuses on London, where there is also an efficient system of local transportation. The road system is dense, and an expressway system is nearing completion. Internal air services are developed only between major cities. The chief ports are London, LIVERPOOL, HULL, and BRISTOL.

Government and History. England is governed from Westminster (London) as part of the United Kingdom. For information on English history, see GREAT BRITAIN, HISTORY OF.

England, Church of

The Church of England is the established church in England. It is divided into two provinces, York and Canterbury. The monarch is technically at the head of the ecclesiastical structure, and the archbishops of Canterbury (see CANTERBURY, ARCHBISHOP OF) and York are next in line.

The beginnings of the Church of England date at least to the 2d century, when merchants and other travelers first brought Christianity to Britain. It is customary to regard Saint AUGUSTINE OF CANTERBURY's mission in 597 as marking the formal beginning of the church under papal authority, as it was to be throughout the Middle Ages. In its modern form, the church dates from the English REFORMATION of the 16th century, when royal supremacy was established and the authority of the papacy repudiated. With the advent of British colonization, the Church of England established churches on every continent and achieved international importance. In time, these churches gained independence but retained connections with the mother church in the Anglican Communion.

The Church of England is identified by adherence to the threefold ministry of bishops, priests, and deacons and by a common order of worship found in the BOOK OF COMMON PRAYER. The church is also characterized by a common attitude of loyalty to Christian tradition, while seeking to accommodate a wide range of people and views. It holds in tension the authorities of tradition, reason, and the Bible, but asserts the primacy of the Bible. It thus seeks to comprehend Catholic, humanist, and reformed elements, historically represented by Anglo-Catholics (high church), Liberals (broad church), and Evangelicals (low church).

The established status of the Church of England means that all episcopal appointments are made by the crown, and all revisions of the liturgy must be approved by Parliament. In modern times, however, Parliament has been composed of non-Anglicans as well as Anglicans, and this places the church in an awkward position. This has resulted in efforts, such as those represented by the OXFORD MOVEMENT, to maintain the church's integrity by separating it from the state. On the other hand, it has also spurred efforts to comprehend other Christians in the national church.

England, John

John England, b. Ireland, Sept. 23, 1786, d. Apr. 11, 1842, was the first Roman Catholic bishop of Charleston, S.C. After serving several poor parishes in Ireland, he was appointed (1820) to the new diocese in South Carolina. England's diocese, which included all the territory between Virginia and Florida, had only 5,000 church members, five priests, and hardly any buildings in which to worship. He established (1822) the *United States Catholic Miscellany*, the first U.S. Catholic newspaper and quickly became a national figure by arguing that his denomination had a legitimate and rightful place in American life.

English art and architecture

English art and architecture have had a continuous if varied history from the 6th century AD. Usually they have echoed developments on the European continent, although at various times from the 8th to the 13th century and again in the 18th and 19th centuries the English school made an original contribution. Two characteristics seem to distinguish English art and architecture from other European schools: a feeling for line and atmosphere as opposed to three-dimensional form, and a high degree of dependence, since the 16th century, on private rather than public patronage.

Anglo-Saxon Period. Despite the presence of earlier Celtic and Roman art in Britain (see CELTIC ART; ROMAN ART AND ARCHITECTURE), the history of English art and architecture may be said to begin with the Anglo-Saxons, who came from north Germany in the 5th and 6th centuries and reestablished Christianity. In the late 6th century, missions began arriving in the southeast, directly from

One of the finest and largest extant examples of Anglo-Saxon architecture is the church of All Saints, Brixworth, Northamptonshire. The structure was built during the 7th century and partially remodeled during the 9th and 10th centuries after damage by Viking raiders. Brixworth's most interesting feature is the apsidal east end, with its semicircular interior and polygonal exterior. A rectangular extension, probably used as a choir, separates the nave from the chancel.

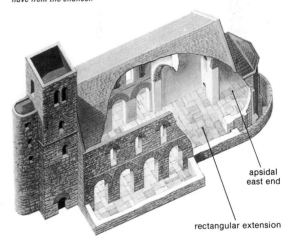

apsidal
east end

rectangular extension

Rome, and in the north, from Ireland.

The Roman missionaries brought with them religious books, church plate, and vestments. They also introduced the techniques of building in stone. Beginning in the 7th century, ABBEYS and CATHEDRALS AND CHURCHES were erected all over Anglo-Saxon England, although most of them have long since disappeared or been rebuilt many times.

The finest artistic achievements of the Anglo-Saxon period were monumental carved stone CROSSES and ILLUMINATED MANUSCRIPTS (religious books made in monasteries, the pages containing both text and exquisite watercolor ornamentation). In the beginning these were produced mainly in the north, particularly in northern Ireland, a region that in the late 7th and early 8th centuries was one of the most civilized in Europe. The masterpieces of the Hiberno-Saxon school, as it is called, are the Ruthwell (Dumfriesshire) and Bewcastle (Cumbria) crosses, both late 7th century, and two superb illuminated manuscripts: the *Lindisfarne Gospels* (*c.*700; British Museum, London), made by the monks of Holy Island off the Northumberland coast, and the BOOK OF KELLS (*c.*800; Trinity College, Dublin), begun on the island of

Iona and finished at Kells, northern Ireland. These and other English manuscripts down to the 13th century were admired and imitated on the Continent.

In the 10th century the emphasis shifted to the south, where a reform of the monasteries gave rise to a new school of manuscript illumination; it was called the Winchester School, although it flourished at Canterbury and other places as well. The manuscripts created by this school, which were influenced by CAROLINGIAN ART, are characterized by broad leaf forms, often arranged symmetrically, and by bolder figures than are found in Hiberno-Saxon work. An example is the *Benedictional of Saint Aethelwold* (975–80; British Museum, London).

Norman Period. With the Norman Conquest in 1066, England became an integral part of medieval Europe (see NORMAN ARCHITECTURE). Architecture in particular was transformed by the energies of the new regime, whose French-born bishops demanded much larger and better-designed cathedrals than had existed before. These cathedrals are the earliest major buildings in England to survive more or less in their original form. While the first examples, such as Saint Albans Abbey (*c.*1080), Hert-

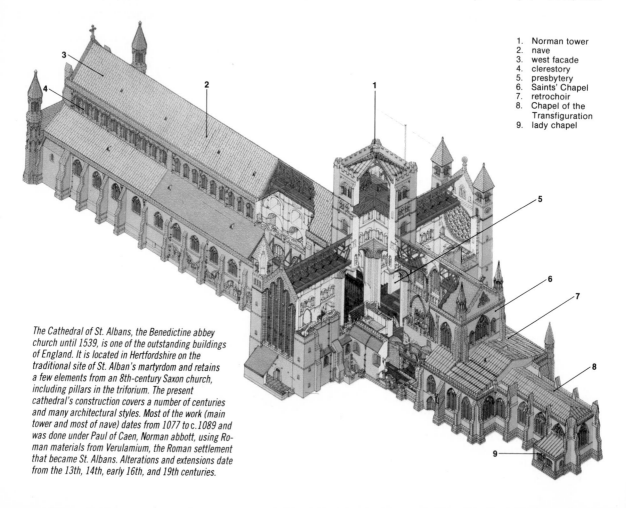

1. Norman tower
2. nave
3. west facade
4. clerestory
5. presbytery
6. Saints' Chapel
7. retrochoir
8. Chapel of the Transfiguration
9. lady chapel

The Cathedral of St. Albans, the Benedictine abbey church until 1539, is one of the outstanding buildings of England. It is located in Hertfordshire on the traditional site of St. Alban's martyrdom and retains a few elements from an 8th-century Saxon church, including pillars in the triforium. The present cathedral's construction covers a number of centuries and many architectural styles. Most of the work (main tower and most of nave) dates from 1077 to c.1089 and was done under Paul of Caen, Norman abbott, using Roman materials from Verulamium, the Roman settlement that became St. Albans. Alterations and extensions date from the 13th, 14th, early 16th, and 19th centuries.

Salisbury Cathedral (1220–60) is one of very few extant buildings in England erected entirely during the 13th century. Its shift from the earlier Anglo-Norman style is apparent in a more vertical style, with more steeply pitched roofs, wider windows and thinner piers and spires, all of which combine to achieve a dignified simplicity. Although the cathedral shows English recognition of French Gothic architecture, the more spread-out look of Salisbury Cathedral is peculiarly English. The cathedral has the highest spire in England, measuring 123 m (404 ft) in height.

(Far right) Decorated ribs and vaults hang from the ceiling in this characteristic English Gothic fan vault in King's College chapel, Cambridge.

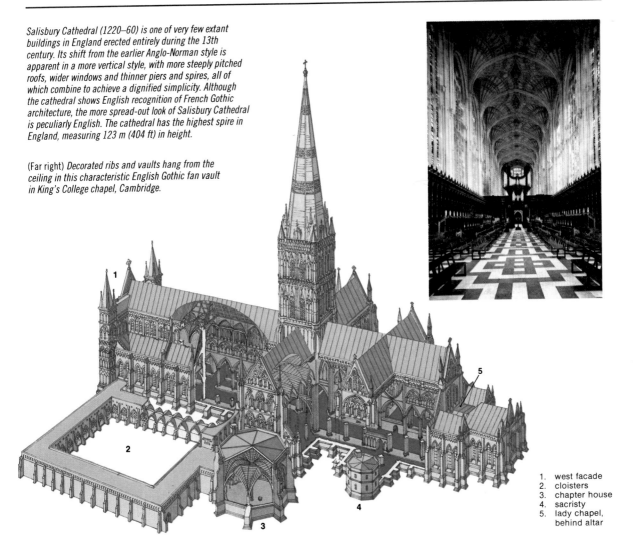

1. west facade
2. cloisters
3. chapter house
4. sacristy
5. lady chapel, behind altar

fordshire, closely followed Norman models, within 30 years the Norman style as developed in England—the equivalent of continental ROMANESQUE ART AND ARCHITECTURE—had acquired a distinct character of its own, best seen in Durham Cathedral (1093–1133). Durham shares with Romanesque cathedrals everywhere the Latin cross plan (a plan with choir, transepts, and nave in the form of an elongated cross), the use of round arches, and generally massive construction. Durham is unusual, however, in the rich decoration of its interior, in the grandeur of its nave arcade, and, above all, in having a stone rib-vault (see ARCH AND VAULT), the first in Europe. The Normans also introduced new kinds of abbeys, which spread throughout England in the 12th century due mainly to the CISTERCIANS (see MONASTIC ART AND ARCHITECTURE), and CASTLES.

English sculpture of the 11th and 12th centuries is relatively unimportant, but manuscript illumination con-

tinued to flourish in the south. Magnificent Bibles with brightly colored initials and busy, expressive figures are characteristic of this phase, for example, the *Winchester Bible* (mid-12th century; Winchester Cathedral).

Gothic Period. Gothic architecture (see GOTHIC ART AND ARCHITECTURE), like Norman, reached England from northern France. The first major example is the choir of Canterbury Cathedral, started in 1175 and designed by a Frenchman, WILLIAM OF SENS. Quite soon, however, national characteristics once more began to assert themselves. Chiefly, English cathedrals are broader, longer, and lower than French ones; they retain transepts (sometimes two sets); and they have square east ends, giving an opportunity for splendid east windows, and flat west fronts and transept facades. Another typically English feature is the centrally planned (round or polygonal) chapter house, or meeting hall of the cathedral clergy.

English Gothic architecture is traditionally divided into

The intricate leaf motifs and realistic figures of the Pentecost page from the Winchester Pontifical *(late 10th century) are typical of fine achievements of English manuscript illumination. (Municipal Library, Rouen.)*

out from the tops of the wall shafts in the shape of a fan. The most famous example is King's College Chapel, Cambridge, which was begun in 1446 and vaulted between 1508 and 1515.

By the end of the 14th century the great age of new cathedral building was over. Besides parish churches and a few royal chapels, the 15th century is notable for the rise of domestic architecture (see HOUSE, in Western architecture). The centerpiece of a domestic complex was a large hall; its crowning feature was a wooden roof of complicated design, such as hammer-beam. Private houses were either built of brick, following Flemish practice, or were timber-framed, with tall gables and overhanging upper stories. The best surviving work of English Gothic sculpture is the array of standing figures on the west front of Wells Cathedral (mid-13th century). Unfortunately, many religious statues were destroyed either during the Reformation or by the 17th-century Puritans. Most of the stained-glass windows suffered a similar fate.

By the late 13th century Paris had become the acknowledged center of manuscript illumination, but English work continued to be distinguished by the quality of its line and by the vividness of its naturally observed fig-

This equestrian portrait of Charles I of England (c.1635) is by the Flemish baroque painter Anthony van Dyck. (The Prado, Madrid.)

three phases. Early English Gothic, clear and austere in design but rich in color and texture, lasted from the end of the 12th to the late 13th century; its representative buildings are Lincoln Cathedral (1192–1235) and SALISBURY CATHEDRAL (begun 1220). The next phase, preceded by another "French" building, WESTMINSTER ABBEY in London (begun 1245), is Decorated Gothic, characterized by rich carvings on surfaces, gables, and arches, complicated vaulting patterns, and elaborate window tracery— an innovation introduced at Westminster. Decorated Gothic also made extensive use of STAINED GLASS. It was the dominant style from about 1280 to the mid-14th century; its typical buildings include the naves of Exeter Cathedral (begun c.1280) and York Minster (begun c.1290) and the Lady Chapel of Ely Cathedral (1321–49).

The third phase is PERPENDICULAR GOTHIC, which lasted until the Reformation. This style, which first appeared in the choir of Gloucester Cathedral (c.1337–57), was an English invention. Its basis was a grid consisting of repeated vertical strips or bars crossed at wider intervals by horizontals; this was either applied as decoration to a wall or used as a screen to form a vast window. By around 1500 this system culminated in a fan vault, a type of vault in which the ribs, joined by finer cross-ribs, spread

St. Paul's Cathedral (1675–1709) in London is the finest achievement of Sir Christopher Wren, the foremost English architect of the baroque style. The facade's main affinity is with the work of the French baroque architect Claude Perrault.

ures and animals in the page margins, as in the *Luttrell Psalter* (*c.*1340; British Museum, London). Wall paintings exist at Chichester and elsewhere, and panel paintings became a feature for the first time. The finest of the latter is the *Wilton Diptych* (*c.*1400; National Gallery, London), a work in the Gothic International Style. During

the 15th century England increasingly became an artistic backwater.

Renaissance Period. With the coming of the Reformation in the 1530s, the monasteries—the principal workshops of painters and sculptors for 800 years—were dissolved, and religious pictures and statues were forbidden in churches. The court of Henry VIII, unlike courts on the Continent, failed to become a leading source of patronage for secular art. A new national tradition had to find expression in the lesser categories of PORTRAITURE, tomb sculpture, and country houses. Fortunately, these were socially important at the time and in the 18th century were to become artistically important as well. During the later 16th and early 17th centuries, tombs and country houses gradually, if only superficially, absorbed Renaissance influences. Portrait painting was very feeble. However, as taste improved toward the end of the period, Dutch and Flemish artists were brought in, and this remained the normal arrangement until the early 18th century. In one field, however, native English painters excelled: the portrait miniature (see MINIATURE PAINTING), an art form that carried on the delicate linear tradition, using transparent colors, of medieval manuscript illumination. Its most famous exponent was the Elizabethan artist Nicholas HILLIARD.

Baroque Period. The patronage of Charles I brought Sir Anthony VAN DYCK to England (1632–41). Van Dyck was the most gifted and advanced portraitist in northern Europe, and his flattering image of the English aristocracy continued to inspire artists, and perhaps still more their sitters, down to the early 20th century. Charles also patronized Inigo JONES, who played a somewhat similar role in the history of English architecture. In the Banqueting House (1619–22) of WHITEHALL PALACE, subsequently adorned with a series of great baroque ceiling paintings (1629–35) by Peter Paul Rubens glorifying the Stuart

William Hogarth's Shortly After the Marriage *is the second in a series of six paintings titled* Marriage à la Mode *(1743). Like all his scenes, it places characters in tableaux, acting out dramatic narratives. (National Gallery, London.)

The Self-Portrait (1780) was painted by Sir Joshua Reynolds at age 57. The dignity of expression and facility of brushwork are typical of this first president of the Royal Academy. (Royal Academy, London.)

monarchy, Jones created the first building in central London to embody not only the classical orders (columns, capitals, entablatures, and the like; see ARCHITECTURE), correctly used, but also classical systems of proportion. By midcentury his influence was reflected in country houses. It was not until the late 17th and early 18th centuries that the baroque style dominated English art and architecture, and even then it was used with restraint (see BAROQUE ART AND ARCHITECTURE). The leading architect of this phase was Sir Christopher WREN, whose masterpiece is SAINT PAUL'S CATHEDRAL (1675–1709) in London. Wren, with his assistant Nicholas HAWKSMOOR, rebuilt nearly 50 City of London churches following the Great Fire of 1666. Wren also designed, or was involved in the design of, several large public buildings commissioned by the king, such as Greenwich Hospital in London (begun 1698). The German-born Sir Godfrey KNELLER was the principal portraitist of this phase. The climax of baroque sculpture was reached a little later, as in the tomb of the duke of Argyll (1745–49) in Westminster Abbey, by the French-born Louis François Roubiliac.

Rococo and Neoclassical Periods. The late 17th and early 18th centuries had been a period of growing national vigor in science, philosophy, political theory, and war. Now, after trailing behind the Continent for so long, England once more began to make an original contribution to the arts. The Palladian movement in architecture, started about 1715 and masterminded by Richard Boyle, 3d earl of BURLINGTON, introduced a relatively pure, "postbaroque" classicism in the design of country houses—for example, at Holkham Hall (begun 1734), Norfolk, by William KENT—that was unique in Europe at the time. For the interiors of some houses, the ROCOCO STYLE was adopted. A new informal type of garden design, the landscape or English garden, was invented by Capability Brown in the mid-18th century and was imitated all over the Continent (see GARDEN and LANDSCAPE ARCHITECTURE). In painting, William HOGARTH gained an international reputation and was the first English-born painter in oils to do

so. His witty pictures and engravings—Marriage à la Mode, a set of six paintings, (1743-45; National Gallery, London), for example—captured the new secular, satirical, earthy yet morally concerned mood of the age.

As national wealth accumulated further in the second half of the 18th century, the number of artists rose. Portraiture reached a peak in the work of Sir Joshua REYNOLDS and Thomas GAINSBOROUGH. A new, typically English genre emerged—sporting painting—whose greatest exponent was George STUBBS. This period also saw the rise of LANDSCAPE PAINTING in both oils (Gainsborough, Richard WILSON) and watercolors (COZENS family). Such architects as Robert ADAM and such sculptors as John FLAXMAN were contributors to international NEOCLASSICISM. The coming of age of English postmedieval art was crowned by the founding of the Royal Academy (see ACADEMIES OF ART) in 1768, with Reynolds as its first president.

Perhaps the most important single example of neoclassicism in English architecture was the Bank of England (1792–1823, rebuilt 1927) in London, by Sir John SOANE. Neoclassical sculpture is well exemplified in Flaxman's tomb of the 18th earl of Mansfield in Westminster Abbey (1795–1801).

Romantic and Victorian Periods. Painting after 1790 tended more toward ROMANTICISM, especially in landscape, where a bold style and an intense feeling for the moods of nature, demonstrated in the art of J. M. W. TURNER, John CONSTABLE, and many others, made the English school of landscape painting the most vital in Europe. The visionary art of William BLAKE is another manifestation of romanticism.

Victorian art, backed by continuing economic prosperity and an expanding middle class, represents an almost equally vigorous development, even though it was less in touch with the Continent than 18th-century art had been. It found its main architectural expression in the GOTHIC

The Blue Boy (1770) by Thomas Gainsborough, is painted in the style of Sir Anthony van Dyck. This deliberate anachronism includes the Caroline costume of the model. (Huntington Art Gallery, San Marino, Calif.)

English romantic landscape painter J. M. W. Turner's The Last Voyage of the Téméraire *(1838–39) relates a historical event, but its translucent, hazy colors stress the strength of Turner's imagination. (National Gallery, London.)*

(Left) Claudio and Isabella (1850), with its detailed realism, literary symbolism, and simplicity of tone, typifies the work of the major English Pre-Raphaelite painter William Holman Hunt. (The Tate Gallery, London.) (Below) View of Salisbury Cathedral (c.1830) is by John Constable, whose most famous works are views of the English countryside. (Museum of Art, São Paulo, Brazil.)

REVIVAL, seen in a renewal not only of church building but also in railway stations, such as Saint Pancras (begun 1860) in London, by Sir George Gilbert SCOTT, town halls, and the Houses of Parliament (begun 1836) by Sir Charles BARRY and Augustus PUGIN (see WESTMINSTER PALACE). The CRYSTAL PALACE by Sir Joseph PAXTON, built of cast iron and glass in sections erected on site to house the Great Exhibition of 1851 in Hyde Park, London, was a historically significant development.

Victorian popular painting consisted mainly of domestic and historical scenes charged with sentiment and telling an affecting story, but the Pre-Raphaelite Brother-

(Above) *Contemporary British artist David Hockney painted* Two Boys in a Swimming Pool *in 1965. The composition, in which the artist uses a cartoonlike technique, combines elements of popular graphics and the modernism of Francis Bacon. (Collection of Lord and Lady Beaumont.)*

(Left) *In* Locking Piece *(1963–64), British sculptor Henry Moore creates an abstract work of organic shapes that demonstrates his mastery of volume and space interaction. Moore admires pre-Columbian and primitive sculpture. (London.)*

hood (see PRE-RAPHAELITES), founded in 1848 by Holman HUNT, Sir John MILLAIS, Dante Gabriel ROSSETTI, and others, made more serious claims. These artists sought to combine the pure, unaffected spirit of the Italian artists before Raphael with a meticulous REALISM. After 1860, Pre-Raphaelitism became dreamier, suffused with a nostalgia for the Middle Ages, and merged with the ARTS AND CRAFTS MOVEMENT led by William MORRIS. This movement had some influence on Continental ART NOUVEAU and even on the BAUHAUS. The late 19th century also produced one other artist of international importance, the Scottish architect and designer Charles Rennie MACKINTOSH, whose Glasgow School of Art (1898–99) is perhaps the last building of real distinction erected in the British Isles. The recent revival of interest in eclectic architecture has brought the work of Sir Edwin Landseer LUTYENS back to prominence, particularly his romantic country houses and his enormous neoclassic Viceroy's House (1913–31; now President's House) in New Delhi, India.

   Contemporary Period. National decline began to set in around 1900, and English artists have spent the 20th century in a well-meaning attempt to catch up with international developments. Among modern artists, the two dominant characteristics of English art—the romantic tradition and the emphasis on line—may be seen in the sculpture of Henry MOORE and the painting of Francis BACON, David HOCKNEY, and Graham SUTHERLAND. Of the work of contemporary British architects, that of James Frazer STIRLING has perhaps been the most influential.

English Channel   The English Channel (French: La Manche, "the sleeve") is an arm of the Atlantic Ocean extending between southern England and northern France and connecting the Atlantic on the west with the North Sea on the east via the Strait of Dover. The English ports of Plymouth, Southampton, Portsmouth, Folkestone, and Dover and the French ports of Boulogne, Cherbourg, Le Havre, and Calais are on the Channel. It is 34 to 240 km wide (21 to 150 mi), 560 km (350 mi) long, and has an area of 89,900 km^2 (34,700 mi^2). Its maximum depth is 172 m (565 ft). Because of the effect of the Atlantic Ocean waves being forced into the narrow Channel, its tides are strong and unusual, particularly at the new moon. The average speed of the tidal stream is moderate, although tidal races may be rather fast. Weather in the Channel is unpredictable and often windy, cloudy, and rainy; the famous Channel fog is most common during the winter. The Channel has important fishing grounds.

   Historically, the Channel has served as a physical barrier to the invasion of Britain. Although it was crossed by Julius Caesar's legions (55 BC) and Norman forces (1066), both Napoleon and Hitler threatened to cross but did not. The Channel was first crossed by balloon in 1785. The first man to swim across the Channel was Matthew Webb in 1875. Gertrude EDERLE was the first woman to swim it (1926). Transportation across the Channel is supplied by ferry-boat services between several ports, and by a hovercraft service (begun in 1968) between Boulogne and Calais. Great Britain and France began construction of a trans-Channel tunnel in 1987.

English Civil War   The English Civil War, which started on Aug. 22, 1642, really consisted of three wars. The first, between King CHARLES I and Parliament, allied with the Scottish COVENANTERS, lasted until 1646; the second, in which a Scottish army fought for Charles I against Parliament, took place in 1648; and the last, in which the Scots were led by CHARLES II as their king, lasted from 1649 to 1651.

The long-term causes of the wars were the growing wealth of the middle classes (gentry and merchants), who made up a majority in the House of Commons and demanded a larger influence on the government, and the insufficiency of the king's hereditary finances, which made him dependent on the Commons whenever he was involved in the foreign wars. From 1629, avoiding such involvement, Charles had governed without a Parliament. But rebellion in Scotland (the so-called BISHOPS' WARS) compelled him to summon the Short Parliament and then the Long Parliament in 1640.

The Commons were angry over the manner in which Charles I had raised new taxes without their consent and had revived obsolete feudal dues, while the majority of members with Puritan sympathies castigated Charles's church policies. The king made several concessions—including the sacrifice of his ablest advisors, William LAUD, archbishop of Canterbury, and the earl of Strafford—but refused to have his ministers and commanders named for him and rejected the idea of handing over to Parliament the control of the militia, the only armed force in the kingdom. Charles's rejection of these demands, set forth in Parliament's Grand Remonstrance, led directly to war.

In the first two years of war, after both sides had raised armies, the royalists, or CAVALIERS, were more successful. After a drawn battle at Edgehill in Warwickshire (Oct. 23, 1642), the royalists threatened London (Charles's headquarters were in Oxford) but were compelled to withdraw. In 1643 the royalists were victorious in most parts of England except London and the east. Instead of converging his armies on London, Charles resolved to clear his communications with Wales and the southwest by taking Gloucester, but the town was relieved by parliamentary forces (popularly known as ROUNDHEADS), and Charles was defeated at Newbury (Sept. 20, 1643). The tide turned for the parliamentarians in 1644, when the royalists were beaten at Marston Moor in Yorkshire (July 2). In 1645 the royalists were again defeated by Thomas Fairfax's New Model Army at Naseby in Leicestershire (June 14). Oxford fell on June 24, 1646, and Charles, who had surrendered himself to the Scots, was turned over to Parliament and became a prisoner.

The second civil war began after Charles had escaped (November 1647) and concluded a treaty with the Scots. Risings on the king's behalf took place in Essex, Kent, and Wales, while the Scots invaded England and were defeated by Oliver CROMWELL at Preston (Aug. 17–19,

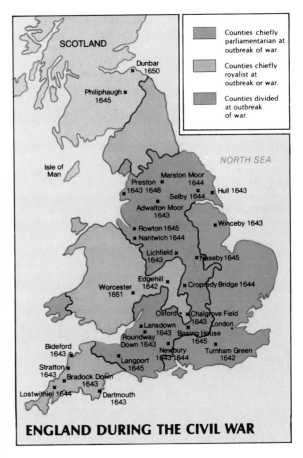

ENGLAND DURING THE CIVIL WAR

Political sympathies varied from county to county during the English Civil War (1642–51), a series of contests between supporters of the monarchy and the allies of Parliament.

1648). After Charles I's execution (Jan. 30, 1649), his son Charles II renewed the war, sustained by royalists in Ireland and Scotland. Cromwell then defeated the Irish and subsequently invaded Scotland, where he crushed the Scots at Dunbar (Sept. 3, 1650).

A year later Charles II led a Scottish army into England but was overwhelmed by a large army at Worcester (Sept. 3, 1651). He fled abroad, while England remained under the republican rule of Oliver Cromwell.

The parliamentarians won the civil wars because of several major advantages. First, they held London and all the richest towns and ports except Bristol, which was held by royalists from July 26, 1643, to Sept. 10, 1645. Second, they had in Thomas Fairfax, 3d baron Fairfax of Cameron, and Oliver Cromwell very capable generals, while Charles I was a poor strategist and did not properly use such able commanders as the marquess of MONTROSE in Scotland and Prince RUPERT. Third, the navy sided with Parliament, which gave it control over foreign trade and many strategic advantages. Last, Parliament's New Model Army was better trained and disciplined than that of the royalists.

English cocker spaniel

The English and American cocker spaniels descend from the same basic stock and are similar in general appearance. The English cocker spaniel is slightly bigger, longer, and leaner than is the American. Males stand 40.6–43.2 cm (16–17 in) at the shoulder and weigh 12.7–15.4 kg (28–34 lb); females stand 38.1–40.6 cm (15–16 in) and weigh 11.8–14.5 kg (26–32 lb). The English cocker spaniel carries less coat than does the American breed. It is an attractive sporting dog, always alert and alive with energy. It has a powerful gait and pendant ears; the tail is docked. English cocker spaniels come in a broad range of colors, solids, and roans, such as blue, liver, red, orange, or lemon as well as black and tan. The breed was recognized officially by the American Kennel Club in 1946.

The English cocker spaniel, which is slightly larger than the American cocker, has longer legs and a longer muzzle and is leaner in appearance. Originally bred for hunting, the English cocker today is bred primarily for show.

English foxhound

The English foxhound is a medium-sized dog with pendant ears, a smooth coat, and a

The English foxhound, bred for its speed and tracking ability, is kept primarily for hunting. Foxhounds have been known in England for centuries, and the English foxhound was used to produce the lighter American breeds.

gaily carried upright tail. Similar in coloring to the beagle, the foxhound is brown, tan, black, or white. The English foxhound stands about 58.4 cm (23 in) at the shoulder, making it slightly smaller and heavier set than the American foxhound. Foxhounds have been bred in England since the 13th century; the modern breed can be traced to before 1800 in official stud books. They are used in packs to run down their quarry while hunters follow on horseback. To do this, the foxhound must have strong legs and feet. In terms of official registrations with the American Kennel Club, the breed is among the rarest.

English horn

The English horn is a woodwind instrument of the OBOE family, sounding a fifth lower than the oboe. It is normally played by the third oboist in modern symphony orchestras. It has a range from E below middle C upwards for about two and one-half octaves. Its slightly conical bore usually ends in a bulbous-shaped bell. All explanations of its name are speculative. Its distinctively dark and plaintive character was prized by orchestral composers in the romantic era.

Before the end of the 17th century, prototypes of the English horn appeared in a form typically curved and leather-covered with holes usually bored at an angle to accommodate the stretch of the fingers. A transposing instrument, the modern English horn sounds a fifth lower than written.

English language

The English language is derived from Germanic (see GERMANIC LANGUAGES), which is derived from Indo-European (see INDO-EUROPEAN LANGUAGES), but it is not definitely known how, when, or even where Indo-European began.

Origins. English carries the story of its own origin, however, as an independent language in its name. The "Engl-" part of the word goes back to the Angles, a Germanic tribe that invaded and colonized much of Britain during the 5th and 6th centuries. The "-ish" part means "belonging to": in this case, the language that belonged to the Angles—the "Angle-ish" language.

The Angles lived in northern Germany alongside a number of kindred tribes, including the Saxons and the Jutes. Beginning about the year 450, members of these three tribes, joining in the widespread barbarian migrations that marked the end of the western Roman Empire, crossed the North Sea to find new homes in Britain. For the next 50 or 60 years the would-be colonizers, aided by reinforcements, fought with the original inhabitants of the island, the Britons, and pushed them back to the north and west into present-day Scotland and Wales. The territory that Angles, Saxons, and Jutes thus carved out for themselves can be called the land of the Anglo-Saxons, or, for short, "Angle-land"—England. Similarly, their language can be called Anglo-Saxon or OLD ENGLISH.

The Britons spoke one of the closely related CELTIC LANGUAGES. The Anglo-Saxons spoke a form of Germanic. Both Celtic and Germanic have a common source language, Indo-European. By the 5th century, however, speakers of these two branches of Indo-European would have been totally unintelligible to each other.

At first the Anglo-Saxons who went to Britain continued to speak the same tongue as their fellow tribesmen whom they had left behind in northern Germany. With each passing generation, however, the speech patterns of the two peoples, now separated by the North Sea, grew less and less alike. After a while it could be said that they spoke different dialects of the same language. Finally, at that time (probably during the 7th century or even later) when the Anglo-Saxons and the people of Germany could no longer understand each other, the English language came into its own: the Anglo-Saxons spoke English—Old English to be precise—and the people of Germany spoke early forms of the German language.

Old and Middle English. Present-day English descends directly from the speech of the Anglo-Saxons. English has, however, changed so much during the course of the past thousand years that today Old English seems like a foreign tongue. The Norman Conquest explains many of the shifts in vocabulary that have taken place since the time of the Anglo-Saxons. Before 1066 only a handful of words had been borrowed from French; since then, tens of thousands of French words have entered the English language. Instead of the Germanic word *rice* (compare present-day German *Reich*), for example, we might say "realm," "dominion," "region," or "possessions," all of which are French loanwords that first appeared in English during the course of the 13th and 14th centuries.

William the Conqueror and his French-speaking court influenced English mostly from the top down. The vast majority of the inhabitants of England continued to speak English after the Conquest, although Henry IV, who succeeded Richard II on the throne in 1399, was the first king since Harold II whose mother tongue was English rather than French. It is not surprising that our words *veal, beef, mutton*, and *pork* for the prepared meats that would have been eaten by the Normans inside their castles are all of French origin, while our names *calf, ox, sheep*, and *swine* for the corresponding animals raised and slaughtered by the English-speaking farmers outside the castle walls are all of Anglo-Saxon origin.

Despite the many French loanwords, English remained English, not a dialect of French. English grammar, as opposed to vocabulary, remained virtually unaffected by French, and grammatical developments that had begun much earlier during Anglo-Saxon times continued without interruption through the Conquest. Even today it is still obvious that the grammatical structure of English resembles that of German far more than it resembles that of French.

Although 1066 in no way marks a change of languages for the people of England, the date nonetheless serves as a convenient divider between two periods of English: Old English and MIDDLE ENGLISH. Middle English is characterized both by its greater French vocabulary and, more important, by the loss of inflections.

Effect of Printing on English. The year 1476, a date not nearly so well remembered as 1066, was every bit as important for the English language. Just as the earlier date can serve as a dividing line between Old English and Middle English, the later date is often used to separate conveniently Middle English from the third and most recent period of our language, Modern English. In c.1476 the first English printer, William CAXTON, set up his press in London. Previously, spelling had changed to reflect changes in pronunciation. Printing froze spelling: we spell essentially the way Caxton did. The Anglo-Saxons wrote *hlaf* because they pronounced the *h*; Chaucer wrote *loof* or *lof* because he no longer did so. Although we do not say "nite," we write *knight* because Caxton still pronounced both the *k* at the beginning of the word and the *gh*, which sounded something like the *ch* in the present-day Scottish pronunciation of *loch*.

Printing had a decisive effect on spelling because until the development of printing all books were copied by hand. Each copy of a book was spelled differently because no two copyists or scribes spoke in exactly the same manner. Thus when Caxton began to turn out dozens or even hundreds of virtually identical copies of a book, his spelling system at once became familiar all over England. Because their readers were accustomed to Caxton's spellings, his immediate successors decided to adapt these spellings for their books. Aside from occasional modifications and reforms, printers have followed the same spelling system ever since—that of Caxton's late-15th-century London.

Pronunciation Shifts. Two far-reaching changes in pronunciation that had nothing to do with the introduction of the printing press also took place in the 15th century: the loss of final unaccented *e*, and what is called the great vowel shift—a series of changes in the pronunciation of the long stressed vowels. The loss of final *e* left Modern English with even fewer inflections than Middle English. The great vowel shift explains many of the most striking differences between Chaucer's pronunciation of English and ours.

English Today. The Modern English period has already lasted longer than either of its predecessors. Old English was used from no earlier than the 7th century until the Anglo-Saxons could no longer understand their German cousins; Middle English covers the 410 years from then, the Battle of Hastings (1066), to the first book printed in England (1476). One cannot know what future event or even what kind of event—a war, an invention, or something else—will mark the end of Modern English and usher in a new era for the language.

Of course it is possible that a new period of English has already begun. Centuries passed before anyone realized the full linguistic significance of the years 1066 and 1476. Specifically, a fourth, "post-Modern" period of English may have originated in 1876 or 1877 with Alexander Graham Bell's invention of the telephone and Thomas Alva Edison's invention of the phonograph. These machines, along with a few others that have followed—radio, talking pictures, television—were able to do for the spoken word what the printing press did for the written word. Before 1876 speakers could be heard only by those within earshot; now, however, a speaker may have a virtually unlimited audience, situated in any time or place.

Just as printing standardized spelling, one result of the latest communications breakthrough has been a leveling of differences in the pronunciation of English. People no longer hear the speech only of those from their own neighborhood or village. Instead, whole nations listen to the same newscasters and entertainers every evening.

British English (the brand of English spoken in Great Britain) and American English (that spoken in the United States) diverged as soon as the American colonies were founded at the start of the 17th century. Nonetheless, because of the constant interchange of people and books across the ocean, American English never developed beyond being a dialect of English. With the advent of records, cinema, radio, and television, the two brands of English have even begun to draw back together again. Britons and Americans probably speak more alike today than they did 50 or 60 years ago.

Canadian English, Australian English, South African English, and the many other dialects of English scattered around the world are coming increasingly to resemble one another. Within each dialect area, subdialects are also losing their distinctive characteristics. Within the United States, for example, the speech of Northerners and Southerners is becoming less obviously distinctive.

Although the English language is becoming more uniform, this does not mean that it will come to a rest once all dialectal differences are gone. Languages never stop changing, and English is no exception. To take a well-known example: at present the indefinite or interrogative pronoun *who* seems to be in the process of assuming all the functions once reserved for the inflected form *whom*. In time everyone, even pedants, may give up saying, "Whom do you wish to see?"

English, once a highly inflected language—though never so inflected as Latin or Greek or many American Indian languages—is now largely uninflected. Unlike the *m* of *whom*, however, most of the few inflections that remain in English show no signs of fading: *-s* for plural and possessive singular nouns, *-s* for the third person present singular of verbs (*I want*, but *he* or *she wants*), *-ing* for the present participle, *-ed* for the past tense and past participle. English also makes grammatical distinctions on the basis of the interior forms of words—*sing, sang, sung*, for example—and most of these distinctions likewise seem as alive as ever.

The American Language

The American language is the name given to the type of English spoken in the United States. American English has dialects of its own—the speech of the South, for instance—but all of its dialects share enough characteristics so that the English found in the United States as a whole can be distinguished from that of other countries, such as Great Britain or Australia.

Until the middle of the 20th century, many commentators believed that the American language would grow increasingly distinct, until it bore a relation to British English similar to the relation between Portuguese and Spanish, or Norwegian and Danish. Lately, however, American and British English are clearly beginning to converge. The most apparent reason for the convergence is the immense influence of the electronic media, but each country has also become more willing to borrow linguistic features from the other.

The essential difference between current American and British English is probably in intonation—an elusive quality consisting of voice timbre, pitch, sentence rhythm, and stress. Almost no syntactical differences are evident between American and British English, and comparatively few differences exist in vocabulary, pronunciation, or spelling. The British, however, do say *rubber* instead of *eraser*, and *vest* instead of *undershirt*. They also drop their *r*'s before consonants—pronouncing *lord* as *laud*, for example—and spell *honour, colour*, and many other words with *-our* instead of *-or*.

Americanisms. Among the first Americanisms—words or usages found in the United States but not in Great Britain—were the names coined to describe the new animals, plants, and landscape features that the British settlers found in North America. *Raccoon* was borrowed from Algonquian, *prairie* from French; *foothill* was a new compound forged from two familiar English words. Later, terms such as *presidential, congress,* and *gubernatorial* were applied to the newly established American political institutions.

The British had no objection to the use of neologisms to describe new phenomena. From the middle of the 18th century, however, they did object, often vehemently, to other kinds of Americanisms. The writer and lexicographer Samuel JOHNSON, for instance, denounced *to wobble, to budge,* and *fun,* because, in his opinion, English already possessed words adequate to express these ideas.

Americans fought back, however. Noah WEBSTER believed that words and usages should be evaluated on their own merits, not on the basis of their place of origin. His *American Dictionary of the English Language* (1828) included thousands of new words, old words with new meanings, new pronunciations, and new spellings—solely on the ground that they were all used by educated American speakers. It was Webster who insisted on *-or* instead of *-our* in words like *honour*; who took the *k* off the end of words like *musick* and *traffick*; and who substituted the suffix *-er* for *-re* in words like *centre*.

English literature   English literature has developed continuously over 15 centuries from the Anglo-Saxon period to modern times. The introduction (*c.*1476) of printing to England by William CAXTON stabilized the language, and Caxton's press, unlike those of other European printers, produced books in the vernacular for the general reader, thus laying the foundation of a literary language that survives fundamentally unchanged to the present day. AMERICAN LITERATURE, AUSTRALIAN LITERATURE, CANADIAN LITERATURE in English, and AFRICAN LITERATURE in English are discussed in separate articles.

The Anglo-Saxon Period

England's oldest literature grew out of the confluence of two traditions: the paganism of the Anglo-Saxons, who

Geoffrey Chaucer (c.1340–1400)

Christopher Marlowe (1564–93)

William Shakespeare (1564–1616)

invaded the island in the 5th and 6th centuries, and the Christian culture introduced to Northumbria by the Irish missionary Aidan and to Kent (in 597) by AUGUSTINE OF CANTERBURY. The invaders' Teutonic heritage stressed the love of battle, fidelity to one's lord, and the implacability of fate. The Christian influence tended to soften this heroic outlook.

Both influences are evident in BEOWULF, the first English EPIC. Although probably composed in Northumbria sometime during the 8th century, the poem is set in 6th-century Scandinavia. No other Old English epic has survived, but a brief 7th-century poem, "Widsith," recounts the travels of a scop—the name given to the professional singers who recited heroic verse to a lord and his retainers while they sat feasting in the mead hall. Accompanying themselves on harps, scops also sang elegiac lyrics such as "The Wife's Lament," "Deor," "The Ruin," "The Seafarer," and the "The Wanderer," of which all but the first are preserved in the EXETER BOOK.

Anglo-Saxon heroic and elegiac verse was characterized by regular stress, free rhythm, end-stopped and unrhymed lines, abundant alliteration, and the use of conventional figures of speech known as kennings. Much of the 7th-century poet CÆDMON's famous "Hymn," for example, is a series of kennings for the word God. Only the fragmentary "Hymn" can be attributed to Cædmon with certainty, but on its strength alone he has been called the father of English song. The 9th-century poet CYNEWULF, who may have come from Mercia, has been credited with writing not only Andreas—the "Christian Beowulf"—but also "The Dream of the Rood," a beautifully imaginative lyrical meditation that anticipates Middle English dream visions. Cynewulf's masterpiece, signed by him, is the saint's life Elene, which includes an account of the discovery of the cross.

Before the reign of Alfred the Great (871–99) prose writers, working in Latin, produced numerous homilies and chronicles. Aldhelm (c.640–709) wrote a number of Latin RIDDLES, later translated into Old English and found today in the Exeter Book. A generation later, BEDE, the greatest Anglo-Saxon scholar, wrote about 40 books, the most famous of which is the Ecclesiastical History of the English People (731).

After Alfred became (871) King of Wessex, he employed court scholars and translated several books into English. It has been said that he thus founded English prose; certainly his versions of Pope Gregory I's Pastoral Care, Saint Augustine's Soliloquies, and Boethius's Consolation of Philosophy increased the prestige of the vernacular. Alfred's reign also saw the beginning of a major national historical record, The ANGLO-SAXON CHRONICLE, which includes such stirring set pieces as the poem "The Battle of Brunanburh."

A century after Alfred, as an outcome of the tenth-century monastic revival, English prose was developed stylistically in the copious writings of the churchmen ÆLFRIC, surnamed "the Grammarian," and Wulfstan (d. 1023). Ælfric's prose in particular has an ease and clarity not achieved again in English until the age of Dryden.

The Anglo-Norman Period

The Norman victory in 1066 at the Battle of Hastings paved the way for the expansion in England of a continental influence that had already begun to make itself felt under Edward the Confessor. But the administrative consolidation and resulting cultural fusion between the Anglo-Saxons and their conquerors was not always evident linguistically: the court continued to speak French, the clerical language remained Latin, and the people continued to speak English.

At Peterborough, The Anglo-Saxon Chronicle was continued in English to the year 1154. But William of Malmesbury (c.1090–c.1143) chose to write his history of the English kings in Latin, and that language was the preeminent one for historians. It was used to greatest effect by the Welsh cleric GEOFFREY OF MONMOUTH, whose partly legendary History of the Kings of Britain (1135) helped to popularize King ARTHUR AND ARTHURIAN LEGEND. The priest LAYAMON's poem, The Brut (c.1205), derived from Geoffrey, is the first truly English version of the story

Ben Jonson (1572–1637)

John Donne (1572–1631)

John Milton (1608–74)

of Arthur, signifying a nationalistic trend also evident in the anonymous metrical romances *King Horn* (*c.*1250) and *Havelock the Dane* (*c.*1310), both based on Norman sources but celebrating English heroes.

Not all Anglo-Norman writers favored the growth of romance. The anonymous author of the English *Cursor Mundi* (*c.*1300) condemns such secular works and proposes scriptural instruction as the appropriate burden of poetry. Didactic writings did indeed flourish, from the metrical homilies of Orm and Robert Mannyng to the anonymous guides *The Pricke of Conscience* (14th century) and *The Ancrene Riwle*. The latter work, composed in the early 13th century as a devotional manual for nuns, expresses the stern asceticism as well as the mysticism of the age.

In spite of such writings and the spread of the somewhat didactic mystery and miracle plays from the 13th century, nonreligious works were also popular. The 13th-century songs "Sumer is icumen in" and the "Cuckoo Song" suggest the attention to seasonal change that is characteristic of the vernacular lyrics of the period; "Alysoun" (*c.*1300) is among the best of the contemporary love lyrics. The late-13th-century beast FABLE *The Fox and the Wolf* and the early-14th-century FABLIAU *The Land of Cockaygne* anticipate Chaucer in their satirical attitude toward social ills. The poem of debate, best represented by the charming *The Owl and the Nightingale* (*c.*1200), mirrors the growth of Norman legal disputation.

The Norman hegemony ensured the deepening of the religious impulse in English writing, while adding to Anglo-Saxon heroic thought the conventions of continental romance. Even the so-called alliterative revival of the second half of the 14th century did not arrest the replacement of stressed verse by rhymed, syllabic verse. Two writers of genius, William LANGLAND and the anonymous Gawain poet, chose the traditional unrhymed, alliterative line. But because they lived in the north or west, away from London, their influence was limited. Langland's apocalyptic dream vision, PIERS PLOWMAN, includes moving accounts of the wretched life of the 14th-century

poor. The Gawain poet takes his name from the chivalric romance *Sir Gawain and the Green Knight*, set in the time of King Arthur, but he also wrote the religious poems *Pearl*, *Purity*, and *Patience*.

The Age of Chaucer

The work of Langland and the Gawain poet marked the end, not the continuation, of a tradition, for neither their language nor their alliterative verse form were destined to survive. It was Geoffrey CHAUCER, writing in a London dialect in rhymed, syllabic verse, who determined the future course of English poetry. Despite the changes in the language that have occurred since Chaucer's time, the educated modern reader has little difficulty understanding his work. His CANTERBURY TALES, begun *c.*1387, portray a wide range of humanity and present a vivid and detailed picture of the England that he knew, depicting not types but individuals. His long narrative poem *Troilus and Criseyde* shows a rare grasp of human character.

Though rarely read today, John GOWER influenced 15th-century verse almost as much as did his contemporary, Chaucer. Gower's long didactic poem, the *Confessio Amantis* (1390), was imitated by Chaucer's London disciples Thomas HOCCLEVE and John LYDGATE, as well as by the Scottish Chaucerians, William DUNBAR and Robert Henryson.

The 15th century also marked the high point in English medieval drama, with mystery cycles such as the Towneley or Wakefield Plays and morality plays such as EVERYMAN. The last medieval chronicler of the Arthurian legends, Sir Thomas MALORY, is thought to have written his prose romance *Morte Darthur* while in prison; he may have died there, a victim of the Wars of the Roses that raged from 1455 to 1485.

During the 16th century, the Renaissance, already established in Italy and France, reached England. Among Henry VIII's courtiers were Sir Thomas WYATT, who introduced the sonnet to England, and Henry Howard, Earl of SURREY. Another poet of the reign was John SKELTON, a vigorous satirist and sometimes a delightful lyricist.

Alexander Pope (1688–1744)   *Jonathan Swift (1667–1745)*   *Henry Fielding (1707–54)*

Saint Thomas MORE, statesman, humanist, and scholar, also wrote poetry but is better remembered for his history, *Richard III* (1513); religious works, notably *A Dialogue of Comfort against Tribulation*, written about 1534 and published in 1553; and UTOPIA, whose title has passed into the language.

The Elizabethan Age

Although King Henry's daughter, Elizabeth I, ascended the throne in 1558, the literary revival that bears her name did not definitely take shape until she was middle-aged. Drama became the chief medium that Elizabethan writers chose, but the earliest English blank-verse play, *Gorboduc* (1561), had little lasting effect.

The poetic drama in England was first successfully launched by a group called the "University Wits"—Robert GREENE, Thomas LODGE, Thomas NASHE, and George Peele. Since the Wits were learned men, their attitude toward the primitive conditions of the English stage was somewhat condescending. Thomas KYD, however, had a natural sense of the theater, and his play *The Spanish Tragedy* continued to fascinate for decades following its production (c.1587).

During that same year Christopher MARLOWE composed *Tamburlaine the Great*, a resoundingly poetic historical melodrama. It was succeeded by his masterpiece *Doctor Faustus* and by *The Jew of Malta* and *Edward the Second*. What Ben Jonson called "Marlowe's mighty line" transformed Elizabethan drama, and an aspiring newcomer who learned from his example was William SHAKESPEARE.

Shakespeare. Shakespeare's life as professional dramatist and, subsequently, as actor-manager lasted from about 1592 until 1616 and moved through the period of his early historical plays, from *Henry VI* to *Richard III*, and his first comedies, such as *The Two Gentlemen of Verona* and The TAMING OF THE SHREW; the period between 1594 and 1599, during which he wrote *Julius Caesar*, ROMEO AND JULIET, A MIDSUMMER NIGHT'S DREAM, The MERCHANT OF VENICE, and his series of later historical dramas; the epoch of his greatest tragedies, HAMLET, OTHELLO, KING LEAR, MACBETH, and some of his most successful comedies; and his last phase, from 1608 to 1616, during which his dramatic method and his attitude toward existence underwent a subtle change. Then, like Prospero in The TEMPEST, he seems to have "drowned his book" and bid his art farewell.

Shakespeare's Contemporaries and Successors. Ben JONSON, Shakespeare's friendly rival, and far more erudite, is remembered for his brilliant VOLPONE, *Every Man in His Humour*, and *The Alchemist* and less for his Roman tragedies *Sejanus* and *Catiline*. Playwrights of the 17th century, such as George CHAPMAN, John FORD, Cyril TOURNEUR, and John WEBSTER, carried on the grand Shakespearean tradition, but they sought to achieve more violent effects. Ford's *'Tis Pity She's a Whore*, for example, explores the tragic consequences of incestuous passion.

Besides Elizabethan and Jacobean drama, the era is noted for its lyric poets, among them such exquisite songwriters as Thomas CAMPION and the famous courtier poet Sir Walter RALEIGH, and writers of moving and mellifluous sonnets, such as Samuel DANIEL, Michael DRAYTON, Philip SIDNEY, and Edmund SPENSER. A major poet, Spenser is best known for his masterpiece, The FAERIE QUEENE, a complex allegorical romance dedicated to Queen Elizabeth.

Elizabethan Prose. In 1597, Francis BACON, a lawyer, politician, and philosopher who announced that he had "taken all knowledge to be my province," published his pithy epigrammatic *Essays*. A more elaborate stylist was Richard HOOKER, the author of a majestic treatise, *Of the Laws of Ecclesiastical Polity*, which attempted in weighty but finely balanced phrases to justify "the eternal law of God." Prominent among the satirists and pamphleteers were Thomas DEKKER and Stephen Gosson. Historians also flourished. Raleigh launched a *History of the World* that he did not live to complete; the works of Raphael HOLINSHED became important source material for Shakespeare's history plays.

William Blake (1757–1827)

William Wordsworth (1770–1850)

George Gordon, Lord Byron (1788–1824)

The Seventeenth Century

The Elizabethan Age was characterized by pride and self-confidence; the 17th century was haunted by doubt and dissension and, between 1642 and 1651, torn by bitter civil war. Early Jacobean prose is seen at its best in the Authorized Version of the Old and New Testaments (1611), the joint work of 47 scholars, which was not only the mainstay of the Protestant faith but an eternal linguistic resource.

The Metaphysical Poets. The career of John DONNE spans the Elizabethan and Jacobean eras. During his youth he wrote a series of strikingly original love poems. During middle age, however, he renounced the pleasures of the world, wrote magnificent religious sonnets, and, having joined the Anglican church, became a powerful preacher. Donne was the most famous of the metaphysical poets (see METAPHYSICAL POETRY), a group that included Abraham COWLEY, Richard CRASHAW, Andrew MARVELL, Henry Vaughan, and Henry King. Poets of ideas, attracted by the achievements of philosophy and science, they probed deeply into the origins of human feelings, employing complex allusive images. More simple and direct were the devotional poems of George HERBERT, the pastoral lyrics of Robert HERRICK, and the courtly verses of two cavalier poets, Richard LOVELACE and Sir John SUCKLING.

Prose. Modern English prose did not begin to develop until the second half of the 17th century. Before, the Elizabethan tradition had not yet lost its hold, and erudite information was compiled for its own sake. Robert BURTON produced *The Anatomy of Melancholy,* a vast encyclopedia of fact and fantasy, with lengthy quotations from earlier writers and a wealth of picturesque tales. Izaak WALTON also compiled what pretended to be a learned treatise, *The Compleat Angler; or, the Contemplative Man's Recreation.* It is, however, far more literary than scientific, including numerous decorative digressions woven around its central theme. The greatest prose writer of the epoch undoubtedly was Sir Thomas BROWNE, the author of the humanistic *Religio Medici* (1642).

A very different conception of Christianity inspired John BUNYAN. His famous allegory PILGRIM'S PROGRESS (1678) was one of over 50 works; from a 20th-century point of view, his spiritual autobiography, *Grace Abounding* (1666), has an even stronger interest. His style is plain, with few pretensions to elegance, and, in this sense, modern.

The same impression of modernity is given by John AUBREY, an inimitable anecdotalist and author of unforgettable portrait sketches, and by philosophers and theorists such as Thomas HOBBES and John LOCKE. The diarists John EVELYN and Samuel PEPYS also strike an altogether modern note. Each was a member of the newly founded Royal Society and took a keen interest in the scientific experiments conducted there.

Restoration Literature. For writers who lived into the second half of the 17th century, the civil wars were a tragic interlude, dividing them from, in John Dryden's phrase, the "giant race before the flood." Nonetheless, one great poet, John MILTON, who had published his earliest poems during the reign of Charles I and played an active political role during the time of the Commonwealth, wrote his noblest work, PARADISE LOST, after the Restoration of Charles II in 1660.

Both in glorious verse and in well-knit controversial prose, Milton towered over his contemporaries; even his mighty successor John DRYDEN did not reach so high a level. Dryden was distinguished, however, by his amazing versatility. A master of prose and a grandly effective satirist, he was also an accomplished lyric poet and dramatist. Thomas OTWAY and Dryden were the last English playwrights to handle blank verse with Shakespearean strength and ease.

Even as tragedy declined, however, a new type of comedy, the fashionable "comedy of manners," emerged. Dramatists such as William CONGREVE, Sir George ETHEREGE, Sir John VANBRUGH, and William WYCHERLEY delighted Restoration playgoers, when the London theaters, closed by a Puritan government in 1642, were reopened under royal patronage (see RESTORATION DRAMA).

John Keats (1795–1821)

Percy Bysshe Shelley (1792–1822)

Sir Walter Scott (1771–1832)

The Augustans

The 18th century in English literature has been called the Augustan Age, the Neoclassical Age, and the Age of Reason. When Dryden died in 1700, he left a vacant throne, and it remained vacant until Alexander POPE boldly took his place.

Alexander Pope. In 1711, Pope published his *Essay on Criticism*, and in 1712, *The Rape of the Lock*, a brilliant mock-heroic poem. Next he translated the *Iliad* and the *Odyssey*, and then embarked on *The Dunciad*, a ferocious literary satire, and set out to satirize society as a whole with a succession of poems called *Moral Essays*. In all these undertakings, Pope made a finely polished weapon of the heroic couplet.

Pope's Contemporaries and Successors. The Augustan Age, apart from Pope, was a period of minor poets—John GAY, whose greatest achievement was the lively *Beggar's Opera*; James THOMSON (1834–82), author of *The Seasons*, a pleasing but conventional tribute to the British landscape; and William COLLINS and William COWPER, who focused on quiet domestic themes. Only Thomas GRAY showed a touch of real genius. His methods of composition were so hesitant and tentative, however, that his ELEGY WRITTEN IN A COUNTRY CHURCHYARD took him eight years to complete.

William Blake. While Gay, Thomson, and the others were all much admired and widely read, William BLAKE, a poet, visionary, painter, and engraver, was writing and printing his "Prophetic Books" and his lyric poems. *The Marriage of Heaven and Hell* (1790), his greatest prophetic work, was preceded by *Songs of Innocence* (1789) and followed by *Songs of Experience* (1794). Blake was exceptional; he rebelled against his age, rejecting moral and aesthetic standards that 18th-century writers readily embraced. They believed that their age was one of steady progress, comparable to the most civilized period of the Roman Empire.

Early 18th-Century Prose. Poetry had declined since Pope's death, but prose flourished under many different guises. Daniel DEFOE pioneered the realistic modern novel with ROBINSON CRUSOE (1719) and *Moll Flanders* (1722), and Pope's friend and contemporary Jonathan SWIFT enchanted the world with GULLIVER'S TRAVELS (1726). Joseph ADDISON and Sir Richard STEELE collaborated to improve the art of essay writing. Their tone was carefully light; Addison's aim, he said, was to bring philosophy out of the library and lead her to the tea table.

The Rise of the Novel. In 1740 the 18th-century novel received a further impetus. The middle-aged printer Samuel RICHARDSON achieved fame with the long novel *Pamela; or, Virtue Rewarded*, followed by the even longer *Clarissa Harlowe* (1747–48). His subjects were always women, their temptations, tragedies, and triumphs; his stories, told in the form of letters, are a remarkable blend of effusive emotionalism and acute psychological analysis. Laurence STERNE, too, introduced not only a new impressionistic way of writing but a revolutionary mode of feeling. Under his influence the adjective *sentimental* became a term of high praise. *The Life and Opinions of Tristram Shandy, Gentleman* (1760–67) is a picturesque medley of autobiographical details, cynical reflections on life, and sentimental and romantic musings.

Compared with Richardson and Sterne, Henry FIELDING, Tobias SMOLLETT, and Oliver GOLDSMITH are straightforward storytellers. Fielding's greatest novel, TOM JONES (1749), gives an exciting and frequently ludicrous account of a young man's progress through the world, enlivened by digressions. Smollett's *Peregrine Pickle* (1751) and *Humphrey Clinker* (1771) also have peripatetic heroes who come into violent contact with innumerable odd, outrageous characters. Goldsmith's *Vicar of Wakefield* depicts the victory of domestic virtue over fashionable vice and therefore appears a little contrived to modern readers, but the easy simplicity of its prose style delighted contemporaries.

Later 18th-Century Prose. Excepting Blake's poetry, the greatest triumphs of the late 18th century were in prose. James BOSWELL claimed of his LIFE OF SAMUEL JOHNSON that "my mode of biography is the most perfect that can

Jane Austen (1775–1817)

Charles Dickens (1812–70)

William Makepeace Thackeray (1811–63)

be conceived." The claim was justified; his portrait of Samuel JOHNSON is the first full-scale modern biography. Earlier biographers tended to envisage their subjects from a historical or moral viewpoint; Boswell's attitude toward Johnson is intensely personal, passionately concerned with the man whom he describes—not only with his genius and moral worth, but also with his human errors. Had Boswell failed to complete his book, Johnson would be remembered for his dictionary, as a versifier and essayist, and as the author of two poems, "London" and "The Vanity of Human Wishes," and *Lives of the Poets*; but his fame would not have been worldwide.

Meanwhile, Edward GIBBON, the founder of modern historiography, had launched his magnum opus, The DE-CLINE AND FALL OF THE ROMAN EMPIRE. The opening volume, published in 1776, found its way, the author informs us, to "every table" and "almost every toilette." The last volume did not appear until 1788.

Among the *Decline and Fall's* keenest admirers was the Scottish philosopher David HUME, who, like Gibbon, was a cultivated agnostic and a brilliant stylist. He believed that philosophy was an important branch of literature and that the philosophic writer should address himself to the ordinary educated person. His *Treatise of Human Nature* (1739–40), *Enquiry Concerning Human Understanding* (1749), and his six-volume *History of England* (1754–61) are all distinguished by lucidity of diction and occasional ironic touches.

Equally celebrated as prose writers were Adam SMITH, whose *Inquiry into the Nature and Causes of the Wealth of Nations* helped found the new science of political economy, and Edmund BURKE, "the Demosthenes of England," statesman, pamphleteer, and master of rhetorical eloquence.

Drama and Later Novels. English literature during the latter 18th century also had a less solemn aspect. Richard Brinsley SHERIDAN revived the comedy of manners with *The Rivals* and *The School for Scandal*. Horace WALPOLE produced an incomparable history of his own age under the guise of private letters that he required the re-

cipients to send back, and his fantastic dream novel, *The Castle of Otranto* (1764), was the precursor of the GOTHIC ROMANCE. In a similar vein, William BECKFORD composed *The History of the Caliph Vathek*, a haunting Arabian fairy tale for sophisticated readers. Finally, Fanny BURNEY gave English fiction a delicately feminine turn. The earliest woman novelist, Burney owed much of her success to the fact that, although a gentlewoman and daughter of the famous musicologist Charles Burney, she dared to write of low life. Her first and best novel, *Evelina; or, a Young Lady's Entrance into the World* (1778), is now appreciated mainly as a period piece; but her record of life at the gloomy Court of George III is a minor masterpiece.

The Nineteenth Century

The 19th century, like the 17th, was a period of change and conflict. Especially in 1848, the year of European revolutions, violent clashes between "the two nations," as Benjamin DISRAELI called the rich and the poor, frequently seemed close at hand. Industrial progress had altered the face of the country, and parliamentary reform shifted the balance of power; but new social problems replaced the old. In literature a series of eloquent prophets, notably John RUSKIN and Thomas CARLYLE, thundered against the purblind materialism of the money-mad Industrial Age.

The Romantic Movement. Meanwhile, ROMANTICISM, already in evidence before the century began, had transfigured English literature. In 1798, Samuel Taylor COLERIDGE and William WORDSWORTH had issued a joint volume, LYRICAL BALLADS. Coleridge contributed The RIME OF THE ANCIENT MARINER, and Wordsworth wrote a series of poems on subjects "chosen from ordinary life," using the "real language" of ordinary people. The keynotes of romantic poetry were its cult of youth and freedom, its reliance on the sovereign force of love, and its sense of a close relationship with nature, which the Augustans had tended to regard as merely a decorative background. Wordsworth's *Ode: Intimations of Immortality from Recollections of Early Childhood* appeared in 1807; however, after *The White Doe of Rylstone* (1815), his verses lost their youth-

Charlotte Brontë (1816–55)

George Eliot (1819–80)

Robert Louis Stevenson (1850–94)

ful fire. His masterpiece, *The Prelude*, the story of his poetic education, was never published in his lifetime. Coleridge's best-known poems, including "Kubla Khan," were written before he had reached 30.

With the emergence of George Gordon, Lord BYRON, John KEATS, and Percy Bysshe SHELLEY, English romantic poetry regained its youthful zest. The triumphant publication in March 1812 of the first two cantos of *Childe Harold* established the 24-year-old Byron as the most dazzling poet of his era, and he remained an international celebrity until his death. Byron had many faces, however. His favorite master was Pope. Besides the exuberant strength of feeling that characterized his earlier poems and that rose to a superb height in *Childe Harold III and IV*, he possessed a vein of satirical and cynical humor that irradiated DON JUAN, his long seriocomic narrative of a young man's life and loves.

Neither Shelley nor Keats lived long enough to enjoy the fame that they deserved. Shelley was ecstatic and visionary; Keats, who took little interest in public affairs, was a quiet, steadily creative spirit. Undeterred by the failure of his first volume, *Poems* (1817), and of *Endymion* (1818), Keats painfully practiced his art until he could publish (1820) his third volume, which contains the famous odes "The Eve of St. Agnes" and his unfinished masterpiece, "Hyperion." Shelley's most productive period was confined to the last three years of his life. In 1819 he wrote the verse tragedy *The Cenci* and the lyric drama *Prometheus Unbound*, in which the heroic giant represents the human soul victimized by tyranny and superstition.

The English romantic writers cannot be called a school. Byron, for example, liked Shelley as a man but had a low opinion of his writings. A poet he respected, however, was George CRABBE, "Nature's sternest painter, yet the best." Crabbe, a poet and storyteller combined, was a realistic, but unexpectedly romantic, chronicler of the bleak East Anglian landscapes where he had been born and raised.

The 19th-Century Novel. In the 18th century the novel had not ranked high as a form of literary expression; during the 19th century, thanks to circulating libraries and the growth of popular education, it became immensely powerful. Sir Walter SCOTT, who had begun his career in verse in 1805 with *The Lay of the Last Minstrel*, occupied himself between 1814 and 1823 with the Waverley novels, a series of historical romances that continued from *Waverley* to *Quentin Durward*.

Jane AUSTEN appealed to very different tastes. Fanny Burney's *Evelina* had shown what a woman novelist could do; but Austen's acuteness of observation and delicacy of literary delineation left her predecessor far behind. PRIDE AND PREJUDICE, *Sense and Sensibility*, and *Northanger Abbey* had all been written and put aside before the 18th century ended. *Sense and Sensibility* appeared only in 1811; *Pride and Prejudice* and *Mansfield Park* were published in 1813 and 1814; and *Emma*, which many critics consider her most accomplished work, appeared in 1816. *Persuasion*, the last of her completed novels, was published posthumously in 1818.

Jane Austen was largely unconcerned with the events and social problems of her day, but the British prime minister Benjamin Disraeli won distinction as a socially concerned writer. Although his first novel, *Vivian Grey* (1826), was a romantic tale, he produced a series of political narratives—*Coningsby* (1824), *Sybil* (1845), and *Tancred* (1847)—in which he set forth an ambitious program of reform and exposed the evils and dangers of the contemporary system.

The constellation of great Victorian novelists Charles DICKENS, Elizabeth Cleghorn GASKELL, William Makepeace THACKERAY, and Anthony TROLLOPE were all committed writers and had a sense of responsibility for the welfare of their fellow human beings. Gaskell, the wife of a Unitarian minister, undertook such themes as the condition of the modern industrial towns and the plight of unmarried mothers. Thackeray's more general attack on society satirized the selfishness of moneyed society. Of his four major novels—VANITY FAIR, *Pendennis, Henry Esmond*, and *The Newcomes*—*Vanity Fair*, the skillfully executed por-

Robert Browning (1812–89)

Alfred, Lord Tennyson (1809–89)

Thomas Hardy (1840–1928)

trait of a thoroughly amoral woman, is the most enduring.

Thackeray used a comparatively plain and direct style. Dickens's method of storytelling, as in the opening passages of *Bleak House*, has a baroque extravagance. The London he describes is a haunted labyrinth through which fantastic personages wander. He had a moral purpose, and many of the evils to which he drew attention were ultimately swept away. Dickens was a prodigious worker. His most important novels, beginning with *Oliver Twist* and *Nicholas Nickleby* and ending with GREAT EXPECTATIONS, *Our Mutual Friend*, and the unfinished *Mystery of Edwin Drood*, were written in the space of 27 years.

Anthony Trollope was the least pretentious, and apparently the most prosaic, of all the great Victorian novelists. He treated storytelling not as an art but as a craft, and, unlike Dickens, he never beautified or grossly sentimentalized his characters. His object was merely to chronicle his age. This he did, first in the Barsetshire novels, which portrayed the busy inhabitants of an English cathedral city, and then in a series of political narratives that took his readers behind the scenes of aristocratic and government life.

Dickens, Thackeray, and Trollope were Londoners. Charlotte, Emily, and Anne Brontë (see BRONTË family) sprang from a lonely Yorkshire parsonage. Charlotte's *Jane Eyre* is a bewildering blend of maturity and rawness. *Villette*, based on an unhappy love affair Charlotte herself experienced, is a wholly satisfactory book. It falls far short, however, of Emily's WUTHERING HEIGHTS, one of the most remarkable novels and wildest love stories ever written. Even Charlotte found Emily's fantastic tale of "perverted passion and passionate perversity" disturbing. Over its pages, she declared, there brooded a "horror of great darkness."

Charlotte and Emily Brontë were solitary figures, whereas Mary Ann Evans, who adopted the pseudonym George ELIOT, played an active part in the London intellectual world. She was concerned with political and moral questions and with the oppressive effect of the established social system on the men and women she described. After *Adam Bede* and *The Mill on the Floss*, she produced her boldest work, MIDDLEMARCH, a panoramic view of England in a period of rapid change. Among the subjects discussed are parliamentary reform, the growth of railways, female emancipation, marriage, economics, and the state of medicine.

Other typical Victorian novelists were Charles KINGSLEY, whose brand of Christian Socialism ruffled many 19th-century critics; George MEREDITH, author of *The Ordeal of Richard Feverel*, his first success, and the originator of a writing style that endeavored to give modern prose the lyrical quality of great verse; and Robert Louis STEVENSON, storyteller par excellence, equally at home in *Kidnapped*, a rousing tale of adventure, and in DR. JEKYLL AND MR. HYDE, his imaginative analysis of a split personality. The Victorian novelists include two rebels, Samuel BUTLER (1835–1902) and George Robert GISSING. Butler's utopian *Erewhon*, a revolutionary vision of the world as it ought to be, attracted little notice when it appeared in 1872. His posthumously published autobiographical novel *The Way of All Flesh* is more interesting from a sociological than from a literary point of view. Each novelist was recording his own experience—Butler, his early struggle against a tyrannical domestic background; Gissing, the grinding effects of poverty, as he recorded them in *New Grub Street* (1891) and *The Private Papers of Henry Ryecroft* (1903).

Victorian Essays. Not all 19th-century writers were attracted to the novel. Walter Savage LANDOR, besides writing one or two unforgettable lyrics, poured out his views of the past and present in a series of literary dialogues, *Imaginary Conversations*. Charles LAMB became an accomplished essayist in the Addisonian style, while William HAZLITT was a more penetrating essayist and critic. Thomas DE QUINCEY, a victim of the opium habit, published *Confessions of an English Opium-Eater* (1821), an account of his lonely youth and of the sublime dreams and appalling nightmares that had haunted him.

The essayist and historian Thomas CARLYLE, a preju-

Rudyard Kipling (1865–1936)

James Joyce (1882–1941)

D. H. Lawrence (1885–1930)

diced theorist and inveterate sermonist, developed a half-biblical, half-Germanic style. He made his mark with *Sartor Resartus* (1833–35), in which he proclaimed his personal despair but enunciated a gospel of the "Everlasting Yea," and then embarked on *The French Revolution* (1837), in which he exercised his dramatic talents to the full, although his historical conclusions were often biased. His later studies, *Cromwell* and *Frederick the Great*, are ponderous and ill digested.

Thomas Babington MACAULAY, on the other hand, strove to make history simple and pleasant reading. He believed in modern progress, the supremacy of Whig ideals, and the virtues of parliamentary government. His *History of England* reflected a temperate optimism that possessed a strong appeal for the cultivated middle classes.

John RUSKIN, one of the most eloquent of the Victorian prophets, combined a passionate interest in art with a determination to reform society. His first book, *Modern Painters*, was a tribute to the genius of his favorite artist J. M. W. Turner. It was followed by *Seven Lamps of Architecture*, devoted to the Gothic cathedrals, and *The Stones of Venice. Unto This Last* (1862) was a fierce attack on the Victorian doctrine of laissez-faire. From that moment the tone of his writings became more and more prophetic and increasingly diffuse, until his autobiography, *Praeterita* (1885–89), which showed all his former mastery.

Victorian Poetry. Later 19th-century poets carried on the tradition of their romantic predecessors; in 1846, Elizabeth Barrett and the relatively obscure poet Robert BROWNING formed their celebrated partnership. Today, Elizabeth Barrett BROWNING's fame has declined, and "the man who married Elizabeth Barrett" has overshadowed her. His two-volume work *Men and Women* (1855) reveals his talents at their highest point. An intellectual, speculative, and discursive poet who showed a novelist's preoccupation with the complexities of human character, he was also a fine lyric poet.

Alfred, Lord TENNYSON succeeded Wordsworth as poet laureate in 1850, but by that time his best work had been done. The spirit of pagan melancholy that breathes through his early poems, for example "The Lotus Eaters" (1832), had largely disappeared, and the feelings of poignant personal sorrow that inspired *In Memoriam* had been stilled.

With Matthew ARNOLD and the Pre-Raphaelite poets—Dante Gabriel ROSSETTI, his sister Christina ROSSETTI, William MORRIS, and Algernon Charles SWINBURNE—the English romantic movement reached a not inglorious close. Arnold had a distinguished career as a poet, during which he produced "Dover Beach" and "The Scholar Gypsy," poignant lamentations over the plight of the faithless modern world; later, he became an influential modern critic. *Culture and Anarchy* is a brave defense of the standards he valued—beauty and reason, "sweetness and light"—against a new barbarian invasion.

All the Pre-Raphaelite artists—and Rossetti was himself a painter—took their subjects from an imaginative vision of the Middle Ages, which Morris, an ardent socialist reformer, compared favorably with the modern industrial civilization. Of this group, however, only Christina Rossetti and Swinburne made any lasting contribution to the art of English verse. Christina Rossetti was the finest religious poet to appear in England since the 17th century. Swinburne's *Poems and Ballads* (1866), a succession of wild, erotic dithyrambs, offended conventional piety with its outspoken sensuality and atheism.

The most original poet of the late Victorian period, the Jesuit priest Gerard Manley HOPKINS remained almost completely unknown until the second decade of the 20th century. He broke with the traditions of the past both in his vocabulary and in his peculiar rhythmic methods. Like a modern poet he sought to rarify and condense rather than diffuse and explicate his meaning.

French literature was now exerting an important influence. Ernest DOWSON and Arthur Symons were both followers of the *"poète maudit"* Paul VERLAINE. Oscar WILDE, almost as much at home in Paris as in London, preached the gospel of AESTHETICISM which he had absorbed from

Virginia Woolf (1882–1941)

Dylan Thomas (1914–53)

Graham Greene (1904– 91)

Walter PATER. Of Wilde's fashionable comedies, the most brilliant was *The Importance of Being Earnest* (1895).

The Twentieth Century

Until the outbreak of World War I, fiction was still dominated by a group of novelists who had already achieved distinction during the Victorian Age—Thomas HARDY, the Anglo-American Henry JAMES, George MOORE, Joseph CONRAD, Rudyard KIPLING, H. G. WELLS, John GALSWORTHY, and Arnold BENNETT. Except for Hardy, who had abandoned the novel in disgust, after the unfriendly reception of *Jude the Obscure*, all remained extremely active. Though James and Moore were literary perfectionists and had a somewhat limited appeal, all addressed themselves to the widest public they could reach. None of these novelists found it necessary to indulge in technical experiments. Even E. M. FORSTER, though his approach to his subject was new, gave his stories a conventional framework. In drama George Bernard SHAW and James BARRIE continued to dominate. Shaw presented a coruscating flow of ideas, sometimes valuable, sometimes foolish and perverse. Barrie possessed a splendid command of stagecraft and sentimental gusto.

The framework of the Victorian novel was finally disrupted by the Irish novelist James JOYCE, whose revolutionary novel ULYSSES (1922) described the events of a single day and made bold use of the interior monologue. On a much smaller scale, Virginia WOOLF adopted a similar technique. She tended to discard plot and incident, concentrating on the analysis of individual characters by resurrecting their secret memories and delving deep into their subconscious minds.

Although D. H. LAWRENCE's *Sons and Lovers* (1913) gives a realistic picture of his own youth, he dwelt more and more on the subconscious aspects of the human personality. Lawrence had a mystic message to deliver and preached the salvation of the modern world through a return to more primitive beliefs and feelings.

A similar revolution occurred in poetry. The Georgian poets and their immediate predecessors, Robert BRIDGES,

A. E. HOUSMAN, and, in his earlier works, William Butler YEATS, all spoke in a language that Tennyson and Arnold might have understood. During the 1930s, however, they were eclipsed by the appearance of the Sitwell confraternity (see SITWELL family), Osbert, Edith, and Sacheverell; by a group of new poets, W. H. AUDEN and his close friends Stephen SPENDER, C. Day LEWIS, and Louis MacNEICE; and, finally, by the rise of Dylan THOMAS, a wild Welsh bard, whose displays of pyrotechnic word spinning gained him extraordinary renown.

Evelyn WAUGH and Graham GREENE, although undoubtedly among the most important novelists of the last 40–50 years, are by no means technical innovators but instead show a deep respect for literary tradition. Younger writers also exhibit little enthusiasm for experiment—although some of the novels by William GOLDING, Doris LESSING, and Anthony BURGESS use science-fiction techniques to good effect. Other important contemporary British writers include Kingsley AMIS and Iris MURDOCH, as well as playwright Tom STOPPARD and poets Seamus HEANEY, Ted HUGHES, and Philip LARKIN.

English music English music has followed an often idiosyncratic, stop-and-go course of development. Fertile periods of native composition and performance (including early-15th- and later-16th-century church music; vocal and instrumental consort music concentrated in the Elizabethan Age; and a 20th-century musical "renaissance") have alternated with long periods dominated by Continental musicians and influences, especially in the 14th, 18th, and 19th centuries. At other times musical development has been interrupted by political and religious upheavals—notably, the break between the Anglican and Roman churches in 1529, and the turmoil of the 17th-century Civil Wars and Commonwealth period. Most of the greatest English composers, particularly such early figures as John Dunstable, John Taverner, and Henry PURCELL, assimilated European techniques while bringing native idioms to a unique level of artistry. The standard musical period labels (baroque, classical, and so on), which have evolved to distinguish historical stylistic qualities primarily in Italian, German, and French compositions, often prove less meaningful when applied to English music. Frequently more revealing are relationships between musical developments and contemporary British political, social, and artistic currents.

Middle Ages. PLAINSONG was brought to the British Isles from the Continent in the late 6th century. The first important center of English sacred POLYPHONY was the cathedral in Winchester. The Winchester Troper, two 11th-century manuscripts containing more than 170 examples of two-voice organum (the earliest type of polyphony), is the oldest large collection of polyphonic music. A unique 13th-century example of secular song is the anonymous *Sumer is icumen in*, an ingenious four-part CANON with two additional voices fitted to English and Latin texts.

The 15th century marked a high point in the development of English polyphonic techniques and of English musical influence in Europe. The major source for this repertoire is the Old Hall manuscript, which contains about 150 Mass movements, motets, and nonliturgical devotional music written between 1350 and 1420 by Dunstable, Lionel Power, and other English composers. These works feature distinctively English stylistic qualities that would be widely imitated elsewhere: a more harmonic (less polyphonic) orientation; a preference for full-sounding sonorities, notably in the use of continuous parallel thirds and sixths in many passages; and a partiality to what one would call the major mode over other modal variants, suggesting early steps in the centuries-long evolution of TONALITY. During the same period secular songs finally took hold in England. Dunstable's 60 known works, which cover all of the major genres and forms of his time, include several secular examples. A unique English medieval and early Renaissance genre of both

A consort, or ensemble of the 16th and 17th centuries, performs the early chamber music of Elizabethan England.

monophonic and polyphonic song was the CAROL.

Tudor Church Music. Composers of the Tudor era (1485–1603) produced much of the finest English sacred music, often expanding conventional European four-part textures to five or six vocal lines.

A three-way struggle for control of the Anglican church between "mainstream," Roman Catholic, and Puritan factions—the latter demanding simple, functional worship music—resulted in abrupt shifts in English liturgical music throughout much of the 16th and 17th centuries. Thomas TALLIS and William BYRD wrote exquisite choral works for both Roman Catholic masses and Anglican services. An important English genre of the 11th through 18th centuries was the choral ANTHEM, the musical centerpiece of many Anglican services and similar in function to the Roman Catholic motet.

Secular Music of the Renaissance and Restoration. The 15th and 16th centuries, and especially the Elizabethan era (1558–1603), were a golden age of English instrumental music and secular song. English consort music—for homogeneous or mixed instrumental ensembles of two to eight strings and/or winds, by such composers as Byrd and Orlando GIBBONS—was renowned throughout much of Europe. Keyboard dances, variations, and similar works by the English virginalists (including Byrd, Thomas Morley, and John BULL) achieved comparable recognition. The English MADRIGAL flowered briefly but brilliantly at the end of the Elizabethan Age in clever part-songs by Morley, Thomas Weelkes, Byrd, Gibbons, and others. Similarly engaging solo songs with lute accompaniment were written by John DOWLAND.

The Civil Wars (1642–48) and the repressions of the Commonwealth (1649–60) severely disrupted English musical life. Polyphonic sacred music and theatrical productions were banned by Oliver Cromwell's government, and most church organs were destroyed. During the artistically more open Restoration period that followed, FRENCH MUSIC was in favor, and Italian forms, dominant on the continent, were fully mastered only by Purcell, who wrote the sole English baroque operatic masterpiece, *Dido and Aeneas*, as well as much incidental music for MASQUE and serious dramatic productions.

After Purcell, English music was dominated by Continental techniques and foreign musicians for almost 200 years. The one vibrant native tradition was the English ORATORIO of George Frideric HANDEL (notably *Messiah*), combining operatic elements with English choral traditions.

The only 19th-century British works to gain a wide following outside of England were the 14 satirical operas of GILBERT AND SULLIVAN.

20th Century. A revival in native English art music began with the romantic orchestral works of Frederick DELIUS and Sir Edward ELGAR. Though thoroughly schooled in German and French techniques, both Ralph VAUGHAN WILLIAMS and Gustav HOLST sought inspiration in the traditions of English folk song and Tudor music. More recent British music has been characterized by a stylistic eclecticism and a special interest in theatrical genres. Benjamin BRITTEN excelled at opera and other vocal genres. Michael TIPPETT, though most familiar in America for his

Benjamin Britten, an influential English composer of the 20th century, is best known for his operas, song cycles and choral works. A Ceremony of Carols (1942), the opera Peter Grimes (1945), and the War Requiem (1962) are among his best-known works.

orchestral works, has also contributed significantly to the renewal of British opera. Peter Maxwell Davies and Harrison Birtwistle have developed highly personal musical styles while drawing freely from English musical practices from the Middle Ages to the present day.

Since the 1890s, British scholars and performers have played a leading role in the revival of historically faithful performances of music from the Middle Ages through the early 19th century. Many of today's finest ensembles and soloists specializing in period performances (a notable example is the Academy of Ancient Music) are resident in and around London. Other evidence of the vitality of current English musical life can be seen in the yearly festivals of opera and other genres throughout the country and in the support by London audiences for four major symphony orchestras.

English setter The English setter is the product of crosses between early pointers and spaniels. The modern English setter traces its origins to Edward Laverack and R. L. Purcell Llewellin, who bred the animal in the early and middle 19th century. The breed is valued highly by hunters for its keen nose and retrieving, for its speed, and for its willingness to enter water.

English setters are large, long-coated dogs standing 61–68.6 cm (24–27 in) at the shoulder. They are white with black, blue, lemon, orange, or liver markings, and breeders prefer that the markings be flecked uniformly over the entire body. The coat should be flat and silky. The chest, legs, and tail should be moderately feathered.

English sparrow see SPARROW

English springer spaniel The English springer spaniel is one of the oldest varieties of hunting spaniels. It was officially recognized as a breed by the English Kennel Club in 1902. In the United States the English springer spaniel Field Trial Association was founded in 1924 to promote the breed, and the American Kennel Club admitted it to its official stud book in 1932. The ideal springer male is 50 cm (20 in) at the shoulder and weighs 22–25 kg (49–55 lb). Females are slightly smaller. The springer is medium sized and compact, with pendant ears and a docked tail. Its coat is moderately long, with feathering on the ears, chest, and legs. The springer is usually liver and white or black and white. The markings may form a full blanket over the body, with white legs, shoulder collar, muzzle, and blaze, and color on the head and ears; or the markings may be spots or patches on a white background.

(Above) The English springer spaniel is bred to flush, or "spring," game birds from their coverts. Larger than the cocker, the English springer makes an excellent retriever on land or in water.

(Left) The English setter is a large hunting dog, standing approximately 63 cm (25 in) at the shoulder and weighing about 27 kg (60 lb). Valued for its ability to "point" hidden game for hunters, the setter was originally trained to crouch, or "set," before its quarry.

The English toy spaniel is believed to have originated in the Orient and imported into England, where it became popular with the Tudor aristocracy. The four types of English toy spaniel differ in color but each exhibits a short nose, domed head, and silken hair.

English toy spaniel The English toy spaniel comprises four color types known as the King Charles, Ruby, Blenheim, and Prince Charles. They weigh 3.6–6.3 kg (8–14 lb), smaller than the general spaniel type, and have pendant ears and a docked tail. Their large, well-domed heads are so full over the eyes that the bulging forehead appears to almost meet the short, upturned nose.

The toy spaniel's coat should be long, silky, soft, and wavy, but not curly. The four color types are grouped into two show varieties: broken colors and solids. The King Charles and Ruby types are solids; the former is black and tan (considered a solid color), the tan occurring over the eyes and on the muzzle, chest, and legs; the latter is red. The Blenheim and Prince Charles types are broken-colored; the Blenheim is white with red patches; the Prince Charles is tricolored—white with black patches and tan markings.

engraving Engraving is a technique of printmaking in which the design to be printed is cut into a plate made of wood or metal. When the plate is inked, the ink collects in the cut lines of the design; the rest of the plate is wiped clean before printing. The printing process itself requires the application of heavy pressure so that the paper can actually be forced into the inked incisions.

Engraving belongs to those printmaking techniques collectively called intaglio. They are distinguished from relief techniques—such as the woodcut—by the fact that intaglio designs are incised below the surface of the plate. Other intaglio processes include lithography and PHOTOENGRAVING.

The tool used to cut the design into the plate in the engraving process is called a burin—a metal instrument consisting of a bent rod that is square or diamond-shaped in section. The plate into which the design is cut may be one of various types of metal, although copper and zinc are the most common. The burin cuts into the metal at varying depths according to the pressure applied on it by the engraver—the deeper the cut, the wider the engraved line. The metal burr raised by the burin at the edge of the engraved line is scraped off before prints are pulled from the plate. This is in contrast to drypoint, in which the burr is left on the plate, giving the finished print a characteristic fuzziness of outline. By contrast, the engraved line is sharp and precise. To get more variation of texture, light, and shadow than is normally achieved with engraving, the artist may use engraving along with other techniques, such as ETCHING or AQUATINT, all on the same plate. In such instances the engraved line usually will be the strongest line on the finished print.

The final print is made by inking the plate and then carefully wiping the unengraved surface clean of ink. The inked plate is positioned faceup on the press bed. Dampened paper is placed on top of the plate, and the plate and paper are passed through the press roller. On the resulting print the ink has been transferred from the plate to the paper. The print will be a mirror image of the design drawn on the plate. Many prints can be pulled from a single plate, although excessive use will coarsen the lines.

Engraving was first used in Germany in the 15th century, and achieved its major impact on the history of northern European art in the work of Albrecht DÜRER in

Engraving techniques require precisely angled tools to incise furrows of varying width or subtlety. A stipple graver (A) creates a dot, or stipple. Differing geometric points (B) of the burin (C) produce lines of corresponding delicacy or breadth. The dry point (D), a steel needle, is used in the technique of the same name. A scraper (E) removes the burr, or metal residue, from the line engraving; the burr remains on the dry point engraving to impart a velvety quality. (Right) Plates, usually of copper, rest on a leather cushion while being incised.

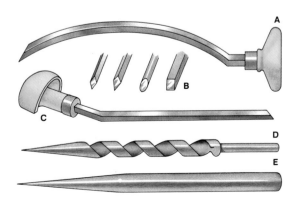

Dürer's Knight, Death, and the Devil *(1513) reveals his skill in copperplate engraving. His manipulation of line enabled him to express complex allegorical themes with stunning effect. (Museum of Fine Arts, Boston.)*

the 16th century. Italian printmakers of the 15th century included Maso Finiguerra, Antonio Pollaiuolo (see POL-LAIUOLO family), and Andrea MANTEGNA. Engraving was an important technique for illustrating books and was widely practiced throughout Europe from the 16th to the 19th century.

Enid [ee'-nid]   Enid (1990 pop., 45,309), a city in north central Oklahoma, is the seat of Garfield County and an important distribution and processing center for wheat, cattle, poultry, and oil. Philips University (1906) is there, and Vance Air Force Base is nearby. Once a watering place on the Chisholm Trail, the town was settled very quickly in 1893, when the Cherokee Strip was opened by "runs" of settlers.

Eniwetok [en-i-wee'-tahk]   Eniwetok is an atoll that comprises a ring of 40 low coral islets in the western Pacific. Located at the northwest extremity of the Ralik Chain of the MARSHALL ISLANDS, it was part of the U.S. Trust Territory of the Pacific Islands until 1986. The atoll has a circumference of 80 km (50 mi) and an area of 5 km^2 (2 mi^2). It was recaptured from the Japanese in 1944 and designated (1947) a proving ground by the

U.S. Atomic Energy Commission. The 146 Micronesian inhabitants were removed, and in 1948 and in the 1950s, Eniwetok was used as a testing site for atomic and hydrogen weapons. The atoll was decontaminated in 1976–80 and reopened to settlement.

Enki   see EA

enlarger   In photography, an enlarger is a type of projector that throws the image from a small negative onto sensitized paper; this operation is part of the process of making an enlarged positive print. The enlarger mechanism is enclosed in an enlarger head, which is mounted on a supporting column and can be moved toward or away from a baseboard easel, which holds the paper. The head contains a light source, the negative in a holder, and a focusing lens on a bellows; the bellows permits finer adjustments in the distance between the lens and the printing paper to be made.

The principal distinction between types of enlargers lies in the quality of the light that is passed through the negative. In a diffusion enlarger, the light is diffused through a plate of frosted or cloudy glass, which spreads illumination evenly over the negative. Prints made with diffused light often lose detail and have a rather soft quality. In a condenser enlarger, two convex lenses gather and control the light in a concentrated beam. Condensers produce sharper, more well-defined images and are preferred for work with small negatives.

See also: PHOTOGRAPHY.

Enlightenment   The Enlightment is a name given by historians to an intellectual movement that was predominant in the Western world during the 18th century. Strongly influenced by the rise of modern science and by the aftermath of the long religious conflict that followed the Reformation, the thinkers of the Enlightenment (called *philosophes* in France and *Aufklärer* in Germany) were committed to secular views based on reason or human understanding only, which they hoped would provide a basis for beneficial changes affecting every area of life and thought. The more extreme and radical of them—Denis DIDEROT, Claude Adrien HELVÉTIUS, Baron d'HOLBACH, the Marquis de CONDORCET, and Julien Offray de La Mettrie (1709–51)—advocated a philosophical RATIONALISM deriving its methods from science and natural philosophy that would replace religion as the means of knowing the nature and destiny of humanity; these men were materialists, pantheists, or atheists. Other enlightened thinkers, such as Pierre BAYLE, VOLTAIRE, David HUME, and Immanuel KANT, were more moderate. They set limits to human knowledge and, while anticlerical, were either agnostic or left room for some kind of religious faith.

All of the philosophes saw themselves as continuing the work of the great 17th-century pioneers—Francis BACON, GALILEO, DESCARTES, Isaac NEWTON, and John LOCKE—who had developed fruitful methods of rational and empirical inquiry and had demonstrated the possibility of a world remade by the application of knowledge for human benefit. This was an incentive to extend scientific methods into every field of inquiry, thus laying the groundwork for the development of the modern social sciences.

The enlightened understanding of human nature was one that emphasized the right to self-expression and human fulfillment, the right to think freely and express one's views publicly without censorship or fear of repression. Voltaire admired the freedom he found in England and fostered the spread of English ideas on the Continent. He and his followers opposed the intolerance of the established Christian churches of their day, as well as the European governments that controlled and suppressed dissenting opinions. In the realm of economics, this concern for freedom resulted in the laissez-faire philosophies of the PHYSIOCRATS and Adam SMITH; in politics it helped prepare the way for the AMERICAN REVOLUTION and the FRENCH REVOLUTION. More conservative enlightened thinkers, concerned primarily with efficiency and administrative order, favored the "enlightened despotism" of such monarchs as Emperor JOSEPH II, FREDERICK II of Prussia, and CATHERINE II of Russia.

Enlightened political thought expressed demands for equality and justice, and for the legal changes needed to realize these goals. Set forth by Baron de MONTESQUIEU, the changes were more boldly urged by the contributors to the great *Encylopédie* edited in Paris by Diderot between 1747 and 1772, by Jean Jacques ROUSSEAU, Cesare BECCARIA, and finally by Jeremy BENTHAM, whose UTILITARIANISM was the culmination of a long debate on happiness and the means of achieving it.

Everywhere the Enlightenment produced restless men impatient for change but frustrated by popular ignorance and official repression. This gave the enlightened literati an interest in popular education. They promoted educational ventures and sought in witty, amusing, and even titillating ways to educate and awaken their contemporaries. The stories of Bernard Le Bovier de Fontenelle or Benjamin FRANKLIN, the widely imitated essays of Joseph ADDISON and Richard STEELE, and many dictionaries, handbooks, and encyclopedias produced by the enlightened were written to popularize, simplify, and promote a more reasonable view of life.

The Enlightenment came to an end in western Europe after the upheavals of the French Revolution and the Napoleonic era (1789–1815) revealed the costs of its political program and the lack of commitment in those whose rhetoric was often more liberal than their actions. Nationalism undercut its cosmopolitan values and assumptions about human nature, and ROMANTICISM attacked its belief that clear intelligible answers could be found to every question asked by people who sought to be free and happy. The skepticism of the philosophes was swept away in the religious revival of the 1790s and early 1800s, and the cultural leadership of the landed aristocracy and professional men who had supported the Enlightenment was eroded by the growth of a new wealthy educated class of businessmen, products of the INDUSTRIAL REVOLUTION. Only in North and South America, where industry came later and revolution had not led to reaction, did the Enlightenment linger into the 19th century. Its lasting heritage has been its contribution to the literature of human freedom and some institutions in which its values have been embodied. Included in the latter are many facets of modern government, education, and philanthropy.

Enlil   see MARDUK

Ennius, Quintus [en'-ee-uhs, kwin'-tuhs]   Quintus Ennius, 239–169 BC, often considered the father of Latin literature, is best known for his long epic poem, the *Annales*, a history of Rome from its origins to his own time. Born in southern Italy, then strongly influenced by Greek culture, Ennius was brought to Rome from Sardinia by Cato the Elder.

Quintus Ennius wrote in a startling variety of genres—tragedy, comedy, satire, philosophy—and even a work on food, "The Delicatessen." Only fragments of his writings remain. The *Annales*, written in 18 books, glorified the Roman state. The poem was greatly admired by Cicero and imitated by Lucretius and Vergil.

Enoch [ee'-nahk]   Enoch was the name of two biblical characters. In Genesis 4, Enoch was the son of CAIN and grandson of ADAM. In Genesis 5, Enoch was the father of METHUSELAH. The latter is described as a holy man who "walked with God" (Gen. 5:24). For this reason, he was an important figure in popular tradition.

Enoch, Books of   see PSEUDEPIGRAPHA

Enormous Room, The   E. E. CUMMINGS's *The Enormous Room* (1922) is perhaps the most highly regarded American novel of World War I. Serving in an ambulance corps in France during the war, Cummings was arrested by the French without being charged and incarcerated in a concentration-camp–like detention center. In revolutionary prose that inaugurates a new era in American fiction—that of the Lost Generation—*The Enormous Room* realistically evokes that experience and the chaos of the era. It remains a powerful antiwar statement.

Ensenada, Zenón de Somodevilla, Marqués de la [en-say-nah'-dah, thay-nohn' day soh-moh-day-veel'-yah, mar-kays' de lah]   The marqués de la Ensenada, b. June 2, 1702, d. Dec. 2, 1781, was chief minister of Spain from 1743 to 1754. He rose to prominence as an administrator and diplomat and in 1734 organized an expedition to put PHILIP V's son Charles (later CHARLES III of Spain) on the throne of Naples. In 1743, after negotiating an alliance with France, he became the chief minister to Philip V, who was succeeded (1746) by FERDINAND VI. Ensenada strengthened the fleet and the army, corrected abuses in the tax and customs systems, and promoted agriculture, commerce, and public works. His anti-British foreign policy led to his dismissal in 1754.

James Ensor's Les Masques singuliers *(1892) well represents the garish color, supple line, and sinister atmosphere that pervade his work. (Musées royaux des Beaux Arts, Brussels.)*

Ensor, James [en'-sur]   The Belgian artist James Ensor, b. Apr. 13, 1860, d. Nov. 19, 1949, was one of the great precursors of modern expressionist art (see EXPRESSIONISM). In paintings, etchings, and drawings he expressed a savage criticism of society with powerful clashes of color and aggressively distorted forms. His most important work, *The Entry of Christ into Brussels* (1888; J. Paul Getty Museum, Malibu, Calif.), is a sweeping condemnation of modern society and contemporary art movements.

Ensor's first exhibitions were warmly received, but critical hostility developed as he increasingly disregarded traditional rules of form and color. His passion for light and intense color led him to ignore academic formulas for the sake of personal expression. His sense of alienation from society is expressed in many works, notably his *Self-Portrait Surrounded by Masks* (1899; private collection, Antwerp). The mask, signifying falseness and deception, became one of his primary symbols. Despite his isolation, Ensor took part in the leading Belgian avant-garde exhibition groups of his time, Les Vingt (1883–93) and La Libre Esthétique (1894–1914).

Many of Ensor's works have a disquieting, hallucinatory effect. Works such as *Two Skeletons Fighting over the Body of a Hanged Man* (1891; Royal Museum of Fine Arts, Antwerp) have been cited as forerunners of SURREALISM. Skeletons and masks reflect Ensor's preoccupation with death and hypocrisy; a gentler aspect of his personality is represented by many still-life paintings and landscapes. The *Still Life with Blue Pitcher* (1890–91; Staatsgalerie, Stuttgart) includes a pickled herring, which he made his trademark because it was a pun on his name (*l'art* Ensor, from *hareng saur*, meaning "preserved herring"). After 1900 his art became largely repetitive.

entablature [en-tab'-luh-chur]   An entablature is a horizontal structural element supported by a colonnade in classical buildings. The term is derived from the Italian word *intavolatura*, meaning "something laid upon a table" (literally, "something laid flat upon something else"). An entablature consists of three distinct sections, which are, in ascending order, the architrave, frieze, and cornice. The architrave rests upon the capital of the column. The form of the entablature depends upon the style of classical architecture used—Ionic, Doric, Corinthian, or other.

Entamoeba [ent-uh-mee'-buh]   *Entamoeba*, a genus of Protozoa belonging to the class Rhizopoda, is parasitic in the oral cavity and digestive tract of humans and animals. Medically, *E. histolytica* is the most important entamoeba. It causes AMEBIASIS, or amoebic DYSENTERY, in humans. In tropical regions, especially where poor sanitation prevails, the incidence of this disease is high. Other members of the genus appear to be nonpathogenic.

Entebbe [en-teb'-uh]   Entebbe, a city in Uganda (1980 pop., 21,289), is located on a peninsula that extends into Lake Victoria. Situated just south of the equator, it has an elevation of 1,146 m (3,760 ft).

Entebbe was founded in 1893 by the British, and it was Uganda's capital from 1894 to 1962. Many government offices remained there, and the city joined nearby KAMPALA as cocapital of the country in the mid-1980s. Entebbe is Uganda's chief port and has an international airport. In 1976 it was the scene of a daring rescue of hijacked airplane passengers by Israeli commandos.

Entente Cordiale   see TRIPLE ENTENTE

enteritis [en-tur-y'-tis]   Enteritis is any chronic or acute inflammation of the lining of the small intestine. Such inflammation may be caused by bacterial or viral infections, by hypersensitivity to certain foods, or by various toxins; in many cases the cause remains unknown. Enteritis is marked by such nonspecific symptoms as abdominal pain, nausea and vomiting, and diarrhea, and may be difficult to diagnose. Treatment addresses the cause, if identified, and may include a bland diet, avoidance of any allergens, or antibiotics. Other medications may be prescribed for pain relief. In severe cases, when fluid and electrolyte loss is significant, intravenous feeding may be required.

Other types of inflammatory diseases of the intestines include COLITIS, CROHN'S DISEASE, and enterocolitis (inflammation of both the small intestine and the colon).

■

Enterobacter [en-tur-oh-bak'-tur]   *Enterobacter* is a genus of bacteria in the family Enterobactiaceae; it is noted for its wide distribution, particularly in water and sewage and sometimes in the secretions of animals. Its presence is an indication of fecal pollution of waterways. Some species can cause CYSTITIS and SEPTICEMIA.

enthalpy   see THERMODYNAMICS

entomology   see INSECT

■

entoproct [ent'-uh-prahkt]   The Entoprocta include about 60 species of small invertebrate animals. They are marine, except for one freshwater genus, *Urnatella*. Living attached to rocks, pilings, and other marine organisms, all are filter feeders. Entoprocts are usually colonial, and individual organisms are small, less than 5 mm (0.2 in) long, with a cuplike calyx, or body, containing organs. The calyx is supported by a stalk by which the organism is attached to the substrate.

■

entrapment   Entrapment refers to the doctrine in criminal law that a person is relieved from criminal liability if officers or undercover agents of the government have induced that person to commit a crime he or she had not contemplated committing. It is not generally considered entrapment if the officer or agent merely furnishes an opportunity to a person "predisposed to commit the crime." This doctrine is most often applied in cases involving the so-called victimless crimes, such as gambling and narcotics offenses.

■

entropy [en'-troh-pee]   Entropy is the scientific term for the degree of randomness or disorder in processes and systems. In the physical sciences the concept of entropy is central to descriptions of the THERMODYNAMICS, or heat-transfer properties, of molecules, heat engines, and even the universe as a whole. It is also useful in such diverse fields as INFORMATION THEORY and the social and life sciences.

Entropy was first defined by the German physicist Rudolf CLAUSIUS in 1865, based in part on earlier work by Sadi Carnot and Lord Kelvin. Clausius found that even for "perfect," or completely reversible, exchanges of heat energy between systems of matter, an inevitable loss of useful energy results. He called this loss an increase in entropy and defined the increase as the amount of heat transfer divided by the absolute temperature at which the process takes place. This basic principle is known as the Second Law of Thermodynamics. The Second Law implies that all processes must operate at less than 100% efficiency due to the inevitable entropy rise from the rejection of waste heat. For example, large coal-fired electric power plants inevitably waste about 67% of the energy content of the coal. Other heat engines, such as the automobile engine and the human body, are even less efficient, wasting about 80% of available energy.

Another manifestation of entropy is the tendency of systems to move toward greater confusion and disorder as time passes. Natural processes move toward equilibrium and homogeneity rather than toward ordered states. For example, a cube of sugar dissolved in coffee does not naturally reassemble as a cube, and perfume molecules in the air do not naturally gather again into a perfume bottle. Similarly, chemical reactions are naturally favored in which the products contain a greater amount of disorder (entropy) than the reactants. Such reactions will not spontaneously reverse themselves. This tendency toward disorder gives a temporal direction—the "arrow of time"—to natural events.

A consequence of nature's continual entropy rise may be the eventual degrading of all useful energy in the universe. Physicists theorize that the universe might eventually reach a temperature equilibrium in which disorder is at a maximum and useful energy sources no longer exist to support life or even motion. This "heat death of the universe" would be possible only if the universe is physically bounded and is governed as a whole by the same laws of thermodynamics observed on Earth.

■

Enuma Elish [en-oo'-muh el'-ish]   The *Enuma Elish* is a Babylonian creation epic (see CREATION ACCOUNTS). Although it exists only in later copies, it was probably composed at Babylon in the Kassite period to celebrate Babylon's victory (*c.*1450 BC) over the Sealand. Many of the mythological motifs in the story were borrowed from earlier Canaanite myths about BAAL.

The text consists of seven tablets. It tells how MARDUK, the god of Babylon, was chosen king of the gods to defeat Tiamat, the personified sea representing chaotic evil. After killing her, Marduk split her in two, created the world from her corpse, and stationed the various gods in their appropriate spheres. Then he created the human race from the blood of the rebel god Kingu to be the slaves of the gods. Finally he established Babylon, and the text ends with the gods praising Marduk by reciting his 50 names.

A similar myth is found in Psalms 74:12–17, and the creation account of Genesis contains a similar ordering of a primeval watery chaos. The biblical writer, however, adapted his sources to reflect his own monotheism.

enuresis   see BED-WETTING

■

environment   The term *environment* broadly indicates the surroundings of an individual organism or a community of organisms, ranging on up to the entire BIO-

SPHERE, the zone of Earth that is able to sustain life. By surroundings is meant all the nonliving and living materials that play any role in an organism's existence, from soil and air to what the organism feeds on and the organisms that may feed on it. Any other factors acting on the organism, such as heat and light and gravitation, make up its environment as well. In the case of human beings, cultural factors may also be included in the term.

The environmental science of ECOLOGY is the observation and analysis of the interactions of organisms with their environment. Because of the complexity of the subject matter, workers in this field call upon a wide range of disciplines in the physical and life sciences—for example, geology, meteorology, and microbiology, among many others. These separate disciplines themselves often incorporate areas of environmental specialization, as, for example, environmental geology, which deals with the effects of human actions on landforms. The word *environment* is in fact most commonly encountered in association with the adverse effects of human activities on their surroundings and society's efforts to prevent or alleviate the damage.

See also: ENVIRONMENTAL LAW; ENVIRONMENTAL MOVEMENTS; POLLUTION, ENVIRONMENTAL.

▬

environmental art The term *environmental art*, in general, refers to avant-garde works that are consciously designed to surround or include the viewer as participant, thereby fostering a direct emotional and sensory experience. The term relates specifically to those works created since the late 1950s which attempt to cloud the distinctions between art and life. Precedents exist in Kurt SCHWITTERS's *Merzbau* (1920s), in the BAUHAUS theater (1930s), and, more recently (1950s), in the ABSTRACT EXPRESSIONIST paintings that virtually surround the spectator with the enormousness of the canvas.

By the late 1950s the first HAPPENINGS occurred, produced by such artists as Jim DINE, Allan KAPROW, and Claes OLDENBURG as semistructured performances incorporating players and audience in artist-designed settings. These experiments led to the "total environments" of the 1960s, interior spaces created by the artist through alteration or manipulation, as in the converted storefront that became Oldenburg's *Store* (1961–62), and later to works like the playful constructions of Red GROOMS in the 1970s and '80s.

Size limitations imposed by interiors led to expansive works created out-of-doors by such earthwork artists as Robert SMITHSON. Some cooperated with the natural environment; others altered or contradicted it. Viewers could often walk around, through, or on the artworks, thereby incorporating into the experience both artificial and natural elements.

▬

environmental impact statement An environmental impact statement is a report on the probable environmental effects of proposed projects, such as highways, large-scale residential or commercial construction, power plants, or dams, which might significantly alter the environment. The National Environmental Policy Act, which became effective in 1970, requires every U.S. government agency to issue a statement on any project it plans to undertake, regulate, or fund. The ENVIRONMENTAL PROTECTION AGENCY reviews all federal environmental impact statements to ensure that they comply with the law. The use of such statements has spread to many state and local governments.

▬

environmental law Environmental laws attempt to prevent or limit the adverse effects of pollution and environmental degradation, normally by requiring or encouraging those who harm the environment to alter their activities. These laws address problems such as the control of hazardous air pollutants, the reclamation of surface-mined land, and the protection of biological diversity.

People have a reasonable expectation that government will provide a safe and habitable environment. At the least, they assume that government will protect its citizens against such ills as toxic wastes, polluted water, or excessive radiation. Yet damage to the environment is often the result of governmentally sanctioned activities that create jobs and sustain economic growth. (See POLLUTION, ENVIRONMENTAL; POLLUTION CONTROL.)

Decisions about acceptable levels of environmental damage are not based solely on scientific or medical evidence; political and economic considerations also play a major role. Lawmakers are forced to make value judgments about which segments of the population should be protected. Making these kinds of choices requires considerations of the societal costs and consequences of environmental laws.

Lawmakers face still another significant problem in deciding how best to respond to environmental problems. The environment is as complex as it is interrelated, which suggests the desirability of a single, comprehensive law that addresses different, but ecologically related, problems in a well-integrated manner. This kind of law would require that policies affecting water pollution, as an example, would also consider the consequences on air pollution, soil erosion, the disposal of toxic wastes, and so on. However desirable such a single, organic law might be, governments characteristically have separate and, occasionally, contradictory laws directed at different sources of environmental harms.

Environmental laws in the United States serve as good illustrations of these general traits. Hundreds of state and national environmental laws address virtually the entire range of environmental problems, from ocean dumping and coastal-resource management to the use of pesticides and the control of air and water pollution. The first versions of these laws, notably in the areas of air- and water-quality management, placed responsibility for implementation and enforcement with state and local governments. As the wide geographic scope of pollution became more evident and as public expectations for action increased, so also did the national government gradually increase its role in environmental management. Amendments to many of the original laws authorized the national government (eventually through the ENVIRONMENTAL PROTECTION AGENCY) to establish nationally applicable goals and pollution standards, to sue recalcitrant polluters, and to require the states to devise strategies to reduce pollution to mandated levels. Today the pattern of state implementation of national programs is common in many areas of environmental law.

One other notable feature of U.S. environmental laws involves the opportunities for citizen participation in the enforcement process. Prior to the 1970s, environmental interest groups were often frustrated in their efforts to gain judicial relief from the harms of pollution. Judges would typically dismiss their complaints because the groups could not demonstrate that they had a specific, direct interest in the issue at hand—that is, they lacked what lawyers term "standing" to sue. Lack of standing is rarely a barrier today because many U.S. environmental laws now allow any citizen to sue an agency administrator who commits unauthorized actions or who fails to perform legally mandated obligations.

environmental movements

Environmental movements are social movements concerned with the protection of natural surroundings from overuse and degradation by humans. They are primarily a post–Industrial Revolution phenomenon initiated mainly in the United States and Europe by educated members of society following major spurts of industrial expansion and resource exploitation. Such movements initially focused on population growth and resource depletion; more recently the concern has been with human-generated pollution and the preservation of natural environments.

Malthus, Ricardo, and Mill. Concern with the Earth's natural resources was first manifested in England during the early years of the Industrial Revolution. Burgeoning industries and the factory towns they spawned combined with the enclosure acts and a declining death rate to transform the country from an agrarian society to an increasingly urban and more densely populated one. The economist Thomas Robert MALTHUS put forth his ideas regarding the future of this technologically sophisticated yet crowded new world in a monumental treatise of 1798, *An Essay on the Principle of Population, As It Affects the Future Improvement of Society.* He believed that a geometrically increasing population would eventually outstrip food supplies with calamitous results. Barring a voluntary reduction in the birthrate, only disease and wars would spare the world from death by starvation. Two decades later, his disciple David RICARDO wrote along similar lines in his 1817 study *Principles of Political Economy and Taxation.* At mid-century, political theorist John Stuart MILL, though more sanguine than the Malthusians as to humanity's ability to check population growth and to better utilize resources, nevertheless introduced a concept that would be especially relevant to the 20th century—the notion that the pleasures to be derived from solitude and natural beauty might be impaired through population growth and industry.

Clear-cut logging has shaved the forest cover off a vast patch of land on an island off Canada's Pacific coast. Clear-cutting creates the conditions for erosion and land degradation.

During the remainder of the 19th century, interest in the environment was further stimulated by Henry David THOREAU, whose WALDEN (1854) marked a revolution in the perception of nature.

The Conservation Movement. Spanning the period 1890 to 1920, the American conservation movement was closely identified with the personality and politics of President Theodore Roosevelt. By the end of the 19th century, Americans were concerned that the rapid pace of social and industrial progress and the closing of the frontier would lead to the extinction of the nation's natural resources, especially its forests. Under Roosevelt's programs, the protection of forests, rangeland, and mineral and water resources began to evolve in piecemeal fashion. Administration officials such as Chief of the U.S. Forest Service Gifford PINCHOT and Secretary of the Interior James R. Garfield, however, argued for a more unified policy of natural-resource planning. Though Congress was unsympathetic, a successful appeal was made to the public for political support, and the drive for resource protection developed into something of a moral crusade.

A more radical ecological approach was taken by the naturalist-founder of the Sierra Club, John MUIR, who favored resource preservation. The prevailing theme of the era, however, was one of conservation or the restrained and efficient use of natural resources. The conservation movement, while not rejecting capitalist development of resources, did call for an end to speculative profiteering from resource exploitation. The most significant legacy of the conservation movement was its application of science to natural-resource management. In order to administer scientifically based management, major federal and state conservation laws were passed, and new agencies such as the Forest Service, the Geological Survey, the National Park Service, and the Bureau of Reclamation were created.

The Modern Environmental Movement. The publication in 1962 of Rachel CARSON's *Silent Spring* marks the beginning of the modern environmental movement. Carson, a successful author and former U.S. Fish and Wildlife Service biologist, warned of the environmental dangers posed by such recently developed pesticides as DDT. This inspired a spate of books calling attention to other threats to the environment, among which were Paul EHRLICH's *The Population Bomb* (1968), Barry Commoner's *The Closing Circle* (1971), and *Limits to Growth* (1972), written by a research team from the Massachusetts Institute of Technology (MIT). These works engendered almost immediate grass-roots sentiment for improving environmental quality. Support for change was particularly strong on college campuses, where the first Earth Day was celebrated Apr. 22, 1970.

National organizations such as the SIERRA CLUB, the Audubon Society, the National Wildlife Federation, and the Wilderness Society have brought litigation and lobbied for stricter laws dealing with almost every aspect of the environment. These laws include the National Environmental Policy Act of 1969, the Clean Water Act of 1972, the National Forest Management Act of 1976, the Clean Air Act amendments of 1977, and the National Acid Precipitation Act of 1980, as well as the creation (1970) of the ENVIRONMENTAL PROTECTION AGENCY.

In the 1980s and '90s public interest was further strengthened by such events as the ACID RAIN controversy, the CHERNOBYL nuclear catastrophe in the Soviet Union, giant OIL SPILLS in Prince William Sound and the Persian Gulf, tropical deforestation in Central and South America, the harvesting of old-growth timber in Alaska and the Pacific Northwest, and the discovery of the possibility of global warming. In Europe, environmentalist sentiment was translated into political action with the formation of "green" movements throughout the continent.

The organizations participating in the environmental movement are as diverse as the problems they undertake to solve. Some concentrate on specific areas (Save the Redwoods League); some do restorative work (Adopt-a-Stream Foundation); some gather and disperse information (Worldwatch Institute); some lobby or bring suit (Environmental Defense Fund); and a few (GREENPEACE, Earth First!) take direct, sometimes confrontational, action.

Environmental Protection Agency

The Environmental Protection Agency (EPA) was established in 1970 as an independent agency in the executive branch of the U.S. government "to permit coordinated and effective government action on behalf of the environment." The EPA consolidates in a single body the administration of all federal environmental legislation, ranging from the Refuse Control Act of 1899 to the most recent statutes concerning environmental pollution. The agency monitors environmental quality and seeks to control the pollution caused by solid wastes, pesticides, toxic substances, noise, and radiation. It has established special programs in air and water pollution, hazardous wastes, and toxic chemicals, and sponsors research in the technologies of pollution control. Ten regional offices facilitate coordination of pollution control efforts with state and local governments.

See also: ENVIRONMENTAL LAW; ENVIRONMENTAL MOVEMENTS; POLLUTION, ENVIRONMENTAL; POLLUTION CONROL.

enzyme [en'-zym]   Various kinds of protein molecules known as enzymes serve to accelerate, or catalyze, the chemical reactions of living CELLS. Without enzymes, most biochemical reactions would proceed too slowly to effectively carry on life processes.

The manufacture of these enzymes is regulated by the cell's genetic material, deoxyribonucleic acid (DNA), through the process of PROTEIN SYNTHESIS. The potential of a cell to grow and divide is determined largely by the number and different kinds of enzymes it contains. Certain cells also perform specialized functions, such as transmitting nerve impulses or producing hormones, that are regulated by enzymes. Several hundred different reactions may proceed simultaneously within a cell, each one catalyzed by one or more enzymes.

Enzymes differ from inorganic catalysts, such as platinum and palladium, in two important ways: the sequence of amino acids in an enzyme molecule is specific to that enzyme and essential for the molecule's catalytic action; and each enzyme exerts its catalytic action only on specific substances in specific reactions. A nonbiological catalyst, by contrast, catalyzes a wide variety of chemical reactions.

History

The term *enzyme* is derived from the Greek and literally means "in yeast" or "leavening." It was coined in 1878, when it was generally but erroneously believed that the yeast enzymes responsible for fermenting wine could function only in living cells. The belief was proved wrong in 1897 when Eduard BUCHNER showed that enzymes isolated from yeast cells were capable of fermenting sugar. Buchner's work ushered in a new era of biology in which most functions of cells have been shown to occur—and can be studied—in the test tube.

In 1926, James Sumner first isolated an enzyme, urease, in crystalline form and showed that it was a protein. Biochemists thereafter realized that the solution to the mysteries of enzyme structure, and how that structure promotes catalysis (see CATALYST), lay in unraveling the chemical structure of proteins.

The first enzymes that yielded clues to structure and function were the protein-digesting enzymes chymotrypsin, trypsin, and carboxypeptidase, and the RNA-splitting enzyme ribonuclease. The first enzyme for which the entire amino-acid sequence has been elucidated is pancreatic ribonuclease. It is a protein containing 124 amino-acid units in a linear sequence. Although the amino acids are lined up end to end, various forces within the molecule cause it, like almost all proteins, to take the shape of a badly tangled ball of yarn.

The three-dimensional tangling, or folding, of an enzyme is called its tertiary structure. All experiments suggest that the information required for the correct folding is contained in the amino-acid sequence, which is dictated by the information encoded in DNA. All experiments also indicate that the catalytic activity of an enzyme is determined largely by its amino-acid sequence and tertiary structure.

Catalysis

The defining property of all catalysts is that they increase the speed of a chemical reaction without being used up or appearing as one of the products of the reaction.

Before the end of the 19th century, chemists understood that molecules must obtain extra energy before they can interact. The extra energy, or energy of activation, may be supplied when one molecule collides with another, or it may be supplied by an external source of energy, such as heat or ultraviolet radiation. The primary barrier to interaction, therefore, is the energy of activation, which is sometimes called the energy barrier. The higher the energy barrier, the fewer the molecules that will pass over it, and thus the slower the rate of the reaction.

In 1889 the Swedish chemist Svante ARRHENIUS suggested that a catalyst (C) acts as follows: it first forms an intermediate compound (CS) with the reactant, or substrate (S); the compound CS then enters a so-called transition state, which presents a lower energy barrier to chemical reaction; finally, CS decomposes into C, which is unchanged, and the product, P, of the reaction. The catalyst can then participate in the reaction again and again.

If the word *catalyst* is replaced by the word *enzyme* (E), the fundamental equation of enzyme catalysis is:

$$E + S \rightleftharpoons ES \rightarrow E + P$$

This equation is often called the Michaelis-Menton equation, and ES is called the enzyme-substrate complex. In forming the complex, enzymes reduce the activation energy, or energy barrier, for a biochemical reaction. Enzymes are far more effective than inorganic catalysts in reducing activation energies; thus, they permit biochemical processes to take place at temperatures compatible with life.

Factors Affecting Enzyme Activity

One factor affecting enzyme function is temperature. Too high a temperature (50°–60° C/122°–140° F) can destroy an enzyme. Below that critical range, enzyme activity increases as the temperature does; and, like other chemical reactions, enzyme-controlled reactions are about doubled in rate by each increase of 10 C degrees (18 F degrees). Another affecting factor is acidity. Each enzyme functions only within a narrow range of its optimum pH (see pH). Pepsin works only in a very acid medium (pH of 2), whereas trypsin requires an alkaline medium (pH of 8.5). Most intracellular enzymes operate best near neutrality (pH of 7) and will not function in either a distinctly acid or alkaline medium. If temperature and acidity are kept constant, the level of activity of an enzyme system is determined by the relative concentration of enzyme and substrate. If there is an excess of substrate, the rate of catalytic reaction is directly proportional to the amount of enzyme present. If enzyme concentration is kept constant, the rate of reaction is proportional to the amount of substrate present.

Types of Enzymes

The enzymes associated with digestion (lactase, lipase,

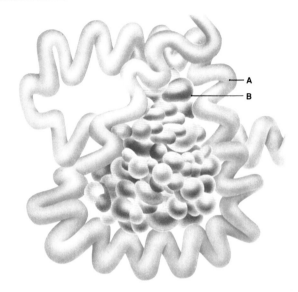

Enzymes are protein molecules that catalyze, or accelerate, biological reactions. They consist of long chains (A) of amino acids folded into an elaborate three-dimensional structure. Each enzyme can interact with only a specifically shaped substrate molecule (B), which binds to the enzyme at its active site. According to the induced-fit theory, the enzyme changes its shape around the substrate molecule; the realigned molecules bind together to form the enzyme-substrate complex necessary for catalysis of the reaction.

pepsin, and so forth), called hydrolases, split larger compounds into smaller ones by the addition of water molecules to their substrates. Another group of enzymes, called ligases, join smaller molecules (nucleotides, amino acids, and so forth) into larger ones, such as polynucleotide chains. The transferases catalyze reactions involving the transfer of a chemical group from one molecule to another. Thus, hexokinase catalyzes the transfer of a high-energy phosphate group from ATP to a molecule of glucose, thereby energizing the glucose for further enzymatic reactions. There are also enzymes, called oxidoreductases, that are involved in the transfer of electrons from one atom or molecule to another. These oxidation-reduction reactions play a larger role in obtaining energy from food. Recently scientists have found that RNA molecules can also act as enzymes. These "ribozymes" cleave specific sites on RNA strands and will soon be used to manipulate RNA for GENETIC ENGINEERING.

Enzyme Cofactors

Some enzymes, such as many of the hydrolases, carry out their catalytic functions without the aid of other compounds. A large number of enzymes, however, require the presence of additional chemical components called cofactors. For a given enzyme the cofactor may be an inorganic ion, or it may be a complex organic molecule called a coenzyme. Whereas each enzyme is substrate-specific and will catalyze a given chemical reaction of only one particular substance, a cofactor is not substrate-specific and will function with many different enzymes. Each cofactor is specific for the transport of a particular substance needed in a given enzymatic reaction.

How Enzymes Work

Formation of the enzyme-substrate complex depends on a special relationship between the surfaces of the two substances. In 1894, Emil Fischer compared that relationship to a template, or key-in-lock; that is, the enzyme contains a certain sequence of atoms called the active site, and only a particularly shaped substrate can bind to the enzyme at that site. The binding of substrate to enzyme causes the enzyme to curl and twist in what is termed a conformational change; this brings about the contact necessary to catalyze the reaction. This concept is often called the induced-fit theory.

The theory that enzymes function by means of an active site is now supported by considerable evidence, but it is still unknown whether the full catalytic activity of the enzyme resides in the protein structure as a whole or in a small part associated with the active site. Thus, for example, the enzyme ribonuclease loses little of its activity when it is partially degraded. The molecule has also been broken into a large part and a small part that are inactive separately but become active when they are put in solution together.

Perhaps the best evidence that only part of the molecule may be necessary for enzymatic activity is supplied by the protein-splitting enzyme papain. When papain is treated with another enzyme that removes amino acids from one end of the linear sequence, two-thirds of the 180 amino-acid units may be removed and papain will still retain its enzymatic activity.

Enzymes and Metabolism

Living organisms must possess the means of regulating both the kinds of metabolic reactions that are to take place at any given time and the rates at which the reactions should occur. One of the primary methods of regulating METABOLISM is through controlling the amount of activity of enzymes. Such control may take one of three forms: induction or repression of enzyme synthesis; so-called feedback inhibition of enzyme activity; and proenzyme activation.

Enzyme Induction. Bacteria, for example, can vary their enzymatic composition widely when grown under different nutritive conditions. In particular, the specific enzymes required for utilizing a given nitrogen or carbon source are usually made only during growth in the presence of that compound. Such responses have come to be known as induced enzyme formation. Thus, the presence of the sugar lactose "induces" the bacteria *Escherichia coli* to synthesize the enzyme beta-galactosidase, which permits these bacteria to use the sugar as fuel for energy.

Enzyme Repression. The addition of amino acids generally causes cells to cease forming the several enzymes necessary for producing those amino acids. In other words, the end product of a series of metabolic reactions, or pathway, evidently plays a special role in regulating the synthesis of the enzymes of its own pathway. This mechanism is more precisely termed end-product repression, and it involves complete shutdown of the DNA-directed synthesis of an enzyme.

Feedback Inhibition. In feedback inhibition, as in end-product repression, the end product of a metabolic pathway may block the activity of enzymes in the same pathway. But inhibition involves the inactivation of enzymes, not the cessation of DNA-directed enzyme synthesis. When the end product reaches a certain concentration, it decreases the rate of its own synthesis by preventing the previous synthesis of substances necessary for its manu-

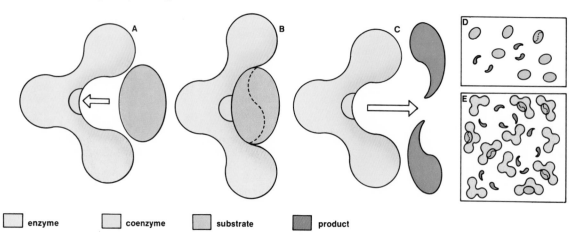

These diagrams represent the catalysis of a reaction by an enzyme and its associated coenzyme. A coenzyme is a relatively small organic molecule required by certain enzymes for the catalytic process. Coenzymes often bind to the enzyme at the active site; they frequently include B-complex vitamins as essential components. The substrate binds (A) to the enzyme and coenzyme and undergoes the reaction (B). The release of products (C) frees the enzyme to bind another substrate molecule. Without the presence of an enzyme, a reaction would proceed very slowly (D); enzyme molecules, however, speed this reaction (E) considerably by reducing the required energy of activation.

□ enzyme   □ coenzyme   ■ substrate   ■ product

facture. The inhibitory action occurs when the end product binds with a previous enzyme in the pathway and so alters its shape as to inactivate it. This type of control is also called allosteric regulation.

Proenzyme Activation. Enzymes may be produced in an inactive form called a proenzyme or zymogen and activated only when they are needed. Thrombin, for example, is an enzyme that causes blood to clot by catalyzing the conversion of the soluble protein, fibrinogen, to the insoluble fibrin. Blood normally contains the inactive precursor of thrombin, prothrombin; clotting occurs only when it is converted to thrombin.

Enzymes in Disease

A number of diseases involve an inherited enzyme abnormality. PHENYLKETONURIA, for example, is a congenital deficiency of the enzyme phenylalanine hydroxylase, which causes brain damage and mental retardation in newborns. This can be prevented by a diet low in the amino acid phenylalanine.

Another inherited defect is deficiency of the enzyme glucose-6-phosphate dehydrogenase, which can cause a breakdown of red blood cells when one of a large number of drugs is ingested. TAY-SACHS DISEASE is an inherited enzyme-deficiency disorder that leads to early neurologic deterioration. ALBINISM is due to a lack of the enzyme tyrosinase. In the muscle disorder known as McArdle's disease, there is a lack of the enzyme glycogen phosphorylase.

Studies of enzyme levels in the blood are a sensitive index of disease and are often used in medical diagnosis. Myocardial infarction, or destruction of heart tissue due to insufficient blood supply, may be indicated by elevated serum levels of certain enzymes. The elevations are due in part to enzyme leakage from destroyed cells. Acute kidney injuries may be associated with increased outputs of enzymes that originate in the kidneys, many of them in cellular debris.

Blood concentrations of enzymes produced in the liver may be used to assess liver function. One enzyme test measures the concentration of acetylcholinesterase, which is made exclusively by liver cells. Serum alkaline phosphatase may be elevated when specific portions of the liver are damaged.

Scientists have created artificial enzymes from antibodies. These "abzymes" may soon be used to dissolve blood clots, remove scar tissue, and act as antiviral agents.

See also: GENETIC DISEASES.

Eocene Epoch   see EARTH, GEOLOGICAL HISTORY OF; GEOLOGIC TIME

eohippus   see HORSE

EOKA   EOKA (National Organization for the Cyprus Struggle) was a Greek Cypriot organization founded in 1954 to achieve *enosis,* or union, of Cyprus with Greece. Led by Georgios Grivas (1898–1974), it engaged in terrorist activities against the British government of the island until 1959, when Cyprus became an independent republic under the presidency of MAKARIOS III. After Grivas's death, his successor as head of EOKA, Nikos Sampson, led a coup on July 15, 1974. A Turkish force soon occupied northern Cyprus, and Sampson fled abroad. Makarios returned to power in December. EOKA disbanded in 1978.

Eos [ee'-ahs]   In Greek mythology, Eos, goddess of the dawn, was mother of the west wind Zephyr and of the morning star Eosphorus. Among the handsome young men whom she carried off as her lovers were ORION and Tithonus. Eos asked ZEUS to give Tithonus immortality but forgot to include eternal youthfulness with her request. When Tithonus grew old and feeble, Eos tired of him and changed him into a grasshopper. In Roman mythology, Eos was known as Aurora.

Epaminondas [e-pam-i-nahn'-das]   Epaminondas, d. 362 BC, was a Greek general of Thebes. Representing Thebes at a peace congress with Sparta in 371, he refused to allow the other cities of Boeotia a separate voice. As a result Thebes was excluded from the peace and attacked by Spartan forces. The Theban victory at Leuctra (371), however, established Thebes' dominance in mainland Greece. His later victories over Sparta won independence for Arcadia and Messenia. He commanded a fleet against the Athenian navy in 364 and in 362 returned to Arcadia to lead the Boeotians against Sparta at Mantinea, where he died in battle.

ephedra [uh-fed'-ruh]   *Ephedra,* or joint fir, is the generic and common name for about 40 species of small bushy shrubs in the family Ephedraceae. They are native to dry areas of the Northern Hemisphere and South America. *Ephedra* are GYMNOSPERMS, and in their peculiar appearance—jointed and apparently leafless green stems—they resemble horsetails.

Asian species of *Ephedra* have been cultivated for several centuries as a source of the drug EPHEDRINE, which is now produced synthetically. In the United States, Ephedra is sometimes planted in dry locations as ground cover or for its green-stemmed clumps. The drab green, jointed stems, which lie almost flat on the ground, grow up to 60 cm (2 ft) long. The leaves of the plant are actually small scales, with two or three scales appearing together. Male or female cones also grow from the scale sites. The cones are inconspicuous, but some species have scarlet, fleshy seeds.

ephemeris   see CELESTIAL MECHANICS

Ephemeroptera   see MAYFLY

Ephesians, Epistle to the [i-fee'-zhuhnz]   The Epistle to the Ephesians is a book of the New Testament in the BIBLE. The text states that it was written by Saint

PAUL while in prison (3:1, 4:1; 6:20), but most scholars attribute it to a later follower of Paul. It uses much Pauline terminology in an unusual rhetorical style and has, with COLOSSIANS, ideas that seem later than Paul. The reference to the Ephesians (1:1) is missing in some manuscripts, and the epistle may have been a circular letter to several churches.

Ephesians proclaims the unity of all people and the universe in Jesus Christ, and describes the church as a body and a building with the apostles and prophets as a foundation (2:20). It also proposes the relationship of Christ to the church as a model for marriage relationships.

Ephesus [ef'-i-suhs]

Ephesus was an ancient city on the coast of western Anatolia, located midway between the Mediterranean and the Dardanelles, slightly northeast of the island of Samos. In ancient times its favorable location at the mouth of the Caÿster River made it the foremost commercial city of a coastal region that also included the cities of MILETUS, Smyrna (now IZMIR), and PERGAMUM, but the silting up of its harbor gradually resulted in the loss of this preeminence. The city was an Ionian colony formed after 1000 BC; its character was Greco-Oriental. Its ancient cult dedicated to ARTEMIS (or DIANA) was famous in antiquity and is vividly alluded to in Acts 19–20 in connection with St. Paul's extended ministry at Ephesus. The Temple of Artemis was one of the SEVEN WONDERS OF THE WORLD.

Like other Helleno-Oriental cities of the Greek colonized coast of Aegean Anatolia, Ephesus came to be ruled by CROESUS of LYDIA in the mid-6th century BC; it passed to the Persians after 546 BC. It joined the DELIAN LEAGUE after the PERSIAN WARS. In 334 BC it fell to ALEXANDER THE GREAT and subsequently to his successors: LYSIMACHUS, who replanned the city in 286, and the SELEUCID dynasty after 281. Later it was controlled by Pergamum, passing eventually into Roman hands in 133 BC. Sacked by the Goths in AD 262, Ephesus was the site of the third ecumenical council in 431. The temple and parts of the city have been excavated, its extensive remains being chiefly from the later Roman period.

Ephesus, Council of

The Council of Ephesus (431), the third ecumenical council of the Christian church (see COUNCIL, ECUMENICAL), was significant for its dogmatic decrees on the position of the Virgin MARY in the celestial hierarchy and on the nature of the incarnation of JESUS CHRIST. It was convened by the Eastern Roman Emperor THEODOSIUS II to respond to the teachings of Nestorius that Mary be considered only the "mother of Christ" and not the "mother of God" (see NESTORIANISM). The pope's representative, CYRIL OF ALEXANDRIA, reached an accord rejecting this view. The council also declared the human and divine aspects of Jesus to be two separate natures perfectly united in Christ.

In 449 another council, known in history as the *latrocinium*, or Robber Synod, met in Ephesus. It approved the doctrines of EUTYCHES, which were subsequently condemned (451) at the Council of CHALCEDON.

ephors [ef'-urz]

Ephors were the chief magistrates of ancient SPARTA and of other Dorian Greek states. In Sparta, five ephors were elected annually, the senior one giving his name to the year. They generally controlled the two kings, whom they could prosecute before the Gerousia (council of elders), and arrived at decisions by majority vote. The ephorate lasted from the 8th century BC until at least AD 200, though it was abolished briefly (227–222 BC) by CLEOMENES III.

Ephraem the Syrian, Saint [ee-fray'-em]

Ephraem, c.306–373, was a Syrian Christian theologian and poet, considered one of the Doctors of the Church. He settled (363) in Edessa, where there was a noted theological school, and there wrote most of his known works. Ephraem's fame rests on his metrical homilies and hymns, which are still used in the liturgy of the NESTORIAN CHURCH. He was deeply devoted to the saints, especially Mary, whom he regarded as the new Eve. Feast day: Jan. 28 (Eastern); June 9 (Western).

Ephraim [ee'-free-uhm]

Ephraim was the younger son of the biblical patriarch Joseph. He was given the blessing of the firstborn by his grandfather, Jacob, and became the ancestor of the Israelite tribe of Ephraim (Genesis 41, 46, 48). Centered on the sanctuaries at Shiloh and Shechem, the Ephraimites dominated their neighbors both economically and politically. Thus the entire northern kingdom of the Israelites was sometimes called Ephraim.

Ephrata [ef'-ruh-tuh]

Ephrata (1990 pop., 12,133) is a borough in southeast Pennsylvania and the trading center for a prosperous agricultural region. The present town grew around a German Protestant monastic community founded in 1732 by Johann Conrad BEISSEL. A press there (established 1746) produced the first music printed in the American colonies.

epic

The term *epic* (from Greek *epos*, "word" or "tale") is applied to a wide variety of imaginative works, ranging from the earliest oral narrative poems to certain modern novels. An epic is a long narrative poem or prose work, retelling important events in the life of a central hero or heroine, who is usually seen as representative of his or her culture. The earliest epics were composed before the invention of writing, in a verse form developed by many generations of oral bards, who combined original narrative with stock formulaic phrases. Normally episodic, these poems deal with type characters rather than well-rounded ones and contain elaborate similes and extended digressions. These early oral poems are storehouses of myth in

Gilgamesh, hero of the Mesopotamian Epic of Gilgamesh, sought the secrets of immortality from Utnapishtim, who, like the biblical Noah, built a ship and escaped humankind's destruction by flood. Throughout his life Gilgamesh faced many tests, often against animals, as depicted in this 8th-century Assyrian relief. (Louvre, Paris.)

which human heroes interact with gods.

The forms SAGA and ROMANCE are closely related to epic. Sagas, related to the Scandinavian EDDAS, are prose narratives of the great families of Norway and Iceland. Romances are verse tales of chivalry from medieval France. Saga and romance are more firmly rooted in history than epic, which looks back to an age of heroes, yet they too tend to draw the central figures larger than life. Epics may be broadly divided into primary (oral) and secondary (written) texts, and the secondary epics may be further divided into classical epic, Renaissance epic, mock heroic (see MOCK EPIC), epic novel, epic theater, and modern epic poetry and film.

The earliest known primary epic, the ancient Sumerian Epic of GILGAMESH, includes versions of the flood and creation myths. The opening books of the Hebrew Bible form a similar chronicle, combining mythical and historical elements. The Western European tradition begins with the two Greek epic poems attributed to Homer, the ILIAD and the ODYSSEY, the first a tragic poem of war, the second an adventure narrative. Vergil's Latin AENEID combines elements of the *Iliad* and *Odyssey* to describe the origins of Rome. This first great secondary, or literary, epic is marked by a new allusiveness and psychological awareness. Its Renaissance successors include Ariosto's *Orlando Furioso*, Tasso's *Gerusalemme Liberata*, Spenser's *The Faerie Queene*, and Milton's *Paradise Lost*. Old English literature already had the epic *Beowulf*. Other national epics include the Hindu *Mahabharata*, the Spanish epic of the warrior *el Cid*, *Poema del Cid*, the German *Nibelungenlied*, and the Finnish *Kalevala*. The 18th century in England produced the mock-heroic poems of Alexander Pope and the digressive novels of Henry Fielding and Laurence Sterne. Other epic novels that draw on the *Odyssey* include Cervantes's *Don Quixote*, Herman Melville's *Moby-Dick*, and James Joyce's *Ulysses*. The epic novel has been especially successful in the hands of the Russians Fyodor Dostoyevsky, Leo Tolstoi, Boris Pasternak, and Aleksandr Solzhenitsyn. Epic theater was a form first developed by the German writer Johann Wolfgang Goethe and modernized by Bertolt Brecht. There have been notable epic films, particularly the Russian ones of Sergei EISENSTEIN.

The 19th and 20th centuries have produced a number of epic poems in a more autobiographical or discursive mode, including Lord Byron's *Don Juan*, William Wordsworth's *Prelude*, Robert Browning's *Ring and the Book*, Walt Whitman's *Leaves of Grass*, T. S. Eliot's *Four Quartets*, William Carlos Williams's *Paterson*, Charles Olson's *Maximus*, Ted Hughes's *Crow*, and David Jones's *The Anathemata*. Perhaps the greatest modern verse epic, Ezra Pound's *Cantos*, is a worthy successor to the *Odyssey*, Ovid's *Metamorphoses*, and Dante's *Divine Comedy*.

See also: separate articles on most of the authors and individual works referred to.

epic theater Epic theater is a form of episodic, didactic, and parabolic drama that is distinct from and opposed to more traditional plot-oriented drama. German in origin, epic theater was an outgrowth of post–World War I theatrical EXPRESSIONISM. Its greatest proponents were the stage director Erwin PISCATOR and the playwright Bertolt BRECHT, who later repudiated the term in favor of the Marxist-flavored *dialectical theater*.

Epic theater shattered the unities of Aristotelian drama and the tidy plotting and emotional intensity of the so-called well-made play and realistic drama. Its aim, according to Piscator and Brecht, was to make the audience think and reflect objectively on predominantly social, historical, documentary, and political material. The use of spare settings, undramatic acting, documentary films, projected titles, and interpolated music was calculated to distance spectators from the emotional content of the play. Piscator's production of Jaroslav Hašek's *The Good Soldier Schweik* (1928), on which he collaborated with Brecht and others, took place on a bare stage that eventually filled with satirical caricatures. Other productions that used the epic style included Piscator's staging of Ehm Welk's *Storm over Gothland* (1927) and Brecht's staging of his own *Mother Courage* (1949). Epic theater eventually engendered the THEATER OF FACT, or documentary theater.

Epictetus (philosopher) The philosopher Epictetus (about AD 50–c.130) was a Roman slave who became a leading representative of STOICISM in Rome. His *Manual* and *Discourses* stress his opinion that philosophy is a way of life rather than an art of using words. He held that since the events of the world are all determined by providence and thus beyond human control, individuals must try to accept whatever happens calmly and dispassionately. Epictetus also argued, however, that individuals are totally responsible for their deeds and must learn how to judge their actions by rigorous daily self-examination. The "wise man" will recognize that he has a duty toward society and his fellow humans, for all humans are alike and entitled to basic rights.

Epicureanism [ep-ik-yur-re'-uhn-izm] Epicureanism is the philosophical teaching about nature and ethics that was derived from the writings of Epicurus and developed by enthusiastic pupils such as the Roman poet LUCRETIUS and Diogenes of Oenoanda (fl. AD 200). Epicureans based their theory of knowledge on sense perception, asserting that sensations are invaribly good evidence of their causes. They worked out a complex account of how objects produce sense impressions and explained error by positing the disruption of causal effluences in transit.

Epicureans established a physical theory on the same basis. According to the theory, nothing comes from or returns to nothing; change must result from a rearrangement of persisting bodies. The basic elements of things are invisible atoms, moving in a void, which produce phenomenal objects by combination. The human soul is made of particularly small, mobile atomic bodies; there is nothing incorporeal or immortal about it. (See ATOMISM.)

In ethics the main thesis of Epicureanism is that seeking pleasure and avoiding pain are the supreme good and the principal goal of life. People should therefore forget their fears of gods and of punishment after death (both of which have no logical basis) and live for pleasure. Epicurean HEDONISM urges the avoidance of worldly distractions, and the pursuit of *ataraxia*, freedom from disturbance and pain, should be sought instead.

Epicurus [ep-i-kyur'-uhs] Epicurus, 341–270 BC, was a Greek philosopher who founded the system known as Epicureanism. He studied with followers of PLATO and DEMOCRITUS before opening his school in Athens. The school, later called the Garden, accepted women and slaves. This, coupled with Epicurus's teachings concerning pleasure, led to public criticism of the school as a scene of debauchery. In reality, life there was fairly austere. Most of the writings of Epicurus have been lost. Fragments from his most important work, *Peri physeōs* (On Nature), were recovered from the charred papyri of Herculaneum, buried by an eruption of Vesuvius in AD 79.

Epidaurus [ep-ih-dawr'-uhs] The ancient Greek city of Epidaurus, on the northeast coast of the Peloponnesus, was famous for its sanctuary of the legendary Greek physician ASCLEPIUS, which functioned as an international

The theater at Epidaurus, designed (c.*350 BC*) by Polyclitus the Younger, is among the largest and best-preserved ancient theaters in Greece. The circular construction and the pitch of the seats permit nearly perfect acoustics.

healing spa from the 5th century BC through Roman times. It was also the site of the *Asclepieia*, a quadrennial athletic and dramatic festival.

The sanctuary includes temples, colonnades, hospitals, hotels, gymnasia, and the best-preserved theater of ancient Greece. The last, a 4th-century structure, has seating for 14,000 and nearly perfect acoustics. The *tholos*, a rotunda built c.360–320 BC, houses an underground maze whose function is unknown. In a long porticoed building, the *abaton*, patients would sleep to dream of cures prescribed by the god. Rare surgical instruments, votive gifts and inscriptions, and sculptures from the site are preserved in a local museum.

epidemiology [ep-i-dem-ee-ahl'-uh-jee] Epidemiology, traditionally, is the description of epidemics, which are occurrences of diseases that significantly affect various groups of people. It studies such factors as an illness attack rate, which describes the number of people ill in a population at risk of being ill. Historically, epidemiology has been applied to studies of INFECTIOUS DISEASES, but in more recent times epidemiologists have also studied major noninfectious diseases, such as cancer and heart disease, and other important health problems. Pandemics are epidemics that encompass large regions or large numbers of people (see PUBLIC HEALTH).

Investigators using epidemiological techniques have been able to describe diseases in great detail years before the causative agent was identified. For example, epidemiological studies resulted in detailed descriptions of hepatitis, and Legionnaires' disease before their causative agents were identified. The correlation between smoking and lung cancer was obtained from epidemiological studies, as well. Much epidemiological research is now devoted to AIDS (see AIDS).

The foremost epidemiological technique is the descriptive approach: the disease or situation is defined in terms of time, place, and person. Long-term and short-term trends in the disease's occurrence are considered. The place where the causative agent and the person had contact is noted; for example, someone may eat a contaminated meal in a restaurant and become ill at home, but the contact point was the restaurant. The patient's age, sex, socioeconomic status, occupation, nutritional status, and other factors are also noted.

In an epidemiological investigation, the existence of an epidemic first must be confirmed by examining individual cases and verifying the diagnosis. The number of cases is then estimated, and the clinical data are collected and analyzed. A case definition is developed that is then used to identify other cases. Appropriate laboratory specimens are obtained and processed, and the data are analyzed in terms of time, place, and person. The source of the causative agent, its mode of transmission, and the risk factors that explain why some people became ill and others did not are determined. A hypothesis is advanced as to why the outbreak occurred, and investigators try to prove or disprove the hypothesis. Once the cause is identified, appropriate control and prevention measures can be instituted. Such public-health organizations as the CENTERS FOR DISEASE CONTROL and the WORLD HEALTH ORGANIZATION investigate and attempt to control epidemics.

epidermis   see SKIN

—

epigram   In ancient Greece, an epigram was an inscription on a monument. Later the term was associated with short satirical poems, such as MARTIAL produced in the 1st century AD. From the 18th century it has denoted a concise, usually witty or ingenious statement in prose, verse, or speech. An excellent example is Oscar WILDE's "Experience is the name everyone gives to their mistakes."

epigraphy   see INSCRIPTION

—

epilepsy   Epilepsy is a general term for at least 30 chronic disorders of BRAIN function, with paroxysms of impaired consciousness and in some cases CONVULSIONS. Most forms of epilepsy may be classified as either idiopathic or focal. Idiopathic forms have no evident cause, whereas focal varieties are associated with certain kinds of brain damage.

The most common idiopathic epilepsies are grand mal seizures and petit mal seizures. Grand mal seizures involve loss of consciousness, spasms of the muscles, and rapid jerking of various body parts. Petit mal seizures are

brief attacks of impaired consciousness—so-called twilight states—with flickering of the eyelids and twitching of the mouth.

Focal epilepsies may occur as a result of a scar, a circumscribed region of brain damage caused either by trauma during the birth process, by cerebral EDEMA in infancy or childhood, or by accident, infection, or tumor. Focal seizures may involve hallucinations and strong sensations of fear, elation, depression, and foul odors, as well as impaired consciousness and muscle spasms. The somnambulistic type of patient performs complicated acts naturally and efficiently but has no subsequent memories of the events.

The beginning of an epileptic seizure may be anticipated by a so-called aura—a peculiar feeling in the stomach, flashes of light, noises in the ear, or vertigo. The mechanisms that initiate a seizure are not yet understood. During the seizure, neurons in the brain are observed to be firing simultaneously to a highly unusual degree.

Seizures are often controllable by drugs. Phenytoin, the most commonly used, has several undesirable side effects. Long-term risks for two other drugs, carbamazepine and valproic acid, have not yet been established, but one study suggests that pregnant women who take carbamazepine may give birth to infants with birth defects. In some young children with seizures uncontrollable by drugs, PET scans revealed that only half of the

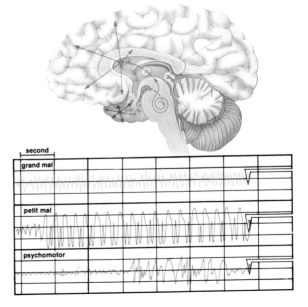

An epileptic attack results from excessive discharges by nerve cells in the brain; it appears in an electroencephalogram (EEG) as abnormal wave patterns. A grand mal seizure exhibits a widespread EEG abnormality in both cerebral hemispheres. The EEG of a petit mal attack shows three bursts, or cycles, of activity per second. Both seizures may originate from the diencephalon, or rear forebrain. Psychomotor epilepsy, a type of focal epilepsy, often results from a lesion in or near one temporal lobe.

brain exhibited epilepsy-related phenomena. When the malfunctioning tissues were removed, the seizures ended. Such radical methods are not used on older persons, whose brains have diminished powers of recovery.

epinephrine   see ADRENALINE

Epiphany [ee-pif'-uh-nee]   The Epiphany is a feast of the Christian calendar celebrated on January 6. The word comes from the Greek and means "manifestation," "appearance," or "revelation." The observance originated in the Eastern church, and at first celebrated the total revelation of God in Christ. When the observance of January 6 spread to the West, it became associated with the visit of the MAGI to the infant Jesus (Matthew 2:1–12), an event that in the West originally formed part of the CHRISTMAS observance.

In medieval and post-Reformation times, January 6 marked the final day of the 12 days of Christmas, a midwinter season of festivity.

---

epiphany   In Christian theology, an epiphany is a spiritual illumination, as in the Feast of the Epiphany. In modern literary criticism, epiphany means a writer's aesthetic illumination. In James Joyce's terms, epiphany was the sudden "revelation of the whatness of a thing" when "the soul of the commonest object seems to us radiant." The artist is charged with these revelations, communicated to the reader through the experiences of his characters. Joyce originated this usage in *Stephen Hero* (written c.1904), his first draft of *A Portrait of the Artist as a Young Man* (1916).

---

epiphyte [ep'-i-fyt]   Epiphytes are plants that normally grow on other plants rather than in soil. They are not parasitic, however, and do not use the host plant as a source of food. Because epiphytes do not derive their nourishment from the supporting plant, they also may be found on telephone wires, fences, and other nonliving objects. Epiphytes occur among flowering plants, ferns, mosses, lichens, and algae. Often called air plants because they appear to live on air, epiphytes require moisture and food to survive. Depending on the type of epiphyte, sufficient moisture may be obtained from dew, mist, or rain. Such moisture may be absorbed immediately by the roots or by specialized leaves, or it may be first collected into small pools in pockets formed by the epiphyte or in cavities in the host plant. The green parts of the epiphyte produce simple foods (sugars) by photosynthesis, while additional nutrients are carried by wind or rain and absorbed by the plant. Examples of epiphytes are SPANISH MOSS and the staghorn fern, genus *Platycerium*.

Epirus [eh-py'-ruhs]   Epirus was an ancient region of Greece, located in what is now Albania and northwestern Greece, with Illyria to the north, the Pindus mountains to the east, and the Gulf of Ambracia to the south. The region was barbarous in early Greek times and famous primarily for its oracle of Zeus at Dodona. It did not become important until Alexander, king of Molossia (in Epirus), unified the Epirotes. Alexander invaded Italy in 333 BC, conquering much of southern Italy, but was finally defeated and killed in 330.

When PYRRHUS (319–272) ascended the throne, Epirus was dependent on Macedonia. He made his country independent and increased its territory at Macedonia's expense. He, too, invaded Italy brilliantly but unsuccessfully. His failure weakened the kingdom, which fell c.232. Epirus was subsequently drawn into the Roman-Macedonian wars, and in 167 the Romans sacked the country and enslaved 150,000 Epirotes.

Epirus languished under Roman rule, was subdued by ALARIC by the end of the 4th century AD, and in 1081 was conquered by the Norman crusader ROBERT GUISCARD. It survived as a vassal state of the BYZANTINE EMPIRE until conquered by the Ottoman Turks in the 15th century.

Episcopal church   The Protestant Episcopal church in the United States is a part of the worldwide ANGLICAN COMMUNION. The history of the Episcopal church began with the English exploration and colonization of North America. Although the New England colonies were established by Puritans opposed to Anglicanism, large numbers of Anglicans settled in the southern colonies, and the Church of England (see ENGLAND, CHURCH OF) became the established church in the Carolinas, Maryland, and Virginia. The American Revolution severed ties between the Church of England and the church in the colonies. Thus in 1789 the Protestant Episcopal church began its separate existence, determined to preserve its Anglican heritage but also committed to such American ideals as the separation of church and state.

The character of the Episcopal church was influenced during its early years by the struggle between the Low church party, led by William WHITE, the first bishop of Pennsylvania, and a High church party, led by Samuel SEABURY, bishop of Connecticut. Seeking to resolve the struggle, the Episcopal church established a polity in which a democratic, lay-dominated church structure was set in tension with the aristocratic, episcopally dominated government structure. A general convention was established, composed of a house of bishops and a house of clerical and lay deputies, and chartered to meet triennially. Further tension was to exist between this national convention and the local dioceses and missionary districts, which resisted interference by the national body. Unity has been maintained by commonly held traditions embodied in a constitution and canon law, the BOOK OF COMMON PRAYER, and the threefold ministry of bishops, priests, and deacons, and through an agreement to coexist.

In 1919 the general convention created the national council, later called the executive council. In 1976 the general convention approved both a revision of the Book of Common Prayer (previously revised in 1892 and 1928) and the admission of women to the ordained ministry.

These actions caused some members to leave for other churches or to establish a new church, the Anglican Church of North America. The consecration of Barbara HARRIS as the first woman bishop in 1989 provoked the formation of the Episcopal Synod of America, a dissenting group supported by several Episcopal bishops.

epistemology [i-pis-tuh-mahl'-uh-jee]

Epistemology is the branch of PHILOSOPHY that studies the nature and limits of knowledge; it examines the structure, origin, and criteria of knowledge. Epistemology also deals with a number of related problems: sense perception, the relation between the knower and the object known, the possible kinds of knowledge and the degrees of certainty for each kind of knowledge, the nature of truth, and the nature of and justification for inferences. The word *epistemology* comes from the Greek words *episteme* ("knowledge") and *logos* ("theory"). Hence, a common definition of epistemology is theory of knowledge.

Greek Origins. Epistemology began in Greece with the SOPHISTS, who challenged the possibility of knowledge. The Sophist PROTAGORAS, an epistemological subjectivist who held that appearances are the only reality that can be known, maintained that each individual is the measure of all things. He explained that since all knowledge is dependent on a person's experience, for which that individual alone is judge, knowledge is relative to each individual.

The philosophies of SOCRATES and PLATO were responses to this epistemological relativism. Socrates was the first to attempt to explicate the concept of definition that he believed gave the essential characteristics of a thing rather than being the relative opinions of individuals. He also presented a method for discovering definitions that involved examining several particular aspects of the thing in question and looking for what is common to each. This method was later called INDUCTION, although it was not the term used by Socrates. Plato's epistemological objectivism (the theory that the object of knowledge is independent of the knowing subject) was also a response to the Sophists. In the *Theaetetus*, Plato examined several definitions of knowledge. He rejected the view that knowledge is perception, arguing that the sensation involved in a perception seems to be subjective insofar as it depends for its existence and nature on the state of the perceiver, whereas the object perceived is not so dependent.

Starting with the assumption that knowledge must be unchanging and have reality as its object, Plato developed the theory of Forms in the *Republic*. Because the world of sense experience is constantly changing, it cannot be the object of knowledge—and hence cannot be real. Since there is knowledge, there must be another unchanging realm that is the object of knowledge. This realm, consisting of substantivized Socratic definitions called Forms, or Ideas, can only be known by reason. For Plato, knowledge was having true belief justified by an account. The justification or account was given by appealing to the Forms. This basic definition of knowledge as justified true belief was not challenged until the 1960s.

Later Developments. ARISTOTLE accepted this structure of justified true belief while rejecting the theory of Forms. He said that justification was through sense experience, and he provided a detailed method for learning and presenting knowledge in his LOGIC, which was the standard for philosophical argument for 2,000 years. In the 3d century AD, Sextus Empiricus revived the SKEPTICISM of the Sophists by accepting Plato's criticism of perception (skepticism of the senses) and by accepting Aristotle's rejection of pure reason (skepticism of reason) as means of gaining knowledge. He concluded that knowledge was impossible. In the medieval period, the questions were not about whether knowledge is possible but about the sources of knowledge and the presuppositions of knowledge. These tended to be either Aristotelian or Platonic.

Modern Approaches. From the 16th to the 19th century, epistemological questions were primarily about methodology. As mathematics and physical science acquired a new importance, rivalry developed between the methodologies of pure reason (RATIONALISM) and sense experience (EMPIRICISM) as the means for gaining knowledge. The methodologies were used to set the limits of knowledge; only what could be discovered or what originated from the accepted methodology would be genuine knowledge, all else being merely opinion or belief. Rationalists such as René DESCARTES, Baruch SPINOZA, and G. W. von LEIBNIZ thought the source and final test for knowledge was deductive reasoning based on self-evidently true axioms. This explained the certainty of knowledge but did not account for erroneous beliefs. Empiricists such as John LOCKE, George BERKELEY, and David HUME thought that knowledge originated in and was tested by sense experience. Although they could account for error, they could not provide certainty for judgments about the world. Hume even provided a critique of induction by showing that because one's knowledge of causes of events is based on perception, which is always subject to error, one can never be certain that a particular cause will always have its expected effects—even for the most basic laws of science (see CAUSALITY).

In the 19th century John Stuart MILL attempted to formulate inductive methods for the justification of causal and mathematical laws. The German philosopher Immanuel KANT had attempted to overcome the drawbacks of these methodologies by combining elements of each. He thought that one could have certainty about the world of experience (phenomenon) because one constructs that world but that one could have no knowledge of the world as it really is (noumenon). Since the world of one's experience is constructed according to mathematical and causal laws, there is no need to justify the universal application of these laws to experience.

Following Kant, both REALISM and IDEALISM reemerged. Neorealists such as G. E. MOORE accepted the view that things are just what they seem to be. For the idealists, who maintained that everything is in the mind, the meaning of truth became a problem. They accepted a coherence theory of truth, in which the standard of truth is the logical consistency of a proposition with a larger system of propositions. This view of truth has been rejected by philosophers such as Ludwig WITTGENSTEIN because a system of false beliefs can also be internally consistent. Wittgenstein accepted a correspondence theory of truth, in which truth is viewed as a relation between an idea or proposition and its object. ANALYTIC AND LINGUISTIC PHILOSOPHY, PHENOMENOLOGY, and PRAGMATISM are other attempts to deal with the questions of epistemology, raising once again the question of the nature of knowledge.

epistle [ee-pis'-ul]   An epistle is a letter addressed to a specific person or persons but intended for a general audience. The most famous examples of ancient epistles are those in books of the New Testament. Modern examples, modeled on Greek and Roman epistles, are the poetic epistles of Alexander Pope and Voltaire. Epistolary novels, consisting of letters, include Samuel Richardson's *Clarissa Harlowe* (1747–48) and Jean Jacques Rousseau's *La Nouvelle Héloïse* (1761).

epitaph   An epitaph is an inscription on a tombstone or a poem written as if it were such an inscription. Epitaphs are usually terse and witty, occasionally even humorous, and address a reader directly. They are concrete, earthy, and ironic in a way that elegies, eulogies, and other genres of poetry for the dead are not. Typical of the epitaph are these lines from Ben Jonson's "Epitaph for Elizabeth Lady H.":

Underneath this stone doth lie
As much beauty as could die.

epitaxy   Epitaxy is the artificial growth, on a solid surface, of a thin, crystalline layer of atoms or molecules, whose geometric structure imitates that of the solid substrate. In liquid-phase epitaxy a heated solution of a chemical substance is cooled while in contact with the substrate, and a crystalline layer is deposited. In vapor-phase epitaxy and molecular-beam epitaxy, gaseous beams of atoms or molecules interact with and are deposited on the substrate. Epitaxial processes play an important role in the manufacture of functional, layered silicon chips that serve as SEMICONDUCTORS.

epithelium   The epithelium is one of the basic kinds of tissues constituting the bodies of animals (see TISSUE, ANIMAL). It is the protective layer covering external body surfaces (see SKIN) and lining most internal surfaces (mucous membranes and other epithelial tissues). The epithelium is involved in the absorption of substances from the environment and their loss to it. According to the body site, these processes are called excretion, respiration, and digestion (see DIGESTIVE SYSTEM; EXCRETORY SYSTEM; RESPIRATORY SYSTEM).

As the animal kingdom evolved, the epithelium was the first kind of specialized tissue to appear. In growing embryos it is also the first tissue to develop, arising from either the ectoderm, mesoderm, or endoderm in different animals (see DEVELOPMENT). Epithelial tissue usually consists almost entirely of closely packed flat or columnar cells, with little intercellular material. The epithelium is well supplied with nerve structures for sensing the environment, but except at a few specialized sites it lacks a vascular system for conducting body fluids. One or more layers may be present.

epoxy resins [ep-ahk'-see]   The group of synthetic RESINS called epoxies produces the strongest ADHESIVES in current use, as well as PLASTICS and corrosion-resistant coatings. Epoxy adhesives are thermosetting; that is, after initial hardening, they cannot be remelted by heat. They have excellent resistance to solvents and weathering agents, and high electrical and temperature resistance. Their adhesion to almost any type of surface is unmatched.

Epoxies are usually made by reacting epichlorohydrin and Bisphenol A to produce a polymer chain. The end of the chain is an epoxy group from epichlorohydrin; the resulting plastic receives its name from the end epoxy group.

The unmodified epoxies are brittle; however, the properties of the cured resin can be varied widely by the selection of a suitable resin, curing agent, filler, and curing procedure. Most epoxy formulations have two components that are mixed for curing. Unlike most thermosetting plastics, epoxies shrink only slightly during curing and so can be used as filler-adhesives. The epoxies can also be used as molding and potting compounds, reinforced plastics, and surface finishes.

epsom salts   Originally, epsom salts was the salt obtained by evaporating water from Epsom spring, a mineral spring in Surrey, England. The salt was primarily made up of magnesium sulfate, $MgSO_4 \cdot 7H_2O$; "epsom salts" is now the common name for magnesium sulfate, however prepared. Epsom salts was first used as a laxative. Magnesium sulfate is used in dyes and bleaches, fertilizers, matches, explosives, and mineral water; to fireproof fabrics; and as an anticonvulsant in medicine.

Epstein, Jacob   Sir Jacob Epstein, b. Nov. 10, 1880, d. Aug. 19, 1959, was a British sculptor noted for his bold, highly personal works in bronze or stone. Born in New York City of Jewish parents, he moved to London in 1905 and began to make the impressionistic, multifaceted portrait busts for which he is well known. The subjects of these works included family members, friends, and famous personalities, such as Joseph Conrad, Albert Einstein, Jawaharlal Nehru, Paul Robeson, and George Bernard Shaw. Epstein also began at this time to create the monumental public works that continued to arouse scandal and controversy throughout his career. The boldness and modernity of his *Strand Statues* (1907–08), 18 marble figures for the British Medical Association Building in London, were misunderstood by a public still accustomed to a more academic sculptural tradition. His winged figure over the grave of Oscar Wilde, commissioned (1911) for the Père Lachaise Cemetery in Paris, also aroused anger.

In 1912, Epstein met Constantin Brancusi, Jean Baptiste Armand Guillaume, Amedeo Modigliani, and Pablo Picasso in Paris. The following year in London he became a founder of VORTICISM, an avant-garde group of sculptors and painters interested in abstract forms of the machine age. Later, working independently, Epstein produced a number of monumental sculptures, mostly in stone, characterized by powerful carving in an expressionistic mode. Among his best-known late works are the marble Trade Unions Council War Memorial (1958; London); *Christ in Majesty* (1957; Llandaff Cathedral, Wales), which was cast in aluminum; and *Madonna and Child* (1952; Convent of the Holy Child Jesus, London).

Epstein-Barr virus   see CANCER; HERPES; MONONUCLEOSIS

▬

equal opportunity   Equal opportunity is the name of a U.S. government program intended to eliminate DISCRIMINATION in employment, education, and housing on the basis of race, color, sex, religion, national origin, or age. It originated with the passage of the CIVIL RIGHTS ACT of 1964, which established the Equal Employment Opportunity Commission (EEOC). The program was redefined and elaborated by a combination of other legislation (such as the ban against mandatory retirement in 1986), executive orders of the president, and decisions of the Supreme Court.

Previous federal policies had forbidden active discrimination in employment, housing, education, and voting rights, but the new program required that employers take AFFIRMATIVE ACTION to create equality in fact. Employers who contract or subcontract with the federal government may be required to take affirmative action to increase the proportion of women and minorities in their work force. The courts have held that when the proportion of such employees is less than their proportion in the available and qualified labor pool, a presumption of discrimination arises. In such cases, the employer must demonstrate that the under-utilization of women and minorities is not the result of discrimination. Many state and local governments have established similar guidelines.

In 1980 the EEOC issued regulations prohibiting sexual harassment, either physical or verbal, of workers by their supervisors. It declared that employers had an "affirmative duty" to eliminate sexual harassment. The Court subsequently held that such harassment is illegal discrimination.

Efforts to carry out equal-opportunity policies have led in many cases to the establishment of quotas or goals for minorities and women, and to "preferential hiring" of people from those groups. These in turn have been criticized as creating new forms of discrimination. Employers and universities have been charged with discriminating against white males. The issue reached the Supreme Court in 1978 in the case of UNIVERSITY OF CALIFORNIA V. BAKKE, which resulted in a decision against the use of quotas. Much uncertainty remained about what kinds of affirmative action were permissible. The Supreme Court resolved this somewhat by upholding the use of affirmative-action quotas by private employers and unions in the case of UNITED STEELWORKERS OF AMERICA V. WEBER (1979). In 1987 the Court ruled that women may also receive preferential treatment. Several Court rulings in 1989 and 1990, however, seemed to restrict the application of affirmative action.

▬

equal protection of the laws   The 14th AMENDMENT to the Constitution of the United States requires that state laws grant "equal protection of the laws" to all persons. This important clause has been used to invalidate practices of racial discrimination (see BROWN V. BOARD OF EDUCATION OF TOPEKA, KANSAS, 1954); unequal treatment of aliens (as in *Yick Wo* v. *Hopkins*, 1886); discrimination based on sex (as in *Reed* v. *Reed*, 1971, and *Frontiero* v. *Richardson*, 1973); and other distinctions, such as in the cases of the handicapped. The equal-protection clause has also been used to rectify inequities in apportionment and to limit the use of racial quotas in AFFIRMATIVE ACTION programs (see UNIVERSITY OF CALIFORNIA V. BAKKE, 1978). The Supreme Court, however, has determined that differences in interdistrict public school financing caused by reliance on varying property-tax revenues does not violate the equal-protection clause (*San Antonio Independent School District* v. *Rodriguez*, 1972), and that mandatory retirement plans are also not in violation of the clause.

▬

Equal Rights Amendment   The Equal Rights Amendment (ERA), proposed as the 27th Amendment to the CONSTITUTION OF THE UNITED STATES and intended to outlaw discrimination based on sex, states that "equality of rights under the law shall not be denied or abridged by the United States nor by any State on account of sex." Originally drafted by Alice PAUL of the National Woman's party and introduced in Congress in 1923, the ERA lay dormant until 1970, when a groundswell of support for it was generated by the NATIONAL ORGANIZATION FOR WOMEN (NOW). The ERA was approved by the House of Representatives in 1971 and by the Senate in 1972. The deadline for ratification was originally March 1979, but in 1978 it was extended 3 years. On June 30, 1982, ratification of the ERA fell 3 states short of the 38 needed. On July 14, 1982, the ERA was reintroduced in Congress. Efforts to regain congressional approval of the proposal, however, were defeated in the House of Representatives on Nov. 15, 1983.

equation An equation, in mathematics, is a statement expressing that two quantities, or expressions, are equal to one another. For example, the equation $a = b$ states that the quantities a and b are equal; the symbol $=$ indicates this equality. The expressions in an equation may sometimes be identical. For example, in the equation $3 = 1 + 2$, 3 and $1 + 2$ are always equivalent. Such a statement is known as an *identity*, for which a triple-bar symbol $\equiv$ may be used. An identity may also contain VARIABLES, as in $3d = e + 2f$, but it is an identity only if the statement is true for all possible values of the variables d, e, and f. Otherwise, as with all other equations, the statement is termed a *conditional equation*, or simply an *equation*. A linear equation has the form $ax + b = 0$, where a and b are numerical constants. The solution occurs when $x = -b/a$. It is an equation of the first degree, or power, because the highest EXPONENT on the variable x is 1. A quadratic equation has the form $ax^2 + bx + c = 0$. It is an equation of the second degree, or power, because the highest exponent on the variable x is 2. The equation has two solutions, given by $x = (-b \pm \sqrt{b^2 - 4ac}/2a$

Linear and quadratic equations are special cases of polynomial equations, which include other degrees, or powers. They take the form $a_n x^n + a_{n-1} x^{n-1} + ... + a_0 = 0$ for given constants $a_0, a_1, ... , a_n$. The fundamental theorem of algebra states that a polynomial equation of degree n may be factored (broken down to a product of FACTORS) in the form $a_n x^n + ... + a_0 = (x - \lambda_1)(x - \lambda_2)... (x - \lambda_n)$. Each of the numbers $\lambda_1, ... , \lambda_n$ is a solution, or ROOT, of the equation and may be either a REAL NUMBER or a COMPLEX NUMBER, even if the coefficients $a_0, ... , a_n$ of the polynomial are all real. The multiplicity of the solution is the number of times the root is repeated in the factored expression. For example, if the expression is $(x - 3)(x - 5)(x - 5)$, then 3 is a root of multiplicity 1, and 5 is a root of multiplicity 2. If multiplicities are counted as separate roots, the fundamental theorem of algebra states that a polynomial of degree n has exactly n roots.

A polynomial equation of degree greater than 1 is an example of a nonlinear equation in a single variable, usually written as $f(x) = 0$ (see FUNCTION). A given nonlinear equation may have no solution, a unique solution, a finite number of solutions, or an infinite number of solutions. For example, the equation $e^x = 0$, where e^x is an exponential function, has no solution; $e^x = 1$ has a unique solution, $x = 0$; a polynomial equation has a finite number of solutions; and the equation $\sin x = 0$ has an infinite number of solutions.

Even if an equation has solutions, it may be difficult or impossible to find them exactly. For example, an equation as simple as a polynomial equation of degree 5 cannot be solved, in general, by elementary rational operations—only approximate solutions can be obtained. Perhaps the most basic approximation technique is called Newton's method of approximation. This method, for the equation $f(x) = 0$, involves a repetitive process that yields approximations of greater and greater accuracy with each repetition.

equation of time see DAY

equator The equator is an imaginary great circle drawn around the Earth equidistant from the two poles. It divides the globe into northern and southern hemispheres. LATITUDES are measured north or south of this line. The celestial equator is the great circle represented by the intersection of the Earth's equatorial plane and the CELESTIAL SPHERE.

Equatorial Guinea [gin'-ee] Equatorial Guinea is a tiny country in west central Africa. It consists of a mainland area, Mbini (formerly Río Muni), wedged between Cameroon and Gabon; and five islands, including BIOKO (named Macías Nguema Biyogo from 1972 to 1979 and Fernando Po before 1972) and Pagalu (formerly Annobón). The largest cities are the capital, MALABO (formerly Santa Isabel), on Bioko, and Bata in Mbini.

Land, People, and Economy

Mbini, on the continent, has a littoral strip of mangrove swamps. Inland, the terrain is rolling and rises to elevations of up to 1,200 m (4,000 ft) in the heavily forested foothills of the Crystal Mountains. Bioko, like the other islands, is volcanic; it rises to 3,008 m (9,869 ft) at Pico Santa Isabel, the highest point in the country. Tropical rain forests predominate. Malabo has a fine natural harbor. The climate is humid subtropical, with average annual rainfall of 1,905 mm (75 in) and an average temperature of 27° C (81° F).

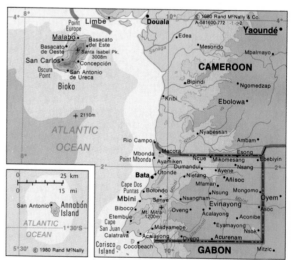

EQUATORIAL GUINEA

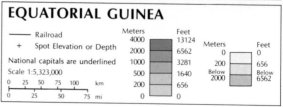

	Meters	Feet		
——— Railroad	4000	13124		
+ Spot Elevation or Depth	2000	6562	Meters	Feet
			0	0
National capitals are underlined	1000	3281	200	656
Scale 1:5,323,000	500	1640	Below 2000	Below 6562
0 25 50 75 100 km	200	656		
0 25 50 75 mi	0	0		

AT A GLANCE

REPUBLIC OF EQUATORIAL GUINEA

Land: Area:28,051 km² (10,831 mi²). Capital and largest city: Malabo (1983 est. pop., 37,500).

People: Population (1990 est.): 368,935. Density: 13.2 persons per km² (34.1 per mi²). Distribution (1989 est.): 60% urban, 40% rural. Official language: Spanish. Major religions: Roman Catholicism, Protestantism, traditional religions.

Government: Type: republic. Legislature: House of Representatives. Political subdivisions: 7 provinces.

Economy: GNP (1987): $103 million; $293 per capita. Labor distribution (1984): agriculture—73%. Foreign trade (1988 est.): imports—$50 million; exports—$30 million. Currency 1 C.F.A. = 100 centimes.

Education and Health: Literacy (1985): 39% of adult population. Universities (1989): none. Hospital beds (1982): 3,200. Physicians (1985): 5. Life expectancy (1990): women—52; men—48. Infant mortality (1990): 118 per 1,000 live births.

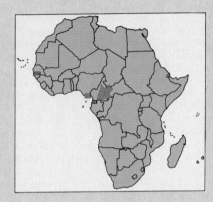

In Mbini the major ethnic group is the FANG, who constitute more than 80% of the population and live mainly in the interior. Coastal tribes include the Combe, Benge, and Bujeba. On Bioko the major groups are the Bubi, who arrived from the mainland between the 10th and 15th centuries, and the Fernando, descendants of Europeans and mainland slaves freed by the British in the 19th century. Equatorial Guinea, formerly a Spanish colony, is the only Spanish-speaking nation in Africa; French became compulsory in the schools in 1988.

Since independence, the economy has reverted largely to subsistence agriculture, with rice, cassava, bananas, and palm nuts the chief crops. The export trade with Spain—cacao from estates on Bioko and coffee grown in Mbini—was virtually destroyed in the 1970s. The country joined the Franc Zone in 1985 and sought French investment.

History and Government

The Portuguese, who claimed suzerainty over the territory about 1471, transferred their rights to Spain in 1778. Spain, however, did not seriously explore the area until the last half of the 19th century and did not effectively control the hinterland of Mbini until 1923. The present provinces were established in 1959. Limited self-government was introduced in 1963, and independence was achieved on Oct. 12, 1968.

Following an abortive coup in 1969, President Francisco Macías Nguema, a Fang, turned the country into a one-party state and became president for life in 1972. His regime became increasingly repressive. An estimated 20% of the population died, and an even larger number

fled the country before he was overthrown in a coup (August 1979) led by Lt.-Col. Obiang Nguema and executed. A Supreme Military Council ruled until 1982, when a constitution was approved by voters, providing for direct presidential elections after a seven-year transition under President Obiang Nguema. Uncontested parliamentary elections were held in 1983 and 1988, and Obiang Nguema was reelected in 1989.

equestrian arts   see RIDING

equilibrium   see BIOLOGICAL EQUILIBRIUM; CHEMICAL KINETICS AND EQUILIBRIUM; STATICS

equinox [ee'-kwin-ahks]   The equinoxes are the two points of intersection between the ecliptic (the Sun's apparent annual path) and the celestial equator (the equator of the CELESTIAL SPHERE). The two moments in the year when the Sun is exactly over the equator, and day and night are hence of equal length, are the times of these equinoxes. In the Northern Hemisphere the vernal, or spring, equinox occurs about March 21, and the autumnal equinox occurs about September 23. In the Southern Hemisphere the seasons are reversed.

equity (finance) [ek'-wit-ee]   Equity is the monetary value of a property less any claims against it. A homeowner's equity, for example, is the value of the home less any mortgages or other claims. In corporate finance, equity is the capital furnished by the owners or stockholders (see STOCK) of a business firm as distinguished from debt, or funds supplied by the firm's bondholders and other creditors. On the firm's financial statements (see ACCOUNTING), equity is equal to its net worth. When the company's entire debt has been paid, the owners of equity become entitled to all of the company's remaining earnings and property.

equity (law)   Equity is a branch of Anglo-American law that was developed as a supplement to traditional COMMON LAW to handle certain civil cases. In medieval England the courts had restricted powers and could not handle every case that arose. When a person could not go to the regular courts for relief, he or she would petition the king for relief, and the king would refer the matter to his chancellor, the next most important government official. In the late 15th century the chancellor began to decide these extraordinary cases directly or through assistants called masters, and the Court of Chancery developed. The purpose of that court was to supply a remedy when the regular common-law courts could not or would not do so. The law it developed became known as equity, to distinguish it from the law applied in the regular common-law courts. This is the function of equity today. Some states apply both legal and equitable principles in the same courts; others assign judges to sit either as equity judges or as law judges.

Equity offers a wide variety of remedies; law has only one basic remedy. In cases at law the basic remedy is money damages. Sometimes, however, money is not a satisfactory remedy. Equitable principles permit the court to order the defendant to do or not to do a given act. Orders to perform a contract (specific performance), to tear down a spite fence (mandatory injunction), and to stop excessive smoke or noise (injunction) are examples of equitable, nonmonetary remedies. The penalty for refusing to obey an equitable order is a possible citation for contempt of court. Equitable principles also apply when a contract must be reformed to reflect the true understanding of the parties and when a contract must be rescinded because it was the result of fraud.

Another application of equitable principles is in enforcing duties imposed by relationships of trust and confidence, such as the duties of a trustee to the beneficiaries of a trust, the duties of the executor of an estate of a deceased person, and the enforcement of the duties of a partner to a partnership or a director to a corporation.

There is no right to a jury trial when a case is based on equitable principles. The judge finds both the law and the facts. The reason for this is purely historical. There was no jury in the English Court of Chancery, and U.S. federal and state constitutions guarantee jury trial only in the kinds of cases that were entitled to a jury trial when the nation was founded. Therefore, even where the distinction between equity and law has been abolished, it is still necessary to determine which principles apply in order to know whether the parties are entitled to trial by jury.

equivalent weight   Equivalent weight, or equivalent, or gram equivalent weight, is the amount of substance that, in electrolysis, will react with or produce the AVOGADRO NUMBER (one mole) of electrons (see ELECTROCHEMISTRY). In an acid-base reaction, equivalent weight is the amount of substance that will react with one mole of hydrogen ions, H^+, or hydroxide ions, OH^- (see ACIDS AND BASES).

Erasmus, Desiderius [ir-az'-muhs, des-i-deer'ee-uhs]   The Dutch scholar Erasmus, b. c.1466, d. July 12, 1536, was the greatest classicist of the RENAISSANCE in northern Europe. Erasmus lived at a time when the breakup of feudalism and the increasingly obvious abuses within the church created widespread anxiety, fanaticism, and violence. Faced with the disintegration of medieval Europe into disputatious national and religious factions, he sought peace, reconciliation, and unity.

His works, combining piety and scholarship, attempted to reconcile faith and reason and bring together Christianity and the culture of ancient times. He was sharply critical of the corruptions of the church and the absurdities of scholasticism, but he did not repudiate the past in a blaze of reforming zeal, as Luther had done. Instead, he tried to reform the church through gentle reason and toleration but was swept aside by the passions unleashed by the Reformation and Counter-Reformation.

Erasmus's literary endeavors were more successful. In one of his most influential works, *Encomium moriae* (1509; *The Praise of Folly,* 1549), which he wrote while staying in England with Sir Thomas MORE, he attacked the superstition, vulgarity, and foolishness of his day with merciless wit. In 1516 he published the work that established him as the major humanist of his generation: an edition of the Greek version of the New Testament ac-

The Dutch scholar Desiderius Erasmus was the foremost classicist of the northern Renaissance. His erudite, humanist works, exemplified in Adages (1500) and The Manual of the Christian Knight (1503), advocated charity and moderation. He appears here in a portrait by Hans Holbein the Younger.

companied by an elegant new Latin translation. In many of his works Erasmus emphasized the literary beauty and moral content of the classics. He saw Latin as a unifying language that could counteract the divisiveness of the vernacular tongues. He largely ignored the value of empirical science, however, and the prestige he lent to a consequently one-sided concept of HUMANISM contributed in later centuries to the dichotomy between the two cultures.

Erastianism [ir-as'-tee-uhn-izm] The idea of absolute state primacy over the church is known as Erastianism. The doctrine derives its name from Thomas Erastus (1524–83), a Swiss Protestant theologian and physician involved in a controversy over the right of Calvinist religious leaders to excommunicate sinners or doctrinal deviates. He held that only the state could punish such offenders because civil authorities had final jurisdiction in all areas, even in matters such as excommunication. The theory of church-state relations, to which the name Erastianism is given, usually goes well beyond the authority Erastus would have granted to the state.

Eratosthenes of Cyrene [air-uh-tahs'-thuh-neez, sy-ree'-nee] The Greek geographer Eratosthenes, c.276–195 BC, is best known for his accurate calculation of the Earth's circumference. He originated a mathematical system, known as Eratosthenes' sieve, for determining prime numbers, and determined the inclination of the ecliptic to the celestial equator. Eratos-thenes served as chief librarian of the museum at Alexandria, Egypt. His method of measuring the Earth's circumference (see EARTH, SIZE AND SHAPE OF) reflects the Hellenistic penchant for mathematical solutions evident, for example, in the work of ARCHIMEDES.

erbium [ur'-bee-uhm] Erbium is a chemical element, a shiny metal of the LANTHANIDE SERIES. Its symbol is Er, its atomic is number 68, and its atomic weight is 167.26. The six naturally occurring erbium isotopes—^{162}Er, ^{164}Er, ^{166}Er, ^{167}Er, ^{168}Er, and ^{170}Er—are not radioactive. The numerous synthetic isotopes of erbium are all radioactive. Erbium was first identified in nature by C. G. Mosander in 1842. Because of its capacity to absorb neutrons, erbium is widely used in manufacturing nuclear control rods. It is also used in magnetic alloys.

Erebus [air'-i-buhs] In Greek mythology, Erebus was the mysterious darkness through which the dead passed on their way to HADES. Personified, Erebus was the son of CHAOS and the brother of Night (Nyx) by whom he sired Aether (Air) and Day.

Erebus, Mount [air'-i-buhs] Mount Erebus is a volcano on Ross Island of Antarctica and has an elevation of

4,023 m (13,200 ft). One of its three cones is active. James C. Ross discovered it in 1841 and named it for one of his ships. Men under T. W. E. Davis of Ernest Shackleton's party climbed it in 1908. In 1957–58 it served as a base for U.S. activities during the International Geophysical Year.

Erechtheum see ACROPOLIS

Erewhon see BUTLER, SAMUEL (1835–1902)

Erfurt [air'-foort] Erfurt, with a population of 217,961 (1987 est.), is the capital of Erfurt state in central Germany. A commercial center, Erfurt still has many old buildings. Most noted are the cathedral (1154–1476), the church of Saint Severus (13th–15th century), the Augustine monastery where Martin Luther spent several years as a monk, the Old University (founded 1392; suppressed 1816), and the former governor's palace (1711–20). The Merchants Bridge (1325), lined with shops and houses, spans the Gera. The city is known for its seed production and horticultural showgrounds and has a large chemical industry.

Erfurt is the site of a bishopric founded by Saint Boniface in 742. It later became a Frankish administrative center that fell to the archbishop of Mainz about 1000. The city joined the Hanseatic League in the 15th century, but in 1664 it was again taken by the archbishop of Mainz. It became part of Prussia in 1802. Erfurt was the site of a meeting between Napoleon I and Emperor Alexander I of Russia in 1808, of an ill-fated Prussian Union parliament in 1850, and of a noted German socialist assembly in 1891.

erg [urg] In the cgs (centimeter-gram-second) system of units, an erg is the unit of ENERGY or work, defined as the work expended by a force of one DYNE acting through a distance of one centimeter. An erg is a relatively small amount of energy, equal to 10^{-7} (one ten-millionth) joules, 7.4 x 10^{-8} foot-pounds, or 2.8 x 10^{-14} kilowatt-hours.

ergonomics Ergonomics, the "science of work," is a field of technology that considers human capabilities and limitations in the design of machines and objects that people use, the work processes that they must follow, and the environments in which they operate. The time and motion studies of Frederick W. TAYLOR and Frank and Lillian GILBRETH laid the groundwork for the field. Then called "human factors engineering," it grew in influence during World War II.

Health and safety features are foremost in ergonomic design. Other considerations, such as information processing and perceptual limitations, must be taken into account in the design of communications devices, computer displays, cockpit gauges, and numerous other applications. The needs of HANDICAPPED PERSONS are a major focus of the field.

See also: ANTHROPOMETRY; INDUSTRIAL DESIGN; INDUSTRIAL PSYCHOLOGY.

ergot [ur'-guht]   Ergot is a disease of cultivated cereals, caused by fungi of the genus *Claviceps.* The most prevalent form is produced by *C. purpurea,* which infects rye grain. Humans and domestic animals that eat contaminated grain develop ergot poisoning, which has such symptoms as convulsions, gangrene, and hallucinations. Great epidemics of the Middle Ages—Saint Anthony's fire, for instance—were caused by ergot poisoning. Drugs produced from ergot include ergotamine, used to treat migraine; ergotoxine, which stays uterine bleeding; and ergonovine, a lysergic acid derivative. LSD-25 (D-lysergic acid diethylamide) is derived from ergot.

Erhard, Ludwig   Ludwig Erhard, b. Feb. 4, 1897, d. May 5, 1977, is regarded as the architect of West Germany's economic recovery after World War II. He worked in a market-research firm before the war but lost his job when he refused to join the Nazi party. Plucked from obscurity during the Allied occupation after the war, he was instrumental in abolishing postwar economic controls. As minister of economic affairs (1949–63) in the Christian Democratic government of the Federal Republic he became identified with the German "economic miracle." He succeeded Konrad ADENAUER as chancellor on Oct. 16, 1963, but economic and political difficulties led to his resignation on Dec. 1, 1966.

Eric the Red   Eric the Red discovered Greenland, where he established the first European settlement in the New World. Born Erik Thorvaldsson, in Norway in the mid-10th century, Eric the Red was descended from Viking chieftains. He went to Iceland as a child, when his father was banished from Norway. A violent man, Eric himself was banished from Iceland for homicide, and then sailed westward and discovered Greenland about 981. After three years during which he explored the island, he returned to Iceland and led an expedition of 25 ships to settle (c.985) in southwestern Greenland. This settlement survived until the late 15th century. Eric himself settled at Brattahlid (Tunigdliarfik) in Greenland, where he died sometime after 1000. The church built at Brattahlid by Eric's wife was excavated in 1962. Eric's son, LEIF ERIKSSON, discovered VINLAND.

Eric XIV, King of Sweden   Eric XIV, b. Dec. 13, 1533, d. Feb. 25, 1577, king of Sweden, set that country on the path to empire. A brilliant scholar and Renaissance man who once courted Elizabeth I of England, Eric succeeded his father, GUSTAV I, as king in 1560. He im-

mediately sent an army to occupy Livonia, and from 1563, he was caught in a major struggle with Denmark. His mind snapped under the pressure in 1567. His brothers deposed him in 1568, and he died in prison.

Ericsson, John   The Swedish-American inventor and naval engineer John Ericsson, b. July 31, 1803, d. Mar. 8, 1889, designed the first ship with an armored, revolving gun-turret. In 1826 he went to London and designed and constructed numerous mechanical devices, including a locomotive engine (1829), caloric engines, and a screw propeller.

Ericsson went to the United States in 1839, where he lived for the rest of his life; he became a citizen in 1848. He designed the *Princeton* (built in 1844), the first warship with a screw propeller and with engines placed below the waterline. In 1861 he designed for the U.S. Navy an armored ship that had a revolving gun turret. Such a ship, the *Monitor*, was launched early in 1862, and on Mar. 9, 1862, it was involved in the first naval engagement between ironclad warships—with the Confederate ship familiarly known as the *Merrimack* (see MONITOR AND MERRIMACK). After the Civil War, Ericsson experimented with solar energy, torpedoes, and steam engines.

Ericsson, Leif   see LEIF ERIKSSON

Eridu [ay'-rid-oo]   Eridu (modern Abu Shahrain), situated 315 km (196 mi) southeast of Baghdad, Iraq, was the earliest known city of SUMER (southern Mesopotamia) and is the site of an important sequence of temples. Eridu was associated with Enki (EA), god of the waters that were essential to fishing and irrigation; the city may have been linked to the sea by a series of waterways. The earliest village settlement (c.5000 BC) had grown into a substantial city of mud-brick and reed houses by c.2900 BC. Eighteen superimposed mud-brick temples at the site underlie the unfinished ZIGGURAT of Amar-Sin (c.2047–2039 BC). The apparent continuity of occupation and religious observance at Eridu provide convincing evidence for the indigenous origin of Sumerian civilization.

Erie (Indian tribe) [ir'-ee]   The Erie were one of several large North American Indian tribes exterminated by Five Nations IROQUOIS raiding parties in the 17th century. Known to their HURON neighbors as the *Yenresh* ("Panther People"), they were a populous agricultural group, numbering more than 15,000 at the time of their destruction. Their lands extended along the southern shore of Lake Erie from the Miami to the Allegheny rivers and probably included most of present-day Ohio.

The Erie spoke an Iroquoian language that was similar to one of the Huron dialects. Huron refugees fleeing their own devastated villages sought asylum among the Erie in 1654 and pressed their hosts to seek revenge against the Iroquois. Threatened by Iroquois expansion, the Erie precipitated a war in which, by 1656, they were totally defeated. Some Erie refugees may have fled to the southeast, where they may have been known as the Black Minqua before they too disappeared.

Erie (Pennsylvania)   Erie (1990 pop., 108,718), a port of entry on Lake Erie, is the third largest city in Pennsylvania and the seat of Erie County, in the northwestern corner of the state. Railroads and truck lines converge on its excellent harbor, which is almost completely landlocked by the 3.1-km-long (2-mi), curving Presque Isle peninsula. Erie is Pennsylvania's only port on the St. Lawrence Seaway and is a shipping point for iron, coal, oil, lumber, grain, and the many heavy manufactured goods produced there. Beyond the busy waterfront and industrial areas are spacious tree-lined streets. The sandy beaches and conservation areas at Presque Isle State Park attract vacationers.

The French built a fort on Presque Isle in 1753. Often destroyed and rebuilt, it changed hands from French to English (1759) to American (1794). The city was laid out in 1795 on the site of the French fort. Commodore Oliver Hazard Perry built his fleet in Presque Isle Bay and sailed from there in 1813 for the Battle of Lake Erie during the War of 1812.

Erie, Lake   Lake Erie, fourth in size of the five North American GREAT LAKES, is situated between Ontario, Canada, to the north, and the United States—abutting New York, Pennsylvania, Ohio, and Michigan. The lake is 388 km (241 mi) long and 92 km (57 mi) across at its widest point. Its surface area is 25,720 km² (9,930 mi²). The shallowest of the five lakes, it has a mean depth of 18 m (58 ft). Numerous rivers flow into Lake Erie, including the Detroit, the Huron, the Sandusky, the Grand, and the Cattaraugus. The lake discharges into the Niagara River, which flows over Niagara Falls and into Lake Ontario.

Lake Erie provides an important link in transportation routes. The Erie Canal links the Hudson River with Lake Erie; the canal ends at Tonawanda, near Buffalo, on the Niagara River, 13 km (8 mi) from the lake. Lake Erie is also an essential part of the St. Lawrence Seaway.

The lake is named for the Erie Indians. In 1669, Louis Jolliet explored the lake, and subsequently both the French and British built forts along its shores. After the American Revolution, many Loyalists moved north of the lake. During the War of 1812, U.S. Adm. Oliver H. Perry defeated the British on Lake Erie, cementing U.S. control.

Industrial cities grew up along the lake, including Cleveland and Toledo, Ohio; Erie, Pa.; and Buffalo, N.Y. By the 1960s, Lake Erie was the most polluted of the Great Lakes, and most organisms in the lake had died. A 1972 agreement between the United States and Canada to stop polluting the water has resulted in a partial recovery.

Erie Canal   The Erie Canal is an important inland waterway in New York State and the principal canal of the New York State Canal system. It connects New York City, via the Hudson River, with Lake Erie at Buffalo, N.Y., and the other Great Lakes. The original canal was 584 km (363 mi) long, 1 m (4 ft) deep, with 83 locks. By 1862 the canal had been enlarged to a depth of 2 m (7 ft), and by 1918 Erie was part of the Barge Canal and was 549 km (341 mi) long and 4 m (12 ft) deep, with 36 locks. Today the canal can accommodate barges carrying up to 2,000 U.S. tons. Although freight traffic has declined, the total number of vessels using the canal increased from about 50,000 in 1979 to more than 100,000 in 1989.

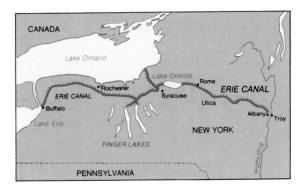

Gov. DeWitt Clinton of New York initiated construction of the canal, and it was built by the state between 1817 and 1825. It was immediately successful; within 10 years, the building costs were paid through the collection of tolls from users. The canal contributed to the dominance of New York as a port city, as well as opening Minnesota, Wisconsin, Michigan, and the other Great Lakes states to settlement by immigrants, who were then able to ship produce, primarily grains, east via the canal and receive manufactured goods in exchange. By the 1850s the canal could not compete with the newly built railroads, and it went into a decline until improvements and expansion of the canal system were begun early in the 20th century.

Erigena, John Scotus [air-ij'-in-uh, skoh'-tuhs]
John Scotus Erigena, *c.*810–877, was an Irish scholastic philosopher and theologian (see SCHOLASTICISM). He spent most of his life in Paris where he directed the court school of Charles II. His thought was based on NEOPLATONISM, which stemmed mainly from his translation of the complete works of DIONYSIUS THE PSEUDO-AREOPAGITE from Greek into Latin. A manuscript of the corpus of these Greek works—four treatises and ten letters—was sent (827) to Emperor Louis I by Byzantine Emperor Michael II. By 850, Erigena had made a complete and accurate translation that was widely used in the Middle Ages.

Erigena's greatest original work, *Periphyseon,* or *De divisione naturae* (On the Division of Nature), presented a fourfold division of reality: (1) God who creates all things from himself (*ex seipso*), (2) Platonic ideas, which are created and in turn create, (3) creatures, which are created but do not create, and (4) the return of all things to God, or the fulfillment of God in his theophany, which neither creates nor is created.

Erikson, Erik   Erik Homburger Erikson, b. June 15, 1902, is a German-American psychoanalyst who has had a major influence on the behavioral and social sciences. In his classic study, *Childhood and Society* (1950; 2d ed., 1963), Erikson introduced his theories of identity, identity crisis (which term he popularized), and psychosexual development. Erikson holds that people grow through experiencing a series of crises. They must achieve trust, autonomy, initiative, competence, their own identity, generativity (or productivity), integrity, and acceptance.

Erikson's main contribution has been to bridge the gap between the theories of PSYCHOANALYSIS on the problems of human development, which emphasize private emotions, and the broader social influences that bear upon the individual.

Erikson was among the first psychoanalysts to study the way a healthy person functions. In later years he turned his attention to history, writing some of the groundbreaking works of PSYCHOHISTORY. In *Young Man Luther* (1958) he analyzes Martin Luther's coming to terms with his own identity crisis. In *Gandhi's Truth* (1970), Erikson discusses Mahatma Gandhi's personal development.

Eriksson, Leif   see LEIF ERIKSSON

Eris [ee'-ris]   In Greek mythology, Eris was the goddess of discord and sister of ARES, god of war. She initiated the series of events that led to the Trojan War by tossing an apple marked "for the fairest" among the gods.

Eritrea [air-it'-ree-uh]   Eritrea, a historic province in northern Ethiopia, is an arid region consisting of a high plateau and a coastal plain. The climate is extremely hot and dry along the coast and somewhat cooler and more humid on the inland plateau, where wheat, coffee, and cotton are grown. Salt and copper are the major mineral resources. Erosion is a serious problem.

The inhabitants are mostly Semitic, Tigrinya-speaking peoples, but Afars are also a large part of the population of 3,127,492 (1989 est.). About 50% are Muslim, and the rest are Ethiopian Orthodox Christian. ASMARA is the capital.

Eritrea has been successively overrun by Portuguese, Turks, Ethiopians, Egyptians, and Italians, but only the latter gained a long-lasting control (1890–1941). Eritrea was federated with Ethiopia in 1952 and ten years later was forcibly annexed. After that time a secessionist war raged; war and drought drove many Eritreans into Sudan. During years of military stalemate, the rebels built a network of underground houses, schools, and hospitals. The government declared much of Eritrea an autonomous region in 1987. Despite a string of rebel victories, subsequent peace negotiations made little progress.

Erlander, Tage [air'-lahn-dur, tah'-geh]   Tage Fritiof Erlander, b. June 13, 1901, d. June 21, 1985, was prime minister of Sweden for 24 years (1946–69). He was elected to the lower house of Parliament in 1933 and served as minister of social affairs (1938), minister without portfolio (1944–45), and minister of education (1945–46).

In October 1946, Erlander was chosen leader of the Social Democratic party and prime minister. During his premiership, Sweden's welfare state was consolidated. Medical and retirement benefits were greatly increased; compulsory education was extended to nine years; and the universities were expanded. The country enjoyed a growing economy and full employment, although the welfare state imposed a heavy burden of taxation. Erlander retired as prime minister in 1969 but remained in Parliament until 1973. He was succeeded by his protégé Olof PALME.

ermine [ur'-min]   The ermine, *Mustela erminea*, is a short-tailed WEASEL, or stoat, whose white winter fur was

The ermine, whose range is the subarctic regions of the Old and New Worlds, is a type of weasel. Its winter coat, still valuable fur, has been prized for centuries.

used as a badge of royalty in Europe. *M. erminea* is found in North America, Europe, and Asia. In warmer areas it may retain its brownish summer coat throughout the year or become only partly white in winter. *Ermine* refers to the white winter fur of several other species of weasel and to the white winter phase of the weasels themselves.

Ernst, Max The German painter-poet Max Ernst, b. Apr. 2, 1891, d. Apr. 1, 1976, was a member of the DADA movement and a founder of SURREALISM. He studied philosophy at the University of Bonn (1909–11) and in 1913 visited Paris, where he first met his lifelong friend Jean ARP and other avant-garde artists of the time. A self-taught artist, he formed a Dada group in Cologne, Germany, with Arp and Johannes Baargeld in 1919. Like his fellow Dadaist Kurt Schwitters, he evolved a technique based on assemblage, or COLLAGE. He pioneered a method akin to brass rubbing called *frottage,* in which a sheet of paper is placed on the surface of an object and then penciled over until the texture of the surface is transferred.

In 1922, Ernst moved to Paris, where he collaborated with the French surrealists Louis Aragon, André Breton, Paul Éluard, and Philippe Soupault on the review *Littérature.* He showed at the first surrealist painting exhibition in Paris in 1925. His vivid imagination was constantly

In his Elephant of the Celebes *(1921), Max Ernst uses distorted figures to express the subtle threat of the illogical. A pivotal figure in the transition of Dadaism to surrealism, Ernst is known for his works of absurd reality. (Tate Gallery, London.)*

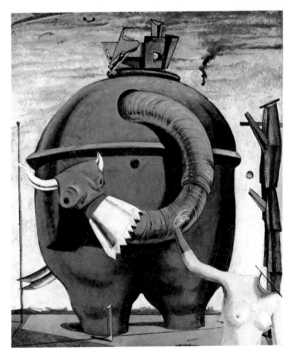

provoked by absurdities, and his work is full of disturbing images—often of fantastic birds and animals set in bizarre landscapes—that reflect his fascination with the art of the insane. While in Paris he painted *L'Éléphant celebes* (1921; Tate Gallery, London) and created collages composed entirely of ready-made printed fragments. His two important collage books, *La Femme 100 têtes* (The Woman with 100 Heads; 1929), with an introduction by Breton, and the equally ambiguous *Une Semaine de bonté* (A Week of Goodness; 1933) are full of irrational, often erotic, imagery of an intensely private nature.

After being interned in southern France (1939–40), Ernst spent World War II in the United States, where he completed *Europe after the Rain* (1940–42; Wadsworth Atheneum, Hartford, Conn.). In New York he worked with Breton and Marcel Duchamp on the magazine *V V V,* which published the work of European exiles from Nazi Germany. In 1948 he wrote *Beyond Painting.* He returned to Paris in 1949 with his fourth wife, the painter Dorothea Tanning. Important retrospective exhibitions have since established him as one of the great masters of the 20th century.

Eros (astronomy) [air'-ohs] Eros is a minor planet, or ASTEROID, discovered in August 1898 by Carl Gustav Witt. It was the first minor planet found to travel almost entirely within the orbit of Mars; at its closest approach it is less than 2.3×10^7 km (14 million mi) from the Earth.

Eros (mythology) In Greek mythology and philosophy, Eros played many roles. In the *Theogony* of Hesiod (*c.*750 BC), Eros impregnated GAEA (mother earth), and their offspring were URANUS (heaven), the sea, and mountains. *The Birds* of Aristophanes contains another theogony, in which CHAOS and darkness first existed. Then night laid an egg in darkness, and Eros was hatched. Finally, Eros fertilized Chaos, who gave birth to ocean, heaven, earth, and all the gods. Among some early Greek philosophers, Eros was love, the force responsible for all creation—if present—and for all destruction—if absent.

As a young, playful god, he was often referred to as a son of APHRODITE and was frequently depicted as causing love by shooting a gold-tipped arrow. Many of his antics are related in the *Aeneid* of Vergil and in the *Metamorphoses* of Ovid. In art, he is usually depicted with wings, carrying a bow and wearing a quiver of arrows. In Roman mythology he is known as Cupid or Amor.

erosion and sedimentation Erosion and sedimentation, in geology, are complementary processes that wear away rock materials, removing them from one area of the Earth's surface and depositing them in another. Before being deposited, the eroded material is usually transported for some time and distance, often by the same agent. Human practices have caused massive SOIL erosion over historical time.

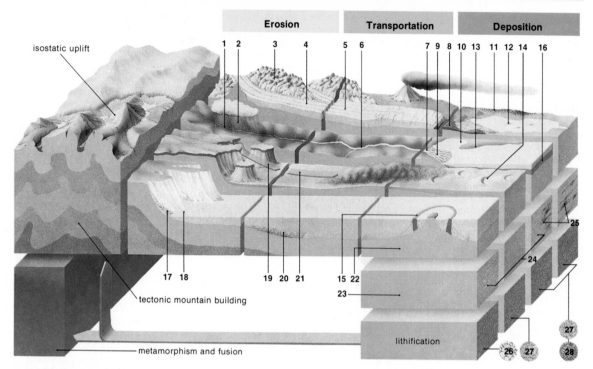

Land erosion involves rivers (1), rain (2), frost (3), glaciers (4), gravity (17), waves (18), and wind (19). Eroded debris may be transported by glaciers (5), rivers (6), turbulent sea currents (20), and winds (21). Deposits include river-carried sand (7), glacial tills (8), delta mud (9), lagoon-evaporated salts (10), wind-borne volcanic material (11), lacustrine mud flats (12), shoreline spits and bars (13), desert sands (14), coral reefs (15), shallow water deposits (16), deep-sea sedimentation, or ooze (22), organic material (23), calcium carbonate from seashells (24), and carbon from coal (25). New minerals form from fragmented materials by recrystallization (26) or by lithification involving cementation (27) and compaction (28). Lithified material may be fused, metamorphosed, or uplifted into mountains by tectonic movements or by isostatic effects.

Modes of Erosion

Subaerial erosion includes all erosion that occurs on land exposed to the ATMOSPHERE. Exposed rock materials are subject to alteration by chemical or mechanical processes (WEATHERING) and then transported, principally by gravity, running water, ice (mainly in glaciers), wind, and near-shore ocean WAVES.

Gravity erosion is often called mass wasting. It occurs where land-surface irregularities such as hillslopes allow gravity to transport weathered rock debris downhill. Running-water, or fluvial, erosion includes erosion performed by the solvent action of water, by the force of moving water, and by the abrasive effects of rock particles in moving water. In humid, vegetated lands, the solvent action occurs beneath the mat of vegetal cover and along watercourses that develop to drain surplus water. The force of running water in humid lands is greatest along stream channels where flow is rapid and perennial. In deserts, where vegetation is sparse, fluvial erosion is virtually unrestricted. Water is rapidly lost by evaporation and infiltration, but there is an almost limitless supply of rock debris. Running-water erosion in deserts mainly occurs, however, during and shortly after violent local THUNDERSTORMS. Water in sheetwash and flash floods quickly picks

up large amounts of solid sediment. Later, runoff volume losses may convert stream runoff into MUDFLOWS, which eventually solidify and cease to move.

Glacial meltwater erodes rock debris and carries it away from the margins of moving ice masses, or glaciers. Ice erosion, or glaciation (see GLACIERS AND GLACIATION), is mainly accomplished by the movement of glaciers, which carve U-shaped valleys and CIRQUES. Glacial erosion by continental ice sheets tends to be more broadly expressed on the land. During the Pleistocene Epoch (see ICE AGES) it produced plains of glacial scour, dotted in many places by lakes, DRUMLINS, and MORAINES. The Great Lakes of North America seem to be products of deep glacial scour of relatively soft rocks beneath continental ice sheets.

Erosion by wind action occurs mostly on beaches and in deserts, where there is no continuous groundcover of vegetation. Except for rare high-velocity tornadic winds, air currents can readily move only rock particles less than 2 mm in diameter. Most sand in desert SAND DUNES and on beaches is smaller than this, as are the finer silt and clay that blow out of deserts during dust storms (see SANDSTORM AND DUST STORM). Most desert sand originates in dry watercourses, although some is freed each time fine-grained fractions of soils blow away following climatic changes from humid to arid. Wind can pick up rock particles by the process known as deflation and may thereby create depressions on the land surface. Where winds are strong, particles bounced and rolled along the surface may abrade and erode rock surfaces as well as polish them. On the dry surfaces of planets such as Mars, and in a few places on Earth, extremely strong winds have carved entire landscapes of elongate, streamlined hills and depressions.

Wave erosion, which occurs along BEACHES AND COASTS, is caused by the impact of breaking waves and the abrasion of wave-transported sediment. It is responsible for shaping the bedrock in headlands along ocean shores to form sea cliffs.

Subaqueous erosion results from the action of water currents on the bottoms of bodies of standing water. It can occur where strong currents develop because of lunar TIDES or differences in water density. In the deep oceans, strong currents may develop in narrow constrictions between land areas or where masses of sediment slump from elevated plateaus or continental margins and move into the abyssal depths. The latter movements, called turbidity currents (see DENSITY CURRENT), may have been responsible for the erosion of some of the deep notches in continental margins called SUBMARINE CANYONS.

Processes of Sedimentation

Sedimentation, the process of sediment accumulation, occurs when a transporting agent is forced to deposit its load of sediment. Deposition may occur for physical reasons, as when a sediment mass moving downhill by gravity reaches the base of the slope, when a current of air or water slows down, or when the ice of a glacier melts; it may occur for chemical reasons, as when materials dissolved in water are precipitated; or it may occur for biological or biochemical reasons, as when organisms act to entrap or induce sediment accumulation.

Gravity deposition of sediment almost always occurs at the bases of hills or cliffs where slopes are too low to permit further downward movement. Deposits include soil and rock mixed by downslope creep (colluvium), fragmental rock (talus), and chaotic mixtures of soil, rock debris, and plant material (LANDSLIDE deposits).

Running-water, or fluvial, deposition of solid sediment occurs when currents slacken. In humid areas this occurs in deep, quiet pools, on the inner margins of stream bends, in slack water areas after overflow, and at stream mouths, where flow enters the standing water of seas, lakes, or swamps. In SWAMPS, some sedimentation occurs by vegetal entrapment.

Chemical and biochemical deposition occur when water containing dissolved solids becomes subject to conditions that reduce solubility. Cooling reduces the solubility of water flowing from HOT SPRINGS, causing deposition of siliceous or calcareous sinter. Agitation at falls and stream rapids may drive off dissolved carbon dioxide gas and cause calcium carbonate to precipitate, forming calcareous sinter, or travertine. Similar processes may occur in bodies of standing water. Evaporation in CAVES may induce deposition of LIMESTONE; in seas it may cause deposition of salt and GYPSUM. Many organisms extract dis-

solved material from water to use in building their skeletons. Fragments of these skeletons may in turn accumulate to form bioclastic SEDIMENTARY ROCK.

Glacial deposition of sediment mainly results from the melting and other forms of wastage of immobilized ice masses. Rock debris accumulated in this way is unsorted (TILL) and not layered, in contrast to sediment deposited by air or water, which tends to be divided into fractions of distinct sizes (sorted) and is also often layered. Sediment deposited by glacier meltwater closely resembles that formed by other streams and rivers.

Wind deposits particles of different sizes in different ways. Sand (1/16–2 mm in diameter) forms sand dunes in deserts and on beaches. Silt (1/256-1/16 mm) blows out of deserts and is trapped by vegetation in humid lands or bodies of water immediately downwind. Clay-sized sediment (less than 1/256 mm) moves readily and settles out of quiet air, often over distant lands and seas.

Standing-water deposition occurs in oceans, lakes, and seas when gravity causes particles of solid sediment to settle out and form layers on the bottom. In oceans, the most common particles include shells of microorganisms that live near the surface (PLANKTON); air-borne dust from deserts, burning meteors, and volcanic eruptions; and fine-grained sediment introduced by rivers and turbidity currents.

——

erotica   *Erotica* is the name given to any artwork—written, pictorial, or performed—that portrays sex explicitly yet possesses enough value to escape condemnation as PORNOGRAPHY. The name derives from Eros, the Greek god of physical desire, whom the Romans called Cupid. But the word *erotica* is a 19th-century invention, devised by booksellers who wished to lend respectability to items that might be seized by the police.

Numerous modern novels, including James Joyce's ULYSSES (1922), D. H. Lawrence's *Lady Chatterly's Lover* (1928), and Vladimir Nabokov's *Lolita* (1955), were deemed pornographic when they first appeared and discovered later to be erotic. In many cases the artist's intention is used as the primary criterion. If the work is intended merely to titillate, it can be dismissed as trash; if the artist means to explore human sexuality, the work deserves to be called erotica. Such matters are vague, however. The public furor over the 1989 and 1990 exhibitions of Robert Mapplethorpe's homoerotic photographs indicates how vexed the issue remains.

It is also chiefly a Western issue. Several non-Western cultures possess ancient traditions of erotic art, which 20th-century Westerners have turned into erotica by publishing pictures of it in expensive books. The highly realistic stone carvings in the state of Orissa, in eastern India, date from at least the first centuries of the Christian era. They are associated with the cult of Krishna, which also generated traditions of erotic painting, poetry, and dance. The KAMASUTRA, a Sanskrit treatise on love written between the 4th and 7th centuries AD, became booksellers' erotica when Sir Richard Burton translated it into English in 1883.

The Chinese and Japanese erotic traditions are also quite old, though chiefly secular rather than sacred. In Japan the Edo period (17th–19th centuries) saw a burgeoning of erotic poetry, novels, and paintings. Chinese erotic fiction and visual art date from the 16th century and earlier. There is also a good deal of erotic imagery in medieval Islamic poetry.

Ancient Greek culture produced much nude statuary, though little of it portrays sexual activity. Vase painting, however, especially from the 5th and 4th centuries BC, offers a wide range of explicit sex acts both homosexual and heterosexual. Until recently, such jars and pots—ordinary household articles for the Greeks—embarrassed modern curators. In ancient Greek eyes, however, they seem to have represented nothing more than scenes of everyday life. Greek comedies, such as Aristophanes' *Lysistrata* (411 BC), employed blunt sexual language chiefly for satiric purposes.

Roman culture must have known a similar volume of explicit art, most of which was destroyed either by time or by Christian authorities after the 4th century AD. The cities of Pompeii and Herculaneum, however, were buried by an eruption of Mount Vesuvius in AD 79 and survived intact to be unearthed by modern excavators, starting in the 18th century. They found wall-paintings in brothels and nuptial chambers, evidently intended to inspire the occupants, along with much phallic art, including earrings and amulets molded in phallic shape. Their purpose seems to have been to ensure fertility. For the Romans, like the Greeks, nudity in itself was not in itself erotic.

Roman civilization also produced a certain amount of erotic literature that survived Christian censorship. The *Songs* of Catullus and the poems in Ovid's *Art of Love* (both 1st century BC) are often explicitly sexual. In Petronius's *Satyricon* and the epigrams of Martial (both 1st century AD), and in the satires of Juvenal (1st–2nd century), the sexual excesses of Roman society are portrayed with great explicitness.

Christianity, with its mistrust of the body, produced no erotica and did what it could to destroy surviving ancient examples. At the very end of the Middle Ages, in the poems of the troubadours (12th–13th centuries), secular love returned to literature, but such works are only incidentally erotic. The rediscovery of ancient learning in the Renaissance led to the widespread imitation of classical models; many paintings of nudes by Titian and Rubens, along with sculptures by Bernini and many others, possess obvious erotic qualities.

Until the 20th century, high artistic intentions continued to mask the presence of erotic elements in pictorial and plastic art, while written works that treated sex explicitly were relegated to the closed shelf or the pornographic underground. In the 20th century, however, all such distinctions broke down, and a burgeoning industry of erotica developed in all art forms. Anaïs Nin, Henry Miller, and Pauline Réage (*The Story of O*, 1954; Eng. trans., 1970) wrote intensely erotic fiction. Pablo Picasso drew and painted erotic nudes, while Georgia O'Keeffe gave erotic overtones to paintings of lilies and steers' skulls. Director Bernardo Bertolucci verged on the pornographic in his film *Last Tango in Paris* (1972). Martha Graham made a decades-long career of erotically tinged choreography; and even in music, Maurice Ravel's *Bolero* became an erotic hit thanks to its use in Blake Edwards's 1979 film *"10"*.

To these must be added a vast array of sex manuals, headed by *The Joy of Sex* (1972), with its *Gay* and *Lesbian* adjuncts and its sequel, *More Joy*—along with mass-circulation magazines such as *Playboy, Penthouse*, and *Honcho*. Cable TV has brought erotica to that medium, while fear of AIDS has meant a boom in erotic conversation on telephones and computer networks.

---

error   In science and mathematics, the term *error* refers to a deviation from a true value. Thus, if a quantity p whose true value is unknown is approximated by a computed value X, the error of value X—its deviation from p, if any—is the difference $X - p$. The error is a measure of the goodness of the approximation. Many quantities in engineering and science have mathematical expressions whose numerical value cannot be exactly determined. For example, p may be the solution of a complicated set of equations that cannot be solved algebraically. Methods for approximating p by simpler expressions are central to applied mathematics. Any method of approximation must be accompanied by an estimate (usually an upper bound) on the error made. In a broader sense, the error $X - p$ may arise because X is a measurement of p made with imperfect instruments (MEASUREMENT error), or because X is a statistical estimate of p based on a sample from a larger population (SAMPLING error), or because only a limited number of significant digits were used in numerical calculation of p (round-off error). Mathematicians usually use error in the first sense given above. (See NUMERICAL ANALYSIS.)

Ershad, Hussain Muhammad   Lt. Gen. Hussain Muhammad Ershad, b. Feb. 1, 1930, Bangladesh's army chief of staff since 1978, took control of the country in a bloodless coup in 1982. He charged that the civilian government had failed to restore order after the 1981 assassination of President Ziaur Rahman. In 1983, Ershad assumed the presidency. He campaigned against corruption, stabilized the economy, and encouraged local participation in development programs. In 1985 a referendum approved his policies. In October 1986, Ershad won a presidential election boycotted by the opposition. Martial law was suspended the following month, but Ershad retained tight control. In December 1990, amid mounting opposition, he suddenly resigned. He was subsequently arrested.

Erskine, Thomas, 1st Baron Erskine   Thomas Erskine, b. Jan. 10, 1750, d. Nov. 17, 1823, was a British lawyer who won fame as an eloquent champion of personal liberties. He was first elected to Parliament in 1783 and served briefly (1806–07) as lord chancellor but is remembered primarily as a trial lawyer. In 1781, Erskine defended Lord George Gordon, who was charged with treason for instigating the Gordon Riots in London. By winning Gordon's acquittal, Erskine helped destroy the doctrine of implied treason. In 1792, Erskine unsuccessfully defended Thomas Paine against a sedition charge arising out of the publication of *The Rights of Man*. His defense of other radicals during the 1790s restricted the definitions of sedition and libel and thus limited the effects of the repressive policies pursued by the British government in reaction to the French Revolution.

Ervin, Sam, Jr.

Samuel James Ervin, Jr., b. Morganton, N.C., Sept. 27, 1896, d. Apr. 23, 1985, won national recognition in 1973 as chairman of the Senate Select Committee on Presidential Campaign Activities. He presided with wit as the committee heard testimony by White House and federal government officials relating to the WATERGATE scandal that led to the resignation of President Richard M. Nixon on Aug. 9, 1974. Ervin was a country lawyer who held local and state offices and was a judge on the North Carolina Supreme Court (1948–54) before serving in the U.S. Senate (1954–74) as a Democrat.

Erving, Julius

Julius Winfield Erving, b. Hempstead, N.Y., Feb. 22, 1950, was an American basketball star whose acrobatic moves on the court won him many fans and the nickname "Dr. J." As a 6-ft 7-in (2-m 1-cm) forward, Erving averaged more than 25 points and 20 rebounds per game as a University of Massachusetts sophomore before joining the Virginia Squires of the now-defunct American Basketball Association (ABA). In his 5-season ABA career, first with the Squires and then with the New York Nets (whom he led to 3 ABA titles), Erving averaged 28.7 points per game and was the league's Most Valuable Player 3 times. In his career (1976–87) with the National Basketball Association's Philadelphia 76ers, he led them to the NBA finals 4 times; they won the championship in 1983. Erving was voted the NBA's MVP award in 1981—the first non-center since 1964 to gain that honor. He was an All-NBA 1st-team selection 5 times, averaging 22 points, 6.7 rebounds, 3.9 assists, and 1.8 steals per game.

erythema

[air-uh-thee'-muh] Erythema is skin redness that is symptomatic of such disorders as ALLERGY, HISTOPLASMOSIS, and RHEUMATIC FEVER; sarcoidosis, coccidioidomycosis, rubella (German measles), Mediterranean fever, and ulcerative colitis; as well as a number of more familiar conditions including sunburn, chemical poisoning, sensitivity to certain oral contraceptives, and emotional excitement. Such malignancies as LEUKEMIA and lymphoma may also be accompanied by erythema.

Erythema is due to increased amounts of blood in the deeper layers of the skin as a result of the dilation of capillaries. Reddening may be restricted to a small area of the body or may be general over the body surface. The reddened areas turn white when pressed by a finger. In allergy or sunburn erythema disappears within a few days or progresses into some other type of symptom. In such conditions as Mediterranean fever, coccidioidomycosis, histoplasmosis, ulcerative colitis, and sensitivity to oral contraceptives, skin reddening is accompanied by a nodule that is painful to the touch.

See also: SKIN DISEASES.

erythromycin   SEE ANTIBIOTICS

Esarhaddon, King of Assyria

[ee-sahr-had'-uhn] Esarhaddon, king of Assyria (680–669 BC), rose to power after the murder of his father, SENNACHERIB. He seems to have been a good general and administrator. After ensuring the allegiance of Babylonia, conquering Media, and strengthening the frontiers of his empire, Esarhaddon attacked Egypt in 675. Four years later he captured Memphis and established Assyrian rule in Egypt.

Esau

[ee'-saw] Esau, also called EDOM, was the first son of the biblical patriarch ISAAC and the supposed ancestor of the Edomites. With their mother's help, his younger twin brother JACOB deceitfully usurped both the elder's birthright and their father Isaac's blessing. These stories in Genesis 25 and 27 illustrate the relationship of the Israelites (Jacobites) to the neighboring Edomites. The story of the brothers thus reflects the larger and later political hostilities.

escalator

A 20th-century invention whose purpose is to move large numbers of people between the levels of a multistory building, the escalator is an endless belt of pivoted moving steps. The steps are carried by two parallel sets of chains, which are propelled by electric-motor–driven sprockets at the top of their rise and are returned by idler sprockets at the lower end. Balustrades define the escalator width. A continuous belt traveling on each balustrade provides a handhold for passenger support and balance. The movement of these belts is synchronized with that of the stairs. The steps are pivoted and machined to form a solid bank of treads and risers, without cracks in which heels or fingers could be caught. At the top and bottom the steps disappear into and emerge from heavy cast-metal "combs," which also protect riders from injury. Safety equipment includes brakes that are automatically applied when the driving motor stops for any reason, a governor that cuts off the motor in case of excessive or too low speed, and readily accessible emergency-stop buttons.

Escalators are manufactured in two standard widths, 81 cm (32 in), rated to carry up to 5,000 persons an hour, and 122 cm (48 in), rated at 8,000 riders an hour. The standard angle of rise or fall is 30° from the horizontal.

The escalator's simple mechanism provides continuous service at comparatively low operating and installation costs. The principal drawbacks of escalators are their slow speed and their large floor-space requirement, due to the necessarily shallow angle of rise.

escallonia [es-kuh-lohn'-ee-uh]   Escallonia comprise about 39 species of ornamental, mostly evergreen shrubs and small trees of South American origin in the family Saxifragaceae. Suited to light, well-drained soil near the seashore, escallonia can withstand only mild frost. Leaves are alternate; white, pink, or red flowers are borne in terminal clusters or, occasionally, in the leaf axils.

Evergreen shrubs of the genus Escallonia *are native to South America, primarily the Andes. They are widely cultivated in yards and parks, where they grow quickly and bloom frequently.*

escape velocity   Escape velocity is the minimum speed that a projectile or spacecraft must attain in order to escape the gravitational field of a celestial body such as a planet.

The concept is also important in determining whether a planet can retain an atmosphere. The value of the escape velocity depends on the mass of the planet and varies with the distance from the planet. It is calculated by the equation

$$V_{esc} = \left[2 \frac{GM}{(R+h)} \right]^{1/2}$$

where G is the gravitational constant, M the mass, R the radius of the planet, and h the altitude above the Earth's surface from which escape is attempted. The exponent denotes the square root of the entire quantity. Ignoring atmospheric drag effects, this value is greatest at the planet's surface.

SURFACE ESCAPE VELOCITY

Planet	km/sec	mph
Mercury	4.15	9,278
Venus	10.23	22,883
Earth	11.18	25,008
Moon	2.4	5,400
Mars	5.02	11,229
Jupiter	60.15	134,548
Saturn	36.45	81,529
Uranus	22.02	49,267
Neptune	25.04	56,020
Pluto	1.0	2,237

escarole   see ENDIVE

escarpment   An escarpment, or scarp, is a long, continuous cliff or steep slope that faces in one general direction and that separates two level or gently sloping areas. Scarps are the result of faulting or EROSION. FAULT scarps are produced by movements of the ground along faults activated by EARTHQUAKES. Scarps form by erosion along one side of uniclinal structures, or homoclines, that consist of rock formations to which a regional tilt has been imparted. In desert areas, erosion of such structures produces an asymmetrical, scarp-bordered landform called a cuesta (see LANDFORM EVOLUTION).

eschatology [es-kuh-tahl'-uh-jee]   Eschatology, a term of Greek derivation meaning literally "discourse about last things," typically refers to the Judeo-Christian doctrine of the coming of the kingdom of God and the transformation or transcendence of history. Old Testament messianism looked for a transformation within human history, whereas New Testament apocalypticism looks for a transcendence of history—the total dissolution of the world at the last judgment. The New Testament concept appears to refer to a literal SECOND COMING OF CHRIST that will bring an evil world to judgment before SALVATION. Both of these, however, are different from the cyclical return to a primordial world outside history as is found in the eschatologies of non-Western religions such as Buddhism and Hinduism.

In the 20th century there have been several interpretations of biblical eschatology, including the "consistent eschatology" of Johannes Weiss and Albert SCHWEITZER, the "realized eschatology" of C. H. Dodd and Rudolf OTTO, the "dialectic eschatology" of Karl BARTH and Rudolf BULTMANN, and the "death of God" eschatology of Thomas J. Altizer.

See also: ANTICHRIST; APOCALYPTIC LITERATURE; BIBLE; DANIEL, BOOK OF; HEAVEN; HELL; IMMORTALITY; MESSIAH; MILLENARIANISM; MYTHOLOGY; REVELATION, BOOK OF; THEOLOGY.

Escher, M. C. [esh'-ur]   The Dutch graphic artist Maurits Corneille Escher, b. June 17, 1898, d. Mar. 27, 1972, explored a strange world of optical illusion, visual puns, and distorted perspectives in his work. He dealt with the theme of metamorphosis and change in such prints as *Verbum* (1942) and *Metamorphosis* (1939–40), which portray a gradual transformation of one shape into another. Escher created a visual paradox in the lithograph *Relativity* (1953) by combining three separate perspectives into a unified, coherent whole. His work has become increasingly popular because of its unique combination of humor, logic, and meticulous precision with visual trickery.

Escherichia [esh-uh-rik'-ee-uh]   *Escherichia* is a genus of rod-shaped BACTERIA, in the family Enterobacteriaceae. Named for Theodor Escherich (1857–1911), a

German bacteriologist, the only species, *E. coli,* is found in large numbers as a normal inhabitant of the large intestine of warm-blooded animals. Whenever they leave their usual habitat, these organisms can cause urinary-tract infections, peritonitis, endocarditis, and other diseases. Some strains cause severe gastroenteritis. *E. coli* has been widely used as a model in molecular biology studies.

Escobedo v. Illinois [es-kuh-bee'-doh]   In the case of *Escobedo* v. *Illinois* (1964) the U.S. Supreme Court held that the refusal of the police to allow an accused to consult his lawyer was a violation of his constitutional rights. The case was decided one year after *Gideon* v. *Wainwright,* in which the court had held that the guarantee of the right to counsel of the 6th Amendment applied to the states through the DUE PROCESS clause of the 14TH AMENDMENT.

Danny Escobedo's brother-in-law had been fatally shot, and despite the repeated requests by Escobedo and his retained lawyer that they be permitted to consult, they were not given the opportunity to do so during the course of a prolonged interrogation. Without informing Escobedo of his absolute right to remain silent in the face of an accusation of murder, the police persuaded him to make a statement that became a major part of the evidence used to obtain a conviction.

In a 5-4 opinion written by Justice Arthur J. Goldberg, the Court reversed Escobedo's conviction. It held that once a suspect requests and is denied the opportunity to see a lawyer and has not been warned of his right to remain silent, he has been denied the assistance of counsel guaranteed by the 6th Amendment and made obligatory upon the states through the 14th Amendment. Therefore, no statement elicited by the police during such an interrogation may be used against an accused person at a criminal trial.

See also: MIRANDA V. ARIZONA; SELF-INCRIMINATION.

Escoffier, Auguste [es-kaw-fee-ay' oh-goost']   The French chef Georges Auguste Escoffier, b. Oct. 28, 1846, d. Feb. 12, 1935, modernized and simplified the elaborate cuisine created by the 18th-century master chef Marie Carême. Escoffier trained under a celebrated Parisian chef and served as chef at the Grand Hotel in Monte Carlo. From 1883 until his retirement, Escoffier's association with the hotelier César Ritz brought fame to every hotel they were connected with: the Savoy and the Carlton House in London and the Ritz hotels in Paris and New York City, among others. A generation of fine chefs were trained in Escoffier's kitchens. For establishing French COOKING as the standard for Western cuisines, Escoffier was awarded (1920) the Légion d'Honneur.

Escorial [ays-kohr-ee-ahl']   The Escorial, a vast building complex in New Castile, near Madrid, in central Spain, was the most important architectural monument of the Spanish Renaissance. Begun in 1562, the project was conceived by King Philip II, who wanted a building to serve the multiple purposes of a burial place for his father, Emperor Charles V, a Jeronymite monastery, and a palace. The first architect, Juan Bautista de Toledo, designed the ground plan on a gridiron scheme, recalling the grill on which St. Lawrence, patron of the building, was martyred. After Toledo's death, Juan de HERRERA took up work on the project. Arranged within a quadrangle, the buildings include the church (1582); the monastery, royal palace, and college (1584); and the library (1592). The interior of the Escorial was decorated by many notable Spanish and Italian artists of the 16th and 17th centuries, including Federico Zuccaro (see ZUCCARO family) and EL GRECO.

escrow [es'-kroh]   An escrow is a conditional delivery of money or other possessions to a holder, to be delivered subsequently to a third person upon the occurrence of an agreed-upon condition. Once an item is deposited in escrow, the depositor has no control over it. If the particular condition is not fulfilled within the time specified by the escrow agreement, the item must be returned to the depositor. The most common use of escrow is in real-estate transactions when a seller deposits a deed with an escrow holder to be delivered to a purchaser upon payment of the full purchase price. In its original meaning, the escrow was the deed rather than the money deposited. The term can also refer to money given to a bank to use in payment of taxes.

Esdraelon, Plain of [es-druh-ee'-luhn]   The Plain of Esdraelon in northern Israel and northwestern Jordan is also known as the Valley of Jezreel. The Hebrew name Jezreel became, in Greek, Esdraelon ("God will sow"). Triangular in shape, the plain is 40 km (25 mi) long. Formerly swampy, it was drained in the 1920s and '30s, and its fertile soil now makes it important for agriculture. The plain has been the scene of many battles, especially around MEGIDDO.

Esdras   see PSEUDEPIGRAPHA

Esenin, Sergei Aleksandrovich   see YESENIN, SERGEI ALEKSANDROVICH

Eshkol, Levi [esh'-kohl]   Levi Eshkol, b. Oct. 25, 1895, d. Feb. 26, 1969, was Israel's third prime minister (1963–69). Throughout his life he worked on financial and economic affairs for the Zionist movement and for the Palestine Jewish community. Born in Ukraine, and originally named Shkolnik, he went to Palestine at the age of 19. In 1920 he helped found the kibbutz Dagania Bet. During World War II, Eshkol was secretary of the Mapai (Labor) party, and from 1948 to 1963 he headed the Jewish Agency settlement department. Elected to the Knesset in 1951, he became minister of agriculture and development, then finance minister under David BEN-

Gurion, whom he succeeded as prime minister. Despite disagreements with Ben-Gurion, he retained control through the period of the third Arab-Israeli War (Six-Day War of 1967) and died in office.

___

esker [es'-kur]   An esker is a long, sinuous, low ridge composed of glacial drift, chiefly layered sand and gravel. These materials were deposited by a subglacial meltwater stream that flowed through tunnels in or near the base of a glacier or an ice sheet and, later, on the ground, as the ice retreated. Eskers range in height from 3 to 50 m (10 to 160 ft), in width from 10 to 200 m (30 to 660 ft), and in length up to hundreds of kilometers.

___

Eskimo   The Eskimo are the native inhabitants of the seacoasts of the Arctic and sub-Arctic regions of North America and the northeastern tip of Siberia. Their habitation area extends over four countries: the United States, Canada, the USSR, and Greenland. Of at least 120,000 Eskimo in this region, the greater part live south of the Arctic Circle, with approximately 42,000 on the Aleutian Islands and in Alaska; 25,000 in Canada; 1,500 in Siberia; and 50,000 in Greenland.

The word *Eskimo* is not an Eskimo word. It means "eaters of raw meat" and was used by the Algonquin Indians of eastern Canada for these hardy neighbors who wore animal-skin clothing and were adept hunters. The name became commonly employed by European explorers and now is generally used, even by Eskimo. Their own term for themselves is *Inuit* (the Yupik variant is *Yuit*), which means the "real people."

Their land is mostly tundra—low, flat, treeless plains where the ground remains permanently frozen except for a few inches of the surface. Most Eskimo traditionally have lived primarily as hunters of maritime mammals (seals, walrus, and whales), and the structure and ethos of their culture have been fundamentally oriented to the sea.

One of the most striking aspects of traditional Eskimo culture is its relative homogeneity across more than 8,000 km (5,000 mi). The main patterns of the culture—religious, social, and economic—are much the same. The language is divided into two major dialectical groups, the Inupik speakers (Greenland to western Alaska) and the Yupik speakers (southwestern Alaska and Siberia).

Traditional Way of Life

The ability of the Eskimo to adapt successfully to a cold

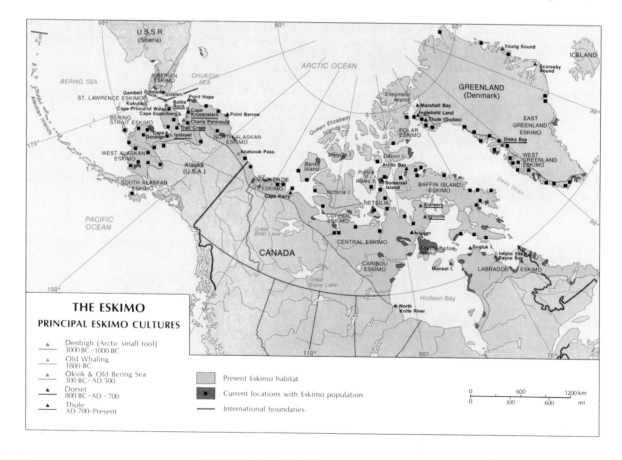

THE ESKIMO

PRINCIPAL ESKIMO CULTURES

- ▲ Denbigh (Arctic small tool)
  3000 BC–1000 BC
- ▲ Old Whaling
  1800 BC
- ▲ Okvik & Old Bering Sea
  300 BC–AD 500
- ▲ Dorset
  800 BC–AD 700
- ▲ Thule
  AD 700–Present

▨ Present Eskimo habitat

■ Current locations with Eskimo population

— International boundaries

An artist's illustration depicts everyday life in a small, 20th-century Eskimo encampment. A successful hunter (foreground), armed with a spear and a modern rifle, has returned to camp with a caribou. A more traditional mode of food-gathering is practiced by another hunter (top left), who waits for a seal to surface at its breathing hole in the ice. Women of the camp are engaged in activities customarily reserved for adults of their gender: child rearing and the preparation of hides. The Eskimo's shelters— in this case, wood-framed canvas tents—are temporary dwellings; they will be dismantled and carried along when the Eskimo break camp and move on in search of game. Blocks of ice are arranged around the shelter's base to cut the piercing Arctic winds, and filleted fish, probably Arctic char, hang from the rafters to dry. The Eskimo have long depended on sleds and dog teams for transportation; but this is slowing changing with the increased use of gas-powered snowmobiles.

and harsh environment depended on a highly inventive material culture (clothing sewn from skins, the toggle harpoon fashioned from ivory or antler and fitted with stone blades, the well-known igloo, or snow house) and particular values and psychological traits. Broad cultural values stressed the importance and excitement of hunting. Courage and hardihood were emphasized in the training of young Eskimo, as was a strong sense of fatalism.

Settlement. Settlement patterns varied according to the location, the time of year, and subsistence opportunities. Permanent villages of stone houses existed in Greenland and in Alaska; along the Siberian shore villages were made up of houses composed of driftwood and earth. In the central areas there were no such settled communities, although a given group might well return to the same fishing or hunting site year after year.

In all Eskimo areas an annual cycle took place in which groups spent the winter together in a larger settlement and then dispersed into smaller, family-sized bands during the summer for seal hunting, for fishing, or for

collecting birds, eggs, and plants. The igloo (from an Eskimo word meaning "home") was constructed of packed snow and used only during the winter, when villages of these structures were built on the firm ocean ice to facilitate seal hunting. Igloos were also used as temporary structures in Greenland and in parts of Canada and Alaska.

Subsistence. During summer, when the sea was free of ice, small groups of families traveled to their camps by open boat. In late spring and throughout the summer they hunted the northward-migrating caribou herds by killing them at river crossings or by driving them into large corrallike structures. Fish swimming upstream for spawning were netted or speared, especially in weirs, net enclosures set in waterways.

The traditional method of hunting seals during winter was most typical of the Eskimo of north central Canada. Since seals are mammals and must breathe air, they scratch a number of holes through the ice as it begins to freeze. The Eskimo hunter stood over a hole, perhaps for hours, with a poised harpoon, awaiting the quivering of a slender piece of baleen, or whalebone, stuck through the thin ice surface that would signal a seal surfacing. The head of the seal harpoon, constructed so as to embed itself and remain fixed in the fat layer of the stricken animal, connected to a float of inflated sealskin by a line about 10 m (33 ft) long that would not only mark the location of the wounded animal but would also hamper its escape. The *utoq* method of hunting seals in the spring was also distinctive of the more northerly Eskimo. Seeking warmth, seals often climb onto the surface of the ice to bask in the sun. A hunter would slowly creep toward a sleeping animal, either pushing a white shield of skin before him or else dressed and acting in such a manner that to the seal he would look like another animal. He would get close enough to fix a harpoon (or, after contact with Europeans, shoot with a rifle) before the seal sensed danger.

Clothing and Transportation. Traditionally, nearly all parts of animals killed by the Eskimo were used. Eskimo clothing was made from skins of birds and animals (seal, caribou, and polar bear). Sewn with sinew thread and bone needles, hooded jackets, pants, and waterproof boots were well adapted to cold and wet climatic conditions. Skins were also processed into tents and boats, and bones were made into weapons.

Two kinds of boats were common. The umiak was a large open boat consisting of a wooden frame covered usually with walrus hide; it was used both to transport people and goods and, especially in northern Alaska, to hunt whales. The other type of craft distinctive of the Eskimo and their cultural relatives, the ALEUTS, was the kayak, a one-man hunting vessel.

Everywhere the Eskimo depended on the DOGSLED as a mode of winter transportation over both land and the frozen sea. The sled was drawn by 2 to 14 huskies and was usually made from wood; where wood was unavailable, dried salmon was sometimes used as structural material. In recent years, snowmobiles have largely replaced the dogsled.

Social Organization. There were no tribes in traditional Eskimo society. Generally a group of people was known by

An Eskimo woman prepares a seal hide. The hides of Arctic mammals, including caribou, seal, and bear, are used by the Eskimo to make clothes, shelters, and watertight boats.

A pair of Eskimo hunters in Greenland haul in a freshly harpooned walrus. These massive marine mammals are hunted as a source of food, fuel, oil, and ivory.

a geographic term to which was added the suffix *miut*, meaning "people of." The basic unit of social organization in most areas was the extended family—a man, his wife and unmarried children, and his married sons and their wives and children. Usually several family groups would join together and exploit the animal resources of a given area. The leader of the group would be the eldest male still capable of hunting.

The traditional kinship system of most Eskimo groups resembled that of American society. They called the same kinds of relatives "cousins" and generally practiced bilateral descent, by which they recognized both the mother's and the father's side of the family equally.

Religion and Art. Eskimo religion was animistic. It imputed spirits, or souls, to most animals and to important features of the landscape. Human beings had several souls, or spiritual substances, one of which was the name. To avoid their hostility, souls of the important subsistence animals—seals, walrus, whales, and polar bears—were propitiated through extensive honorary customs and taboos. Most groups believed in a supreme ruler of the sea animals and in a vague deification of the forces of nature. The central religious figure was the SHAMAN.

Arts and crafts were expressed mainly in etched decorations on ivory harpoon heads, needlecases, and other tools; in carved sculpture in ivory, tooth, or soapstone; in skin sewing; in dancing and the composition of songs; and in storytelling. Elaborate wooden masks were also made by the Alaskan Eskimo. (See INDIANS OF NORTH AMERICA, ART OF THE.)

History

The origin of Eskimo culture is disputed. Some scholars have traced it to Late Paleolithic cultures of Europe; others have suggested a New World origin, such as the region west of Hudson's Bay. In coastal areas of the Bering Sea and southward along the Siberian shore, artifacts have been found that give persuasive evidence of earlier cultures adapted to maritime hunting from which Eskimo culture could have evolved. The so-called Arctic Small Tool tradition, best known from CAPE DENBIGH, Alaska, and dated from around 5000 to 3500 BC, was one such precursor culture, as was the Old Whaling culture, dated at about 1800 BC.

Fully developed Eskimo cultures that focused on seal and walrus hunting included the OKVIK and Old Bering Sea cultures; artifacts found in Siberia and on Saint Lawrence Island are dated at around the beginning of the Christian Era. At about the end of the 1st millennium, Thule culture, in which whaling became a central focus, developed in Alaska and began to spread eastward to Greenland. It was characterized by whale, walrus, and seal hunting, dogsled traction, and permanent stone or dirt houses. It was the prevalent cultural type when the Eskimo were first encountered by Europeans.

The Vikings were the first Europeans to contact the Eskimo. From the 10th to the 15th century Norse settlements existed in southwestern Greenland based on farming, cattle, and sheep raising. They disappeared as a result of the effects of sickness and depredation by the Eskimo. Modern contact began in the 18th century, with missionaries establishing education, government, and trade relations.

The Canadian Eskimo were first contacted by European explorers and whaling ships beginning in the 18th century, while in the west, the Alaskan Eskimo were first encountered by the Russians. They were followed by other European explorers and then, during the 1800s, by commercial whaling ships. Such ships traded rifles, whiskey, and other goods for whalebone, oil, hides, and ivory. The Eskimo became closely involved in a monetary economy, and institutional features of their social life were deeply influenced by contacts with Western culture.

Eskimo Life Today

Wherever they live—Alaska, Canada, Greenland, Siberia—the Eskimo are now much involved in the modern world, but traditional practices and beliefs have not so thoroughly changed that most Eskimo can be termed assimilated or acculturated, especially in matters relating to social organization and child rearing.

Significant changes were first apparent in Greenland. Major shifts in subsistence patterns followed the decline of maritime animals in offshore waters. A fishing industry concentrated the formerly dispersed hunters into larger settlements. Education, medical services, and local self-government began in the 19th century as part of a program of protective governance by Denmark. Extensive intermarriage occurred between Greenland Eskimo and Danes, and in the early 1950s, Greenland became a Danish county, with representatives in the Danish Parliament. Since 1979—though still an integral part of Denmark—Greenland has had home rule and its own legislature. Consequently, there has has been a rise in political

This soapstone bear sculpture is typical of Eskimo art. Traditional sculpture was carved in ivory, stone, wood, or bone and served a religious or utilitarian purpose.

consciousness among the Greenland Eskimo.

The Eskimo living in the USSR have been involved in a planned program of modernization since the early 1930s. They still hunt walrus, seals, and whales, but they do so as members of mechanized hunting work-groups called collectives.

At the beginning of this century, the Alaskan Eskimo were still mostly following a traditional way of life. Until the 1930s fox trapping was a major source of income, and schools and limited medical facilities were provided by the government. Health conditions, however, remained well below those of the rest of the United States. World War II and subsequent developments related to national defense created many opportunities for employment in construction and other jobs. Numerous Eskimo settled permanently in the larger towns of western Alaska. Many live in substandard housing and at marginal economic levels and exhibit many characteristics of social pathology. Statehood (1959) and the passage of the Alaska Native Land Claims Settlement Act (1971) have set in motion major changes in landholding patterns and economic potential for the Eskimo and in part have symbolized the considerable rise in political activity on the part of Alaskan natives. The exploitation of petroleum and natural gas resources, as well as extensive exploration for other minerals throughout Alaska, has had significant effects on the lives of the Alaskan Eskimo.

Although in some isolated areas hunting and trapping are still carried on, most Canadian Eskimo have congregated in towns and settlements in search of wage labor as well as to take advantage of modern facilities. The federal government in 1984 concluded a land-claims agreement with the Eskimo and in 1989 negotiated another land-claims agreement-in-principle that was expected to be finalized in the early 1990s. Ongoing talks also have been concerned with the division of the Northwest Territories in order to give both the Eskimo and the Indians greater control of their respective regions.

Eskimo dog   The Eskimo dog is one of the basically similar group of Arctic sled dogs, which are often given local names. The Eskimo dog as recognized by the Canadian Kennel Club is believed to have originated in eastern Siberia. As in all sled dogs, its body is protected by a heavy double coat. The soft, dense undercoat grows up to 6 cm (2.5 in) long; the harsh, shaggy outer coat, up to 15 cm (6 in) long. Colors vary greatly and have not been standardized. Eskimo dogs average about 34 kg (75 lb) in weight and stand about 61 cm (24 in) high at the shoulder. A smaller, white-coated breed, known as the American Eskimo, or spitz, is recognized in the United States by the United Kennel Club. It stands up to 51 cm (20 in) high at the shoulder and weighs about 14 kg (30 lb).

Eskimo language   see INDIAN LANGUAGES, AMERICAN

esophagus   see HUMAN BODY

ESP   see EXTRASENSORY PERCEPTION

espalier [es-pal'-ee-ur]   Espaliering is the art of training plants and trees so that a limited number of branches are oriented in a flat, vertical plane. The espaliering technique exposes a greater proportion of the branch surface to the Sun, stimulating proportionally heavy flowering and more annual fruiting. Apple and pear trees are the most common subjects for espaliering.

Trees to be espaliered are planted along a basic support, such as a wall or a trellis. Pruning and training are done during seasons of rapid shoot growth. The terminal growth of all branches is cut back each spring and summer. During the growing season the side shoots on all branches are cut back to encourage development of fruiting spurs and flower buds.

Esperanto [es-pur-ahn'-toh]   Esperanto is an artificial language designed to serve internationally as an auxiliary means of communication among speakers of different languages. The creation of Ludwik Lazar Zamenhof, a Polish-Jewish ophthalmologist, Esperanto was first presented in 1887 (see LANGUAGES, ARTIFICIAL). An international movement to promote its use has continued to flourish and has members in more than 80 countries.

Esperanto is used internationally by at least one million people, particularly in specialized fields. It is used in personal contacts, on radio broadcasts, and in a number of publications as well as in translations of both modern works and classics. Its popularity has spread from Europe—both East and West—to such countries as Brazil and Japan. It is, however, in China that Esperanto has had its greatest impact. It is taught in universities and used in many translations (often in scientific or technological works). *El Popola Cinio* (From People's China), a monthly magazine in Esperanto, is read worldwide. Radio Beijing's Esperanto program is the most popular program in Esperanto in the world.

Esperanto's vocabulary is drawn primarily from Latin, the Romance languages, English, and German. Spelling is completely regular. A simple and consistent set of endings indicates grammatical functions of words. Thus, every noun ends in *o*, every adjective in *a*, and the infinitive of every verb in *i*. It has a productive system of constructing new words from old, for example: *ami*, to love; *malami*, to hate; *malamemo*, the tendency to hate.

Espinel, Vicente Martínez [ays-peen-el']   Vicente Martínez Espinel, b. December 1550, d. Feb. 4, 1624, was a Spanish writer of his country's Golden Age and the eponym of the octosyllabic ten-line stanza, the *espinela*. Best known in his day for his poetry (*Diversas rimas*, 1591), he is now chiefly remembered for his autobiographical picaresque novel, *La Vida del Escudero Marcos de Obregón* (1618; *The Life of the Squire Marcos de Obregon*, 1816).

espionage   Espionage is the practice of spying to acquire information. It involves gaining access to the desired information, actually acquiring the information, and then conveying it to an intelligence agency for evaluation. Although espionage is only one aspect of INTELLIGENCE OPERATIONS, it is an important source of information for any government attempting to learn the secrets of other nations. Industries also use it to gain the fruits of another firm's research, and political factions use it hoping to preempt and undermine their rivals.

Methods. Espionage is chosen over other means of intelligence collection when physical acquisition of a document or object is required, or when only an on-the-spot observer can procure the information desired. Agents can install wiretaps or "bugs" (concealed microphones), steal, buy, or transcribe documents, steal equipment, or simply observe with their own eyes.

There are several different types of espionage agents. The professional spy popularized in fiction is often an "illegal" who passes himself off as a fictitious person complete with forged identity papers. The "illegal" may work alone or establish a spy ring. Another type of agent is the part-time spy who maintains an open, legal existence (often as a diplomat or businessman) and conducts espionage on the side. A "plant" is an agent who is positioned within the target organization for an extended period of time. The "insider" or "recruit" is a member of the target organization who has shifted loyalties and who produces information on a regular basis. Historically, the "insider" is probably the most productive type of agent. "Insiders" can be recruited by ideological appeals, by offers of money, or by blackmail.

Counterespionage. Counterespionage is the prevention and thwarting of hostile espionage. The best method of crippling an adversary's espionage program is by planting one's own agent (a "mole") into the hostile espionage organization. Another successful practice is to capture hostile spies and turn them into "double agents" who channel false information to their original employers. The

FEDERAL BUREAU OF INVESTIGATION (FBI) is responsible for counterespionage in the United States.

History. Espionage has been practiced throughout history. The Old Testament reports that both Moses and Joshua employed spies. The Chinese philosopher Sun Zu wrote knowingly of spies around 400 BC. Modern espionage had its origins with Sir Francis WALSINGHAM, the spymaster for Queen Elizabeth I of England, whose agents infiltrated the courts of Europe. The spies who appear in early American history, such as Nathan HALE in the American Revolution, as well as Belle BOYD and Elizabeth Van Lew in the Civil War, were generally amateur volunteers.

Espionage had little impact in World War I. During World War II, however, some very impressive feats of espionage took place. Soviet espionage groups such as the *Rote Kapelle* ("Red Orchestra") and the Richard Sorge ring penetrated the German and Japanese high commands, respectively. On the other hand, German attempts to infiltrate England backfired when British counterespionage made double agents out of 40 German spies (the "Double Cross" operation).

The Cold War brought the United States fully into the world of espionage. Although it has proven very difficult to introduce spies into certain closed societies, defectors and "insiders" have, from time to time, conducted valuable espionage on behalf of the Western powers. After its division into eastern and western halves, Germany, where the cultural homogeneity of the two nations facilitated infiltration, became a focal point of cold-war espionage.

The Soviet Union's cold-war espionage program utilized every type of agent against the Western powers—highly professional "illegals," masses of part-time spies doubling as diplomatic personnel, and a seemingly endless supply of "insiders." These "insiders" included ideologically motivated agents, such as Julius and Ethel ROSENBERG (though their case remains controversial), and agents whose sole motive was money, such as those involved in the John A. Walker case in the mid-1980s.

Esposito, Phil [es-puh-zee'-toh]   Hall of Fame member Philip Anthony Esposito, b. Sault Ste. Marie, Ontario, Feb. 20, 1942, is a hockey player who in the 1968–69 National Hockey League (NHL) season became the first player to score more than 100 points when he tallied 126. In 1970–71 he scored a record 76 goals in 78 games, with a total point mark of 152; these records have since been broken, however. Esposito, who played center for the Chicago Black Hawks, Boston Bruins, and New York Rangers in his 18-year career, was the NHL's Most Valuable Player twice (1969, 1974) and scoring leader five times (1969, 1971–74). He retired during the 1980–81 season, at that time the second most prolific scorer in NHL history (1,590 points).

essay   The essay, the most flexible of all literary forms, offers writers maximum freedom with respect to choice of subject, length of composition, and style of expression.

An essay can be formal or informal, personal or impersonal, highly organized or rambling, playful or didactic, serious or satirical.

Michel de MONTAIGNE, whose highly individualistic reflections on the vicissitudes of life and the world around him were embodied in two volumes called *Essais* (Attempts, 1580), not only gave rise to the term but is also generally considered the originator of the form. Using the discursive, intimate approach, he established the model for the informal, familiar essay that proved as congenial to James Thurber and E. B. White in the mid-20th century as it did to Thomas De Quincey in the 19th. Sir Francis Bacon, keeping the reader at some distance in the brief, polished, and informed discussions that constitute his *Essays* (1597, 1612, 1625), set the tone for the other major type, the formal essay.

The variety of forms that the essay can assume and something of its commodiousness are suggested by a few disparate examples: John Dryden's *Essay of Dramatic Poesy* (1668), which established the essay as a vehicle for literary criticism; Alexander Pope's *Essay on Man* (1734), which is presented in heroic couplets rather than prose; Jonathan Swift's *A Modest Proposal* (1729), a brutal satire on contemporary economic theory; many meditative passages in Thomas Mann's novel *The Magic Mountain* (1924) on art, love, and history, which are, in fact, essays; and, of course, newspaper editorials.

In 18th-century England, Joseph ADDISON and Sir Richard Steele, with their diverting pieces in *The Tatler* and *The Spectator*, perfected the kind of informal essay popularized by Montaigne. Such periodicals as *The Rambler* and *The Idler* also served as forums for the pessimistic, elegant, essentially moral arguments of the formidable Samuel Johnson.

In the 19th century a profusion of talents on both sides of the Atlantic excelled at the genre: Charles LAMB, whose humorous anecdotal treatment of everyday life in the whimsical *Essays of Elia* (1823 and 1833) perhaps finds an American counterpart in the travel sketches in Mark Twain's *The Innocents Abroad* (1869); William HAZLITT, whose portraits of eminent contemporaries in *The Spirit of the Age* (1825) are matched by Ralph Waldo EMERSON's *Representative Men* (1850); and Thomas Babington Macaulay, whose *Critical and Historical Essays* (1843) exalts human liberty, as does Henry David Thoreau in WALDEN (1854).

Literary criticism has contributed more than its share of outstanding examples of the essay, from George Bernard Shaw's *Dramatic Opinions and Essays* (1907) to T. S. Eliot's *Essays Ancient and Modern* (1936) and Ezra Pound's *Literary Essays* (1954). In France, Paul Valéry and Jean Paul Sartre continued the distinguished tradition of the literary essay set in the 19th century by Charles Augustin Sainte-Beuve.

Essen [es'-en]   Essen, a major industrial city in the RUHR district of North Rhine–Westphalia, Germany, lies between the Ruhr River and the Rhine-Herne Canal, about 80 km (50 mi) north of Bonn. It has a population of 615,400 (1987 est.). The city is surrounded by rich iron deposits and coalfields, which supply raw materials for its huge industries. Principal among these are the manufacture of iron and steel, chemicals, machinery, textiles, glass, furniture, and electricity.

The city developed around a Benedictine convent established in 852, and the convent's abbesses governed the town as an imperial city until 1802. Authority was ceded to Prussia in 1815, at about the time the KRUPP family began to build its industrial empire in Essen. Today the family home, Villa Hügel, is used by the city for concerts, conventions, and exhibitions. The Krupp complex became especially noted for its production of heavy armaments; because of its presence, Essen was heavily bombed during World War II. Most of the city's historic buildings were destroyed, but the restored cathedral (the former convent church) is still standing.

Essenes [es'-eenz]

The Essenes were members of an ascetic Jewish sect of the 1st century BC and the 1st century AD. Most of them lived on the western shore of the Dead Sea. They are identified by many scholars with the QUMRAN community that wrote the DEAD SEA SCROLLS. They numbered about 4,000 members. Admission required two to three years of preparation, and new candidates took an oath of piety, justice, and truthfulness.

According to Philo of Alexandria and other writers of the 1st century AD, the Essenes shared their possessions, lived by agriculture and handicrafts, rejected slavery, and believed in the immortality of the soul. Their meals were solemn community affairs. The main group of Essenes opposed marriage. They had regular prayer and study sessions, especially on the Sabbath. Transgressors were excluded from the sect.

The similarity between a number of Essene and Christian concepts and practices (kingdom of God, baptism, sacred meals, the position of a central teacher, titles of officeholders, and community organization) has led some people to assume that there was a close kinship between the groups. It is possible that after the dissolution of the Essene community some members followed John the Baptist or joined one of the early Christian communities, but any other direct connection seems unlikely.

essential oils

Essential oils are aromatic substances produced by certain plants. Most of these oils, which are extracted, concentrated, and used as perfume scents or food flavorings, have been known since ancient times. They are called essential because it was thought that each oil represented the essence of the plant from which it was obtained. Chemically complex, they are a mixture of organic compounds, primarily terpenes.

There are some 200 commercially produced essential oils, all obtained from the oil-bearing leaves, flowers, bark, seeds, or wood of aromatic plants. Steam distillation is the most common method of extraction: hot steam is passed over the plant tissues, the volatile compounds evaporate, and they are then condensed. Citrus oils are expressed from flavor sacs in the fruit rind. Some flower petals, whose oils are destroyed by steam processing, are treated by enfleurage: the blossoms are placed on a layer of cold fat, which absorbs the oil; fresh blossoms are added until the fat is totally oil saturated; and the resulting substance, called a pomade, is washed with alcohol to remove the oil.

With the exception of pine oil and oil of turpentine, which are manufactured in great volume, essential oils are produced in relatively small quantities. (It requires, for instance, some 1,600–1,800 kg/3,500–4,000 lb of rose petals to distill 28 g/1 oz of attar of rose.) The high cost of many of these oils has prompted a search for synthetic substitutes. A few of the important constituents of essential oils have been synthesized and are used as artificial flavorings. These, however, lack many of the subtle odors present in the natural oils. The complex mixtures of constituents have so far proved impossible to duplicate.

See also: FATS AND OILS; FLAVORS AND FRAGRANCES; HERBS AND SPICES.

Essex

Essex, a county in southeastern England just north of London, is bordered by the North Sea on the east and the River Thames on the south. The county has a population of 1,529,500 (1988 est.) and covers 3,672 km^2 (1,418 mi^2). The low eastern coastline gives way to fertile, undulating farmland, where wheat, barley, and vegetables are grown for London markets. Heavy industry is found in the south, in the greater London area, and in COLCHESTER, Chelmsford (the county town), and Basildon. Oystering and tourism are important along the coast. Many southern towns are suburban communities.

Several Roman settlements were located in Essex, which, in the early 6th century, became a Saxon kingdom. In the 9th century the Danes took Essex, but in the 10th century it was retaken by the English and became an important earldom.

Essex, Robert Devereux, 2d Earl of

Robert Devereux, 2d earl of Essex, b. Nov. 10?, 1567, d. Feb. 25, 1601, was a favorite of Queen ELIZABETH I of En-

Favored courtier of the English queen Elizabeth I, Robert Devereux, 2d earl of Essex, was a military adventurer who engaged in several controversial expeditions.

gland. Following the death (1576) of his father, the 1st earl, Robert was brought up by his stepfather, Robert Dudley, earl of LEICESTER, who introduced him at court. Handsome and dashing, Essex attracted the Queen's attention, and after Leicester's death in 1588 he became her favorite courtier despite the great difference in their ages. Essex made a reputation as a military leader; he was the hero of an expedition that captured Cádiz in 1596. In 1599 he was placed in charge of an English campaign to suppress the rebellion of the earl of TYRONE in Ireland, but he returned to England without permission and was imprisoned. In 1601 he attempted to lead a rebellion against the officials of Elizabeth's government. When this failed he was convicted of treason and was beheaded. Essex was a friend of Sir Francis Bacon and a rival of Sir Walter Raleigh and Robert Cecil, 1st earl of Salisbury.

Estaing, Jean Baptiste Charles Henri Hector, Comte d' [des-tan'] The comte d'Estaing, b. Nov. 24, 1729, d. Apr. 28, 1794, was a French admiral who served in India and as governor of the Antilles (1763–66) before commanding the French fleet dispatched to assist the American colonists in the American Revolution. Although he failed to engage English squadrons on the Atlantic seaboard in battle in 1778, he took Grenada (in the Caribbean) for France and was wounded (1779) in an unsuccessful attack on Savannah, Ga. He supported the French Revolution but was guillotined for royalist leanings.

estate An estate is the property to which a person is lawfully entitled. In traditional law, the word referred to property in land; a person's estate consisted of the interest or rights that the person held in land. Courts in the United States have ruled that the word *estate* covers everything a person owns, both real and personal.

In traditional common law, an estate in *fee simple* meant complete ownership of real property. The owner was allowed to sell it or dispose of it in any way he or she chose. An estate in *fee tail* gave possession during the owner's lifetime, though not the power to sell it; when the owner died, the property passed to the owner's descendants. These terms are still used in legal documents.

A common form of estate is the life estate, in which the possessor has an interest only in his or her lifetime. Afterward, it passes to a designated person or reverts to the former owner or to his or her heirs. For example, a person making a will may bequeath property to one person, with the stipulation that upon that person's death, it goes to yet another.

Estates-General see STATES-GENERAL

Este (family) [es'-tay] The Este family ruled Ferrara, Italy, from 1264 to the end of the 16th century, and Modena and Reggio from the late 13th to the late 18th century. Coming to power on the fall of the imperial vicar Ezzelino da Romano in 1256, the Este sought to keep Ferrara free from the domination of Venice and Milan in a series of wars fought in the 14th century. In the next century the Este were made dukes of Modena and Reggio by Holy Roman Emperor Frederick III and of Ferrara by Pope Paul II.

Ercole I (1431–1505) gathered many major painters and poets at Ferrara and established a brilliant court culture. He strengthened his position as a prince by marrying his children into royal houses of Italy and the rest of Europe. In 1598, Pope Clement VIII took direct control of Ferrara, leaving only Modena and Reggio to the Este, who collected a rich library at Modena. They were driven out by Napoléon Bonaparte in 1796, but a branch of the family returned (1815) to govern Modena until it was united with the Kingdom of Sardinia (later Italy) in 1859.

ester Esters are organic compounds formed by the reaction of an alcohol with an acid, acid anhydride, or acid chloride. Polyhydric alcohols (polyols) may also be used. The general formula of a simple ester is RCOOR', where R and R' are any organic groups. Esters are named in a manner comparable to inorganic salts, where the named alcohol replaces the metal atom (ethyl acetate, glyceryl tripalmitate). Esters of lower molecular weight are colorless liquids with a limited solubility in water that decreases as the molecular weight of either the acid or alcohol increases. Melting points and boiling points increase with molecular weight.

Most lower-molecular-weight esters have a pleasant, fruity odor. Higher-molecular-weight esters are odorless and have a waxy appearance and touch; many simpler ones occur in fruits and flowers. Naturally occurring vegetable oils and fats are esters of glycerol. Esters undergo hydrolysis to restore the acid and alcohol. They are used as solvents for paints and lacquers and in drugs (including aspirin), cosmetics, perfumes, artificial food flavors, plasticizers, plastics (alkyd resins), and explosives (poly-nitro esters).

Esterházy (family) [es'tur-hah-zee] The Esterházys were a Hungarian family who played a significant role in Hungarian and Austrian history. While unsubstantiated family traditions take their origin back to Attila the Hun, genealogists trace it only to the 12th century. The founder of the greatness of the family was **Miklós**, b. Apr. 8, 1582, d. Sept. 11, 1645, who—through his loyalty to the Habsburgs—became a baron (1613) and then a count (1626). He was also elected (1625) Hungary's palatine (regent) and was given huge estates, including the fortress of Fraknó (Forchtenstein) in Austria. His son **Pál**, b. Sept. 7, 1635, d. Mar. 26, 1713, continued Miklós's pro-Habsburg policies, and in 1687 he was made an imperial prince. Pal's grandson, **Miklós**, b. Dec. 18, 1714, d. Sept. 28, 1790, is known primarily for his patronage of artists, including Franz Josef Haydn, and for his building of the Versailles-like palace of Eszterháza in Fertöd, Hungary.

Estes, Richard

Estes, Richard [es'-teez]   American painter Richard Estes, b. Kewanee, Ill., May 14, 1932, is one of the leading superrealists or photorealists (see PHOTOREALISM). His studies of streets and automobiles are done with the aid of photographs and concentrate on the interplay of reflections in windows and chrome. Pop art painters employed similar subject matter, but Estes is more interested in surface detail and in the ambiguity that makes his works paintings of photographs as well as paintings of real scenes. Estes studied at the Art Institute of Chicago in the 1950s.

Esther, Book of

Esther, Book of   Esther is a book in the Old Testament of the BIBLE. It recounts the deliverance of the Jews from persecution in the Persian Empire, a deliverance accomplished by the timely actions of two Jewish members of the foreign court: Queen Esther and her cousin and foster father, Mordecai. Popular tales from Persian times about a recalcitrant native queen, a Jewess who became queen of a foreign nation, and deadly rivalry among courtiers were worked into the account. The book was intended to strengthen Jews under persecution during the Maccabean wars and, in particular, to authorize celebration in Palestine of the Feast of PURIM, otherwise unknown in the Old Testament. Jews in the Diaspora may earlier have observed this festival of deliverance from foreign persecutors.

The anti-Semitic temper, the murder of many Gentiles, and the apparently forced conversion of others described in the book indicate that it was written during the reign of John Hyrcanus, the Hasmonean Jewish king (c.135–105 BC; see MACCABEES). The absence of the name of God, which led to religiously motivated additions of 107 verses to the Greek version of the book (forming a separate book in the APOCRYPHA), may be the result of wisdom influence or of a secularizing trend in the Hasmonean circles that introduced the Feast of Purim to Palestine.

estivation

estivation   see HIBERNATION

Estonia

Estonia   Located on the northeastern shore of the Baltic Sea, Estonia borders on the Gulf of Finland in the north, the Russian Federated Soviet Socialist Republic in the east, Latvia in the south, and the Baltic Sea in the west. It has an area of 45,215 km² (17,413 m²), and its population is 1,537,000 (1989). The capital city is TALLINN, with a population of 482,000 (1989). From 1940 to 1990, Estonia was a Soviet Socialist Republic, one of the 15 constituent republics of the USSR. Its current political status is ambiguous and transitional. In March 1990, its freely elected parliament declared Soviet rule illegal and proclaimed independence to be achieved by a gradual process. In May 1990 it changed its name to the Republic of Estonia, and in March 1991 a large majority of the Estonian people voted for independence.

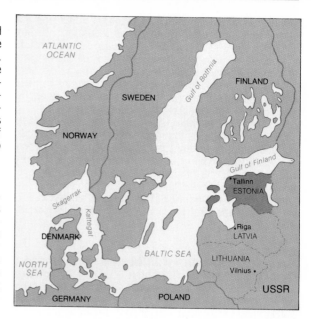

Land and People.   Estonia's landscape is of glacial origin, dotted with lakes and rivers. Forests constitute 35% of its territory. Its Baltic coastline is 1,240 km (744 m) long and contains many inlets. About 10% of Estonia's territory consists of islands in the Baltic Sea. The Gulf of Finland provides a number of ice-free harbors, of which Tallinn is the most important. The highest elevation is 317 m (1,040 ft).

The Estonians, a Finno-Ugric people whose language is related to Finnish, formed 89% of the population at the beginning of Soviet rule. By 1989 the proportion had been reduced to 61.5%. During the same period the proportion of Russians increased tenfold by immigration to 30%. Smaller groups include Ukrainians, Belorussians, Latvians, and Jews. Nearly 90% of the Russians live in cities and towns, as opposed to about half of the Estonians. The largest cities, in addition to Tallinn, are TARTU (1989 pop., 114,000), NARVA (1989 pop., 83,000), and Kohtla-Järve (1989 est. pop., 60,000). Ethnic Estonians are predominantly Lutheran in religion.

Economy.   The main natural resources are oil shale (which provides most of Estonia's energy needs) and phosphates. More than two-thirds of Estonia's gross national product comes from industry, less than one-fifth from agriculture. Industrial products include machinery, textiles, and paper; some of the main agricultural products are meat, dairy products, cereal grains, flax, and potatoes. Estonia possesses a well-developed fishing industry and has oceangoing fishing fleets. It has good networks of hard-surface roads and railways.

History.   The Estonian people have lived on the shores of the Baltic since ancient times. In the 13th century they were conquered by the Germanic Knights of the Sword, who introduced Christianity. The area was dominated by Sweden in the 16th and 17th centuries and was annexed by Russia in 1704. The Protestant Reformation reached Estonia in 1523 through its German merchants and landowners, who remained the ruling class under the Russian tsars. A national awakening in the 19th century led ultimately to independence with the collapse of the Russian Empire in 1918. Two decades of freedom ended when the Soviet Union occupied and annexed Estonia in 1940. During World War II, for 3 years, 1941–44, Estonia was occupied by the Germans.

Soviet rule was harsh. Well over 100,000 of Estonia's population either were deported or perished in labor camps. The country was industrialized and collectivized, and government-sponsored Russian immigration substantially changed the ethnic balance of its population. In the late 1980s the PERESTROIKA policy of Soviet president Mikhail Gorbachev afforded an opportunity for change. Beginning in 1988, the non-Communist People's Front promoted democratic and national goals by organizing the masses and winning electoral majorities. Estonian was restored as the official language, and the Communist monopoly of power was abolished at the end of 1989. Press censorship was abolished, religious freedom allowed, and private farming legalized. In 1990, Estonia began negotiations with Moscow on its proposed separation from the USSR. In March 1991, just two weeks before a USSR-wide plebiscite on maintaining the current union, the Estonian people voted overwhelmingly for independence.

Estonian language   see URAL-ALTAIC LANGUAGES

Estrada Cabrera, Manuel [es-trah'-dah kah-bray'-rah, mahn-wel'] Manuel Estrada Cabrera, b. Nov. 21, 1857, d. Sept. 24, 1924, was dictator of Guatemala from 1898 to 1920. Having held various government offices, he assumed the presidency on the assassination (1898) of President José María Barrios. His corrupt and repressive administration favored the wealthy while ignoring the plight of the poor. Economic conditions were improved by the involvement of foreign investors (notably the American United Fruit Company) in the sugar and banana industries. In 1920 a revolution led by Carlos Herrera overthrew Estrada Cabrera; he died in prison.

Estrada Palma, Tomás [es-trah'-dah pahl'-mah] Tomás Estrada Palma, b. July 9, 1835, d. Nov. 14, 1908, was an activist in the Cuban independence movement and the first president (1902–06) of Cuba. He became a general during the TEN YEARS' WAR and was captured and later exiled by the Spanish. Estrada Palma was originally elected president as a compromise candidate, but his reelection provoked (1906) a revolt by the liberal faction. U.S. forces then intervened at Palma's request; he resigned, and Charles E. Magoon, a Washington-appointed governor, ruled Cuba until 1909.

Estremadura [es-truh-muh-door'-uh] Estremadura, a historic region in central Portugal, lies along the Atlantic coast. Many important cities, including LISBON, SINTRA, and Setúbal, are in the region. Estremadura is a productive agricultural area drained by the TAGUS RIVER; fruits, grains, and olives are grown, and wine is produced. Along the coast, called the Portuguese Riviera, fishing and tourism are important.

Visited by the Phoenicians, Estremadura subsequently became part of the Roman province of Lusitania. Visigoths conquered the region in the 6th century, and by 715 it had been conquered by the Moors, who held it until 1147, when it became part of Portugal.

estrogen   see SEX HORMONES; STEROID

estrous cycle [es'-trus] The estrous cycle is the periodic sequence of change in the female reproductive system of mature mammals in response to variations in the level of female hormones. It coincides with ovulation, which occurs midway in each cycle, at which time the female is receptive to the male. At ovulation, a distinct period of "heat" is apparent in animals other than humans. MENSTRUATION occurs toward the end of each cycle. In higher primates, the menstrual cycle developed from the estrous cycle, which lasts about 28 days in most women.

Ovulation and menstruation are controlled by several hormones whose levels rise and fall during the cycle. In the human female during the first 2 weeks of the cycle, one or more ova mature in a follicle located in the ovary in response to follicle-stimulating hormone (FSH) from the pituitary gland, and estrogen hormones from the ovary prepare the lining of the uterus for implantation should fertilization occur. After the ovum is released and passed toward the uterus, a portion of the ruptured follicle, the corpus luteum, secretes the hormone progesterone, which further develops the uterine lining. If fertilization does not occur, the corpus luteum degenerates about 12 days after ovulation. The loss of progesterone triggers menstruation, which lasts 3 to 7 days. If fertilization occurs, the corpus luteum is maintained by the hormone chorionic gonadotropin secreted by the developing placenta.

estuary [es'-choo-air-ee] Estuaries are drowned coastal river valleys in which fresh water and SEAWATER mix. Drowning occurs as a result of either worldwide rise in SEA LEVEL or subsidence of the land.

Estuaries along the Atlantic coast of the United States (Chesapeake Bay is the largest) have an average depth of about 4 m (13 ft) and a much deeper central channel. Estuarine embayments—providing protected harbors, access channels to the ocean, and connection with a landward river system—are sites of many of the world's major ports. They are also the habitat of an important source of seafood—shellfish that live in brackish (moderately salty) water.

In the inner portions of estuarine embayments, water circulation is stratified, with less dense river water flowing out over a wedge of denser seawater. Vertical mixing along the turbulent boundary between the two kinds of water causes some of the seawater to be carried upward and then back toward the sea. More seawater is drawn inward along the bottom to replace that lost by mixing.

Where little sand is available, an estuary mouth may be wide and open. With abundant sand and strong tidal flow, it may be constricted by linear sand ridges. In the Gironde River estuary in France, sand ridges partially separate ebb and flood channels, reducing the extent of stratification and modifying the pattern of circulation. Estuary mouths may also be constricted along coasts on which sand is being actively transported by longshore drift (see BEACH AND COAST).

Sediments in an estuary have both a river and an ocean source. Sand is carried into an estuary by oceanic tidal currents. Coarser, river-borne sediments drop out near the head of the estuary as current velocities decrease. Finer river sediment also tends to accumulate in the upper reaches of estuaries.

Nearly all the river-borne sediment carried into an estuarine embayment is trapped there, causing embayments to slowly fill. As an embayment becomes shallower, wave and tidal action begin to dominate circulation and sediment movement. As a result, circulation tends to become restricted to the main channels.

etching

Etching is one of the intaglio processes of printmaking. It is similar to ENGRAVING in many respects. The main distinction is that in the engraving process the line is cut directly into the metal plate by the engraver, who applies pressure to the burin to cut away the metal; in the etching process the line is cut by the action of acid acting on metal. As a result, the etched line can be more varied in depth, width, and texture than the engraved line.

The metal plate, usually of copper or zinc but sometimes of other metals, is first coated with an acid-resis-

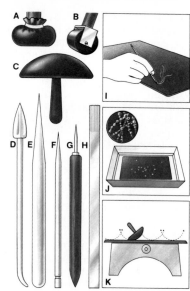

In the execution of an etching, the plate is cleaned, then heated to facilitate the application of the ground, applied with a silk-covered dabber (A) or a hard roller (B). A mushroom-shaped dabber (C) applies ink to the finished work. A scraper (D), burnisher (E), and etching needles (F, G, H) are shown here. After the design is completed (I), the plate is immersed in an acid bath (J), where the acid bites into the exposed lines on the plate. When the process is completed, the plate is cleaned, inked with a dabber (K), and printed.

tant material, usually wax-based, called a ground. The design is drawn onto the ground with an etching needle or other drawing instrument. The needle scratches away the ground, leaving the metal plate exposed. When the design is complete, the entire plate is immersed in a bath of acid, usually nitric or hydrochloric acid. The acid eats away the metal where it has been exposed, forming a cut-in line in the plate. The plate is kept in the acid until the desired depth and width of line have been bitten into the metal. The plate is then removed from the acid, and the ground is removed. After being cleaned, the plate is ready for printing. As in engraving, the plate is inked, then wiped clean of surface ink; damp paper is placed on the surface of the plate, and the plate and paper are passed through the rollers of a press under pressure.

A very wide variation of effects can be achieved by the use of different types of ground, acid, and etching tools, and by varying the time the plate spends in the acid bath. The amount of ink left on the plate after wiping can also alter the effect of the finished print. For these reasons the technical aspect of etching is an integral part of the artistic process, and slight variations in technique can completely alter the finished effect of a given print.

Etching emerged as the primary printmaking technique in the 17th century. Many of the greatest artists have used the etching technique, including notably Francisco de Goya, Pablo Picasso, Giovanni Battista Piranesi, and Rembrandt. Etching is frequently used in conjunction with other techniques such as engraving, DRYPOINT, or AQUATINT to allow the maximum degree of tonal and textural variation.

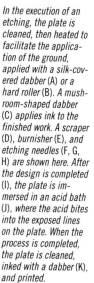

Jacques Callot made his series of etchings, Beggars, *while he was at the Florentine court of Grand Duke Cosimo II (from 1611 to 1621). Accustomed to working on an extremely small scale, Callot invented a new, "hard" ground for the etching plate, and with it obtained far more detail and finer lines.*

Ethan Frome

[eeth'-uhn frohm] The simplest and least typical of Edith WHARTON's works, *Ethan Frome* (1911) became the society novelist's most popular story.

The novella presents a bleak picture of Massachusetts farm life, with characters who lead lives of almost unmitigated isolation. As a result, they are narrow, emotionally distorted, and never able to approach their full potential. Ethan Frome, as a young farmer, had shown traces of warmth and intelligence, but years of poverty and marriage to Zeena, a whining invalid, have made him desperate. When his wife's young cousin, Mattie, comes to live with them, he responds to her youth and liveliness, and they fall in love. Suspecting this, Zeena forces Mattie to leave. Ethan and Mattie attempt suicide rather than part, but instead of being killed, they are crippled for life. Ironically, it is then Mattie who becomes the nag, while Ethan's wife develops patience in her role as nurse.

ethane [eth'-ayn] In organic chemistry, ethane, CH_3CH_3, is an ALKANE. It is a colorless, odorless gas. Ethane occurs in natural gas. It is used in some two-stage refrigeration systems and in the preparation of ETHYLENE.

ethanol see ETHYL ALCOHOL

Ethelbert see ÆTHELBERT, KING OF KENT

Ethelred II see ÆTHELRED II, KING OF ENGLAND

ether (chemistry) [eeth'-ur] Ethers are a class of organic compounds in which an oxygen atom is bonded to two organic radicals, R-O-R. The ether may be a gas, a liquid, or a solid, depending on the size of the organic radicals. The two most widely used ethers are diethyl ether (or ethyl ether, or simply ether, $C_2H_5OC_2H_5$) and tetrahydrofuran (or THF, $(CH_2)_4O$), a heterocyclic compound. Diethyl ether, a low-boiling liquid (bp 35° C), was the anesthetic first used in surgery. Because it is extremely flammable, however, it has been displaced by other anesthetics.

Both ether and THF (bp 64° C) are widely used SOLVENTS in organic chemistry. Because diethyl ether is only slightly soluble in water, or water in diethyl ether, a mixture of the two separates into two layers, the less dense ether layer rising to the top. After separation of the layers the volatile ether is easily evaporated, and materials that have been removed from the water by the ether may be recovered.

Chemically, ethers are relatively inert but may be split at the oxygen atom by strong acids such as hydriodic acid, HI. When exposed to air, ethers react slowly with oxygen to form peroxides that are explosive and sensitive to heat.

Methyl ethers, CH_3OR, are widespread in nature. Quinine and reserpine, for example, are physiologically active methyl ethers. Cyclic ethers (heterocycles) also occur in such compounds as morphine and the anthocyanins (flower pigments).

The chlorine-substituted phenyl ethers 2,4–D and 2,4,5–T are widely used herbicides for broad-leaved plants; they have little effect on grasses.

ether (physics) In 19th-century physics the ether was a hypothetical medium that supported the transmission of LIGHT through space, much as mechanical vibrations are supported in a steel bar. The ether was supposedly at rest in an absolute sense, and the speed at which light traveled relative to the ether was the constant c. Observers on Earth ought to have been able, by observing the speeds of light waves moving in different directions, to determine their own absolute motion.

A sensitive experiment designed by A. A. Michelson and E. W. Morley and performed in 1881 and 1887 failed, however, to detect an absolute motion of the Earth (see MICHELSON-MORLEY EXPERIMENT). This unexpected result was ultimately explained by Albert Einstein's theory of RELATIVITY and led to a rejection of the ether concept.

Etherege, Sir George [eth'-uh-rij] The first of the great English writers of RESTORATION drama, Sir George Etherege, b. c.1635, d. May 10, 1692, found success with *The Comical Revenge; or, Love in a Tub* (1664) and set the pattern of genteel comedy with the rakish and witty *Man of Mode; or, Sir Fopling Flutter* (1676). Etherege's own life and exploits were reflected in those of his dissolute and amoral characters. His sparkling dialogue depicts the amours and fashion of his time.

Ethical Culture Ethical Culture is a religious movement based on the motto "Deed, not creed." Felix Adler (1851–1933), trained as a rabbi, founded (1876) the Society for Ethical Culture in New York City; other U.S. societies were soon formed, and they joined (1887) in the American Ethical Union. The first ethical society in England was established (1886) by Adler's associate Stanton Coit (1857–1944). The American Ethical Union is affiliated with the International Humanist and Ethical Union.

Adler held that the supreme goal of human life is ethical endeavor, a goal that should be kept independent of religious dogma. Ethical societies therefore are strictly nonsectarian and devote themselves to social reform (Stanton Coit introduced the settlement-house movement in the United States) and education.

ethics Ethics, or moral philosophy, the branch of philosophy concerned with conduct and character, is the systematic study of the principles and methods for distinguishing right from wrong and good from bad. Ethics is connected with metaphysics, the study of reality, and epistemology, the study of knowledge; this may be seen in such questions as whether there is any *real* difference between right and wrong and, if there is, whether it can be *known*.

Experiences that have led to ethical inquiry are uncertainty or conflicts of opinion about what ought to be done; the sometimes painful consequences of an action that earlier seemed perfectly acceptable; and awareness of differences in norms and practices among different societies. These experiences give rise not only to questions of practical ethics (What should I do?) but also to questions of theoretical ethics (Is any one of these standards really right or are they all just arbitrary?). Such experiences are also the main source of moral skepticism—along with the fact that moral judgments appear unverifiable by observation, because there seems to be nothing in experience corresponding to the rightness of an action.

Metaethics. Metaethics (literally "about ethics") is the analytical study of the discipline of ethics itself. Metaethics attempts to determine the meanings of normative terms, such as *right, good, ought, justice,* and *obligation,* to determine their interconnections and whether any of these concepts is basic. A question of some prominence in recent discussions is whether an *ought* can be deduced from an *is* and just what the relation is between facts and values.

These are questions of both metaethics and prescriptive—or normative—ethics, and the importance of the distinction between metaethics and normative ethics is itself controversial, some writers regarding it as essential, others as not. The question at issue is whether it is possible to analyze moral concepts and judgments without at the same time presupposing moral beliefs. If so then metaethics can be morally neutral, otherwise not.

Among the main approaches in metaethics are views called naturalism, cognitivism, intuitionism, and subjectivism. Naturalism (represented in different ways by Herbert SPENCER and John DEWEY) maintains that moral terms name complex matters of fact and that moral judgments can be established by scientific or factual investigation; nonnaturalistic theories (such as that of G. E. MOORE) deny this. A cognitivist theory maintains that moral judgments can be true or false and can, in principle, be subjects of knowledge or cognition; noncognitivist theories deny this. These two categories overlap, and a cognitivist theory can be naturalistic or nonnaturalistic.

Intuitionists such as H. A. Prichard and W. D. Ross claim that the sort of knowledge humans have of right and wrong is immediate and self-evident. Reaction to intuitionism has led to subjectivism, emotivism, and imperativism. Subjectivists maintain that moral judgments state only subjective facts about attitudes and make no assertion about the object; thus if one says that something is wrong one is saying only that one disapproves of it or that society does. The emotive theory (A. J. AYER, C. L. Stevenson) claims that moral judgments do not state anything that is capable of being true or false, even subjectively, but merely express emotions; moral terms, according to this view, have only emotive meaning, like oaths or exclamations. Imperativism (Rudolf CARNAP) claims that moral judgments are commands in disguise (so that "You ought to do that" means simply "Do that!") and hence incapable of truth or falsity. Imperativism and emotivism are forms of noncognitivism. Subjectivism, however, is not, although it cannot usefully be classified as cognitivist either.

Any theory that maintains that moral principles cannot be proved, that there are no moral truths, that morality has no rational basis, or that the difference between right and wrong is merely a matter of taste or convention, is a form of moral skepticism. Subjectivism, imperativism, and emotivism are thus forms of skepticism. Cognitivist theories, on the other hand, are usually incompatible with it.

A widespread and familiar form of skepticism is ethical relativism, the view that there is no one correct moral code for all times and peoples, that each group has its own morality relative to its wants and values, and that all moral ideas are necessarily relative to a particular culture. According to this view, cannibals are justified in eating human beings by the standards of their own culture even if not by the standards of Western culture, and there can be no basis for claiming that the standards of Western culture are superior to theirs. Relativism seems to be supported by the most cursory observations of the diversity among cultures and constitutes a problem both for metaethics and for normative ethics. For if there is no right or wrong that can be determined apart from the conventions of one's own culture, the question arises of what ought to be done when different cultures come into conflict.

Normative Ethics. Among the questions of normative ethics are: What makes right actions right? How can we tell what is right? Why should I be moral? Major theories are usually classified as consequentialist (teleological) or nonconsequentialist (deontological). Consequentialism maintains that the morality of an action is determined solely by its consequences. Deontological theories claim, variously, that the morality of an action depends on its intrinsic nature, or on its motives, or on its being in accordance with some rule or principle, and either not at all or only partly on consequences.

Teleological theories vary in their determination of what consequences are relevant and in how the value of the consequences is to be determined, but all interpret moral judgments as dependent on values and evaluation, hence on value theory. One such value theory is HEDONISM, the view that only pleasure is good as an end, and teleological theories are commonly classified as hedonistic or nonhedonistic. UTILITARIANISM (Jeremy BENTHAM, John Stuart MILL), the theory that the greatest happiness of the greatest number is the test of right and wrong, is hedonistic, since it interprets happiness as a balance of pleasure over pain. A nonhedonistic form of consequentialism is the "ideal utilitarianism" of G. E. Moore and Hastings Rashdall, which maintains that one ought to do that act of all those available in the circumstances that would produce the most good. Another rival to utilitarianism is self-realizationism, or perfectionism (ARISTOTLE, Thomas Hill Green), which holds that the ultimate end is the full development or perfection of the self. This is a form of teleological theory, but it is not hedonistic.

Some theories do not readily fall under the above classification. One such is the theological (or divine command) theory that it is the will of God that determines whether an action is right or wrong. On this view (Saint AUGUSTINE, William Paley) the morality of an act depends on neither its consequences nor its essential nature nor its motive, but solely on whether it is in accordance with the will of God. Such theological theories have had wide acceptance and correspond closely to what many religious though nonreflective people uncritically think is the truth about morality. Religion, however, does not necessarily commit one to the theological theory, which has received as much criticism by theists (Richard Whately) as by nontheists (Moore).

In the philosophy of Immanuel KANT, for one's action to be morally right one must be able to will one's maxim to be a universal law, that is, be willing to have everyone act in the same way. Kant introduced the concept of moral worth, insisting that one's action, even if right, has moral value only if one's motive for acting was to do what is right. Moral worth, then, depends on one's motive or intention, and not on what is actually done.

EGOISM (Thomas HOBBES), basing itself on the idea that everyone acts always out of self-interest, maintains that an action is right only if it is in the interest of the agent. This view is consequentialist, but it is not utilitarian; on the utilitarian view of what is right in conduct everyone's interest must be given equal weight. Egoism, however, is not just another version of normative theory; it is, rather, a challenge to ethical theory itself. The challenge of egoism is that it raises the questions Why should I be moral? What's in it for me?, which rest on the idea that if there is no advantage in being moral, the agent can have no reason to be. Theological theories find it extremely easy to answer this question; others find it more difficult. The attempts to answer it have led to many inquiries into the basis of human motivation, the sanction for morality, the possibility of disinterested action, and the proper organization of society.

Situation ethics, which has come into prominence only recently, claims that the morality of an action depends on the situation and not on the application of a law to the case. This is a form of particular-case intuitionism and is opposed to utilitarianism and Kantianism as well as the divine-command theory. The original idea can be traced back to Aristotle, who held that the decision in a particular case "rests with perception," and the idea can be found in Ross (an intuitionist and nonnaturalist) as well as in Dewey (a naturalist and consequentialist).

Religious Ethics. One of the main problems of moral philosophy is the connection between morality and religion. Religious moralists tend to claim that there can be no morality without religion, because without God there can be no reason to be moral. Philosophers (with exceptions) tend to deny this, even take the opposite view. Philosophers as opposed as Mill and Kant held that religion rests on morality, since religion itself depends on the distinction between good and evil, an ethical concept.

Social Ethics. Some philosophers distinguish between personal ethics and social ethics. Personal ethics is taken as comprehending how one should act in relation to oneself, social ethics how one should act in relation to others. Such a distinction rests on differentiating between duties to oneself and duties to others, and one standard question of ethics is which of these is primary. Other thinkers (Dewey, for instance) regard the distinction as spurious, however, and regard all morality as essentially social, as

comprehending problems that arise in a social setting.

In recent years some moral philosophers have returned to considering the questions of ethics in closer relation to those of political and legal philosophy. A paramount question is that of the justice of social institutions, especially (though not solely) the law. John RAWLS's *A Theory of Justice* (1971), which takes the basic structure of society as the primary subject of justice and attempts to derive laws for individual conduct from the principles for institutions, has sparked great debate. In the process new interest has developed on the nature of a just law, on whether one has a moral obligation to obey the law, and on whether law itself can be defined independently of morality. These are questions both in moral philosophy and in philosophy of law, as is the question of whether morality can be legislated, which is involved in disputes over racial integration and over legal restrictions on sexual relations and abortion.

Normative and Professional Ethics. In recent years, owing to rapid social change and unprecedented technological developments, there has been a great resurgence of interest in normative ethics. One aspect of this is the attention given by scientists, engineers, lawyers, physicians, journalists, and others to the ethical problems involved in the practice of their professions.

New fields of ethics, such as bioethics, engineering ethics, and environmental ethics, dealing with issues not previously contemplated and with problems of concern to all, are now developing rapidly. Abortion and euthanasia are familiar examples of moral problems in medicine becoming moral problems for the wider society. Another area of serious debate concerns the propriety and limits of experimentation on both human subjects and animals (see ANIMAL RIGHTS). Thus current discussions exemplify the interplay between theory and practice, in this case in the area of ethics, that has always been most fruitful for both.

See also: CONSCIENCE; DETERMINISM; MEDICAL ETHICS; NATURAL LAW.

Ethiopia [eeth-ee-oh'-pee-uh]   Ethiopia, a country in eastern Africa bordered by Somalia and Djibouti to the east, Kenya to the south, and Sudan to the west, was one of the earliest world centers of agricultural innovation. Unlike most African nations, it was never a European colony, and it has been important to the modern history of Africa as a symbol of independence. Its capital, ADDIS ABABA, is the headquarters of the ORGANIZATION OF AFRICAN UNITY (OAU).

Land and Resources

Ethiopia's landforms are highly varied. Highlands above 1,500 m (5,713 ft) cover about 40% of Ethiopia's land area and make up almost half of Africa's highland area; the nation's highest point is Ras Dashen (4,620 m/ 15,157 ft). The central highland plateau is dissected by deep gorges and broad valleys; it descends sharply to the east into the GREAT RIFT VALLEY. Near the border with Sudan, the highlands drop off into hot grasslands adjoining the Nile Valley.

AT A GLANCE

PEOPLE'S DEMOCRATIC REPUBLIC OF ETHIOPIA

Land: Area: 1,221,900 km^2 (471,778 mi^2). Capital and largest city: Addis Ababa (1988 est. pop., 1,412,515).

People: Population (1990 est.): 51,666,622. Density: 42.3 persons per km^2 (109.5 per mi^2). Distribution (1989 est.): 11% urban, 89% rural. Official language: Amharic. Major religions: Islam, Ethiopian Orthodox Christianity.

Government: Type: one-party state. Legislature: National Shango (Parliament). Political subdivisions: 24 administrative regions, 5 autonomous regions.

Economy: GDP (1989 est.): $6.6 billion; $130 per capita. Labor distribution (1988): industry—3%; agriculture—90%; services—7%. Foreign trade (1988): exports—$418 million; imports—$1.1 billion. Currency: 1 birr = 100 cents.

Education and Health: Literacy (1988): 60% of adult population. Universities (1990): 3. Hospital beds (1988): 11,000. Physicians (1986–87): 1,241. Life expectancy (1990): women—52; men—49. Infant mortality (1990): 116 per 1,000 live births.

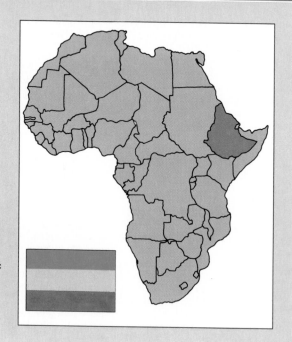

Ethiopia's river systems rise in the highlands (where Lake TANA, the country's largest lake, is located) and carry water and fertile topsoil to its neighbors. The Genale (Juba) and Wabe Shebele rivers of the southwest bring water to Somalia. In the north and west the Blue Nile (Abay in Ethiopia), Tekeze, Baro, and Mereb (Gash) rivers join the NILE RIVER system.

Ethiopia's climate is determined by elevation. The highest zone (4,000–2,300 m/13,123–7,546 ft) has a mean annual temperature of 10°–15° C (50°–59° F). The lowest zone (below 1,500 m/4,921 ft) has a range of 20°–25° C (68°–77° F). The hottest areas are along the borders; the coolest are in the central highlands. Hail, morning frost, and even snow are common in the higher elevations. Rainfall, which varies tremendously but also follows elevation, ranges from 800–1,200 mm (31–47 in) annually in the central highlands to 400 mm (16 in) or less in areas below 1,500 m (4,921 ft). Almost 75% of the annual precipitation falls between mid-June and early September. The slow drying of Africa's SAHEL region also affects eastern and northeastern Ethiopia, where the frequency of droughts has increased in the past two decades.

Broad-leaved forests cover about 20% of the country, including the southwestern highlands, where coffee trees originated and still grow wild. Another 34% is more open woodland savannah, although the northern highlands have been rapidly deforested in the 20th century. The re-

mainder of the country, especially the lowlands, is grassland and semidesert. Ethiopia's volcanic soils range from highly fertile black cotton soil to reddish sandy loam. Ethiopia historically had abundant wildlife. Species found nowhere else in the world include the simen fox and the walia ibex. Baboons, wild pigs, and porcupines abound in the highlands, and the country has Africa's largest livestock population (cattle, sheep, and goats). Few mineral resources exist, although gold is mined in the south and west.

People

More than 80 languages are spoken in Ethiopia, with the greatest linguistic diversity found in the southwest. Amharic (a Semitic language), Oromominya, Tigrinya, and Somali are spoken by more than two-thirds of the population. Ethiopian Orthodox Christianity and Islam are each adhered to by about 40% of the population. The remainder of the people are Protestants, Roman Catholics, and followers of local religions. Ethiopia is also home to the FALASHAS, a small group who practice a form of Judaism.

The population is overwhelmingly rural, with the highest population densities in the central highlands. The largest cities are Addis Ababa, ASMARA, and Dire Dawa. Urban growth is 5.5% annually. Educational and health facilities are limited and concentrated in urban areas.

Historically, the Semitic AMHARA and Tigray peoples of the northern highlands have dominated political and economic life in the region. These groups were predominant-

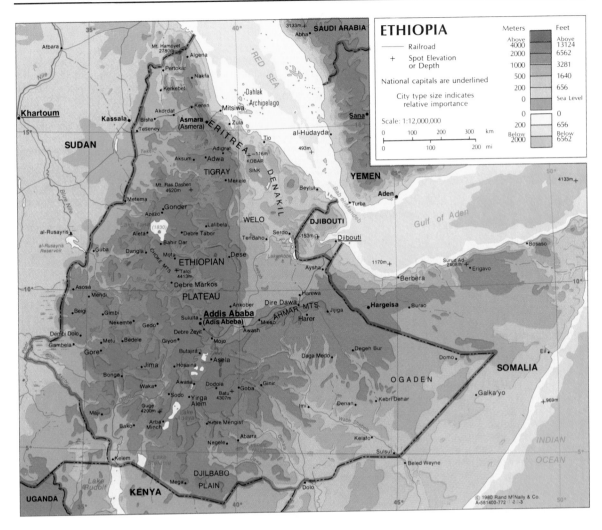

ly Ethiopian Orthodox and constituted the population of the land that outsiders called Abyssinia until the 1930s. The largest single group in Ethiopia, however, is the Oromo, who invaded highland Ethiopia from the south in the 16th century and pushed as far north as Tigray. Today they occupy much of central, southern, and eastern Ethiopia. Because of drought and war, there were as many as 700,000 refugees from Sudan and Somalia in Ethiopia and as many as 1.5 million Ethiopian refugees in Sudan and Somalia by 1989.

Economic Activity

Agriculture accounts for 40% of Ethiopia's gross domestic product (GDP) and 90% of all export earnings. Industry, concentrated in Addis Ababa and Asmara, mainly comprises the processing of agricultural raw materials. The country's major export is coffee.

After the 1974 revolution, which overthrew Emperor HAILE SELASSIE, Ethiopia's central government attempted to reorganize the economy along socialist lines. Although 90% of Ethiopia's food is produced on peasant farms, most government investment went to inefficient state farms and cooperatives. In 1984 the government began to resettle northern famine victims in the south; more than 500,000 people were resettled, some forcibly, raising international opposition. To reorganize the rural population, the government began a controversial policy of "villagization" in 1987, forcing farmers to move into new village sites. These policies were unsuccessful and agricultural production has declined rapidly. In 1990 the government announced changes in its farm policies to allow private investment.

Major famines occurred in 1972–74, 1984–85, 1987, and 1989–90, killing perhaps two million people. In each case international donors provided millions of tons of food aid. The causes of these famines are complex. Extensive, long-term agriculture on much of the northern highlands led to deforestation and soil erosion.

The Organization of African Unity, headquartered in Addis Ababa, was founded in 1963 to promote pan-African cooperation and eradicate colonialism on the continent.

The combined effect of government policy, civil war, climatic change, and an exhausted agricultural base has contributed to famine in the regions of ERITREA, Tigray, Welo (Wollo), and Gonder.

Government

Ethiopia is a one-party state headed by a president who also serves as general secretary of the nation's Communist party, renamed the Ethiopian Democratic Unity party in 1990. MENGISTU HAILE MARIAM, a young military officer who founded the party and became its first leader, came to power after the 1974 revolution and a series of bloody purges. The military group (called the Dergue) converted itself to a civilian ruling party with a national constitution in 1987, when it declared Ethiopia the People's Democratic Republic of Ethiopia. Civil war and discontent within the armed forces have made the government's hold on power tenuous.

History

To the ancient world, Ethiopia meant all lands south of Egypt. Ethiopia's northern highlands were the site of the empire of AKSUM (Axum) (established in the 1st century AD), which controlled the Red Sea coast and had trade and cultural contacts with southern Arabia, Egypt, Rome, and Greece. In the 5th century, migrants from Syria converted Aksum's Emperor Ezana to Christianity. Aksum then used its power to spread Christianity across the central highlands. Late in the 7th century, Islam penetrated the region from the Red Sea coast and took hold in eastern Ethiopia. The major theme of the history of ancient and medieval Ethiopia was the efforts of Christian highland kingdoms to extend their control over the territory and trade routes of their lowland neighbors. At the same time Ethiopia's efficient ox-plow system of agriculture spread across most of the region's highland zones.

Modern Ethiopia's borders are the result of the late-19th-century expansion under Emperor MENELIK II. In 1896 his armies defeated a modern Italian army at the Battle of Adowa (Adwa) to assure Ethiopia's independence. Political and economic modernization took place

under Emperor Haile Selassie. Italy invaded and occupied Ethiopia in 1935; Haile Selassie resumed the throne in 1941 and remained in power until he was overthrown by the Dergue in 1974.

Ethiopia's new leaders began a program of socialist development. In Eritrea, an Italian colony from 1889 to 1941, the Eritrean Peoples Liberation Front (EPLF) has fought to secede from Ethiopia since 1962, when Ethiopia forcibly annexed Eritrea. Tigray has had an increasingly effective insurrection since 1974, which seeks to overthrow the central government. Other antigovernment groups have been active in areas inhabited by Somali and Oromo peoples; an invasion from Somalia in 1977–78 in support of indigenous Somali rebels in the OGADEN brought arms and military aid from the Soviet Union and Cuba and strained relations with the United States. The government's control of northern Ethiopia has gradually weakened, and the nation's political and economic future will depend largely on how these conflicts are resolved.

---

ethnic minorities   An ethnic minority is a group of people who differ in language, race, or color or in national, religious, or cultural origins from the dominant group—usually the majority population—of the country in which they live. The differing identity of an ethnic minority may be displayed in any number of ways, ranging from distinctive customs, life-styles, speech patterns and accents, dress, or food preferences to the particular attitudes, value systems, and economic or political beliefs espoused by members of the group. Frequently, ethnic minorities are discriminated against by members of the dominant group. The position of the ethnic minority may be a result of past wars of conquest or of emigration patterns that are centuries old. It is estimated that about one-quarter of the world's population belongs to some kind of ethnic minority.

Ethnic minorities vary greatly in relative size. In the Soviet Union, for example, about 52% of the population (known as Great Russians) politically dominate the rest of the population, which includes more than 15 major ethnic groups, each numbering 1 million or more, and many smaller ethnic minorities, each with at least 100,000 members. In South Africa, nonwhites constitute more than 80% of the population, but they have minority status insofar as their political and civil rights are concerned. In Japan, on the other hand, the ethnic Ainu are less than 1% of the total national population.

Most ethnic minorities constitute between 15% and 35% of the populations of their countries. In the United States about 18.8% of the population qualify as belonging to an immigrant ethnic minority. When the 12% of the U.S. population that are black is included, the U.S. ethnic population is 29%. In Canada nearly 25% of the national population are of so-called ethnic origin. When the French Canadians are included, the ethnic minority (meaning mainly those of non-British origin) adds up to about 50% of the total national population. This also includes American Indians and Eskimo, who together represent about 2% of the population.

In the United States the Bureau of the Census has identified more than 30 separate groups of people of foreign ancestry that have more than 100,000 members. They stem from Austria, Belgium, Canada, China, Cuba, Czechoslovakia, Denmark, Finland, France, Germany, Greece, Hungary, Ireland, Italy, Japan, Korea, Lithuania, Mexico, the Netherlands, Norway, the Philippines, Poland, Romania, Spain, Sweden, Switzerland, Turkey, the United Kingdom (English, Northern or Protestant Irish, Scots, and Welsh), the USSR, Vietnam, and Yugoslavia. In addition to these there are AFRICAN AMERICANS, HISPANIC AMERICANS, American Indians, Eskimo, and Jews.

Types of Minorities in North America

Five distinct types of ethnic minorities have appeared in the United States and Canada since 1600.

(1) Colonial ethnics of non-English origin arrived between 1683 and the onset of the American Revolution in 1775. Most important among them were the Germans, the Scots-Irish, a few Dutch, and some Swedes and Moravians. The majority sought either religious freedom or land. Those who sought religious freedom were generally slowest to assimilate into the mainstream American culture; those whose motives were primarily commercial or agricultural soon lost their ethnic identity, except in the most superficial sense.

(2) Work ethnics arrived largely between 1850 and 1920. Among them were Italians, Poles, Hungarians, Slovaks, Serbo-Croatians, Russians, Ukrainians, Chinese, Japanese, and Jews. Many were recruited by agents of major U.S. corporations to work in the mines, mills, and factories. They mostly sought economic opportunity. A few fled political persecution. Many have been incorporated into the mainstream of American life, although some still retain strong ethnic identification.

(3) More recent ethnics have arrived in the wake of the two world wars and later conflicts. Many were refugees from Nazi, Fascist, Communist, and other political or ethnic oppression; they include Armenians, Jews, Baltic peoples, Chinese, Vietnamese, Cambodians, and Cubans. Other groups, including Greeks, Turks, Puerto Ricans, Mexicans, various Central and South American groups, and Koreans, have sought economic opportunity much as did those who came between 1880 and 1910. These recent arrivals by and large have retained the strongest ethnicity of all such groups.

(4) Subjugated ethnics include peoples who have been conquered either by the Americans or by the British Canadians over the past three centuries. Among them are French Canadians, who were conquered in 1763, American and Canadian Indians and Eskimo, Mexican Americans in the American Southwest, and African Americans who were brought to the New World as slaves mostly between 1620 and 1820. These groups generally have not succeeded in becoming well integrated into the dominant culture. Some, like the French Canadians, Indians, and Eskimo, have resisted integration. Many have faced widespread discrimination and prejudice.

(5) Socioreligious ethnics sought freedom in North America but often did not want to move into the cultural mainstream. These have included such devout groups as the Amish, the Mennonites, the Doukhobors, and many Orthodox Jews.

North American Ethnic Generations Compared

The following brief survey of ethnic groups in North America reveals some broad patterns of adaptation.

First-generation ethnics, those born abroad of peasant or working-class families, usually arrived in North America penniless and had to concentrate on surviving economically. They usually spoke little or no English and lived in ethnic enclaves, or GHETTOS, avoiding contact with the dominant culture. They tended to be very ethnocentric.

Second-generation ethnics, the first generation born in the New World, attended the public schools and learned English. Many concealed the fact that they still spoke the language of the old country. This generation sought to come to terms with the dominant culture in order to gain a secure place in society. Its members were often about equally American (or Canadian) and Old World in outlook.

Third-generation ethnics were inclined to slough off their Old World roots and to become as Americanized as possible. They often dropped the use of the old language and thought of themselves simply as Americans or Canadians. Many Anglicized the pronunciation of their names or translated them into English. Many also rejected most of their native culture and moved away from the old ethnic neighborhoods.

Fourth-generation ethnics usually completed the Americanization or Canadianization process begun by the preceding generation. Many actively rejected their cultural past in order to move into the cultural mainstream of American and Canadian society without any of the old impediments, retaining only a few vestiges, such as old-country Christmas and Easter observances.

Fifth-generation ethnics (and subsequent generations) usually felt so secure that they simply ignored their ethnic heritage rather than try to conceal it. Sometimes they even tried to regain it by learning the ancestral language and resuming some of the old customs. Many have also shown a resurgence of ethnic (but not ethnocentric) pride in their origins. At the same time they have moved to the suburbs and into the American and Canadian middle classes, or beyond in some instances. Some descendants of Old World work ethnics have shifted their traditional political allegiance from the U.S. Democratic and the Canadian Liberal parties to the U.S. Republican and the Canadian Conservative parties or else have become political independents. In fourth- or fifth-generation families a college education may be offered to all the children, whereas second- or third-generation ethnics usually sent only their sons to college.

Since 1950 the U.S. and Canadian governments have largely eliminated the legal bases for discrimination against ethnic minorities. Prejudice still remains against many of them, however. Added to this are differences in economic power and educational attainments that work against equality of opportunity and reinforce patterns of ethnocentrism.

See also: ASIAN AMERICANS.

ethnocentrism [eth-noh-sen'-trizm] Ethnocentrism is the tendency to regard the beliefs, standards, and code of behavior of one's own culture or subculture as superior to those found in other societies. Ethnocentrism thus may serve the socially useful function of encouraging cohesion and solidarity among group members; it may also contribute, however, to attitudes of superiority, intolerance, and even contempt for groups with different customs and lifeways.

ethnography [eth-nahg'-ruh-fee] Ethnography is a field of anthropological research based on direct observation of and reporting on a people's way of life. As such, ethnography is the core method of cultural anthropology (see ANTHROPOLOGY). Ethnographic subjects are usually cultural groups, such as communities, tribes, or dialect groups. However, classes or institutions within complex urban societies are also subjects of study. Ethnography consists of two phases: the process of observing and recording data, usually called fieldwork, followed by the preparation of a written description and analysis of the subject under study.

Early ethnographic studies often included random anecdotes and facts about "primitive" peoples whose way of life was thought to be disappearing. As the field of anthropology became more professional, however, ethnography became more systematic, and ethnographers attempted to interrelate the various aspects of a way of life. In recent years ethnography has become more specialized. Sometimes it involves studying small segments of large societies or focuses on specific, practical, or theoretical problems in anthropology.

ethnohistory [eth-noh-his'-tuh-ree] Ethnohistory is a subfield of ANTHROPOLOGY in which historical materials are used in conjunction with ETHNOGRAPHY to reconstruct past periods of a culture. Like ethnographers, ethnohistorians make field observations, but they also cull data from documentary, archaeological, and oral sources. These include historical materials such as the accounts of explorers, traders, missionaries, and government officials; information from old persons; and oral traditions. The term has also been used to mean folk history, a group's traditional explanation of their past.

ethnolinguistics see ANTHROPOLOGICAL LINGUISTICS

ethnology see ANTHROPOLOGY

ethology [eth-ahl'-uh-jee] Ethology is the science of the behavior of animals in their natural, or wild, state. Thus, ethology mainly concerns instinctive or inherited behavior rather than learned behavior. The ultimate goal of ethologists is to discover how instinctive behavior among related species evolved and now serves to enhance survival. The first ethologists, in the early 1900s, believed that their studies would reveal the origins of human ethics; hence, they borrowed the term *ethology* from philosophy, where it refers to the evolution of human values. The term remains popular in Europe, but American counterparts of European ethologists prefer the term SOCIOBIOLOGY, behavioral biology, or comparative psychology.

The basic procedure in ethology is the formation of an ethogram—a detailed description of all the behaviors exhibited by the subject species. The ethologist postulates various theories to explain the cause, development, and adaptive function of each behavior. Finally, experiments are conducted to confirm or refute the theories. For example, Konrad LORENZ found that the newly hatched greylag goose followed any large moving stimulus presented shortly after hatching. The function of this process, termed IMPRINTING, is to secure the association between parent and offspring.

Many of the behaviors described in the ethogram consist of fixed action-patterns, which are inherited, stereotyped behaviors, or instincts. These patterns are stimulated by specific cues, called releasers or sign stimuli, from the environment and are carried out by the innate releasing mechanism, or nervous system. Releasers are especially important in social behaviors such as aggression and courtship.

See also: ANIMAL BEHAVIOR; ANIMAL COURTSHIP AND MATING.

ethyl alcohol [eth'-ul] Ethyl alcohol, CH_3CH_2OH, also known as ethanol and grain alcohol, is a colorless, flammable liquid. It boils at 78.5° C and has a pleasant odor and burning taste. It is miscible with water in all proportions and soluble in other polar solvents. The product of enzymatic fermentation of carbohydrates, including cellulose, it is present in all alcoholic beverages (see ALCOHOL CONSUMPTION). Ethanol undergoes all of the reactions of a primary ALCOHOL. It oxidizes to form acetaldehyde. a reaction that occurs rapidly in the human body. Ethanol is used as a solvent, an ANTIFREEZE, and a fuel (see GASOHOL); in the preservation of organic specimens; in the preparation of pharmaceuticals and esters; and, diluted, as a beverage. It can be DENATURED (made unfit for human consumption) by the addition of other compounds.

ethylene [eth'-ul-een] Ethylene, or ethene, $CH_2{=}CH_2$, is a colorless, flammable gas and is the most important hydrocarbon used in chemical processes. It is the simplest member of the ALKENE family of hydrocarbons and is highly reactive. Ethylene has relatively few direct industrial uses but serves as a starting material for a variety of other products, including polyethylene plastic, polyvinyl chloride (PVC), ethyl alcohol, styrene, and synthetic rubber. Most ethylene is made from PYROLYSIS of natural and oil-refinery gases.

Ethylene also functions as a plant hormone (see HORMONE, PLANT). Its ability to hasten fruit ripening makes it commercially important.

ethylene dibromide   see EDB

---

etiolation [eet-ee-oh-lay'-shuhn] Etiolation is the blanching, or whitening, of a plant that results when the plant is grown in darkness. Generally, the green pigment CHLOROPHYLL develops only when a plant is exposed to light. Keeping the plant in darkness usually prevents it from turning green. In farming, white asparagus and similar vegetables are produced through a form of etiolation.

---

etiquette [et'-i-ket] Etiquette, the codes of rules that govern social behavior, probably takes its name from the 17th-century court of Louis XIV, where courtiers were given *une étiquette* (a ticket), a list of elaborate rules prescribing acceptable behavior for every situation that might be encountered at court. Louis himself wrote a book on court ceremony. The earliest known book of manners is the ancient Egyptian *Instructions of Ptah Hotep,* in which a father advises his son on proper conduct. Such books have been written in all sophisticated societies and reached a height of popularity in 19th-century England and the United States, as the upwardly mobile tried to remedy their ignorance of the manners of the rich. In 20th-century America, books such as *Etiquette: The Blue Book of Social Usage,* by Emily POST, have been perennial best-sellers, although interest in codified lists of behavior has declined.

Etna, Mount Mount Etna, the highest active volcano in Europe, is on the eastern coast of Sicily, 29 km (18 mi) north of Catania. Its height, which varies with major eruptions, is currently 3,262 m (10,703 ft). Active since the end of the Tertiary Period, about 2 million years ago, Etna has the structure of a truncated cone, with more than 200 secondary cones caused by lateral eruptions. The Valle del Bove, a chasm nearly 1,220 m (4,000 ft) deep, is an inactive fissure. Snowcapped except in late summer, the top of the volcano is covered with lava and volcanic ash and supports little vegetation. Below 2,000 m (6,500 ft) is the forest zone. Agriculture on the gentle slopes below 915 m (3,000 ft) consists of vineyards and nut trees in the higher, temperate zone and olive and citrus trees in the lower, subtropical zone. These lower slopes, with their rich volcanic soils, are densely populated agricultural regions. Of the more than 250 recorded eruptions, the most violent occurred in 475 BC—according to accounts by Pindar and Aeschylus—and in 1669, when Catania was inundated by lava flow.

Eton College [eet'-uhn] Founded by King Henry VI in 1440, Eton College is a private secondary school for boys in Eton, Berkshire, England. Eton's academic and social prestige are so great that children are registered at birth for admission. Many of England's most illustrious men were educated there. Eton has a tutorial system similar to the systems at Oxford and Cambridge universities, in which each student studies under a tutor. The school is well known for its late Gothic architecture.

Etowah Mounds [et'-uh-wah] The Etowah Mounds are a series of prehistoric earthen burial mounds located in the southern Appalachian Mountains, near Cartersville, Ga. Forming part of a fortified village complex, they constitute one of the largest of the MOUND BUILDER sites in the southeastern United States.

Extensive excavations at the site from 1925 to 1928 yielded copper axes, engraved copper and shell objects, incised pottery, and other artifacts, as well as stone sarcophagi called stone-box graves. The Etowah Mounds site was occupied from about AD 1200 to 1700. An assemblage of artifacts dated *c.*1300 is associated with the Southern Death Cult, so named because the designs on characteristic ritual objects suggest a preoccupation with violence and death. This cultural tradition appears to have spread to mound sites in northwestern Georgia from the eastern Oklahoma site of Spiro Mound.

Etruria   see ETRUSCANS

Etruscans [ee-truhs'-kuhnz] The Etruscans were an ancient people of central Italy who flourished from about the 8th to the 1st century BC in an area known as Etruria bounded by the Arno and Tiber rivers and by the Apennines and the Tyrrhenian Sea. Within this area developed a number of independent Etruscan city-states, including

Ancient Etruria occupied an area of west-central Italy between Florence and Rome. At the height of the Etruscans' power in the 6th century BC, however, their influence spread north to the Po River, east to the Adriatic Sea, and south into Campania.

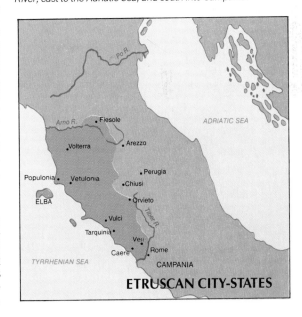

ETRUSCAN CITY-STATES

This detail of a wall painting (c.400 BC) from the Tomb of Orcus in Tarquinia shows the head of Velia, a member of the aristocratic Velcha family.

Etruscan tomb art expressed religious beliefs that centered on a death cult. This 7th-century BC wall painting in the Tomb of the Augurs in Tarquinia portrays two mourners in priestly garments. The doorway symbolized entry into the other world.

Caere (Cerveteri), CHIUSI, TARQUINIA, VEII, Clusium, Orvieto, Perugia, Volterra, Fiesole, Vulci, Arezzo, Populonia, and Vetulonia. The Etruscans adopted much from Greek civilization, including their alphabet, and they turned Rome into a city, although the Romans eventually assimilated the Etruscans and brought an end to their culture.

Origins. The mystery surrounding the origins of the Etruscans stems from the isolation of their language, which is not Indo-European and is apparently unrelated to any other language in Europe or the Mediterranean (except for that appearing on a 6th-century BC tombstone from Lemnos, in the Aegean Sea). Etruscan was written

The Etruscans were one of the few cultures that used terracotta widely in their artwork. This sarcophagus of an Etruscan couple from Caere dates from the late 6th century BC. (Villa Giulia Museum, Rome.)

in the Greek alphabet, and it is known principally from 11,000 short inscriptions of funerary, magic, and religious texts; no Etruscan literature survives.

Ancient historians argued about the origins of the Etruscans. Herodotus reported that they came from Lydia, in Anatolia; Dionysius of Halicarnassus, writing in the 1st century BC, thought they originated in Italy. Archaeological evidence supports the autochthonous (native) theory, proving continuity between the Etruscans, who can be traced to the 7th century BC, when they began to write, and their predecessors, the VILLANOVANS. Most scholars today speak of a development of the Etruscan people, perhaps including small groups from the East, such as the Tursha, mentioned in Egyptian records as one of the SEA PEOPLES of the 13th century BC.

History. Etruria's great wealth was based on its fertile land and rich mineral-ore resources, particularly the iron found on Elba and at Populonia. Excellent harbors encouraged trade, and most cities were protected against piracy by their distance of roughly 8 to 16 km (5 to 10 mi) from the coast. Famous for their seamanship, the Etruscans formed an alliance with the seafaring Phoenician colony of Carthage. In the 6th century BC they colonized the Po Valley to the north and Campania to the south; the last three kings of Rome (the Tarquin dynasty) were Etruscans, and King LARS PORSENA of Clusium also played a part in early Roman history.

Expansion by the Etruscans was checked by their rivals, the Greek cities of southern Italy and Sicily, who defeated them in two battles (524 BC and 474 BC) near the Greek colony of CUMAE. The 5th century saw the decline of their flourishing trade with Greece and the beginning of their struggle with other neighbors in Italy: the Gauls to the north and the increasingly powerful Romans. The Etruscans formed a league of 12 cities, each apparently ruled by a king, and in 413 BC helped the Athenians in their disastrous expedition against Syracuse. Etruria suffered further raids by the Gauls in the 4th century and Veii fell to the Romans in 396 BC. In the following century the Romans, together with Umbrians, Samnites, and Gauls, conquered Caere (273 BC) and sacked Volsinii (265 BC), carrying away 2,000 Etruscan bronze statues.

Rome received contributions from the still-wealthy Etruscan cities during the Second PUNIC WAR (218–201 BC), for the Etruscans had by then become a part of the Roman world. After the Roman general Sulla devastated the Etruscan cities in 80 BC, the remaining Etruscans became Roman citizens. Thereafter, Etruscan culture virtually disappeared, although the language continued to be used for certain religious and magic formulas until the fall of the Roman Empire. Rome derived several features of its culture from the Etruscans, including the Capitoline wolf, still the city's symbol; the *fasces*, the symbol of a general's authority; the Cloaca Maxima, the sewer that drained the Forum; gladiatorial games; and many words.

Etruscan Art. The Etruscans were great technicians, whose architectural skill is evident in their roads, bridges, canals, and temples. In art they specialized in luxury items and in magnificent painted and sculpted works intended for religious and funerary purposes. Few cities have been excavated because most of them are buried under modern cities, but much has been learned of the Etruscans' culture from their richly furnished tombs. Tombs carved out of the native rock reproduced the architecture and furnishings of the houses of the living and formed a city of the dead on the outskirts of each city. Wealthy families or clans had many-chambered tombs to accommodate children and dependents of several generations. Each city-state developed a distinctive artistic tradition.

The art of the 7th century BC, executed in the local Villanovan style or in the Greek Orientalizing style current in the Mediterranean, exhibits contemporary Greek as well as Near Eastern influence. Subsequently, Etruscan art, though highly original, follows the stylistic phases of Greek art: archaic (c.550–450 BC), classical (c.450–350 BC), and Hellenistic (c.350–1st century BC).

The painted interiors of Etruscan tombs provide rare examples of large-scale ancient painting. Among the best preserved is the series from Tarquinia, dating from the late 7th to the 1st century BC. Human forms figure prominently in the lively and naturalistic scenes, which depict daily activities, funeral celebrations, and themes relating to the afterlife.

Etruscan vase painting imitated Greek imported models and included Italo-geometric, Italo-Corinthian, black-figure, and red-figure styles. Numerous Greek vases have been found in Etruscan tombs, including the famous Chigi jug, François vase, and Euphronios krater. About 550 BC the Athenians took over the lucrative Etruscan market, and the so-called Pontic vases, Caeretan hydriae, and Chalcidian vases were probably made in Etruria by Greek immigrant artisans. The most notable Etruscan local pottery was the shiny black *bucchero* ware produced (c.700–500 BC) at Chiusi and Caere.

The highly developed art of sculpture often served to represent or memorialize the dead. Caere and other southern cities specialized in works of TERRA-COTTA, while in the north local limestone, sandstone, volcanic tufa, and alabaster were worked.

Funerary portrait sculptures of men and women were produced from the 7th century BC, as exemplified in life-size stone statues from the Pietrera tomb in Vetulonia and the famous reclining couple on a terra-cotta sarcophagus lid from Caere (late 6th century BC; Villa Giulia Museum, Rome). In Chiusi, cinerary urns were sculpted in the form of a bust representing the deceased whose ashes they contained; in southern Etruria and Latium, miniature hut-shaped urns were used. During the archaic and classical periods such extraordinary works were produced as the Apollo from Veii (c.510 BC; Villa Giulia Museum) and the powerfully realistic heads from the tomb of Orcus at Tarquinia (450–300 BC). Relief stone stelae of the 5th century BC from Fiesole, Volterra, and Felsina (Bologna) typically depict the deceased on the journey to the underworld.

Bronze sculpture, produced chiefly in the northern cities, was an Etruscan speciality. Notable examples include the early-5th-century BC Capitoline Wolf (Capitoline Museum, Rome), the late-5th-century BC Chimaera (Archaeological Museum, Florence), and the 4th-century BC Mars of Todi (Etruscan Museum, Vatican City). Perugia and Vulci produced bronze-relief decorative plaques for furniture or chariots, and Volterra, Perugia, and Chiusi were noted in the Hellenistic period for stone, terra-cotta, or alabaster urns decorated with relief scenes.

Fine metalwork included bronze reliefs; statues and statuettes; lamps; vases and other vessels; engraved bronze mirrors; and intricate gold jewelry, in which the technical virtuosity of Etruscan metalwork is best revealed.

étude [ay'-tued]   A piece of music designed to improve a particular technical skill of an instrumental performer is called an étude (French: "study"). Études are usually longer than finger exercises, which serve the same purpose with less musical interest. Composer-teachers from the time of Muzio CLEMENTI (1752–1832) wrote volumes of études for piano and various other instruments, many of them still in use as study material. Concert études for piano were first written by Frédéric CHOPIN in 1829; these pieces, in addition to demonstrating the facility of the performer, possess intrinsic musical value.

etymology   see LINGUISTICS

Euboea [yoo-bee'-uh]   Euboea (Greek: Évvoia), the second largest island of Greece, is at its nearest point (Chalcis) 38 m (125 ft) from the east coast of the Greek mainland. Euboea has an area of about 3,654 km^2 (1,411 mi^2) and a population of 185,626 (1981). The island is mostly mountainous, with its highest peak, Dhirfis, reaching 1,742 m (5,715 ft). Iron and copper have been mined, but magnesite, lignite, and marble are more important today. Conquered by the Athenians in 506 BC, the island came under Roman rule in 194 BC. It fell to the

Turks in 1470 and became part of Greece with that country's independence in 1830.

eucalyptus [yoo-kuh-lip'-tuhs]   Eucalyptus trees are broadleaved evergreen trees of the myrtle family, Myrtaceae, and are native to Australasia. About 540 species exist, ranging from shrubs 3 m (10 ft) tall to giant trees; specimens over 90m (300 ft) have been reported.

Eucalyptus trees are the dominant vegetation in Australia and the most important timber trees there; the *jarrah* forests consist of Australian eucalypti with wood similar to mahogany. (These forests are currently threatened by a root-rot fungus.) The trees have lance-shaped, leathery leaves and bell-shaped flowers. They are adapted to a wide range of environmental conditions but cannot survive in climates with rigorous winters. Almost all species produce a gum called kino; thus, many eucalypti are called gum trees.

Species of eucalypti have been planted extensively in tropical and subtropical areas around the world, notably California and Ethiopia. They make good shade and windbreak trees; their wood is used for ships, railroad ties, telegraph poles, fencing, and piers; and the leaves are the almost exclusive food of the Australian KOALA. An oil extracted from the leaves, oil of eucalyptus, is used as an antiseptic, nasal decongestant, and deodorant.

The most commonly cultivated species in California as well as worldwide is the blue gum, *Eucalyptus globulus,* a very tall tree with a straight trunk and narrow crown. The bark peels off in long, thin strips and becomes smooth and grayish. Two other common eucalypti in California are the red ironbark, *E. sideroxylon,* with coal-black bark and blue green foliage, and *E. ficifolia,* a spectacular tree with broad, dark leaves and brilliant crimson flowers.

The Murray red gum, *E. camaldulensis,* is a tall evergreen tree with a slender symmetrical crown and slender drooping branches. The bark is dark gray, rough, and furrowed near the base. It has been extensively planted in

The red-flowering gum eucalyptus is a small, rough-barked evergreen with broad, lance-shaped leaves. Its red flowers grow in clusters of three to seven and mature into egg-shaped fruits.

subtropical regions of California, southern Arizona, southern Texas, and Florida.

eucaryote   see EUKARYOTE

Eucharist [yoo'-kuh-rist]   Since early Christian times, the word *Eucharist,* from the Greek *eucharistia* ("thanksgiving"), has been used to describe the SACRAMENT that Jesus Christ instituted at the LAST SUPPER. Four accounts of the origin of the Eucharist are given in the New Testament (Matthew 26:26–29, Mark 14:22–25, Luke 22:15–20, and 1 Corinthians 11:23–26). There are minor variations, but all accounts agree that on the night before his crucifixion, Christ met with his disciples for a Last Supper. After solemn ritual acts he spoke of the bread as his body and the wine as his blood of the new COVENANT. In the earliest written account, that of Saint Paul to the Corinthians, and in Luke, it is recorded that the disciples were instructed to continue the rite in remembrance of their Lord's death. The celebration of the Eucharist is variously described as the Lord's Supper, Holy Communion, and the MASS. Christians of all traditions, with very few exceptions, regard the observance of the sacrament as a binding obligation.

Interpretations of the meaning of the Eucharist vary. Some Christian writers of the 2d century held that the Eucharist consists of two realities, an earthly and a heavenly. In the Middle Ages, the doctrine of transubstantiation was developed; it has remained the official doctrine of the Roman Catholic church. According to this position, the substance, or inner reality, of the bread and wine are changed into the substance of the body and blood of Christ, but the accidents, or external qualities known through the senses (color, weight, taste), remain unchanged. Protestant positions range from the Lutheran view of consubstantiation, which holds that Christ is present along with the unchanged reality of the bread and wine, to the symbolic interpretation of the Eucharist as a memorial of Christ's death.

euchre [yoo'-kur]   Euchre is a trump card game for two to four players, using 24 of the highest cards of a standard 52-card deck, with ace ranked high; when four play, 32 cards are used. Each player is dealt five cards face down; the next card is turned face up, and the players, in turn, accept or reject the turned card's suit as trump. Once a player accepts, the dealer takes the turned card and replaces it with one from his hand. When trump is determined, the jack of that suit becomes the highest trump, called right bower, and the jack of the same-colored suit, called left bower, becomes the second-highest trump. The rules of play are the same as those for WHIST. To win, the player (or team of partners) who names the trump suit must collect at least three of the five tricks in the play of one hand. If unsuccessful, he is *euchred.* When one side wins all five tricks, it scores a *march,* worth two points. A game is usually played to a total of five points.

Euchre is descended from a short, simple, 16th-century card game called triomphe, which gave rise to a widespread family of games. Three of them have at some time been considered "national" games: écarté in France, Napoleon in England, and euchre in the United States.

Euclid [yoo'-klid]   Euclid, fl. c.300 BC, is one of the most famous mathematicians of all time despite the fact that little is known of his life, save that he taught at Alexandria, Egypt. Euclid's *Elements,* an introductory work on elementary GEOMETRY and other topics, superseded other works of its kind. The *Elements* begins with definitions, postulates, and axioms, including the famous fifth, or parallel, postulate that one and only one line can be drawn through a point parallel to a given line. Euclid's decision to make this an indemonstrable assumption led to Euclidean geometry. The fifth postulate was later modified in order to develop NON-EUCLIDEAN GEOMETRIES.

While Euclid is not known to have made any original discoveries, and the *Elements* is based on the work of his predecessors, it is assumed that some of the proofs and the excellent arrangement are his. Euclid's other works include *Data, On Divisions of Figures, Phaenomena*, and *Optics.*

Euclid, shown studying a geometrical construction, wrote the mathematics textbook Elements. *A basic work for more than 2,000 years, it set a standard for deductive reasoning. Euclid, a Greek teacher and mathematician, also wrote treatises on optics and music.*

Euclidean geometry   see GEOMETRY

Eudoxus of Cnidus [yoo-dahk'-suhs ny'-duhs]
Eudoxus of Cnidus, c.408–c.355 BC, was a Greek scholar known for his work in mathematics, astronomy, geography, philosophy, and law. His theory of proportions solved the crisis in Greek mathematics that had arisen with the Pythagorean discovery of irrational numbers. His work on the method of exhaustion was the forerunner of INTEGRAL CALCULUS. His most influential contribution is the system of concentric spheres centered on the Earth, which he used to describe the apparently irregular motion of the planets. ARISTOTLE adopted this geometric system as the basis of his cosmology. None of Eudoxus's works survives.

Eugene   Eugene, the seat of Lane County in western Oregon, has a population of 112,669 (1990), which makes it the state's second largest city. It lies on the Willamette River, about 170 km (105 mi) south of Portland in the fertile valley formed by the Cascade Mountains to the east and Oregon's coastal range to the west. A center for the timber and wood products industries, as well as food processing, Eugene is the home of the University of Oregon (1872) and hosts numerous horse shows. Named for its first settler, Eugene Skinner, who arrived in the 1840s, the city has grown steadily since the arrival of the railroad in 1870.

Eugene of Savoy   Eugene of Savoy, b. Oct. 18, 1663, d. Apr. 20, 1736, was one of the many outstanding generals of foreign birth who served the Austrian Habsburgs in the 17th and 18th centuries. Unattractive and frail-looking, the prince grew up in France but could not obtain a commission in Louis XIV's army. In 1683 he sought his fortune with Emperor LEOPOLD I and fought in the army that lifted the Turkish siege of Vienna.

In subsequent campaigns to free Hungary from Ottoman control, Eugene displayed such remarkable courage and leadership ability that he was soon commanding armies of his own. He won three crushing victories against the Turks, at Zenta (1697), at Peterwardein (1716), and at Belgrade (1717).

During the War of the SPANISH SUCCESSION (1701–13), Eugene cooperated with the brilliant English general John Churchill, 1st duke of MARLBOROUGH, in a joint command; in 1714 he negotiated the Peace of Rastatt. Eugene was celebrated throughout Europe as a soldier, statesman, and patron of the arts.

Eugene Onegin   see PUSHKIN, ALEKSANDR; TCHAIKOVSKY, PETER ILICH

Eugene III, Pope   Eugene III, d. July 8, 1153, was pope from 1145 to 1153. A Pisan named Bernardo Paganelli, he was a Cistercian monk and abbot and a friend of Saint Bernard of Clairvaux. Eugene helped to promote the Second Crusade and worked to reform clerical behavior. Political problems with the Roman senate and with ARNOLD OF BRESCIA, a reformer and head of the senate, caused Eugene to absent himself from Rome frequently. He was beatified in 1872. Feast day: July 8.

---

eugenics [yoo-jen'-iks]   Eugenics, a science concerned with the control of hereditary traits through selective human mating, is also defined as the deliberate control, by law or social pressure, of the perpetuation of human genetic traits.

Charles DARWIN's theory (1859) of evolution by NATURAL SELECTION initiated modern eugenics as both a science and a social movement. By influencing reproduction, societies can affect both the direction and the rate at which human genetic evolution occurs. Sir Francis GALTON was the intellectual father of modern eugenics, a word he coined in 1883. As a social movement, eugenics encompasses all efforts to modify selection in order to bring about genetic change in a desired direction. Galton contended that the purpose of eugenics was not to copy the blind way in which selection often operates, but to deliberately change selection in a humane way.

Eugenics programs are classified as positive if their aim is to increase reproduction of individuals considered most valuable to society. One such program, AID (Artificial Insemination by Donor), uses sperm of a donor who is not the woman's husband; physicians usually select donors with well above average mental ability and physical health. Several thousand AID babies are born each year in the United States and Western Europe. The Repository for Germinal Choice, a unique facility founded in 1979 on similar concepts, stores the sperm of Nobel Laureates who agree to donate. Another eugenics-related measure was adopted by Singapore in 1983, when it afforded educational advantages to children born of educated women. In general, rapidly developing disciplines and technologies such as genetic counseling, GENETIC ENGINEERING, and AMNIOCENTESIS enable couples to take the lead in making their own decisions to achieve eugenic goals.

Negative eugenics programs seek to decrease reproduction by individuals with serious genetic handicaps. Most commonly this has taken the form of compulsory sterilization of such individuals. Nazi Germany took these practices to a terrible extreme in support of its theory of Nordic superiority to other races.

Eugénie [yoo-jee'-nee] Eugénia María de Montijo de Guzmán, b. May 5, 1826, d. July 11, 1920, was empress of France (1853–70) as consort of NAPOLEON III. Daughter of the Spanish conde de Montijo, she married Napoleon in January 1853. Eugénie's beauty, intelligence, and extravagance enlivened the court. Consulted on state affairs, she supported the disastrous project of making MAXIMILIAN emperor of Mexico in 1861. After Napoleon's deposition (September 1870) Eugénie went with him and their son, Louis Napoleon (1856–79), into exile in England.

Euglena [yoo-gleen'-uh] Euglenas, genus *Euglena,* comprise some 150 species of spindle-shaped eukaryotic (having a membrane-bound nucleus) organisms whose classification is uncertain. According to recent classification systems they belong to the phylum Euglenophyta of the kingdom Protista. In other systems they are considered protozoans of the phylum Mastigophora, because they have one, rarely two, flagella for locomotion and usually one nonemergent flagellum in the gullet. They have also been claimed by botanists for the kingdom Plantae. Nutrition is by photosynthesis occurring in chromatophores. Food is stored in starchlike glucose polymers (polysaccharides) called paramylum. A red eyespot, or stigma, is located at the anterior end. Euglenas have no cell wall; protein strips, in a helical arrangement, constitute the thin cell membrane. Reproduction is asexual, by longitudinal splitting in two. Euglenas are the common cause of the green or red color in ponds or rivers.

eukaryote [yoo-kair'-ee-oht] A eukaryote, or eucaryote, is any life-form consisting of one or more CELLS that contain a membrane-bound nucleus and organelles separate from the plasma membrane enveloping the cell. Cells of higher plants and animals are eukaryotic, whereas organisms such as bacteria and blue-green algae have cells without membrane-bound internal structures and are called prokaryotes. Life-forms called ARCHAEBACTERIA share some characteristics of both. Eukaryotes apparently evolved from prokaryotes somewhere back in Precambrian time.

Eulenspiegel, Till [oy'-len-shpec-gul] Till Eulenspiegel is the peasant hero of the oldest German chapbook (cheap, popular pamphlet) in prose. A supposedly historical figure of the 14th century, he appears in literature as a scapegoat clown and prankster of rustic simplicity whose practical jokes are aimed at craftsmen, innkeepers, nobles, and clergy. He is considered to personify Low German humor. The anonymous collection of farcical tales in which he figures as hero first appeared about 1480 and was soon translated into High German, Dutch, English, and French.

Euler, Leonhard [oy'-lur, lay'-ohn-hart] Leonhard Euler, b. Apr. 15, 1707, d. Sept. 18, 1783, was the most prolific mathematician in history. His 866 books and articles represent about one-third of the entire body of research on mathematics, theoretical physics, and engineering mechanics published between 1726 and 1800. In pure mathematics he integrated Leibniz's and Newton's works on DIFFERENTIAL CALCULUS into mathematical analysis, refined the notion of a FUNCTION, made common many mathematical notations, and introduced various TRANSCENDENTAL FUNCTIONS. He also worked on the calculus of variations, TOPOLOGY, and NUMBER THEORY. In physics he articulated Newtonian dynamics and laid the foundation of analytical mechanics. He elaborated continuum mechanics, also setting forth the kinetic theory of gases with the molecular model. In addition, he did fundamental research on lunar theory, elasticity, acoustics, optics, and hydromechanics.

Euler was born in Basel, Switzerland. His father, a pastor, wanted his son to prepare for the ministry and sent him to the University of Basel, but geometry soon became his favorite subject, so he changed his major to mathematics. He joined the Saint Petersburg Academy of

Science in 1727. When funds were withheld from the academy, he served as a medical lieutenant in the Russian navy from 1727 to 1730. He became professor of physics at the academy in 1730 and professor of mathematics in 1733. His reputation grew after the publication of many articles and his book *Mechanica* (1736–37), which extensively presented Newtonian dynamics in the form of mathematical analysis.

In 1741, Euler joined the Berlin Academy of Science, where he remained for 25 years. During his stay in Berlin, he wrote more than 200 articles, as well as three books on mathematical analysis. In 1755 he was elected a foreign member of the Paris Academy of Science.

In 1766, Euler returned to Russia, after Catherine the Great had made him a generous offer. In Russia, Euler became almost entirely blind after a cataract operation but continued to work, dictating various scientific treatises. At his death in 1783, he left a vast backlog of articles, which were published posthumously for nearly 50 more years.

Eumenes II, King of Pergamun Eumenes II, d. 159 BC, was the son of ATTALUS I, whom he succeeded as king in 197 BC. As his father had done, he adopted a policy of alliance with the Romans. Eumenes took advantage of the Roman wars in the East to extend his kingdom, acquiring much of Anatolia from ANTIOCHUS III. He played some part in bringing on the Third Macedonian War (171–168 BC), which ended in the Roman annexation of Macedonia, but thereafter lost the confidence of Rome. Under Eumenes, PERGAMUM reached the height of its prosperity as an independent state. The city, embellished by Eumenes' public buildings, became a major cultural center.

Eumenides see FURIES

euphonium see TUBA

Euphrates River [yoo-frayt'-eez] The Euphrates, with the TIGRIS RIVER, was the cradle of civilization in ancient Mesopotamia. The river begins at the confluence of the Kara Su (or Western Euphrates) and the Murat (or Eastern Euphrates), at Keban Dam in east central Turkey. From there it flows south, then southeast through Syria and Iraq. Above Basra, in southern Iraq, it joins the Tigris to form the SHATT-AL-ARAB, which flows about 160 km (100 mi) to the Persian Gulf. In the first third of its total length of 2,735 km (1,700 mi) the Euphrates drops steeply through the foothills of the Taurus Mountains to Syria, where it is joined by the Balikh and the al-Khabur rivers. The river's course narrows between limestone cliffs in Iraq until it reaches the town of Hit, where it enters a silt-covered alluvial floodplain with a hot, arid climate. Here, where irrigation canals, embankments, and two major reservoirs conserve and direct the river's waters, cereal grains and dates are cultivated by the FELLAHIN (Arab peasantry), and livestock is raised by the nomadic BEDOUIN. The river floods twice each year.

EURATOM see EUROPEAN COMMUNITY

Eureka [yoo-ree'-kuh] Eureka (1990 pop., 27,025), a Pacific port city on Humboldt Bay in northern California, is the seat of Humboldt County and a commercial center. Its industries include lumbering, fishing, shipping, and tourism. Eureka offers many examples of ornate Victorian architecture, a museum notable for Indian relics, an 18-ha (44-acre) redwood park, and an island wildlife refuge. Founded in 1850 by Canadian settlers, the city was incorporated in 1856.

eurhythmics [yur-rith'-miks] Eurhythmics (Greek: good rhythm) is a system of rhythmic education evolved by Émile Jaques DALCROZE from about 1897, first gaining public recognition in 1905. Originally developed as an aid to the musician, the system is based on the thesis that the source of musical rhythm is in the body and that the fullest experience of rhythm is achieved through physical expression. Dalcroze believed that the memory of rhythmic experience persists in the body's muscles after the original motor experience is past. To perfect his system he selected movements that systematically develop the student's musical ability. Thus the study of eurhythmics teaches the student to express musical rhythm creatively in spontaneous body movements accompanied by percussion or other musical instruments. Eurhythmics places emphasis on what Dalcroze called "plastic movement," or movement that flows freely from the music and the individual personality.

Eurhythmics had a profound effect on the early development of modern dance, and on physical education and physical therapy.

Euripides [yur-ip'-i-deez] Euripides, youngest of the three great Greek tragedians, was born c.485 BC, possibly on Salamis, and died in Macedonia in 406. Though he was scarcely a generation younger than SOPHOCLES, his world view better reflects the political, social, and intellectual crises of late 5th-century Athens. All but one of his surviving tragedies were written during the Peloponnesian War, which eventually destroyed Athens. Of the 92 plays he wrote, 19 survive intact—more than the combined total for AESCHYLUS and Sophocles—including the satyr play *Cyclops* and the possibly spurious *Rhesus*.

Anecdotes about Euripides' life are important in two ancient sources, a recently discovered biography by Satyrus and the comedies of ARISTOPHANES, particularly *The Acharnians*, *The Thesmophoriazusae*, and *The Frogs*, in which the playwright is frequently satirized. He was friendly with the philosophers Anaxagoras and Socrates and with Sophists such as Protagoras and Prodicus, and his plays reflect contemporary ethics, rhetoric, and science. He may have been prosecuted for impiety by the demagogue Cleon. Shortly after 408 he left Athens for the court of Archelaus, king of Macedon, and there wrote one of his greatest plays, *The Bacchae*.

Euripides, a great Athenian tragedian of the 5th century BC, addressed the moral questions of divine fallibility and human frailty in his plays. His unheroic representation of gods and mortals led to a charge of blasphemy, and eventually he fled Athens to live in Macedonia.

Medea (431), *Hippolytus* (428), *Hecuba* (c.425), and *Heracles* (c.430–423), written early in the Peloponnesian War, are plays of passion and revenge; *The Children of Heracles* (c.430), *Andromache* (c.426), and *The Suppliant Women* (c.422) are patriotic plays; *Iphigeneia in Tauris, Helen,* and *Ion* (all c.414–412) are romantic melodramas in which long lost loved ones discover each other; the plays of Euripides's last period (409–406)— *The Phoenician Women, Orestes, Iphigeneia at Aulis,* and *The Bacchae*—exhibit increasingly episodic structure, greater irony, and a mood suggestive of the dissolution of values then taking place.

Of the three great classical writers of TRAGEDY, Euripides is the least classical. Aristotle, in his *Poetics,* however, called him "the most tragic" because of his powerful depictions of pathos and suffering. In *The Trojan Women, Alcestis, Medea, Hippolytus, Heracles,* and *The Bacchae,* Euripides portrays violent emotion, erotic passion, and insanity with almost clinical insight. Medea's vengeful infanticide, Phaedra's incestuous passion and Hippolytus's vehement prudishness, the madness of Heracles, and the delusions of Pentheus and Agave in *The Bacchae* lay bare the sordid side of ambition and the coexistence of conflicting emotions. Euripides could also depict tenderness and love, as in Alcestis's self-sacrifice for her husband and children and the recognition scenes of *Iphigeneia in Tauris* and *Ion.*

Less reverent than Aeschylus or Sophocles, Euripides criticized traditional religion and shocked contemporaries by representing mythical figures as everyday, unheroic people or even as abnormal or neurotic personalities. His heroes are often victims of divine cruelty. Considered a misogynist because of his unsparing analysis of feminine passion, he was in fact highly sympathetic to the plight of women in 5th-century Athens.

Euripides' enormous range spans contradictory tendencies: he was both a rationalist and a romanticist; he both criticized the traditional gods and celebrated religious phenomena like the Maenadism of *The Bacchae;* he was the author of both patriotic and antiwar plays, and of plays with happy endings and of the bitterest tragedies.

He incorporated the new intellectual and scientific movements into his works but also conveyed the irresistible power of the irrational. Original and experimental, he parodied the conventions of tragedy and also used new theories about the illusionistic and deceptive powers of language. He created tragicomic plots (*Ion, Helen, Iphigeneia in Tauris*) that foreshadowed the so-called New Comedy. His deheroization, psychology, and use of the *deus ex machina* (see NARRATIVE AND DRAMATIC DEVICES) colored later drama. He was especially popular in the centuries after his death and profoundly influenced Seneca's tragedies.

Eurodollar [yur'-oh-dahl-ur]   U.S. dollars that are held or loaned by foreign banks outside the United States are called Eurodollars. Originally Eurodollars were almost exclusively European bank deposits or loans, but they quickly became a global phenomenon with large amounts in Japan, Canada, and the Middle East. Eurodollars are not subject to the U.S. Federal Reserve System regulations applied to dollars held within the United States. The result is that Eurodollars—one of several similar currencies collectively called Eurocurrency—acquire a life of their own, financing international commerce, unifying monetary systems, and obstructing the exercise of coherent national monetary policies.

Europa (astronomy) [yur-oh'-puh]   Europa, a satellite of the planet JUPITER, has a diameter of 3,126 km (1,942 mi). It is the smallest of that planet's four Galilean satellites, so called because they were discovered by Galileo in 1610. Compared to most solid planets and satellites, Europa is as smooth as a billiard ball. Its bright surface is crisscrossed by darker lines up to 70 km (45 mi) wide and 1,000 km (600 mi) long. Some are flat, and others are ridges or grooves that vary by only a few hundred meters from the rest of the surface. There are also smaller streaks, and regions of mottled terrain. Only a few low craters exist, which means the surface is relatively young.

Because Europa has a density 3.04 times that of water, it probably consists mostly of rock, with a mantle of water ice only about 75 to 100 km (45 to 60 mi) thick. Because of the lack of craters, astronomers speculate that Europa was covered with an ocean of water until its frozen surface formed. Because ice is less dense than water, the surface then expanded and cracked to form the fine lines. Some astronomers suggest that Europa will remain warm enough for a few hundred million more years to maintain a liquid sea sandwiched between the surface and the core.

Europa (mythology)   In Greek mythology, Europa, the daughter of Agenor and sister of Cadmus, was loved by the god Zeus. Disguised as a beautiful white bull, he persuaded Europa to mount his back and then swam to Crete with her. Europa bore three sons by Zeus—Minos, Rhadamanthus, and Sarpedon. Eventually she married Asterius, king of Crete.

AT A GLANCE

EUROPE

Area: 10,531,623 km² (4,066,281 mi²); 7.0% of the world's land area.
Population: 684,800,000 (1988 est.); 13.5% of the total world population. *Density*— 65 persons per km² (168.4 per mi²).
Coastline: 80,500 km (50,000 mi).
Elevation: *Highest*—Mount Elbrus, 5,633 m (18,481 ft); *lowest*—Caspian Sea, 28 m (92 ft) below sea level.
Northernmost Point: North Cape, Norway, 71°10'20"N.
Southernmost Point: Cape Tarifa, Spain, 36°01'N.
Westernmost Mainland Point: Cape Roca, Portugal, 9°30'W.
Easternmost Point: Ural Mountains, USSR.
Principal Rivers: Danube, Volga, Rhine, Dnepr, Po, Elbe, Oder, Vistula, Dvina, Donets, Don, Dnestr, Ebro, Loire, Thames.
Principal Seas: Mediterranean Sea, North Sea, Black Sea, Baltic Sea, Caspian Sea.
Principal Mountain Ranges: Alps, Caucasus, Carpathians, Pyrenees, Apennines, Urals.
Political Divisions: 31 entire separate countries, part of the USSR, part of Turkey, Faeroe Islands (self-governing part of Denmark), various dependencies.

Europe   Europe, including the European portion of the USSR, ranks sixth in size among the continents; only Australia is smaller. Covering 10,531,623 km² (4,066,281 mi²), Europe is one of the most densely populated land areas of the Earth. It has a population of 684,800,000 (1988 est.), including the European USSR, or an average of 65 people per km² (168 per mi²).

Water bounds Europe on the north (BARENTS SEA), west (ATLANTIC OCEAN), and south (MEDITERRANEAN SEA). The eastern land boundary is traditionally defined by a line following the URAL MOUNTAINS, southeast to the CASPIAN SEA, then across to the BLACK SEA south of the CAUCASUS MOUNTAINS, and cutting through the BOSPORUS, Sea of MARMARA, and the DARDANELLES. Actually, Europe is a large peninsula of the Eurasian landmass. The eastern boundary of Europe is also sometimes defined as the western border of the USSR.

Peninsulas, bays, islands, and fjords give the southern, western, and northern areas of Europe irregular coastlines. Consequently the coastline is unusually long for the total area and is estimated at 80,500 km (50,000 mi), longer than that of Africa. In Norway alone the north-south distance is about 1,770 km (1,100 mi), but the coastline, with its numerous fjords and approximately 150,000 islands, is nearly 20,125 km (12,500 mi) long. Great Britain, Ireland, and Iceland are the major islands of Europe. Smaller groups include the ORKNEYS, SHETLANDS, FAEROES, and the CHANNEL ISLANDS. All except Iceland and the Faeroes are on the European continental shelf.

Europe is complex and diverse in physical, economic, historical, political, and social makeup. The Alpine mountain system is the most outstanding physical feature; it dominates the south central portion of the continent and is the source of many major European rivers.

Historically, Europe has held an importance in the world that far exceeded its relative size and population. Many world social movements, economic systems, and political ideas have begun in Europe. In the 20th century, however, the continent has suffered several setbacks. At the end of World War II the countries of Europe were greatly weakened economically and politically. Moreover, as the COLD WAR era began, the continent was divided between the countries in the Soviet bloc and those aligned with the United States. The latter received massive economic aid through the MARSHALL PLAN, and many of them entered the NORTH ATLANTIC TREATY ORGANIZATION (NATO; established 1949). Another factor that weakened European world-power status after World War II was the loss of colonial territories by the British, French, Dutch, Belgians, and, more recently, the Portuguese.

The concept of economic union was implemented to offset the disadvantages of loss of resources and political and economic power by the individual European nations. The European Economic Community (Common Market, or EEC) was formed in Western Europe in 1958. Its goal is to pool resources, production, and labor into one large market by abolishing all customs barriers, and in general to promote European unity. The elimination of trade barriers has proceeded gradually over a period of decades,

Arctic Circle
3734m +
+ 2952m
North Cape
Hammerfest
BAR
S

ICELAND
Akureyri
Reykjavik
Hvannadalshnúkur
+ 2119m

Tromsø
Lofoten Islands
+ Kebnekaise
2111m
LAPLAND

NORWEGIAN
SEA

FAEROE
ISLANDS
(Den.)

Shetland Is.

Trondheim

West Fjord
Storsjön
Luleå
Oulu
SWEDEN
FINLAND

ATLANTIC

OCEAN

Hebrides
Orkney Is.
Ben Nevis
1343m +
Devils Hole
239m +

Glasgow
Edinburgh
Belfast
IRELAND
Newcastle
Dublin
Liverpool Manchester
Cork
St George's Channel
Irish Sea
UNITED
KINGDOM
Cardiff Birmingham
Land's End
London

153m +

+ 5080m

Bergen
NORWAY
+ Glittertinden
2472m
Oslo
Stavanger
Kristiansand

+ 46m
DENMARK
Ålborg
Århus
JUTLAND
Copenhagen
Fyn
Zealand
Bornholm
Rostock

Tampere
Turku Helsinki

Stockholm
Hiiumaa
Saaremaa
Åland
Tallinn
(Reval)
Lake
Peipus
Ler

Gulf of Bothnia
Lake
Vänern
Lake
Vättern
Mälaren
Göteborg
Gotland
Öland
Gulf of
Riga
Riga

BALTIC
SEA
Neman
Western Dvina

+ 15m
Malmö

Kalininrad
(Königsberg)
Min

Gdańsk
(Danzig)
POLAND
Warsaw

NORTH SEA

Frisian Islands
Hamburg
NETHERLANDS
Amsterdam
Rotterdam
Antwerp
BELGIUM Essen
Lille Brussels Cologne
Channel
Islands
(U.K.)
Le Havre Bonn
LUXEMBOURG

Berlin
Poznań
Warta
Vistula

Brest

English Channel
Str. of Dover

GERMANY
Frankfurt
am Main
Main

Leipzig
Wrocław
Katowice
Kraków
(Cracow)
Lvov

Paris
Nantes
Loire

Strasbourg
Stuttgart
Munich

Prague
Ostrava
CZECHOSLOVAKIA
Gerlach Pk.
2655m
CARPATHIAN MOUNTAINS

5098m +

Bay
of
Biscay

FRANCE
Zurich
Bern
SWITZERLAND LIECH.
MASSIF
CENTRAL
Lyon
Mt. Blanc
4807m
ALPS

Lake
Constance
Vienna
AUSTRIA
Graz
Budapest
Debrecen
HUNGARY
Balaton
Cluj-Napoca

Cape Finisterre
La Coruña
CORDILLERA CANTABRICA
Bilbao
Bordeaux
Toulouse
PYRENEES
Aneto Peak
3404m ANDORRA
Porto
Duero
PORTUGAL

Marseille
MONACO
Turin
Genoa
Milan
Bologna
Venice
Zagreb
Moldoveanu
2543m
ROMANIA
Bucharest
Belgrade
YUGOSLAVIA
Danube

40°

Lisbon
Madrid
SPAIN
Barcelona
Guadiana
SIERRA MORENA
Valencia
Seville
Mulhacén
3478m SIERRA
NEVADA
GIBRALTAR
(U.K.)
Tangier

Balearic Islands
(Spain)
Palma
Majorca
CORSICA
(Fr.)
Ajaccio
Elba
SARDINIA
(Italy)
Cagliari

APENNINES
ITALY SAN
MARINO
Rome
Naples + Vesuvius
1277m
Bari
ALBANIA
Tiranë
Split
ADRIATIC SEA
Ligurian Sea
TYRRHENIAN
SEA

Ionian Islands
Skopje
Salonika
Mt. Olympus +
2917m
GREECE
Lesbos
Chios
AEGEAN

BULGARIA
Sofia

2887m +

MEDITERRANEAN
SEA

Palermo
Mt. Etna
3323m
SICILY

IONIAN
SEA

Patras
Athens
PELOPONNESUS

Rabat
Casablanca
Oran
Algiers
Tunis

MOROCCO
ATLAS MOUNTAINS
ALGERIA
TUNISIA
Valletta
MALTA
+ 4135m
Crete
Iráklion

Strait of Gibraltar
Sierra de Sevilla

© 1980, 1991 Rand McNally & Co.
A-550090-772
WEST 0° EAST

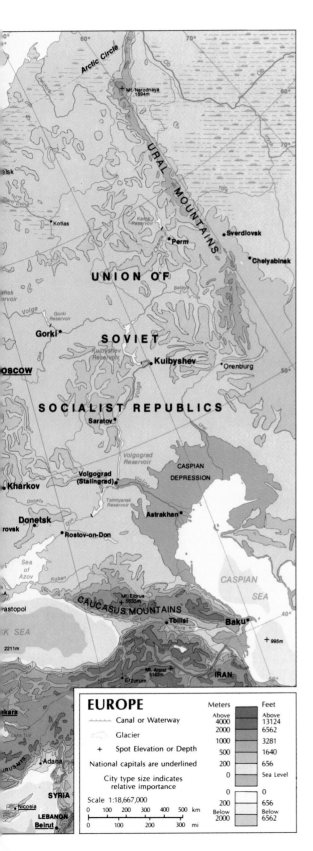

The Houses of Parliament, the seat of the United Kingdom's legislature, are situated along the northern bank of the Thames River in London.

and is scheduled to be completed by the end of 1992. The EUROPEAN COMMUNITY (EC)—established in 1967—has provided the EEC nations with common political institutions, such as the European Parliament, which meets in Strasbourg, France, and the powerful European Commission, headquartered in Brussels. The eventual aim of the EC is the political unification of its member countries.

Somewhat comparable institutions, the WARSAW TREATY ORGANIZATION and the COUNCIL FOR MUTUAL ECONOMIC ASSISTANCE (Comecon), were established in Eastern Europe after World War II by the USSR, but these ceased to be of great significance when the Soviet satellite system broke up in 1989–90.

The disappearance of the Eastern European Communist regimes, the reunification of Germany, and the radical transformation of the USSR under Mikhail Gorbachev dramatically altered the European political picture in the early 1990s. The IRON CURTAIN that had divided East from West since the 1940s suddenly vanished, and where Communism had been supreme, one country after another began turning toward a free-market economy.

Land and Resources

Geology and Landforms. Europe can be divided into two major areas—western peninsular Europe and eastern continental Europe—each characterized by its differing landforms. The western and southern portions have a complex pattern of mountains, valleys, plateaus, and lowlands. In contrast, eastern Europe, including the Soviet Union, consists largely of a stable geologic platform with limited amounts of local relief. The northern third of the continent was much altered by continental glaciation during the PLEISTOCENE EPOCH (from about 2,000,000 to 10,000 years ago); the massive ice sheets of the Ice Age left the area only 10,000–12,000 years ago. The mountains of Scotland and Scandinavia were rounded by ice scouring, and glacial debris was deposited in old valleys. Glacial disruption of drainage left much poorly drained land

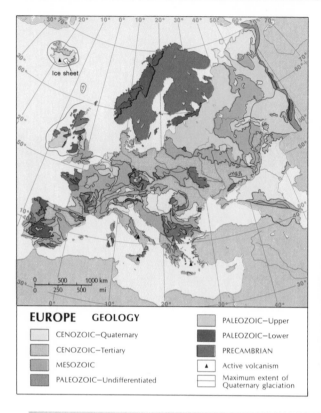

EUROPE GEOLOGY

- CENOZOIC–Quaternary
- CENOZOIC–Tertiary
- MESOZOIC
- PALEOZOIC–Undifferentiated
- PALEOZOIC–Upper
- PALEOZOIC–Lower
- PRECAMBRIAN
- ▲ Active volcanism
- Maximum extent of Quaternary glaciation

(Above) *The Alps, Europe's most important mountain system, extends across the south central portion of the continent between southeastern France and northwestern Yugoslavia.*

(Left) *The Dordogne River valley in southwestern France is an agricultural district noted for the growing of cereal crops.*

(Below) *The lowlands bordering the North Sea in the Netherlands are commonly used for pasture.*

(Above) *The Mediterranean coast of Monaco, a small independent principality bordering southeastern France, is famed for its beaches.*

(Right) *A mountain stream courses through Telemark, a rugged province in southeastern Norway.*

(Below) *Thera, or Santorini, is the southernmost of the Cyclades, a group of Greek volcanic islands in the Aegean Sea.*

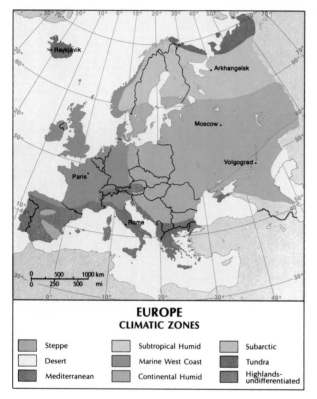

EUROPE
CLIMATIC ZONES

Steppe		Subtropical Humid		Subarctic	
Desert		Marine West Coast		Tundra	
Mediterranean		Continental Humid		Highlands-undifferentiated	

The Northwest Highlands of Scandinavia and Finland have a subdued mountain topography. This landscape was formed over millions of years by repeated uplifting and erosion, with the more recent leveling and rounding of landforms by continental glaciation. The geologically younger highlands formed by the Hercynian orogeny consist of the high plateau of the Iberian Peninsula (the Meseta), the Bohemian highlands of Czechoslovakia, the MASSIF CENTRAL and VOSGES mountains of France, and the mountains and plateaus of central and southern Germany. The Alpine system is a series of geologically young mountains with sharp peaks and deep, narrow valleys. In addition to the Alps themselves, this system includes the CARPATHIANS, Balkan Mountains, Transylvanian Alps, DINARIC ALPS, Pindus Mountains, APENNINES, and the SIERRA NEVADA of southern Spain. The central lowlands, which have a level to gently undulating relief, begin in southeast England and northern France and stretch to the east across Germany and Poland, finally widening to include most of eastern Europe.

Climate. Europe has four dominant types of climate: maritime in the west, continental in the east and north, Mediterranean in the south, and mountain in the highlands. The maritime climate has moderate temperatures in both summer and winter. The temperatures at LA CORUÑA, in northwestern Spain, average 18° C (64° F) in July and 10° C (50° F) in January. This area also has a relatively long growing season, except in its northern reaches in the British Isles and Norway. Precipitation of 510–1,015 mm (20–40 in) is distributed evenly throughout the year, although the weather is subject to frequent changes. The winters in northwestern Europe are moderated by the warming effect of the North Atlantic Drift, which is a continuation of the GULF STREAM.

The continental climate is characterized by extreme differences between winter and summer temperatures. Temperatures in MOSCOW average -12° C (10° F) in January and 16° C (60° F) in July. A precipitation maximum occurs in summer with storms caused by convection of air that has been heated over the land. The growing season is short, and annual precipitation averages about 635 mm (25 in).

The regions on the Mediterranean coast have dry, hot summers (the average July temperature is about 22° C/72° F) and cool to mild, rainy winters (the average January temperature is about 8° C/46° F). Rainfall averages from less than 760 mm (30 in) in the lowlands to over 1,015 mm (40 in) in the highlands. Highland areas, notably in the Alps and Caucasus, have a large range of climatic conditions depending upon their height and orientation in relation to the prevailing winds. Generally, temperatures range from -4° C (25° F) in January to 16° C (60° F) in July. Rainfall averages from 510 mm (20 in) in the hills to more than 2,030 mm (80 in) in the mountains.

The climate of Europe, especially in the west, is far more moderate than that at the same latitude in eastern North America. This is due to the marine influences of the relatively warm waters of the North Atlantic Drift, which are brought on shore by the prevailing westerly winds. The major air pressure systems include the Icelandic Low, dominant in winter but influential all year, which

in the north of Europe, and melting ice filled many lakes. The deep fjords of Norway were formed by glacial action eroding old river valleys. The high mountains in the south, such as the ALPS, PYRENEES, and Caucasus, bore glaciers that deepened the valleys and sharpened the peaks.

The highest elevations in Europe are found in the Caucasus Mountains (Mount ELBRUS, 5,633 m/18,481 ft) and the Alps (Mont BLANC, 4,807 m/15,771 ft). The Pyrenees rise to a high point of 3,404 m (11,168 ft); the JOTUNHEIMEN in Scandinavia reaches an elevation of 2,472 m (8,110 ft), and BEN NEVIS in Scotland (1,343 m/4,406 ft) is the highest point in the British Isles. Many of Europe's coastal regions are at, or only slightly above, sea level. The lowest point of the continent, the surface of the Caspian Sea, is 28 m (92 ft) below sea level. Denmark's highest point is below 175 m (570 ft), and this is typical of the elevations of the large glaciated plain of central Europe. Western Europe is fortunate in having considerable areas of lowland plains located between its numerous highlands as well as the glaciated plains of the northern and central regions of the continent.

The four major physiographic divisions that constitute Europe are: the Precambrian resistant rocks of the Northwest Highlands; the varied Hercynian Highlands of central Europe; the rugged Alpine system of southern Europe (the Pyrenees and Caucasus are of similar geologic age and landform character); and the recent sediments due to glacial or riverine deposition in the European Lowlands.

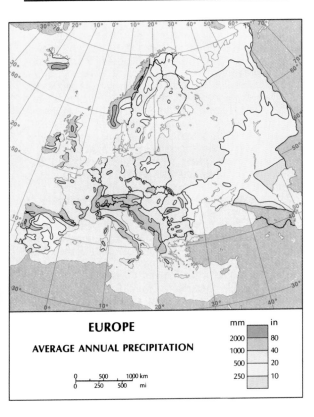

EUROPE

AVERAGE ANNUAL PRECIPITATION

	mm	in
	2000	80
	1000	40
	500	20
	250	10

0 500 1000 km
0 250 500 mi

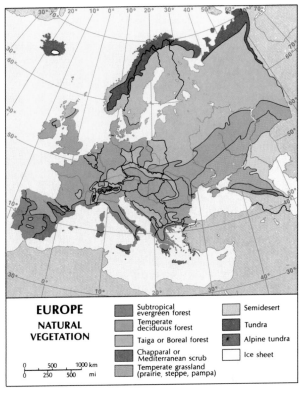

EUROPE

NATURAL VEGETATION

- Subtropical evergreen forest
- Temperate deciduous forest
- Taiga or Boreal forest
- Chapparal or Mediterranean scrub
- Temperate grassland (prairie, steppe, pampa)
- Semidesert
- Tundra
- Alpine tundra
- Ice sheet

0 500 1000 km
0 250 500 mi

is the origin of the cyclonic storms so important in the changing weather conditions in western and northern Europe. The Azores High, dominant in the summer, extends over southern Europe and is responsible for the hot, dry, stable weather of the Mediterranean region. The Siberian High, dominant in the winter, extends the cold, dry air of the interior of the Eurasian landmass over eastern and central Europe. The Southwest Asian Low, dominant during the summer, pulls the moist marine air from the Atlantic into Europe and furnishes the precipitation necessary for agricultural production. The Alps prevent much of this northern, moist air from entering the Mediterranean regions in the summer.

Drainage. Most major rivers of western Europe originate in the Alps or in the central European mountain systems. These include the RHINE, RHÔNE, SAÔNE, PO, DANUBE, ELBE, and VISTULA. Rivers of eastern Europe, flowing mostly to the south, include the DNEPR, Donets, and VOLGA. All the rivers of Europe, with the exception of those in the Mediterranean region, have a rather even flow due to the even distribution of precipitation throughout the year. The rivers of the Scandinavian Peninsula, the Alps, and other highlands generate large quantities of hydroelectric power for Europe's industries.

Soils and Vegetation. The complex patterns of soils and vegetation in western Europe are related to the variety of landforms, rock structures, and climates. The soil characteristics of regions that were covered by continental

glaciation vary, depending on the amount of sand, gravel, clay, and organic material (as in peat) found in that particular type of glacial deposit.

The TUNDRA region of the northern Scandinavia Highlands has a predominantly moss, lichen, and dwarf-birch vegetation growing in a thin, acid, poorly drained soil, which is of low fertility. To the south of this is a broad zone of coniferous trees, the taiga, which extends from Scandinavia across the northern USSR. It has a podzol soil that is gray in color, highly leached, has little organic matter, and is low in fertility. The deciduous forest region that constitutes much of western Europe has, to a large extent, been denuded to make way for agriculture. Forests are predominantly hardwood, with beech and oak being most typical. This region has a deep layer of brown forest soil that is leached and contains a considerable amount of decayed organic material and is relatively fertile. In the Mediterranean area, the natural vegetation is xerophytic, or drought resistant, and consists of cypress, cork oak, scrub evergreen, olive, and low bushes. A vegetation of trees and scrub brush in this region is called maquis. The soil is often reddish in color, indicating a high iron content. The low amounts of precipitation in this region result in little leaching of the soil, and the humus content is low from lack of leaf fall.

In eastern Europe, the vegetal progression from north to south is tundra, coniferous, mixed coniferous and deciduous, deciduous forest, wooded steppe, prairie grasses, and semiarid shrub vegetation. The humus content and degree of leaching of the soil increase southward; thus the color changes from gray to brown and black (prairie) and then back to brown and gray (dry areas). The black prairie soils (chernozems) of the steppe regions are the most fertile in Europe, but precipitation is unreliable, and consequently agricultural production often suffers.

Fauna. The native animal life of Europe has been greatly disturbed in types, numbers, and distribution by man's long occupation of the continent. Reindeer graze the moss and lichen in the high plateau areas of the far north. Numerous fur-bearing animals such as wolves, marten, foxes, bears, and beavers are found in the cold forest and mountain regions. Deer are common in most forested areas. Also common are many types of small mammals such as rabbits, squirrels, otters, moles, marmots, lemmings, and hedgehogs. The lakes, rivers, and coastal waters are rich in a variety of fish life. Cod, herring, halibut, haddock, and mackerel are abundant in the continental shelf waters of the North Sea and west of the British Isles and Norway. Tuna and sardines are common in the Mediterranean Sea and the Bay of Biscay and sturgeon in the Black and Caspian seas. Freshwater fish such

as salmon and trout are found in the coastal rivers of Scandinavia and Scotland. Birdlife is varied and widespread and includes storks, seabirds, ravens, and eagles.

Mineral Resources. Europe is fortunate in possessing considerable amounts of two of the necessities of an industrialized society, namely, coal and iron ore. Nevertheless, western Europe has traditionally had inadequate supplies of natural gas and petroleum. This situation is changing, however, with the development of NORTH SEA oil and natural gas reserves. The continent's hilly-to-mountainous terrain and reliable precipitation create a good hydroelectric power potential that is highly utilized in the Scandinavian countries as well as in and around the Alpine mountain system.

Coal deposits are widespread throughout Europe, with the exception of the Scandinavian and the Mediterranean countries. Europe produces about one-third of the world's anthracite and bituminous coal. The best quality deposits are in the RUHR area of Germany, northern France, and southern Belgium; the Saar field on the French-German border; the flanks of the PENNINE Chain in Great Britain; the Silesian field of southern Poland and northern Czechoslovakia; and in several areas of the European USSR, in-

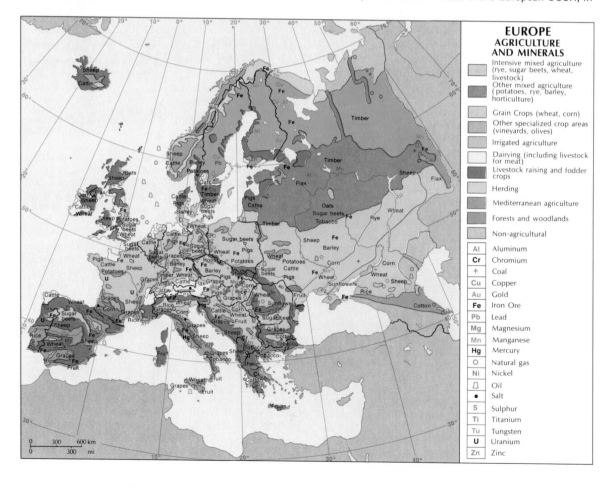

EUROPE AGRICULTURE AND MINERALS

- Intensive mixed agriculture (rye, sugar beets, wheat, livestock)
- Other mixed agriculture (potatoes, rye, barley, horticulture)
- Grain Crops (wheat, corn)
- Other specialized crop areas (vineyards, olives)
- Irrigated agriculture
- Dairying (including livestock for meat)
- Livestock raising and fodder crops
- Herding
- Mediterranean agriculture
- Forests and woodlands
- Non-agricultural

Al	Aluminum
Cr	Chromium
+	Coal
Cu	Copper
Au	Gold
Fe	Iron Ore
Pb	Lead
Mg	Magnesium
Mn	Manganese
Hg	Mercury
O	Natural gas
Ni	Nickel
◊	Oil
•	Salt
S	Sulphur
Ti	Titanium
Tu	Tungsten
U	Uranium
Zn	Zinc

The Eiffel Tower, a 300-m (984-ft) landmark designed by Alexandre Gustave Eiffel for the Centennial Exposition of 1889, dominates the skyline of Paris.

cluding the DONETS BASIN. Low-quality brown coal, or lignite, is found in Germany. The industrial burning of coal, especially in some eastern European countries, has caused severe pollution problems.

The major iron ore deposits are found in Lorraine in northeastern France, northern Sweden, KRIVOI ROG (the Ukraine), and the southern Urals (MAGNITOGORSK) in the USSR. With the exception of those in northern Sweden, iron ore and coal deposits are located near one another and relatively near population centers. Europe produces about two-fifths of the world's iron ore.

Europe's major areas for the production of oil and natural gas are the North Sea, the Russian fields around the Caspian Sea, and the northern plains of the European USSR. Smaller fields are found in southwestern France, the Po Valley of Italy, in the Netherlands and Germany, and in Romania. Europe supplies only a small percentage of its own oil and natural gas needs.

Two other minerals of major importance in Europe are bauxite in southern France, Yugoslavia, Hungary, and the Urals; and potash in France, Germany, Spain, and the European USSR. A variety of other minerals are mined, including copper, lead, zinc, ferro alloys, and precious metals such as gold and silver. Europe is fortunate in that much of its total mineral resources is located near industrial and population centers or is easily accessible by land and water transportation.

Water Resources. Western Europe normally has sufficient surface and groundwater supplies due to its well-distributed precipitation, extensive river network, and numerous lakes in areas of continental glaciation. The reliability of the water supply decreases eastward and becomes deficient in the regions north of the Caspian Sea and during the summer in the areas with Mediterranean climate. Irrigation is widely practiced in Greece, Italy, southern France, Spain, Portugal, and the southern Euro-

pean USSR. The production of hydroelectric power depends on the regularity of water flow and the vertical fall of rivers. Thus, Europe is relatively well furnished with hydroelectric power, the Alps and the Scandinavian Highlands being the principal production areas along with the Volga and other rivers in the European USSR. Also, many rivers throughout the continent have been dammed to supply power. Large portions of the Mediterranean, as well as many of Europe's major rivers, have been seriously polluted, industrially and otherwise.

Arable Land. Despite the numerous highland areas of western and southern Europe, the continent has large areas of arable land. The countries with the highest percentages of land under cultivation are the United Kingdom, Denmark, the Netherlands, and France, all of which have large areas of plains. Most countries of western Europe have nearly 50% of their land arable, except the Scandinavian states, where the percentages are low due to extensive highlands and cold climates. Eastern Europe does not have a large area of highlands, but wetlands and forests preclude cultivation in many areas.

Forest Resources. Two principal forest areas supply much of the forest-product needs of the European people. The coniferous forests that extend from the Scandinavian Peninsula into the northwestern USSR are an excellent stand of commercial pines, spruces, and hemlock. The slopes of the Alps and the other mountainous areas of central and southern Europe, containing coniferous and deciduous trees, are the only other major forest resources of the continent. Some major forests, such as the Black Forest of Germany, have suffered the effects of acid rain.

People

Ethnic Groups, Languages, and Religions. The diversity of ethnic groups in Europe is indicated by the large number of small political units. During the nationalistic peri-

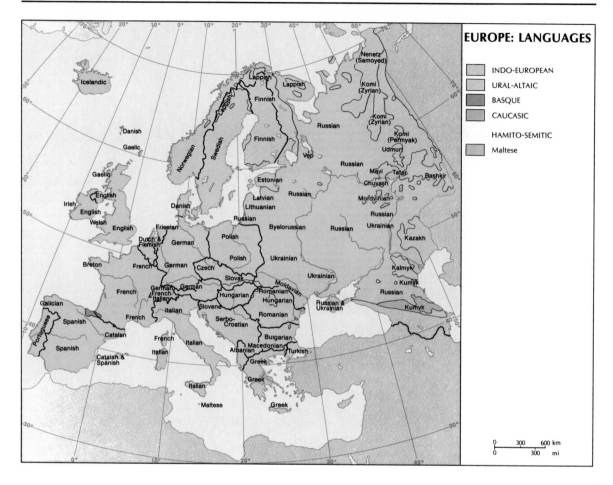

EUROPE: LANGUAGES

INDO-EUROPEAN

URAL-ALTAIC

BASQUE

CAUCASIC

HAMITO-SEMITIC

Maltese

ods of the 19th century, an attempt was made to draw boundaries around ethnic, linguistic, and cultural groups, with the result that today there are more autonomous political divisions than there were 100 years ago. Even

though nearly all the people are classified as Caucasian, there are major differences in color of skin, hair, and eyes. Light or fair pigmentation is dominant in northwestern Europe, including northern Russia, and darker pigmentation is common in southern Europe.

Most of the languages of Europe fall into the INDO-EUROPEAN classification, the major groupings of which include the Germanic, Romance, and Slavic families. The Germanic group is found in Germany, Austria, Switzerland, the United Kingdom, the Netherlands, Belgium, Norway, Sweden, and Iceland. The Romance group is found in France, Iberia (Spain and Portugal), Italy, southern Belgium, the western part of Switzerland, and Romania. Slavic languages dominate in eastern Europe and include Russian, Belorussian, and Ukrainian in the Soviet Union; Czech and Slovak in Czechoslovakia; Polish; Bulgarian; and Serbo-Croatian in Yugoslavia. Greece has a Hellenic language; Albania, a Thraco-Illyrian. A Baltic language group exists east of the Baltic Sea. The Celtic language is found in Brittany in France and in the western parts of Wales, Ireland, and Scotland. The Basque language is spoken by a small group on the Spanish-French border. The non-Indo-European languages, found in Hun-

A view of Rome as seen from Saint Peter's Basilica, the largest Christian church in the world, overlooks the Piazza de San Pietro, a vast, colonnaded courtyard.

(Top row) *A gentlemen* (left) *attending the Burghley Horse Trials wears a bowler hat, a fashion associated with traditional British businessmen. A farmer* (center) *from a rural Italian district uses his donkey to bring produce to market. A young woman* (right) *in Poland wears a traditional folk costume worn by generations of her ancestors.* (Bottom row) *A Lapp girl* (left) *in Sweden poses at the entrance to her parents' tent. The age-creased features of a Romanian woman* (center) *testify to her long years of labor in the fields. An elderly Greek farmer* (right) *prunes grapes in his vineyard near Manos.*

gary, Finland, and the Baltic states, belong to the Finno-Ugric group of URAL-ALTAIC LANGUAGES; they probably reflect the movement of people out of the Ural Mountain region.

Roman Catholic, Protestant, and Orthodox churches dominate in Europe. Protestant sects are found mostly in Germany, the Netherlands, the United Kingdom, and the Scandinavian countries. Roman Catholics are predominant in Ireland, Belgium, France, Iberia, Italy and the eastern European countries that were included in the Holy Roman Empire. The Orthodox church was established by the Byzantine Empire and is the majority religion in the countries of southeastern Europe and the European USSR. Pockets of Islam are found in the Balkan Peninsula, and Judaism is common in urban areas, especially in western Europe.

Education and Health. Europe has long been a world center of educational progress and a generator of new ideas. Three universities in Italy and one each in France and England were established before 1200. Italy and France continued as centers of university development until 1500, and Spain and Germany also developed centers of higher learning. After 1500, universities appeared in northwestern and eastern Europe and European Russia. The literacy rates are very high in western, central, northern, and eastern Europe. Illiteracy is higher in the southern European countries.

The patterns indicating the level of health roughly follow those of educational and industrial development. The highest life expectancy, nutritional levels, and availability of doctors and health care facilities are found in western and northern Europe and decrease southward toward the Mediterranean countries. The highest life expectancy, over 70 years, is found in Scandinavia, and the lowest, in southern and eastern Europe.

Demography. Europe is one of the most densely populated and urbanized regions of the world, with the majority of its people living in cities or villages. Even the agricultural population in southern, eastern, and central Eu-

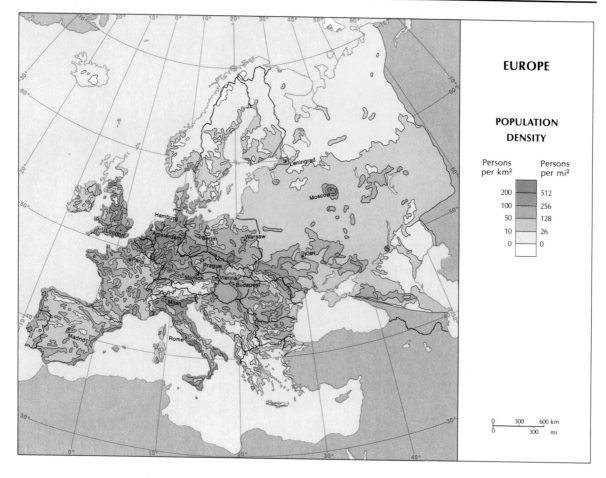

EUROPE

POPULATION DENSITY

Persons per km²	Persons per mi²
200	512
100	256
50	128
10	26
0	0

rope lives in nucleated villages. The isolated farmstead is the more common rural settlement pattern in northwestern Europe. Population densities are greatest in the highly industrialized areas of western Europe where agriculture is also well developed.

Both the internal and overseas movements of people have been extensive in recent European history. Some of these migrations have been forced, such as the movement of 15,000,000 ethnic Germans into the new German borders at the end of World War II. Other groups have moved out to escape political or religious persecution or in the hope of finding better economic opportunities elsewhere. Millions of Europeans left the continent during the 19th and early 20th centuries, migrating to the Western Hemisphere, particularly the United States and Canada. Others moved in large numbers to Australia, New Zealand, South America, and South Africa. The development of colonial empires during the 17th, 18th, and 19th centuries by western European nations lured many people to the colonized areas. More recent internal movements have been from rural to urban areas. Of great importance in recent decades has been the regional migra-

tion from northern marginal areas south to urbanized, industrial regions, and north from the less industrialized areas of Mediterranean and Balkan Europe.

More than 60% of the population in most European countries is classified as urban, with the highest proportion (95%) of urban dwellers in Belgium. Europe's largest cities are Moscow (8,675,000; 1988 est.), LONDON (6,735,400; 1988 est.), BERLIN (3,307,021; 1988 est.), ROME (2,816,474; 1988 est.), and PARIS (2,057,000; 1988 est.). Most countries have one city that dominates in population, economy, and culture. Examples are COPENHAGEN in Denmark, OSLO in Norway, Paris in France, and ATHENS in Greece.

The population of Europe as a whole increased by 80% between 1845 and 1914. From 1914 to 1975, the increase was 40%. The highest growth rates now are in the Roman Catholic countries of southern Europe, Ireland, and, to a lesser extent, eastern Europe. Because of the recent greater affluence throughout Europe, emphasis on birth control policies, and individuals' desire to control family size, the annual growth rates are likely to continue their decline.

The Ruhr River valley in Germany, the single largest industrial complex in Europe, developed in an area with extensive deposits of coal and iron ore.

Economic Development and Commerce

Industrial Development. Europe was the cradle of the Industrial Revolution, and manufacturing developed rapidly throughout the continent after 1850. Today in most of the countries, manufacturing employs the largest percentage of the working population. Heavy industry, which produces iron and steel, basic chemicals, and metal products, is concentrated principally in the large industrial countries of Western Europe—the United Kingdom, Germany, France, and the Low Countries—as well as in the USSR and in Eastern Europe. Urban areas have grown rapidly along with industry. The industry of both the northern European and the Mediterranean countries consists more of processing raw materials such as fruits, agricultural products, minerals, wood, and fish. Each European country has developed industrial specializations based on the skills of its people and its resources.

In most countries the emphasis in industrial development has changed from the manufacturing of such primary products as iron and steel to more finished products such as machinery, textiles, chemicals, and a variety of consumer goods. Much of Western Europe now has a postindustrial economy, and a large percentage of people are employed in the service industries.

The Industrial Revolution began in Great Britain and put to use inventions such as the steam engine and the power loom. Coal was the major source of power, and industry was drawn to locations on or near the coalfields. Consequently, the major urban and industrial areas in the British Isles, with the exception of London, are found on the coalfields in the Scottish Lowlands, in fields flanking the Pennine Chain, and in south Wales. The same pattern was true on the continent, with large industrial urban populations developing in and around coalfields of the Ruhr and the Saar.

The industries that grew up to the north and south of core regions of west central Europe were based more on hydroelectric power than on coal. Mountains of the Alpine system, the Pyrenees, and the highlands of Scandinavia supplied the necessary water power. More recently natural gas and petroleum have become important sources of power. Deposits of natural gas were discovered in the Netherlands in the late 1940s, and since then important reserves have been found in the British and Norwegian sectors of the North Sea. Nuclear power is being developed but at present supplies only a very small percentage of the total requirements.

Agriculture, Forestry, and Fishing. Many of the world's food crops and agricultural practices were developed in Europe and spread elsewhere. Pastoral and crop agriculture have existed in the Mediterranean region for thousands of years. As the urban populations grew, farming practices became more intense and scientific, and the specialization in various crops developed as transportation between large markets improved.

The farms of Europe average 10 ha (25 acres) or less in western Europe, but the state and cooperative farms of the USSR may be thousands of hectares in size. However, the average European farm has been getting larger as a result of the increasing use of machinery. Yields continue to be higher in western Europe where the precipitation is more reliable and scientific farming methods are better developed.

Wheat is a major crop throughout most of Europe. Barley, oats, sugar beets, rye, potatoes, and hay are also common. The low summer temperatures preclude the maturing of maize (corn) in western Europe except in the Low Countries, but it is found in the Danube Valley and in irrigated areas of the Mediterranean countries. Citrus fruits, olives, and grapes are also grown in the Mediterranean as are a variety of vegetables and deciduous fruits,

Mechanized farming is not economically feasible for small, owner-operated concerns like this vineyard in northwestern Italy.

many of which find a market in the densely populated areas of industrial northern Europe. Livestock grazing is common in the many mountainous and hilly areas as well as in the moist, marine-climate regions of western Europe. Dairying is found in all countries, but Denmark and the Netherlands in particular are highly specialized in dairying and hog production. Sheep are raised extensively in the British Isles, and sheep and goats are raised in the drier Mediterranean countries.

The principal commercial forest regions are the coniferous forests of Norway, Sweden, Finland, and the USSR and, to a lesser extent, the lower slopes of mountains in central and southern Europe.

Fishing is a major activity in the waters along all the coasts of Europe. The most productive areas are the North Sea, the coastal waters of Norway, and the northern North Atlantic, including the areas around Iceland, the Faeroe Islands, and Greenland. Cod and herring are the two principal species caught, but plaice, haddock, coalfish, halibut, salmon, sea trout, and mackerel are also common. Tuna and sardines are important along much of the Mediterranean coastline and the Atlantic shores of the Iberian Peninsula. Norway, Denmark, Spain, Iceland, and the United Kingdom are the leading fishing nations in western Europe, but Poland, Germany, and the USSR frequent the waters off Europe for large catches. Of all European countries, Iceland relies most upon fishing, with a heavy dependency upon fish exports. Most countries are now adopting the 320-km (200-mi) limit for fishing rights off their coasts.

Transportation. Europe has an excellent network of rail, road, and air transportation facilities. The lowland topography of much of the densely settled central and western Europe facilitated rail, highway, and waterway development. Even the major mountain barriers such as the Alps can be crossed at passes or have been penetrated by road and railroad tunnels.

Because of the extensive coastline of Europe, water transportation has always been important. Most western European countries have large merchant marines; those of the United Kingdom and Norway are notable. Many rivers originating in central Europe, such as the Rhine, Oder, Elbe, and Danube, are large, slow flowing, and heavily utilized for passenger and freight traffic. In the lowlands many canals have been built to connect navigable rivers. An extensive water network exists in such countries as France and Germany. Air travel is common throughout the continent, and all countries have one or more international airports and national airlines.

The large number of political subdivisions causes problems in coordinating control of transportation. The Rhine River, for instance, flows through four countries; so an international organization has formed to advise on all problems and policy. Similar situations exist for the Danube and other rivers. Most of the railroads throughout Europe are state owned and operated and are generally heavily subsidized. In 1986, British and French leaders approved a plan to build a railroad tunnel under the English Channel. Scheduled for completion in 1993, this "Chunnel" will be a major new link between Britain and the Continent.

Trade. Europe generates more international trade than any other continent. The large, technologically advanced society needs to import much of its food and raw material supplies. Europe sends a large variety of manufactured products to all parts of the world. Countries surrounding the North Sea are a major focus of world imports and exports, much of the trade taking place with immediate neighbors and the United States.

Since World War II, the trade of Europe has largely been controlled by international organizations such as the European Economic Community (Common Market, or EEC), Council for Mutual Economic Assistance (CMEA or Comecon), and the EUROPEAN FREE TRADE ASSOCIATION

(EFTA). The primary objective of each of these is to eliminate the tariffs on goods crossing the boundaries of member nations, thus increasing the size of the markets and facilitating trade. The EEC consists of 12 nations: Italy, France, Germany, Belgium, the Netherlands, and Luxembourg—the original six—and Great Britain, Ireland, Denmark, Greece, Spain, and Portugal. By the early 1990s the dominant EEC had come to overshadow both Eastern Europe's Comecon and the EFTA (Austria, Finland, Iceland, Norway, Sweden, and Switzerland). In 1989, Austria applied for membership in the EEC.

The major commodities flowing into Europe are petroleum, food products, industrial raw materials, and manufactured products. The major exports are machine products and other manufactured goods. A large volume of international trade also flows within Europe, particularly between industrialized countries and the lesser-developed regions.

The tourist industry has had tremendous impetus since World War II and is becoming increasingly important to the economy of Europe. In some countries, especially those bordering the Mediterranean, tourism constitutes well over half the national income.

European Atomic Energy Community   see
EUROPEAN COMMUNITY

European Coal and Steel Community   see
EUROPEAN COMMUNITY

European Community   European Community (EC) is the collective name given to the European Economic Community (EEC, or Common Market), the European Coal and Steel Community (ECSC), and the European Atomic Energy Community (EURATOM), together with their common political and administrative organs. The members of The EC are Belgium, Denmark, France, Germany, Great Britain, Greece, Ireland, Italy, Luxembourg, the Netherlands, Portugal, and Spain.

A plan for a united Europe was first put forward by the French statesman Jean MONNET after World War II. In 1950, French foreign minister Robert SCHUMAN proposed a plan for joining the coal and steel industries of France and West Germany to foster peace between the two countries. As a result, the European Coal and Steel Community was established in July 1952 by Belgium, the Netherlands, Luxembourg, France, West Germany, and Italy. Trade barriers in coal and steel among the six member nations were abolished, and coal and steel workers were allowed to work anywhere within the community. By 1955 a fully operating, successful common market for coal and steel had been achieved, setting a precedent for the formation of the EEC. On Mar. 25, 1957, the Treaty of Rome was signed by the six ECSC nations, establishing the EEC and EURATOM, effective as of Jan. 1, 1958. At the core of the EC is the EEC.

European Economic Community
The European Economic Community was established for the purpose of integrating the economies of Western Europe and was the most important step toward the creation of the EC.

Freeing of Trade among Members. During the EEC's first decade, the member countries abolished all tariffs and many other restrictions on trade in manufactured goods among themselves. At the same time, they established a common, uniform tariff against the rest of the world. The removal of tariffs on member-country trade was an important stimulus to economic growth within the EEC, as evidenced by the substantial increases in domestic production and incomes in the EEC countries during the 1960s, as well as in their international trade in manufactured goods.

Domestic agriculture had long been protected against import competition in individual EEC member countries, and these countries were reluctant to lower their barriers. After long and difficult negotiations, the EEC worked out a Common Agricultural Policy (CAP) in 1962 to cover imports of wheat, dairy products, and other foodstuffs. Imports from nonmembers were subject to a tax. The CAP made the EEC self-sufficient in almost all farm goods that could be grown locally.

Other Common Problems. The EEC also adopted policies to increase the mobility of resources. These included freeing the movement of labor and capital among member countries. One result was the employment of large numbers of Italian workers in the late 1950s and 1960s in the other EEC member countries, especially in West Germany. Steps were also taken to harmonize the tax systems, standardize social insurance and welfare programs, and stimulate economic development in some of the more backward regions of member countries. Finally, common policies were adopted for transportation and for the development and use of nuclear energy.

Associates and New Members. In 1961, Great Britain, Ireland, Norway, and Denmark began negotiating for admission into the EEC. Great Britain was concerned, however, that EEC membership should not unduly harm Commonwealth, EUROPEAN FREE TRADE ASSOCIATION (EFTA), and British agricultural interests. In 1963 and 1967, French president Charles DE GAULLE blocked the membership bids because of his desire to retain French preeminence in the EEC, to protect French agriculture, and to avoid any loss of French national sovereignty in a larger organization. Negotiations were begun again in 1970, and in 1973, Great Britain, Denmark, and Ireland became full-fledged members of the EEC. (Norway's voters rejected membership in a referendum in 1972.) These countries were given until 1978 to align their tariffs and other policies with those of the other six EEC member countries.

The EEC has worked out special reciprocal arrangements to provide associate status for several less developed countries. These arrangements were made available to Greece in 1963, to Turkey in 1964, to Malta in 1971, and to Cyprus in 1973. Beginning in 1965, arrangements were also made with 64 African, Caribbean, and Pacific countries. These associated states were given preferential access for their exports to the EEC, and they in turn agreed to give preferential access for EEC exports to their markets. Minor arrangements were made with other countries in the Mediterranean region and with EFTA, Canada, Latin America, and Asian countries.

Greece became a full member in 1979, and Spain and Portugal joined in 1986. The reunification of Germany on Oct. 31, 1990, brought the population and economy of the former East German state into the EEC.

Economic and Political Integration. Monetary integration of the EEC, begun in 1972, involved moving toward unification of national currencies by narrowing the allowable margins of exchange-rate fluctuations and led to the establishment of the European Monetary System (EMS) in December 1978. In addition to providing internal exchange-rate stability, the EMS created an official European currency unit (ECU).

In 1985, EEC leaders approved changes in the Treaty of Rome that allowed more decisions to be made by majority (instead of unanimous) vote, with the aim of eliminating the remaining trade barriers among members by 1992.

Joint Institutions

Although the three communities (EEC, ECSC, and EURATOM) were established by two separate treaties, their central institutions were merged in July 1967. These include the Council of Ministers, the Commission, the European Parliament, the Court of Justice, and the European Council.

The Council of Ministers, the main decision-making body of the community, is made up of one representative appointed by the government of each member country—usually its foreign minister. The council, with offices in Brussels, is aided in its work by the Committee of Permanent Representatives.

The Commission, also in Brussels, has 14 members appointed by the council, no more than 2 of whom may be nationals of the same state. The Commission initiates proposals to the council and implements the council's decisions. Jacques DELORS (France), who became president of the Commission in 1985 and was reappointed in 1989, is a strong proponent of European integration.

The European Parliament, which meets in either Luxembourg or Strasbourg, France, consists of 518 representatives elected by the voters of the member countries. The Parliament serves as a general deliberative body and supervises the executive organs. It has the power to dismiss the Commission on a motion of censure approved by a two-thirds majority. Reforms enacted in 1985 allow the Parliament and the Commission jointly to overrule the Council of Ministers.

The Court of Justice, with one judge from each member country, adjudicates disputes arising out of the application of the treaties and community legislation. It is also located in Luxembourg.

The European Council is composed of the heads of government of the member states. It meets for informal discussion three times a year.

European Economic Community   see EUROPEAN COMMUNITY

European Free Trade Association   The European Free Trade Association (EFTA) was created in 1959 to promote free trade among several Western European countries. Its original members were Austria, Denmark, Great Britain, Norway, Portugal, Sweden, and Switzerland. Iceland joined in 1970, and Finland, an associate member since 1961, became a full member in 1986. EFTA's headquarters are in Geneva, Switzerland.

Great Britain and Denmark withdrew from EFTA when they joined the EUROPEAN COMMUNITY (EC) in January 1973; Portugal did the same in 1986. At the time of the British and Danish withdrawals, the remaining members of EFTA negotiated an arrangement with the enlarged EC for mutual tariff removal on all industrial products by January 1984.

European Organization for Nuclear Research   The European Organization for Nuclear Research (originally, Conseil européen pour la recherche nucléaire, or CERN) is an international center for research in high-energy physics. Founded in 1954, its laboratory is located near Geneva, Switzerland. It is funded by Austria, Belgium, Denmark, France, Germany, Greece, Italy, the Netherlands, Norway, Sweden, Switzerland, and the United Kingdom.

The major research facilities are large proton accelerators in the GeV energy range (see ACCELERATOR, PARTICLE). Two CERN physicists, Carlo RUBBIA and Simon VAN DER MEER, adapted an accelerator for collisions of protons with antiprotons, discovering the elusive W and Z particles in 1983 and the top quark in 1984. An enormous electron-positron collider, now being built at CERN, is scheduled for completion in the early 1990s.

European Parliament   see EUROPEAN COMMUNITY

European prehistory   European prehistory has conventionally been studied in light of the Three Age system—Stone Age, Bronze Age, and Iron Age—ending with the start of written history. The periods covered in this article date from the spread of farming to Europe before the 6th millennium BC to the Roman conquests about the beginning of the Christian Era. For the prehistory of Greece and Italy, see AEGEAN CIVILIZATION; ETRUSCANS; GREECE, ANCIENT; and ROME, ANCIENT.

Neolithic Period

The NEOLITHIC PERIOD marked the introduction of agriculture and settled life in Europe. Of all the major domesticated plants and animals, only cattle were native to Europe. Sheep, goats, wheat, and barley were introduced from the Near East. The new farming economy spread over several millennia from southeast Europe to the north and west, perhaps limited by mountain ranges and by temperate climates.

Eastern and Central Europe. The earliest Neolithic sites in southeast Europe date from before the 6th millennium

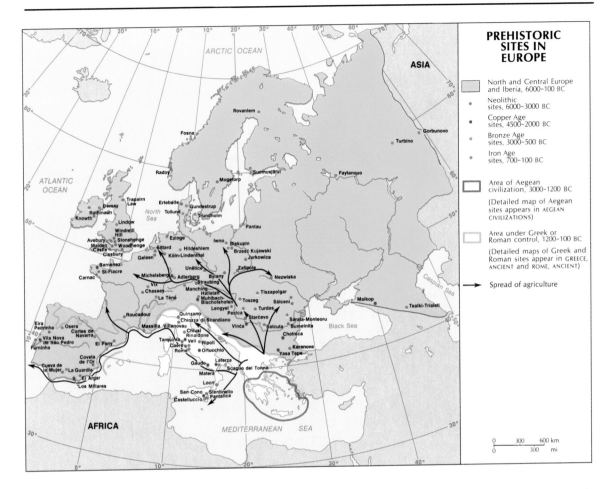

PREHISTORIC
SITES IN
EUROPE

North and Central Europe
and Iberia, 6000–100 BC

Neolithic
sites, 6000–3000 BC

Copper Age
sites, 4500–2000 BC

Bronze Age
sites, 3000–500 BC

Iron Age
sites, 700–100 BC

Area of Aegean
civilization, 3000–1200 BC

(Detailed map of Aegean
sites appears in AEGEAN
CIVILIZATIONS)

Area under Greek or
Roman control, 1200–100 BC

(Detailed maps of Greek and
Roman sites appear in GREECE,
ANCIENT and ROME, ANCIENT)

Spread of agriculture

BC and are located in areas with the most easily workable soils. Constant settlement on the same location produced tells, or settlement mounds, that measure up to 30 m (100 ft); successive phases of the Balkan Neolithic are named for two such tells, Starčevo and Vinča, near Belgrade. Barley and several varieties of wheat were grown, and domesticated breeds of sheep, goats, cattle, and pigs were raised. The houses were small, rectangular single-roomed structures of timber, many with wattle-and-daub (woven twigs plastered with clay) walls. Pottery skills were highly developed, and numerous objects were produced, including a wide variety of figurines.

In central Europe farming began with the Danubian or Linear Pottery culture, so called because of the decorated ceramics it produced. This culture, which began in the 5th millennium BC and stretched from Hungary to Holland, exhibited remarkable homogeneity. Cattle were more important than sheep or pigs, and in addition to wheat and barley, other crops such as peas, beans, and flax were grown. The settlements, such as Bylany, Czechoslovakia, and Köln-Lindenthal, Germany, were frequently large, and the people were sheltered in massive timber longhouses up to 30 m (100 ft) long. In the 4th millenni-

um BC a greater variety of pottery, buildings, and burial types began to appear. The 3d-millennium settlements of the Michelsberg culture, which extended from the Rhineland to Belgium, are distinguished by enclosure ditches.

Western Europe. In Italy, southern France, and Spain the Impressed Ware culture introduced farming in the 6th millennium; however, stone tool manufacture and the occupation of caves continued. Subsistence, not yet based primarily on agriculture, was still dependent on hunting and fishing; deer, wild boar, and fish and shellfish were important sources of food.

Farther north in France, the earliest Neolithic culture, c.4000 BC, is named for the site at Camp de Chassey. Settlements were located in a wide variety of areas, including caves and fertile river terraces; crop production and animal husbandry, especially cattle, were the basis of the economy. In Switzerland, at a series of settlements called LAKE DWELLINGS, agriculture was adapted to the Alpine environment, with emphasis on cattle and legumes and fruit in addition to wheat.

In northern Europe and Scandinavia the earliest Neolithic culture was the Funnel-beaker culture. In some areas, as in the Mesolithic Ertebølle culture of Denmark,

The artifacts shown are representative of a diverse cross section of European prehistoric cultural periods. The selection includes: (1) a red-deer antler pick and an ox shoulder-blade shovel, both used as flint mining tools (England, 3500–500 BC); (2) an amber animal carving, which typifies Maglemosian art and dates from the Mesolithic Period (Denmark, 8000–5000 BC); (3) a pottery model of a cart found in a grave in Hungary, from the Copper Age (c.2000 BC); (4) a battle-axe made by the Fatyanov culture of the Late Copper to Early Bronze Age (USSR, 2000–1000 BC); (5) a Copper Age, terracotta, anthropomorphic figurine found in Romania (3800–3500 BC).

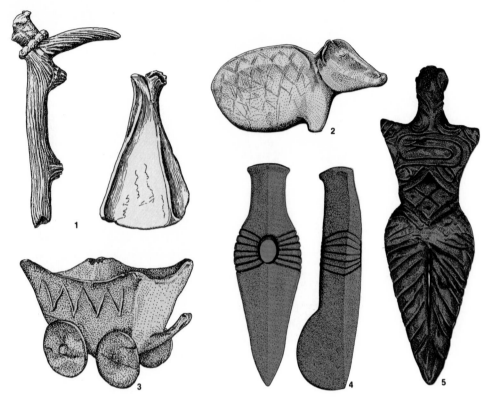

older traditions of hunting and fishing survived alongside agriculture. In the 3d millennium BC, the Corded Ware and Battle-Axe cultures developed new single-grave burial rites.

The beginning of the Neolithic in Britain and Ireland, dated from the later 4th millennium BC, is marked by extensive clearance of the forest for agriculture. The earliest monuments are collective tombs, such as the wedge-shaped graves in Ireland called court cairns and the earthen long BARROWS in England. Settlements were rare until the 3d millennium. In the late 3d millennium, major ceremonial monuments were constructed, including AVEBURY, WOODHENGE, and the first phase of STONEHENGE. In Britain, as on the continent, flint and other stone sources suitable for tools were traded over long distances.

Megalithic Culture. The collective burial rite represented in the long barrows occurred more widely in the megalithic tomb tradition that extended from Portugal to the north of Scotland and across northern Europe to Germany and Denmark. These MEGALITHS, the earliest of which are in Brittany and date from before 4000 BC, were constructed in a variety of external forms with an assortment of different internal chamber constructions. The latest are the most complex, such as the passage graves in the Boyne Valley, Ireland, at KNOWTH. Recent research suggests that some of these tombs, whose construction demanded a high degree of social organization, were astronomically aligned for viewing the winter solstice.

Bronze Age

Beginnings of Metallurgy in Europe. The BRONZE AGE is marked by the first appearance of metallurgy. The development of this new technology was a long process, from the simple use of native copper (natural nuggets of pure metal) through cold hammering and the discovery of smelting and casting, to the use of a tin alloy to make bronze. Copper objects occur widely in some late Neolithic cultures, and this phase lasted so long in some regions that it is sometimes referred to as the Copper Age, or Chalcolithic Period.

The earliest copper objects in Europe appeared in the Neolithic Vinča culture of the Balkans, perhaps as early as 5000 BC—substantially earlier than in the Aegean, suggesting an independent invention of metallurgy in Europe. By 4000 BC smelting and casting had been mastered, and metallurgy soon became an integral part of the economy. Other independent centers of metallurgy were in Spain and possibly in Italy. The dissemination of early metal technology is particularly linked with the BEAKER CULTURE. Typical Beaker grave goods included pottery, a small copper knife, and in some cases, small ornaments of gold. The great difference in wealth visible from these graves is evidence for the emergence of social ranking.

Emergence of Bronze Industries. The art of smelting copper with tin to produce the harder alloy bronze had been learned in the Balkans in the early 3d millennium

BC and, soon after 2000 BC, was well established throughout Europe. Axes and daggers were among the most common objects produced. The wealth of early Bronze Age society is seen in richly furnished graves of the WESSEX CULTURE in southern England, from sites in Brittany, and from the Únetiče culture of central Europe.

The skill of the bronzesmiths progressed throughout the 2d millennium, as more complex techniques of casting were mastered. The daggers of the early Bronze Age were transformed into rapiers and swords of varied forms. A wide range of local bronze ornaments, especially pins and bracelets, were also produced.

Toward the end of the 2d millennium, a number of important cultural and social changes were underway throughout Europe. The so-called Urnfield burial rite of flat-grave cremation was widely adopted in central and western Europe. The bronze industry became increasingly specialized and centralized, with improved systems of collecting raw materials and distributing finished products. New techniques were introduced, including sheet-metal working, which was used especially for armor, and for buckets and bowls. New sword types used for slashing rather than stabbing became common, which together with the body armor suggest that new fighting methods were introduced. The horse was also more widely used, for traction if not for riding.

Social Developments. Many of these changes affected the highest levels of contemporary society, suggesting an increase in the social ranking already apparent in the earlier Bronze Age. Further evidence for this social development is seen in the appearance of hillforts (fortified hilltop enclosures) in many parts of central Europe and western Britain. The construction of such defenses at the same time as the adoption of new fighting methods was a result of increased aggression, possibly from competition for mineral and agricultural resources. Certainly, many areas overexploited in the Neolithic and earlier Bronze Age were abandoned, and the appearance of the first field systems suggests a more controlled use of available land. All of these social, political, and economic changes mark

An artist's illustration depicts daily activities in the Neolithic settlement site of Habasesti in Romania, dating from about 3000 BC. Villages of this type were set on low promontories and defended by a bank and ditches. Habasesti had 44 longhouses, which averaged 15 by 7 m (50 by 25 ft) and were built according to a rectangular plan. The settlement's population of some 20 extended families is estimated to have numbered 500 persons. The houses were built with timber and clay walls, constructed on a framework of tree branches, with reed and thatch roofs. Each house had an individual hearth; communal top-draught kilns were elsewhere on the site. The people of Habasesti cultivated wheat, barley, and millet and kept domesticated animals, which included cattle, sheep, and pigs. Stone hoes and edged axes were found, as well as some copper ornaments and tools, which may have been copied from items imported from Bronze Age Anatolia. The sophisticated, painted pottery bears a distinctive S-shaped or spiral design applied over a red or white ground.

The Hallstatt culture, named for the cemetery at Hallstatt in Austria, marked the first period of the Iron Age in Europe. (Left) This Hallstatt bronze statue of a warrior dates from the 8th-5th century BC. (Museum of Natural History, Vienna.) The burial customs of the Hallstatt peoples included distinctive methods of tomb construction and inhumation of the dead. Burial mounds covered timber chambers containing the body and costly goods. (Right) A reconstruction of a Hallstatt tomb at Vix, in eastern France, shows the body of an upper-class woman wearing various types of jewelry, including a gold diadem decorated with animal motifs. She is lying in a dismantled, four-wheeled wagon. Because of the trade routes used during the 6th century BC, many imported artifacts were found in the tomb, including 6th-century Attic Greek vases and Etruscan bronzes. The most unusual piece is an enormous Greek bronze crater (c.500 BC), the largest such vessel to survive from the ancient world. Food and wine containers placed in the tomb suggest that members of the Hallstatt culture believed in an afterlife.

a significant turning point in European prehistory in the late 2d millennium BC.

Iron Age

The IRON AGE in Europe is conventionally divided into an earlier period (700–450 BC), named for the cemetery at HALLSTATT in Austria, and a later period (450 BC–1st century BC) named for the site of LA TÈNE in Switzerland.

Hallstatt Period. In many areas Bronze Age traditions continued relatively unchanged during the Hallstatt period, especially in pottery styles and patterns of settlement, economy, and social structure. The most obvious change was in the metal industry, with iron gradually replacing bronze during the 7th century BC, especially for weapons and tools. However, bronze was still used for many small castings and sheet-metal work. It was once thought that when iron was first introduced into Europe, it was rapidly adopted because of its superiority to bronze, but it is now apparent that iron was worked widely throughout Europe during the Bronze Age; it is therefore probable that the replacement of bronze was due primarily to economic factors that made iron cheaper.

Changes also occurred in burial customs, especially in central Europe, where inhumation in a barrow once again became common. For some of the richest burials a new rite appeared—that of burying the dead with a four-wheeled wagon in a wooden mortuary chamber under a

barrow, a custom that had a long tradition in Asia. Such wagon burials were particularly common from eastern France through Switzerland to Bohemia.

From the 8th century BC, the Greeks had been first trading and then settling throughout the Mediterranean area; by the 6th century there were Greek colonies from Syria and the Black Sea to Spain. The quest for metal ores and other raw materials was one of the main reasons for this expansion; the ensuing trade with barbarian Europe had profound effects. A rich civilization flourished among the Dacians and Thracians in present-day Romania and Bulgaria, with many Greek influences absorbed from the Black Sea colonies. The most important colony in the west was Massilia (Marseille), founded about 600 BC. In the 6th century extensive trading links developed from central Europe to Marseille via the Rhone Valley and also across the Alps with the Etruscans.

In return for the goods supplied from Europe (mainly raw materials), Mediterranean luxury goods flowed northward, especially Greek painted pottery and Etruscan bronzes. Many of the imports, such as jugs and cups, were concerned with the drinking of wine, which was also imported from Marseille in large jars. This trade was controlled by the Iron Age aristocracy, whose members in eastern France and southern Germany inhabited a series of small fortified hilltop settlements, complete with associated rich cemeteries. The best-excavated is the

Heuneburg, on the upper Danube in Germany, which produced a great variety of imported luxury goods and at one stage even adopted a Mediterranean style of defense, with mud-brick walls and bastions. The nearby barrows have yielded many rich grave goods, including a wagon, bronze cauldrons, and oriental silk. Mont Lassois, in eastern France, was a similar site, as was the nearby Vix burial.

La Tène Period. About 500 BC many of these sites declined. In the following La Tène period, the main centers that profited from the Mediterranean trade, now mostly with the Etruscans, were located further north. Richly furnished burials, usually in the form of inhumations under barrows, have been found in the highland areas containing metal ores and salt that extend in a crescent from the Champagne region of France through the Rhineland to Austria and Bohemia. These graves often contained imported Mediterranean items, two-wheeled chariots, and gold and bronze objects of local manufacture. New fashions emerged in weapons and ornaments, including torcs (neck rings), and a new art style using geometric motifs and plant elements derived from classical prototypes appeared; this new tradition is sometimes called CELTIC ART, because the La Tène culture is identified with the CELTS.

Few such burials were made after 400 BC, and in the next two centuries there were few signs of such wealth or of contacts with the Mediterranean. Later burial rites were more uniform; men were buried with their weapons, shield, spear, and sword, and women were buried with their ornaments, especially brooches, bracelets, and torcs. Contact did not cease entirely, however; in the 3d century BC the first gold coins were struck, copying those of Philip II of Macedonia.

The La Tène culture reached its final development in the 1st century BC before the Roman conquests, when the sites known to the Romans as *oppida* (towns) flourished from central France to Hungary. They were fortified sites, mainly on hilltops, although in Germany they were frequently in river valleys. Excavations at Staré Hradisko, Czechoslovakia, and at Manching, Germany, have shown that these were densely occupied towns, functioning as markets and centers of industrial production for such items as iron, bronze, glass, leather, wood, and pottery. Coins were minted, including small denominations for everyday transactions, and goods were again imported from the Mediterranean—especially wine in *amphorae* (pottery jars for bulk transport) and Italian bronze jugs. Evidence of political developments suggests that kings gave way to government by council and magistrates.

Few of these Iron Age developments affected northern Europe, although some associated objects have been found there, such as the famous silver cauldron from Gundestrup, Denmark. A new form of ritual sacrifice and burial occurred in northern Europe; it is still poorly understood (see TOLLUND MAN). In Britain, Hallstatt and La Tène fashions in weapons and ornaments were copied, as was La Tène art in an insular version. Beginning about 50 BC, however, a similar urban pattern emerged: some of the towns in the west developed from long-established hillforts such as MAIDEN CASTLE; in the southeast, however, new sites such as Colchester appeared. As on the con-

The Celtic peoples borrowed much from their contemporaries in the Mediterranean area. This 3d-century BC gold coin bears the likeness of the Macedonian king Philip II. (Bibliothèque Nationale, Paris.)

tinent, these *oppida* were local market and industrial centers. Extensive trade with the Romans also took place, with such items as grains, furs, and slaves exchanged for wine and other luxuries.

See also: EUROPE, HISTORY OF; PREHISTORIC ART; STONE ALIGNMENTS.

The typical dwelling of the native Briton during the Celtic Iron Age was a tentlike structure made of timbers and embedded in a round or oval ring of stone and earth. The door, which was fashioned out of interlaced branches, led into a central floor space, an area that was excavated to a depth of 46 cm (18 in) to increase headroom. Rafters placed around the periphery were plastered with mud and covered with such materials as reeds, straw, heather, and turf. The stone chimney extended through the house's roof.

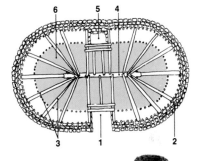

(Left) A floor plan of the Celtic dwelling shows:
(1) entrance;
(2) outer ring of stone and earth;
(3) rafters;
(4) central ridgepole;
(5) fireplace with stone chimney;
(6) central floor space.

European Recovery Program see MARSHALL PLAN

European Southern Observatory The European Southern Observatory (ESO) is an international astronomical project initiated on Oct. 5, 1962 by five European countries. Six member states—Belgium, Denmark, France, Germany, the Netherlands, and Sweden—now participate. Administrative headquarters are located in Garching, near Munich; the observatory itself is situated at La Silla, Chile, 960 km (600 mi) north of Santiago. Beginning in 1964, several telescopes were constructed at this site. ESO also manages other telescopes for national institutes.

European Space Agency The European Space Agency (ESA) is a multinational organization formed to develop space technology and to conduct research. ESA members are Austria, Belgium, Denmark, Finland, France, Germany, Ireland, Italy, the Netherlands, Norway, Spain, Sweden, Switzerland, and the United Kingdom; Canada participates with observer status. ESA was formed in 1975 when the European Space Research Organization (established in 1962) and the European Launcher Development Organization (1964) were merged. Each member determines its annual contribution and the projects it will support. No member may undertake a project without inviting the participation of ESA. In return, ESA issues contracts on a pro rata basis.

Most ESA space payloads are launched by ARIANE rockets from a pad at Kourou, French Guiana. Besides producing communications, geophysics, and astronomy satellites, ESA owns and operates SPACELAB. In 1985, ESA sent the spacecraft *Giotto* toward a successful flyby of HALLEY'S COMET. Future projects include Eureca, an experiment platform to be orbited by the Space Shuttle; Hermes, or an alternative reusable space plane to be launched by a new generation of Ariane rockets; and the designing of modules and related service systems for the future NASA SPACE STATION.

europium [yur-ohp'-ee-uhm] Europium is a chemical element, a metal of the LANTHANIDE SERIES, in Group IIIB of the periodic table. Its symbol is Eu; its atomic number is 63; and its atomic weight is 151.96. Two isotopes of europium occur naturally, ^{151}Eu and ^{153}Eu; both are stable. Many radioactive, artificial isotopes of europium have been created. The existence of europium was first postulated by Sir William CROOKES in 1889. In 1896, E. A. Demarçay discovered the element and named it for Europe. Europium, a soft metal, is the most reactive of the lanthanides, and many of its properties are more like those of calcium, strontium, and barium. Europium oxide is used as the red phosphor in cathode-ray tubes for color-television receivers. Because europium easily absorbs neutrons, it is used in control rods for nuclear reactors.

Eurydice see ORPHEUS

Eurynome [ue-rin'-ah-mee] In Greek mythology, Eurynome was the name of the following characters: (1) the mother of BELLEROPHON; (2) the daughter of Tethys and Oceanus who with THETIS, mother of ACHILLES, welcomed HEPHAESTUS to the bosom of the sea when HERA cast him down from Olympus; (3) a sea nymph and the third wife of ZEUS; (4) an ancient goddess who, with the TITAN Ophion, ruled Olympus before CRONUS; and (5) an old and faithful servant in the household of ODYSSEUS.

Eusebius of Caesarea [yoo-see'-bee-uhs sez-uh'ree-uh] Eusebius, *c.*260–*c.*340, was the first historian of the Christian church. Around 315 he was elected bishop of Caesarea, in Palestine, and became embroiled in the controversy over ARIANISM, in which he took the side of Arius. At the Council of Nicaea (325) he eventually signed the approved formula, largely in deference to Emperor Constantine.

Eusebius's *Chronicle* (*c.*303) and *Ecclesiastical History* (*c.*324) are principle sources of early Christian history. The *History* is both a political theology and a theology of history, the first major attempt to explain the association of Christianity with the Roman Empire and to take a historical approach in describing the development of the church.

Eusebius of Nicomedia [nik-oh'-mee-dee-uh] Eusebius, d. *c.*342, was a leader of ARIANISM, a Christian heresy denying the divinity of Jesus Christ. Although he signed the formula approved at the Council of Nicaea (325; see NICAEA, COUNCILS OF), afterward Eusebius advocated the views of Arius with renewed zeal. He used his increasing political and ecclesiastical ascendancy to procure the banishment of ATHANASIUS, one of the leaders at Nicaea, in 335. In 337 he baptized Constantine, the first Christian emperor, and in 339 he became bishop of Constantinople.

Eustace, Saint Saint Eustace, traditional patron of hunters, was a legendary martyr of the 2d century. According to legend, he was a Roman general who was converted to Christianity when a vision of a crucifix appeared between the antlers of a stag he was hunting. He was roasted to death for not praying to the Roman gods. Feast day: Nov. 2 (Eastern); Sept. 20 (Western; abolished in 1969).

eustachian tube see EAR

eutectic point see PHASE EQUILIBRIUM

euthanasia [yooth-uh'-nay-zhuh] Euthanasia (Greek, "easy death") is the act of inducing a gentle, painless death. In recent decades the term has come to mean deliberately terminating life to prevent unavoidable suffering. Passive euthanasia is discontinuing life-sustaining treatment of the ill or stopping so-called extraordinary treatment. Active euthanasia, or mercy killing, is putting to death a person who, due to disease or extreme age, can no longer lead a meaningful life; the term can also include an act of voluntary euthanasia, or SUICIDE, for similar reasons.

Passive Euthanasia. Many physicians consider it good medical practice not to prolong artificially the life of a suffering person whose disease is inevitably fatal. Instead, they provide comfort and relief while the patient awaits death. Passive euthanasia, however, has only recently gained legal support. In 1976 the New Jersey Supreme Court ruled that doctors may disconnect a mechanical respirator that is keeping a comatose patient alive because it prevents the patient from dying with decency and dignity. In 1977 "right to die" bills were introduced into several state legislatures. Since then, more than 30 states have passed laws that confer the authority to withdraw life support from a patient upon a designated relative, friend, legal or religious advisor, or court. In 1990 the U.S. Supreme Court ruled that people who make their wishes known have a constitutional right to have life-sustaining treatment discontinued. In the cases of permanently unconscious persons who have left no clear instructions, however, the state may deny the request by family members to terminate treatment. This ruling gave legal backing to the living will, which provides evidence of a person's desire not to be kept alive by artificial means should that person become terminally ill and incompetent.

Passive euthanasia continues to raise many legal problems, however, such as in cases in which parents and doctors decide not to pursue drastic life-saving measures for children born with severe birth defects. An enduring ethical question is also raised by the Hippocratic oath, which requires physicians both to relieve suffering and to prolong life. The problem is intensified because the definition of death has become blurred. Formerly a person was considered dead when breathing and heart action ceased. Since these functions can be maintained artificially now, a definition of death that includes brain death—lack of electrical activity for a period long enough to make return to functioning virtually impossible—is widely accepted (see DEATH AND DYING).

Active Euthanasia. In the United States taking active measures to end someone's life is a serious crime, punishable by as much as life imprisonment. In some countries active euthanasia is treated as a special crime with lighter penalties, but only in Uruguay is mercy killing not considered a crime. Those who oppose legalizing it argue that medically justifying mercy killing might lead to the kinds of abuses that occurred in Nazi Germany.

eutrophication [yoo-troh-fi-cay'-shuhn] Eutrophication is an aging process in the life cycle of a lake (see LAKE, body of water), pond, or slow-moving stream. It is caused by the gradual accumulation in the water of the nutrients needed to sustain aquatic plants and animals, accompanied by an increase in the number of organisms in the water. Geologically a young lake is one containing water that is cold and clear and that has a plentiful supply of oxygen but little organic material. Over time, the content of nitrogen, phosphorus, and other nutrients increases as organic materials are deposited by streams feeding into the lake and by erosion from banks of the lake. The growth rate of algae and other aquatic plants increases, as does that of the fish and organisms that feed on them. When these organisms die, they sink to the lake bottom and decompose, adding still more organic material to the water and forming an ever-growing layer of silt. Decomposition, however, decreases the amount of dissolved oxygen in the lake. Eventually the lake is overwhelmed by plants life growing in its shallower waters, or by silt, and a marsh forms.

The natural aging of a lake may take many thousands of years to complete. Some lakes—those which are particularly deep or cold or which have limited drainage—never undergo eutrophication. In recent years, however, the eutrophication of many bodies of water has been accelerated by environmental pollution, for example, the introduction of nutrients from the leaching of agricultural fertilizers, from sewage, and from the widespread use of detergents containing phosphorus.

Eutyches [yoot'-i-keez] Eutyches, c.378–454, was archimandrite of a monastery in Constantinople, inclined to MONOPHYSITISM in the doctrinal controversy over the person of Jesus Christ. His vigorous opposition to NESTORIANISM, and his refusal in 433 to accept the formulary of reunion that restored unity between the churches of Alexandria and Antioch, led to his condemnation at a synod in 448 on a charge of heresy.

Pope LEO I sent a dogmatic letter condemning Eutyches's denial of Christ's human nature. However, at the so-called Latrocinium (Robber Synod), convoked (449) at Ephesus by Emperor THEODOSIUS II, Leo's letter was not read out and Eutyches was declared orthodox. At the Council of Chalcedon (451; see CHALCEDON, COUNCIL OF) Eutyches was condemned, deposed, and exiled.

Evangelical and Reformed Church   see UNITED CHURCH OF CHRIST

Evangelical United Brethren Church   The Evangelical United Brethren Church came into existence in 1946 through the merger of the Church of the United Brethren in Christ and the Evangelical Church. Both denominations were products of religious revival among the German-speaking populations of Pennsylvania and Maryland at the turn of the 19th century. The Church of the United Brethren in Christ arose in 1800 through the efforts of Philip OTTERBEIN of the German Reformed Church and Martin BOEHM, a MENNONITE bishop. The organization that later became the Evangelical Church was begun by Jacob ALBRIGHT in 1807. His followers adopted the names Evangelical Association in 1816 and Evangelical Church in 1922.

Albright, Otterbein, and Boehm were close associates

of Francis Asbury, the founder of American Methodism. With him, these leaders shared a commitment to the Arminian theology of grace (see Arminianism), pietistic spirituality, and episcopal church organization. Only the language barrier prevented their followers from becoming Methodists. In 1968 the Evangelical United Brethren Church finally joined with the Methodists to establish the United Methodist Church.

evangelicalism *Evangelicalism* is the term applied to a number of related movements within Protestantism. They are bound together by a common emphasis on what they believe to be a personal relationship with Jesus Christ and a commitment to the demands of the New Testament. Evangelicalism is usually associated with a type of preaching that calls on the hearer to confess his or her sin and believe in Christ's forgiveness.

During the late 17th century and throughout the 18th, Pietism was the mainspring of the so-called evangelical revival in Germany. Its counterpart in Great Britain and the United States was Methodism, which contributed to the series of revivals called the Great Awakening that swept 18th-century America. The common purpose of evangelical movements was to revitalize the churches spiritually.

In the late 18th and early 19th centuries, Evangelicals in the Church of England—especially William Wilberforce and other members of the group known as the Clapham Sect—played a leading role in the movement to abolish slavery in the British colonies.

Since about 1950 the term *evangelical* frequently has been applied in the United States to the inheritors and proponents of Fundamentalism.

Evans, Sir Arthur The English archaeologist Sir Arthur John Evans, b. July 8, 1851, d. July 11, 1941, excavated (1900–35) the palace at Knossos, in Crete, and was a leading authority on that island's Bronze Age civilization, which he named Minoan. He was also an ex-

In this painting (1907), Sir Arthur Evans, a British archaeologist, is surrounded by Minoan artifacts unearthed on the island of Crete. Evans's excavations at Knossos (1900–35) revealed an ancient palace complex erected by a previously unknown Bronze Age civilization. (Ashmolean Museum, Oxford.)

pert on Dalmatia (now part of Yugoslavia), where he earlier investigated Roman antiquities and supported local efforts for independence from Austria-Hungary.

The son of Sir John Evans, a distinguished amateur archaeologist, Arthur studied modern history at Oxford, where he served (1884–1908) as keeper of the Ashmolean Museum. He was responsible for the expansion and modernization of the museum, which he enriched with his father's sizable archaeological collections, the Fortnum collection of Italian majolica and bronzes, and his own gifts of Cretan antiquities.

Evans, Dame Edith Dame Edith Evans, b. London, Feb. 8, 1888, d. Oct. 14, 1976, a British actress, made her London stage debut in 1912 and performed more than 100 parts. Although she acted in many modern dramas, she was best known for her Shakespearean roles, notably as the nurse in *Romeo and Juliet*. Evans also appeared in many films.

Evans, Frederick Henry Frederick Henry Evans, b. June 26, 1853, d. June 24, 1943, an English photographer renowned for his photographs of cathedrals and landscapes, was a leader in the artistic photography movement at the turn of the century. His platinum prints, concerned with the qualities of light and spirit, used straight, unmanipulated photography to achieve poetic results. Evans was a member of the Linked Ring, a photographic society opposed to the conservatism of the Royal Photographic Society. His work was reproduced in *Camera Work*, a quarterly established in 1903 and edited by Alfred Stieglitz.

Evans, Mary Ann see Eliot, George

Evans, Oliver Oliver Evans, b. Newport, Del., Sept. 13, 1755, d. Apr. 15, 1819, designed the first automated factory and pioneered (1801) in the development of the high-pressure steam engine. Evans constructed (1784) a water-powered flour mill, patented in 1790, in which grain was moved automatically through the various processes by a series of conveyors that became fundamental in factories. He patented his high-pressure steam engine in 1804 and used it that same year to power a dredge (see Dredging), *Orukter amphibolos* ("amphibious Digger")—the first powered land vehicle in the United States. Between 1807 and 1817, Evans built more than 100 steam engines for industry and for Western steamboats. He proposed numerous technical advances, including artificial refrigeration that used a steam pump to volatilize ether.

Evans, Rowland, Jr., and Novak, Robert Rowland Evans, Jr., b. White Marsh, Pa., Apr. 28, 1921, and Robert Novak, b. Joliet, Ill., Feb. 26, 1931, are a team of newspaper columnists who achieved fame and sparked controversy after beginning their collaboration in 1963. Their columns were exposés rather than statements of opinion, and their conservative viewpoints sometimes infuriated liberals. Evans and Novak collaborated on *Lyndon B. Johnson: The Exercise of Power* (1966), *Nixon in the White House: The Frustration of Power* (1971), and *The Reagan Revolution* (1981). Both have appeared on television.

◼

Evans, Walker   Walker Evans, b. St. Louis, Mo., Nov. 3, 1903, d. Apr. 10, 1975, was an influential photographer whose spare images depict the richness of the American experience. From 1935 to 1937 he made many of his best-known photographs for the Farm Security Administration. In 1936, Evans accompanied James AGEE to Alabama and did the photography for Agee's brilliant prose commentary about tenant farmers, *Let Us Now Praise Famous Men* (1941). After a show (1938) at the Museum of Modern Art and a lengthy series (1938–41) of candid subway portraits, Evans worked (1945–65) for *Fortune* as a photographer and writer. He taught photography at Yale University from 1965 to 1975.

◼

Evans-Pritchard, Sir Edward   Sir Edward Evan Evans-Pritchard, b. Sept. 21, 1902, d. Sept. 11, 1973, was an influential English social anthropologist. In the 1920s and '30s he conducted extensive ethnographic fieldwork in Africa. He was a professor of anthropology at Oxford University from 1946 to 1970. Evans-Pritchard's book entitled *The Nuer* (1940), which describes the economy and society of a pastoral people, is a classic in ethnological interpretation. His other major writings include *Theories of Primitive Religion* (1965) and *The Azande: History and Political Institutions* (1971).

◼

Evanston   Evanston (1990 pop., 73,233) is a residential city in northeastern Illinois on the shore of Lake Michigan just north of Chicago. It is the seat of a number of institutions of higher learning, including NORTHWESTERN UNIVERSITY, long a major factor in the community's economic, social, and cultural life. A quiet city with an air of academic dignity, Evanston has preserved the natural beauty of its residential sections, parks, and shoreline.

Jacques Marquette and Louis Jolliet stopped at Evanston in 1674, near a natural harbor later known as Grosse Point. The first settler, Major Edward Mulford, arrived in 1826 and built a tavern. In 1854, Evanston was mapped out around Northwestern University, which opened in 1855; the town was named for Dr. John Evans, a founder of the university. Evanston was incorporated as a city in 1892.

◼

Evansville   A port on the Ohio River in southwestern Indiana, the city of Evansville is the seat of Vanderburgh County. It has a population of 126,272 (1990). It is a shipping, industrial, and commercial center in a coal, oil, and farm region.

During the 19th century, when the amount of steamboat traffic on the Ohio River was substantial, Evansville was a prominent port of call. For many years it served as a vital link between farmers in the North and the markets of the South. Today, with its modern terminal facilities, Evansville retains an air of Southern leisure. The University of Evansville and the University of Southern Indiana are located there. Evansville was founded in 1812, with Col. Hugh McGary and Gen. Robert Evans playing prominent roles in its development.

◼

evaporation   Evaporation is the conversion of a liquid substance into the gaseous state (see HYDROLOGIC CYCLE). If the liquid is in an open container, eventually it will evaporate completely. If a liquid is placed in a closed container of larger volume, some molecules leave the liquid and go into the excess space. This process continues until an equilibrium is reached, in which the molecules of vapor return to the liquid at the same rate as they evaporate. The pressure exerted by the vapor in equilibrium with its liquid is called the vapor pressure; it is a characteristic property of each substance at a given temperature, and it increases as temperature increases.

Evaporation causes a decrease in the temperature of the liquid; to maintain a constant temperature, heat must be supplied. The secretion and evaporation of sweat are the principal mechanisms by which the human body gets rid of excess heat. High humidity hinders evaporation; in conjunction with high temperature, it causes a person to feel uncomfortable.

◼

evaporite   Evaporites are SEDIMENTARY ROCKS formed from brines (salt-saturated bodies of water) concentrated by evaporation. The major minerals that precipitate to form evaporite rocks are the sulfate minerals ANHYDRITE and GYPSUM and halite, or rock salt. These accumulate to form bedded deposits, along with large amounts of associated LIMESTONE, DOLOMITE, and small quantities of magnesite, BARITE, and CELESTITE (see CARBONATE MINERALS).

The ions in SEAWATER are the most common source of major evaporite accumulations. Because they are present in minute amounts, more than 200 m (about 660 ft) of seawater must evaporate to precipitate a mineral deposit 1 m (3 ft) thick.

Sites of Formation. Evaporites may form in the arid interiors of continents or in the deepest parts of enclosed marine basins, such as the RED SEA. Continental deposits may form in regions of interior drainage such as PLAYAS or salars (saline or alkaline lakes, such as the Great Salt Lake and the northern Sahara of Algeria and Morocco) or in continental sabkhas (salt or alkaline marshes, such as those found in Egypt, Libya, and Algeria).

Evaporites are mined on every continent except Antarctica, especially throughout Europe and the Middle East, and over large areas of Australia. In the United States the leading producers are Michigan, New York, Iowa, and California.

Economic Importance. Evaporites are commonly found

Evaporites are layers of salt deposits that form in dry, arid regions from evaporation of salt water in constricted ocean gulfs or inland lakes. As surface water evaporates from confined gulfs, the concentrations of salts increase until eventually they precipitate. The least-soluble salts, calcium and magnesium carbonates (A), are deposited first, followed by calcium sulfate (B), sodium chrloride (C), calcium-sodium sulfate and potassium-magnesium-calcium sulfate (D), and finally the more soluble magnesium, potassium, and sodium borates and fluorides (E). Thick deposits are formed when subsidence, or sinking, of the basin floor occurs (F). Dissolved salts brought into the inland lakes by rivers (G) are deposited around the drying edges of the lake (H).

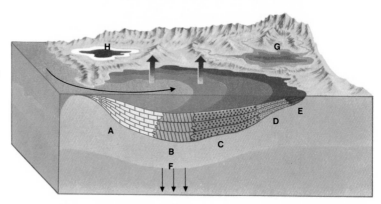

in association with oil and gas deposits, where they serve both to form suitable structures for accumulation and as seals to hold in the fluids as they develop (see SALT DOME). Evaporite minerals are used in the construction, fertilizer, and chemical industries, in the preservation and flavoring of food, and for other applications.

evapotranspiration

Evapotranspiration is the combined water loss by EVAPORATION from a SOIL or water surface and transpiration from vegetation. It is responsible for the return to the atmosphere of an estimated two-thirds of the PRECIPITATION that falls on the land areas of the Earth. Hydrologists distinguish between potential and actual evapotranspiration, defining the former as the amount of water that would be lost from an extensive, closed (no bare spots), homogeneous (all growing to the same height) vegetation cover that never suffers from a lack of water. Potential evapotranspiration depends only on the climatic factors of solar energy, WIND, and HUMIDITY. Actual evapotranspiration depends on soil moisture content—a variable quantity, especially in semiarid areas—as well as on climatic factors, the type of vegetation cover, the type of soil, and land-management practices. In summer, rates of potential evapotranspiration average close to 5 mm (0.25 in) per day across the United States.

See also: DROUGHT; HYDROLOGIC CYCLE; IRRIGATION.

Evarts, William Maxwell

[ev'-urts]   William Maxwell Evarts, b. Boston, Feb. 6, 1818, d. Feb. 28, 1901, was a noted U.S. lawyer and diplomat. He was the government's counsel in the indictment for treason of Jefferson Davis in 1867. His successful defense of President Andrew Johnson in the impeachment trial of 1868 won him an appointment as U.S. attorney general that year. He was a U.S. counsel in the arbitration of the Alabama Claims in 1871–72. The Republican attorney for Rutherford B. Hayes in the disputed 1876 presidential election, Evarts became Hayes's secretary of state (1877–81) and established the principle of U.S. control over any canal built across the Isthmus of Panama. Evarts was also a U.S. senator from New York (1885–91).

Evatt, Herbert Vere

[ev'-uht, veer]   A brilliant Australian lawyer and leftist political leader, Herbert Evatt, b. Apr. 30, 1894, d. Nov. 2, 1965, was a member of the New South Wales legislature (1925–30) before becoming a judge of the High Court of Australia. In 1941 he was appointed attorney general and minister for external affairs in the Labor government. He helped write the United Nations Charter and led (1946–48) the Australian delegation to the UN General Assembly. Later president of the Assembly (1948–49), he championed the rights of small nations. He headed the Australian Labor party from 1951 to 1960, when he retired from politics to become chief justice of New South Wales.

Eve

According to the Bible, Eve was the first woman—the mother of Cain, Abel, and Seth. God created her from the rib of ADAM to be his wife. She and Adam lived in the Garden of EDEN until they were expelled for eating the forbidden fruit from the tree of knowledge (Genesis 2–4).

See also: ORIGINAL SIN.

Evelyn, John

[eev'-lin]   The English writer John Evelyn, b. 1620, d. Feb. 27, 1706, is remembered primarily as a diarist. Covering the years 1641 to 1706, his diary gives a valuable insight into political events during that time. It was first published in 1818, and modern editions were published in 1955 and 1983.

After study at Oxford and military service abroad, Evelyn devoted his life to scientific pursuits. He was a founding member of the Royal Society and was its secretary in 1672. His many works include translations of Lucretius (1656, in verse) and Saint John Chrysostom (1659). An enthusiastic gardener, Evelyn also wrote a book on the cultivation of trees, *Sylva* (1664).

evening primrose

Evening primroses constitute about 80 species of herbaceous plants in the genus *Oenothera*, family Onagraceae. *O. biennis*, the best-known species, is a robust, biennial weedy herb. Its roots

The evening primrose, also called the sundrop, grows wild in North America and Europe. Other evening primrose species are prized by gardeners for their evening flowers, which have a sweet fragrance.

are large and fleshy, often 5 cm (2 in) in diameter at the crown, and its stems, 0.9–1.2 m (3–4 ft) high, are usually simple or branched. Its yellow flowers open in the evening. Native to the Western Hemisphere, *O. biennis* has been introduced into most of Europe.

Everest, Mount   Mount Everest, the world's highest mountain, rises in the eastern HIMALAYAS between Nepal and Tibet, about 160 km (100 mi) northeast of Katmandu. A young, limestone mountain not yet worn by erosion, it has two peaks, one of which reaches 8,848 m (29,028 ft; new measurements were undertaken in the late 1980s). Everest is covered with snow except for its bare, gale-swept summits. Many glaciers, including spectacular Rongbuk, feed rivers that rise near Everest's base. The mountain supports little life, although spiders and insects have been found as high as 6,100 m (20,000 ft). The mountain's name, given in 1865, honors Sir George Everest, the British surveyor general of India who established the location and approximate altitude of the mountain. The Tibetan name *Chomolungma* means "goddess mother of the world."

Climbing attempts began in the early 1920s, and several expeditions came within 300 m (1,000 ft) of the top. Success was achieved after the development of special equipment to cope with the low oxygen supply, high winds, and extreme cold. On May 29, 1953, Edmund HILLARY of New Zealand and Tenzing Norgay, a Sherpa, members of a British expedition led by Col. John Hunt, reached the top. Everest has since been climbed many times. The first U.S. success was in 1963.

Everett, Edward   Edward Everett, b. Dorchester, Mass., Apr. 11, 1794, d. Jan. 15, 1865, was a U.S. statesman and orator. He was a professor of Greek literature at Harvard (1819–25) and editor of the *North American Review* and later served as a congressman (1825–35), governor of Massachusetts (1836–40), minister to England (1841–45), president of Harvard (1846–49), and secretary of state (1852–53). Elected to the Senate in 1853, he resigned in 1854 under criticism for his compromising views on slavery. Everett ran for vice-president in 1860 on the slate of the CONSTITUTIONAL UNION PARTY. On Nov. 19, 1863, he made the keynote speech at the dedication of the Gettysburg National Cemetery, the occasion that also called forth Abraham Lincoln's famed Gettysburg Address.

Everglades   The Everglades are extensive marshlands in southern Florida. They originally extended about 160 km (100 mi) from Lake OKEECHOBEE south to the Gulf of Mexico. More than 64 km (40 mi) wide in some sections, they have an area of 10,360 km² (4,000 mi²). The northern part of the Everglades has been drained by a complex system of canals and dikes, and its rich soils are now used for farming. The southern part has been preserved as the 566,795-ha (1,400,533-acre) Everglades National Park, established in 1947. Only about 200 SEMINOLE Indians, the original inhabitants of the area, now remain in the Everglades.

The Everglades were formed in a flat, shallow basin with a limestone floor that slopes very gradually to the Gulf of Mexico. The area receives more than 1,400 mm (55 in) of rain annually. Water accumulates on the surface because the porous limestone floor has been sealed by peat deposits formed by decomposing vegetation. Evaporation and drainage to the Gulf of Mexico regulate the water level.

The Everglades support a unique pattern of vegetation characterized by plains of saw grass and thick hummocks of pine, cypress, and mangrove trees. The mangrove may grow as high as 21–24 m (70–80 ft). Animal life includes alligators, manatee, and cougars. Birdlife is plentiful and varied, including herons, ibis, kites, and turkey vultures.

A typical Everglades swamp contains low islands that support such trees as the bald cypress. Water hyacinth floats on the water's surface and Spanish moss hangs from trees. The Everglades support a varied fauna of birds, mammals, and reptiles.

The park is the home of many rare species, such as the Florida panther.

A unique ecological system, the Everglades are under threat from 100 years of dredging, draining, and land clearing. The flow of water across the area and into the Biscayne Aquifer has been drastically reduced; seawater has intruded into the aquifer; and fertilizer runoff has encouraged the growth of algae and of nonindigenous flora. A major rescue effort has begun, involving the restoration of natural water courses throughout the Everglades.

Tennis star Chris Evert was one of the greatest women players in history. By the time she retired in 1989, Evert had won 18 Grand Slam singles titles and 157 professional singles titles overall, the latter an all-time record.

Evergood, Philip   Philip Evergood, b. New York City, Oct. 26, 1901, d. Mar. 11, 1973, was an American artist whose paintings during the 1930s dealt with hunger, war, and the Great Depression. His early paintings—biblical subjects, literary themes, and fantasy— were exhibited in his first one-man show in 1927 in New York City. His later subject matter was often more symbolic in content. In *My Forebears Were Pioneers* (1940; Georgia Museum of Art, Athens), Evergood depicts a stiff-backed old woman in a rocking chair beside an emaciated hound.

evergreen   Evergreens are trees and shrubs that are never completely without leaves. The leaves are not all shed at one time but at intervals as new leaves are formed, and they persist for as long as 15 years. The leaves often have a heavy cuticle, or waxy coating, and may have stomata deep within the epidermis. Leaf retention may be beneficial during winter or drought, when absorption of water is difficult and heavy transpiration detrimental. CONIFERS are a major evergreen group.

everlasting   Everlastings are flowers that retain their form and color when dried. They are often used in winter bouquets. Most are members of the family Compositae, and their lasting qualities are produced by their brightly colored bracts—modified leaves surrounding the bases of the flowers—which resemble petals and are strawlike in texture. The most popular everlastings are *Helichrysum bracteatum* and *Helipterum roseum*, both called strawflowers, and the daisy, *Xeranthemum annuum*.

Evers [family] [ev′-urz]   The Evers brothers of Decatur, Miss., became prominent in the black civil rights movement in the 1960s. **Medgar Wiley Evers,** b. July 2, 1925, d. June 12, 1963, was the first field secretary of the National Association for the Advancement of Colored People in the state of Mississippi. During the late 1950s and early 1960s he registered black voters and organized boycotts of firms that practiced racial discrimination. He was shot and killed by a sniper in front of his home. **James Charles Evers,** b. Sept. 11, 1922, continued his brother's work in the NAACP. Between 1969 and 1989, when he switched parties from Democrat to Republican, he served four terms (not all continuous) as mayor of Fayette, Miss.

Evert, Chris   Christine Marie Evert, b. Ft. Lauderdale, Fla., Dec. 21, 1954, was the outstanding woman tennis player of the 1970s and early 1980s. Noted for her excellent ground strokes, consistency, and mental toughness, Evert played world-class tennis from 1969 to 1989. Along the way she won 18 Grand Slam singles titles—6 U.S. Opens (1975–78, 1980, 1982), 3 Wimbledon crowns (1974, 1976, 1981), 2 Australian Opens (1982, 1984), and a record 7 French Opens (1974–75, 1979–80, 1983, 1985–86)—a total surpassed only by Margaret Court (24) and Helen Wills Moody (19). In 56 lifetime Grand Slam appearances, Evert failed to reach the semifinals only 4 times, and for 13 consecutive years (1974–86) she won at least one Grand Slam title, a record that may never be equaled. Evert was ranked number one in the world a total of 7 times (1974–78, 1980–81).

Everyman   *Everyman* (late 15th century), written by an unknown Dutch author and soon adapted into English, is the best and the most famous example of the MEDIEVAL DRAMA form the morality play. An allegory, it is often revived and redramatized. The play portrays a carousing Everyman who is informed by Death of his approaching end. When Fellowship, Worldly Goods, Beauty, and other companions are unwilling to accompany him, he understands the transience of earthly life and the importance of eternity. With the help of Knowledge and Good Deeds, Everyman repents, regains his faith, and is saved. Vexing the Devil, he then steps into his grave calmly.

evidence   Evidence is a legal term meaning the information that a jury is permitted to consider in resolving disputed questions of fact. Evidence includes the oral statements of witnesses produced by the parties to the litigation; documents such as deeds and written contracts; objects such as an axe allegedly used in a slaying; and data gathered from scientific tests, such as blood grouping, and technical appliances, such as police radar equipment, if the test or appliance has been authenticated to the court's satisfaction. Scientific tests and appliances inevitably involve experts, but expert testimony is not limited to tests and appliances. As a general rule, the opinions and conclusions of a witness judged to be an expert will be allowed in evidence whenever the expert is better qualified than the jury to assess the facts of a particular situation.

Direct and Circumstantial Evidence

Evidence is either direct or circumstantial. Direct evidence, if true, immediately establishes the fact that was to be proved, while circumstantial evidence, even if true, still requires that the fact be inferred. Thus, the statement "I saw John and Jane married in a magistrate's office 20 years ago" is direct evidence of the marriage; if true, this evidence immediately establishes the fact of marriage. On the other hand, "John and Jane have lived in our community as man and wife for 20 years" is only circumstantial; the fact of marriage remains to be inferred.

The principal requirement of evidence is that it be relevant. The information offered must have some tendency to prove or disprove some disputed question of fact. Direct evidence is always relevant. The offer of circumstantial evidence, on the other hand, forces a court to examine its probative quality. In some instances, the decision to admit circumstantial evidence will turn altogether on precedent. In prosecutions for murder, for example, courts long ago determined that evidence of flight may tend to prove a consciousness of guilt, and consciousness of guilt in turn may tend to prove guilt itself.

Rules Excluding Evidence

The requirement of relevance has obvious advantages. It concentrates the jury's attention on the problem at hand, saves valuable time, and, most important, minimizes the possibility that the jury's verdict will be influenced by prejudice or bias. But relevance is not the only criterion applied to determine if evidence may be admitted. Most of the law of evidence has to do with various exclusionary rules that keep a jury from hearing admittedly relevant evidence. The reasons for these rules vary. The three principal ones involve hearsay, privilege, and evidence obtained illegally.

Hearsay. The best known, and perhaps least understood, of the exclusionary rules is that dealing with hearsay. The Federal Rules of Evidence define hearsay as "a statement, other than one made by the declarant while testifying at the trial or hearing, offered in evidence to prove the truth of the matter asserted." First, then, hearsay is a statement not made at a trial or a hearing but merely reported there. But the second requirement of hearsay is even more important: the reported statement will be hearsay only if it is offered in an attempt to prove the truth of the matter asserted. Thus, in a prosecution of B for assaulting A, an investigating officer might testify that A said that B assaulted him or her. If this report is

offered for the purpose of showing that B did in fact assault A, it is plainly hearsay. But if it is offered merely to establish A's physical condition at the time in question (for example, that he or she was able to speak) the evidence is not hearsay; it does not matter that the reported remark was made outside the courtroom, because the accuracy of the remark is of no consequence.

Hearsay is not always rejected. The law recognizes a number of situations in which evidence may be considered sufficiently trustworthy even though it is plainly hearsay.

Privilege. Much relevant evidence is not allowed because it would violate the various rules involving privilege. Privilege may arise from a particular relationship, such as that between husband and wife or attorney and client, or it may relate to a particular fact, such as how one voted at the last election.

Of the various relationship privileges, the most widely recognized is that between husband and wife. Other privileges frequently met with involve attorney and client, priest and penitent, and doctor and patient.

Even when a privilege is recognized, it is not absolute; it may always be waived by the party entitled to claim it. Moreover, the privilege will often be in some degree inapplicable. For example, if a husband or wife is prosecuted for assaulting his or her spouse, he or she has no privilege to request that the spouse not testify to the assault. The assaulted party has a privilege in the sense that he or she may refuse to testify *against* the spouse, but the assaulted may be compelled to be a witness *for* the spouse.

Privilege is increasingly coming to be looked on with disfavor. An exception is the important privilege against SELF-INCRIMINATION constitutionally guaranteed by the 5th Amendment. This privilege, which extends to nonjudicial proceedings such as legislative investigations, is most often invoked in court by a criminal defendant who chooses not to testify. This is his or her privilege, and a jury is not allowed to draw adverse inferences from the defendant's mere failure to testify.

Evidence Obtained Illegally. The third especially important group of rules excluding clearly relevant evidence of obvious probative value has to do with evidence obtained illegally. Since the 1960s the overall prohibition against illegally obtained evidence has commonly been called the exclusionary rule. For the most part, this group of rules is thought to be required by the 4th and 5th amendments to the Constitution or, if not actually required, highly desirable to enforce the guarantees of those amendments. The 4th Amendment requires "probable cause" for search warrants and prohibits "unreasonable searches." To enforce these provisions, the Supreme Court has ruled that evidence obtained by their violation is inadmissible. Similarly, the due-process and self-incrimination clauses of the 5th Amendment prohibit the use of illegally obtained confessions.

The widely known MIRANDA V. ARIZONA case laid down rules that the police must follow whenever a suspect is taken into custody or otherwise deprived of his or her freedom. The suspect has a right to remain silent and to have an attorney, and, if the suspect cannot afford one, to request that an attorney be appointed for him or her. Before any of these rights can be disregarded, the suspect must make a knowing and intelligent waiver. Evidence obtained in violation of these rules is summarily rejected. Even where the *Miranda* warnings have been given, a confession will be ruled inadmissible if for any reason it appears to be involuntary.

Other sources of illegally obtained evidence include impermissibly suggestive police lineups and the suggestive handling of photographs where a prospective witness, usually the victim of a crime, is asked to make an identification. To insure the fairness of such procedures, the suspect's counsel must be present.

evil eye   The evil eye, the ability of certain people to convey misfortune through their gaze, is a feature of traditional belief in many regions of the world. Associated since antiquity with the Mediterranean area and the Muslim peoples of the Middle East, it also occurs among the Yucatán Maya and the Ugandan Lugbara. Individuals in these societies often wear protective AMULETS to ward off its ill effects. The possessor of the evil eye may unintentionally cause harm to others, although he or she is usually said to be motivated by envy. A belief in the evil eye may thus discourage envy and underline boundaries of acceptable behavior, both for those suspected of possessing the evil eye and for their potential victims.

evolution   Evolution is the process by which all living things have developed from primitive organisms through changes occurring over billions of years, a progression that includes the most advanced animals and plants. Exactly how evolution occurs is still a matter of debate, but that it occurs is a scientific fact. Biologists agree that all living things arose through a long history of changes shaped by physical and chemical processes that are still

taking place. It is plausible that all organisms can be traced back to the origin of life from inanimate matter.

The most direct proof of evolution is furnished by the science of PALEONTOLOGY, or the study of life in the past through fossil remains or impressions, usually in rock. Additional evidence comes from comparative studies of living animals and plants, including their structure (comparative anatomy), biochemistry, EMBRYOLOGY, and geographical distribution. Approximately 2 million different species of organisms are now living, but it is estimated that at least 99.9 percent of the species that have ever lived are now extinct and that some 2 billion species have evolved during the past 600 million years.

Changes occur in living organisms that serve to increase their adaptability, or potential for survival and reproduction, in the face of changing environments. Evolution apparently has no built-in direction or foreordained purpose. A given kind of organism may evolve only when it occurs in a variety of forms differing in hereditary characteristics, or traits, that are passed from parent to offspring. Purely by chance, some varieties prove to be ill adapted to their current environment and thus disappear, whereas others prove to be adaptive, and their numbers increase. The elimination of the unfit, or the "survival of the fittest," is known as NATURAL SELECTION because it is nature that discards or favors a particular variant. Basically, evolution takes place only when natural selection operates on a population of organisms containing diverse inheritable forms. Recently natural selection was demonstrated for the first time outside of the laboratory when scientists observed guppies change their reproductive behavior over an 11-year period in direct response to being transferred to a new environment that had different predators.

History

Until the mid-19th century, naturalists believed that each species was created separately, either through a supreme being or through spontaneous generation—the concept

Charles Darwin (left) *and Alfred Russel Wallace* (right) *presented their papers on natural selection to the Linnaean Society of London on July 1, 1858. Darwin published a more complete statement of his theory in* On the Origin of Species; *the title page of the first edition is shown* (center). *Darwin's and Wallace's theories laid the basis for research on the evolution of plants and animals.*

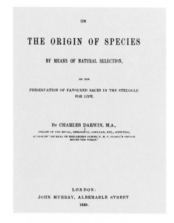

ON

THE ORIGIN OF SPECIES

BY MEANS OF NATURAL SELECTION,

OR THE
PRESERVATION OF FAVOURED RACES IN THE STRUGGLE
FOR LIFE.

By CHARLES DARWIN, M.A.,
FELLOW OF THE ROYAL, GEOLOGICAL, LINNÆAN, ETC., SOCIETIES;
AUTHOR OF 'JOURNAL OF RESEARCHES DURING H. M. S. BEAGLE'S VOYAGE
ROUND THE WORLD.'

LONDON:
JOHN MURRAY, ALBEMARLE STREET.
1859.

that organisms arose fully developed from soil or water. The work of the Swedish naturalist Carolus LINNAEUS in advancing the classifying of biological organisms focused attention on the close similarity between certain species. Speculation arose as to the existence of a sort of blood relationship between these species. These questions—coupled with the emerging sciences of geology and paleontology—gave rise to hypotheses that the life-forms of the day evolved from earlier forms through a process of change. Extremely important was the realization that different layers of rock represented different time periods and that each layer had a distinctive set of fossils of life-forms that had lived in the past.

Lamarckism. Jean Baptiste LAMARCK was one of several theorists who proposed an evolutionary theory based on the "use and disuse" of organs. Lamarck stated that an individual acquires traits during its lifetime and that such traits are in some way incorporated into the hereditary material and passed to the next generation. This was an attempt to explain how a species could change gradually over time. According to Lamarck, giraffes, for example, have long necks because for many generations individual giraffes stretched to reach the uppermost leaves of trees; in each generation the giraffes added some length to their necks, and they passed this on to their offspring. New organs therefore arise from new needs and develop in proportion to the extent that they are used; conversely, disuse of organs leads to their disappearance.

Later the science of GENETICS disproved Lamarck's theory: it was found that acquired traits cannot be inherited. No evidence exists that acquired traits can alter genetic makeup and be passed to succeeding generations.

Darwin and Wallace. After more than 20 years of observation and experiment, Charles DARWIN presented his theory of evolution through natural selection to the Linnaean Society of London in 1858. He presented his discovery simultaneously with another English naturalist, Alfred Russel WALLACE, who independently discovered natural selection at about the same time. The following year Darwin published his full theory, supported with enormous evidence, in *On the Origin of Species*. Darwin's triumph was in seeing the relationship between natural selection and heritable variations in populations, although he never understood how heritable changes occurred or resulted in variation.

Genetics. The principal contribution of genetics to the understanding of evolution has been the explanation of the inheritance of variability in individuals of the same species. Gregor MENDEL discovered the basic principles of inheritance in 1865, but his work was unknown to Darwin. Mendel's work was "rediscovered" by other scientists around 1900. From that time to 1925 the science of genetics developed rapidly, and many of Darwin's ideas about the inheritance of variations were found to be incorrect. Only in the years since 1925 has natural selection again been recognized as essential in evolution. The modern, or synthetic, theory of evolution combines the findings of modern genetics with the basic framework supplied by Darwin and Wallace, creating the basic principle of POPULATION GENETICS, which describes, in mathematical terms, the consequences of heredity on a population—a group of interbreeding individuals—rather than on a single individual. Modern population genetics was developed largely during the 1930s and '40s. According to the synthetic theory, variability among individuals in a population of sexually reproducing organisms is produced by mutation and genetic recombination. The resulting genetic variability is subject to natural selection in the environment.

Individuals with characteristics making them more successful in using the resources of the environment are more likely to survive and reproduce, whereas the others with less favorable characteristics are less likely to reproduce. The hereditary patterns controlling the more favorable characteristics are therefore passed on in greater frequency to the next generation. The resulting change in the genetic makeup of the population in the next generation constitutes evolution.

New Species

New species may evolve either by the change of one species to another or by the splitting of one species into two or more new species. Splitting, the predominant mode of species formation, results from the geographical isolation of populations of species. Isolated populations undergo different mutations, recombinations, and selection pressures and may evolve along different lines. If the isolation is sufficient to prevent interbreeding with other populations, these differences may become extensive enough to establish a new species (a group of organisms that does not successfully interbreed with any other group). When a single group of organisms diversifies over time into several subgroups by expanding (radiating) into the available niches of a new environment, it is said to undergo ADAPTIVE RADIATION.

DARWIN'S FINCHES, in the Galápagos Islands, west of Ecuador, illustrate adaptive radiation. They were probably the first land birds to reach the islands, and, in the absence of competition, they occupied several ecological habitats and diverged along several different lines. Such patterns of divergence are reflected in the biologists' scheme of classification of organisms, which groups together animals that have common characteristics. An adaptive radiation of great importance followed the first conquest of land by vertebrates.

Natural selection can also lead populations of different species living in similar environments or having similar ways of life to evolve similar characteristics. This is called convergent evolution and reflects the similar selective pressure of similar environments. Examples of convergent evolution are the eye in cephalopod mollusks, such as the octopus, and in vertebrates; wings in insects, extinct flying reptiles, birds, and bats; and the flipperlike appendages of the sea turtle (reptile), penguin (bird), and walrus (mammal).

Molecular Evolution

An outpouring of new evidence supporting evolution has come in the 20th century from molecular biology, an unknown field in Darwin's day. The fundamental tenet of

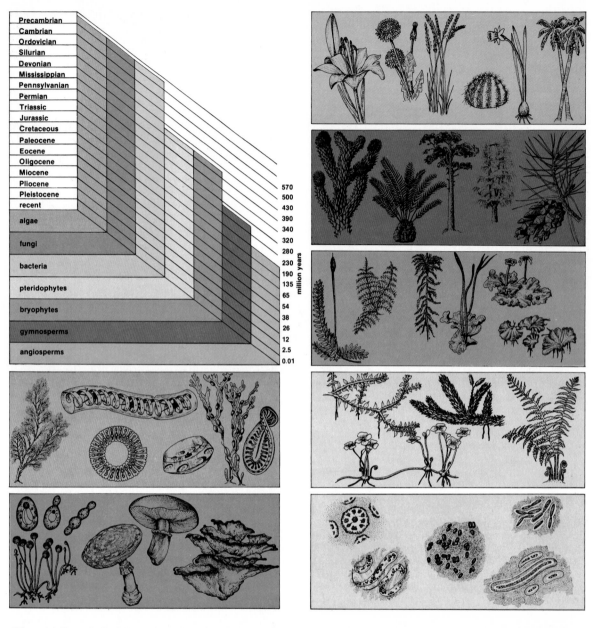

This graph indicates the fossil history of bacteria, fungi, and various groups of multicellular plants. Bacteria apparently originated over three billion years ago. Unicellular algae evolved perhaps 1.5 billion years ago, and multicellular forms emerged later in the Precambrian. Not many fossils have been found of the fungi, today represented by yeasts, molds, and mushrooms. Bryophytes, including mosses and liverworts, appear in the Devonian fossil record. Pteridophytes, which include ferns, horsetails, and club mosses, dominated the Devonian land flora. Gymnosperms, such as cycads, conifers, and ginkgos, became dominant in the drier climates of the Mesozoic Era (Triassic through Cretaceous). Angiosperms, or flowering plants, originated in the Jurassic and spread explosively during the Cretaceous Period.

molecular biology is that genes are coded sequences of the DNA molecule in the chromosome (see GENETIC CODE) and that a gene codes for a precise sequence of amino acids in a protein. Mutations alter DNA chemically, lead-ing to modified or new proteins (see TRANSPOSON). Over evolutionary time, proteins have had histories that are as traceable as those of large-scale structures such as bones and teeth.

Plant Evolution

Biologists believe that plants arose from the multicellular green algae (phylum Chlorophyta) that invaded the land about 400 million years ago. Evidence is based on modern green algae having in common with modern plants the same photosynthetic pigments, cell walls of cellulose, and multicellular forms having a life cycle characterized by ALTERNATION OF GENERATIONS. Photosynthesis almost certainly developed first in bacteria. The green algae may have been preadapted to land. Adaptations present in most plants today include the cuticle, which slows water evaporation; the waxy coating; the stomata, pores that allow carbon dioxide to enter leaves and stems during photosynthesis; and the protective cells around the sex organs to prevent desiccation.

The two major groups of plants are the bryophytes and the tracheophytes; the two groups most likely diverged from one common group of plants. The bryophytes, which lack complex conducting systems, are relatively small and are found in moist areas. The tracheophytes are vascular plants with efficient conducting systems; they dominate the landscape today. The seed is the major development in tracheophytes, and it is most important for survival on land.

Fossil evidence indicates that land plants first appeared during the Silurian Period of the Paleozoic Era (425–400 million years ago) and diversified in the Devonian Period. Near the end of the Carboniferous Period, fernlike plants had seedlike structures. At the close of the Permian Period, when the land became drier and colder, seed plants gained an evolutionary advantage and became the dominant plants.

Plant leaves have a wide range of shapes and sizes, and some variations of leaves are adaptations to the environment; for example, small, leathery leaves found on plants in dry climates are able to conserve water and to capture less light. Also, early angiosperms adapted to seasonal water shortages by dropping their leaves during periods of drought.

Evidence for Evolution

FOSSIL RECORDS furnish important insights into the history of life. The order of fossils, starting at the bottom and rising upward in stratified rock, corresponds to their age, from oldest to youngest.

Deep Cambrian rocks, up to 570 million years old, contain the remains of various marine invertebrate animals—sponges, jellyfish, worms, shellfish, starfish, and crustaceans. These INVERTEBRATES were already so well developed that they must have become differentiated during the long period preceding the Cambrian. Some fossil-bearing rocks lying well below the oldest Cambrian strata contain imprints of jellyfish, tracks of worms, and traces of soft corals and other animals of uncertain nature (see EDIACARAN FAUNA).

Paleozoic waters were dominated by bizarre arthropods called TRILOBITES and large scorpionlike forms called eurypterids. Common in all Paleozoic periods (570–230 million years ago) were the NAUTILOIDS, which are related to the modern nautilus, and the BRACHIOPODS, or lamp-

shells. The odd GRAPTOLITES, colonial animals whose carbonaceous remains resemble pencil marks, attained the peak of their development in the Ordovician Period (500–430 million years ago) and then abruptly declined. In the mid-1980s researchers found fossil animal burrows in rocks of the Ordovician Period; these trace fossils indicate that terrestrial ecosystems may have evolved sooner than was once thought.

Many of the prominent Paleozoic marine invertebrate groups became extinct or declined sharply in numbers before the Mesozoic Era (230–65 million years ago). During the Mesozoic, shelled ammonoids (see AMMONITE) flourished in the seas, and insects and reptiles were the predominant land animals. At the close of the Mesozoic the once-successful marine ammonoids perished and the reptilian dynasty collapsed, giving way to birds and mammals. Insects have continued to thrive and have differentiated into a staggering number of species.

During the course of evolution plant and animal groups have interacted to one another's advantage. For example, as flowering plants have become less dependent on wind for pollination, a great variety of insects have emerged as specialists in transporting pollen. The colors and fragrances of flowers have evolved as adaptations to attract insects. Birds, which feed on seeds, fruits, and buds, have evolved rapidly in intimate association with the flowering plants. The emergence of herbivorous mammals has coincided with the widespread distribution of nutritious grasses, and the herbivorous mammals in turn have contributed to the evolution of carnivorous mammals.

Fish and Amphibians. During the Devonian Period (390–340 million years ago) the vast land areas of the Earth were largely barren of animal life, save for rare creatures such as scorpions and millipedes. The seas, however, were crowded with a variety of invertebrate animals. The fresh and salt waters also contained a highly diversified and abundant assemblage of cartilaginous and bony FISH. From one of the many groups of fish inhabiting pools and swamps emerged the first land vertebrates, starting the vertebrates on their conquest of all available terrestrial habitats.

Prominent among the numerous Devonian aquatic forms were the Crossopterygii, lobe-finned fish that possessed the ability to gulp air when they rose to the surface. These ancient air-breathing fish represent the stock from which the first land vertebrates, the amphibians, were derived. Scientists continue to speculate about what led the crossopterygians to venture onto land. The crossopterygians that migrated onto land were only crudely adapted for terrestrial existence, but because they did not encounter competitors, they survived.

Lobe-finned fish did, however, possess certain characteristics that served them well in their new environment, including primitive membranous lungs and internal nostrils, both of which are essential for atmospheric breathing. Such characteristics, called preadaptations, did not develop because the crossopterygians were preparing to migrate to the land; they were already present by accident and became selected traits only when they imparted an

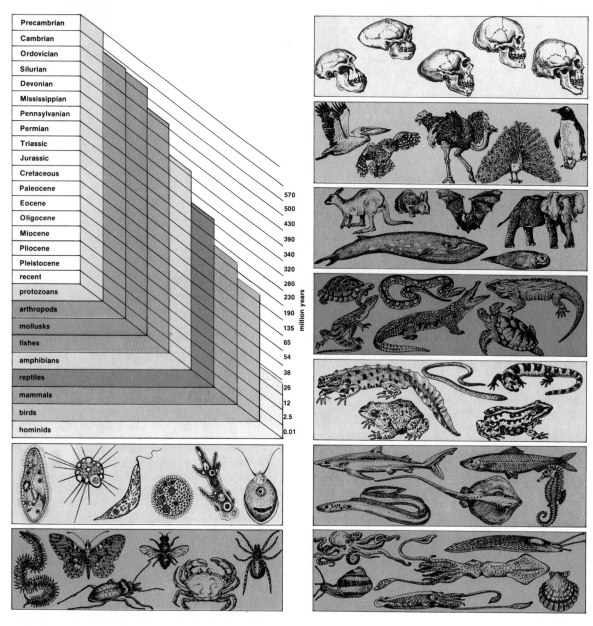

	million years
Precambrian	
Cambrian	
Ordovician	
Silurian	
Devonian	
Mississippian	
Pennsylvanian	
Permian	
Triassic	
Jurassic	
Cretaceous	
Paleocene	570
Eocene	500
Oligocene	430
Miocene	390
Pliocene	340
Pleistocene	320
recent	280
protozoans	230
arthropods	190
mollusks	135
fishes	65
amphibians	54
reptiles	38
mammals	26
birds	12
	2.5
hominids	0.01

Protozoan history dates from the Precambrian. Among the multicellular animals, many invertebrate groups were already diversified in the Cambrian Period, including arthropods and mollusks, both of which remain successful groups today. Fishes, the first vertebrates, appear in the fossil record during the Ordovician; they became abundant by the Devonian. Amphibians arose from lobe-finned fishes in the late Devonian. Reptiles, adapted to a terrestrial life, are known from the Pennsylvanian and later dominated the Mesozoic land fauna. The earliest mammals evolved from small therapsid reptiles in the Triassic. The oldest undisputed bird fossil is known from the Jurassic. Skulls dated from the Miocene to the present indicate the relatively recent divergence of hominids (humans and related species) from apes.

advantage to the fish on land.

The early land-dwelling amphibians were slim-bodied with fishlike tails, but they had limbs capable of locomotion on land. These limbs probably developed from the crossopterygians' lateral fins, which contained fleshy lobes that in turn contained bony elements. The ancient amphibians never became completely adapted for existence on land. They spent much of their lives in the water, and their modern descendants—the salamanders, newts, frogs, and toads—still must return to water to deposit their eggs. The elimination of a water-dwelling stage, which was achieved by the reptiles, represented a major evolutionary advance.

The Reptilian Dynasty. Perhaps the most important factor contributing to the emergence of reptiles from the amphibians was the development of a shell-covered amniotic egg that could be laid on land. This development enabled the reptiles to spread throughout the Earth's landmasses in one of the most spectacular adaptive radiations in biological history.

Like the eggs of birds, which developed later, reptile eggs contain a complex series of membranes that protect and nourish the embryo and help it breathe. The space between the embryo and the amnion (a thin membrane loosely enclosing the embryo) is filled with an amniotic fluid that resembles seawater; a similar fluid is found in the fetuses of mammals, including humans. This fact has been interpreted as an indication that life originated in the sea and that the balance of salts in various body fluids did not change very much in subsequent evolution. It is also significant that the membranes found in the human embryo are essentially similar to those in reptile and bird eggs. The human yolk sac remains small and functionless, and the allantois exhibits no elaborate development in the human embryo. Nevertheless, the presence of a yolk sac and allantois in the human embryo is one of the strongest pieces of evidence documenting the evolutionary relationships among the widely differing kinds of vertebrates. This suggests that mammals, including humans, are descended from animals that reproduced by means of externally laid eggs that were rich in yolk.

The reptiles, and in particular the DINOSAURS, endured as the dominant land animals of the Earth for well over 100 million years. The Mesozoic Era, during which the reptiles thrived, is often referred to as the Age of Reptiles.

In terms of evolutionary success, the larger the animal, the greater the likelihood that the animal will maintain a constant BODY TEMPERATURE independent of the environmental temperature. Birds and mammals, for example, produce and control their own body heat through internal metabolic activities (a state known as endothermy, or warm-bloodedness), whereas today's reptiles are thermally unstable (cold-blooded), regulating their body temperatures by behavioral activities (the phenomenon of ectothermy). Most scientists regard dinosaurs as lumbering, oversized, cold-blooded lizards, rather than large, lively, endothermic animals with fast metabolic rates; some biologists, however, assert that a huge dinosaur could not possibly have warmed up every morning on a sunny rock and must have relied on internal heat production.

The reptilian dynasty collapsed before the close of the Mesozoic Era. Relatively few of the myriad Mesozoic reptiles have survived to modern times; those remaining include the CROCODILES, LIZARDS, SNAKES, and TURTLES. The cause of the decline and death of the large array of reptiles is obscure, but their demise is usually attributed to some radical change in environmental conditions (see EXTINCTION).

Like the giant reptiles, most lineages of organisms have eventually become extinct, although some have not changed appreciably in millions of years. The opossum, for example, has survived almost unchanged since the late Cretaceous Period (more than 65 million years ago), and the HORSESHOE CRAB, genus *Limulus*, is not very different from fossils 500 million years old. Scientists have no adequate explanation for the unexpected stability of such organisms; perhaps they have achieved an almost perfect adjustment to a relatively unchanging environment. Such stable forms, however, are not dominant today. The human species, one of the dominant modern life-forms, has evolved rapidly in a relatively short time.

The Rise of Mammals. The decline of the reptiles provided evolutionary opportunities for birds and mammals. Small and inconspicuous during the Mesozoic Era, mammals rose to unquestionable dominance during the Cenozoic Era (beginning 65 million years ago).

The mammals diversified into marine forms, such as the whale, dolphin, seal, and walrus; fossorial (adapted to digging) forms living underground, such as the mole; flying and gliding animals, such as the bat and flying squirrel; and cursorial animals (adapted for running), such as the horse. These various mammalian groups are well adapted to their different modes of life, especially by their appendages, which developed from common ancestors to become specialized for swimming, flight, and movement on land.

Although there is little superficial resemblance among the arm of a person, the flipper of a whale, and the wing of a bat, a closer comparison of their skeletal elements shows that, bone for bone, they are structurally similar. Biologists regard such structural similarities, or homologies, as evidence of evolutionary relationships. The homologous limb bones of all four-legged vertebrates, for example, are assumed to be derived from the limb bones of a common ancestor. Biologists are careful to distinguish such homologous features from what they call analogous features, which perform similar functions but are structurally different. For example, bird and butterfly wings are analogous; both types are used for flight, but they are entirely different structurally. Analogous structures do not indicate evolutionary relationships.

Closely related fossils preserved in continuous successions of rock strata have allowed evolutionists to trace in detail the evolution of many species as it has occurred over several million years. The ancestry of the horse can be traced through thousands of fossil remains to a small terrier-sized animal with four toes on each front foot and three toes on each hind foot. This ancestor lived in the Eocene Epoch, about 54 million years ago. From fossils in the higher layers of stratified rock, the horse is found to have gradually acquired its modern form by eventually evolving to a one-toed horse almost like modern horses and finally to the modern horse, which dates back about 1 million years.

Primate Radiation. PRIMATES, the order of mammals to which humans belong, underwent adaptive radiation in Cenozoic times. Except for humans, who are fully adapted for life on the ground, primates are primarily tree dwellers. Many primate characteristics evolved as adaptations to arboreal life.

There is almost universal agreement that the APES are

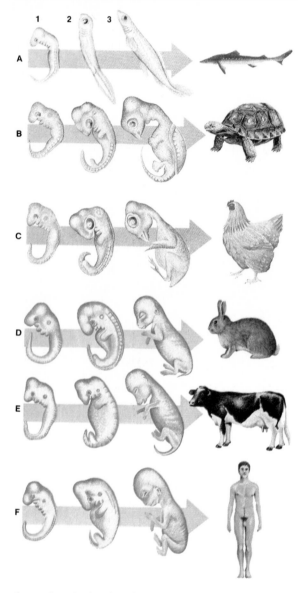

Comparative embryology shows that early stages of vertebrate embryos resemble one another more closely than do later stages. This is cited as evidence of a common ancestor. The young embryos (column 1) of a fish (A), tortoise (B), chicken (C), rabbit (D), cow (E), and human (F) are difficult to distinguish; each has a fishlike tail and gill slits. As development proceeds (columns 2 and 3), distinctive features of each group become evident, first among distantly related groups and later among more closely related species.

the closest living relatives of humans and that the line that ultimately led to the human form diverged from the ape line during the Tertiary Period (65–2 million years ago). Several humanlike fossils dating from this period have been proposed as possible human ancestors (see PREHISTORIC HUMANS). Comparisons of genetic material suggest a divergence only about 5 million years ago, an estimate at variance with prevailing interpretations of the fossil record. The resolution of this matter awaits the unearthing and analysis of further remains from the time period in question.

Relatively few anatomical and physiological differences exist between modern humans and the living great apes. Their close relationship can be clearly demonstrated by comparing the amino-acid sequences in their fibrinopeptide molecules, which in different mammalian species have undergone rapid and numerous changes. The differences between humans and other primates can be counted as follows: chimpanzees, none; orangutans, 2; gibbons, 5; Old World monkeys, 5; New World monkeys, 9 to 10; and prosimians such as the slow loris, 18. Humans and African apes are in fact more closely related to each other than either is to the Asian orangutans.

The most pronounced differences between human beings and apes have to do with locomotor habits and brain growth: humans have a fully upright posture and gait and a much larger brain. The cranial capacity of a modern ape rarely exceeds 600 cm^3 (37 in^3), while the average human being has a cranial capacity of 1,350 cm^3 (82 in^3). The superior intelligence of humans, gradually acquired through evolution, has helped them master a wide variety of different environments.

Social Behavior. Many species of higher organisms, particularly birds and mammals, exhibit highly structured social interactions. Since cooperative social behavior helps members of the group to survive, it is reasonable to assume that behavioral dispositions have evolved just as morphological and physiological traits have evolved. While the evolutionary process generally tends to select organisms that are optimally designed for individual reproduction, however, in many species social behavior has evolved that promotes the reproductive advantage of certain members of the population but is generally detrimental to individual reproduction. In social insects, for example, a female worker bee refrains from breeding and devotes her entire life to assisting the queen bee. Evolutionists do not yet fully understand how it is possible to select for behavior disposition that is beneficial to the species as a whole but that is costly to the individual.

Punctuated Equilibria

Because evolutionary events in the past are not amenable to direct observation or experimental verification, the processes of evolution over the course of Earth's history must be inferred. Most students of evolution hold the view that evolution in the past was guided by the same evolutionary forces being witnessed in operation today, and that small genetic variations have gradually accumulated in evolving lineages over periods of millions of years. Were a complete set of fossil specimens of a lineage somehow to be recovered, it would be expected to exhibit a graded series of forms changing continuously from the antecedent to the descendant species. In this view, a lack of transitional fossil forms between some given ancestral and descendant populations represents merely the imperfect nature of the fossil record, comparable to a book with random pages missing.

In recent years, Stephen Jay GOULD of Harvard University and Niles Eldredge of the American Museum of Natural History have challenged this conventional view. They argue that the fossil record shows that most lineages do not change much for long intervals of geologic time; they can be said to remain in stasis, or "equilibrium." Significant evolutionary changes instead are concentrated into geologically brief periods, or "punctuations," during which the lineages actually split or branch. Under this hypothesis, known as "punctuated equilibria," the apparent gaps in the fossil record are actually a faithful rendering of the evolutionary process. Perhaps the best documented illustration of the concept is the study made in 1981 of fossil snails in the Lake Turkana region of Africa. The thick fossil beds there contain lineages of at least 19 snail species, several of which remained exceptionally stable for 3 to 5 million years. When morphological changes in shell shape did occur, they were concentrated in brief periods of 5,000 to 50,000 years; these newly evolved populations of snails thereafter persisted relatively unchanged until they became extinct.

The punctuated-equilibria hypothesis has been criticized by other scientists. In the matter of the Lake Turkana snails, for example, the observation has been made that while changes over a period of 50,000 years might appear instantaneous to a paleontologist, a geneticist would probably view 50,000 years as a quite sufficient period of time for morphological changes in snail populations to accrue gradually rather than dramatically. Evolutionists in general are doubtful that punctuational changes dominated the history of life, although recognizing a role for sudden transitions.

Neutral Evolution

A more recent controversy over theory has arisen in the field of molecular evolution. When amino acids of proteins were first compared from an evolutionary viewpoint, it was assumed that differences between two species were preserved by natural selection because each form of a protein was best in some way for its own species. Further study, however, showed that some amino-acid substitutions were not likely to produce either an evolutionary advantage or disadvantage. The mutational changes responsible for such unimportant substitutions might then be viewed as neutral and preserved by sheer chance rather than by natural selection. The major advocate of this view is Japanese geneticist Motoo Kimura, who holds that different species may have different amino-acid residues at a particular protein region not because it matters to the operation of the molecule but precisely because it does not matter. This position remains unacceptable to so-called selectionists, who ascribe all amino-acid substitutions to natural selection.

evolution, human   SEE PREHISTORIC HUMANS

Évora [e'-voh-ruh] Évora (1988 est. district pop., 174,300), the capital of Alto Alentejo province, Portugal, is situated about 115 km (70 mi) east of Lisbon. A market center for olives, cork, and livestock, it also produces iron products, textiles, rope, and flour. Historical landmarks include a Roman temple, the cathedral (begun 1186), and the 16th-century buildings of a former university (now housing a high school). Settled by Romans as a military center, Évora was taken by Moors in 712. In 1166 it was captured by the Portuguese.

Evren, Kenan Kenan Evren, b. 1918, led a military coup that overthrew the civilian government of Turkey in September 1980 and later was named (Oct. 27, 1980) president of the country. Evren was educated at the Turkish Military College and attained the rank of general in 1964. He became a leader of the National Security Council, the organization of army officers who eventually overthrew the government, abolished the constitution, imposed severe press censorship, and banned all political parties. Evren remained president until 1989, when he was succeeded by Turgut Ozal.

Ewald, Johannes [ay'-vahl] Johannes Ewald (or Evald), b. Nov. 18, 1743, d. Mar. 17, 1781, was a Danish poet and dramatist whose early writings were heavily dependent on French classicism. He gradually turned for inspiration to themes and figures from his own Scandinavian culture. *Rolf Krage* (1770) is a play about a legendary 6th-century Danish hero. Considered the first original Scandinavian tragedy on a native theme, it was based on a work by Saxo Grammaticus. *The Death of Balder* (c.1773–74; Eng. trans., 1886), a verse drama, concerns the Norse god of light and peace. Ewald collaborated with others on *Fiskerne* (The Fishermen, 1779), an operetta that contains the Danish national anthem, "King Christian Stood by the Lofty Mast."

Ewe [ay'-vay] The Ewe are a West African people, numbering about 1.5 million in the mid-1980s, in Benin, southern Togo, and southeastern Ghana. They speak various dialects of Ewe, which belongs to the Kwa subfamily of the Niger-Congo languages. Their traditional government was a confederation of many small kingdoms governed by a council of chiefs.

The Ewe are subsistence farmers, fishermen, craftsmen, and traders. Descent is traced through the paternal line. Marriage may include more than one wife and involves both payment of bride-price and premarital bride service by the prospective husband. Ewe religion centers on a creator god and a host of lesser deities; its cults are similar to those of the Fon and Yoruba, as is the culture's close tie between religion and art.

Ewell, Richard S. A Confederate general, Richard Stoddert Ewell, b. Georgetown, D.C., Feb. 8, 1817, d. Jan. 25, 1872, graduated from West Point in 1840 and served in the U.S. Army until resigning in 1861 to join the Confederacy. Ewell was a capable officer until he lost a leg at the Second Battle of Bull Run in 1862. He returned to duty in 1863 as a corps commander, but he lacked initiative in his higher position and is often held responsible for the Southern defeat at the Battle of GETTYSBURG. He led his corps into the fierce fighting of the Wilderness campaign of 1864, but his health failed, and he was put in command of local defense troops. After the war Ewell farmed in Tennessee.

Ewing, Maurice William Maurice Ewing, b. Lockney, Tex., May 12, 1906, d. May 4, 1974, was a geophysicist and oceanographer whose studies of the ocean floor provided much of the data upon which current understanding of PLATE TECTONICS is founded. After graduating from Rice University (Ph.D., 1931), Ewing applied terrestrial geophysical methods to the study of continental margins. Toward the end of World War II, Ewing joined the faculty of Columbia University (1944–74), helping to found LAMONT-DOHERTY GEOLOGICAL OBSERVATORY (1949), one of the most comprehensive Earth-science institutions in the world. He was the first to demonstrate the relationship between the MID-OCEANIC RIDGE and EARTHQUAKE epicenters, and his controversial ideas about periodic glaciation in the Northern Hemisphere (see ICE AGES) stimulated research in paleo-oceanography.

Ex parte Milligan Growing out of the Civil War, the case of *Ex parte Milligan* (1866) involved a major restraint on presidential use of military force against civilians. Milligan, a citizen of Indiana and not a member of the military forces, had been arrested at home by order of the military commander of Indiana and tried by a military commission on charges of affording "aid and comfort to rebels" and inciting "the people to insurrection." He was found guilty and sentenced to be hanged.

The Supreme Court, speaking through Justice Davis, invalidated the conviction in an opinion that made three points: first, that Milligan, a civilian, should have been tried by the Circuit Court of Indiana; second, that his right to a trial by jury guaranteed by the 6th Amendment had been violated; and third, that Milligan had been illegally denied the privilege of a writ of HABEAS CORPUS (the right to seek a hearing and be given reasons for one's confinement).

ex post facto law An ex post facto law is a retroactive law that has the effect of prejudicing the rights of a person in a criminal proceeding. The U.S. Constitution prohibits Congress and the states from enacting such laws. Ex post facto laws include those which make an act criminal after it has already been committed, increase the gravity or punishment of the offense, or prejudicially alter criminal procedure in a case—for example, by allowing less or significantly different evidence to be admissible to convict a person. Retroactive criminal laws that serve to benefit an accused are not considered to be ex post facto, nor are retroactive civil laws.

examination, medical The periodic medical examination is one of the most effective methods of detecting and diagnosing illness. Such examinations date back to ancient times, when physicians listened to heart sounds, examined the urine, and observed the pulse. Percussion—tapping of the chest or abdomen to elucidate fluid levels and the size of organs—was introduced in 1761; it was enhanced by the invention of the STETHOSCOPE in 1819. Inspection of the eye, throat, larynx, stomach, bladder, and other organs by means of mirrors and lenses began in the mid-19th century, following the development of ENDOSCOPES. Another basic diagnostic tool was added early in the 20th century with the development of medical X RAYS. Today's physicians can make use of a wide range of instrumentation.

Basic Procedures. Every examination begins with a thorough recording of the patient's medical history. The physician then attempts to elucidate the state of the patient's health and the nature of any symptoms, such as pain or sudden and prolonged weight loss. In evaluating the origin of symptoms, the doctor may ask about the patient's workplace and home environment, any medicines the patient may be taking, and the occurrence of certain diseases in the patient's family.

Physical examination follows the oral history. This includes listening to the rate and regularity of heartbeats, measuring blood pressure, percussing the abdomen and back, and testing simple reflexes. An inspection of the skin can reveal alterations such as extreme dryness, growths, ulcers, and discoloration. The breasts, prostate, and genitals are palpated to detect tumors, and endoscopic examination of the rectum and colon may be appropriate in older persons.

Laboratory Tests. Blood and urine samples are routinely taken for laboratory testing. Trained technologists count blood cells to determine whether any one component is present in excessive or diminished amounts. A high number of white blood cells, for example, could be an indication of bacterial infection; a sample of blood can be placed in a nutrient medium to search for infectious agents. The doctor may also order a measurement of the ability of the patient's blood to clot. At least two or three times during a person's early life, the amount of cholesterol in the blood should be measured. In addition, the presence of certain enzymes in the blood can confirm a suspected diagnosis of heart attack or viral angina. The urine is examined for such things as sugar, often found in diabetes; proteins, present in some kinds of kidney damage; and acid levels.

Special Techniques. Radiographic investigations may take place when other findings suggest certain conditions (see RADIOLOGY). Perhaps the most common is the X ray for detecting broken bones. An ELECTROENCEPHALOGRAPH can be taken if the doctor wants to see the patient's brain waves. One of the newer diagnostic techniques is the sleep examination, in which the patient spends one or more nights sleeping in a controlled environment while being electronically monitored.

exchange rate   An exchange rate is the rate at which one country's currency may be exchanged for that of another. Exchange rates have been governed in recent years primarily by the forces of supply and demand. The demand for a currency may come from sources such as importers and exporters, tourists, the military, private investors, or international corporations. If the total demand for a particular currency in the money market is greater than that for dollars, the value of the other currency tends to rise.

Until recently governments preferred to keep exchange rates stable. Under the GOLD STANDARD, which prevailed from the 1870s to 1914, the value of each currency was fixed in terms of gold. If the demand for a currency exceeded the supply, banks shipped gold bullion to satisfy their clients' requirements for the scarce currency. A flow of gold into a country increased its money supply, raising prices and making its goods more expensive. This, in turn, reduced foreign demand for its currency.

After World War I, the gold standard was replaced by other devices, some of which adversely affected international trade. The INTERNATIONAL MONETARY FUND was created (1944) in an effort to stabilize exchange rates without interfering with the healthy growth of trade. Currency values were still defined in terms of gold, although the place of gold in international transactions was, to a large extent, taken by the dollar. The supply of dollars was provided by a deficit in the U.S. BALANCE OF PAYMENTS averaging several billion dollars a year during the 1950s and '60s.

In 1971 the United States left the gold standard, announcing that it would no longer stand ready to convert the dollars held by foreign central banks into gold. Since 1973 all major industrial countries have allowed their currencies to "float"—that is, to find their own values in relation to each other, except for occasional intervention by CENTRAL BANKS to prevent large short-term fluctuations.

exchequer [eks-chek'-ur]   The exchequer, in Britain, is the accounting and auditing department in the government's treasury. Its name is derived from the checkered cloth on which accounts were originally worked out. Today, the exchequer and audit department is headed by the comptroller and auditor general, appointed by the crown; its independence of the executive is preserved by specific statutory provisions. Since 1866 the department has had two functions: to ensure that the collection and spending of tax revenue are properly handled and to audit departmental and other accounts. The British minister of finance is known as the chancellor of the exchequer.

exclusion principle   The exclusion principle formulated by Wolfgang PAULI is a rule used for predicting atomic and molecular structure. In its simplest form, it states that no two electrons in an atom can have all of four quantum numbers the same; at least one must be different. The state of an electron in an atom may be labeled with four quantum numbers: n, the principal quan-

tum number; l, the orbital quantum number; m, the azimuthal quantum number; and m_s, the spin quantum number. Each electron must be assigned a unique set of these numbers. More generally, the exclusion principle states that the allowed states of a system must be antisymmetric with respect to interchange between any two electrons or other FERMIONS.

See also: QUANTUM MECHANICS.

exclusionary rule   see EVIDENCE

excommunication   Excommunication is the formal expulsion of a member from a religious group. Although the censure has been used in some form by practically every church or religion, it is generally associated with the Roman Catholic church. The grounds for excommunication, as established by canon law, include heresy and the deliberate violation of church law, as, for example, in the procuring of an abortion. The effect of the excommunication is exclusion from the sacraments, especially the Eucharist. The intent of excommunication, however, is always for purposes of correction rather than punishment. Excommunications are normally automatic, but some require a judicial process. The authority to lift excommunications once imposed may fall to the pope or a bishop, depending on the seriousness of the offense and the provisions of the law itself.

excretory system   Excretory systems are special structures in organisms through which waste products of METABOLISM are rid and the proper balance of water and salts in the blood and other body fluids is maintained at the same time. Defecation is the elimination of undigested material from the body and is a function of the DIGESTIVE SYSTEM.

Urinary System

The major excretory organs in vertebrates are the KIDNEYS, which are two paired organs, one on each side of the body. The kidneys and associated organs that store and eliminate urine are collectively called the urinary system. The kidneys dispose of toxic wastes, such as ammonia, urea, and uric acid, and excess salt and water in the form of urine. The heart, in a sense, pumps blood blindly, but the kidneys monitor the quality of blood so that the organism is not poisoned by the end products of its own metabolism and the proper volume and composition of its body fluids are maintained.

The kidneys continually form urine by filtering many materials from the blood or body fluids and then returning some of these as necessary. Just what the kidneys do and how they do it varies from one vertebrate to another. In general, however, a two-way traffic route prevails between the blood, for example, and urine-forming units in the kidney. The bulk of water extracted from the blood is put back into the bloodstream, as are necessary nutrients and salts. At the same time, wastes are removed and added to

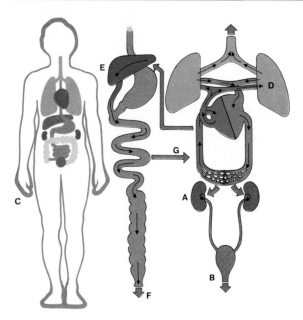

The main excretory route from the body is by way of the kidneys (A) and the bladder (B), which disposes of urine. Urine is composed of excess water, salts, toxic chemicals, urea, and uric acid. Uric acid, water, and salt are also excreted by sweat glands of the skin (C). The lungs (D) rid the body of water and carbon dioxide when a person breathes out. Bile pigments, which are products of hemoglobin breakdown, are excreted by the liver (E) in the form of bile. These pigments are either eliminated with the feces through the intestines (F) or are absorbed into the blood (G) and excreted in the urine.

the now much-concentrated urine.

The urine-forming unit of the kidney is called the nephron, which is a coiled tubule full of complicated twists and turns and too small to be seen by the naked eye. Each human kidney contains approximately 1 million nephrons, and the total filtering surface of a single kidney is as large as the surface of the entire body. The tubules of the various nephrons empty urine into collecting tubules, which in turn empty into the central cavity of the kidney, or kidney pelvis. In frogs and other amphibians, birds, and reptiles, a large duct finally empties the urine into the cloaca, which is a common chamber for eliminating urine and feces and for copulation. Mammals have no cloaca; instead, ducts, called ureters, drain into the urinary bladder. The bladder is a storage organ that is periodically emptied to the outside through another duct, the urethra.

Other Excretory Organs

Vertebrates also use the RESPIRATORY SYSTEM, special glands, and the SKIN to eliminate water, salt, and carbon dioxide, which is a relatively harmless end product of metabolism. Carbon dioxide and some excess water are discharged through the lungs; the sweat glands of mammals get rid of salts and water; many marine fish eliminate excess salt through their gills; and a rectal gland in the shark eliminates excess salt. Seabirds, such as gulls, albatrosses, and penguins, take in large quantities of salt

with their food. They can also drink seawater, which no mammal can do. For these birds, the excess salt is not eliminated through the kidneys but through specialized glands in the head. These glands have a structure entirely different from that of the kidney and can excrete a salt solution up to twice the concentration of seawater. The solution flows into the nasal cavity, runs out through the nostrils, and drips from the tip of the beak. Large sea turtles and marine iguanas of the Galápagos Islands have similar salt glands close to the eyes, and the ducts open into corners of the eye.

The Problem of Toxic Waste

All organisms share the problems of maintaining enough water to flush away the toxic by-products of metabolism. No major excretory difficulties occur with the utilization of carbohydrate and fat by the body, because these are broken down to carbon dioxide and water; the carbon dioxide is readily eliminated, and the water may be an asset. The breakdown of protein in metabolism, however, produces large quantities of highly toxic ammonia, which must be removed rapidly.

Ammonia Excretion. Ammonia excretion depends on the species and the adaptations it has made to its environment. Some organisms excrete the ammonia itself, whereas others excrete it as less toxic urea or uric acid.

Ammonia readily dissolves in water and requires large amounts of fluid for rapid elimination. In many aquatic animals, such as protozoans, sponges, coelenterates, and freshwater fish, ammonia is simply washed out by the copious supplies of water in the environment. The gills of freshwater fish, for example, are excellent devices for flushing out ammonia.

Flatworms, such as planaria and tapeworms, have developed special systems for expelling water with its dissolved ammonia and carbon dioxide. These animals possess tubes running down either side of the body and opening to excretory pores; wastes are swept from the coelom into the tubules by the beating of hairlike cilia contained in a series of flame cells. Flame cells are so called because the beating cilia gave a flickering, flame-like appearance.

Urea Excretion. Most terrestrial organisms have only a limited supply of water and therefore rapidly convert ammonia to far less toxic UREA or uric acid, and then excrete it. Mammals, amphibians, and, paradoxically, marine fish excrete urea, which also readily dissolves in water and must be expelled in a watery urine. Marine fish, however, are in constant danger of desiccation; they are much less salty than the sea, and, by OSMOSIS, water tends to flow from their bodies into the sea.

Almost all fish excrete large amounts of very watery urine, but urination reduces to a relative trickle in land animals, which must conserve their water. Humans lose approximately a liter of water daily in urine, or about 2 percent of their weight. Amphibians, such as frogs, absorb large quantities of water through their skin and can produce a substantial portion of their weight in urine daily, as can earthworms, which, although terrestrial, live in moist places.

Uric Acid Excretion. Birds, insects, and many reptiles excrete uric acid instead of urea. Unlike urea, uric acid is almost insoluble in water and, therefore, may be expelled as an almost dry pellet of urine, with very little loss of water. The urine of these animals is liquid at first, but the uric acid crystallizes out from solution, and most of the water is reabsorbed in the body. Uric acid crystals are expelled with the feces, and the droppings of birds, for example, have a dark portion of fecal matter and a whitish mass of uric acid.

The excretion of uric acid, besides conserving water, is vital because these animals lay eggs enclosed in a relatively impermeable shell. If chick embryos, for example, excreted urine containing ammonia and urea, they would rapidly be poisoned. Uric acid in solid form, however, may be safely stored in the egg. The mammalian embryo, by contrast, easily rids itself of urea through the mother's excretory system.

executive branch

executive branch The executive branch of any government is that which carries out the laws and conducts public and foreign affairs. The PRESIDENT OF THE UNITED STATES heads the executive branch of the U.S. government. The other two branches of the U.S. government are the legislative (Congress) and the judicial (courts). In each state government, the executive branch is headed by a governor.

executive privilege

executive privilege Executive privilege is the right claimed by members of the executive branch of the U.S. government to immunity from congressional investigation and judicial procedures. The claim, based on the constitutional provision of separation of powers, has long been the subject of controversy. In 1974 the U.S. Supreme Court unanimously ruled that President Richard M. NIXON must obey a subpoena to surrender tape recordings pertaining to the WATERGATE scandal. This decision invalidated claims for absolute executive privilege but affirmed the legitimacy of a limited executive privilege.

Exekias

Exekias [ek-sek'-ee-uhs] Exekias, active *c.*545–525 BC, was a Greek potter and vase painter renowned as the greatest artist to work in the so-called Black Figure style. He signed 2 vases as painter and 11 as potter; numerous other vases have been attributed to him. As a potter Exekias popularized several new vase shapes and may have invented the calyx krater. In vase painting his use of negative areas in composition was totally new, as was his interest in spatial depth. His sophisticated balances and rhythms, as in his cup *Dionysus on a Ship* (Staatliche Antikensammlungen, Munich), were outstanding.

exemplum

exemplum [eg-zem'-pluhm] An exemplum was a tale told to teach a moral lesson in a medieval sermon, or one of a collection of tales, such as the *Gesta Romanorum* (13th century), for the use of preachers or for personal edification. Often these exempla contained allegories of the Seven Deadly Sins. Chaucer's "Nun's Priest's Tale," a beast fable about a rooster, is an exemplum.

exercise

exercise Exercise is physical exertion for the purpose of improving physical fitness or for the sake of enjoyment. The primary physiologic event in exercise is contraction of skeletal muscle, or so-called voluntary muscle; this requires the greatest activity of circulatory and respiratory functions.

When a muscle contracts it compresses the blood vessels in it, but between contractions flow in exercising muscle is increased as much as 30-fold; thus, extra oxygen must be carried to active cells, and carbon dioxide away from them, at high rates. Contracting muscle cells, moreover, may increase total heat production 10 to 20 times and thus place severe demands on the mechanisms that regulate body temperature. These interrelationships between METABOLISM and the circulatory, respiratory, and nervous systems present challenging problems for physiologists and physicians.

Physical Benefits

In view of the current vogue for jogging and other forms of exercise (see RUNNING AND JOGGING), it is first worth noting that one of the clear-cut benefits of exercise is psychological. Persons who exercise regularly appear to feel better. Beyond this there is evidence that the person who exercises regularly reduces the risk of developing coronary

Exercises that increase flexibility are important in preventing disease and improving blood circulation and muscle tone.

heart disease. A 1989 study found that even mild exercise—as little as a half-hour walk daily—can delay mortality caused by cardiovascular disease and cancer in men and women of all ages.

The proven physical benefits of exercise have been observed in many studies of athletes. Trained athletes have a larger stroke volume and slower heart rate at rest than do untrained persons, and they tend to have larger hearts. During exercise, their stroke volume and heart rate increase, but a given increase in cardiac output can be effected with a smaller increase in heart rate. The maximum possible increase in cardiac output is also greater in athletes, and there is an approximately threefold increase in the oxygen extraction (uptake of oxygen from arterial blood). The increased oxygen extraction permits the athlete to boost oxygen consumption in muscle as much as a hundred times.

These results, however, depend on the kind of exercise being pursued. Jogging and other endurance exercises are called aerobic (oxygen-using); they enhance the ability of muscle to use oxygen in producing energy-rich biochemicals. Endurance-trained muscle also oxidizes less carbohydrate and more fat than does untrained muscle. Weight-lifting, sprinting, and other exercises requiring brief spurts of intense effort, however, overload the metabolic reactions that supply oxygen to muscle. Other biochemical reactions are called into play, so such exercises are called anaerobic (occurring without oxygen). These exercises quickly build up compounds in the muscles that lead to fatigue and exhaustion. Although they improve muscle strength, they do not serve much purpose in terms of cardiovascular health.

Body Temperature

Prolonged exertion markedly increases body temperature. Rectal temperatures of 41.1° C (106° F) are not uncommon in long-distance runners. An important question is, how does an athlete tolerate such body temperatures? When researchers attempt to raise the rectal temperature of a resting individual to 40° C (104° F), the sweating mechanism vigorously resists. Thus, dehydration and perhaps heat exhaustion may occur before this temperature is exceeded. Other data indicate that the rise of temperature with exercise is independent of environmental temperature, except at extreme ranges, but dependent on increased metabolism. Thus, in exertion, as in fever, the body's heat-dissipating mechanisms may be activated at a higher temperature. This issue is still unresolved, however.

A second question concerns body temperature: does increased body temperature enhance physical performance? There is some evidence that skeletal muscle works more efficiently at temperatures above 37° C (98.6° F). A higher temperature lowers blood viscosity and may also slightly reduce the resistance to blood flow in the muscles. The diffusion of oxygen, carbon dioxide, and metabolites to and from tissues is likewise enhanced by temperature increases. Higher temperature, on the other hand, may be the athlete's worst enemy. A combination of high environmental temperature and elevated internal heat production may cause serious dehydration

due to profuse sweating. If fluids are not replaced, shock may ensue and lead to physiological collapse.

Exercise Versus Inactivity

Exercise as a necessity for health and well-being is still a matter of considerable debate among scientists. Hereditary and environmental and behavioral factors are intricately involved and difficult to isolate in the matrix of influences that have to do with developing and maintaining a general state of health and a sense of well-being in a given individual. By and large, however, the data speak clearly in favor of habitual exercise as a life-style component and against habitual physical inactivity.

Table 1 compares the individual differences in certain variables associated with morphological and physiological determinants of fitness and performance in athletes, in sedentary individuals, and in sick or vulnerable persons. One can thus better understand the possible interactions between the individual's genotype and environmental factors. Current research indicates that the champion athlete not only has a high genetic endowment in terms of specific structural and physiological determinants of performance, but also has paid the high price of systematic and rigorous exercise in order to develop his or her potential and meet the demands of high performance.

In general, therefore, the long-term effects of exercise and training are the opposite of physical, physiological, and clinical phenomena occurring during physical inactivity and degenerative diseases.

Exercise and Degenerative Diseases

In North America the principal cause of death is cardiovascular disease. Granted the predisposing factors asso-

TABLE 1: EFFECT OF EXERCISE ON CARDIOVASCULAR SYSTEM

Variables	Champion Athlete*	Sedentary Individual (age 30–40)	Grossly Unfit Individual
Percent body fat	1.5	18–22	>30
Vital capacity (liters)	8.5	4.0–5.0	3.0–3.5
Maximum vital capacity (liters)	264	90–120	<80
Heart volume (cc)	1,700	500–800	>1,000†
Heart volume/body weight (cc/kg)	19.2	9–13	variable
Maximum oxygen uptake (ml/min/kg)	93.2	30–40	<20
Maximum cardiac output (liters/min)	42.3	15–20	<15
Maximum stroke volume (ml/beat)	212	80–120	<70
Maximum oxygen debt capacity (liters O_2)	22.8	6–8	<5
Systolic blood pressure at rest (mm Hg)	115	140	160
Diastolic blood pressure at rest (mm Hg)	70	85	95
Serum cholesterol (mg%)	120	140–150	>260

*Highest value reported or optimal value found in champion athletes.
†Pathological cardiomegaly.

TABLE 2: GUIDELINES FOR COOPER'S 12-MINUTE TEST

	Under 30	30–39	40–49	50 and Up
		Running—by Age group		
Men				
Very poor	Under 1.0 mile	Under 0.95 mile	Under 0.85 mile	Under 0.80 mile
Poor	1.00–1.24	0.95–1.14	0.85–1.04	0.80–0.99
Fair	1.25–1.49	1.15–1.39	1.05–1.29	1.00–1.24
Good	1.50–1.74	1.40–1.64	1.30–1.54	1.25–1.49
Excellent	Over 1.74	Over 1.64	Over 1.54	Over 1.49
Women				
Very poor	Under 0.95 mile	Under 0.85 mile	Under 0.75 mile	Under 0.65 mile
Poor	0.95–1.14	0.85–1.04	0.75–0.94	0.65–0.84
Fair	1.15–1.34	1.05–1.24	0.95–1.14	0.85–1.04
Good	1.35–1.64	1.25–1.54	1.15–1.44	1.05–1.34
Excellent	Over 1.64	Over 1.54	Over 1.44	Over 1.34

ciated with heredity, sex, and age, there is no doubt now that the following factors are also associated with a high risk of coronary heart disease: overweight and obesity, hypercholesterolemia and hypertriglyceridemia, hypertension, chronic exposure to stress, smoking, and physical inactivity.

Adaptation and Training

When the body is at rest and in a sitting position, basal metabolism consumes only about 250 to 300 milliliters of oxygen a minute. This value increases by a factor of 20 in, for example, an endurance runner or a cross-country skier performing at peak exertion, and oxygen consumption rises to more than 6 liters a minute. Since 1 liter of oxygen consumed corresponds to about 5 kilocalories of metabolic energy, the peak oxygen consumption implies an energy output of 1,500 to 1,800 kilocalories an hour. Heavy demands are obviously also made on all body systems. Pulmonary ventilation may increase from less than 10 liters to more than 150 liters a minute; the heart rate commonly increases by a factor of 3 (4 in athletes), that is, to rates around 190 beats a minute. The stroke volume of the heart, the cardiac output, the peripheral resistance, the venous return, the buffer system of the blood, and an amazing matrix of metabolic and enzymatic reactions, in the blood as well as within the cells, all contribute to optimizing the strength and duration of muscular contraction. At the same time, homeostasis, or the state of the internal environment, is kept within the biological limits set for the species.

The most striking adaptations to exercise occur in the cardiovascular system. An average healthy individual who adopts an exercise regimen designed to increase endurance will experience decreased heart rate and systolic blood pressure, ventilation requirement, oxygen intake, and lactate-pyruvate production during submaximal effort; and an increase in maximal oxygen uptake of up to 40 percent.

Additional benefits include an increase in capillarization of muscle; an increase in the diastolic (rest) period of the heart; an increase in arteriovenous oxygen difference at rest and in exercise; and a decrease in the daily work of the heart. Lowering the resting heart rate from, say, 75 to 65 beats a minute saves up to 100,000 beats a week.

Exercise Programs

The main objective of an exercise program is the maintenance of an efficient oxygen-transport system. Also important is maintaining a reasonable amount of body fat. The percentage of body fat should not exceed 16 to 18 percent in men and 18 to 22 percent in women. Muscle tone, which implies muscle strength and endurance, particularly of the abdominal and back regions, is attained through exercise, as is improved posture. A person who exercises regularly is also more likely to detect nervous tension and to take steps to lessen it.

No magic formulas can guarantee fitness. One gets what one trains for. Exercising at least three times a week at an intensity that is commensurate with a heart rate of 75 to 80 percent of the maximal heart rate for the age is considered basic. A field test based on a 12-minute run has been developed by Dr. Kenneth H. Cooper, comparing indivuals of the same age and sex (see Table 2).

See also: SPORTS MEDICINE.

Exeter (England)   Exeter is the county seat of Devon in southwestern England and has a population of 98,800 (1987 est). Located on a broad ridge overlooking the River Exe, it is best known for its magnificent cathedral (built 1275–1365) with twin Norman towers. Joined by a canal to the mouth of the Exe, it is an agricultural and shipping center. Exeter is an ancient center of learning and is the seat of Exeter School (first founded in 1633) and the University of Exeter (1955); the Cathedral Library contains many old manuscripts and books.

The site was probably settled before Roman times—perhaps as early as 200 BC. As a Roman trading center and fort it was called Isca Dumnoniorum. It was captured by the Danes in 1003 and by the Norman William I in 1068. Its many historic buildings include the Priory of Saint Nicholas, dating from 1080; the ruins of Rougemont Castle, begun by William I; and the 14th-century Guild Hall.

Exeter (New Hampshire)   Exeter (1990 pop., 12,481) is the seat of Rockingham County in southeastern New Hampshire. It is located on the Exeter River, 20 km (12 mi) southwest of Portsmouth. Founded in 1638 by John Wheelwright and other outcasts from Boston, the town served as the capital of New Hampshire from 1774 to 1784 and led the state in revolt from British control. It is the site of Phillips Exeter Academy, founded in 1781.

Exeter Book   The Exeter Book (*Codex Exoniensis*) is a manuscript collection of Anglo-Saxon poetry transcribed about 975 and presented to Exeter Cathedral a century later by Leofric, its first bishop. The codex contains some of the greatest poetry, including most of the extant lyrics, of the Old English period (8th–11th century), including "Christ," "Guthlac," "The Phoenix," "Juliana," "The Wanderer," "The Seafarer," "Deor," and "The Ruin," as well as riddles and precepts. The poems are characterized by their alliteration, kennings, and blend of Christian values and Germanic fatalism.

See also: ENGLISH LITERATURE.

exfoliation   Exfoliation is a form of WEATHERING that strips thin, concentric layers from a rock outcrop, producing a pattern similar to that of a peeling onion. The process may be initiated by rapid temperature changes, chemical reactions, or the sudden release of pressure through the removal of overlying material. Exfoliation is particularly common in massive rocks, such as GRANITE, and on a large scale the process has helped shape spectacular features, such as Half Dome in Yosemite Park, Calif., and Sugar Loaf in the harbor of Rio de Janeiro.

exhaust system   An automobile exhaust system directs combustion products away from the passenger compartment, attenuates combustion noise, and often reduces harmful pollutants in the exhaust stream. The principal components of the system are the engine's exhaust manifold, the muffler, the pipes connecting them, and exhaust-purifying CATALYTIC CONVERTERS.

An exhaust manifold does more than link the engine exhaust ports to the rest of the exhaust system. It reduces combustion noise and transfers heat downstream to promote the continued oxidation of unburned hydrocarbons and carbon monoxide. The manifold therefore supplies some emissions control before the exhaust reaches a catalytic converter that may be fitted farther downstream.

The muffler's main function is to reduce engine noise to an acceptable level. Engine noise is a jumbled collection of its fundamental firing frequencies, which range from about 100 to 400 hertz (1 Hz = 1 cycle/sec); overtones of these; and an extended range of "white noise" caused by resonance of the various components.

A muffler attenuates noise in three ways. Interior compartments called Helmholtz tuning chambers are tuned to set up canceling resonance of specific frequencies. Oth-

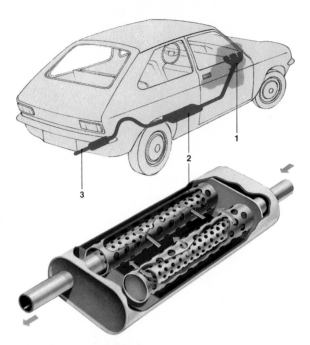

An automobile's exhaust system consists of manifold pipes (1) that conduct hot, high-pressure waste gases from the cylinders through a muffler (2) and out a tail pipe (3). The muffler reduces temperature and pressure (and thus noise level) by circulating the gases and allowing them to expand through a series of perforated pipes.

ers, called broadband dissipators, are designed to reduce the energy of sound pulses and thus to attenuate a wide range of frequencies. Finally, the muffler's absorptive surfaces function like sound-deadening wall and ceiling panels to absorb noise. In a typical "three-pass" design, the exhaust stream changes direction twice as it passes through separate compartments, each tuned to attenuate certain frequencies. When the exhaust gases finally pass out of the exhaust system through the tail pipe, their temperature, pressure, and noise have been greatly reduced.

See also: POLLUTION CONTROL.

exhibitionism   Exhibitionism is deriving sexual gratification from exposing the genitals to unexpecting, unwilling observers. When adults mutually desire exposure, this is not exhibitionism. Exhibitionism is considered a psychosexual problem (see PSYCHOPATHOLOGY) because satisfaction is obtained vicariously rather than through a sexual act with a consenting partner. Virtually all exhibitionists are male, and their victims are female. About half the victims are under the age of 16. Exhibitionists are likely to be passive individuals with feelings of masculine inadequacy.

existentialism   Existentialism is the popular name of a philosophical focus on human freedom, personal responsibility, and the importance of the individual's need to make choices. Søren Kierkegaard is the chief exponent of religious existentialism, a very personal approach to religion that emphasizes faith and commitment, and tends to minimize theology and the place of reason in religion. Kierkegaard attacked the theologians of his day for attempting to show that Christianity was a thoroughly rational religion, claiming instead that faith is important precisely because it is irrational, and even absurd. The important thing, he argued, is not the objective question of whether God in fact exists, but the subjective truth of one's own commitment in the face of an objective uncertainty.

Although Kierkegaard's work inspired an influential school of 20th-century religious existentialists (including Paul TILLICH, Martin BUBER, Karl BARTH, and Gabriel MARCEL), the existentialist attitude is perhaps more often associated with atheistic thinkers to whom religious belief seems like an act of cowardice, or, as Albert CAMUS calls it, "philosophical suicide." Friedrich NIETZSCHE's attack on Christianity and Christian morality is based on his suspicion that these are in fact crutches for weakness, instruments for the weak and mediocre to use against the strong and self-reliant. They are products of what he calls "the herd," the legacy of a slave morality that prefers safety and security to personal excellence and honor. But both Nietzsche and Kierkegaard attacked the Christianity of their day as hypocritical, insisting that it was an expression of the herd instinct and personal weakness.

Twentieth-century existentialism is largely defined—in its form if not its expression—by the movement known as PHENOMENOLOGY. Martin HEIDEGGER borrowed the phenomenological focus on experience and applied it to personal problems—questions about how human beings should live, what they are, and the meaning of life and death. His work *Being and Time* (1927; Eng. trans., 1962) is nominally concerned with metaphysics, but in fact it is a radical reassessment of what it means to exist as a human being. Heidegger rejects the classical Cartesian concept of consciousness ("I think, therefore I am") and replaces it with the neologism "*Dasein*," a word that literally means "being there." In his view there is no separation of mind and matter, no consciousness separate from the world. One finds oneself in the world "abandoned." The problem is to find out what to do with oneself or, as Nietzsche said, how to become what one is. Phenomenology, for Heidegger, becomes a method for "disclosing one's [essential] being."

Jean Paul SARTRE combined existentialism with Marxism. Following both Husserl and Heidegger, he used the phenomenological method to defend his central thesis that humans are essentially free, free to choose (though not free not to choose) and free to negate the given features of the world. One may be cowardly or shy, but one can always resolve to change. One may be born Jewish or black, French or crippled; it is an open question what one will make of oneself, whether these will be handicaps or advantages, challenges to be overcome or excuses to do nothing. Camus borrowed from Heidegger the sense of being abandoned in the world, and he shared with Sartre

the sense that the world does not give meaning to individuals. But whereas Sartre joined Heidegger in insisting that one must make meaning for oneself, Camus concluded that the world is "absurd," a term that has (wrongly) come to represent the whole of existentialist thinking. For Sartre, however, the heart of existentialism is not gloom or hopelessness, but a renewed confidence in the significance of being human.

When Sartre died in 1980, existentialism as such died with him, but the existentialist emphasis on the individual, the personal, and the importance of freedom and responsibility continue to represent an essential ingredient of philosophical thinking.

exobiology   SEE LIFE, EXTRATERRESTRIAL

Exodus, Book of   Exodus, the second book of the BIBLE, derives its name from the narrative's main theme, Israel's exodus from Egypt. Picking up where GENESIS left off, the first 15 chapters of Exodus describe Egypt's harsh policy toward Israel and the escape of the Israelites from their bondage. The narrative follows the career of MOSES from his marvelous birth through his exile in Midian. It continues with his final victorious contest with Pharaoh, in which Moses is God's spokesman, and ends with the Egyptian debacle at the Reed (traditionally Red) Sea. Chapters 16–40 describe the march of the Israelites through the wilderness to Mount Sinai, where God descends on the mountain, gives the law to Moses, and establishes a quickly broken COVENANT with Israel that must be reestablished after AARON makes the GOLDEN CALF.

Many important events are recorded in Exodus: the revelation of God's name as Yahweh in 3:11–15; the institution of the PASSOVER in 5:1–12:36; and the giving of the TEN COMMANDMENTS, directives for the construction of the TABERNACLE, and other religious and ceremonial legislation in 19–40. The authorship of the book has been ascribed traditionally to Moses, but it is actually a composite work of much later date, containing the same literary strands found in Genesis.

exogamy   [ek-sah'-guh-mee] Exogamy (from the Greek, *x*, "outside marriage") is the social rule that a person must marry a spouse from outside a culturally defined group (almost universally, the nuclear family) or groups of which he or she is a member. The exogamous nature of the nuclear family is a correlate of the INCEST taboo. Depending on its social structure, a culture may define as exogamous various other groups, such as lineage, clan, or moiety groups.

exorcism   Exorcism is the ritual act of expelling DEMONS, or evil spirits, from persons or other creatures. In former times most sickness was believed to have been caused by the activity of such spirits. Traditionally, various levels of demonic possession have been believed to occur, and the rites of exorcism have varied accordingly.

In the strict meaning of exorcism, the level of possession is such that the personality of the person possessed is completely taken over by the personal presence of the devil. Cases of involuntary as well as voluntary possession have been claimed; in other words, the evil spirits choose their victims in some cases without their cooperation.

Exorcism is practiced in many religions throughout the world. In Islam it is called *da'wah*. In Roman Catholicism, the practice is regulated by canon law, and must be authorized by a bishop. Traditional Judaism has a large body of literature dealing with the exorcism of evil spirits *(dibbukim)*. In Japan, Nichiren Buddhist monks perform exorcisms based on the teachings of the *Lotus Sutra.*

exosphere   The exosphere is the outermost portion of the Earth's ATMOSPHERE, at altitudes beyond 450–600 km (280–370 mi). Atoms of atmospheric gas in this region readily escape into space after colliding with each other. Helium is the most abundant exospheric gas. Atomic hydrogen is more common than atomic oxygen above 850 km (530 mi), and molecular nitrogen (N_2), molecular oxygen (O_2), and argon become quite rare with greater altitude. The temperature of the exosphere is about 700° C (1,300° F), but it can vary from only 300° C (570° F) during SUNSPOT minimums to as high as 1,700° C (3,090° F) at sunspot maximums.

exothermic reaction   See THERMOCHEMISTRY

exotic shorthair cat   The exotic shorthair cat is one of the most recently accepted breeds in the United States. Its fur has Persian texture but is as short as that of the Abyssinian and will not mat. Colors are the same as for the Persian. The nose should be short and snub and the legs low. This cat is produced by breeding any shorthair, usually the American shorthair, with a Persian.

The exotic shorthair cat is a recent breed, produced by crossing a domestic shorthair with a long-haired Persian.

expatriation   Expatriation is the giving up of citizenship, usually on a voluntary basis. Most countries now recognize the right of a citizen to change allegiance from one country to another, although some, including France and the USSR, require that the government of the native country give its permission. Under U.S. law a person who becomes a citizen of a foreign state or serves in its military forces is automatically expatriated. A person who has become a U.S. citizen by naturalization may be expatriated if he returns to live in his native country for two years or lives outside the United States for five years.

experimental theater   See IMPROVISATIONAL AND EXPERIMENTAL THEATER

expert system   An expert system is a computer program that acts like an expert consultant in predicting the outcomes of events or diagnosing problems. It does this by referring to a large DATABASE of specific knowledge in a given area, and by using structured rules of inference to draw conclusions. An outgrowth of ARTIFICIAL INTELLIGENCE research, the first expert system—Dendral, a program useful in chemical analysis—was developed by Edward Feigenbaum at Stanford University in the mid-1960s. In 1975, Mycin, a program that diagnoses bacterial infections, was introduced. By the end of the 1980s, a few thousand expert systems had been designed for such diverse applications as assessing credit risks, configuring computer networks, and advising mechanics.

exploration   Exploration is a quest for the unknown. Earliest records show evidence of humanity's unquenchable curiosity about unknown places and peoples, and in more than 3,000 years of recorded history, men and women have explored most of the Earth's surface. This article will survey that exploration. It will not include deep-sea, underground, and space explorations, which are more recent and continue today.

The concept of world exploration is used in a European context: from the eastern Mediterranean in ancient times; from western Europe in the 15th and 16th centuries; and from Europe or areas of European culture in the 18th, 19th, and 20th centuries. Explorers have been motivated by curiosity, by a desire to find riches, and by the need to find a place for surplus populations. Some have explored by accident, others as a result of military campaigns, but most have explored by design. Colonization has frequently resulted in further exploration, and in modern times the quest for scientific knowledge has sometimes spurred explorations.

Ancient and Medieval Explorations

The early Egyptians, whose civilization centered on the Nile River, were aware of and used the Mediterranean Sea. The Assyrians, whose civilization was based on the Tigris and Euphrates rivers, followed those rivers to the

Persian Gulf; they also went overland to the Mediterranean. The Minoans on the island of Crete sent ships at least as far as Sicily before 1500 BC. The Phoenicians, from their base in what is now Lebanon, ranged throughout the Mediterranean, establishing trading posts at Carthage and Gades (now Cádiz, Spain). They also are thought to have made a 3-year voyage around Africa about 600 BC. The Carthaginians certainly sailed beyond Gibraltar to establish trading posts on the West African coast.

By the 8th century BC the Greeks had moved into the Black Sea and also sailed widely on the Mediterranean, establishing colonies in Libya, on Sicily, and at Massilia (Marseille, France). ALEXANDER THE GREAT of Macedonia marched to the east to defeat the Persians and then went farther into Asia, finally reaching India in 326 BC. Pytheas, a Greek from Massilia, ventured westward beyond the Mediterranean about 325 BC. He visited the British Isles and went farther north to a place he called Thule, probably Norway or Baltic territory.

Active exploration declined during the period of Roman dominance (1st century BC–4th century AD), and even more so during the early Middle Ages, but the Crusades brought a revival of European interest in Asia. The Muslim Arabs, against whom the Crusaders fought, had contacts with India and China, and the rise of the Mongols in Central Asia made possible relatively safe travel for Europeans. Pope Innocent IV sent Giovanni da Pian del CARPINI eastward by land. Between 1245 and 1247 he reached Karakorum in Mongolia and returned with a travel account that aroused much interest. Niccolò and Maffeo Polo went from Venice to Beijing and back between 1260 and 1269. They returned to Asia in 1271, taking Niccolò's young son Marco, by way of the overland SILK ROAD. They remained for 24 years, while Marco held responsible posts under Kublai Khan. The Polos returned to Europe, mostly by sea, in 1295, and Marco POLO's account of his travels became widely known. IBN BATTUTA, a Muslim judge from Tangier who traveled widely in the Islamic world between 1325 and 1354, also reported on his travels.

Centuries earlier the VIKINGS had sailed from Scandinavia eastward through the Baltic to Russia and southward to what are now the British Isles, France, and Sicily. They also went westward across the North Atlantic, reaching Iceland about 870, where they found some Irish monks. From Iceland they moved farther west to Greenland in the 980s, after which voyages were made to VINLAND and other sites in North America. Efforts to settle Vinland failed, and eventually the Greenland colony died out. These Norse explorations seem to have had little effect on later explorations.

Age of Discovery

The great Age of Discovery is dated from 1415, when western Europeans, beginning with the Portuguese, began to venture into the Atlantic Ocean, down the African coast and to the west. Prince HENRY THE NAVIGATOR, a younger son of King John I of Portugal, devoted his life to the cause of exploration: to opening a sea route for trade with India and to locating PRESTER JOHN, the legendary Christian ruler, in Africa. Although Henry never left Portugal, he sent ships down the African coast and worked to improve the ships, their instruments, and maps. By his death in 1460, the Portuguese had rounded the bulge of West Africa and reached the Guinea coast. The Portuguese crown continued to support exploration. In 1488, Bartolomeu DIAS finally rounded the southern tip of Africa and reached the East African coast. Vasco da GAMA left Portugal in 1497 on an expedition around Africa and across the Indian Ocean to Calicut in India; he opened a sea route, making possible further Portuguese advances into Asia and a Portuguese overseas empire.

Between the voyages of Dias and da Gama, a Genoese who had been in Portugal went to Spain and in 1492 persuaded ISABELLA I of Castile to fund a voyage to reach Asia by sailing west. Christopher COLUMBUS had underestimated the distance; he thought it was about 4,800 km (3,000 mi). He sailed on August 3 from Palos and landed on Oct. 12, 1492, in the Bahamas. From San Salvador (Watling Island) he sailed to and discovered Cuba and Hispaniola, before returning to Spain. In succeeding years, still searching for the Asian mainland, Columbus made three more voyages and discovered many of the Caribbean islands, the mainland of South America, and Central America. Other explorers soon sailed westward. Amerigo VESPUCCI, of Florence, made two or more voyages, reached South America, and had his name given to the New World by a German mapmaker named Martin Waldseemüller. The second Portuguese fleet to India, led by Pedro Álvares CABRAL, took too wide a tack in the South Atlantic and, blown even farther west by storms, reached Brazil in 1500.

A Portuguese, Ferdinand MAGELLAN, sailing under the Spanish flag, sought to prove the Spice Islands were on the Spanish side of the line of demarcation between Spanish and Portuguese spheres of interest established (1494) by the Treaty of TORDESILLAS. He sailed west in 1519, found the Strait of Magellan near the tip of America, crossed the Pacific, and was killed in the Philippines. One of his captains, Juan Sebastian del Cano, brought his ship, the *Victoria*, back to Spain, completing in 1522 the first world circumnavigation.

Other early explorers of the Americas were John CABOT, a Genoese who sailed under commission from Henry VII of England, reaching Newfoundland in 1497. His son Sebastian CABOT also served Henry VII, spent many years in Spanish service, and then returned to England to supervise exploration for the Northeast Passage. A Florentine, Giovanni da VERRAZANO, sailed under French commission. He reached the Carolina coast in 1525 and, moving northward, sighted New York harbor and then sailed on to Maine. Jacques CARTIER, a Frenchman who served his own country, reached the lower St. Lawrence River in 1534, and on a second voyage in 1535 got past Quebec's site and as far inland as what is now Montreal. A third voyage helped to pave the way for Samuel de Champlain's expeditions.

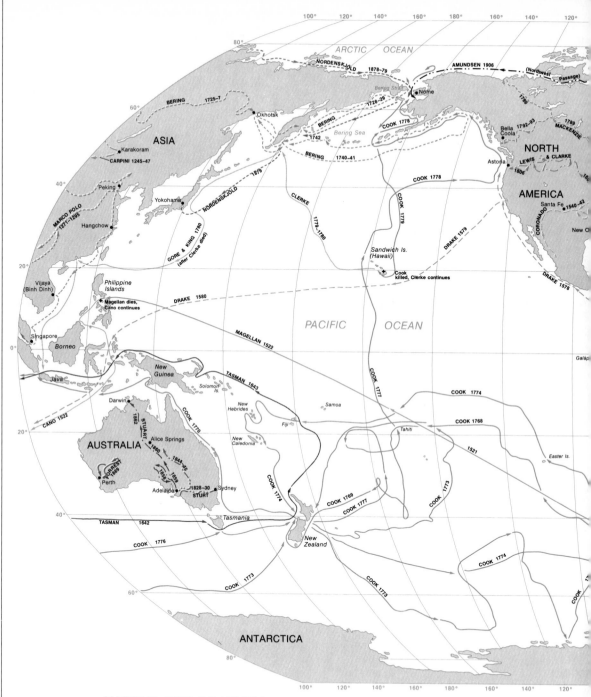

WORLD EXPLORATION
Principal sea voyages and selected land explorations

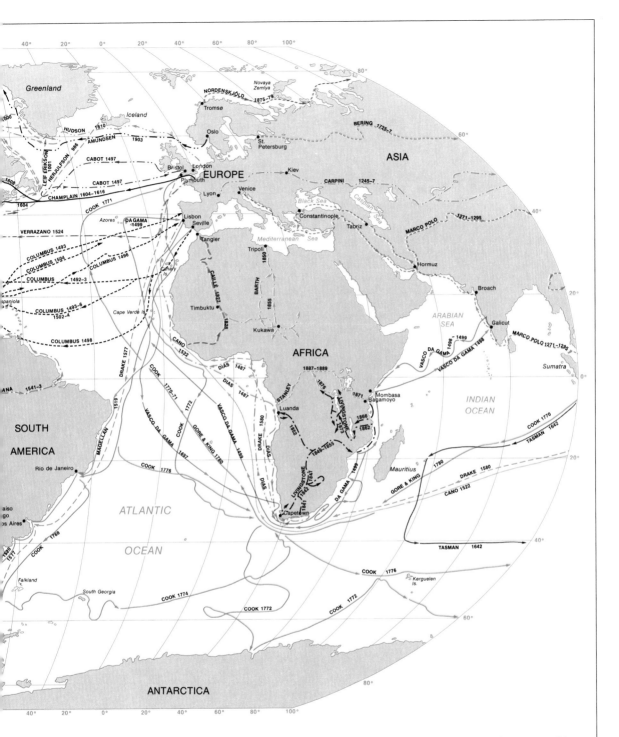

The era of European discovery was stimulated by the 13th-century visits of Giovanni del Carpini and Marco Polo to the courts of the Mongol khans; their accounts of the Orient's wealth spread throughout Europe. The Portuguese led the way in opening new maritime trade routes and thus circumvented the Arab overland trade monopoly with the Orient. By the end of the 15th century, Portuguese and Spanish explorers had reached India and had discovered the New World. The Dutch, English, and French soon entered the competition for trade monopolies and colonial acquisitions. By the end of the 19th century, exploration had resulted in the mapping of nearly all the Earth's land area.

Later Maritime Explorations

It was the search for a NORTHWEST PASSAGE that brought Cartier into the St. Lawrence River in 1534. Subsequent early attempts included the voyages of Sir Martin FROBISHER and John Davis, exploring west of Greenland in the 1570s and 1580s, that of Henry HUDSON reaching Hudson Bay in 1610, and that of William BAFFIN, who sailed into Baffin Bay in 1616. Not until the 19th century was another major effort mounted to find the Northwest Passage.

The search for a NORTHEAST PASSAGE was begun in 1553 by the English Muscovy Company. Richard CHANCELLOR reached the White Sea and then went overland to Moscow. A Dutchman, Willem BARENTS, discovered Spitsbergen in the 1590s and got to the Kara Sea. In 1607 and 1609, Henry Hudson was stopped by ice. Russians worked from the Pacific side. Semyon I. Dezhnev (c.1605–1673) went in 1648 from the Arctic coast of Siberia through the Bering Strait to the Pacific, while Vitus BERING, a Dane sailing under the Russian flag, explored the region in the 1720s.

From PTOLEMY's time (AD 150) a great southern continent was thought to exist. The idea was revived in the mid-16th century. Early Spanish and Portuguese voyagers to the South Pacific could not find it. Sir Francis DRAKE, on his circumnavigation (1577–80), reached some islands south of Cape Horn, but the Dutch made the major discoveries. Willem Janszoon went to New Guinea and found Australia in 1606. Abel TASMAN discovered Tasmania and New Zealand in 1642 and sailed around Australia on the south, proving it an island. In 1769–70 the British Captain James COOK circumnavigated both islands of New Zealand and surveyed and mapped approximately 3,200 km (2,000 mi) of previously unknown east Australian coast. None of these voyages, however, located the great southern continent. The Antarctic mainland was not found until 1820, when Nathaniel B. PALMER and Edward BRANSFIELD made separate sightings.

By the time of Captain Cook's voyages, the value of scientists accompanying exploring expeditions was recognized. Cook's pioneering work in this respect, aided by the British government and the Royal Society, was followed in the 1830s by the voyage (1831–36) of the H.M.S. *Beagle*, on which Charles DARWIN traveled as the official naturalist. Between 1838 and 1842 a U.S. exploring expedition led by Lieutenant Charles WILKES, and accompanied by a team of scientists, drew charts of the South Pacific that were used for more than a century. The French had been active in scientific exploration in the 18th century, when Louis Antoine de BOUGAINVILLE, an officer and scientist, completed the first French-sponsored circumnavigation between 1766 and 1769. Bougainville's explorations in the South Pacific were particularly noteworthy.

Land Explorations

Exploration over land was more complicated than sailing the seas. Natural obstacles had to be overcome, and expeditions could be mounted only after reaching newly discovered regions by sea. The Spanish, who lacked the great Portuguese seagoing tradition, were more adept on land, largely because of military expertise.

The Americas. Spanish settlements and colonies in the Americas were begun in the time of Columbus. In 1513 survivors of several Spanish efforts to settle in the Panama region were led across the isthmus to the Pacific Ocean by Vasco Núñez de BALBOA. This was the first crossing of the American continent, and it set the scene for Magellan's voyage and Francisco Pizarro's conquest of Peru. Juan PONCE DE LÉON traveled twice (1513, 1521) from Puerto Rico to Florida, where he was mortally wounded. However, it was Hernán CORTÉS's conquest (1519–21) of Mexico that opened much of North America to Spain. In 1540, Francisco de CORONADO was sent north from Mexico to find the fabled Seven Golden Cities of CÍBOLA. After discovering the Grand Canyon, he got as far as Kansas, but without finding treasure. The following year, Hernando DE SOTO, who had crossed from the Tampa, Fla., area, reached the Mississippi River near Memphis, Tenn. He went on into the Ozarks but returned and died on the Mississippi.

Far to the north, French claims to Canada were secured by land explorers' activities. The first governor of New France was Samuel de CHAMPLAIN. His explorations took him (1615) as far west as Lake Huron, from which he returned by way of Lake Ontario. His lieutenant Jean NICOLET reached Lake Michigan in 1634. The French also sent explorers to trace the Mississippi: Louis JOLLIET and Jacques MARQUETTE in 1672 and the Sieur de LA SALLE in 1681.

Land exploration of the far western parts of North America included efforts (1731–49) by the Sieur de LA VÉRENDRYE and his sons, who went as far west as the Dakotas. After Canada became a British territory, Alexander MACKENZIE was sent west in 1789 and 1793. He mapped the Mackenzie River to the Arctic Ocean and then crossed the Rockies and reached the Pacific. In the United States, President Thomas Jefferson sent two army officers, Meriwether LEWIS and William CLARK, to explore the territory of the LOUISIANA PURCHASE. Between 1804 and 1806 the LEWIS AND CLARK EXPEDITION went up the Missouri River, crossed the Rockies, and descended the Columbia River to the Pacific. In the succeeding decades many other American explorers—among them Zebulon PIKE, Stephen LONG, Jedediah SMITH, and John FRÉMONT—explored the West, establishing routes across the interior to the Pacific.

Exploration of South America began with Francisco PIZARRO's expedition by sea from Panama to Ecuador and then by land to Peru, where the Inca empire was conquered (1531–33). It was from Peru that Diego de ALMAGRO in 1535 and Pedro de VALDIVIA in 1540 began the conquest of Chile. Another expedition of the same period, led by Francisco de ORELLANA, went north from Peru, crossed the Andes, and followed the Amazon River to the Atlantic. Many other Spaniards and Portuguese explored the interior of South America during the 16th century. The main features became known, but exploration and discovery continued into the 20th century. Major advances were made by the German geographer Alexander von HUMBOLDT in 1799–1803.

Africa. The exploration of the interior of Africa was also a slow process. Between 1768 and 1773, James BRUCE, a Scot, had gone through Abyssinia (Ethiopia) and located the source of the Blue Nile. Another Scot, Mungo PARK, explored part of the Niger River in 1795–96 and again in 1805, but the river's course was not finally determined until John and Richard Lander sailed down it in 1830. The best-known African explorer of the 19th century was David LIVINGSTONE, a Scottish medical missionary who worked chiefly in the Zambesi region. Livingstone, who lost contact with the outside world for a time, was found in 1871 by Henry M. STANLEY, a journalist writing for New York and London newspapers. In an expedition in 1874–77, Stanley sought to continue Livingstone's explorations and followed the course of the Congo River to the sea. The Royal Geographic Society, founded in 1830, supported the search conducted by British explorers for the source of the White Nile. The first major expedition was that of Richard BURTON and John H. SPEKE in 1857–59. Together they discovered Lake Tanganyika; then Speke alone discovered Lake Victoria and claimed it as the source of the White Nile. Burton disagreed. In 1862, Speke and James Grant found where Lake Victoria emptied into a river. That this was the Nile was confirmed by Samuel W. BAKER, who came up the river from the Sudan in 1864.

Asia. In the mid-19th century attempts were made to increase knowledge of Central Asia. Russians took a lead in this endeavor. Aleksandr Middendorf (1815–94) worked in Siberia in the 1840s. Nikolai M. Przhevalski (1839–88) crossed the Gobi Desert, explored Mongolia, reached Tibet, and explored in the Kuen Lun in the 1870s and 1880s; he also discovered the wild camel and the Mongolian wild horse, now called Przhevalski's horse. In the 20th century, Aurel Stein explored in Central Asia, and Roy Chapman ANDREWS led an expedition to Mongolia that discovered prehistoric reptile eggs.

Arabia was another area relatively unknown to Europeans. Portuguese ships had touched the South Arabian coast, and an English adventurer, Henry Middleton, reached Mocha on the Red Sea in 1610. In 1761, King Frederick V of Denmark sponsored a scientific expedition, led by Carsten Niehbur (1733–1815), that traveled widely in Arabia; Niehbur alone survived. Other Europeans who traversed interior Arabia in the 19th century included Richard Burton.

Australia. English settlement in Australia began soon after Captain Cook's voyage, but exploration of the interior came somewhat later. Charles STURT explored the river systems of southeastern Australia in 1828–30, and Thomas Mitchell continued the same type of work between 1831 and 1836. Ludwig Leichhardt (1813–c.1848) overcame terrible hardships to cross tropical northern Australia in 1844–45, but he disappeared on a cross-Australian expedition in 1848. Robert O'Hara BURKE and W. J. Wills, who used camels, almost succeeded in crossing Australia from south to north in 1860; John McDouall STUART finally made the crossing on his third try (1861–62) from Adelaide to the site of Port Darwin. More recently, automobiles and airplanes have been used to explore the remote interior regions of Australia.

Polar Expeditions

Polar exploration had its beginnings in the 16th-century quest for a northern passage to Asia. Richard Chancellor, Willem Barents, Henry Hudson, and others searched for a Northeast Passage but were blocked by ice. Martin Frobisher, John Davis, Henry Hudson, and others searched for the Northwest Passage. Sir Francis Drake and, later, Captain Cook and Captain George VANCOUVER searched for the Northwest Passage from the Pacific side. In the 19th century intensive search for the northern passages was resumed. The disappearance (1845) of Sir John FRANKLIN in the Arctic focused attention on the Northwest Passage, which was finally traversed by Roald AMUNDSEN in 1903–06. Meanwhile, the Northeast Passage was sailed by Adolf Nordenskjöld from east to west in 1878–79.

The quest for the North Pole also became serious in the 19th century. William E. PARRY tried to reach it by sledge in 1827. Between 1893 and 1896, Fridtjof NANSEN froze his ship, the *Fram*, into the sea ice in the hope that currents would carry it to the Pole. He and Fredrik Hjalmar Johansen left the ship and tried for the Pole on foot. They were rescued ultimately from Franz Josef Land. Robert E. PEARY and his associate Matthew A. Henson are generally credited with reaching the North Pole by dogsled on Apr. 6, 1909. They had conducted a series of polar expeditions lasting 11 years. Although much of the Arctic region still remains unknown, and explorations continue, access to the North Pole has become relatively easy. Richard E. BYRD flew to the North Pole from Spitsbergen in 1926. In 1958 the U.S.S. *Nautilus*, a nuclear-powered submarine, reached the Pole under the ice.

Captain James Cook was the pioneer of Antarctic exploration. His work was followed by naval exploring expeditions from many nations as well as by sealing voyages. On an expedition in 1819–21 the Russian Adm. Fabian von BELLINGSHAUSEN circumnavigated the Antarctic continent. Charles Wilkes in 1838–42 and Sir James ROSS in 1839–43 made major sightings. Although an American whaling captain, John Davis, landed on the continent in 1821, a second landing, by Norwegians, did not occur until 1895. Many expeditions followed. Ernest SHACKLETON failed to reach the South Pole in 1909 and failed also in an attempt to cross the Antarctic continent in 1914–16. Another Englishman, Capt. Robert F. SCOTT, followed Shackleton's route to the Pole, reaching it on Jan. 16, 1912. However, he found that the Norwegian explorer Roald Amundsen had arrived there before him, on Dec. 14, 1911; Scott's entire group perished on the return journey. Air travel has made Antarctica more accessible; explorations there have continued. In 1989–90, a multinational team led by Will Steger became the first to cross the continent by dogsled.

Conclusion

Explorers now seem to have reached most parts of the Earth's surface. The availability of increasingly sophisticated scientific techniques, however, including photographs taken from space satellites, undoubtedly will continue to show that areas of the Earth have not yet been explored, or fully explored. The quest for knowledge, of which exploration is a part, continues.

See also: ANTARCTICA; ARCTIC; OCEANOGRAPHY; SPACE EXPLORATION.

Explorer Explorer is the name of a series of scientific satellites sponsored first by the U.S. Army and later by the National Aeronautics and Space Administration (NASA). *Explorer 1*, the first U.S. artificial satellite—named for the high-altitude balloon flights of the 1930s—was launched from Cape Canaveral on Jan. 31, 1958, by a Juno 1 rocket. Since then, numerous other satellites have been launched that are in the Explorer class of lighter scientific satellites, as contrasted to the heavier satellites in the observatory class. In variety and purpose, the Explorers are similar to the Soviet COSMOS series.

explosives An explosive is a stable material that, upon proper stimulation, rapidly changes from a solid or liquid into a hot, expanding gas. The pressure exerted on the surrounding materials by the expanding gas constitutes an explosion.

Confining an explosive greatly increases its propensity to detonate by increasing the speed of the reaction. For example, GUNPOWDER, or black powder, confined within the paper wrapping of a firecracker explodes when ignited, but the same powder sprinkled in the open simply burns when ignited because the pressure of the hot gases does not increase fast enough to have an explosive effect.

Although many substances in various forms can be exploded (gasoline vapors, hydrogen, and finely dispersed coal or grain dust are all explosive substances, for example), only those substances specifically intended to produce an explosion are generally called explosives. They can be divided into two types: propellant explosives, such as gunpowder, and detonating explosives, such as TNT and dynamite.

Propellant Explosives. Gunpowder, which was developed by the Chinese in the 10th century and by the Arabs, independently, soon afterward, was the first explosive to be used in FIREARMS. In 1845 a nitrocellulose explosive called GUNCOTTON was introduced, but it proved too potent for its intended use as a firearms propellant. Breakthroughs in the 1880s, however, resulted in satisfactory smokeless powders that, within 20 years, virtually supplanted black powder as a propellant. With the advent of the space age, many specialized explosives were developed for use as rocket propellants.

Detonating Explosives. Detonating explosives may be subdivided into initiating explosives and high explosives.

Initiating explosives, which must be handled with extreme care, are the more sensitive of the two. Materials such as fulminate of mercury explode instantly when burned or ignited, which makes them desirable for use in blasting caps.

High explosives are less sensitive and can burn without producing an explosion. They can only be detonated by a severe shock, which is delivered by another explosive (usually a blasting cap) placed in or near the high explosive. Therefore large amounts can be moved and handled safely.

In 1846 the Italian Ascanio Soberro invented NITRO-GLYCERIN, an explosive so sensitive that it was virtually unusable. It became important later, however, when in 1867 the Swedish inventor Alfred NOBEL combined it first with siliceous earth and later with wood pulp to produce dynamite.

TNT (trinitrotoluene), which was first used in the early 1900s, has become the standard by which all other explosives are measured. It is used either by itself or mixed with other ingredients and explosives to produce many subtypes with differing performance characteristics.

Modern Explosives. Modern detonating explosives include PETN (pentaerythrite tetranitrate), which is used in blasting caps and detonating cord; RDX (also known as cyclonite), which is combined with other explosives and waxes to produce what are popularly known as plastic explosives; ammonium nitrate, an explosive of low detonating velocity that is used when a slow push or heave is more desirable than a shattering effect; and amatol, a mixture of ammonium nitrite and TNT that is used as a bursting charge.

Explosives are used in a wide variety of civilian and military tasks. Tunnel construction, obstacle clearing, and open pit and underground mining employ large quantities of explosives. They are also used as propellants for firearms and ROCKETS; as bursting charges for BOMBS, MINES, ARTILLERY projectiles, TORPEDOES, and hand GRENADES; and for general engineering and demolition work. Small explosive charges have wide uses in industry, as well. In metallurgy, metals can be pressed into dies, extruded, or welded together by means of explosions, and new metal alloys have been created by such means. Explosives are also used in the production of diamond dust from graphite.

exponent [eks'-pohn-ent] In mathematics, an exponent is a number that indicates how many times a FACTOR, or base, is multiplied by itself to form a product. For example, in 4^2 the superscript 2 is the exponent. It indicates that the product is $4 \cdot 4$ or 16. In the same way, $4 \cdot 4 \cdot 4$ is written as 4^3, and so on. The exponential form of a product can be applied only when the factors that constitute it are the same. The exponent is also called the power. Thus x^2 can be stated as x raised to the second power (or x squared). In general, x^n is stated as x to the nth, or the nth power of x.

Exponents may also be zero, negative, and fractional. Any nonzero quantity to the zero power equals 1 ($a^0 = 1$ for $a \neq 0$). A base with a negative exponent equals the reciprocal of the base with the positive exponent, that is, the base with the positive exponent, divided into 1; for example, $y^{-3} = 1/y^3$. A fractional exponent indicates a ROOT of the base; for example, y raised to the ½ power equals the square root of y. Calculations involving exponents can be done using the following basic properties of exponents.

1. To multiply exponential factors having the same base and different powers, the powers (exponents) are added, that is, $a^r a^s = a^{r+s}$.
2. To raise an exponential factor to a power, the exponents are multiplied, that is $(a^r)^s = a^{rs}$.
3. To divide exponential factors having the same base and different powers, the exponents are subtracted, that is, $a^r/a^s = a^{r-s}$.

—

Export-Import Bank   The Export-Import Bank (Eximbank) was established in 1934 to facilitate U.S. exports and to aid in their financing. It extends long-term loans to borrowers outside the United States who want to purchase U.S. goods, usually industrial equipment; guarantees export credits offered by U.S. commercial banks; and insures credits given by U.S. exporters to foreign buyers against possible defaults. Eximbank is authorized to have up to $40 billion outstanding at any one time in the form of loans, guarantees, and insurance. For this purpose it employs a capital stock of $1 billion and may borrow up to $6 billion from the U.S. Treasury.

exposition   see WORLD'S FAIRS

exposure meter   see ACTINOMETER

—

expressionism   Originally a term used by a group of early-20th-century German artists to describe their aesthetic principles and their art, the word *expressionism* has since been applied to works in fields as disparate as literature, music, and the cinema. In its loosest sense, the term applies to any artistic work in which objective reality is distorted to represent the mental condition of the artist.

As a distinct artistic movement, German expressionist painting of the early 1900s evolved in reaction to the inert academic standards of the previous century. It rejected refined pictorial naturalism in favor of direct emotional expression characterized by bold distortions of form and violent color. The first expressionist painters, a group called DIE BRÜCKE (The Bridge) was formed in Dresden in 1905. Their manifesto asserted the value of emotional experience as a test of moral and artistic values. Die Brücke drew encouragement from the contemporaneous French movement known as FAUVISM, and from the earlier artists Paul GAUGUIN, Vincent VAN GOGH, Henri de TOULOUSE-LAUTREC, and Edvard MUNCH.

A second expressionist group, Der BLAUE REITER (The Blue Rider), was formed in Munich in 1911. Its name was taken from a painting by one of its leading spirits, Wassily KANDINSKY, who, with Franz MARC, formulated new aesthetic aims for the group. From the first, the

The exuberance of movement in Emil Nolde's Dancing the Boogie (1912) is emphasized by the blurred figures and brilliant, chaotic color. Nolde's work epitomizes the exploration of mind and emotion characteristic of expressionism. (Private collection.)

movement was marked by an international scope and a pronounced degree of intellectualism. Der Blaue Reiter ceased to be a unified group after 1914, when World War I dispersed its members and claimed the lives of Marc and of another member, August MACKE. Expressionism as a movement, however, proved to be an enduring force in 20th-century art, exercising a strong influence on New York painters of the 1940s and 1950s (see ABSTRACT EXPRESSIONISM).

In poetry and drama, expressionism represented a reaction to the sentimentality of late-19th-century romanticism. Expressionist poets, writing in Germany and Austria in the years just before and after World War I, were influenced by Freudian theories of the subconscious, the anti-rationalism of Friedrich Nietzsche, and the psychologically profound novels of Fyodor Dostoyevsky. The poems of Gottfried BENN, Ernst TOLLER, Johannes Becher, and Georg Trakl are characterized by their chaotic, frenzied imagery and vehement tone. Certain qualities of expressionism are also found in the prose of Franz KAFKA, but the movement was strongest in the dramatic works of August STRINDBERG and Frank WEDEKIND and their followers among early-20th-century German-language playwrights. Expressionist drama, with its disturbing incident, terse dialogue, and exaggerations and distortions, left its mark on the silent cinema, especially in the films of Fritz LANG, F. W. MURNAU, and Robert Weine, whose *Cabinet of Dr. Caligari* (1919) epitomizes the expressionist film.

—

extended family   The extended FAMILY, an enlargement of the NUCLEAR FAMILY, comprises at least three generations, the core members of which are linked by ties of unilineal descent, or descent that is traced through one side of the family (see KINSHIP). The extended family is also called the joint family, the composite family, and the consanguineal family.

—

extinction (in geology)   Extinction, in geological history, is the complete disappearance of a species of living organism. This occurs when the number of deaths begins to exceed the number of births among members of the species over its geographical range, and the trend is not interrupted or reversed. Episodes of mass extinction are distinguished by the simultaneous, worldwide disappearance of many different species.

Major Extinctions. Extinctions of individual species have occurred throughout GEOLOGIC TIME (see FOSSIL RECORD). The first recorded mass extinction of the Paleozoic Era came at the end of the Cambrian Period, when numerous families of invertebrate marine life disappeared. Primitive families of fish disappeared during a wave of mass extinction at the end of the Devonian Period, which also claimed many species of corals and TRILOBITES. More than 90 percent of all species of marine life disappeared at the end of the Permian Period, making this the greatest mass extinction in Earth history.

The most recent mass extinction of geologic time occurred at the end of the Mesozoic Era, in the late Cretaceous Period, about 65 million years ago. The disappearance of the DINOSAURS was the most spectacular feature of this climactic portion of the fossil record, but more than 50 percent of the marine invertebrate species disappeared as well—including the AMMONITE cephalopods that had existed for 325 million years.

Possible Causes. Extinctions of species, even on a massive scale, can be accounted for in part by the usual processes of competition and of the slow environmental change that characterizes UNIFORMITARIANISM. Thus, one explanation of the mass extinction at the end of the Permian derives from the CONTINENTAL DRIFT theory, according to which all the continents fused into one huge landmass, Pangea, thereby reducing the area of shallow marine habitats essential to most of the then-existing families of marine fauna. The Cretaceous extinction, however, has raised speculations that are reminiscent of the discredited theory of CATASTROPHISM.

Evidence that the Cretaceous extinction may have had a catastrophic, extraterrestrial origin has been uncovered by geochemical studies of a layer of clay that occurs at the Cretaceous-Tertiary stratigraphic boundary in many parts of the world. The iridium content of this clay is much higher than in other crustal materials and resembles, instead, the iridium content of meteorites (see METEOR AND METEORITE). This has led some scientists, such as Luis ALVAREZ and his son Walter, to suggest that the Earth was hit by an asteroid or comet at the end of the Cretaceous. A cataclysmic impact of such magnitude would have thrown enough dust into the atmosphere to have reduced incoming solar radiation for months and perhaps years. The worldwide drop in temperatures that ensued would have disrupted food chains (see ECOLOGY), causing starvation and mass extinction.

Indirect support for this neocatastrophist theory has been provided by statistical analyses of extinctions among marine faunas over the past 250 million years. A pattern of extinctions occurring roughly every 26 million years was demonstrated by this work, with the Cretaceous extinction as one of ten episodes in this pattern. Many geoscientists, however, dispute these apparent results,

pointing out the complex problems involved in setting up statistical models over such a long time period with the kinds of data available. As for the Cretaceous, they argue that mass extinctions were occurring among dinosaur groups long before the end of the period, and that the iridium record of that time could be accounted for equally well by very active volcanism.

extortion see BLACKMAIL

---

extraction Extraction is a process used in organic chemistry to separate mixtures. Solvents are used in which the component to be extracted is highly soluble. After treatment of the mixture with the solvent, which now contains the extracted material, the desired substance may be isolated by removal of the solvent through DISTILLATION or evaporation. The extraction process most frequently used involves the treatment of a solution with a second solvent. The two solvents must be mutually insoluble (immiscible) in each other, allowing them to form two layers that can be separated.

---

extradition Extradition is the surrender of an alleged criminal by one political jurisdiction to another jurisdiction having authority to try the charge. There are two kinds of extradition, interstate and international. Interstate extradition is the surrender of individuals between states in a federal system of government. Extradition among the states is provided for under the U.S. Constitution. The Uniform Criminal Extradition Act has been adopted by most states.

International extradition is generally governed by treaties, and by statutes within the countries involved. Some countries do not allow extradition of their own citizens, and many make special provisions for those accused of political crimes. Depending on the terms of the relevant treaties and the nature of the political offense, some countries may grant asylum but agree to prosecute the extradited person.

---

extragalactic systems [eks-truh-guh-lak'-tik] Extragalactic systems are the enormous assemblages of stars found outside the Milky Way Galaxy. They may be normal galaxies, radio galaxies, or QUASARS, which are believed to be extremely active nuclei of very distant galaxies. Normal galaxies have diameters ranging from 2,000 to nearly 800,000 LIGHT-YEARS, masses ranging from 1 million (10^6) to 10 trillion (10^{13}) solar masses, and luminosities ranging from 1 million to 100 billion suns. (Our own Milky Way system is a large galaxy with a visible diameter of about 100,000 light-years; see GALAXY, THE.) Quasars may be more than 100 times more luminous than the brightest known galaxies, and yet are much smaller. They range in distance from 700 million light-years to perhaps 15 billion light-years, if their red shifts are proportional to their distances, as with other galaxies.

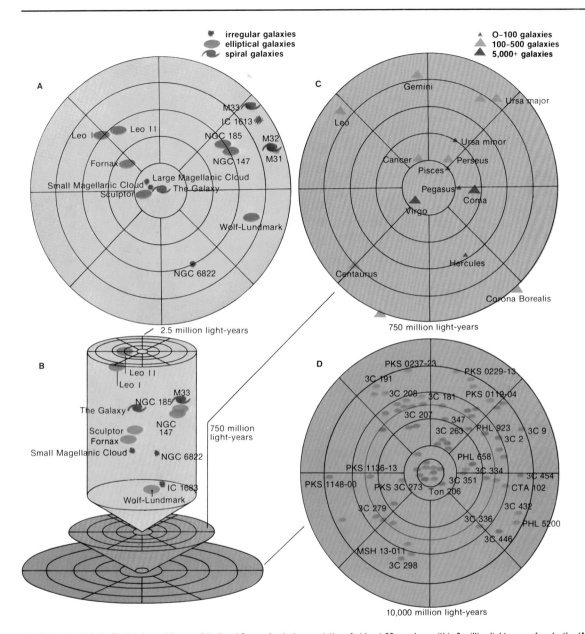

The Galaxy in which the Earth is located is part of the Local Group of galaxies consisting of at least 28 members within 3 million light-years of each other (A). The most important of these galaxies are our own, the Andromeda (M 31) and Triangulum (M 33) spirals, and the Clouds of Magellan. The positions of some of these galaxies in three-dimensional space relative to The Galaxy is illustrated in diagram B. In all directions beyond the Local Group, similar but larger groups of galaxies (C, D) are found, their numbers increasing as their distance from Earth increases. The distance scales are progressively expanded in diagrams C and D, such that the Local Group would be a dot in the center of C and the entire group of clusters in C falls within the smallest circle in D. The blue circle in diagram D represents the present distance of about 5 billion light-years at which normal galaxies can be identified optically. Beyond this limit, only quasars, which appear as blue, starlike points of light through the largest telescopes, are identifiable from red-shift data as possible galaxies.

Discovery of Other Galaxies

As early as 1755, Immanuel Kant speculated that the faint cloudy patches, or NEBULAE, that were elliptical in form might be systems of stars analogous to the Milky Way. Only in the early 20th century, after a great deal of confusing and discordant data was sorted out, was it proven that this was indeed the case.

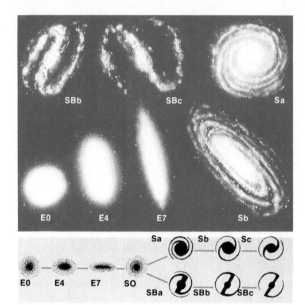

Edwin Hubble's classification scheme for galaxies divides them into three major classes according to their forms: elliptical, spiral, and irregular. Elliptical galaxies (E) are subdivided into eight types, varying from a spherical, or E0 type, to an elongated ellipse, or E7 type. Normal (S) and barred (SB) spirals are each separated into three types, according to the size of the nucleus and the degree of openness of the arms. Thus Sa and SBa types have large, bright nuclei and tightly coiled arms; Sc and SBc types have small nuclei and prominent, open arms. S0 type galaxies resemble normal spirals, but arms are absent.

All of the arguments came to a head in a great debate beween the astronomers Harlow Shapley and H. D. Curtis, which took place before the U.S. National Academy of Sciences on Apr. 26, 1920. Shapley argued that the Milky Way was 300,000 light-years in diameter, that the Sun was far from the center in the direction of a point in the constellation of Sagittarius on the galactic equator, and that the spiral nebulae were part of the Milky Way system. Curtis advanced arguments that the Milky Way was about 30,000 light-years in size with the Sun at, or close to, the center and that the spirals were distant island universes. Each protagonist was only partly right. What was needed was a reasonably reliable distance to one or more of the nearer galaxies.

Edwin P. Hubble of Mount Wilson Observatory filled the need for reliable distances by using Cepheid variables—unstable, pulsating giant and supergiant stars whose light varies in a characteristic way by a factor of 2 in periods ranging from about a day up to about 50 days. If these objects could be found in a spiral nebula, their periods could be observed, and the luminosity of the Cepheid calculated from the period-luminosity relation. When the luminosity was determined, the distance could be determined by comparing the luminosity, or absolute magnitude, with the apparent magnitude.

In December 1924, Hubble presented a paper before the American Astronomical Society showing that the spi-

rals M 31 and M 33 and an irregular galaxy NGC 6822 were at distances of about three-quarters of a million light-years. Although Hubble's distances were too small by a factor of 3, they proved the existence of extragalactic systems. Within about half a dozen years Hubble had extended his breakthrough into what he called "the realm of the nebulae" by a factor of nearly 1,000 to what then seemed to be the edge of the observable universe.

Distance determination is of utmost importance to extragalactic astronomy, and several reliable methods are now used, including Cepheids and RED SHIFTS (see DISTANCE, ASTRONOMICAL). In particular, Hubble's finding in 1929 that red shifts were closely proportional to the distances had profound implications. It demonstrated that the universe was expanding, that it possibly originated in a BIG BANG some billions of years ago, and that the distance of any isolated, extremely distant object could be determined from its red shift.

The linear relation between the radial velocity V of a galaxy and its distance D can be put in the form of a simple equation known as Hubble's law (see COSMOLOGY, HUBBLE'S CONSTANT).

Characteristics of Extragalactic Systems

Whereas one star image on a photographic plate looks like any other star image, except for differences in brightness, galaxies have complex shapes and can be classified usefully into a logical sequence on this basis.

Classification. The three broad categories of galactic shapes are elliptical (E), spiral (S), and irregular (Irr). Elliptical galaxies are further classified as E0 through E7, where E0 is circular and E7 highly elliptical. The shape

Extragalactic systems called faint blue objects appear to populate the farthest reaches of the universe. They are revealed in this photograph of a tiny area of sky obtained through lengthy exposures and advanced data-processing.

M 82, an irregular galaxy found in the constellation of Ursa Major, appears to be exploding. Huge filaments of hydrogen gas can be seen shooting out from the center of the galaxy at tremendous speeds.

depends, however, on the galaxy's orientation to the observer. Spirals are subdivided into two types: normal (S) and barred (SB). (An intermediate type between ellipticals and spirals is called SO. Such SO galaxies are not yet well understood, but some show characteristics of both spirals and elliptical galaxies.) Two sequences follow: (1) Sa, Sb, and Sc and (2) SBa, SBb, and SBc. The subdivisions a, b, and c refer to the decreasing prominence of the nucleus and tightness of the arms. About one-quarter of all spirals are barred spirals, in which the arms terminate at the ends of a central bar, which rotates as a unit.

More than two-thirds of the brightest, most conspicuous galaxies are spirals, about 3% are irregulars, and the rest are ellipticals. In the universe as a whole, elliptical galaxies are far more numerous. Because of their low luminosity, dwarf elliptical galaxies are difficult to discover but are probably the most numerous type of galaxy in a given volume of space. Elliptical galaxies are both larger and more luminous and also smaller and less luminous than spirals.

Clusters of Galaxies. Galaxies come in pairs, triples, groups, and clusters. Clusters of galactic clusters also exist. The LOCAL GROUP OF GALAXIES contains 22 known members and is spread out over a region about 3 million light-years in diameter. Among the group are 3 spirals, 13 ellipticals (including 9 dwarf ellipticals), and 6 irregular galaxies. The largest galaxy in the group is the Andromeda galaxy, an Sb about 30% larger than the Milky Way, which is either an Sb or SBb spiral. The Local Group is near the edge of a supercluster of galaxies, revolving about its center at about 400 km/sec (240 mi/sec). The supercluster, which has a diameter of about 130 million light-years, also contains the great Virgo cluster of about 2,500 galaxies, and evidence exists that the supercluster itself may in turn be part of a much larger supercluster of tens of thousands of galaxies called the "Great Attractor."

George ABELL cataloged 2,713 rich clusters of galaxies on the Palomar Sky Survey plates. These clusters group into superclusters typically 300 million light-years in diameter. Rich galaxian clusters are composed almost entirely of elliptical galaxies. The brightest galaxies in a cluster of galaxies are supergiant elliptical galaxies, perhaps ten times as luminous as the Andromeda; from the red shift evidence they are nearly identical from cluster to cluster in both their size and luminosity.

Normal Galaxies. A typical galaxy has a central nucleus of closely packed stars. The star density in the nucleus may exceed 1 million times that of the rest of the galaxy. It contains chiefly old, hot, low-mass stars known as population II stars. Outside of the nucleus, absent in elliptical galaxies but increasing in prominence in the spirals as they become more open, are the young, massive, and hotter stars of population I, usually found in connection with gas and dust. Population I stars are also found in the halo of a galaxy—the large, circular region surrounding—where the globular clusters are located. (See POPULATION, STELLAR.)

Cosmological theories attempt to account for the observed structures of galaxies. According to the standard big bang theory, matter came to predominate over radiation about one million years after the big bang and eventually fragmented into clouds of hot gas, the protogalaxies. The clouds contracted gravitationally and began to take a disk form if their spin was fast enough. Unincorporated gas formed a galactic halo of stars. Later generations of metal-enriched stars were formed in the disk as INTERSTELLAR MATTER was recycled through the stars. The young blue supergiant stars in the disk are short-lived (see SUPERNOVA) and are continuously being formed. The observation in 1989 of a vast cloud apparently forming into a galaxy about 65 million light-years away suggests, however, that the time limit placed by standard theory on galaxy formation may have to be extended.

Standard theory also suggests that elliptical galaxies

The so-called Sombrero galaxy, or M 104 in Messier's list, is found in the direction of the Virgo constellation. It is a good example of a Hubble-type Sa spiral galaxy seen almost edge-on.

took their different form because they had little initial rotation. Stars were formed in an initial burst, and the shape of such galaxies changed very little over time. Some astronomers propose instead that elliptical galaxies may be the product of collisions between spiral galaxies, accounting for the greater average massiveness of ellipticals and their lack of interstellar matter, most of which was converted into stars through the collision process.

A normal galaxy may shine for many billions of years until all its available gas and dust are contained in heavier elements, WHITE DWARFS, NEUTRON STARS, and possibly BLACK HOLES. According to standard theory, no new material will be left that is capable of forming new stars, so the galaxies may eventually cool and fade away.

Active Galaxies, Radio Galaxies, and Quasars. Galaxies that exhibit abnormalities are generally classified as active galaxies. The abnormalities may range from extreme luminosity to variation in optical and radio brightness and colliding and exploding galaxies. Radio galaxies emit up to 10 million times more energy at radio wavelengths than normal galaxies. (See RADIO ASTRONOMY.) Seyfert galaxies are galaxies that have extremely active, energetic nuclei, as do the so-called starburst galaxies, whose nuclei radiate strongly in the infrared and are thought to be sites of large-scale star formation. Quasars and BL Lacertae objects have very active nuclei and may be closely related to radio galaxies. Astronomers have suggested that all galaxies, from normal ones to quasars, may form an evolutionary sequence in which massive black holes, at the centers of the galaxies, play a critical role.

Mass of Galaxies. Gravitational forces between galaxies are enormous. The mass of the local supercluster, for example, acts at a distance 4 trillion times greater than the distance between Earth and the Sun. Yet it causes the Sun (and Earth) to move in space 13 times faster than the Earth moves around the Sun. The masses of individual galaxies can be calculated from the velocities they induce on objects outside and within themselves. Thus, in our own Galaxy, the Sun moves in a nearly circular orbit about the galactic center, 32,600 light-years distant, with a velocity of 250 km/sec (155 mi/sec). A straightfor-

ward calculation indicates that our Galaxy contains 150 billion solar masses. When detailed corrections are made—allowing for the unequal distribution of mass in the Galaxy—the galactic mass is estimated to be about 200 billion solar masses. Calculating the masses of other galaxies becomes more difficult because of their distance, but the effects of pairs of galaxies on one another can be used, as can the observation of bright objects within the nearer galaxies. The dispersion in galactic velocities within a cluster of galaxies can also be employed in estimating the total mass of the cluster.

One major issue of modern cosmology is that of the total mass of the galaxies and other matter in the universe, because whether the universe will continue to expand or will collapse upon itself depends on its average density. Current astronomical models call for a great deal more mass than has actually been observed. Some astronomers propose that this "missing mass" might be accounted for by the existence of many dim galaxies as yet unobserved. A few such dim galaxies have already been detected.

extrasensory perception Extrasensory perception (ESP) means the perception of objects, thoughts, or events without the mediation of the known human senses. Such perceptions, collectively called psi phenomena, are grouped in four main categories: telepathy, or mind-to-mind communication; clairvoyance, or the awareness of remote objects, persons, or events; precognition, or the knowledge of events lying in the future; and retrocognition, or the knowledge of past events in the absence of access to information about those events.

Scientific theory explains modes of perception that are mediated by the sense organs and other body systems (see SENSES AND SENSATION), so ESP by definition lies outside the realm of scientific explanation. Claims for the occurrence of ESP therefore remain controversial. In the 20th century, attempts at controlled study of ESP phenomena have been undertaken by various persons and groups (see PARAPSYCHOLOGY). Such researchers often claim that ESP experiences can be induced by hypnosis, chemicals, or other artificial means so that they can be measured precisely under laboratory conditions. The scientific community as a whole does not accept ESP research reports, because it does not find them verifiable or reproducible.

extraterrestrial life   see LIFE, EXTRATERRESTRIAL.

extraterritoriality In international law, extraterritoriality is the principle that allows certain citizens or property of a nation or an international organization to be exempt from the laws of a host nation. The premises and grounds of a diplomatic mission are considered part of the territory of the sending state, and hence that state's laws apply to the personnel of the mission. This doctrine forms an exception to the general rule of international law that a country has jurisdiction over people and things within its territory.

Among those benefiting from extraterritoriality are heads of foreign nations who travel abroad. There is some dispute as to whether their families and entourages are accorded similar protection. Ambassadors and certain other diplomatic personnel are also given immunity from local jurisdiction. Like a head of state, an ambassador is secure against both civil and criminal prosecution in the receiving state. Also, his or her residence cannot be entered by local police or affected by judicial process. Consular officers, however, enjoy immunity only with respect to acts connected with their official functions. Extraterritoriality is also usually applied to members of armed forces invited to a foreign country, public ships in foreign waters, and United Nations personnel.

extreme unction   see ANOINTING OF THE SICK

---

extroversion-introversion   Extroversion and introversion are concepts that were invented by Carl JUNG to describe psychological personality types; they have since become familiar everyday words. Extroversion typifies people whose interests and attention are directed outward from themselves, who feel easy in social situations, and who feel free to carry out appropriate actions in the open. Introversion describes opposite tendencies. Introverts direct their attention inward upon themselves, tend to withdraw from social situations, and tend to be self-reliant. The mental or psychic energy responsible for producing both extroversion and introversion Jung called the libido. The extroversion-introversion dimension probably represents a collection of slightly related variables: everyone has tendencies to both extroversion and introversion, though one will predominate. Jung did not intend either term strictly and narrowly to define an individual's personality.

---

extrusion   Extrusion is a method of forming metals and plastics by forcing them through a die to produce various shapes. The method has been widely used since the 19th century. Plastics are extruded in a molten form, usually using an ARCHIMEDES' SCREW to feed the material into the die after compression.

The three general types of metal extrusion are direct, indirect, and impact. In the direct-extrusion process, the metal ingot or billet is placed in a confined cylinder that may be heated. A dummy block is placed behind the ingot, and a die (the tool that will determine the shape of the extrusion) is placed ahead of the ingot. Pressure is applied to the ingot, causing it to move forward to extrude metal through the restricted orifice of the die.

During indirect extrusion, the ingot position is fixed, and a ram containing the die moves into the ingot from one end. The other end is closed by a plate. The extruded metal passes through the hollow die stand.

Impact extrusion is a combination of extrusion and

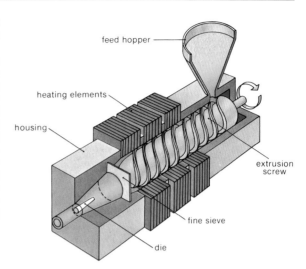

feed hopper
heating elements
housing
extrusion screw
fine sieve
die

Plastic-extrusion processes involve melting a thermoplastic polymer and forcing the melt through a die shaped to give an object the desired form. A typical extruder contains a hopper through which polymer pellets are fed onto a rotating extruder screw, which is enclosed in a steel housing. The rotating screw forces the polymer toward the die at a uniform rate and pressure. Heat generated by the rotating screw and by external electrical heating elements melts the polymer by the time it reaches the die. The melted polymer is forced through a fine sieve to remove solid contaminants and then through a die. The extruded polymer is immediately air-cooled to solidify it.

forging in a single operation so that the process is sometimes referred to as extrusion forging. In this process, the piece to be extruded, called the slug, is placed in a shallow die. The slug is then struck an impacting blow by a punch or former, which causes the metal to flow up over the punch and the sides of the die to form a cup-shaped part.

Extruded metal shapes are used extensively in automobiles, containers, construction, and appliances. The most commonly extruded metals are aluminum, magnesium, copper, brass, lead, and tin. Extruded plastics are used for pipe, wires, and many domestic purposes.

See also: METALLURGY.

extrusive rock   see IGNEOUS ROCK

Eyck, Jan van [ike, yahn vahn]   Jan van Eyck, the most famous and innovative Flemish painter of the 15th century, is thought to have come from the village of Maaseyck in Limbourg. No record of his birthdate survives, but it is believed to have been about 1390. In 1425 he was made court painter and *valet de chambre* to Duke Philip the Good of Burgundy; he signed and dated a number of paintings between 1432 and 1439. According to documents, he was buried on July 9, 1441.

Van Eyck has been credited traditionally with the invention of painting in oils, and, although this is incorrect, there is no doubt that he perfected the technique. He used the oil medium to represent a variety of subjects with striking realism in microscopic detail; for example,

The Flemish master Jan van Eyck's attention to detail is obvious in this wedding portrait of Giovanni Arnolfini and Jean Cenami (1434). Van Eyck surpassed all contemporaries in the technique of oil painting and is therefore among the most influential painters of the 15th century. (National Gallery, London.)

he infused painted jewels and precious metals with a glowing inner light by means of subtle glazes over the highlights. Van Eyck carefully selected and arranged his subject matter so that it would contribute deeper symbolic meaning to his painting. The meticulous attention to detail in his paintings of architectural interiors and landscapes is also evident in his portraits, painted with unrelenting, dispassionate accuracy.

Van Eyck's most famous and most controversial work is one of his first, the Ghent altarpiece (1432), a polyptych consisting of twenty panels in the Church of St. Bavo, Ghent. On the frame an incomplete inscription in Latin identifies the artists of the work as Hubert and Jan van Eyck. Scholarly conflict over the identity of Hubert cast doubt on attribution of the panels, which vary somewhat in scale and even in style. Equally famous is the wedding portrait of Giovanni Arnolfini and his wife (1434; National Gallery, London), which the artist signed "Johannes de Eyck fuit hic 1434" (Jan van Eyck was here), testimony that he witnessed the ceremony. Other important paintings are the *Madonna of Chancellor Rolin* (1433–34 Louvre, Paris) and the *Madonna of Canon van der Paele* (1436; Groeninge Museum, Bruges).

eye   Almost all animals can perceive and respond to light, but eyes are as varied as the animals that possess them.

Eyes that form definite images are found only in some mollusks, mainly squids, octopuses, and cuttlefish; in a few worms; in most arthropods, including insects, spiders, lobsters, and crabs; and in vertebrates. Except for most insects, these animals have eyes that are similar in structure and function to a camera. The eye uses a single LENS to focus a picture on a surface of densely packed cells called photoreceptors. The receptor surface, called the retina, functions like a piece of film. An external object is pictured on the retina like the points of a newspaper photograph. The picture later received in the BRAIN, however, is not the same simple point-by-point image. Exactly what this picture is remains unknown, but PERCEPTION is a process that takes place in the brain, not in the eye. Information from the eye, like the piece of a puzzle, is analyzed in the brain and fitted into meaningful forms.

Most insect eyes are built on an entirely different principle from that described above and are called compound eyes. Thousands of densely packed lenses are spread like a honeycomb over a spherical surface so that a mosaic image is formed. Each lens is associated with relatively few receptor cells, and the entire unit is called an ommatidium. No structure, therefore, is strictly analogous to the retina of other animals. What kind of image this arrangement conveys to the insect depends on the complexity of the structure.

Evolution

At least three times during evolution, eyes with lenses have developed independently in animals as widely different as insects, mollusks, and vertebrates. Fish move the whole lens closer to the retina when focusing on distant objects. Mammals, including humans, have evolved a more complex method of focusing by changing the curvature of the lens—flattening it for close objects, thickening it for distant ones. Predatory birds have an effective strategy of keeping the prey in focus while sweeping down on it: instead of adjusting the lens, they quickly change the curvature of the more flexible structure called the cornea, which is a transparent membrane covering the lens and also supporting the eyeball.

Another essential refinement, color perception, also evolved independently several times. Among mammals, only humans, primates, and a few other species can recognize colors clearly. Birds, on the other hand, have a color perception superior to that of humans. Among insects, honeybees can be trained to distinguish colors, but they are color-blind to red. Similar training experiments have shown that at least some teleosts, or bony fish, can discriminate colors, but elasmobranches, such as sharks, cannot.

Finally, evolution resulted in the gradual development of binocular vision—the shifting of the eyes' position from the side of the head to the front; this permitted the fusion of the images in each separate eye into a single, three-dimensional image in the brain.

Invertebrates

The light receptors of many invertebrates do not form definite images; they simply register light or dark or the direction of a source of light. The simplest such eyes are the light-sensitive patches found on the flagella, or limblike projections, of the protozoan *Euglena* and the eyespots of certain flatworms called planaria. Some organisms that have evolved true eyes have also retained simple photoreceptors of this type. Examples are the so-called ocelli found in the tails of lobsters and in the brain area

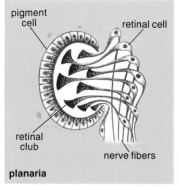

planaria

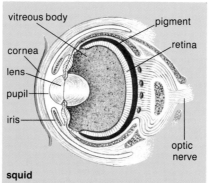

squid

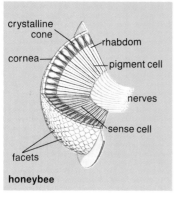

honeybee

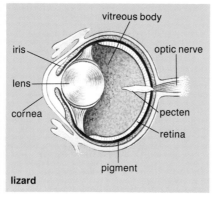

lizard

The eyes of different animals vary greatly in structure and complexity. Most lower animals, such as the planaria (top left), a flatworm, do not possess image-forming eyes but simple photoreceptors, or light-sensing organs. In the eye spots of a planaria, retinal clubs transmit information to the cerebral ganglia, or brain, from the light-absorbing pigment cells that form the outer layer of the spots. This information enables the animal to detect different degrees of light intensity and to locate the source of a light stimulus. More advanced animals have image-forming eyes, in addition to or instead of such simple light-sensitive organs. Insects, such as the honeybee (bottom left), typically have compound eyes composed of many individual facets, each of which is a photoreceptor unit linked by a nerve to the brain. Light entering the crystalline cone behind the cornea is focused on the rhabdom, or light-sensitive zone; the result is a mosaic and, in some cases, a combined image. Eyes of most other higher animals are cameralike in function and similar in structure, sometimes providing striking instances of convergent evolution. Thus the eyes of an invertebrate such as the squid (top right), a mollusk, and of a vertebrate such as the lizard (bottom right) arose in separate ways over the course of geological time; but many of the structures of the eyes, and their functions, are practically the same.

under the skull; these organisms can perceive light even when their true eyes have been removed.

Detection of Light

Despite the variety of types of eyes, the chemical process that transforms light into nerve impulses in the eye is basically similar in all land vertebrates and marine fish, and in some insects. In 1967, George Wald of Harvard shared a Nobel Prize for physiology or medicine for discovering the details of the first step, which occurs in the retina or ommatidium.

The substances in the retina that detect light are called photosensitive, or visual, pigments. The major pigment in the eye is rhodopsin, or visual purple, which is composed of two distinct parts: a protein molecule called opsin, and a molecule made from vitamin A called retinene. When light strikes rhodopsin, the retinene portion is split away, or bleached, from the opsin portion; this leads, through a cascade of chemical reactions, to nerve impulses that relay visual information to the animal's brain.

In the dark, and with the aid of chemical energy obtained from metabolism, retinene and opsin are recombined and rhodopsin is reconstituted. In very intense light, visual purple may be split faster than it can be reconstituted. Vision may then become impaired, for example, as in so-called snow blindness. Vision may be similarly impaired if vitamin A is deficient in supply, and a shortage of retinene results in so-called night blindness. (See EYE DISEASES.)

Vitamin A has the structure of one-half molecule of β-carotene, a pigment found in almost all plants. It cannot be made by animals and must be present in the food or be made from plant carotene. In plants carotene seems to be responsible for the growth toward light, and it also plays a role in photosynthesis, the process by which sunlight and water are combined to produce organic nutrients. Remarkably, evolution has adapted this almost universal plant pigment to animal vision.

Structure of the Eye

The eyes of vertebrates differ in some details, yet they are all built to a common plan. More is known about the human eye than about that of any other vertebrate, and it may therefore serve as an example.

Protecting the eyeball is a bony socket called the orbit. Each eye is suspended within its orbit and is surrounded by a cushion of fat and blood vessels and motor and sensory nerves, including the optic nerve. There are six small muscles attached to each eye to allow coordinated movement of the pair. The eyelids provide some protection in the front and also serve to keep the cornea lubricated by spreading the tear fluid with each blink, as well as an oily fluid produced by Meibomian glands in the lid. The tear fluid is produced by the lacrimal glands near the outer portion of each eyebrow and is collected and drained through tiny canals within the upper and lower lids near the nose. The tears eventually flow into the nasal passages and are swallowed.

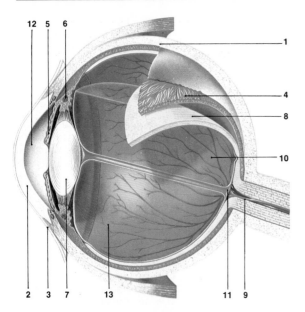

The eye is composed of three membrane layers. The outer white layer, or sclera (1), helps the eye keep its spherical shape. The transparent part of the sclera, or cornea (2), is protected by the conjunctiva (3). The middle layer, the choroid (4), supplies the eye with blood. The iris (5), which is colored, and ciliary body (6), which holds the lens (7) in position, are part of this layer. The inner layer, or retina (8), receives light and sends nervous messages to the brain by way of the optic nerve (9). The fovea (10), or focal point, and blindspot (11) are located on the inner surface. The aqueous humor (12), a fluid, and vitreous humor (13), a jelly, fill the cavities of the eye.

The adult human eye is a hollow globe with a diameter of approximately 2.5 cm (1 in). The wall of the globe is composed of three coats. The outer coat, called the fibrous tunic, supplies the basic support of the eye and gives it shape. The fibrous tunic is divided into the cornea, which is the transparent, exposed membrane in front of the lens, and the sclera, the firm, white coat of the eye to which is attached the muscles that move the eyeball. The middle, or vascular, coat is composed of three regions. The choroid layer is pigmented black and carries blood vessels to and from the eye. In mammals other than humans, it has an iridescent layer that increases the retina's sensitivity to low-intensity light. The ciliary body consists of a ring-shaped muscle, which can change the lens shape, and ciliary processes to which the lens is attached. The iris, which contains an opening, the pupil, is colored and has a sphincter and a dilator muscle, called a contractile diaphragm. The innermost coat is the retina, which lies behind the lens. It contains the optic disk, or blind spot, which is the junction of nerve fibers passing to the brain. The retina also contains rods and cones, light-sensitive cells. The lens is a biconcave, transparent structure.

The Eye as a Camera. Light is excluded or permitted to enter by the eyelids, the equivalent of the camera shutter. Once admitted, the amount of light is further regulated by a variable opening, the pupil, which is like the aperture of

a camera. The diameter of the pupil is controlled by the expansion and contraction of muscles in the iris. If a bright light is shone into the eye, the pupil immediately constricts. This is the light reflex, the purpose of which is to protect the retina from too intense illumination. As time passes, the retina adapts to the new level of light and the pupil returns to its original size.

Light rays are focused by a lens system composed of the cornea and a crystalline lens, and an inverted image is projected on the retina. To prevent the blurring of images by internal reflection, the inner walls of the camera—the choroid layer—are painted black. The process by which the lens focuses on external objects is called accommodation. When a distant object is viewed, the lens is fairly flat. As the object moves nearer, the lens increasingly thickens, or curves outward. Lens shape is controlled by the ciliary body. A blurred image elicits reflex impulses to the ciliary body that promote contraction or relaxation until the image is sharp.

The Retina. The retina is made of several layers of nerve cells and one layer of so-called rods and cones. Together these constitute the photoreceptors that translate light energy into nerve impulses. The rods and cones are farthest removed from the light entering the front of the eye. Light must first pass through the nerve cells, strike the rods and cones, and then pass back to the nerve cells in order to generate nerve impulses. Because of this, the

Accommodation involves the unconscious adjustment of the eye for seeing far and near objects by changing the curvature of the lens. In order to focus on a far object (A), the ciliary body, to which the lens is attached, relaxes and pulls the lens flat. The eye focuses on a closer object (B) by contracting the ciliary body, and the highly elastic lens becomes more curved to accommodate the object. In both cases, upside-down images of the objects are sharply focused against the retina, and later are reversed to the correct visual pictures by the brain.

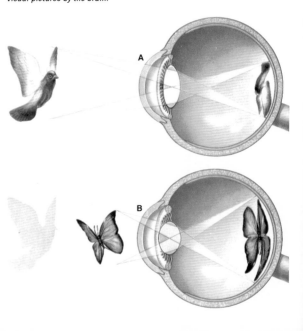

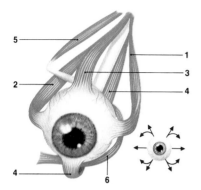

The eye has muscles that allow it great freedom of movement. The eyeball moves side to side by the actions of the lateral (1) and medial (2) rectus muscles. The superior (3) and inferior (4) rectus muscles as well as the superior (5) and inferior (6) oblique muscles control all other eye movement (bottom right).

retinas of vertebrates are said to be inverted, and another problem of the evolution of the eye is that of accounting for the origin of the inverted retina.

The rods contain rhodopsin, are sensitive to dim light, and are important in black-white vision and the detection of motion. Cones are responsible for color vision and for the perception of bright images. Little, however, is known about their conversion of light to electrical impulses. The greatest concentration of cone cells is found in a tiny depression in the center of the retina called the fovea. Only cones are present there; rods are absent. Because of this dense accumulation of cones, vision is most acute at the fovea.

Nerve fibers from the retina eventually collect in one region and form the optic nerve, which relays visual information to the brain. Where this nerve leaves the eye, somewhat off-center, it interrupts the continuity of the rods and cones.

The Role of the Brain

The optic nerve enters an area on the underside of the brain called the lateral geniculate body, which partially processes the data before passing it to the visual cortex at

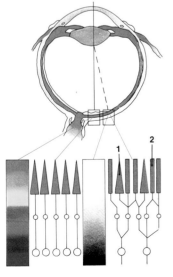

The eye perceives color and tint by means of light-sensitive cone (1) and rod (2) cells, which are located in the retina. Cones and rods translate photons of light into nerve impulses, which travel to the brain. Cones are sensitive to strong light and color, especially greens and yellows of the spectrum. Cones cease to respond in dim light, and rods, which are sensitive to low levels of light, come into play. Rods respond best to white light, to black, and to shades of gray.

the rear of the brain. The degree of such processing varies with the species. Frogs, for example, have very complex retinas containing specialized cells for detecting the characteristic shapes and movements of insects. The retinas of humans and other primates are less complex, and less processing occurs in their eyes. The difference is also correlated with the presence of a visual cortex in the brain or the degree of its development; the frog has no visual cortex, whereas primates have a well-developed cortex.

The nerve fibers connecting the retina and the brain are so arranged that the right half of a field of vision "crosses over" and registers in the left half of the brain, and the left half of a field registers in the right half of the brain. The brain is able to smoothly superimpose the "left" picture of the external world on the "right" picture. Both halves of the picture are seen right side up, though the retinas receive inverted images.

eye diseases   Eye diseases are a common cause of human disability. In most developed countries, major eye problems are generally errors in refraction—that is, in the optical system of the eye—whereas in developing nations, infective and nutritional diseases cause most impaired vision and BLINDNESS.

Defects. Many people suffer from errors in refraction. With MYOPIA, or nearsightedness, distant objects appear blurred. With hyperopia, or farsightedness, an individual has difficulty focusing for near objects. Astigmatism causes some parts of an object to be in focus while others are not. Presbyopia is a condition that arises in later life in which the lens of the eye loses its ability to change shape and thus cannot focus well for near objects. Nystagmus is an involuntary, rapid oscillation of the eyes, and STRABISMUS, or cross-eye, occurs when one or both eyes cannot focus on an object.

Photophobia is the inability to tolerate normal levels of illumination. The condition may be a result of eye disease, and occasionally it is symptomatic of various disorders of the central nervous system. About 8% of all men and less than 0.5% of women have COLOR BLINDNESS, or difficulty in recognizing one or more colors. Total absence of color vision is very uncommon. Most color-vision defects are caused by abnormal genes for three light-absorbing molecules that are components of pigments of retinal cones, although some can be acquired as a result of certain systemic diseases or medications. NIGHT BLINDNESS is the inability to see when illumination is dim. This condition can occur as a result of vitamin A deficiency or, more commonly in developed countries, as a hereditary disorder.

Infection and Inflammation. Most individuals will at one time or another during their lives suffer from mild inflammation or infection of the eyes. Blepharitis, in which the eyelids become red or inflamed, is often caused by the bacteria STAPHYLOCOCCUS. A sty is a painful infection of the hair follicles of the eyelashes. Inflammation and infection of the mucous-membrane lining of the eyelids and eyeball, or CONJUNCTIVITIS, can be caused by allergy, chemical pollutants, smoking, or such infectious agents as bacteria or viruses. Infections or inflammations of the opaque outer white coat of the eye, or sclera, are called scleritis; those of the clear outer coat, or cornea, are keratitis. Both can lead to clouding of the clear cornea and distorted or blurred vision. Disorders of the iris, ciliary body, and choroid are named, respectively, iritis, cyclitis, and choroiditis.

One of the leading causes of blindness in the world is TRACHOMA, an infection caused by the bacteria *Chlamydia trachomatis.* This disease initially affects the lids and conjunctiva and eventually the cornea; it most frequently occurs in dry climates and is associated with overcrowding and unsanitary conditions. RIVER BLINDNESS is caused by a parasitic worm transmitted by flies. It is common in parts of Africa, Central America, and South America.

Degenerative Diseases. A major cause of visual loss in the United States and Europe is CATARACT, an opacity of the lens most frequent with aging or certain metabolic diseases. Recent evidence has linked some forms of cataracts with defective genes. A cataract can be removed surgically. Another common eye disease is GLAUCOMA, an elevation of the intraocular pressure in the eye. This disease can be treated either medically or by surgery.

Another cause of visual impairment is a vascular disease of the retina associated with diabetes—diabetic retinopathy. It is possible in some cases to halt or reverse diabetic retinopathy by the use of laser coagulation. Macular degeneration is a condition that affects the central retina and is a common cause of visual loss in the elderly. Retinal detachment, a condition in which the retina separates from the underlying retinal pigment epithelium, is most frequently found in nearsighted individuals, in people sustaining eye injury, and in those who have had cataract surgery.

Retinitis pigmentosa is an inherited disorder caused by a defective gene. Its first symptom is decreased night vision, and it may also be associated with hearing loss and a variety of metabolic diseases. Perhaps the leading cause of visual impairment in children is a vitamin A deficiency known as xerophthalmia, which occurs mainly in developing countries and leads to corneal degeneration and impairment of night vision.

Treatment. Such refractive-error conditions as myopia, hyperopia, astigmatism, and presbyopia can all be corrected with EYEGLASSES. CONTACT LENSES, both soft and hard, can also be used to correct refractive errors—including aphakia, a condition that most commonly follows the removal of a lens during cataract surgery. Surgical distortion of the cornea to correct for extreme myopia—an operation known as radial keratotomy—is increasingly being practiced but remains controversial and is discouraged by many ophthalmologists. An opacified or markedly distorted cornea now can be replaced, and eye banks have been established for the provision of donor material in cases where corneal transplantation is required. Optometrists can prescribe glasses and contact lenses for some visual defects and certain medications in some states. Only ophthalmologists, who are physicians, can treat eye diseases by means of surgery.

eye worm   Eye worm disease, or loiasis, is caused by a parasitic roundworm, *Loa loa.* The disease, one of a class of parasitic infestations called FILARIASIS, occurs only in western and central Africa. Eye worm is usually transmitted by the bite of deer flies. Humans, baboons, and possibly monkeys can harbor the parasite. The filamentous adult worms continuously migrate through the connective tissues below the skin and cause itching and sometimes localized inflammatory swellings. Occasionally a worm can be seen moving beneath the conjunctiva of the eye. The worms mate within the tissues; larval offspring are carried by deer flies to new hosts. The drug diethylcarbamazine can kill both adult and larval worms.

eyeglasses   Eyeglasses, also called spectacles, consist of a pair of lenses (see LENS) mounted in a frame and worn over the eyes to aid vision. Although the 13th-century Englishman Roger BACON is sometimes credited with their invention, they probably developed in many places over a long period of time. Half of the U.S. population wear eyeglasses; 95 percent of the population over age 45 use eyeglasses for reading and close work.

The purpose of eyeglasses is to correct errors of refraction in the lens of the EYE itself. Farsightedness hyperopia—the inability to focus on nearby objects—results from the front of the eyeball (cornea) being too close to the layer that receives the image (retina); it can be corrected by using a convex lens. Nearsightedness (MYOPIA) usually results from the retina's being too far back optically from the cornea, and it is corrected by a concave lens. Simple farsightedness and simple nearsightedness may be corrected by convex or concave lenses that are spherically uniform. Farsightedness or nearsightedness that is not uniform results in the condition called astigmatism and must be corrected by adding a cylindrical component to the spherical lens.

With advancing age the power of the eye to focus at many distances gradually diminishes, and the individual can no longer see clearly for close work. This gradual and progressive reduction in the amplitude of accommodation, known as presbyopia, usually develops after the age of 45 and is often corrected by the use of bifocals, lenses that have a spherical lens added to part of them. One part corrects for near vision, and the other part for distant vision. The progressive-addition lens eliminates the line in conventional bifocals that separates distance- from close-focus; the new lens provides instead for a gradual change in focus.

Eyeglass frames are fitted by measuring interpupillary distances so that the lenses will be centered correctly. Temple length is determined by measuring from the top of the ear to the end piece of the frame or mounting and adding 5 cm (2 in). The horizontal width of the lens is determined by the shape of the head, by the distance between lenses required by the bridge, and by considerations of lens weight.

Special, shatterproof glasses, which may be made of

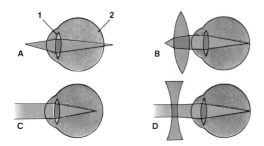

The human eye contains a lens (1) that normally focuses light from an object directly on the retina (2) to produce a sharp image. If the eye lens converges the light rays to a focus behind the retina (A), the eye is said to be farsighted. This defect is corrected by the use of a convex lens (B) that combines with the eye lens to focus the image onto the retina. If the eye lens focuses the light in front of the retina (C), the eye is nearsighted and is corrected with use of a concave lens (D) that decreases the refraction of the eye lens.

plastic materials or case-hardened glass, give protection against flying particles. Polarizing lenses and antireflective lenses reduce glare from smooth surfaces such as roads and bodies of water. Photochromic glasses contain tinted lenses that become darker in bright sunlight and lighter in a dark room. Depending on their color and the depth of the tint, sunglasses block a proportion of sunlight from entering the eyes. ULTRAVIOLET LIGHT, which can damage the lens and the retina, is a component of sunlight. A new labeling system on some sunglasses will tell consumers what percentage of ultraviolet light is blocked.

See also: CONTACT LENS; EYE DISEASES.

Eyre, Edward John [air]   Edward John Eyre, b. Aug. 5, 1815, d. Nov. 30, 1901, was a British explorer and colonial administrator. As a young man he immigrated to Australia, where he explored (1840) the interior north of Adelaide, discovering the lake named for him, and crossed (1840–41) the Nullarbor Plain to Western Australia. In Australia he gained a reputation for protecting the aborigines.

Leaving Australia in 1845, Eyre held a series of administrative posts in New Zealand and the West Indies before becoming governor of Jamaica in 1864. There he brutally suppressed a black uprising that began at Morant Bay in October 1865; more than 400 people were executed, and the Jamaican constitution was suspended. Eyre's conduct caused a major controversy in England, and he was recalled in 1866.

Eyre, Lake   Lake Eyre is a shallow, saline lake in central South Australia, covering 9,325 km² (3,600 mi²). The drainage point for central Australia, it is 14 m (46 ft) below sea level, making it the lowest point in Australia. In dry years it is a muddy waste covered by a salt crust up to 38 cm (15 in) thick. On rare occasions, it is completely filled to a depth of 2 to 4 m (7 to 13 ft). The lake is named for Edward John Eyre, who discovered it in 1840.

Ezekiel, Book of   The Book of Ezekiel in the Old Testament of the Bible is one of the books of the Major Prophets. Its name is drawn from Ezekiel, a priest-prophet who lived in Jerusalem and was one of the Jews deported by Nebuchadnezzar II to Babylon at the beginning of the 6th century BC. The book is divided into three parts: (1) the threats against Judah and Jerusalem before the fall of Jerusalem (chaps. 1–24); the threats against foreign nations (chaps. 25–32); and (3) promises for the future restoration of Israel and the Temple (chaps. 33–48). The Book of Ezekiel describes the prophet's many visions and symbolic actions with vivid literary imagery.

Written during the BABYLONIAN CAPTIVITY (586–38 BC), the book links preexilic Israel and the Judaism of the restoration. Ezekiel stressed the interior qualities of religion, as the earlier prophets had, but in the manner of later writers he looked to the Temple and to cultic observances. He described life in exile and preached a message of hope, striving to sustain his fellow deportees in their faith and traditions. This message culminates in the final vision of the temple in the new Jerusalem and the restoration of Israel.

Ezion-geber [ee'-zee-ahn-gee'-bur]   Ezion-geber (modern Tell el Kheleifeh) was an ancient seaport on the north shore of the Gulf of Aqaba. Founded (c.950 BC) by SOLOMON, it was intended as his major port for Arabian and African trade. Copper slag and the remains of a hand-bellows furnace demonstrate the importance of the site as a unit in Solomon's metalworking complex along the copper deposits of the Wadi-al-Araba. Destroyed by the pharaoh SHESHONK, the site was rebuilt at the instigation of JEHOSHAPHAT of Judah (c.870–848 BC). It was again destroyed in the mid-9th century BC, probably by the Edomites. Afterward, Ezion-geber ceased to exist. When occupation resumed in the 8th century BC, it was under the new name Elath (ELAT). Excavations were conducted at the site in 1938-40.

Ezra and Nehemiah, books of [ez'-ruh, neeuh-my'-uh]   Ezra and Nehemiah are two books of the Old Testament of the Bible, originally one work in the Hebrew canon. Written between 450 and 250 BC and named for two political and religious reformers in the postexilic Jewish community, they relate aspects of Jewish history from 538 BC to about 420 BC. Because of the confused organization of the books, the chronology of the two reformers and their work is uncertain. With some rearrangement of contents, the purposes of scribe Ezra's mission to Jerusalem from the Persian court in 458 BC may be seen to have been to introduce stricter observance of the Law and to dissolve marriages with foreigners; the purposes of Governor Nehemiah's two missions to Jerusalem in 445 BC and 432 BC may be seen to have been to fortify and resettle the city, reform temple organization, oppose mixed marriages, and secure loyalty to these reforms by a covenant.

Ff

GERMAN-GOTHIC	RUSSIAN-CYRILLIC	CLASSICAL LATIN	EARLY LATIN	ETRUSCAN	EARLY GREEK	EARLY ARAMAIC	EARLY HEBREW	PHOENICIAN

F   *F/f* is the sixth letter of the English alphabet. Both the letter and its position in the alphabet derive from the Latin, which in turn derived it from the Greek by way of the Etruscan. The Greeks took the letter from a Semitic writing system, where the name of the sound was *waw*, used for the consonant *w*. The corresponding Greek letter *digamma* probably represented the *w* sound but disappeared before the development of the classical Greek alphabet. Through a series of complex transitions the *digamma* came to represent the *f* sound in Western alphabets—a voiceless, labiodental fricative made by expelling the breath between the lower lip and upper teeth. The voiced counterpart of *f* is *v*, and the two sounds interchange at times, as in the English *of*, where written *F/f* is pronounced as *v*.

F-15 Eagle   see AIRCRAFT, MILITARY

F-16 Fighting Falcon   The General Dynamics F-16 Fighting Falcon is a highly maneuverable, all-weather, multirole jet fighter aircraft. Since reaching combat readiness status in 1980, the F-16 has become a mainstay of NATO air forces. Basic configurations are the single-seat F-16A fighter and the two-seat F-16B fighter/trainer. The F-16A is powered by one turbofan engine with a static thrust of 25,000 lb (11,340 kg), which enables the aircraft to exceed Mach 2, or 1,226 km/h (1,524 mph). Its armament includes a 20-mm multibarrel cannon and the new advanced medium-range air-to-air missile (AMRAAM).

Fa-hsien   see FAXIEN

Fabergé, Peter Carl   [fah-bair-zhay']   Peter Carl Fabergé, b. May 30 (N.S.), 1846, d. Sept. 24, 1920, was a Russian goldsmith whose work has often been compared with that of Benvenuto Cellini. Fabergé inherited (1870) the directorship of the jewelry firm established by his father, Gustave, in 1842. Under his leadership the Fabergé studios achieved fame for the objets d'art created by its artisans, who worked in gold, silver, enamel, and precious stones, set in ingenious designs. The Fabergé firm was in its heyday during the reigns of tsars Alexander III and Nicholas II; it employed more than 500 artisans, with branches in Moscow (1887), Kiev (1905), and London (1906). Some of its most imagina-

tive pieces included decorated enamel Easter eggs that were given as presents by the tsars. The firm did not survive the Revolutions of 1917; it was nationalized and then closed down (1918) by the Bolsheviks. Fabergé died in exile in Lausanne.

Fabian Society   [fay'-bee-uhn]   The Fabian Society is a British organization that was founded in 1883–84 with the aim of spreading socialist ideas among the educated public and ultimately establishing a socialist government. Among its more prominent members have been George Bernard Shaw, Sidney and Beatrice Webb, and Annie Besant. The Fabians rejected revolutionary Marxism, favoring a program of education fostered by research, publications, and seminars. After the appearance (1889) of the *Fabian Essays*, the society became an influential political force. It was a key constituent of the Labour Representation Committee, founded in 1900, which subsequently became the British LABOUR PARTY. It is now a specialized research agency of the Labour party.

See also: SOCIALISM.

Fabius   (family)   [fay'-bee-uhs]   The Roman patrician clan (*gens*) of the Fabi was prominent from the 5th century BC on. Its most famous member was **Quintus Fabius Maximus Verrucosus**, d. 203 BC, who was consul five times (233, 228, 215, 214, 209) and dictator twice (*c*.221, 217). He was nicknamed Cunctator (delayer) for his delaying tactics against HANNIBAL in the Second PUNIC WAR. He first used these tactics of harassing Hannibal's army but not joining battle after the Roman defeat (217) at Lake Trasimene and again, with even greater success, after the Roman disaster at Cannae (216).

Quintus Fabius Maximus Aemilianus, *c*.186–130 BC, was consul in 145, fought Viriathus (145-44), and was the legate (134–33) of Scipio at Numantia. **Quintus Fabius Pictor**, fl. 216 BC, wrote a history of Rome in Greek that traced the beginnings of Rome to Aeneas; now lost, this work set the pattern for Roman historiography.

fable   Although the term *fable*, derived from Latin *fabula*, "a telling," can be applied to any work of fiction, it usually denotes a brief tale in which animals or inanimate objects speak and behave like humans, usually to advance a moral point.

lated moral lessons are less important than the larger fiction, and fable merges with ALLEGORY. Other modern examples of the fable are James Thurber's *Fables of Our Time* (1940) and William Golding's *Pincher Martin* (1950).

fabliau [fa-blee-oh'] The fabliaux (singular, fabliau) constitute a genre of short narrative verse composed in France primarily from the 12th to the 14th century. The conventional form consisted of eight-syllable lines with rhyming couplets.

The narrative formula and subject matter of the fabliau were exploited by Giovanni BOCCACCIO and Geoffrey CHAUCER, among others. The genre is distinct from the FABLE and miracle story in its realism. It is concerned with everyday events, real customs, minor disasters, and human folly. The subjects, often drawn from folklore, are sometimes serious but usually oriented toward comedy and amusing satire, mocking avid monks, imperious women, charlatans and their dupes, and pompous fools.

Fabliaux are thought to represent a reaction to the more serious medieval literary genres such as the epic, lives of the saints, and courtly love lyrics.

fabric   see TEXTILE INDUSTRY

facsimile [fak-sim'-uh-lee] Facsimile, in telecommunications, is the process of transmitting exact copies of

The 17th-century French fabulist Jean de la Fontaine created the tale of the fox and the raven, in which the clever fox tricks the raven out of a piece of cheese. The fable illustrates a moral point within an allegorical framework.

Fables appear in the earliest records of widely separated cultures. In the 16th century, Sanskrit tales came to Europe via Persia. Earlier versions of similar tales, however, had probably reached classical Greece and were reflected in the tales of AESOP (about 6th century BC). They were transmitted into Latin by Phaedrus in the 1st century AD. The medieval beast epic REYNARD THE FOX introduced a cast of animal characters that were adapted by later poets to contemporary situations. Examples are the vain cock Chauntecleer of Geoffrey CHAUCER's "Nun's Priest's Tale" (in the *Canterbury Tales*, c.1387–1400) and the fox and ape in Edmund SPENSER's more openly satirical *Mother Hubberds Tale* (1591).

France, in particular, showed a continuing interest in the fable from the 13th century onward, as seen in the works of MARIE DE FRANCE. This interest culminated in the *Fables* (1668–94) of Jean de LA FONTAINE, which remain popular to the present day. Within natural settings, they comment on human folly, and many may be read as satires—tolerant but shrewd commentaries on French society.

A reaction against La Fontaine was expressed by the German Gotthold LESSING, whose *Fables* (1759) presented a more vigorous moral analysis. Lessing advocated a return to the example of Aesop, in which the story existed primarily for the moral, and he accused La Fontaine of relying too heavily on the charm of the tale itself. The tradition of the fable was continued in the 17th and 18th centuries by such writers as John Dryden and John Gay.

Modern authors often use the expanded fable, a book-length story involving an animal population, such as George Orwell's *Animal Farm* (1945). In these works iso-

In one version of a facsimile system, the document to be transmitted is wrapped around a rotating drum and scanned by a traversing lens-photocell (1). The resulting electric signal is transmitted by telephone line (2) to the receiving facsimile machine, where light reproduces the image on photographic paper. Signals for synchronizing the drive motors (3) and scanning traverses (5) are also transmitted (4).

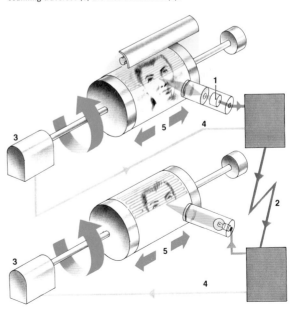

printed and pictorial material over telephone lines, using a machine—a fax, in current jargon—that both sends and receives. The document to be transmitted is inserted into the fax, where an array of photodiodes (see DIODE) scans the image and—in the same way a television picture is scanned—converts it into thousands of picture elements, or pixels. The pixels are transmitted in groups of digital pulses over telephone lines. (Digitized phone lines can handle digital pulses directly; with conventional lines, the pulses must first be converted into electric signals.) The receiving fax prints the incoming image using an array of fine, electrically charged wires that correspond to the photodiode array on the transmitting fax, or, in some cases, by a system resembling the electrostatic printing used in copying machines.

The use of facsimile transmission is ever increasing, for it is the most rapid method for sending printed material. Once the fax has been purchased, the costs of transmission are minimal. Transmission times are almost instantaneous, and the newest fax machines can reproduce photographs and graphics with great fidelity.

----

factor   When a natural NUMBER (1, 2, 3, 4,...) can be written as a product of two or more natural numbers, these numbers are called factors of the given number. Because 12 can be written as 1×12, 2×6, and 3×4, the numbers 1, 2, 3, 4, 6, and 12 are all factors of 12. In general, if a is any natural number, b and c are factors of a if $a = b \times c$.

Any factor of a natural number a is also a divisor of a. Thus, for $a = 12$, we have $12 \div 1 = 12$, $12 \div 2 = 6$, $12 \div 3 = 4$, $12 \div 4 = 3$, $12 \div 6 = 2$, and $12 \div 12 = 1$. Because the only divisors of 12 are 1, 2, 3, 4, 6, and 12, we conclude that the only factors of 12 are 1, 2, 3, 4, 6, and 12.

Any natural number a, except 1, has at least the two distinct factors a and 1. If the number has only these two factors, it is called a PRIME NUMBER. A number that has additional factors is called a composite number.

In algebra, factors of polynomials are defined in a similar manner. Thus, since $2x^2 - 10x + 12 = 2(x - 2)(x - 3)$, the expressions 2, $x - 2$, and $x - 3$ are said to be the factors of $2x^2 - 10x + 12$. The process of breaking an expression into factors is known as factorization.

----

factorial [fak-tohr'-ee-ul]   The product for any positive integer n, $1 \times 2 \times 3 \times ... \times (n - 2) \times (n - 1) \times n$ is called factorial n and is denoted by $n!$ For example, $1! = 1$; $2! = 1 \times 2 = 2$; $3! = 1 \times 2 \times 3 = 6$. Although 0! is meaningless, it is useful to define factorial zero as one ($0! = 1$) for completeness and to simplify expressions that arise in certain mathematical calculations. Expressions containing factorials arise in the SERIES expansions of many quantities, in the BINOMIAL THEOREM, in PERMUTATIONS AND COMBINATIONS, and in PROBABILITY theory.

----

factory farming   Factory farming, or confinement rearing, is a method of raising large numbers of POULTRY or livestock in relatively small areas, under conditions that ensure rapid growth. Confinement practices include bringing feed to the animals rather than allowing them to forage, and controlling feed rations—often through computerization and automation—to attain the most efficient ratio of growth-time to feed cost. In general, factory farming produces meat, milk, or eggs in less time than is possible with traditional ANIMAL HUSBANDRY practices. Confinement facilities range from barns that may contain several hundred pens for VEAL calves to chicken houses holding 100,000 broiler chickens penned in groups of 10,000 or more. Dairy farms may house large numbers of cows in small confined lots; PIGS may be fattened in droves of several hundreds; and cattle feedlots containing up to 100,000 animals are not uncommon. Animals raised in confinement conditions receive rations containing high proportions of protein and high percentages of grains. Cattle ordinarily require 4.5 kg (10 lb) of feed to produce 0.45 kg (1 lb) of weight gain; under confinement they gain 0.45 kg with only 2.7 kg (6 lb) of enriched feed.

The large concentrations of animals in confinement pens or feedlots would once inevitably have caused lethal epidemics of disease. To prevent such epidemics and to improve feed/weight-gain efficiency ratios, minute quantities of various growth stimulants and of antibiotics and other drugs are added to feed or injected directly into the animals. There is widespread controversy about the potential effects on humans of residues of these substances in food. Another problem is the creation of antibiotic-resistant bacteria, such as SALMONELLA, as the result of the routine administration of small quantities of antibiotics to farm animals.

Factory farming has greatly reduced the labor required to raise farm animals. Nevertheless, some farmers are beginning to question the fundamental economics of factory farming. In Europe especially—where concerns over cruelty to animals and the health hazards associated with intensive rearing have been more publicized than in the United States—some studies suggest that although production of meat, poultry, milk, and eggs is greatly enhanced by factory-farming practices, the high costs of erecting buildings and buying equipment and the expenses necessary to chemically maintain herds and flocks may, in the end, erode profits to a level comparable with those obtained under conventional rearing practices.

----

factory system   The factory system is the most advanced of the four principal types of industrial organization. There are three simpler industrial organizations. Of these forms, the simplest and least specialized is the undiversified household, in which members of the family provide for their own needs. The second is the handicraft system, in which skilled independent CRAFT workers, working in small shops or with the assistance of apprentices or journeymen, specialize in making particular products. Third is the domestic, or putting-out system, in which an employer owns the materials and distributes them to various craft workers who carry out the various steps in a production process.

The factory system, when fully developed, differs from the other forms of industrial organization in several important ways. It brings sizable groups of laborers together in rooms wholly devoted to their work. It is marked by an extensive use of power-driven machines. Further, the system is characterized by a high degree of coordination, achieved within the factory by causing the work to flow through processing steps and by imposing supervision on the workers.

The factory system played a key role in the INDUSTRIAL REVOLUTION that originated in Britain. First utilized in the British cotton textile industry during the 1770s, the system was initially slow to move into other industries, largely because of the workers' hostility. As power-driven machinery came to be used more widely, however, the cost advantages of the factory over other forms of industrial organization served to force workers into the factory system, making it the predominant form of industrial organization.

The factory system, which has drastically increased the output of manufactured products, has had important social as well as economic effects. It has led, for example, to the emergence of a capitalist-owner class whose members finance the machinery and equipment. It is responsible both for the decline in the relative importance of self-employed artisans and craft workers and for the emergence of a labor class dependent for income on the sale of their services to employers. The factory system has also contributed significantly to the urbanization of modern society.

See also: ASSEMBLY LINE; AUTOMATION; INDUSTRIAL ENGINEERING; INDUSTRIAL MANAGEMENT; MANUFACTURING, HISTORY OF.

Faerie Queene, The   *The Faerie Queene* is an epic poem by Edmund SPENSER, planned as a chivalric allegory praising England and Queen Elizabeth I (1533–1603). The first installment was published in 1590 in 3 books of 12 cantos each. A dedicatory letter to Sir Walter Raleigh proposes a complete poem of 12 books on the moral virtues followed by 12 on the political.

Each book has its own protagonist, and in each Prince Arthur personifies magnificence, or "greatness of soul." Books 1–3 are devoted to Holiness, Temperance, and Chastity; 4–6 (1596), to Friendship, Justice, and Courtesy. A fragment was published posthumously in 1609 as "Cantos of Mutabilitie" with an indication that it was part of a seventh book on Constancy. The poem is written in Spenserian stanzas—eight lines of iambic pentameter and a final alexandrine, rhyming *a b a b, b c b c, c* (see VERSIFICATION).

Although *The Faerie Queene* is unfinished, it has been said to possess a certain completeness in its present form. *The Faerie Queene* had a powerful influence on later poets, especially Milton and the romantics.

Faeroe Islands [fair'-oh]   The Faeroe Islands, located in the North Atlantic about halfway between the Scottish Shetland Islands and Iceland, constitute a self-governing unit within Denmark. With a total land area of only 1,399 km^2 (540 mi^2), the archipelago comprises 17 inhabited and 5 uninhabited islands. The population is 47,653 (1989 est.). Thorshavn (1988 est. pop., 14,547), on the island of Streymoy, is the capital. The people speak their own language, Faeroese, which is related to Danish.

The Faeroes are volcanic, rocky, and precipitous, with mountains rising to 882 m (2,894 ft). Winters are long and dark, and summer nights are short. Rainfall is heavy, and storms are frequent, but temperatures are mild. Sheepherding, wool working, fowling, and potato growing are still pursued, but deep-sea fishing and fish processing are now the major activities, and tourism is being developed.

The islands were first settled by Irish monks about 700 and by Vikings about 800. They belonged to Norway until 1380, when they were ceded to Denmark. The islands were granted home rule in 1948 and send two representatives to the Danish parliament.

Fahd, King of Saudi Arabia   Fahd ibn Abd al-Aziz, b. 1922, succeeded to the throne of Saudi Arabia upon the death (June 13, 1982) of his half brother King KHALID. One of the many sons of Ibn Saud, founder of the kingdom, Fahd held several official posts before becoming crown prince and first deputy prime minister in 1975. Fahd, who supervised Saudi Arabia's economic modernization, is regarded as a moderate among Arab leaders. After the Aug. 2, 1990, Iraqi invasion of Kuwait, he invited in U.S. forces to defend Saudi Arabia. It was from that country that U.S. and coalition forces, with UN authorization, launched a successful attack against Iraqi forces, ousting them from Kuwait in February 1991 (see GULF WAR).

Fahrenheit scale   SEE TEMPERATURE

faïence [fay-ens' or fay-ahns']   In its broadest sense, faïence describes all glazed, porous earthenware, but the term primarily refers to a kind of tin-glazed earthenware, also called DELFTWARE, that became popular throughout Europe in the 16th century. The term, which was current by 1610, is probably a French corruption of Faenza, an Italian city celebrated for its production of MAJOLICA. In the manufacture of faïence, earthenware is covered with a white enamel glaze that was often left undecorated.

In the 16th century, colors were applied to the white glaze before the piece was fired, but after 1750 a new technique known as *petit feu* was introduced whereby colors were added after the first firing, and then fired a second time at a lower temperature. This technique permitted ornate decoration. Faïence was at the height of its popularity during the early and mid-18th century, when factories in Italy, France, and Holland produced a great variety of wares—including tableware, tiles, and jardinieres. Individual centers of production evolved distinctive styles, and Bologna, Padua, Rouen, Moustiers, and Nevers produced particularly fine pieces.

Fair Deal   The Fair Deal was the name given to the domestic programs of U.S. president Harry S. Truman. First used in 1949, the term generally refers to Truman's entire presidency (1945–53). Included among the Fair Deal programs were a national health insurance plan; extended social security, aid to education, and public housing; higher price supports for farmers; and a fair-employment-practices committee. Only some of these programs were passed during Truman's administration, but many of them later became law in the 1960s as part of the Great Society program of President Lyndon B. Johnson.

Fairbanks   Fairbanks, a city in central Alaska, lies on the Chena River, about 180 km (110 mi) south of the Arctic Circle. Its population is 30,843 (1990). Fairbanks is a transportation and trade center for Alaska's interior; its major industries include mining and lumbering. Fort Wainwright and Eielson Air Force Base are nearby, and the University of Alaska (established 1915) is at College, 5 km (3 mi) to the northwest. Alaskaland, a 16-ha (40-acre) civic and cultural center, includes the Pioneer Museum and a reproduction of an Indian village. Fairbanks was founded in 1902 after gold was discovered in the vicinity.

Fairbanks, Charles Warren   Charles Warren Fairbanks, b. near Unionville Center, Ohio, May 11, 1852, d. June 4, 1918, was an Indiana lawyer who served in the U.S. Senate (1897–1905) and as the 26th vice-president of the United States (1905–09). A conservative Republican, Warren was chosen in 1904 to run for the vice-presidency as a balance to the presidential nominee, Theodore Roosevelt, a progressive.

Fairbanks, Douglas   Douglas Fairbanks was the stage name of Douglas Elton Ullman, b. New York City, May 23, 1883, d. Dec. 12, 1939, an American actor who starred in silent films including *The Mask of Zorro* (1920) and *The Thief of Bagdad* (1924). His most successful sound film was *The Taming of the Shrew* (1929), costarring his wife, Mary PICKFORD. His son by a previous marriage, Douglas Fairbanks, Jr., b. Dec. 9, 1909, also appeared in action films.

Fairfax of Cameron, Thomas Fairfax, 6th Baron   Lord Fairfax, b. England, Oct. 22, 1693, d. Dec. 9, 1781, was one of the principal landowners of 18th-century Virginia. A descendant of the 3d Baron Fairfax (1612–71), who was commander in chief of the parliamentary forces in the English Civil War, the 6th baron inherited about 2 million ha (5 million acres) of land between the Potomac and Rappahannock rivers and settled there in 1747.

fairs   SEE CARNIVALS AND FAIRS; TRADE FAIRS; WORLD'S FAIRS

The painting Titania, Bottom and the Fairies *(1794) by Henry Fuseli depicts a scene from Shakespeare's* A Midsummer Night's Dream. *Fantasy and reality blend in the play when mortal lovers enter an enchanted world ruled by Queen Titania.*

fairy   In folklore a fairy is a preternatural creature that lives on the Earth and may be either helpful or harmful to human beings. Fairies are common to folklore all over the world. They resemble humans but are usually much smaller and possess powers of magic. They can become invisible at will and thus live unseen in the midst of human society.

According to tradition some fairies live in an organized community, called fairyland, which is free of sickness and the passage of time. Mortals occasionally discover fairyland by accident or are abducted and taken there by fairies. Another type of fairy is associated with a particular place, occupation, or household. Nixies live in water, for example, and gnomes are subterranean creatures; leprechauns are shoemakers, and trolls are smiths. Household fairies, such as elves and goblins, play mischievous pranks but also help with domestic chores. Some fairies bewitch humans; they may also steal human babies and leave fairy changelings in their place. Other fairies promote the welfare of people, as does the fairy godmother in CINDERELLA. Love or marriage between fairies and mortals rarely ends happily.

Fairies were traditionally identified as fallen angels or as the first inhabitants of the Earth. Modern scholars have suggested that they represent discarded gods, spirits of the dead, or the personification of primitive nature spirits.

See also: FAIRY TALE; FOLKTALE.

fairy tale The fairy tale includes two distinct narrative types: the folk fairy tale, best known in the West through the works of the brothers Grimm (see GRIMM'S FAIRY TALES); and the literary fairy tale, popular in France and Germany since the 18th century. Although each form has its own history and style, the two forms share important traits: both represent a distinct art form, and both evoke a sense of wonder and enchantment.

The folk fairy tale belongs to the oral tradition of the FOLKTALE but differs in several respects from other types, such as the FABLE, anecdote, legend, and myth. It is complex, with several episodes; it takes place in a world outside of time, space, and causality; its hero or heroine has neither historical nor mythical significance; it does not pretend to be true; and it aims not to instruct but to entertain.

Folk fairy tales have appeared at different times in many countries of Europe, Asia, and North Africa, and many date back centuries in oral tradition. The earliest collections with motifs of the European folk fairy tale are the *Gesta Romanorum* (about 14th century), the ARABIAN NIGHTS (c.1450), Giovanni Francesco Straparola's *The Facetious Nights* (1550–53; Eng. trans., 1901), Giovanni Battista Basile's *Pentamerone* (1634–36; Eng. trans., 1893), and Charles PERRAULT's *Tales of Mother Goose* (1697; Eng. trans., c.1729).

Working with polarities—good and bad, beautiful and ugly—the folk fairy tale tells of the wondrous adventures of a hero or heroine who, after a series of tasks or struggles with supernatural forces, attains his or her wish and lives happily ever after. The protagonists blindly follow their destiny. Such tales create an abstract world of a higher reality, the truth of which is what Bruno BETTELHEIM calls "the truth of the imagination."

In contrast, the literary fairy tale has no set pattern of

The fairy tale is a synthesis of oral and written folktale traditions. Charles Perrault published 80 tales from European oral tradition, popularly known as the Tales of Mother Goose *(1697). One of his tales is illustrated here: a 19th-century illustration by Gustave Doré of* Little Red Riding Hood.

plot, character, or motif. It was popularized in Germany by GOETHE and Christoph Martin WIELAND before becoming canonized by the romantics, for whom it was synonymous with poetry. Using terms such as *fairy tale of nature*, *metaphysical fairy tale*, and *fairy tale of reality* in tales that often resemble dreams or nightmares, the romantics sought to penetrate the highest and deepest levels of mind and spirit.

But fairy tales have been a source of inspiration for artists of all kinds. Walt DISNEY's animations of "Cinderella," "Sleeping Beauty," and "Snow White" are examples. Many artists have illustrated the Grimms' *Fairy Tales*, which have also inspired operas such as Engelbert HUMPERDINCK's *Hänsel and Gretel* (1893) and Jacques OFFENBACH's *Tales of Hoffmann* (1881). Writers such as Hans Christian ANDERSEN, Lewis CARROLL, Charles DICKENS, and Oscar WILDE have continued the literary tradition.

Faisal, King of Saudi Arabia [fy'-sul] Faisal ibn Abd al-Aziz ibn Abd al-Rahman al Saud, b. c.1906, d. Mar. 25, 1975, succeeded his brother SAUD, who was peacefully deposed from the throne of Saudi Arabia in 1964. He also served as premier from 1953 to 1960 and from 1962 until his death. A moderate reformer, Faisal made Saudi Arabia a leading conservative power in Arab politics, opposing revolutionary movements in the Arab world. He did, however, join left-wing Arab regimes in the 1967 Arab-Israeli War. Thereafter he was more concerned with Arab unity, supporting the Arab oil embargo in the fall of 1973. He was assassinated by his nephew Prince Faisal ibn Masaid and succeeded by his brother KHALID.

Faisal I, King of Iraq Faisal I, b. May 20, 1885, d. Sept. 8, 1933, was the first king of the Iraqi state that emerged after World War I. The third son of HUSAYN IBN ALI of Mecca, he abandoned his youthful vision of a reformed Ottoman Empire to lead his father's armies in the Arab Revolt (1916–18) during World War I; T. E. LAWRENCE was his advisor. Faisal was elected king of Syria in 1920 but was forced to abdicate by the French. In 1921, however, the British installed him as king of Iraq under their mandate. Shrewdly balancing British against local interests, Faisal gained legal independence for Iraq in 1932.

faith healing Faith healing is the cure or relief of physical or mental ills by prayer or religious rituals that may either supplement or replace medical treatment. The practice has been common in most cultures and religious traditions. Primitive peoples turned to a shaman or medicine man to cure their ills. The ancient Greeks and Romans erected temples to Asclepius, the god of medicine. In biblical times, sickness was considered the result of sin or the work of the devil. According to the New Testament, Jesus Christ sometimes brought about physical cures through the forgiveness of sin (Matthew 9:2–7).

The early Christians followed his example and prayed for the healing of the sick (James 5:14–16). A sacrament of healing, the ANOINTING OF THE SICK, developed in the Catholic tradition, and faith-healing services have been a part of the Protestant tradition. One of the best-known Protestant faith healers was Kathryn Kuhlman. LOURDES and other shrines noted for their claims of cures attract thousands of sick people each year. Faith healing is also of interest to those who promote psychosomatic treatment and is related to principles of divine healing followed by CHRISTIAN SCIENCE.

faith   see RELIGION

Faiyum   see AL-FAIYUM

Fakhr al-Din [fah'-kur ahl-deen']   Fakhr al-Din al-Razy, 1149–1209, was a Muslim theologian and philosopher and the author of one of the greatest commentaries on the Koran. Born in Persia, he traveled in Central Asia and later settled in Herat (in present-day Afghanistan). An exponent of orthodox Islam, he wrote *Mafatih al-Ghayb* (The Keys of the Mystery, 1279–89), a 6-volume commentary on the Koran, and set out the bases of Muslim jurisprudence in his *Encyclopedia of the Sciences.*

fakir [fah-keer']   Fakir (Arabic, "poor") refers to a Muslim or Hindu ascetic or mendicant monk who belongs to a religious order but lives by begging and may be adept in magic and miracle working. In Islamic cultures the term is often synonymous with DERVISH.

Falange   see FASCISM

Falashas [fah-lah'-shuhz]   The Falashas are a group of Ethiopians who claim Jewish origin as descendants of Menelik, the alleged son of King Solomon and the Queen of Sheba. Until recently they lived a segregated life in villages north of Lake Tana. The Falashas observe the traditions of Judaism: they practice monogamy, obey the biblical laws of purity and circumcision, observe the Sabbath and biblical holidays, recite traditional prayers, and follow biblical dietary customs. Their Bible, in an Ethiopian translation, includes the Old Testament and some Apocrypha. They do not know the Talmud. The name *Falasha* (Amharic for "stranger") was given to them by other Ethiopians; they call themselves *Beta Israel* ("House of Israel"). In 1984 and 1985, thousands of them were airlifted to Israel in a rescue operation sponsored by the Israeli government.

falcon [fal'-kuhn]   Falcons are any of about 60 species of birds of prey that constitute the family Falconidae in the order Falconiformes, which also includes eagles, hawks, kites, and vultures. The true falcons are typified

The peregrine falcon, once prized for the sport of falconry, ranges throughout the world, particularly in open country. It flies swiftly, diving from high altitudes to attack its prey.

by a bullet-shaped body, long and pointed wings, a medium to long tail, long toes with sharply hooked claws, a short neck, and a short, hooked, and usually notched bill. Coloration may vary widely, but the sexes of any one species are usually similar in appearance, except that the females are larger. Certain species of falcons are also known as caracaras, falconets, gyrfalcons, hobbies, kestrels, and peregrines; somewhat confusingly, a number of falcons are also called hawks.

Falcons are strong, fast fliers with great aerial agility. They seldom soar in the manner of hawks. The peregrine has been clocked at 290 km/h (180 mph) in a dive. This speed and agility make falcons successful hunters of birds, reptiles, and small mammals. Some species, however, are insectivorous or eaters of carrion. Although falcons strike or grasp their prey with their claws, they generally kill the captured prey with their beaks, whereas hawks kill with their claws.

Falcons are usually solitary or live in pairs. They nest in trees or on cliffs and often occupy the nests of other species of birds. Females generally lay two to six eggs, and both the male and female incubate the eggs and care for the young. Falcons seldom live more than 20 years.

The falcons' only serious enemy is humankind. For many years falcons were considered vermin because they were thought to exact a heavy toll on chickens and other livestock. In recent times pesticides have been responsible for decimating and endangering several species. Organochlorine pesticides (DDT, dieldrin) reduce the ability of certain birds to produce sufficient calcium for their eggs; consequently, the eggs are thin-shelled and susceptible to breakage.

The earliest fossil record of the falcon family is from the Miocene Epoch of Argentina, about 15 million years ago.

falconry [fal'-kuhn-ree]   Falconry, or hawking, is the sport of hunting with FALCONS and HAWKS. Believed to have originated in Central Asia about 2000 BC, it has had a devoted following in the Middle East ever since. In Europe it was popular among nobility between the 10th and 17th centuries, but it declined with the introduction of guns. Interest in the sport revived after World War I.

In strict falconry usage, the terms *falcon* and *tiercel* were reserved for the female and male peregrine, respectively, but with qualifying terms they were also applied to falcons such as the gyrfalcon, kestrel, and merlin, and to hawks such as the goshawk and sparrow hawk.

The style of hunting varies, depending somewhat on the kind of hawk available to the hunter. Short-winged hawks, such as the goshawk and Cooper's hawk, hunt ground-level prey from a high perch. Long-winged hawks, such as the peregrine, gyrfalcon, and merlin, hunt from the air and take flying prey. Short-winged hawks are trained to return to the falconer's glove, but long-winged birds are trained to return to a lure—a mock bird swinging on a cord.

Falkenhayn, Erich von [fahl'-ken-hyn, ay'-rik fuhn]   Erich Georg Anton Sebastian von Falkenhayn, b. Sept. 11, 1861, d. Apr. 8, 1922, was chief of the German general staff (1914–16) during World War I. Succeeding Helmuth Johannes Ludwig von MOLTKE, Falkenhayn adopted the strategy of a war of attrition on the western front. Believing that the war would be won there, he opposed the plans of Generals Paul von Hindenburg and Erich Ludendorff for an offensive against Russia but was overruled by Emperor William II. To break the deadlock in the west, Falkenhayn planned a major assault on Verdun, which began on Feb. 21, 1916. Six months later, as the unsuccessful and costly battle continued, he was relieved of his command. He subsequently commanded forces in Romania, Palestine, and Lithuania.

Falkland Islands   The Falkland Islands (Spanish: Islas Malvinas) are a British crown colony, located in the South Atlantic Ocean about 770 km (480 mi) northeast of Cape Horn. There are two large islands, East and West Falkland; about 200 smaller, mostly uninhabited islets; and several other widely scattered islands that are dependencies of the Falklands. The total land area is about 12,000 km² (4,700 mi²). Stanley, located on East Falkland, is the capital. The population of 1,800 (1980) is primarily of British origin. Sheep raising is the mainstay of the economy.

The Falklands were probably discovered by John Davis, a British navigator, in 1592. The first colony was established (1764) by the French, but it soon passed to Spain and, after abandonment, was resettled by Argentina in 1820. The British occupied the islands in 1833. Argentina's claim to sovereignty continued, however, finally prompting UN-initiated negotiations in 1966.

Negotiations were halted when, on Apr. 2, 1982, Argentine troops seized the islands. Britain dispatched a large task force, retook (April 25) the dependency of South Georgia, and, following intense naval and air battles with the Argentines, landed (May 21) several thousand troops on East Falkland Island. Heavy fighting ensued until the Argentines, entrenched at Port Stanley, surrendered on June 14, 1982.

fall line   A fall line, also called a fall zone, is the line at which streams make a sudden descent, for example, over the edge of a plateau. Falls or rapids occur as the waters descend from a zone of erosion-resistant uplands to lowlands or plains composed of softer, less resistant rock. This imaginary line on each river, which usually marks the head of navigation and a source of significant waterpower, is a natural site for settlement. A notable example is found in the eastern United States from New York to Alabama in the zone where the major rivers descend from the Appalachian foothills to the Atlantic coastal plain.

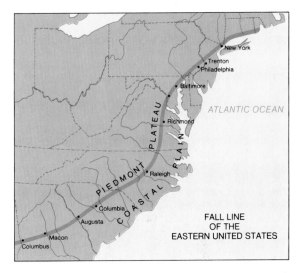

An extensive fall line lies between the Appalachian Piedmont and the Atlantic coastal plain. Waterfalls and rapids occur along this line on such rivers as the Delaware, Potomac, and Savannah.

Fall River   Fall River is a port city in eastern Massachusetts. Its population is 92,703 (1990). Located at the mouth of the Taunton River on Mount Hope Bay, the city harbors the World War II battleship U.S.S. Massachusetts as a war memorial; it also has a marine museum.

First settled in 1656, Fall River was incorporated in 1803. It provided one of the earliest sites for the manufacture of cotton because of its good harbor and the presence of the rapidly flowing Quequechan River to power the mills. Its first cotton mill was constructed in 1811.

The city was hard hit by the Depression of the 1930s and competition from southern textile mills. The current economy is more diversified, but cotton goods and clothing are still manufactured. Plastics are also produced. The murder trial of Lizzie BORDEN was held there in 1892-93.

Falla, Manuel de [fah'-ee-ah, mahn-wayl day]
Manuel de Falla, b. Nov. 23, 1876, d. Nov. 14, 1946, a famous Spanish composer, is admired for his brilliant and colorful evocations of Spain in his music. He studied piano at the Royal Conservatory in Madrid and composition with Felipe Pedrell, who urged Falla to write music of true Spanish character. He spent the years 1907–14 in Paris, where he was befriended and encouraged by Claude Debussy. His only published opera, *La Vida Breve* (The Short Life), was performed at the Opéra Comique in 1914. Thereafter, Falla lived mainly in Granada, which is evoked in the symphonic impressions for piano and orchestra, *Nights in the Gardens of Spain* (1911–15). His greatest successes were two ballets reflecting the dances and folklore of his native province of Andalusia. The first, *El Amor Brujo* (Love, the Sorcerer), composed in 1914–15 and drawn from legends of the Gypsies of Granada, includes "Ritual Fire Dance" and "Dance of Terror," two numbers frequently performed in piano versions. The second, *The Three-Cornered Hat* (1918–19), tells the humorous story of a miller, his attractive wife, and an amorous magistrate.

In *Four Spanish Pieces* (1906–07), for piano, and *Seven Spanish Popular Songs* (1914), for voice and piano, Falla evokes the regional folk music of Spain. With *El Retablo de Maese Pedro* (Master Peter's Puppet Show, 1919–22), he turned to a scene from Cervantes's *Don Quixote*. His concerto for harpsichord and five instruments (1923–26) draws largely on Spanish music of the 16th century. In 1939, Falla went to Argentina. He died there, leaving unfinished a cantata, *Atlántida*, which was completed by his former pupil, Ernesto Halffter, and first performed in 1961.

---

fallacy [fal'-uh-see]   In LOGIC a fallacy is a form of reasoning. A formal fallacy violates the rules of formal logic. An informal fallacy is unsound in less precise ways.

Two common formal fallacies occur in hypothetical reasoning—an inference from a premise of the form "If A, then B." Affirming the consequent occurs when one adds B as a second premise and infers A. For example, from "If all Americans are bald, then all Americans require no hairdressers" and "All Americans require no hairdressers," one infers "All Americans are bald." Denying the antecedent occurs when one adds not-A to the hypothetical and infers not-B.

Two other common formal fallacies are arguing from the undistributed middle—inferring from "All A is B" and "All C is B" that "All A is C," and the conversion of universal positive proposition—inferring from "All A is B" that "All B is A."

Informal fallacies are much more common than formal ones in ordinary discussions, political speeches, and advertising. Some of these involve slipping from one meaning of an ambiguous term to another meaning.

Other major informal fallacies are the *ignoratio elenchi*, that is, arguing for something different from the question asked; and the *tu quoque* argument, in which an unsound argument is justified by claiming the unsoundness of another. These soon degenerate into the argument *ad hominem*, in which the argument of an opponent is countered by pointing to his or her personal faults rather than by considering the substance of the argument; and the argument from authority, which appeals to famous or important people who agree with a particular point of view.

Fälldin, Thorbjörn [fel-deen', toor'-bee-urn]   Nils Olof Thorbjörn Fälldin, b. Apr. 24, 1926, became, in 1976, Sweden's first non-Socialist prime minister in more than 40 years. After working as a farmer, he was elected to parliament in 1958, representing the agrarian Center party. Defeated in the 1964 election, Fälldin was reelected in 1967. He became the Center party leader in 1971 and prime minister when the non-Socialist coalition triumphed in the September 1976 election. Fälldin resigned in October 1978 over a nuclear power plant dispute but again became prime minister in October 1979. In May 1981 a dispute over tax policy led Fälldin to resign; two weeks later he was reappointed. In September 1982 his coalition was defeated in the general elections.

In 1976, Thorbjörn Fälldin led a non-Socialist coalition to victory over Sweden's long-dominant Social Democratic party. Fälldin resigned as prime minister in 1978 but was reelected in 1979. His government was defeated in the 1982 elections.

---

falling star   See METEOR AND METEORITE

---

fallout   Fallout is radioactive material that falls through the atmosphere as a result of natural causes, the explosion of ATOMIC BOMBS or HYDROGEN BOMBS, or possible nuclear accidents (see NUCLEAR ENERGY). Natural fallout occurs when radioactive elements in the Earth's crust diffuse into the atmosphere or when COSMIC RAYS from the Sun produce radioactive isotopes of carbon and hydrogen in the atmosphere.

Fallout produced by bomb explosions is of three kinds:

local, tropospheric, and stratospheric. Local fallout, which occurs in the vicinity of the explosion, is usually heavy but lasts only a short time. Tropospheric fallout is produced by fine radioactive particles from an explosion that becomes trapped in the troposphere, the atmospheric belt that extends from 11 to 16 km (7 to 10 mi) above the Earth. These tropospheric particles fall out well after the explosion and cover a much wider area. Stratospheric fallout results from the largest bombs, which produce particles that may travel above the troposphere to the stratosphere, remain there for years, and later fall all over the Earth. Prominent among the radioisotopes in stratospheric fallout are cesium-137 and strontium-90, which have half-lives of 27 and 28 years, respectively.

Nuclear reactors generally release fission products in such tiny quantities that no significant fallout results. In theory, reactor designs also incorporate safety features to keep fallout to a minimum should some accident occur, such as a loss of coolant, but in the world's worst reactor accident—at the Soviet CHERNOBYL power plant, in 1986—significant fallout spread across parts of Europe.

---

fallout shelter   A major consideration in any CIVIL DEFENSE program is the establishment of a shelter system to protect against the heat, blast, and radioactive fallout that would result from an attack with nuclear weapons. A shelter should ideally be large enough to accommodate at least 50 people, and should have the capacity to reduce radiation by a factor of at least 100 for a two-week period and to protect against heat and blast effects. The protective value of a shelter, however, depends on a large number of variables, among them its distance from the blast center and the length of the half-life of the radioactive elements created by the blast. (No shelter, of course, can protect against ingestion of such long-lived radioactive elements as strontium-90 and cesium-137.)

In some nations, including the United States, shelters of a sort have been created in buildings and such structures as tunnels and mines. The U.S. National Shelter Survey, begun in 1961, has identified sites—principally basements, subways, and the like—that might shelter some 250 million people. Unfortunately, most of these sites are in large urban centers and are not readily accessible to a majority of the population. In addition, shelters should contain at least a two-week supply of food, water, sanitation kits, radiological-monitoring kits, and medical supplies. The federal program that was to assure stocking of shelter sites ended in 1970.

According to estimates by the Federal Emergency Management Agency (FEMA)—which is responsible for integrating federal and state planning for emergencies such as nuclear war—it would cost some $60 billion to build shelters to protect the entire U.S. population.

---

false paca   The false paca, or pacarana, *Dinomys branickii*, in the family Dinomyidae, is a chunky, fat-tailed rodent that resembles a huge guinea pig. The largest false pacas weigh about 15 kg (33 lb), are about 80

The false paca, or pacarana, is a rare species of rodent native to the Andes. It resembles the paca, a forest-dwelling rodent that is also native to South America.

cm (30 in) long, and have a 20-cm (8-in) tail. The coat is brown or black with white stripes and spots. Each of the four digits of every foot is armed with a long, powerful claw. False pacas live on the lower Andean slopes and feed on plants. They are nearly extinct.

---

false teeth   see DENTURES

---

falsetto   [fawl-set'-oh]   Falsetto is the light "head voice" of the male singer, providing a weak addition to the normal vocal range. The effect is achieved by relaxation of the thyroarytenoid muscle. Falsetto is distinct from the sound of the castrato and countertenor voices. It was much used by adult singers in church music of earlier centuries when boys were not available or not skilled enough to sing the treble part. After the middle of the 20th century falsetto singing became common in popular music, with amplification serving to project the sound in large halls and outdoor concerts.

Falwell, Jerry   A Baptist minister and television evangelist, the Rev. Jerry Falwell, b. Lynchburg, Va., Aug. 11, 1933, is a leading advocate of religious and political conservatism in the United States. His "Old Time Gospel Hour," on the air since 1956, has been televised nationally since 1971. Falwell founded (1979) and served as president (until 1987) of MORAL MAJORITY, a conservative political action group, which he expanded into a larger movement, Liberty Federation, in 1986. An upholder of traditional morality, he strongly condemns homosexuality, pornography, and abortion and favors prayer in the public schools. He wrote *Strength for the Journey: An Autobiography* (1987).

---

family   The family, among the oldest and most fundamental of human institutions, consists of a man and a woman who are generally expected to produce children, care for them, and help train them in the ways of their culture. This simple family, known as the conjugal, elementary, or NUCLEAR FAMILY, is present in virtually all known societies.

(Left) *The nuclear family has formed the fundamental unit of nearly all human societies. The nuclear family, as of these Brazilian Indians, serves three important functions: regulating reproduction, caring for and educating the children, and sharing economic duties.*

(Right) *The form and functions of the modern nuclear family in many ways resemble those of its preliterate Indian counterpart.*

Long before the emergence of tribal society, people regulated themselves by elaborating rules governing sexual pairing. These rules were, and remain, extremely diverse, although prohibitions against INCEST have been virtually universal. The incest taboo requires individuals to find and marry mates from outside their own family group, thus reducing the possibilities for serious conflict within the family and also increasing social interaction between family groups.

Generally speaking, all people encounter two families: the family they are born or adopted into, called the family of orientation, and the family they form when they take a spouse, called the family of procreation. KINSHIP bonds link these two families into more complex family systems.

In traditional, preindustrial societies, kinship ties regulate the transfer of property, provide structures of authority, and form the basis for the organization of production and distribution. In such societies the nuclear family tends to be overshadowed by the larger network of kin.

In modern industrial societies, kinship matters less in shaping human lives. Individuals rely on a complex array of institutions—the state, industrial and commercial institutions, churches and schools—to organize their activities into orderly and socially useful endeavors. In such societies the nuclear family tends to be predominant, and kin relations secondary.

Family Structure

All families begin with a mated pair, but they rarely remain so simple in structure. There are two general sources of complexity in family structure. The first originates in the custom of taking more than one spouse. A few preliterate cultures have practiced polyandry, the system by which one woman takes more than one husband. Much more common, and not limited to preliterate societies, has been polygyny, one husband having more than one wife. In many Islamic cultures polygyny is still practiced, and family structures as a result tend to be rather com-

plex. Even in Islam, however, relatively few men in fact practice polygyny, because they cannot afford to maintain more than one wife or one set of children. (See also POLYGAMY.)

The second source of complexity in family structure hinges on how the relations between kin and the nuclear family are ordered. In various societies children are encouraged to remain closely attached to their family of orientation and to bring their spouses to live in or near their parents' home. This arrangement, known as the EXTENDED FAMILY, consists generally of several nuclear families arrayed around parents.

The extended-family structure is well suited to subsistence economies because the expansive network of kin provides any given couple with access to goods and services that they alone could not provide. Once widespread, it is characteristic of almost all preindustrial societies, large or small. In modern industrial societies variations of the extended family and the kin network persist among the poor and within ethnic or religious minority groups, in part because such a family structure helps to sustain individuals in the face of economic hardship and to lessen the demoralization that often accompanies minority status.

Family Functioning

In preliterate cultures, and even in Western society until fairly recently, the family was an all-purpose institution. The network of kin provided the nuclear family with economic assistance; the household was the principal unit of production as well as of consumption; and the complex rules of kinship regulated sexual behavior and helped assure the orderly reproduction of society. The family head was typically also its religious leader and the spokesperson for the family in public matters. Countless aspects of daily life were thus organized in terms of families, kin groups, and the residence and descent rules that prevailed.

In contemporary industrial societies the family is a

much less comprehensive institution. Specialized institutions have taken over many of the responsibilities that were once the family's. For administration and production, the office and the factory have replaced the home. The church and the school carry much of the burden of sacred and secular training. The legal, medical, and other professions provide much of the specialized assistance, counseling, and support that the extended family once supplied. Nevertheless, the family remains the primary group in which intimacy and affection can be freely expressed; it is still the most broadly satisfactory setting for the care of infants. In a sense, the family has become a specialized institution whose unique mission is to provide the emotional support that the larger, more impersonal worlds of education, work, and politics do not provide.

With this transformation in family functioning, momentous changes have occurred in the nature of the husband-wife bond and in relations between parents and children. In traditional societies marked by extensive kin relations, the nuclear family is only a small component of a larger system. Until comparatively recent times, parents had the most powerful voice in deciding when and whom their children would marry. The nuclear family and its members were neither economically nor emotionally self-sufficient. Furthermore, the nuclear family traditionally did not generate the intensely emotional relationships that characterize it today. Infants were indulged to the extent that scarce resources permitted, but at a comparatively tender age children were expected to begin shouldering serious adult responsibilities.

This pattern of family functioning began to unravel with the Enlightenment and the Industrial Revolution. Aspirations for greater personal freedom combined with changing economic conditions to produce a slow but accelerating movement toward more independent nuclear families. The change began among the wealthier and more secure middle classes. With the advance of industrialism and the rapid rise in standards of living, more and more couples broke away from the kin network. Emphasis shifted to the couple and its needs: the nuclear family began to become more self-sufficient in both economic and emotional ways. Husbands and wives were expected to be loving companions, not just helpmates. Children assumed a more prominent place in family relations as attention shifted to themes of emotional maturity and personal development.

Changes that first swept Western societies now also affect non-Western cultures. The practice of child marriage, for example, is no longer officially sanctioned in India; the traditional extended family of China has been almost completely dismantled in favor of nuclear families; and the elderly in Japan can no longer rely on being cared for in the homes of their children. As industry spreads and wage labor replaces subsistence agriculture, the nuclear family begins to predominate, and ties to relatives weaken. Family functions turn inward, focusing more and more on private concerns.

Patterns of Contemporary Family Life

Except during wartime and depressions, the marriage rate in the United States has remained consistently high; more than 90 percent of Americans marry at least once. In selecting a spouse, most people choose from groups of people similar to themselves, a tendency that social scientists term *homogamy*. Such factors as religion and ethnicity continue to play a role in mate selection, although their impact has diminished.

After many decades of earlier and earlier marriages, the average age at first marriage for both men and women began increasing after 1955 so that the pattern today is closer to what it was in the 1890s than to that of the 1950s.

More and more men and women postpone marriage in order to establish themselves in occupational pursuits or simply to enjoy the relative freedom that remaining single offers. The relaxation of norms governing premarital sex

The extended family consists of at least two nuclear families spanning three or more generations and living in or near the parents' home.

and the increased acceptance of cohabitation also reduce pressures that lead to early marriages. Expectations for married life are changing rapidly, and the resulting uncertainties contribute to the growing reluctance to rush into marriage. Rising divorce rates also make people hesitant. These changing patterns have led to three broad trends: greater equality in marital roles; declining size of families; and increasing acceptance of divorce.

Changing Roles. For many generations of American families, the customary role for wives was exclusively that of homemaker and mother, and the primary role of husbands was that of breadwinner. As recently as 1970 the majority of American men, according to public-opinion polls, were opposed to their wives' working outside the home. Declining living standards combined with a growing insistence on equal treatment for women, however, led to rapid change. The majority of American wives now work outside the home. In fact, close to a majority of mothers with preschool-aged children work outside the home. Opinion polls record that most husbands approve of their wives' working, though equal patterns in the performance of domestic duties have been slower to catch on.

A greater flexibility in work habits has gone hand in hand with a smaller number of children for most families. The birthrate has steadily declined to the point where the statistically average American family now has slightly fewer than two children. The continuation of this trend would make the once-standard large family virtually obsolete.

Researchers also report that parents are less inclined to defer their own aspirations in favor of their children's. Whether this reflects a growth in emphasis on personal autonomy and satisfaction, such changes have made families more fragile. This is reflected most obviously in the dramatic increase in DIVORCE in recent years. If the present divorce rate persists, within another generation roughly half of all marriages will end in divorce. Nearly half of all children can now be expected to live some portion of their childhood years in a single-parent family.

The New Diversity. As the family continues to undergo change, new forms of family living as well as alternatives to family living have emerged. Various COMMUNAL LIVING experiments enjoyed a flurry of attention in the 1960s and '70s. Cohabitation has become more common, as has the decision to remain childless. In recent years the number of single-parent families has dramatically increased, reflecting not only rising divorce rates but also a growing tendency not to remarry. Each of these developments raises its own moral, economic, and emotional problems.

In recognition of both its fragility and its importance, many industrial nations have developed comprehensive programs of support for the nuclear family. State-funded DAY-CARE CENTERS and homemaker programs help to make it easier for both husband and wife to work. In some countries, notably Sweden, paid paternity leaves have been introduced so that fathers can assist in caring for their newborn children. Many societies are also attempting to devise ways, apart from institutionalization, to help the elderly be less reliant on their children. The future of the family, whatever else it may hold, will almost certainly depend to a large extent on enlightened support from other institutions in the society.

See also: MARRIAGE; OLD AGE; WOMEN IN SOCIETY; YOUNG PEOPLE.

Family Compact   In Canadian history, Family Compact is the name given to a small oligarchy that ruled Upper Canada (Ontario) in the early 19th century. A group of wealthy men who dominated the governor's council and the legislature, the compact was conservative and pro-British in outlook. Its influence declined in the 1830s. In European history, the name is applied to three treaties (1733, 1743, 1761) between France and Spain, both ruled by branches of the Bourbon dynasty.

family planning   see BIRTH CONTROL; POPULATION

---

famine   A famine is a shortage of food of sufficient duration to cause widespread privation and a rise in mortality. Famine has recurred since at least as early as the beginnings of agriculture, which laid the foundation for settled, civilized society. Very little is known, however, of the frequency and severity of famines in the past. Even within this century the exact number of people who have perished during major famines is unknown.

Natural Causes of Famine. Shortfalls in food availabilities can be of both natural and human-caused origin. DROUGHT is the most common natural cause, although hurricanes and their accompanying floods can cause disaster in intensively cultivated coastal areas. Historically, drought has been most crippling in the more arid portions of densely populated monsoonal Asia, especially in China and India.

Periodic pest infestations and epidemics of plant and animal diseases have also been important natural causes of famine. Among the latter, the potato blight that struck Ireland in the 1840s is the best known. The potato is native to South America. Introduced into Ireland in the 18th century, it proved an ideal crop and by the end of the 1700s supplied some 80 percent of the calories in the peasant diet. The blight, caused by a fungus, appeared three times in the 1840s, each time destroying most of the crop. Relief efforts were only partially effective. Perhaps 1.5 million people died, and an equal number emigrated, reducing the population by about one-fourth. Today, with about 5 million people, Ireland's population remains much lower than its 1840 level.

War-Induced Famines. Warfare from earliest times has been destructive to crops and animals, and blockades and sieges of cities have been responsible for countless famines, as they were for hundreds of thousands of deaths in Leningrad, Warsaw, the Netherlands, and Greece during World War II.

Control of the food supply can also be used by political leaders to force their will during peacetime. The Soviet famine of the early 1930s was the result of a ruthless drive to force a reluctant peasantry onto collective farms.

Few famines are general, in the sense that all people within a given area suffer equally. Rather, food scarcity causes a rise in prices, and the poor find their access to food cut off. The Bengal famine of 1943 had several causes: the conquest of Burma by the Japanese, India's being deprived of a traditional source of surpluses; the removal of rice stocks from rural Bengal to deny them to a potential invader; a series of hurricanes that did heavy damage to the main 1942 harvest; and unprecedented war-induced prosperity in Calcutta. These factors caused about a sixfold increase in the price of rice. People who had jobs in town were little affected. To the rural poor, however, such prices were utterly beyond reach. Estimates of the number who perished range between 1.5 million and 3 million.

Physiological Effects of Famine. The rise in the death rate caused by famine can result either from outright starvation or from diseases that afflict the undernourished (see NUTRITIONAL-DEFICIENCY DISEASES). Studies indicate that if caloric intake is reduced to 50 percent of normal, body weight drops within a few months by about a quarter. Thereafter, a reduced level of activity can be maintained for many months. With prolongation or further drops in intake, however, additional weight losses occur, and the incidence of diseases that traditionally accompany famine, such as typhus, cholera, and the plague, rises. Although starvation will occur mainly among the poor, disease epidemics can afflict all.

With restoration of normal supplies of food, recovery can be rapid, and most adults will show no lasting aftereffects. Young children, however, can be permanently impaired, both mentally and in the height and weight they will ultimately attain. KWASHIORKOR and marasmus are widely prevalent childhood diseases caused by insufficient protein intake.

Scientific and technical advances during the last 150 years have greatly enhanced the ability to grow more food and to move it quickly from abundant to deficient areas. Crop yields per unit area are now many times what they were only 50 years ago, and the potential for additional gains, particularly in the world's poorer regions, remains enormous.

Because famines have always been localized, the effect of improved communications has been especially dramatic. The isolation of most communities formerly could turn a regional crop failure into a calamity. Today assistance can be speedily mounted from substantial distances. That no serious famines occurred in India between 1899–1901 and 1943 is attributable to the construction of that country's rail network; that none occurred in the mid-1960s following the successive crop failure caused by the aftermath of two monsoons was due to the ability of the United States, Canada, and Australia to rush almost 20 million tons of wheat to India's relief.

Obstacles to Relief Efforts. Despite the current abundance of grains and other foods that can be airlifted to countries suffering from famine, political conditions within the starving nations themselves may often frustrate relief efforts. The 1984–85 Ethiopian famine provides examples of many of the problems associated with relief.

The Ethiopian government denied the existence of the famine for many months. When it finally acknowledged the need for help, it seized and held shipments destined for the north of the country, because it was fighting against a separatist movement there. Much of the food was stolen and sold by government officials; much of the rest spoiled before it could reach starving populations. Transport arrangements often broke down. It was only when famine victims fled to refugee camps that it became possible to feed them adequately.

International organizations have discussed various plans for dealing with famine crises when they occur. A fundamental necessity for the prevention of famine would be the establishment of a system of world food reserves.

See also: CLIMATE; DESERT; STARVATION.

---

fan-tan [fan'-dan]   Fan-tan, also known as sevens, parliament, or card dominoes, is a card game for two to eight players. All 52 cards in a standard deck are dealt and each player antes one chip. The player to the dealer's left must place a seven face up in the center of the table or pass and pay a one-chip penalty. The next player tries to build a sequence in the suit played or lay down another seven. Sequences are built downward to the ace or upward to the king. The first to play out his or her hand wins. *Fan-tan* is also the name of a Chinese gambling game that uses beans for counters.

---

fandango [fan-dang'-goh]   Possibly the oldest existing Spanish dance, dating from the 7th century, the fandango is a dance of courtship or of friendly competition in brisk $6/8$ or $3/4$ time. Without touching and with arms held high, two dancers flirt as they stamp their feet and hop in elaborate patterns as counterpoint to the rhythm of castanets and guitar. Sudden pauses punctuate the intricate footwork, which increases in tempo as the dancers challenge one another to greater virtuosic displays.

Faneuil Hall [fan'-yul]   Faneuil Hall was built as a market and meeting hall and given (1742) to the city of Boston by Peter Faneuil, a merchant. It became famous as the "Cradle of Liberty" because it was the site of public protests against British policies before the American Revolution. During the 19th century Wendell Phillips and Daniel Webster addressed antislavery meetings held in the hall. The building was restored after a fire in 1761 by the architect Charles BULFINCH and enlarged in 1805. Designated a national historical landmark in 1967, Faneuil Hall is still in use as a market and for forums.

Fanfani, Amintore [fahn-fah'-nee, ah-meen-tor'-ray]   Amintore Fanfani, b. Feb. 6, 1908, has five times been premier of Italy. Fanfani gained his doctorate in political economy in 1932 and has been a teacher and writer in the field of economic history. In 1946 he was elected to the Constituent Assembly as a Christian Democrat. He served in various ministerial posts from 1947 to 1953. He was premier in 1954, 1958–59, 1960–62, and 1962–63, minister of foreign affairs in 1965 and 1966–68, and president of the Senate from 1968 to 1973 and from 1976 until he again became premier in 1982. (He had been made a life senator in 1972.) Fanfani's most recent coalition government fell in April 1983.

Fang   The Fang are a people of west central Africa who live principally in the rain forest of Gabon and Cameroon and speak a Bantu language of the Benue-Niger subfamily of Niger-Congo stock. A subdivision of the Pahouin peoples, they number about 300,000. Fang live in compact villages led by headmen. They are subsistence farmers who grow primarily root crops and bananas. Because many young men have become migratory workers in the timber industry, the traditional social cohesion has tended to break down.

Descent, inheritance, and residence after marriage are traced through the paternal line. Marriage is polygamous and is arranged by payment of bride price or by sister exchange. Fang have several types of secret societies that play an important role in social and religious rituals. Traditionally the Fang were a warring people, and their exploits and conquests are kept alive in legend. They are known for their poetry, their spectacular dancing, and for various types of woodcarving, especially their blackened *bieri*, or reliquary figures.

Fangio, Juan Manuel [fahn'-hee-oh]   Juan Manuel Fangio, b. June 24, 1911, is an Argentine automobile racer who won the world driving championship five times in the 1950s. Fangio drove mostly American-built cars and was little known until 1948, when he went to Europe to race. Driving Alfa Romeos, he finished second (1950) and first (1951) in the world driving championship. Fangio won again (1954) in a Maserati, in a Mercedes (1955), in a Ferrari (1956), and in a Maserati (1957). He last raced in 1958.

Fanny Hill, or The Memoirs of a Woman of Pleasure   John Cleland's *Fanny Hill, or The Memoirs of a Woman of Pleasure* (1748–49) is a classic erotic novel. Although the author attempted to avoid vulgarity by using poetic diction and euphemisms, the novel was suppressed shortly after its publication because of its frankly sexual scenes. The story of a prostitute, *Fanny Hill* parodies novels of the time, particularly Daniel Defoe's *Moll Flanders* (1722).

Fanon, Frantz [fah-nohn', frahnts]   Frantz Omar Fanon, b. 1925, d. Dec. 6, 1961, a psychiatrist, became involved in the Algerian nationalist movement and wrote several seminal works on racism and colonial liberation. Born on Martinique, he was educated there and in France. After taking a psychiatric post in an Algerian hos-

pital in 1953, Fanon joined (1954) the liberation movement. In 1960 he was appointed ambassador to Ghana by the rebel Algerian government. Fanon's first book, *Black Skin, White Masks* (1952; Eng. trans., 1967), was a study of the psychology of racism and colonial domination. In *The Wretched of the Earth* (1961; Eng. trans., 1968) he called for revolutions to liberate Third World peoples from dehumanizing colonialism.

fantasy (literature)   Fantasy is the treatment of events that the rational mind considers impossible or highly unlikely. As a literary genre, it is hard to define. Writings since ancient times have incorporated elements of myth and legend for purposes ranging from satire and allegory to simple storytelling. The 18th-century movement known as the Enlightenment brought critical attention to bear on the uses of the probable and the possible in fiction. In the early 19th century the English writer Samuel Taylor Coleridge formulated the influential view that "fancy, or fantasy," is a poorer echo of the higher workings of the "imagination." This view is still reflected in the distinction sometimes made between "high" and "low" fantasy, the former taken to include works of literary skill and psychological depth, the latter indicating the so-called "sword and sorcery" books that make up the bulk of titles in the fantasy section of bookstores.

Modern fantasy and its subgenre, SCIENCE FICTION, developed from the GOTHIC ROMANCES of the later 18th century. Equally important were such 19th-century figures as Lewis CARROLL and George Macdonald. Modern writers as disparate as Jorge Luis BORGES, Ray BRADBURY, James Branch CABELL, Italo CALVINO, Lord DUNSANY, Ursula LE GUIN, C. S. LEWIS, H. P. LOVECRAFT, J. R. R. TOLKIEN, and Charles WILLIAMS have all been called fantasists.

fantasy (psychology)   Fantasy is a form of consciousness that lies between ordinary thought processes and an uncontrolled state of awareness. The mind is released from the strictures of objective reality, and the imagination is allowed to roam freely—although usually guided by more or less unconscious urges, concerns, and memories. Such distinctions take time to develop; in children, it is often hard to distinguish between fantasy and other modes of thought. Fantasy is also apparent in the PLAY activities that are part of normal growth. Fantasizing is perhaps most familiar in the form of daydreams, often of a wish-fulfilling nature. Although sometimes called fantasies, night dreams are a distinct phenomenon occurring in a different physiological state (see DREAMS AND DREAMING). Fantasy activity is frequent in creative thought and also helps in rehearsing future actions, but excessive fantasizing is considered a sign of maladjusted personality. Various PSYCHOSES are characterized by an inability to distinguish fantasy from reality, and drug-disoriented persons may similarly experience HALLUCINATIONS. Fantasies are a common object of psychological studies, and personality tests often use fantasizing as a technique. (See also HYPNOSIS.)

Fanti [fan'-tee] The Fanti, or Fante, are an Akan-speaking people of the coastal area of Ghana. Numbering about 500,000, they live in compact villages where they grow vegetables and keep livestock. Descent and inheritance are traced through the mother's line, but the soul is thought to come from the father.

Traditionally the Fanti formed a confederation of small military states that competed with the ASHANTI kingdom to the north in the trade of gold, slaves, and European imports. After the British broke the strong Fanti confederation, the Fanti became (1874) part of the British Gold Coast colony; together with the British, they defeated the Ashanti. Patrilineal, military companies played an important role in the political, social, and religious life of the Fanti states.

Traditional Fanti religious beliefs are concerned with a creator god, a host of lesser deities served through priests, and ancestral spirits. Art forms include a rich body of folklore, woodcarvings, and objects cast in bronze through the lost-wax process.

Fantin-Latour, Henri [fahn-tan'-lah-toor'] Henri Fantin-Latour, b. Jan. 14, 1836, d. Aug. 25, 1904, was a French painter best known for his flower studies executed in a meticulous "Dutch" manner. His works include still lifes, romantic figures, and portrait groups. Believing color to be analogous to sound, Fantin-Latour painted compositions inspired by the music of Hector Berlioz, Robert Schumann, and Richard Wagner. Although his work subsequently appeared regularly at the Paris Salon, he was rejected in 1859 and exhibited at the Salon des Refusés in 1863 with other artists frequently spurned by the Salon jury. Fantin-Latour was friendly with most of the advanced artists of the day, including Édouard Manet and James McNeill Whistler. Though he never exhibited with the impressionists, he painted them. In his best-known group portrait, *Studio in the Batignolles Quarter* (1870; Louvre, Paris), Frédéric Bazille, Claude Monet, and Pierre Auguste Renoir are grouped around Manet.

Far East The term *Far East*, referring to eastern Asia, was first used by Western Europeans in the early 17th century, during the Age of Exploration. It refers primarily to China, Japan, Korea, Mongolia, and eastern Siberia but sometimes includes the countries of the Indochinese and Malay peninsulas (Burma, Cambodia, Laos, Malaysia, Singapore, Vietnam, and Thailand) and the entire Malay Archipelago, comprising Indonesia and the Philippines. The designation is not exact, and the western boundaries, between Central and South Asia and the Far East, are vague.

Farabi, al- [fah-rah'-bee, ahl] Al-Farabi, *c.*870–*c.*950, was the greatest philosopher of Islam before AVICENNA. He wrote commentaries on a number of Aristotelian texts and composed many original treatises on psychology, mathematics, and the occult sciences. In both his commentaries and original compositions, al-Farabi attempted to demonstrate the unity of Plato and Aristotle and to prove the primacy of philosophy. He maintained that, in contrast to philosophy, religion represents the truth in a symbolic form for nonphilosophers. In all his writings, which reveal the influence of a mystical NEOPLATONISM, he attempted to reconcile Islam with philosophy.

farad [fair'-uhd] The farad is the unit of capacitance, named for Michael Faraday. A CAPACITOR has a capacitance of 1 farad (1F) if there is a potential difference of 1 volt between its plates when it is charged to 1 coulomb of electricity on each plate. Thus, 1 farad is 1 coulomb/volt. The farad is a relatively large amount of capacitance, and most of the capacitors used in electronics have capacitances measured in microfarads (μF) or micromicrofarads ($\mu\mu$F).

Faraday, Michael [fair'-uh-day] The English chemist and physicist Michael Faraday, b. Sept. 22, 1791, d. Aug. 25, 1867, is known for his pioneering experiments in electricity and magnetism. Many consider him the greatest experimentalist who ever lived. Several concepts that he derived directly from experiments, such as lines of magnetic force, have become common ideas in modern physics.

Faraday was born at Newington, Surrey, near London. He received little more than a primary education, and at the age of 14 he was apprenticed to a bookbinder. There he became interested in the physical and chemical works of the time. After hearing a lecture by the famous chemist Humphrey DAVY, he sent Davy the notes he had made

Michael Faraday, whose experiments in electrical chemistry and magnetism led to his discovery (1831) of electromagnetic induction, laid the groundwork for the developing field of electromagnetism.

of his lectures. As a result Faraday was appointed, at the age of 21, assistant to Davy in the laboratory of the Royal Institution in London.

During the initial years of his scientific work, Faraday occupied himself mainly with chemical problems. He discovered two new chlorides of carbon and succeeded in liquefying chlorine and other gases. He isolated benzene in 1825, the year in which he was appointed director of the laboratory.

Davy, who had the greatest influence on Faraday's thinking, had shown in 1807 that the metals sodium and potassium can be precipitated from their compounds by an electric current, a process known as ELECTROLYSIS. Faraday's vigorous pursuit of these experiments led in 1834 to what became known as Faraday's laws of electrolysis (see ELECTROCHEMISTRY).

Faraday's research into electricity and electrolysis was guided by the belief that electricity is only one of the many manifestations of the unified forces of nature, which included heat, light, magnetism, and chemical affinity. Although this idea was erroneous, it led him into the field of electromagnetism (see MAGNETISM), which was still in its infancy. In 1785, Charles Coulomb had been the first to demonstrate the manner in which electric charges repel each other, and it was not until 1820 that Hans Christian Oersted and André Marie AMPÈRE discovered that an electric current produces a magnetic field. Faraday's ideas about conservation of energy led him to believe that since an electric current could cause a magnetic field, a magnetic field should be able to produce an electric current. He demonstrated this principle of INDUCTION in 1831. Faraday expressed the electric current induced in the wire in terms of the number of lines of force that are cut by the wire. The principle of induction was a landmark in applied science, for it made possible the dynamo, or GENERATOR, which produces electricity by mechanical means.

Faraday's discovery (1845) that an intense magnetic field can rotate the plane of polarized light is known today as the Faraday effect. The phenomenon has been used to elucidate molecular structure and has yielded information about galactic magnetic fields.

Faraday described his numerous experiments in electricity and electromagnetism in three volumes entitled *Experimental Researches in Electricity* (1839, 1844, 1855); his chemical work was chronicled in *Experimental Researches in Chemistry and Physics* (1858). After suffering from loss of memory, he ceased his research in 1855.

farce Farce is a dramatic form that derives much of its comic appeal from broad physical humor, improbable situations, and exaggerated characters. Its name, from the Latin *farcire*, "to stuff," suggests its often chaotic nature. Unlike more refined and rational COMEDY, farce delights in the theatrical and the fantastic. The typical farce makes us laugh at situations that in real life would cause extreme pain or embarrassment. Thus physical abuse, sexual impropriety, exposure, and even death are staples of farce.

The many forms of farce can be grouped into two categories. The first, characterized by a loose, improvisational structure, is dominated by clowns (often masked), who usually retain the same name or distinctive appearance and behavior in every play in which they appear. Italian COMMEDIA DELL'ARTE takes this form, as in modern times do the films of Charlie CHAPLIN and the MARX BROTHERS. Plays of the second category are more regular in structure, with carefully controlled plots that often seem to reduce the characters to the status of puppets. Shakespeare's *Comedy of Errors* and the bedroom farces of Georges FEYDEAU are examples.

Although elements of farce can be found in the comedies of ARISTOPHANES and PLAUTUS, farce developed as a distinct form both in antiquity and in the Middle Ages. French medieval farces were short and simple, mere interludes between the religious dramas with which they appeared. The more complex commedia dell'arte developed in Italy during the Renaissance; its stock characters were freely borrowed by MOLIÈRE. Farce has never ceased to be popular, but 19th-century France was especially favorable to the genre. Eugène LABICHE and Feydeau developed farce into a complex art of involved plots and absurd situations. In the 20th century farce has been given a serious turn by such writers for the THEATER OF THE ABSURD as Eugène IONESCO and Harold PINTER.

Fargo [fahr'-goh] Fargo is the seat of Cass County, North Dakota, and the state's largest city. It is located on the west bank of the Red River of the North, which separates North Dakota from Minnesota. The city, which has a population of 74,111 (1990), is a trade and distribution center for the wheat and livestock produced in the surrounding region. Local industries manufacture farm machinery, automobile parts, construction materials, electrical equipment, luggage, and fertilizer. North Dakota State University (1890) is there.

Fargo was established in 1871 at the point where the Northern Pacific Railway crossed the Red River. First called Centralia, the name was changed in 1872 to honor William George Fargo, founder of Wells, Fargo and Company and one of the railroad's directors. Low railroad freight rates and the discovery of the land's immense wheat-producing potential attracted settlers.

Fargo, William George William George Fargo, b. Pompey, N.J., May 20, 1818, d. Aug. 3, 1881, was an American leader in long-distance express services. He began carrying mail over a 48-km (30-mi) route when he was 13 years old. After working at a number of jobs, he formed (1844) a partnership, Wells and Company, to operate an express service between Buffalo, N.Y., and Chicago. He helped organize the American Express Company (1850) and WELLS, FARGO AND COMPANY (1852) to provide express service between the East Coast and California. The latter company soon dominated the express business west of the Mississippi. From 1862 to 1866, Fargo was mayor of Buffalo. In the 1870s he was president both of Wells, Fargo and Company and of American Express.

Farm Bureau see AMERICAN FARM BUREAU FEDERATION

Farm Credit Administration The Farm Credit Administration (FCA) is an independent agency of the U.S. government that was established under the Farm Credit Act of 1933. It supervises and coordinates the cooperative Farm Credit System—agencies that provide long-term, intermediate, and short-term credit to farmers, ranchers, and agricultural organizations. These banks and associations were initially capitalized by the U.S. government but are now owned by their users.

There are 12 Farm Credit districts nationwide; each district has a federal land bank, a federal intermediate credit bank, and a bank for cooperatives. The 37th bank in the system is the Central Bank for Cooperatives in Denver, Colo. The policy-making body of the FCA is the 13-member Federal Farm Credit Board. Twelve of the members are appointed by the president for 6-year terms, and the 13th is appointed by the secretary of agriculture.

In 1985 an economically depressed year for U.S. farmers, the system held about one-third of the nation's $210 billion farm debt. Congress that year passed a farm credit bill that established a new unit, the Farm Credit System Capital Corp., to assume responsibility for bad loans as well as for transferring funds from healthier districts to weaker ones. The same legislation authorized the U.S. Treasury to provide a line of credit for the system, and it also strengthened the regulatory powers of the FCA over the system.

farm machinery see COMBINE; FARMS AND FARMING; HARVESTER; PLOW; REAPER; TRACTOR

Farmer, Fannie The American culinary expert Fannie Merritt Farmer, b. Boston, Mar. 23, 1857, d. Jan. 15, 1915, is best known as the author of *The Boston Cooking School Cook Book*, published in 1896 and still consid-

Fannie Merritt Farmer, an American author and teacher, wrote (1896) the popular Boston Cooking School Cook Book *and in 1902 founded Miss Farmer's School of Cookery. Her teaching methods and recipes, intended for unskilled cooks emphasized the use of standard measurements.*

ered by many the most useful cookbook ever written. Modernized for the modern kitchen, and now called *The Fannie Farmer Cookbook*, it is in its 13th edition. Farmer began teaching herself to cook after she suffered a paralytic stroke that forced her to discontinue high school. She enrolled in the Boston Cooking School, and in 1891, two years after graduating, she was named director. Her own school, Miss Farmer's School of Cookery, opened in 1902.

Farmer was the first recipe writer to indicate precise measurements, using standardized measuring implements such as the teaspoon and cup. Her careful description of basic processes enabled even novice cooks to follow her recipes.

Farmer, Moses Moses Gerrish Farmer, b. Boscawen, N.H., Feb. 9, 1820, d. May 25, 1893, was a versatile American inventor who conducted pioneer experiments with electricity and telegraphy. He helped build early telegraph lines in Massachusetts, installed the first electric fire-alarm system in Boston, discovered the principle of multiplexing (see MULTIPLEXER), and developed a process for ELECTROPLATING aluminum.

In 1858–59, anticipating Thomas EDISON by 20 years, Farmer produced electric lamps. He lighted his own house and in 1868 fitted out a house in Cambridge, Mass., with 40 electric lamps and his own patented generator.

Farmer-Labor party The Farmer-Labor party was a Minnesota political party (1918–44) founded to represent the interests of farmers and urban laborers. An offshoot of the NONPARTISAN LEAGUE, the party first placed candidates on the ballot in 1918 and subsequently elected two U.S. senators and three U.S. representatives as well as a number of state and local officials. In 1930 its candidate, Floyd B. Olson, was elected to the first of three terms as governor. The party supported the NEW DEAL policies of President Franklin D. Roosevelt, and in 1944 it merged with Minnesota's Democratic party to form the Democratic-Farmer Labor party.

The Minnesota party had little connection with the National Farmer-Labor party. Its platform called for widespread public ownership of the nation's resources, but its strength was largely limited to such states as Montana, South Dakota, and Washington. It met its eclipse during the 1920s.

---

farms and farming The production of food and fiber from the soil, farming is a slow biological process involving soil cultivation, planting, harvesting, and the disposition of the harvest. Closely related to farming are herding, ranching, the cultivation of orchards, tree farming, and FISH FARMING, or aquaculture.

Throughout history, farming has been the occupation of nine-tenths or more of humankind. Painfully slow progress in farming techniques eventually provided sur-

American farms in moderately hilly areas, such as those in Pennsylvania, are plowed along the natural contours of the land to prevent excessive water runoff and soil erosion.

pluses beyond the needs of the producers, freeing many for the nonfarming pursuits that eventually created societies based on technology rather than food production. The farmer's surplus, then, is fundamental to civilization. Even today, however, more than half the world's population of about 5 billion people are still engaged in farming.

Farming can be carried on only where climate and soil are favorable. It is necessarily limited to areas of productive soils, tillable topography, adequate moisture from precipitation or irrigation, and a growing season long enough for plant germination and maturation. There are a few especially advantaged areas that have the natural resources to build an extensive system of highly productive farms. Taken overall, the United States is one such area.

Within the natural environmental conditions necessary for farming there are wide variations that determine the crops produced, the techniques employed, and the type of farm organization. In addition, regional history, tradition, folk wisdom, level of knowledge, and incentive for gain have multiplied the differences among farming practices from place to place and time to time. Today, however, diminishing isolation has resulted in the diffusion and exchange of plants, animals, tools, and knowledge, and—at least where economic and agricultural conditions are similar—a growing similarity of agricultural practices. Nevertheless, crop belts such as the corn-hog belt in the U.S. Midwest and special niches such as the Rhine vine-

yards of Germany or the rubber-tree groves of Malaysia, along with hundreds of other distinctive farm areas, continue to produce immensely diverse patterns among the world's farms.

Primitive slash-and-burn AGRICULTURE is still practiced in remote areas. Subsistence and small-village farming is the pattern in much of the developing Third World. Mixed or general-family farms with crops and livestock interrelated, and with the resources to reach commercial markets, have dominated agriculture in the developed countries in the 19th and 20th centuries. Plantations producing staple crops for sale in world markets are a feature of tropical and subtropical regions.

Farming is a production process that requires much care and attention, and farms have usually been family operations. Other forms of organization—communes, collective farms, cooperatives, special structures such as the Israeli kibbutz, and corporation farms—have appeared where government authority or cultural or ideological pressure has intervened.

Farming in the Western World

Techniques of farming evolved in response to population pressure, invention, selection of crops and animals, available human and animal or mechanical power, supply of arable land, and, eventually, the pull of market demand.

Beginning with the digging stick, the hoe, the sickle, and the earliest domesticated plants of the NEOLITHIC PERIOD about 10,000 years ago, farming evolved with painful slowness, as animals were domesticated, the ard (a primitive plow) and the flail were invented, fruit and nut trees were cultivated, and irrigation became a standard practice. Shifting slash-and-burn techniques were succeeded in Europe by a two-field system that alternated crops with fallow fields. The succeeding three-field system used late in the Middle Ages increased production nearly 17%. Along the way, the ard was replaced by a real moldboard PLOW made of wood and iron, which turned over rather than simply scratched the earth. The scythe improved upon the sickle, and the horse-collar allowed the quicker horse to replace the ox has a draft animal. The narrow strips of land cultivated by medieval village farmers provided bare subsistence. The ENCLOSURE of these divided fields into larger fields devoted to a single crop led to more efficient production of marketable crops. The enclosure movement eventually brought about the elimination of fallow fields and the introduction of the practice of crop rotation.

19th-Century Farm Technology. The great progress in science and technology during the late 18th and 19th centuries transformed agriculture in Western Europe and North America. Expanded knowledge of agricultural chemistry led to improved practices of fertilization and of livestock feeding. Plant and animal breeding by selection of desirable features increased productivity (see ANIMAL HUSBANDRY). Growing urban markets that could now be reached by canals, railroads, and steamboats spurred farmers to maximize production for material gain. The cotton gin and steam-powered sugar mills and grain-threshing machines transformed methods of growing crops that had once been highly labor-intensive.

A great age of horse-powered farm machinery dominated Western European and American agriculture until early in the 20th century. Horses pulled steel plows, harrows, cultivators, mowers, hay rakes, and reapers; they activated threshing machines and combines and performed many other farm jobs. Elaborate horse-powered farm machinery vastly increased labor productivity and brought new lands under cultivation. Horse power applied to farming had developed as far as it could by the time horses were replaced by the internal combustion engine early in the 20th century.

Mechanical power led to another farming revolution in the developed countries. In the United States between 1910 and 1960 about 36,420,000 ha (90,000,000 acres) were freed from growing the hay that fueled horses and were shifted to other crops. Tractors, autos, trucks, combines, irrigation pumps, milkers, aerial crop dusters, and vegetable harvesters further increased labor productivity and gross volume while allowing farm size to grow and encouraging farm specialization.

At the same time as the mechanical revolution was taking place in farming, the application of biological and chemical science to crop improvement was increasing both the quality and quantity of agricultural output. The science of genetics produced hybrid corn, more productive poultry and dairy cattle, and—since World War II—the "miracle" rices and wheats of the GREEN REVOLUTION. Recently developed techniques of genetic engineering hold promise for still greater gains. Insecticides, fungicides, herbicides, growth regulators, and antibiotics have made farming a high-tech enterprise. Chemical fertilizer applications soared with cheapened production by the petrochemical industries.

The U.S. Family Farm. About 1900 the family farm (at least, the farm that has remained in the American collective memory as the "ideal" family farm) measured about 65 ha (160 acres), was largely self-sufficient, and produced modest quantities of surplus products for sale. The farm family provided most, if not all, of the labor required except during harvest, when a harvesting crew might be assembled from the neighborhood. Horses for power and other livestock were bred and fed on the farm. Established routines allowed for the field rotation of hay, pasture, oats, corn, and wheat that conserved soil resources. Dairy cattle, pigs, and poultry provided salable goods as well as farm food. Livestock manure fertilized the fields. Basic machinery—the plow, harrow, harvester, and mower—was relatively simple, and might be repaired and maintained on the farm itself. Farm structures—house, privy, barn and silo, corn crib, hoghouses, equipment shed, fences—were equally uncomplicated, and some could be built by the farmer and his family. Crop production, the upkeep of harness, machinery, and structures, the care of the animals, milking, and housekeeping kept the family labor force fully occupied and tied to daily and seasonal rounds of toil.

Farm families lived on their farms and not in villages, as was (and is) common in much of Europe and the Third World. When farms averaged 65 ha, the distance between farmhouses was 0.8 km (0.5 mi). Such dispersed settlement isolated farm families. Yet these distances could be overcome by trading labor at harvest time, exchanging special skills such as butchering, and participating in community schools and churches.

The norm primarily in the Midwest for the generations between the Civil War and World War II, the 65-ha family farm exemplified the American ideal of independence. Equally numerous in other sections of the country, however, were small, poor farms on the margins of good land, and tenant farms—particularly in the cotton-raising South—where farmers worked land they did not own in exchange for a share of the crops they raised. Southern sharecroppers vanished following World War II, largely as the result of the mechanization of cotton cultivation. Rental of land for cash, or for a share of the crop, however, is a practice that still persists.

Changes in U.S. Farm Structure. Technological change in farming has proceeded hand in hand with industrialization and urbanization. The increase in field size and farm size to accommodate innovative technologies—such as harvester combines—has meant a decline in the number of farms and a reduction of the farm labor force. Gains in gross production volume and production per worker, per acre, and per animal unit released labor for nonfarm pursuits and provided ample and relatively cheap food for urban populations.

The United States provides the most notable measurements of the changes in farming that have occurred throughout the industrialized West. From 1950 to 1980, U.S. farm output doubled. The average size of farms grew from 87 to 182 ha (215 to 450 acres), the number of farms fell from 5.6 to 2.4 million, and the farm population shrank from 23 to 6 million (from 10.3% to 2.7% of the total population). At the same time, the number of persons supplied with farm products grew from 15 to 65 for each farm worker.

Among the 2.4 million farms that exist at present, the top 20% in terms of size produce almost 80% of farm output. The smallest farms—representing almost 50% of all farms—produce only 10% of total farm output.

Although the decline in the number of farms began to slow after 1980, the number of people who earned their livelihood solely from farming continued to shrink. About one-half of all U.S. farm families now derive more income from nonfarm sources than from the sale of farm products.

Today a successful family farm is a commercialized and specialized business, highly capital- and energy-intensive. It concentrates on the production of one or two commercial crops (corn, for example, or soybeans, pigs, beef cattle, or milk). It utilizes machinery to the fullest extent on ever-larger fields, and depends on borrowed capital for the purchase of equipment, seeds, fertilizer, and pesticides to maximize yields on expensive land. Management skills of a high order are required to succeed in this type of farming. A representative midwestern farmer, for example, could have a capital investment in land and equipment of $1.5 million and sell crops worth $300,000. Net income on such a farm—depending on production costs, weather, market demand, and other factors—might be $30,000 or less.

Commercial family farms are sometimes incorporated to gain tax and management advantages, but they remain family businesses. Public corporations have ventured into specialized farming operations that benefit from expansion of scale. Big corporation farms grow fruits and vegetables in California and cotton in California, Texas, and Mississippi; they fatten thousands of cattle in feedlots and raise poultry in factories.

Changes in Farm Economics. The increase in farm size and productivity has been both the cause and the result of the increased dependence on the input industries that supply machinery, chemicals, and feed and seed. In the United States particularly, the temptation to buy more acreage in order to use farm machinery to its full potential (and to buy larger machinery so that the increased acres can be efficiently cultivated) has brought many farmers close to bankruptcy.

Farm products today are no longer directly consumable goods. Rather, they are raw materials that will be factory processed, packaged, and merchandised. For example, much of the corn grown in the United States is used for livestock feed for the meat-packing and distributing industry. Wheat is shipped long distances to flour mills, then to mass-production bakeries, then to retail stores. Fruits and vegetables—when not processed and canned or frozen—move from the farmer to packers and middlemen handlers before reaching store shelves. In the United States, distribution charges interposed between the farmer and the consumer have reduced the farmer's share of the consumer's food dollar to about 36 cents.

Farming is necessarily a slow process, even where two or three crops can be grown annually. In the United States, one crop a year is the norm in most areas. Trees and vines require three or more years to come into bearing. The pig crop takes nearly a year from breeding to sale weight; beef cattle require two or more years. The farmer's turnover is slow compared to that of commerce and industry, and in addition, the hazards of nature bear heavily on farms.

Unlike industry, in farming increase in size does not necessarily produce increased efficiency. Optimum farm size varies with differing crops and locations. The most efficient U.S. dairy farms in 1984, for example, maintained about 300 cows on about 120 ha (300 acres). Larger herds increase volume but do not raise efficiency or lower costs.

Areas of Specialized Farm Production. Farms tend to specialize according to climatic and soil conditions and according to their location with respect to markets and sources of production materials. Dairy farms are concentrated around the Great Lakes, in the Northeast, and around large cities. Cattle and sheep ranches are located in arid regions from the Rocky Mountains westward and in other regions where there are large supplies of hay and grasses. Specialized wheat farms are found in the Great Plains and in the Northwest.

Corn and soybean production is the foundation of farming on the rich lands of the central region known as the Corn Belt. Many farms specialize in producing only these two grains. Since soybeans and corn are the main feed for hogs and for fattening cattle, however, many Corn Belt farms also produce hogs and import beef cattle for fattening.

Cotton is limited by climate to the southern and southwestern states. Fruits and vegetables are produced mainly where local climate is favorable. Year-round vegetable production is found primarily in Florida and California. Poultry is produced in large specialized units concentrated especially in states that have access both to feed supplies and to consuming centers.

The Role of Government

Farming figures importantly in the governmental policies of most nations. Farms are the source of strategic food supplies, of important raw materials for industry, and of major commodities for trade and commerce. Farming interests may possess considerable political power and influence.

Farm welfare has had the solicitous attention of the United States government for many decades. In the 19th century it was assumed that easy distribution of land would encourage the development of productive farms. This idea culminated in the HOMESTEAD ACT of 1862, which gave 160 acres (65 ha) of public land each to settlers who declared their intention of building farms. By establishing support for research and education, the government hoped to make farms more productive and farm life more fulfilling. The creation of the U.S. Department of Agriculture (see AGRICULTURE, U.S. DEPARTMENT OF) and the passing of the Morrill Land Grant College Act, both in 1862, were followed by the Hatch Act of 1887, which subsidized state agricultural experiment stations, and the Smith-Lever Act of 1914, which supported agricultural extension services in the states.

The disadvantages of small-scale farming in an industrialized economy, especially evident at the time of the Great Depression of the 1930s, gave rise to federal efforts to support farm prices. A program to restrain the production of price-depressing surpluses and to raise prices to parity levels began with the Agricultural Adjustment Act of 1933 and became a central feature of government farm policy. The act declared that farm commodities should have the same purchasing power (parity) as they had in the period 1910–14. For example, the parity price of a bushel of corn should buy as much fertilizer, machinery, or other materials as a bushel of corn would have purchased during the base period. The base period for determining parity has changed several times since 1933, and the 1977 Food and Agricultural Act uses the cost of production rather than parity as a means of setting price supports.

At different times the government has also paid farmers to withhold land from production, has provided commodity loans above market prices to persuade farmers to keep crops off the market, and has paid farmers the difference between the target prices it considers fair and actual market prices. The 1983 PIK (Payment in Kind) program attempted to shrink government surplus commodity holdings by paying farmers who reduced their plantings of wheat, rice, and cotton from government stockpiles of these commodities. The program, which cost about $12 billion, did little to reduce the size of harvests or of government surpluses.

Importance of Farm Exports. Since colonial times, food and commodity exports have bolstered American growth. Tobacco, rice, indigo, and foodstuffs were major colonial exports. Exported cotton, wheat, and livestock products sustained the U.S. economy through the 19th and into the 20th century. After World War II, swelling farm productivity caused a great accumulation of surpluses, which were reduced through the Food for Peace program, begun in 1954, and through subsidized sales to Third World countries. Renewed demand for American wheat and feed grains during the decade 1970–80 moved surpluses abroad at good prices and encouraged U.S. farmers to plant more hectares. The first half of the 1980s, however, saw a U.S. grain embargo imposed against the Soviets in retaliation for their invasion of Afghanistan; a world economic recession; and growing competition from other grain producers, such as Argentina. Wheat farmers, particularly, felt the negative economic effects of shrinking export markets. Nevertheless, one-quarter of U.S. farm production is still exported. Its receipts—$30 to $40 billion—are nearly equal to the cost of oil imported into the United States.

Farming in Western Europe

Western Europe has moved at a slower pace than the United States toward more efficient, larger, commercialized family farming operations. Specialized dairying, livestock, and poultry farmers, especially in Britain and the Netherlands, draw heavily on purchased feed grain, much of it imported from North America. In France and Italy, and most of the other European Mediterranean countries, however, the traditional small holding remains the norm.

The European Economic Community (EEC) was organized in 1958. Its principal purpose was to establish open markets for European products within the European community and to permit more efficient export marketing of farm surpluses. The price subsidies provided farmers by the EEC, combined with more productive farming techniques, have made the EEC a serious competitor with the United States and other food-exporting nations. Price subsidies, however, have also created a surplus problem: the Community holds vast quantities of unsold butter, powdered milk, beef, and wine.

Farming in Eastern Europe

Farming in the centrally planned countries of Eastern Europe is organized in accord with Communist ideology. Big industrialized farms, state farms, and collective farms aim to achieve economies of scale by covering great acreages of cropland with massive machinery and large numbers of workers. Efficiency is elusive under bureaucratic management and is often thwarted by erratic climatic conditions. Production per worker and per acre in the USSR averages about half that of Great Britain's farms. Once a major exporter of grain, the USSR now imports millions of tons of wheat and cattle feed.

Rice, the most important food crop in Asian countries, has been cultivated for thousands of years in wet, tropical areas, such as the Indonesian island of Bali.

Other Types of Farming Organizations

Alternatives to the family farm include the giant communes of China, which became the standard farm organization there after the 1949 revolution. A commune takes in the land and populations of several villages—perhaps 10,000 to 20,000 people. Despite an initial sharp decline in production, China has managed to regain near self-sufficiency in food.

Israel pioneered the KIBBUTZ, a form of cooperative farm that has been highly productive of food and specialty crops both for local consumption and for export. The Mexican ejido is a cooperative village enterprise that leaves production to individual farmers but centralizes purchasing and marketing.

Plantations produce single crops—rubber, coffee, sisal, bananas, palm oil, pineapples, cacao—for sale to distant markets. Today plantation farming is found primarily in tropical and semitropical countries. It is usually organized on a large scale and may be exploitive both of labor and, because only one type of crop is raised, of soil resources. Plantations growing export crops have often displaced peasant farms.

Village farming in the past, and in many regions in the present, has involved peasants cultivating small plots of land intensively, producing a diversity of intertilled food and fiber crops, and sustaining a large rural population. It rarely produces great surpluses. Many areas of subsistence peasant farming are close to maximum land productivity, and many peasant villages may live on the edge of malnutrition.

The green revolution produced high-yielding strains of rice, wheat, and corn and has transformed agriculture in Mexico and India, but the cultivation of these new grains is confined to wealthy farmers with large fields. The development of indigenous plants as crops for food and export, however, offers the possibility of new wealth for village farmers, especially in tropical regions. Little-known tropical fruits (the carambola or the pummelo, for example), the high-protein seeds quinoa and AMARANTH, and desert shrubs such as PRICKLY PEAR and kenaf (a hibiscus grown for its fiber)—as well as many other plants now ignored or grown only in small quantities—might become major crops in the future.

See also: AGRICULTURE, HISTORY OF; AGRICULTURE AND THE FOOD SUPPLY.

Farnese, Alessandro

[fahr-nay'-zay, ahl-es-sahn'-droh]   Alessandro Farnese, 3d duke of Parma, b. Aug. 27, 1545, d. Dec. 3, 1592, was a diplomat and one of the greatest generals of the 16th century. The son of Ottavio Farnese, 2d duke of Parma, and Margaret of Austria, he grew up in the court of PHILIP II of Spain. Farnese fought the Turks in the Battle of LEPANTO (1571) and in 1578 became governor-general of the Netherlands, then in armed revolt against Spanish rule (see DUTCH REVOLT). With the capture (1585) of Antwerp, Farnese subdued the largely Catholic southern Netherlands (modern Belgium). During the French Wars of Religion (see RELIGION, WARS OF), Farnese led Spanish troops into France to aid the Catholics at Paris (1590) and Rouen (1592).

Farnese, Elizabeth

Elizabeth Farnese, b. Oct. 25, 1692, d. July 11, 1766, was the second queen consort of PHILIP V of Spain, whom she married in 1714. Aided initially by the able Cardinal Alberoni (1664–1752), she soon dominated her husband and involved Spain in several wars. As a result of these, her son Charles (later CHARLES III of Spain) became (1734) king of Naples, and her son Philip received (1748) Parma. Elizabeth lost power after the succession (1746) of her stepson FERDINAND VI.

faro

[fair'-oh]   Faro is a card game in which up to ten players bet that a certain card will win or lose. A 52-card deck is used, and the 13 spade cards from another deck are placed face up. Two cards from the deck are exposed. The first card is the loser, the second the winner. All bets on either card are paid. Faro is a 17th-century gambling game named for the pharaoh on French playing cards. Banned (1739) by law in England, it later became the most popular card gambling game in America.

Faroe Islands   see FAEROE ISLANDS

Farouk, King of Egypt

[fuh-rook']   Farouk, b. Feb. 11, 1920, d. Mar. 17, 1965, was king of Egypt from 1936 until July 1952, when he was overthrown in the revolution led by General Muhammad Naguib. Succeeding his father, FUAD I, Farouk was initially popular. His authority crumbled, however, as a result of confrontations with domestic political opponents (especially the powerful Wafd party), of gossip about his lurid private life, and of his ambitious nationalist foreign policy that brought conflict with Britain and the disastrous ARAB-ISRAELI WAR of 1948. By 1952, Farouk symbolized a corrupt, uncaring regime that shamed patriotic Egyptians. Gamal Abdel NASSER, who played a leading role in the coup against the king, soon displaced Naguib as ruler of Egypt.

Farquhar, George

[fahr'-kwur]   The Irish-born English dramatist and actor George Farquhar, b. 1678, d. Apr. 29, 1707, is often considered the last playwright of RESTORATION DRAMA. His popular comedies of manners, notably *The Recruiting Officer* (1706) and *The Beaux' Stratagem* (1707), have often been successfully revived. The first of these draws on Farquhar's own military experiences. The second, with its ingenious plot, middle-class characters, and happy ending, was a success when first produced, yet Farquhar died in poverty during the play's first run.

Farragut, David Glasgow

[far'-uh-guht]   David Glasgow Farragut, b. Stony Point, Tenn., July 5, 1801, d. Aug. 14, 1870, was an American naval officer who led the Union assaults on New Orleans and Mobile Bay during the Civil War. A midshipman at the age of nine, he served on the frigate *Essex* in the War of 1812 and was made prize master of a captured ship. From 1815 until 1861, Farragut had a long but undistinguished record of naval service.

A resident of Norfolk, Va., Farragut left for New York on Apr. 18, 1861, the day after Virginia seceded from the Union. Once satisfied with Farragut's loyalty to the Union, the Navy Department chose him to capture New Orleans,

Admiral David Farragut entered the U.S. Navy at the age of nine and became one of the outstanding naval commanders of the Civil War. Farragut gave the North an important victory in 1862 by capturing New Orleans. Two years later he led a Union fleet into Mobile Bay, sealing off the vital port from Confederate shipping.

a major Northern objective. Farragut boldly led his ships past Forts Jackson and St. Philip, the principal obstacles on the Mississippi River below New Orleans. He arrived at the city on Apr. 25, 1862, and the army occupied it on May 1. Farragut's feat electrified the North, opened the lower Mississippi to Federal forces, and discouraged European intervention on behalf of the Confederacy. It also earned Farragut promotion to rear admiral; he was the first to hold that rank in the U.S. Navy.

On Aug. 5, 1864, Farragut similarly bypassed strongly defended forts in Mobile Bay to attack and destroy the Confederate warships defending Mobile, Ala. Although the city itself was not captured until April 1865, Farragut effectively closed the Confederacy's last major Gulf port. During a critical moment of this assault, when one ship's captain hesitated out of fear of Confederate mines—then called torpedoes—Farragut shouted, "Damn the torpedoes, full speed ahead." Between 1865 and 1870, Farragut was twice promoted, becoming the U.S. Navy's first four-star admiral.

Farrar, Geraldine

Farrar, Geraldine [fuh-rahr'] Geraldine Farrar, b. Melrose, Mass., Feb. 28, 1882, d. Mar. 11, 1967, was one of the most glamorous American operatic sopranos. Farrar studied in Boston, Paris, and Germany, making her operatic debut (1901) in Berlin as Marguerite in Gounod's *Faust.* She also sang in Monte Carlo, Paris, London, and Brussels before her triumphant debut in Gounod's *Roméo et Juliette* at the Metropolitan Opera (1906). Farrar was the Metropolitan's principal lyric soprano for 15 years, appearing in nearly 500 performances, often as a partner to Enrico Caruso.

Farrell, James T.

Farrell, James T. [far'-ul] James Thomas Farrell, b. Chicago, Feb. 27, 1904, d. Aug. 21, 1979, was an American author best known for his novels about Irish-American families on Chicago's South Side. He first received recognition for his Studs Lonigan trilogy (*Young Lonigan*, 1932; *The Young Manhood of Studs Lonigan*,

The American author James T. Farrell became controversial during the later 1930s, because of his Marxist views and the stark realism of his literary style. Farrell's most important work, the Studs Lonigan trilogy, chronicles the brutalization and corruption of a young man growing up in Chicago.

1934; *Judgment Day*, 1935) and subsequently published more than 50 works of fiction, criticism, poetry, and journalism. In the 1930s and '40s he was active in left-wing social causes; *A Note on Literary Criticism* (1936) delineated his brand of independent Marxism.

Farrell's fiction is a part of the tradition of naturalistic writing established by Sherwood Anderson and Theodore Dreiser, and the force of his work derives from the uncompromising realism of his technique. He was especially inspired by the pragmatist thinkers John Dewey and George Mead in his effort to reveal the social basis of human character and destiny in his fiction. Naturalism has been a less influential technique since the end of World War II, but Farrell continued to write in the style he had mastered.

Farrell, Suzanne

Farrell, Suzanne Suzanne Farrell, b. Cincinnati, Aug. 16, 1945, is the archetypal American ballerina. She was trained at the School of American Ballet where she was discovered by George Balanchine. She joined the New York City Ballet in 1961, rising to principal in 1965. After a row with Balanchine over her marriage, she resigned in 1969 and joined Maurice Béjart's Ballet of the 20th Century, before returning to New York City Ballet in 1975. She retired from the company in 1989 and soon after joined the Fort Worth Ballet as an artistic advisor.

farsightedness

farsightedness   see EYE DISEASES

fasces

fasces [fas'-eez] In ancient Rome, fasces were rods of elm or birch tied together with leather thongs around an ax with a projecting blade, used as a symbol of authority. They were carried by lictors (guards) walking in advance of such public officials as praetors, consuls, proconsuls, victorious generals, dictators, and emperors. The Italian Fascist party adopted the fasces as its emblem and took its name from them.

fascism

fascism [fash'-izm] Fascism was an authoritarian political movement that developed in Italy and several other European countries after 1919 as a reaction against the profound political and social changes brought about by World War I and the spread of socialism and communism. Its name was derived from the fasces, an ancient Roman symbol of authority consisting of a bundle of rods and an ax.

Italian fascism was founded in Milan on Mar. 23, 1919, by Benito MUSSOLINI, a former revolutionary socialist leader. His followers, mostly war veterans, were organized along paramilitary lines and wore black shirts as uniforms. The early Fascist program was a mixture of left- and right-wing ideas that emphasized intense NATIONALISM, productivism, antisocialism, elitism, and the need for a strong leader. Mussolini's oratorical skills, the postwar economic crisis, a widespread lack of confidence in the traditional political system, and a growing fear of socialism, all helped the Fascist party to grow to 300,000 registered members by 1921. In that year it elected 35

The fascist dictator Benito Mussolini (center) of Italy reviews an elite corps of German troops with the Nazi leader Adolf Hitler. The alliance of these dictators in the 1930s reflected the close relationship between fascism and Nazism.

members to parliament. Mussolini became prime minister in October 1922 following the "march on Rome" and 3 years of bloody violence. In 1926 he seized total power as dictator and ruled Italy until July 1943, when he was deposed. A puppet Fascist regime with Mussolini at its head nominally controlled northern Italy under the Germans until Mussolini's execution by partisans in 1945 (see ITALY, HISTORY OF).

The Philosophy of Fascism. Fascist ideology, largely the work of the neoidealist philosopher Giovanni GENTILE, emphasized the subordination of the individual to a "totalitarian" state that was to control all aspects of national life. Violence as a creative force was an important aspect of the Fascist philosophy. A special feature of Italian fascism was the attempt to eliminate the class struggle from history through nationalism and the corporate state. Mussolini organized the economy and all "producers"—from peasants and factory workers to intellectuals and industrialists—into 22 corporations as a means of improving productivity and avoiding industrial disputes. Contrary to the regime's propaganda claims, the totalitarian state functioned poorly. Mussolini had to compromise with big business, the monarchy, and the Roman Catholic church. The Italian economy experienced no appreciable growth. The corporate state was never fully implemented, and the expansionist, militaristic nature of fascism contributed to imperialist adventures in Ethiopia and the Balkans and ultimately to World War II.

The intellectual roots of fascism can be traced back to voluntaristic philosophers such as Arthur SCHOPENHAUER, Friedrich NIETZSCHE, and Henri BERGSON and to SOCIAL DARWINISM with its emphasis on the survival of the fittest. Its immediate roots, however, were in certain irrational, socialist, and nationalist tendencies of the turn of the century that combined in a protest against the liberal bourgeois ideas then holding sway in Western Europe. The writings of Gabriele D'ANNUNZIO, Georges SOREL, and Maurice Barrès were particularly influential.

European Fascism. Closely related to Italian fascism was German National Socialism, or NAZISM, under Adolf HITLER. It won wide support among the unemployed, the impoverished middle class, and industrialists who feared socialism and communism. In Spain the Falange Española Tradicionalista played a crucial role in the attack on the republican government that began the SPANISH CIVIL WAR in 1936. Of less importance were the Fascist movements in France and the British Union of Fascists under Sir Oswald MOSLEY. Fascist movements sprang up in many other European countries during the 1930s, including Romania (see IRON GUARD), Belgium, Austria, and the Netherlands. The defeat of Italy and Germany in World War II spelled the end of fascism as an effective, internationally appealing mass movement.

See also: TOTALITARIANISM.

fashion design   The term *fashion* is used to refer to the prevailing mode or style in clothing. The changes in style that influence the public's taste in dress are frequently brought about by the innovations of the major couturiers, or fashion designers, who act as arbiters of current trends.

Paris. Since the 14th century the acknowledged center of the fashion industry has been Paris, largely because of the predominance of fabric manufacturing and the number of merchants of fashionable goods. Much of France's fashion industry, especially silk weaving, was encouraged by the patronage of the king. To promote their wares, the French manufacturers would dispatch dolls, dressed in the latest styles, to cities and courts throughout Europe. By the 17th century, fashion engravings appeared in France, the forerunners of modern fashion magazines.

The first French fashion designer of eminence was Rose Bertin, who by 1776 was modiste to Queen Marie

The elaborate gowns of Queen Marie Antoinette, seen in this 18th-century fashion plate, were designed by the court dressmaker, Rose Bertin. Bertin, designated "Minister of Fashion," was the first notable French fashion designer. (Louvre, Paris.)

Charles Worth's designs were imitated throughout the world. This fashion plate shows different views of the American version of a Worth gown (1874). (Harper's Bazaar.)

Antoinette of France. During the Napoleonic age the designer Louis Hippolyte Leroy created apparel for the Empress Josephine. The man who created the Parisian fashion industry as it is known today, however, was an Englishman working in Paris, Charles Frederick WORTH, who became (1858) the fashion arbiter to the Empress Eugénie. He created the first couture house with its fashion shows, mannequins, sales staff, dressmakers, and Paris labels; the house of Worth continued in the family until 1956.

Paul Poiret created the first revolution in 20th-century dress about 1910, when he freed women from corsets and introduced oriental-style costumes of turbans and hobble skirts. In the 1920s, Coco CHANEL replaced Poiret's exoticisms with simple classic suits and dresses of restrained color. Jeanne Lanvin's career began with her

designs for her daughter's clothes, and this free and innocent effect, which was often created with costly brocades and lamés, became her métier. Madelaine Vionnet cut and sewed her own designs and introduced the bias cut—cutting the fabric against the weave—to create a free-flowing effect, as well as the cowl and halter necklines. Jean Patou brought an end to the 1920s look in 1929, when he introduced a collection with natural waistlines and longer hemlines for daytime dresses and floor-length skirts for evening wear.

The English designer Captain Edward Molyneux and the American Mainbocher were prominent during the 1930s. Molyneux's clothes were elegant and uncomplicated, correct for spectator sports and practical for traveling. Mainbocher's padded shoulders and "wasp" waists anticipated the styles of the 1940s. Lucien Lelong introduced a ready-made department, *robes d'édition*, in 1933. Ready-made clothes had been available from mail-order houses and department stores before 1900, but Lelong's innovation was unique in a Paris *haute couture* ("high fashion") house. Elsa Schiaparelli's designs in bright colors, especially shocking pink, added unusual surrealist-inspired touches to her collection: junk jewelry that glowed in the dark and handbags that lit up inside.

In 1947, Christian DIOR's romantic "New Look," with its slim waist, full bust, and long wide skirt, reaffirmed French domination of the world of fashion. Other French couturiers who brought glamour to postwar Paris were Hubert de Givenchy and Pierre Balmain. The Spanish designer Cristobal BALENCIAGA was renowned for his puffed gowns and unfitted chemises, in vogue during the 1950s.

The 1960s saw the rise of the *prêt-à-porter*, or ready-

Paul Poiret's loosely fitted, brightly colored evening gown (1915), seen in the Gazette du Bon Ton, reveals the influence of the Far East on his designs. Poiret was one of the most innovative couturiers of the early 20th century.

Coco Chanel dominated the haute couture of the mid-20th century with such simple, elegant styles as the "little black dress" (1930) and the tweed suit (1930). Chanel's tailored fashions, designed for office wear, reflected the increasing emancipation of women. (Fashion Institute of Technology, New York City.)

The American couturiere Claire McCardell, seen modeling one of her gowns (1945), created clothing noted for simplicity of both style and construction. (Fashion Institute of Technology, New York City.)

Other notable designers in America include Norman Norell, Pauline Trigère, Valentina, and, more recently, James Galanos, Rudi Gernreich, Halston, Adolfo, Perry Ellis, Calvin Klein, and Donna Karan. Ralph Lauren and Bill Blass have promoted the idea of a whole environment, creating designs for clothing, housewares, eyeglasses, and auto interiors. By the 1980s, fashion catering to the needs of professional working women was a priority for some designers, notably Liz Claiborne. Most international designers now also create clothing for men.

See also: CLOTHING INDUSTRY; COSTUME.

Fashoda Incident [fuh-shoh'-duh]   The Fashoda Incident was a confrontation between Great Britain and France in 1898 that arose from the rivalry of the two powers for territory in Africa. The British aim to link Egypt with South Africa by a Cape-to-Cairo railway was challenged by a French drive to establish a belt across the continent from Senegal to Somaliland. A French military party advancing eastward was met at Fashoda (now Kodok) on the White Nile by a British force under Sir Herbert KITCHENER on Sept. 18, 1898. War was averted when France accepted the watershed between the Congo and the Nile basins as the boundary between its sphere of influence and Britain's.

Fassbinder, Rainer Werner [fahs'-bin-dur, ry'-nur vair'-nur]   Rainer Werner Fassbinder, b. May 31, 1946, d. June 10, 1982, was one of Germany's greatest and most prolific film directors as well as a stage and screen actor and scriptwriter. He joined the Munich Action Theater in 1967 and began making films two years later, using a permanent ensemble of experienced actors. His subject matter ranges from the failure of friends to communicate, as portrayed in *Katzelmacher* (1969), to the dullness of daily existence, depicted in *Die bittren Tränen der Petra von Kant* (The Bitter Tears of Petra von Kant, 1972). Particularly admired are the bittersweet *Der Händler der vier Jahreszeiten* (Merchant of the Four Seasons, 1971), the stylish *Effi Breist,* and *Ali: Angst essen Seele auf* (Ali: Fear Eats the Soul, 1974). Fassbinder's *Faustrecht der Freiheit* (1975), released in English as *Fox and his Friends,* created a new wave of interest in his films in both the United States and Europe. In 1978, he released his first English language film, *Despair,* starring Dirk Bogarde. His most commercially successful film was *The Marriage of Maria Braun* (1979).

to-wear, market. Since the days of Worth couture designers had permitted and profited from a limited copying of their fashions by manufacturers in other countries, particularly the United States. By the 1960s, Yves SAINT-LAURENT had expanded the limits of the fashion house by opening boutiques with inexpensive ready-to-wear clothes, as well as perfumes, cosmetics, and accessories. In Italy, designer Aldo Gucci had founded his own fashion empire, with outposts in major cities worldwide. The 1960s revolutionaries André Courrèges and Pierre Cardin designed for the youth explosion, offering boots, miniskirts, and pantsuits in a space-age style. Also part of the international market were the fashions of Karl Lagerfeld, who designed for Chanel, and Christian Lacroix, who captured attention in the 1980s with his bold colors and innovative silhouettes, particularly the "pouf" or bubble dress.

International Fashions. Since the 1960s other nations—particularly Britain, Italy, the United States, and in the 1980s, Japan—have produced designers with international reputations to match those of the Paris couturiers. Mary Quant of London created (1965) the miniskirt before Cardin or Courrèges adopted it. Among the Italian designers, in addition to Gucci, Emilio Pucci and Valentino have achieved international success, and Japan's Issey Miyake has gained a following with his flowing, unstructured designs.

Designers in the United States have generally taken a less traditional and more practical approach to style. Claire McCardell brought a new practicality and puritanical simplicity to women's clothing; in 1938 she created a dress with no inner construction, years ahead of its time.

fasting   Fasting is the practice of abstaining from food, either completely or partially, for a specified period. It is an ancient practice found in most religions of the world. Recent scientific research suggests that fasting may be healthful and, when engaged in carefully, may bring about heightened states of consciousness and sensibility. Traditionally, fasting has been a widely used form of ASCETICISM and a penitential practice observed for the purpose of purifying the person or of atoning for sins and wrongdoing. Most religions designate certain days or seasons as times of fasting for their adherents, such as LENT, YOM KIPPUR, and RAMADAN.

---

fat   Fat, or LIPIDS, is a family of chemical compounds stored by plants and animals as a source of energy. In most animals fats are stored in special cells that tend to form pads of tissue under the skin and around certain organs and joints, the locations depending on the species. Stored fat, or adipose tissue, serves as a fuel reserve for METABOLISM. Fat protects the body from shocks and jolts and provides insulation. In plants, fats in the form of oil are found in the stems, seeds, and fruit.

All fats are made up of units of GLYCEROL and fatty acids. The kind of fatty acids eaten can affect a person's health. Saturated fatty acids found in butter, milk, and other animal products can raise the level of CHOLESTEROL in the blood, thus leading to ATHEROSCLEROSIS. Evidence exists that suggests the unsaturated fatty acids found in vegetable oils tend to reduce high levels of blood cholesterol.

Fat is a concentrated source of energy. The breakdown of storage fat during metabolism yields fatty acids, the prime source of metabolic energy for muscle contraction. An active energy storehouse, the adipose tissue of the body is in a constant state of buildup and breakdown, thus ensuring a continual supply of fatty acids. It is estimated that a normal human male has about 15 kg (33 lb) of stored fat, which theoretically can support life for about two months. In cases of obesity, 100 kg (220 lb) of fat may be present—a year's supply. Various fats are used as raw materials for many industrial processes. The salts of fatty acids, for example, are called soaps.

See also: NUTRITION, HUMAN.

---

fata morgana   [fah'-tuh mor-gah'-nah]   A fata morgana is a complex MIRAGE that causes distant coastlines and buildings to appear as castles in the sky. It is a combination of an inferior mirage, in which the false image appears below the true position, and a superior mirage, in which a double image appears, one image inverted below the other. The fata morgana is named for the magical powers of Morgan le Fay, the sorceress of Arthurian legend. It was first described in the Strait of Messina, Italy, but also occurs across Toyama Bay, Japan, and on Lake Geneva, Switzerland.

Fates   In Greek mythology, the three Fates, or Moirai, were the offspring of ZEUS and the Titan Themis. Though robed in white, they are described as daughters of the night and equated with the obscure darkness of human destiny. Each had her separate duty to perform: Clotho spun the thread of life; Lachesis fixed the length of the thread as she held it; and Atropos cut the thread with her shears when the span of life was done. In Roman mythology, the Fates were also known as the Parcae.

Fathers of the Church   During the first three centuries of Christian history, only bishops were called Fathers of the Church. The title was later extended to all learned church writers of antiquity recognized for their orthodoxy of doctrine and holiness of life. The last of the fathers are generally considered to be Saint ISIDORE OF SEVILLE (d. 636) in the West and Saint JOHN DAMASCENE (d. c.750) in the East. Some of the preeminent fathers have also been designated as DOCTORS OF THE CHURCH, a title of later origin.

See also: PATRISTIC LITERATURE.

---

fatigue   see MUSCLE CONTRACTION

Fátima (city)   [fah'-tee-mah]   Fátima (1981 pop., 525) is a village in central Portugal located 115 km (70 mi) north of Lisbon. It is one of the world's foremost Roman Catholic pilgrimage centers. In 1917 the Virgin Mary reportedly appeared on several occasions to three children there. Authorized pilgrimages have taken place since 1927 by those seeking cures and offering prayers. A basilica was begun in 1928 and consecrated in 1953.

Fatima (person)   [fat'-i-muh]   Fatima, c.616–33, was the only daughter of the Prophet MUHAMMAD, the wife of ALI, and in Muslim tradition, the ancestor of the Fatimid caliphs and the imams of the SHIITE branch of Islam. The subject of many legends, she is revered by all Muslims, but especially by the Shiites.

Fatimids   [fat'-i-midz]   The Fatimids were an Islamic dynasty that reigned in North Africa and later in Egypt from 909 until 1171. The Fatimid CALIPHATE was the political pinnacle of the ISMAILIS, a group of SHIITES who expected the appearance of a messiah descended from the marriage of ALI, the fourth caliph, and Fatima, the daughter of the Prophet Muhammad.

The Fatimids initially established a North African empire centered in Tunisia, from which they planned to move eastward and supplant the ABBASIDS. Consequently, they conquered Egypt in 969 and created Cairo as their capital. They then extended their influence to Syria, Palestine, and Arabia. They reached the zenith of their power in the reign of al-Mustansir (1036–94). The dynasty enjoyed generally peaceful relations with the Byzantines and cooperated with the Turkish rulers of Syria against the Crusades.

From the mid-12th century the kingdom began to crumble internally, and SALADIN easily ended Fatimid rule in 1171. Despite the religious unorthodoxy of the dynasty, most of its subjects remained orthodox Muslims. In this period Egypt enjoyed extraordinary economic and cultural vitality.

---

fats and oils   Fats and oils constitute an important, diverse class of animal and vegetable compounds used extensively as foods, cleansers, and lubricants. Originally, fats and oils were distinguished by their physical state: fats are solids at room temperature, oils are liquids. Chemists now classify both as fats to avoid possible confusion with petroleum and essential oils.

Chemistry of Fats. Fats are triglycerides—ESTERS comprising three molecules of FATTY ACIDS and one of the alcohol GLYCEROL. Natural triglycerides are usually mixed; that is, they contain more than one kind of fatty acid. Natural fats are composed of different glycerides, the specific composition being determined by the species and the function.

The common fatty acids have between 12 and 20 carbon atoms in even numbers and may be saturated or unsaturated. The unsaturated acids contain one or more carbon-carbon double bonds, which leads to a decrease in the melting temperature. Unsaturation is most often found in the oils. Unlike the saturated fats, the oils are more reactive to oxygen and are therefore less stable and more subject to rancidity.

Sources. A relatively small number of plants and animals yield commercial quantities of fats.

Hogs yield lard from their fatty tissue. Major producers are the United States, Canada, Brazil, France, and Germany. Approximately 14% of the live weight of the hog can be obtained as lard and rendered into pork fat, a somewhat darker grade with a characteristic flavor and better keeping quality. Recently, a process to improve lard as a shortening has been developed, involving the chemical rearrangement of triglyceride structures.

Cow's milk (goat and buffalo in some countries) is the source of the fat in butter. The commercial product contains about 81% butterfat along with small amounts of salt and curd.

Whale oil, in Europe, is used as a substitute for margarine or lard. Its major current application is in soap.

Soybean oil, the world's largest-volume oil product, is a food. Much of the oil, which constitutes about 16% to 18% of the bean's weight, is modified before use. Soybean oil, often a constituent of paints and printing inks, is basic to the preparation of resins and plastics.

Peanut oil is the world's second largest oil product by volume. A high-quality edible oil, it is widely used for cooking, in mayonnaise, or as a salad oil.

Coconut oil, from copra, the dried nutmeat of many palm trees, represents approximately 8% of the world's trade in fats and oils. The Philippines, Ceylon, and Indonesia are the principal producers and exporters of copra. After World War II copra use shifted from food to applications in soapmaking and later to production of chemical detergents, alcohols, amines, and acids.

Linseed oil, derived from flaxseeds grown mainly in Canada, Argentina, and the United States, is a drying oil because of the large amount of unsaturation present. Drying oils are used in protective coatings such as paints and varnishes. Linseed oil is also used in the manufacturing of linoleum and alkyd resins.

Processing. Processes for obtaining fats are of two general types: extraction from the natural source, and processing or modification. Three basic modes of extraction are used. (1) In rendering, the seeds or fatty tissues are heated with water and steam, often under pressure, and the nearly insoluble fat is separated by skimming or centrifuging. Lard from hogs, and whale and olive oils are derived this way. (2) In pressing, mills or screw presses are used to break down the cell walls and liberate the oil. This method is effective for soybean, peanut, coconut, and linseed oils. (3) Extraction takes advantage of the solubility of fats in hydrocarbon solvents. These solvents are volatile and may be removed and recycled. Nuts and seeds of high oil content lend themselves well to pressing and extraction. Soybean, linseed, and peanut oils are obtained by either method.

Raw fat is processed to improve the quality of the product. The number of steps used depends on the type of raw fat and its ultimate application. Refining removes the nonglyceride material consisting mostly of hydrolyzed fatty acids. Their presence imparts a disagreeable taste to foods such as salad oil. The nonglycerides may be removed by treatment with bases such as sodium hydroxide or sodium carbonate. Bleaching makes fat white and can be accomplished chemically, by physical adsorption with activated carbon or clays, or by heating. Winterizing is rapid or slow chilling to remove waxes, stearic acid, or higher-melting glycerides. Peanut-based salad oil is winterized so that it will remain a liquid at cooler temperatures. Hydrogenation, often called hardening, involves the addition of hydrogen to the carbon-carbon double bonds of unsaturated fats. It produces a desirable solid fat for margarine and shortening. Hardened fats have less susceptibility to slow oxidation, which would cause them to turn rancid.

Function. Fats play two principal roles in plant and animal physiology: as sources of stored energy and as protection against thermal and physical injury. Research shows, however, that they are also associated with the sterols, vitamins, and other substances vital to the organism's well-being. The greater solubility of these chemicals in fats assists in their necessary transfer from one location in the organism to another.

See also: CARBOXYLIC ACID; LIPIDS; SAPONIFICATION.

---

fatty acid Certain CARBOXYLIC ACIDS, particularly those with longer carbon chains (12–20 carbon atoms), are often called fatty acids because they are constituents of animal FATS AND OILS. The fatty acids may be released from the fat by HYDROLYSIS. Fatty acids may also be easily prepared from other organic compounds by oxidation of the corresponding alcohol, aldehyde, or unsaturated hydrocarbon. They have the acidic properties and chemical reactivity typical of carboxyl compounds. Salts of long-chain fatty acids (14 or more carbon atoms), or soaps, are important because of their ability to form emulsions with oils.

See also: ACIDS AND BASES; SAPONIFICATION.

Faulkner, Brian [fawk'-nur] Arthur Brian Deane Faulkner, b. Feb. 18, 1921, d. Mar. 3, 1977, was the last prime minister of Northern Ireland under the constitution established in 1920. A Protestant, he was elected to the Northern Ireland Parliament in 1949; he became prime minister in March 1971. Faulkner initiated (1971) the policy of interning suspected members of the Irish Republican Army (IRA), but this had the effect of increasing, rather than decreasing, violence. In March 1972, the British government suspended the constitution and assumed direct rule. On Jan. 1, 1974, Faulkner became head of the new coalition administration, the first in Ulster's history. The coalition was brought down in May 1974 by a general strike organized by Protestant extremists, and the British government resumed direct rule.

Faulkner, William   William Cuthbert Faulkner, b. New Albany, Miss., Sept. 25, 1897, d. July 6, 1962, was one of America's most innovative novelists. He lived most of his life in Oxford, Miss., and his works combine regional traditions and culture with masterful characterization and technical experimentation.

In a career lasting more than three decades, Faulkner published 19 novels, more than 80 short stories, 2 books of poems, and numerous essays. Like Thomas Mann and James Joyce, writers he greatly admired, Faulkner depicted traditional society not only in its own terms but also in terms of ageless human dramas.

Early Life and Works. Faulkner's principal setting is Yoknapatawpha County, a fictional domain loosely based on places and subjects near to him in his youth. His family had played a significant role in Mississippi history. His great-grandfather, the model for the senior John Sartoris of several novels, was a lawyer, soldier, painter, railroad builder, poet, and novelist and was twice acquitted of murder charges. Faulkner grew up surrounded by traditional lore—family and regional stories, rural folk wisdom and humor, heroic and tragic accounts of the War Between the States, and tales of the hunting code and the

The American author William Faulkner, a major figure in contemporary literature, wrote novels and short stories combining stream-of-consciousness narrative with linguistic innovations and vivid characterization. Faulkner's fictional Yoknapatawpha County, although set in his native South, is a microcosm of universal human experience.

Southern gentleman's ideal of conduct. In his lifetime and in his works, Faulkner bore witness to great political, economic, and social changes in the life of the South.

Although Oxford, Miss., was in some ways rural, it was also the seat of the state university, the county government, and the federal district court, and it had ties to major cultural centers. A voracious reader, more schooled than he would ever admit, Faulkner began writing in his early teens. As a young man he produced hand-lettered and hand-illustrated books for his friends, including books of poems, at least one esoteric play, an allegorical story, and a children's tale.

Faulkner's early years were not confined to the countryside that he eventually shaped into Yoknapatawpha. Before the 1918 armistice he trained in Toronto as a fighter pilot with the Royal Air Force. He traveled to New York City, New Orleans, and Europe. He read and wrote, absorbing the modernist influences that were changing the face of 20th-century art. In the mid-1920s, Faulkner lived among writers and artists in the French Quarter of New Orleans and received encouragement for his fiction, most notably from Sherwood Anderson. He had come to New Orleans with a book of poems to his credit, *The Marble Faun* (1924), and he there completed his first novel, *Soldiers' Pay* (1926), about the homecoming of a fatally wounded aviator.

The Mature Years. After travel abroad and the publication of his second novel, *Mosquitoes* (1927), about bohemian life in New Orleans, Faulkner returned to Oxford, Miss., apparently on Anderson's advice, to begin a remarkable decade of writing. *Sartoris* (1929) was his first major exploration of Yoknapatawpha County, what he called his "little postage stamp of native soil," and he exploited it fictionally during the following 24 years, with occasional side trips.

Faulkner's next novel, The SOUND AND THE FURY (1929), displayed startling progress. It showed that he had mastered his material, demonstrated a rich variety of styles, and brought to bear techniques and ideas then pervasive in literature and art. Established as an author, Faulkner continued to write novels, always experimenting with new forms. *As I Lay Dying* (1930) was a tour de force in stream of consciousness. Subsequent works included the tightly knit *Light in August* (1932), the monumentally complex ABSALOM, ABSALOM! (1936), and the episodic *Go Down, Moses* (1942), containing his most famous short piece, "The Bear." *A Fable* (1954) and *The Reivers* (1962) each won the Pulitzer Prize, but Faulkner's later novels are generally considered less successful.

Faulkner set ambitious goals for himself and often considered his books failures because they did not measure up to his expectations. Others thought differently, however. Faulkner received the 1949 Nobel Prize for literature. A humanist, he repeatedly explored the question of human freedom and the obstacles to it—racism, regimentation, shame, fear, pride, and overly abstract principles. In his Nobel Prize acceptance speech Faulkner summed up a lifetime of writing: "The poet's voice need not merely be the record of man, it can be one of the props, the pillars to help him endure and prevail."

fault A fault is a fracture in the Earth's crust along which measurable movement has occurred. Generally, one block of the crust moves past another, the distance moved varying from a few meters to hundreds of kilometers, but because it is usually not possible to say with certainty which block moved and which remained still, geologists can generally describe only the sense of movement, not the direction and magnitude.

Types. Two general classes of faults exist, distinguished by whether the movement is up and down (dip-slip) or parallel to (strike-slip) the fault plane. Dip-slip faults are further classified as normal or thrust (reverse) faults. The difference between these is determined by relative movement. In a dip-slip fault, the fault plane is commonly not vertical. Consequently, one block rests above the other. The block on top is the hanging wall, that beneath is the footwall. If the hanging wall moves down relative to the footwall, the fault is a normal fault; if the hanging wall moves up, the fault is a thrust fault. Normal faults are produced by tensional (pull-apart) forc-

es and result in movement that conforms to the force of gravity. Thrust faults are produced by compressional (push-together) forces and result in movement in opposition to the force of gravity.

Faults are produced by the forces that build MOUNTAIN systems. Major thrust and strike-slip faults are more common than major normal faults, however, because mountain chains are produced by compressional forces. Normal faults may form later, following the compressional, or orogenic, phase of mountain building, as in the BASIN AND RANGE PROVINCE of the western United States. Normal faults also form along COASTAL PLAINS, where fault movement occurs in response to gravitational forces on accumulating sediment.

Fault Movement. Although most faults are inactive, and have been for millions of years, some faults, such as the SAN ANDREAS FAULT in California, have remained active. When such an active fault moves sporadically and suddenly, an EARTHQUAKE results. In the case of the San Andreas, a strike-slip TRANSFORM FAULT, portions are creeping (moving very slowly), while others are locked. Strain ener-

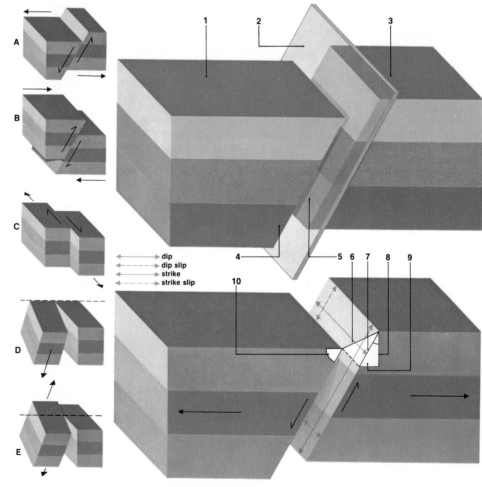

A normal fault (A) results from crustal tension forces that pull apart blocks. A thrust fault (B) results from compressional forces that push one block over another. In strike-slip faults (C), crustal compression causes the blocks to move apart horizontally. Hinge faults (D), or pivotal faults (E), result when one end of a block moves downward on an axis at right angles to the fault, and another end remains level or moves upward.

The terms describing movements of fault blocks include a downthrown block (1), which moves down along a fault plane (2) relative to an upthrown block (3); a hanging wall (4); and a footwall (5). The net slip is the total distance a block has moved (6); the hade, the angle between the fault plane and a vertical plane (7); the throw, the vertical displacement of the blocks (8); and the heave, the horizontal displacement of the blocks (9). The angle of dip lies between the fault plane and the horizontal direction (10).

dip
dip slip
strike
strike slip

gy accumulates in the locked portions, where earthquakes are likely to occur. The largest earthquakes occur along compressional faults that mark the juncture of crustal plates (see PLATE TECTONICS); smaller earthquakes occur along tensional faults. The reason for this is that the force of friction is more easily overcome in a tensional system.

Measurements are made along active faults to determine the rate of movement. Various techniques are employed, some of which involve the use of LASER measuring devices, and others merely an iron bar placed athwart the fault plane and anchored at only one end. Rates of continuous movement on a creeping fault may amount to 1–10 cm (0.4–4.0 in) a year. Active faults that produce earthquakes may not move for several decades, then move a meter (3 ft) or more in less than a second. If averaged over the period of time since the last movement, however, the rate of such movement may be about the same as that of a fault that has been continuously creeping.

Faults that have a history of recent movement or that are still active generally affect the surface TOPOGRAPHY. Offset streams, fault scarps (cliffs coincident with fault planes; see ESCARPMENT), flatirons (truncated ridge spurs), and stream valleys that follow fault traces are all features related to recent fault movement. These features are generally eroded away along inactive faults; resistant rock layers, however, may be offset and brought into relief, forming a fault-line scarp.

Construction along Faults. Construction along faults may pose complex problems. If the fault is active, special building or foundation designs, or both, may be necessary to ensure that the structure withstands seismic shaking or other movement. Large buildings, bridges, or dams are generally not built directly on active faults, although in California many such structures have been built directly on the San Andreas and other active faults.

Construction on inactive faults may present problems of other kinds. GROUNDWATER may open up a fault zone by dissolving crushed rocks bordering the fault plane, allowing the water to percolate upward and form springs and swamps. An ancient fault may have brought rocks of different mechanical properties into contact, posing unique problems for foundation construction.

See also: HORST AND GRABEN; JOINT (in geology); RIFT VALLEYS.

Faunus [fawn'-uhs]   In Roman mythology Faunus was a fertility and woodland god. An agricultural deity, Faunus protected crops, fields, flocks, and shepherds and invented a rustic musical instrument, the shawm. The Roman festival known as the LUPERCALIA was closely identified with Faunus, who, as Lupercus, was worshiped in a temple on the Palatine Hill. Faunus also functioned as a prophetic god.

Fauré, Gabriel Urbain [foh-ray', gah-bree-el']
Gabriel Urbain Fauré, b. May 12, 1845, d. Nov. 4, 1924, was an eminent French composer, organist, and teacher. He attended (1855–65) the Niedermeyer School in Paris,

where he studied with Camille Saint-Saëns. Fauré later became a church organist in Brittany. He served briefly in the French army in 1870 and taught at the Niedermeyer School from 1872. In 1896 he became professor of composition at the Paris Conservatory and principal organist at the Church of the Madeleine. Later he was a music critic for *Le Figaro*. In 1905 he was appointed director of the Paris Conservatory. Many of Fauré's pupils achieved fame, among them Nadia Boulanger, Georges Enesco, Maurice Ravel, and Florent Schmitt.

Fauré's outstanding works include much chamber music, particularly the Piano Quartet in C minor (1879), *Requiem* (1886), and nearly 100 songs. Few other compositions have become popular outside France, despite their excellence, melodic beauty, and harmonic originality. Fauré's music represents the best in the French tradition, in which restraint and balance, simplicity and lyricism, and subtle detail are characteristic. He also wrote two operas; orchestral works, including *Pavane* (1887); and piano pieces.

Faust [fowst]   A Dr. Johann Faust—who lived in Germany in the first half of the 16th century and was a student of magic, astrology, and alchemy—provided the model for the protagonist of *The History of Dr. Johann Faustus* (anon., c.1580). The German book was the first printed collection of the legends attached to the name *Faust*, the scholar who sells his soul to the devil in exchange for knowledge and power. The story, in translation, appeared throughout Europe and inspired—among other, lesser works—Christopher Marlowe's great play *Doctor Faustus* (publ. 1604) and Johann Goethe's dramatic poem *Faust: A Tragedy* (1808–32). For many, the Faust figure embodies a human dilemma, where the search for and possession of knowledge inevitably poisons or corrupts one's relationship to God and nature. Authors such as Heinrich Heine and Thomas Mann, composers such as Hector Berlioz and Thomas Gounod, and Eugène Delacroix and Max Beckmann among artists have all found Faust a tragic symbol of central importance.

Fauvism [foh'-vizm]   At the 1905 Salon d'Automne in Paris a group of painters under the leadership of Henri MATISSE shocked the art world with their paintings characterized by brilliant color, expressive brushwork, and flat composition, as in Matisse's *The Green Stripe, Portrait of Mme. Matisse* (1905; Statens Museum fur Kunst, Copenhagen). The critic Louis Vauxcelles, on visiting the show, called the painters the "Wild Beasts," or "Les Fauves"; the pejorative remark was exploited by hostile critics, and the name stuck.

Vincent VAN GOGH, Paul GAUGUIN, the NABIS, and the neoimpressionists (see NEOIMPRESSIONISM) were the most important influences on the Fauves. Some of them had been students of Gustave MOREAU at the École des Beaux-Arts; these included Matisse, Georges ROUAULT, Albert Marquet, Charles Camoir, Jean Puy, and Henri Manguin. André DERAIN and Maurice de VLAMINCK had painted to-

Maurice de Vlaminck's Street Scene in Marly-le-Roi *(1904) is representative of the style known as Fauvism. The work exhibits the Fauvist combination of spontaneous execution, expressive colors, and distorted composition. (Musée National d'Art Moderne, Paris.)*

gether at Chatou. A contingent from Le Havre, Raoul Dufy, Georges Braque, and Achille Émile Orthon Friesz, joined the group after seeing Matisse's work. Kees van Dongen, a Dutch painter, joined them when he settled in Paris.

The Fauves never issued a theoretical manifesto. By the time Matisse wrote his "Notes of a Painter" in 1908, the peak of Fauvism was over. Matisse himself moved from the spontaneous and exuberant use of color that characterized Fauvism to a more decorative formalism. Although Fauvism was a short-lived movement, it was influential; the German expressionists, particularly Wassily Kandinsky and Alexey von Jawlensky in Munich, and the Die Brücke group in Dresden were heavily indebted to it. (See Expressionism.)

The Fauves represented the first break with the artistic traditions of the past. The movement's emphasis on formal values and expressive use of color, line, and brushwork helped liberate painting from the representational expectations that had dominated Western art since the Renaissance. Fauvism was the first explosive 20th-century art movement.

favorite son In U.S. politics a favorite son is a person favored for nomination by a state delegation to a presidential nominating convention (see Political Convention). Although he or she has little chance of being nominated, the favorite son controls a block of votes that can be released at a crucial moment to gain the election of a preferred candidate.

Fawkes, Guy [fawks, gy] Guy Fawkes, b. Apr. 13, 1570, d. Jan. 31, 1606, was instrumental in the Gunpowder Plot of 1605 to blow up the English Parliament and King James I. In 1604, Fawkes was engaged by the Catholic conspirators who planned to overthrow the Protestant monarchy in England to stow gunpowder barrels in a vault under the House of Lords and to explode them on Nov. 5, 1605, when the king opened Parliament. An anonymous letter warned the government, however, and during a search on Nov. 4, 1605, Fawkes was arrested. Under torture he revealed the plot and was subsequently executed. November 5 continues to be celebrated in England as Guy Fawkes Day.

Faxien (Fa-hsien) [fah-shee-en'] Faxien was a Chinese Buddhist monk and scribe of the 4th–5th century. From 399 to 414, he and several companions made a pilgrimage through India and Central Asia gathering and copying sacred texts of various schools of Buddhism. After returning to China, Faxien began translating the sacred texts into Chinese, with the goal of compiling a complete canon of Buddhist scriptures. His account of his travels *Fo Guo Ji* (*c*.414; Record of Buddhist Kingdoms) is an invaluable source of information on India in the early 5th century. There are several English translations of the work.

Fayetteville [fay'-et-vil] Fayetteville, seat of Cumberland County, is a city in central North Carolina at the head of navigation on the Cape Fear River. It has a population of 75,695 (1990). Settled (1739) by Highland Scots, it was incorporated (1783) from two settlements and named for the marquis de Lafayette. Serving as state capital (1789–93), it was the scene of the state's ratification of the U.S. Constitution (Nov. 21, 1789). The economy is based primarily on textiles and wood products. Fort Bragg and Pope Air Force Base are nearby.

FDIC see Federal Deposit Insurance Corporation

fear Fear is an emotion characterized by unpleasant, often intense feelings and by a desire to flee or hide. Although it is generally believed to be related to anxiety, there is no consensus about how it is related. When recurring fear is out of proportion to any real danger, it is called a phobia. Fear is accompanied by activity of the sympathetic nervous system, the system that shifts blood flow and energy to the functions needed for fight or flight. Electrical stimulation of certain areas of the brain in animals will cause flight.

The most common symptoms of fear are pounding heart, rapid pulse, muscle tension, irritability, dry throat, nervous perspiration, and "butterflies" in the stomach. Some of these symptoms, such as pulse and heart changes, also occur when other emotions are experienced. Other features, though not unique to fear, are more characteristic; among these are increases in muscle tension, skin conductance, and respiration rate. These features are associated with the hormone epinephrine, whereas the symptoms characteristic of anger are associated with the additional action of norepinephrine. Rabbits show more epinephrine; lions, more norepinephrine.

Although most causes of fear are learned, some things cause fear the first time they are seen. Chimpanzees fear the first snake or skull they see. Both chimp and human infants in certain stages show an innate fear of strangers.

feather A feather is a specialized epidermal outgrowth unique to birds. It is composed of pigments and keratin, a protein that constitutes horny substances such as hair, nails, claws, and hooves. Strong, lightweight, and flexible, feathers cover and shape a bird's body, make flying possible, serve as attractive displays in courtship and mating rituals, and provide balance, protective coloration, and insulation.

The main types are body contour feathers, which include flight feathers and wing coverts, down, and filoplumes. All feathers grow from papillae, which are nipplelike structures that anchor the quill. The quill, which is hollow, emerges from a follicle and connects to a shaft, the center of which contains spongy, air-filled cells.

Body contour feathers shape a bird's body into a characteristic form. A contour feather has downy barbs at the shaft's base and a vane at the tip. A typical flight feather has a tightly structured vane, which is the flat, bladelike

Primary (A) and secondary (B) wing feathers, as well as the tail feather (C), are strong enough to lift and guide a bird in flight. Contour feathers (D) define the bird's body shape, and down feathers (E), the first type of feather grown by a young bird, provide insulation. A filoplume (F) is a hairlike feather usually interspersed among contour feathers. Feathers have a hollow quill (1) that is embedded in the bird's skin. The quill extends into a central shaft (2), from which barbs (3) project to form a vane (4). Each barb of the first four types of feather has numerous barbules (5), which hook onto barbules of adjacent barbs. These hooked barbules strengthen the feather for flight. The down and filoplume feathers appear fluffy because they lack hooked barbules. The fluffy down feathers provide warmth.

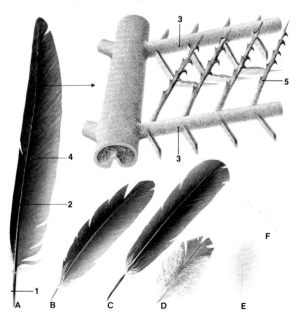

part of the feather. Long rows of barbs constitute a vane and in turn comprise rows of overlapping barbules. The barbules are held in place by hooklike structures known as barbicels. Barbs can be separated from each other and smoothed back into place because barbules and barbicels act somewhat like a zipper. Primary and secondary flight feathers of the wing, as well as tail feathers, allow a bird to control lift, steering, and braking during flight. Wing coverts, which grow over the quills of flight feathers, are similarly structured.

A down feather has barbules that lack hooks and as a result has a loose, fluffy appearance. Down feathers cover all young birds before wing and body feathers grow in and provide insulation to most adult birds. Filoplumes are hairlike feathers that have a slender shaft with few or no barbs.

Birds molt, or shed their feathers, one or more times a year, depending on the species. Chicks molt several times before assuming adult plumage. Some birds molt an equal number of feathers on each wing so they can maintain balance during flight. Many waterfowl, such as ducks, molt their flight feathers all at once and cannot fly until the feathers are renewed.

Coloration results from chemical pigments and from the refraction of light from the structural irregularites of the feathers. Red, yellow, and black colors are due to pigment, and blue and iridescent colors are caused by light refraction.

featherbedding Featherbedding is a method of maintaining the employment of some LABOR UNION members by imposing rules or limitations on employers that result in their retaining or hiring "redundant" workers or that arbitrarily lengthen the period of time in which work is performed. A classic example of featherbedding was the insistence of the railroad unions in the 1960s that firemen continue to ride diesel locomotives, which have no fires to tend. Although unions generally dispute the charge of featherbedding, officials often defend the practice as the only way to protect workers whose jobs may be threatened by improved technology.

feces [fee'-seez] Feces, also called excreta and stool, are the waste products of digestion. They take form as they are moved along the large INTESTINE by involuntary muscular contractions called PERISTALSIS (see also DIGESTION, HUMAN). The normal daily stool of human adults is about 250 g (9 oz). Besides food products, up to 20 percent of this weight is intestinal bacteria. Other constituents are digestive secretions, enzymes, fats, cell debris, electrolytes, water, and small amounts of protein. The characteristic odor of feces is caused by certain organic chemicals.

Medical examination of feces aids in diagnosing many gastrointestinal disorders. Very dark stools, for example, may indicate an ulcerative lesion in the higher digestive tract. Heavy, fat-rich stools can indicate various intestinal and pancreatic disorders, and so forth. Feces are also examined to detect internal parasites.

Federal Aviation Administration   A part of the U.S. Department of Transportation since 1967, the Federal Aviation Administration (FAA) is responsible for regulating the technical aspects of civil air transportation. The FAA establishes safety standards for aircraft and medical standards for personnel, operates and maintains communications equipment and control towers at airports, develops and tests navigation equipment and improved aircraft, and investigates airplane crashes. The FAA also helps plan and develop public airports and provides numerous other technical services. Until 1967 it was called the Federal Aviation Agency.

Federal Bureau of Investigation   The Federal Bureau of Investigation (FBI), a division of the U.S. Department of Justice, is one of the most powerful and influential law enforcement organizations in the world. With more than 8,000 special agents scattered across the country or based at headquarters in Washington, D.C., the FBI is responsible for enforcing federal criminal laws. Its cases include kidnappings and bank robberies, efforts to locate fugitives, and analyses of frauds against the government. It also has jurisdiction over counterintelligence matters (finding and apprehending foreign spies working in the United States). Since World War II, it has been responsible for conducting background investigations of some people under consideration for federal jobs. By the example of its own procedures and the thorough training courses that it conducts, the FBI has a profound influence on local police forces.

The FBI Identification Division, established in 1924, maintains the world's largest fingerprint files. Like those of the agency's scientific laboratory, established in 1932, its services are available to other law enforcement agencies.

Beginning as the Bureau of Investigation in 1908, the FBI originally had few responsibilities. It first attracted notice when new federal laws, such as those forbidding the interstate transportation of stolen motor vehicles, were adopted to deal with problems that had traditionally been handled by the states. The bureau was soon exploited for political purposes. It was used in the Palmer raids (1919–20; see PALMER, A. MITCHELL) to arrest immigrants who were thought to be subversives, and its agents later spied on political adversaries of President Warren G. Harding.

J. Edgar HOOVER was named director of the bureau in 1924 with a mandate to eliminate corruption and to get the agency out of politics. Hoover established professional qualifications for the bureau's members. His own ambitions for national celebrity and the adoption of dozens of federal criminal laws by Congress combined to increase the bureau's prestige. Hoover's death in 1972, however, was followed by the gradual revelation of a series of abuses that occurred both during his tenure and in subsequent years. They included disruptive activities against leftist and civil rights organizations; extensive illegal wiretapping and bugging; the use of agency files for political

purposes by U.S. presidents beginning with Franklin Delano Roosevelt; and the keeping of extensive secret dossiers on politicians and on people perceived as FBI adversaries (for example, Martin Luther King, Jr.).

The agency's reputation was retrieved in part during the directorship (1978–87) of William H. WEBSTER. Webster was succeeded by William S. Sessions.

Federal Communications Commission   The Federal Communications Commission, an independent U.S. government agency, regulates interstate and foreign communications by radio, television, wire, and cable. It grants licenses to radio and television broadcasters and assigns frequencies. The commission is responsible to Congress and is not part of the executive branch of the government; the president of the United States, however, with Senate approval, appoints the five commissioners and designates one of them as chairperson.

The FCC has three main bureaus. The Mass Media Bureau regulates most RADIO AND TELEVISION BROADCASTING. It issues construction permits and operating licenses and oversees cable television operators. The Common Carrier Bureau regulates public services such as telephone, telegraph, and satellite communications. The Private Radio Bureau regulates such services as police and taxicab radios, CITIZENS BAND RADIO, and other short-distance radio communications.

The commission was created by the Federal Communications Act of 1934, succeeding the Federal Radio Commission established in 1927. Its decisions have aided the development of FM and of color television broadcasting, and have determined the amount of regulation and—in the 1980s—deregulation of TV advertising.

Federal Deposit Insurance Corporation   Created in 1933 during the Great Depression, when many banks failed, the U.S. Federal Deposit Insurance Corporation (FDIC) protects depositors by insuring their bank accounts, up to $100,000. All national banks are required to belong, and most state banks are voluntary members. The FDIC has had to assume control of several major insolvent banks since 1989. Of the three board members, one is comptroller of the currency.

Federal Home Loan Bank Board   The Federal Home Loan Bank Board (FHLBB) was established in 1932 to provide credit reserves for savings and loan associations engaged in home mortgage lending. It was dismantled by the extensive savings-and-loan bailout and reorganization legislation of 1989, when its regulatory functions went to the new Office of Thrift Supervision under the Treasury. Until then the FHLBB had directed 12 regional Federal Home Loan Banks. It also had operated the Federal Savings and Loan Insurance Corporation, which in 1989 became the Savings Association Insurance Fund run by the FEDERAL DEPOSIT INSURANCE CORPORATION.

Federal Housing Administration The Federal Housing Administration (FHA) was created in 1934 as a U.S. government agency whose function was to insure MORTGAGES, thus providing (a) banks and other lending institutions with a guarantee that their HOUSING loans would be adequately secured, and (b) the housing industry with a new stimulus during a time when almost no new homes were being built. Because FHA-insured mortgages, and the houses they buy, must conform to certain standards, the agency has had a great influence on the housing and mortgage-lending industries. In 1965 the FHA was incorporated into the new Department of Housing and Urban Development (HUD).

Federal National Mortgage Association The Federal National Mortgage Association—nicknamed Fannie Mae—was created (1938) by the U.S. Congress. Now a private corporation, it seeks to encourage the fluidity of the home-mortgage market by buying and selling mortgages, which helps keep them available to consumers. Its sister organization—Ginnie Mae, or Government National Mortgage Association—was established in 1968. A government-owned corporation under the control of the Department of Housing and Urban Development, it helps finance public-housing programs.

Federal Republic of Germany see GERMANY

Federal Reserve System The Federal Reserve System, nicknamed the Fed, is the CENTRAL BANK of the United States. It has two main functions: to be a "bankers' bank," holding deposits of the commercial banks and operating a nationwide check-clearing system; and to serve as the basic controller of credit in the U.S. economy, thus determining the size of the money supply and the ease or difficulty of borrowing. All national banks must belong to the Federal Reserve System, and many state banks belong voluntarily. The system was established in 1913.

Unlike the central banks of other countries, the Federal Reserve is divided into 12 privately controlled, separate, central banks located in Atlanta, Boston, Chicago, Cleveland, Dallas, Kansas City, Minneapolis, New York City, Philadelphia, Richmond, St. Louis, and San Francisco. Each bank serves a designated district. The system was organized this way to diffuse the power of the central bank. The independence of the Federal Reserve banks is limited, however; power is centralized in a board of governors, with offices in Washington, D.C. The 7 governors are appointed for terms of 14 years by the president of the United States, subject to confirmation by the Senate. The president also nominates a chairperson, who serves a 4-year term.

The governors of the Federal Reserve Board and the presidents of the 12 Federal Reserve banks are often referred to as monetary authorities. They control the issuance of paper currency and coins, regulate the banks that are members of the Federal Reserve System, decide whether member banks may establish branches or buy other banks, and regulate the operations of bank-holding companies.

All member banks are required to maintain non-interest-bearing reserve deposits based on a percentage of their transaction balances at the district Federal Reserve Bank. The monetary authorities implement MONETARY POLICY primarily by changing the size of the reserves. By raising legal reserve requirements, the Federal Reserve tightens credit, that is, reduces the size of the money supply generated by the BANKING SYSTEM. By lowering reserve requirements, it can increase the money supply. More often, however, the Federal Reserve controls reserves indirectly, through the operations of the Federal Open Market Committee (consisting of the 7 governors and 5 of the 12 reserve-bank presidents), which directs the buying and selling of U.S. government securities on the open market. When the Federal Reserve wishes to decrease reserves in this way, it sells federal securities; the checks it receives in payment have the effect of removing funds from the banking system. When it wishes to expand the money supply, it buys securities, issuing checks drawn on itself; these checks enable banks receiving them to obtain increased reserve deposits with their reserve banks, which lets them expand the money supply.

The Federal Reserve regulates the money supply in a third way: through the discount rate, the interest rate at which it lends money to members. In practice, however, changes in the discount rate act as a signal of the Federal Reserve's intentions, which are carried out mainly by changing reserve requirements or through open-market operations.

The Federal Reserve acts as the government's official buyer and seller of foreign currencies. It also holds gold deposited in the United States by other countries and handles purchases and sales of U.S. government securities on behalf of foreign governmental bodies.

Federal Savings and Loan Insurance Corporation see FEDERAL HOME LOAN BANK BOARD

federal style The federal style is a style of architecture, furniture, and decoration produced in the United States in the years 1780 through 1820. The style is best characterized as an aspect of NEOCLASSICISM, influenced by the Scottish architect Robert ADAM, with American motifs added. The original source of the style lay in the architecture and ornament of late Roman antiquity. In 1773, just before the American Revolution, the first volume of *The Works of Robert and James Adam* appeared in London and soon became the most influential manual for architectural design in England and, subsequently, in the newly established United States.

The most important architect of the federal style was Charles BULFINCH of Boston, who designed the Massachusetts State House (1795–98) and various churches and houses in that city before being called to Washington to complete the national Capitol building. Characteristics of the style include light, classical geometry; use of slender Ionic or Corinthian orders, frequently in white against a background of red brick or clapboard; and use of a delicate fanlight (half-circle window with sash bars in the shape of a fan) above doorways.

Federal Theatre Project   A program of the Works Progress Administration, the Federal Theatre Project (1935–39) was developed during the presidency of Franklin D. Roosevelt and employed thousands of theater artists and technicians who were on relief rolls. Under the leadership of Hallie Flanagan, and with a congressional appropriation of $46 million, the FTP staged over 1,200 productions of more than 800 works and published *Federal Theatre Magazine*. Regional playwriting and staging experimentation were encouraged. The FTP also presented circuses, children's programs, and puppetry.

Federal Trade Commission   Established in 1914, the Federal Trade Commission (FTC) is charged with maintaining free and fair competition in U.S. business. It takes action against monopoly, restraints on trade, and unfair or deceptive trade practices by issuing advisory opinions and other guidance materials for business to comply with voluntarily. It also takes legal action in cases where there appears to be a persistent violation of the law. This may begin with the issuance of a formal complaint by the commission, followed by hearings before an FTC administrative law judge. The judge's decision may be appealed by the respondent to the commission itself, to a U.S. court of appeals, and even to the U.S. Supreme Court. The FTC has five commissioners, appointed by the president for 7-year terms.

Federal Writers' Project   The Federal Writers' Project was a federally funded arts program that supported out-of-work writers during the Depression of the 1930s. A project of the Works Progress Administration and directed by Henry G. Alsberg, it began in 1935 and continued for four years. Although the wages were modest, writers flocked to the program, and more than 6,000 were involved during its life. The Federal Writers' Project eventually published 378 books and pamphlets. These include a series of state guidebooks, studies of American folklore, and special individual projects. The state guidebooks are perhaps the most impressive achievement, although *These Are Our Lives* (1939), an oral history of workers' lives during the Depression, received critical acclaim and initiated a genre that is still popular today. Among the writers who participated in the project were John Cheever, Kenneth Patchen, Richard Wright, Tillie Olsen, Nelson Algren, and Studs Terkel.

---

federalism   Federalism is a form of GOVERNMENT in which power is divided between a central government and several formerly independent regional governments. The regional governments maintain partial autonomy after being subsumed into the larger central government. The central government is responsible for matters of mutual concern to all regions, such as foreign affairs, defense, and currency, while the regional governments are entrusted with authority over other matters, such as education. In the United States, for example, the individual states surrender partial sovereignty but retain all rights and prerogatives not specifically assigned the federal government under the Constitution. In all modern federal systems the authority of the central and regional governments is specified in a written constitution, and conflicts of authority between the two are decided by a judicial authority. A federation differs from a confederation, in which the central authority normally has little power over member states and almost none over individuals within those states.

Federalist, The   *The Federalist* is the collective title for 85 essays signed "Publius" and published (1787–88) in various New York newspapers to convince New York voters to support ratification of the new Constitution of the United States. Sometimes called the *Federalist Papers*, they were published in book form in 1788. Although the authorship of certain essays is still disputed, the consensus is that Alexander Hamilton wrote 52; James Madison, 28; and John Jay, 5.

The first 14 are a general discussion of the importance of union to the "political prosperity" of America. Essays 15–22 contain arguments to show the inadequacy of confederations and of the Articles of Confederation, and in 23–36 evidence is presented to show the need for a government "at least equally energetic" as that provided by the Constitution. Numbers 37–51 contain explanations of the republican principles underlying the document, and 52–66 are an analysis of the legislative power and the regulation of elections. The remainder, written by Hamilton, contain the analysis of the executive (67–77) and judicial (78–83) branches and of the question of a bill of rights (84–85).

The essays failed in their immediate purpose, for New York voted against ratification. They endured, however, as the classic analysis of the Constitution and an influential treatise on federalism.

Federalist party   The Federalist party, in U.S. history, is a name that was originally applied to the advocates of ratification of the Constitution of the United States of 1787. Later, however, it came to designate supporters of the presidential administrations of George Washington and John Adams and especially of the fiscal policies of Treasury Secretary Alexander Hamilton.

Until 1795 the Federalists were not a political organization in any modern sense. Rather, Federalism was a frame of mind, a set of attitudes that included belief in a strong and activist central government, public credit, the promotion of commerce and industry, and strict neutrality in the French Revolutionary Wars—all of which were

Alexander Hamilton wrote at least 52 of the 85 essays constituting the Federalist Papers, *published anonymously in 1787-88 to rally support in New York for ratification of the federal Constitution.*

generally reflected in government policy. Opposition arose on all these points, however, and became increasingly organized around James Madison and Thomas Jefferson. Federalists began to adopt the tactics of the opposition Democratic-Republicans in response to attacks on JAY'S TREATY with Britain (1794), which Federalists believed preserved neutrality and Democratic-Republicans charged was anti-French. Although parties were widely regarded as inimical to free government, and although Washington, Hamilton, and Adams deplored their rise (together with the tendency toward a North versus South and pro-British versus pro-French polarization of political opinion), parties were an established fact by the presidential election of 1796.

During Adams's presidency the Federalists attempted to stifle dissent by the ALIEN AND SEDITION ACTS (1798). These, however, had the effect of stiffening the opposition at the time when the Federalists themselves were splitting into "High" and "Low" wings over the issue of the XYZ AFFAIR and the ensuing Quasi-War with France. By the election of 1800, therefore, the Democratic-Republicans gained control of the federal government. The death of Washington in 1799 and of Hamilton in 1804 left the Federalists without a powerful leader, and they proved inept at the highly organized popular politics of the Democratic-Republicans. Although the party continued to have strength in New England, expressing the opposition of commercial interests to the EMBARGO ACT of 1807 and the WAR OF 1812, it never made a comeback on the national level. After the HARTFORD CONVENTION of 1815, the Federalists were a dying anachronism.

See also: DEMOCRATIC PARTY.

fee see ESTATE

---

feedback Feedback refers to a system, process, or machine in which part of the output is returned (or fed back) to the input in order to control, or regulate, the operation. Certain mechanical, electrical, and biological systems may be controlled by feedback. Models that provide for feedback have also been proposed for interper-

sonal COMMUNICATION. When the feedback signal is arranged to oppose the trend of the system, it is called negative feedback. In this case, an increase in the output value is made to decrease the input value and vice versa. When the feedback signal reinforces the trend of the system, the feedback is said to be positive. Negative feedback is employed to stabilize systems. It is used in AMPLIFIERS and is basic to the important fields of AUTOMATION and PROCESS CONTROL. Positive feedback finds an application in OSCILLATORS.

Early applications were in the control of liquid level, flow, and temperature. An early example was James Watt's flyball governor for his steam engine (1788). The device contained two balls that were attached in such a way that they rotated at engine speed and moved in or out by centrifugal force, a force that is proportional to the speed of rotation. The outward motion of the balls controlled the steam inlet valve to the engine, shutting the valve as the speed increased. The feedback consisted of the transmission of ball position (a function of engine speed) to the input valve; deviations from the desired speed were automatically corrected by a change in steam input, and the engine became self-regulating.

More rigorously, it can be said that a negative feedback system is intended to maintain an output equal to a desired value. The system includes a sensing or measuring element at the output, and the output and input are then compared. The error signal resulting from the comparison process is fed back to control the input.

In the 1920s the U.S. telephone industry was seeking an accurate amplifier for use in the long-distance telephone system, where several hundred amplifiers might be

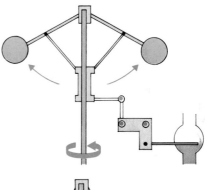

In Watt's flyball governor two heavy balls are linked to the drive shaft of a steam engine and to a control linkage. With increasing speed the weights move out, partially closing the steam valve and slowing the engine.

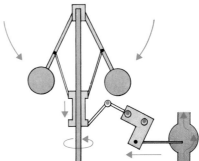

When the steam engine slows down, the heavy balls fall and move inward. The moving weights cause the control linkage to open the valve, allowing more steam to enter the engine and speed it up.

used along a telephone line, and the effects of distortion would be cumulative. Harold S. Black of the Bell Telephone research staff, who was studying the problem, saw that feedback might solve the problem. On Aug. 6, 1927, he developed the mathematical theory of a feedback amplifier, which led to the actual design of a feedback system. He recognized that a sample from the amplifier output should be compared to the amplifier input in such a way that a difference in the waveforms creates an error signal; this signal is put into such a form that when it is fed back to the input, it reduces the error so that the output waveform is made to correspond more closely with the input waveform. The principle is now universally used in transistor power amplifiers and in automatic control systems.

Feiffer, Jules [fy'-fur]

Jules Feiffer, b. New York City, Jan. 26, 1929, is an American cartoonist and writer. His satirical cartoons, first published in the New York *Village Voice* in 1956, have been nationally syndicated in the United States since 1959. Feiffer's writings for the theater include *The Explainers* (1961), a musical revue based on his cartoons; *Little Murders* (1967); *God Bless* (1968); *The White House Murder Case* (1970); and *Elliot Loves* (1990). *Feiffer's America* (1982), a collection of his cartoons, was adapted for the stage in 1988. He has written a novel, *Harry the Rat with Women* (1963), and the screenplays for *Little Murders* (1971) and *Carnal Knowledge* (1971).

Feininger, Lyonel [fy'-ning-ur]

Lyonel Charles Adrian Feininger, b. New York City, July 17, 1871, d. Jan. 13, 1956, was one of America's important expatriate artists. Sent to Germany in 1887 to study music, he studied art instead, and became a successful cartoonist and illustrator in Berlin. Turning to serious painting, he traveled to Paris in 1906–07 and again in 1911, when he came under the influence of the cubists, particularly Robert Delaunay. He soon established a reputation as one of the most lyrical interpreters of the cubist manner. In 1919 he was invited by Walter Gropius to teach at the BAUHAUS and remained there until the Nazis forced its closing in 1933. Four years later he returned to New York, where he worked until he died.

In his most memorable paintings—such as the series of 13 scenes of the village church at Gelmeroda, begun in 1913—Feininger employs the cubist techniques of planar fragmentation and multiple views. He goes beyond cubism, however, in suggesting a haunting, translucent light that seems to dissolve forms even as it defines them, as in *The Church of Gelmeroda XII* (1929; Rhode Island School of Design, Providence). After his return to America, Feininger interpreted the towering skyline of Manhattan—with such works as *Manhattan, Dawn* (1944; Collection Julia Feininger, New York)—in much the same way he had the village church, transforming the modern city into a poetic vision of great subtlety and nuance.

In Woman in Mauve *(1922), the American cubist painter Lyonel Feininger breaks the figural and architectural images into planes of translucent color. (Private collection, Lugano, Switzerland.)*

Feke, Robert [feek]

The first native American artist to create a substantial body of paintings of high merit, Robert Feke, b. Oyster Bay, N.Y., c.1707–52, developed a restrained but eloquent version of the British baroque

Robert Feke, a native-born American painter of the colonial period, painted Isaac Royall and His Family *in 1741. (Fogg Museum, Cambridge, Mass.)*

portrait style. Though largely self-taught, he was influenced in his early work by the painter John Smibert. His group portrait *Isaac Royall and his Family* (1741; Fogg Museum, Cambridge, Mass.) is one of his earliest works and one of the most ambitious by any colonial American artist. His two self-portraits (*c.*1742; Museum of Fine Arts, Boston; and *c.*1750; Rhode Island Historical Society, Providence) are remarkable for their penetrating characterization. Although he traveled widely, Feke painted chiefly in Boston and Philadelphia.

---

feldspar [feld'-spahr] The feldspars are the most abundant and widespread SILICATE MINERALS of the crust, or outermost part, of the Earth. Because of their abundance, feldspars are used in the classification of IGNEOUS ROCKS. They are also abundant in METAMORPHIC ROCKS and in some sediments and SEDIMENTARY ROCKS. Feldspars are also major constituents of most Moon rocks. Feldspars are used in the manufacture of ceramics and ceramic glazes and as mild abrasives. A few varieties, including labradorite and orthoclase, are occasionally used as gems because they show an iridescent play of colors or a milky translucence. Milky varieties are termed MOONSTONE.

Mineralogy. Feldspars are aluminosilicates, containing silicon and aluminum ions bound together by oxygen ions to form a three-dimensional framework of atoms. Other ions, principally potassium, sodium, and calcium, occupy sites within the framework and give rise to the three pure, or end-member species: orthoclase ($KAlSi_3O_8$), albite ($NaAlSi_3O_8$), and anorthite ($CaAl_2Si_2O_8$). Extensive chemical variation, or solid solution, occurs between orthoclase and albite, with potassium and sodium substituting for each other. Feldspars in this range are called alkali feldspars. A complete solid solution between albite and anorthite is also possible, with calcium substituting freely for sodium. Because these two ions have different charges, the proportions of aluminum to silicon in the aluminosilicate framework must also vary to maintain electri-

Plagioclase feldspars, the most abundant minerals in the Earth's crust, are mixtures of sodium and calcium aluminum silicates. Usually gray, pink, or white, they are found as irregular grains or as granular masses.

Microcline feldspar, usually found as yellow, red, or green prismatic crystals, is a potassium aluminum silicate. Translucent blue-green microcline, or amazonite, is a semiprecious stone used in jewelry.

cal-charge neutrality. Feldspars between albite and anorthite in composition are termed plagioclase. There is little solid solution between orthoclase and anorthite.

Feldspars are generally light-colored minerals, white or buff to gray in color. One species, microcline, may also be light brick red or even the green to blue green variety called amazonite. Feldspars are slightly translucent and have a glassy, or vitreous, luster rather like that of glazed porcelain. Because their atomic framework has planes of weakness, feldspars exhibit good cleavage, breaking readily into blocky pieces with smooth sides. On the Mohs mineral hardness scale, feldspars are 6—slightly harder than a steel knife blade and about as hard as porcelain.

Alkali Feldspars. The three different but closely related species of alkali feldspar are sanidine, orthoclase, and microcline. The differences among these feldspars result from details of their atomic structures, principally the different ways in which aluminum is distributed, or ordered, in the aluminosilicate frameworks of each.

Alkali feldspars occur in many rocks. They are abundant in GRANITES, a family of intrusive igneous rocks composed chiefly of alkali feldspars and quartz. Granites constitute the cores of mountain ranges; they are formed by the melting of the Earth's crust as mountains are built. Sanidine is found chiefly in some LAVAS, where it is preserved by rapid chilling. When cooled slowly, sanidine changes to orthoclase. Crude crystals of microcline several feet wide (among the largest of any mineral) are commonly found in PEGMATITES, coarse-grained, granitelike rocks found in mountains. Pockets yield beautiful, sharp crystals, sometimes of the green variety amazonite. Pegmatites in the granite near Pikes Peak in Colorado are famous for such crystal groups.

Alkali feldspars are also common in many metamorphic rocks that have crystallized at high temperatures. MICAS and other minerals common in lower-temperature rocks tend to break down into feldspar as the temperature increases during metamorphism. Alkali feldspars weather to CLAYS, forming important deposits of china clay or kaolin. In arid regions, however, alkali feldspars accumulate in the sand and gravel formed by mechanical breakdown of rock. A SANDSTONE formed from this sand with more than 25 percent feldspar grains is called an arkose.

Plagioclase. Plagioclase feldspars are those ranging from albite to anorthite in composition. Plagioclase feldspars are even more abundant than the alkali species, and are found in many igneous and metamorphic rocks.

Crystallization of plagioclase from a melt or molten-rock MAGMA has been studied in detail. As the melt cools, the feldspar that forms is richer in calcium than the melt itself. On further cooling, feldspar that is richer in sodium forms, and the feldspar already formed tends to react with the melt and become richer in sodium as well. If cooling takes place slowly, the feldspar will be homogeneous and have the same composition as the starting melt. Under conditions of relatively rapid cooling, however, the feldspar grains will not have fully reacted and will be zoned, richer in calcium in the centers and in sodium on the outsides.

Plagioclases are among the most common minerals in igneous rocks. They are the chief constituent of BASALT, a volcanic rock that forms the sea floors and many oceanic islands, including Iceland and Hawaii. Basalt also makes up the mare, or lowlands, of the Moon. ANDESITE, the volcanic rock of the Andes, the Cascades, and many other mountain ranges, also contains substantial plagioclase.

Plagioclase weathers more readily than alkali feldspars and is less common in sediments and sedimentary rocks (see WEATHERING). Albite, considered either an alkali feldspar or a plagioclase, is found in some sedimentary rocks; in some sodium-rich sediments it has actually grown as crystals rather than being detritus from the breakdown of other rocks. Plagioclase is widespread in metamorphic rocks. Albite is characteristic of metamorphic rocks formed below about 500° C; at higher temperatures more calcic species are characteristic. Pure anorthite is found in some highly metamorphosed marbles.

feldspathoid

feldspathoid [feld'-spuh-thoyd] Feldspathoids are a group of SILICATE MINERALS that are typical of rocks relatively rich in the alkali elements sodium and potassium and relatively poor in silica (SiO_2). In such alkaline rocks, as they are called, the feldspathoids occur with, or instead of, the more common FELDSPAR minerals; they are never found in rocks containing the mineral QUARTZ.

Types. Nepheline (Na, K)($AlSiO_4$), the most common of the group, is a white to gray mineral that is distinguished from the feldspars, which it resembles, by its poorer cleavage and slightly greasy luster. It occurs as grains or large masses in many alkaline IGNEOUS ROCKS.

Leucite ($KAlSi_2O_6$), next to nepheline in abundance, is usually found in fine-grained LAVAS in the form of chalky, well-formed, trapezohedral crystals up to several centimeters across.

The sodalite group of feldspathoids (sodalite, noselite, and lazurite) contain sodium and sometimes calcium. In addition, they contain such extra ions as chloride (Cl^-), sulfate (SO_4^{2-}), and sulfide (S^{2-}). They are found, usually

Sodalite, a sodium-aluminum silicate, is closely related chemically to the feldspars; sodalite, however, contains less silica. Sodalite is generally found as transparent-to-opaque rounded masses or as scattered grains.

in small amounts, in many of the rocks that contain nepheline.

Uses. Nepheline is used instead of feldspar in ceramics. Sodalite provides an opaque, purplish blue GEM, and the related species lazurite is the blue LAPIS LAZULI. Most feldspathoids, however, have no commercial uses.

fellahin

fellahin The term *fellahin* (from Arabic *fellāh*, "farmer") is used in Arab lands to refer to peasant agriculturalists as opposed to nomadic desert dwellers (Bedouin). In English usage it more frequently refers to the inhabitants of the Egyptian Delta, the largest agricultural area in the Middle East. More fellahin have gained ownership of land since the Egyptian social revolution of the 1950s and the completion of the ASWAN HIGH DAM, but most remain small-scale farmers whose ancient life-style has only recently begun to change through mechanized cultivation and government-sponsored social services.

Feller, Bob

Feller, Bob Robert William Andrew Feller, b. Van Meter, Iowa, Nov. 3, 1918, was an American baseball pitcher known for his famous strikeout records in the 1930s, '40s, and '50s. Nicknamed "Rapid Robert," Feller reached the major leagues with the Cleveland Indians as a 17-year-old in 1936. That season he struck out 17 men in a single game. He continued to set records, including 3 no-hitters, 12 one-hitters, and 348 strikeouts in a season and 18 in a game, compiling 266 victories before he retired from the Indians in 1956. As he lost his fastball with age, Feller developed into one of the finest all-around pitchers. He is a member of the Baseball Hall of Fame.

Fellini, Federico

Fellini, Federico [fel-lee'-nee, fay-day-ree'-koh] Federico Fellini, Italy's most famous filmmaker, b. Jan. 20, 1920, is the creator of symbolic fantasies that often have the spirit of fairy tales and may express a vision that is flamboyant and grotesque. After starting in Rome as a cartoonist and sketch writer, Fellini turned in 1939 to

The most poetic of Fellini's movies, the early film La Strada (1954) also reveals Fellini's penchant for the grotesque. Here, the heroine awaits a vision of the Virgin Mary, who has already appeared to a small, perhaps lunatic, child.

script writing, collaborating with Roberto Rossellini on the neorealist films *Open City* (1945) and *The Miracle* (1948)—in which he also acted—before becoming a director on his own. *The White Sheikh* (1952), his first solo effort, showed his inventiveness as a comic director, and *I Vitelloni* (1953), an evocation of the Rimini of his youth, demonstrated his insight into the provincial bourgeoisie. *La Strada* (1954), starring his wife, Giulietta Masina, secured his position as a major director. It won him the first of four Academy Awards for best foreign film. Fellini's second Oscar was awarded for *Nights of Cabiria* (1956), again starring Masina.

In later films, Fellini began to explore more fully the relationship between reality and dream. *La Dolce Vita* (1960), a sensational indictment of the indolence and decadence of modern Rome, was followed by the more openly symbolic *8½* (1963), another Oscar winner in which Fellini used Pirandellian techniques to comment on his problems as an artist. It was followed by the gorgeous, if somewhat opaque, *Juliet of the Spirits* (1965), with Masina playing a prosperous, neglected housewife seeking enlightenment. *Fellini's Satyricon* (1969) and *Roma* (1972) were not universally acclaimed, but the director redeemed himself with the splendid, Oscar-winning *Amarcord* (1974), a brilliantly nostalgic portrait of his boyhood in Rimini. This and the television film *The Clowns* (1970) reveal the autobiographical wellsprings of Fellini's art. Later Fellini films seem to lack the magical sheen of his best work: *Casanova* (1976), *City of Women* (1980), *And the Ship Sails On* (1983), and *Ginger and Fred* (1985) were all relatively unsuccessful.

felony　In criminal law a felony is a serious crime that in the United States is punishable by death or confinement in state or federal prison, usually for more than one year. Under the old English COMMON LAW, felons had to forfeit either their lands or their goods or both and were subject to possible capital punishment. Under modern law, forfeiture no longer exists, but felons can temporarily or permanently lose certain legal rights, such as the right to vote or to bear arms. States may follow federal law or modern common law in classifying offenses or may simply declare some crimes to be felonies. Crimes most commonly classified as felonies include murder, manslaughter, arson, burglary, and rape.

felt　Nonwoven felt is a fabric produced from a matted sheet of tangled wool, hair, or fur, often combined with cotton or synthetic fibers. The felting process has been known since antiquity, and felted materials were probably made before woven fabrics. Heat, combined with pressure, moisture, and other chemical action, causes the tangling and shrinkage of the wool fibers. Felts of various materials are used for hats; as padding in apparel, mattresses, and furniture; and as insulation. Woven felts are woven fabrics of cotton or wool that are compressed by shrinkage and then napped on both sides so that the weave is barely discernible.

Felton, William Harrell [fel'-tuhn]　William Harrell Felton, b. Oglethorpe County, Ga., June 19, 1823, d. Sept. 24, 1909, was an American politician who gained fame by battling almost single-handedly the reactionary political machine of Georgia. He was elected to Congress in 1874 in one of the bitterest campaigns in Georgia's history. After defeating the state's Democratic organization, Felton became the central figure in Georgia politics and served three terms in Congress. His wife, Rebecca Latimer Felton (1835–1930), was the first female member of the U.S. Senate, where she served briefly by appointment in 1922.

femininity　see SEXUAL DEVELOPMENT

feminism　Generally, feminism means the advocacy of women's rights to full citizenship—that is, political, economic, and social equality with men. Feminism encompasses some widely differing views, however, including those which advocate female separatism.

Modern feminism, which was born with the great democratic revolutions of the 18th century (American and French), differed from its precursors in applying the democratic implications of "the rights of man and the citizen" to women as a group. Abigail ADAMS asked her husband, John, to "remember the ladies" in framing the Constitution; Mary WOLLSTONECRAFT, inspired by the French Revolution, wrote the premier feminist treatise, *A Vindication of the Rights of Women* (1792). Beginning with the SENECA FALLS CONVENTION (1848), U.S. women schooled in reform struggles began a serious fight for the right of women to control their persons, property, and earnings and for the right to vote (see SUFFRAGE, WOMEN'S). Elizabeth Cady STANTON's Declaration of Rights and Sentiments established a blueprint. U.S. women would not gain the vote until 1920, but throughout the remainder of the 19th century many feminist goals were gradually realized, especially the rights of married women to control their own property (New York State, 1848 and 1860; South Carolina, 1868; and so on).

Throughout the 19th and early 20th centuries the women's movement primarily reflected white middle-class values and never satisfactorily answered the ex-slave Sojourner TRUTH's challenge: "Ain't I a woman?" The goals of black and working-class women remained inseparable from their racial and class oppression. The goals of middle-class women centered on obtaining the opportunities available to men of their own class, such as education, or on reforming society as a whole. Thus some women sought to improve the position of women through temperance (see TEMPERANCE MOVEMENT; WCTU), social reform, and protective legislation for working women. After women won the vote, the women's movement waned, and the first EQUAL RIGHTS AMENDMENT (ERA), introduced by Alice PAUL in 1923, failed to pass.

The women's movement did not reemerge until the 1960s, when the example of the civil rights movement and the dissatisfactions of college-educated women converged. Betty FRIEDAN's *The Feminine Mystique* (1963) called national attention to the plight of women. The founding (1965) of the NATIONAL ORGANIZATION FOR WOMEN provided a focus for the struggle for women's rights. Since the passage of the Civil Rights Act of 1964, women have enjoyed some guarantees for equal opportunity and pay in employment, and in 1973 the Supreme Court's decision in *Roe* v. *Wade* won them the right to ABORTION. During the 1980s, however, the ERA, reintroduced in 1973, was defeated, the right to abortion came under attack, and growing numbers of women were finding the ad hoc employment measures inadequate to guarantee equality. The decline in alimony and child support, combined with a rising divorce rate, made women's rights to economic equality pressing.

Despite differences, most feminists seek equal economic rights; support reproductive rights, including the right to abortion; criticize traditional definitions of gender roles; and favor raising children of both sexes for similar public roles and domestic responsibilities. Many also campaign vigorously against wife battering and rape and against the denigration of women in the media.

fencing   Fencing, once exclusively a form of combat, is now enjoyed as a sport worldwide. Modern fencers frown on identifying their sport with dueling, as in motion-picture sequences portraying acrobatic combatants engaged in reckless, devil-may-care sword play. The sports enthusiast's version of fencing calls for precision, coordination, and strategy, among other skills. First introduced as a sport on a small scale in the 14th century, fencing was one of the few events included in the first Olympic Games in 1896, and it has been included in every Olympic competition ever since.

The basic equipment used in fencing consists of a mask, a padded jacket, glove, and one of three weapons—the foil, épée, or sabre. Techniques and target areas for valid hits differ according to the weapon used. While some fencers may compete in each of the three weapons, generally skills are honed in one particular weapon. Until recently, women were permitted to compete only in foil, but the United States Fencing Association now offers national competitions for women in sabre and épée, and the international federation has added women's épée to the World Championships.

The foil, which is the basic weapon of the sport, is a direct offshoot of the short dress sword introduced in the last half of the 17th century, probably at the court of France's Louis XIV. Weighing about 0.45 kg (1 lb), it has a flexible, rectangular blade, about 89 cm (35 in) in length, and a bell guard to protect the hand. Touches are scored with the point of the blade and must land within

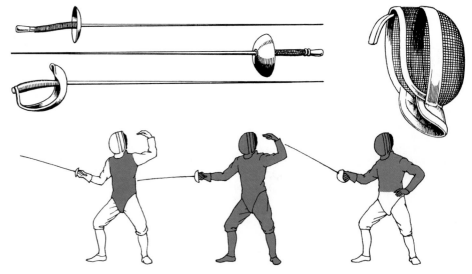

The three basic weapons used in competitive fencing are the foil, the épée, and the sabre. The foil and the épée, or dueling sword, have long, flexible blades and are used for thrusting attacks. The sabre's blade, unlike that of the foil or épée, has two cutting edges and is used for either thrusting or slashing. The diagram of fencers in the on-guard position indicates the differing technique required by each weapon. The shaded portion of the fencers represents the accepted target zones. Fencers are required to wear a face mask and throat bib.

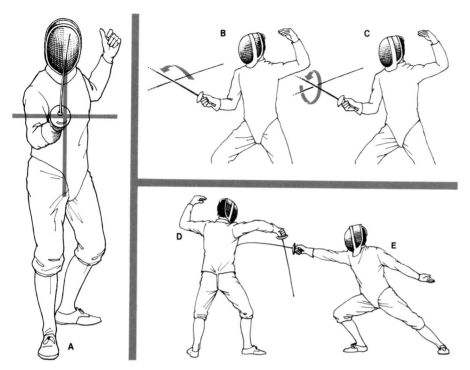

Crosslines imposed over the diagram of a fencer (A) indicate quadrants into which the target area is divided. (Right) Four basic maneuvers of swordsmanship are illustrated. To parry (B), a fencer employs a sideward sweep of his weapon to deflect an attack. The counterparry (C) is used to deflect an attack by means of a rapid circular movement of the weapon. The prime parry (D), which involves a swift, downward sweep of the weapon, is used to fend off an attack to the upper central target area. The lunge (E), the fundamental technique of attack, is executed with a swift forward stride with the right foot in an attempt to reach the opponent before a defensive reaction can occur.

the torso of the body, from the neckband of the fencer's uniform to the hipline, the groin, and back.

The épée is the weapon most closely resembling the old-style dueling sword. It is similar in length to the foil, but it weighs about 0.77 kg (1.7 lb), with a larger hand guard and a stiffer, triangular blade. Touches are scored with the point of the blade, and the entire body is a valid target area.

The sabre has a flexible, rectangular blade with cutting edges along the entire front and along one-third of the back edge. Its hand guard has one section attached to the pommel at the back of the handle. Touches are scored with the point as well as with the length of the blade, and the target area includes the front and back torso, arms, hands, neck, and head.

An electrical apparatus is now used in all fencing matches. For foil and épée, a spring-loaded tip is attached to the point of the weapon and is connected to a wire that runs inside the blade, through the sleeve of the contestant's jacket, and into a central scoring machine that registers hits. In the sabre, a sensor in the hand guard connects to the scoring machine.

Each time a fencer scores a touch, a point is gained. In a fencing bout the objective is to be the first to score five touches on the opponent. Bouts are officiated by a "president" with the assistance of a number of judges. The playing area is the "strip" or "piste," an area 14 m (46 ft) long and 2 m (6.5 ft) wide.

Fénelon, François de Salignac de la Mothe

[fay-nuh-lohn'] François de Fénelon, b. Aug. 6, 1651,

d. Jan. 7, 1715, was a French Roman Catholic churchman, theologian, and writer, whose works had considerable influence on the political and educational theories of the ENLIGHTENMENT. His sympathy for the mystical doctrine of QUIETISM and his treatise *Télémaque* (1699), an implicit criticism of Louis XIV's government, earned him numerous enemies at court and in the church. He also wrote (1687) an important treatise on the education of girls.

Fenian cycle   see IRISH LITERATURE

Fenians

The Fenians, or Irish Republican Brotherhood (IRB), was a revolutionary society founded in 1858 to overthrow British rule in Ireland. Its American wing, which led raids on Canada in 1866 and 1870, was an important center of Irish-American politics in the late 19th century. In Ireland, the brotherhood declined after an abortive rebellion in 1867. Many of its adherents drifted over to the more promising constitutional methods of Charles Stewart PARNELL's Home Rule movement. Nevertheless, the IRB survived to organize the EASTER RISING of 1916, and its spirit lives on in the IRISH REPUBLICAN ARMY.

See also: IRELAND, HISTORY OF.

fennel

Fennel, *Foeniculum vulgare* var. *dulce*, is a perennial herb cultivated as an annual and grown for its small, fragrant fruits (fennel seeds), which are mildly licorice-flavored and are used as a food seasoning. The large-leaf bases of *finocchio*, or Florence fennel, *F. vul-*

gare var. *azoricum*, are eaten as a vegetable. Fennel oil is used in liqueurs, candies, and perfumes. The plant is native to southern Europe and widely cultivated in temperate and subtropical regions.

Fenollosa, Ernest Francisco [fen-uh-loh'-suh]

The American educator and orientalist Ernest Francisco Fenollosa, b. Salem, Mass., Feb. 18, 1853, d. Sept. 21, 1908, pioneered Western studies of Far Eastern art and literature and also made contributions in American art education. Graduated (1874) from Harvard, he taught philosophy and economics at the newly founded Imperial University in Tokyo from 1878 to 1886 and later (1887–90) was on the staff of Tokyo's Imperial Museum. He undertook studies of the traditional arts of the Orient and urged the preservation of ancient art treasures in Japan, then preoccupied with emulating modern Western traditions. With Arthur Dow of Columbia Teacher's College, he later developed a system of art education that incorporated Far Eastern aesthetics, which was implemented in American public schools in the early 20th century.

fer-de-lance [fair-duh-lans']

Fer-de-lance, *Bothrops atrox*, is a venomous pit viper in the family Crotalidae related to the RATTLESNAKE. Its name is derived from the Creole-French *fer-de-lance*, meaning "head of a lance," which refers to the shape of the SNAKE's head. Its habitat extends from southern Mexico into tropical South America, but it is also found in some islands of the Lesser Antilles. Maximum size is 1.5 to 1.8 m (5 to 6 ft). The coloration is olive gray crossed by dark bands with yellow or greenish margins. The young are born live, with up to 70 in a brood.

See also: POISONOUS PLANTS AND ANIMALS; REPTILE.

The fer-de-lance inhabits sugarcane fields and normally feeds on rodents. Its bite is almost always fatal to humans.

feral children (fair'-ul]

Feral children are those said to have been nutured and reared by animals in the wild. Children who have wandered off and survived on their own and children who have been deliberately deprived of human contact may also be described as feral. Females of one species have long been known to adopt the young of another species. It has been hoped that scientific study of feral children would shed light on the origins of language and on the interrelation of culture and biology.

Although there have been more than 40 recorded cases of children being reared by animals—from a 14th-century Hessian wolf child to a gazelle boy in the Spanish Sahara (1966) and a contemporary wolf boy in Sultanpur, India—most of the evidence has been secondhand and lacking in essential detail. No one case has afforded conclusive proof. Because feral children are always severely retarded when restored to human society, it has even been speculated that they are autistic children who have been abandoned by their parents (see AUTISM).

The best documented account of feral children is that of the wolf children of Midnapore, India, who were dug out of a wolf den by an Anglican missionary, the Reverend J. A. L. Singh, in 1920. Singh claimed that he personally rescued the children after having seen them living with the wolves. Although the children developed some social skills and the rudiments of language, they never became completely normal, and they died young. There is, however, no way of knowing to what extent their limitations were due to cultural deprivation.

Ferber, Edna

Edna Ferber, b. Kalamazoo, Mich., Aug. 15, 1887, d. April 16, 1968, was a popular American writer who described the diversity and panorama of American life, from Eastern society to Western pioneers. Many of her works were made into motion pictures, including the Pulitzer Prize–winning *So Big* (1924; films 1932 and 1953); *Show Boat* (1926), adapted by Jerome Kern and Oscar Hammerstein II into a successful musical play (1927; films, 1929, 1936, 1951); *Cimarron* (1930; films 1931 and 1961); *Giant* (1952; film 1956); and *Ice Palace* (1959; film 1960). With George S. Kaufman she wrote such popular stage comedies as *The Royal Family* (1927; film 1930) and *Dinner at Eight* (1932; film 1933).

Ferdinand II, King of Aragon

(Ferdinand the Catholic)   Ferdinand II, b. Mar. 10, 1452, d. Feb. 23, 1516, was king of Aragon (1479–1516) and king of Castile (as Ferdinand V, 1474–1504). He was the second son of John II, king of Aragon. In 1469, Ferdinand was married to ISABELLA I, who in 1474 succeeded her brother Henry IV and became queen of Castile and León. The marriage was a political success that made possible the later unification of Spain.

Ferdinand helped Isabella restore order in Castile after the civil wars of the preceding reign, and he was also the chief architect of the conquest (1492) of Granada, the last Moorish state in Spain. In his native Aragon, he maintained the traditional liberties of his subjects. When he instituted reforms, as in his settlement of the agrarian difficulties in Catalonia (the *Senténcia* of Guadalupe of 1484), he did so by strengthening traditional institutions. Lacking the religious fervor of Isabella, he nevertheless supported the INQUISITION and the expulsion of the Jews (1492) for political reasons.

Although his domestic policies were important for the

Ferdinand II of Aragon and Isabella I of Castile make their triumphal entry into Granada, the last Moorish stronghold in Spain. Ferdinand's victory over the Moors on Jan. 2, 1492, united Spain under the joint rule of the "Catholic kings." (Royal Chapel, Granada, Spain.)

development of Spain, Ferdinand's primary interest was in diplomacy and war. Cold, calculating, and devious, he was one of the models for Machiavelli's PRINCE. His greatest diplomatic achievement was the establishment of Spanish predominance in Italy through a complex series of campaigns (part of the ITALIAN WARS) and negotiations that brought him Naples in 1504 and greatly weakened his archrivals, the French. He also developed an elaborate system of matrimonial alliances to isolate France and prepare for the eventual unification of Spain and Portugal; but these proved less successful.

After Isabella's death in 1504, Ferdinand claimed the regency of Castile on behalf of his daughter JOAN THE MAD but was opposed by her Habsburg husband, PHILIP I, and a majority of the Castilian nobles. When Philip died in 1506, Ferdinand gained his prize but spent the remainder of the reign working against the succession of Philip's son, the future emperor CHARLES V. As Aragon did not recognize descent in the female line, he tried to conceive a son by his second wife, Germaine de Foix, in the hope of detaching his ancestral kingdom from Charles's inheritance. Fortunately for Spanish unity, he failed to do so.

Ferdinand I, Emperor of Austria

Ferdinand I, b. Apr. 19, 1793, d. June 29, 1875, succeeded his father, Francis I (earlier Holy Roman Emperor FRANCIS II) as emperor of Austria in 1835. Subject to fits of insanity, he was an ineffectual ruler, and the empire was governed by a council under Klemens von METTERNICH. Unable to deal with the REVOLUTIONS OF 1848, Ferdinand abdicated in favor of his nephew FRANCIS JOSEPH in December of that year.

Ferdinand I, Tsar of Bulgaria

Ferdinand I, b. Feb. 26, 1861, d. Sept. 10, 1948, was a German prince who was elected ruler of the principality of Bulgaria, then under Turkish sovereignty, in 1887. In 1908 he proclaimed Bulgaria's independence, with himself as tsar. His army fought the Turks victoriously in the first phase of the BALKAN WARS (1912–13), but he turned against his Serbian and Greek allies, and the second phase ended disastrously for Bulgaria. To achieve his expansionist ambitions, Ferdinand joined (October 1915) the Central Powers of World War I. The Bulgarian Army was defeated in September 1918, and Ferdinand abdicated on Oct. 4, 1918.

Ferdinand I, Holy Roman Emperor

Ferdinand I, b. Mar. 10, 1503, d. July 25, 1564, Holy Roman emperor (1558–64) and king of Hungary and Bohemia (1526–64), was one of the most successful of HABSBURG rulers. Born in Spain, he was the younger son of Philip of Habsburg and JOAN THE MAD of Castile. Ferdinand's elder brother, CHARLES V, gave him the Habsburg duchy of Austria and made him his representative in the imperial government of Germany (1522). In 1530, Charles had the German electors designate Ferdinand king of the Romans (heir presumptive to the imperial title).

Ferdinand had already succeeded (1526) through his wife, Anne, sister of LOUIS II of Hungary and Bohemia, to those two crowns. His relations with the local estates remained difficult, but in both countries Ferdinand established effective rule and a hereditary succession. The Turks continued to occupy a large part of Hungary, however, and the prince of Transylvania, John Zápolya, who also claimed the crown as JOHN I, occupied another part. In a bitter quarrel with Charles V, Ferdinand successfully insisted on his succession to the imperial title, against the claims of Charles's son, who became PHILIP II of Spain. In 1555 he negotiated the Peace of Augsburg, by which the German princes were given the right to choose between Roman Catholicism and Lutheranism. Ferdinand died in Vienna, and was succeeded in all his titles by his son MAXIMILIAN II.

Ferdinand II, Holy Roman Emperor

Ferdinand II, b. July 9, 1578, d. Feb. 15, 1637, was Holy Roman emperor from 1619 to 1637 and the principal champion of the Roman Catholic cause in the THIRTY YEARS' WAR. As archduke of Styria he banished the Protestant leaders of the Styrian estates. King of Bohemia from 1617, he crushed the rebellion of the Bohemian Protestants, who elected (1619) the elector palatine, FREDERICK V, as a rival king of Bohemia. This struggle precipitated the Thirty Years' War.

After 1626, Albrecht von WALLENSTEIN organized a huge imperial army that made Ferdinand the virtual military master of Germany. The emperor, however, had failed to think out a consistent policy, and he was content with the restoration of ecclesiastical property through the Edict of Restitution (1629) and with supporting Spanish ambitions in the Netherlands.

The jealous imperial electors blackmailed Ferdinand into dismissing Wallenstein in 1630; but the victories of GUSTAV II ADOLF of Sweden forced him to recall his hated general. After Gustav's death, Wallenstein's enemies accused him of treason and murdered him in 1634. The Spanish-imperial victory of Nördlingen in 1634 led most

German princes to conclude (1635) the Peace of Prague with Ferdinand. By this agreement, the Edict of Restitution was rescinded, but the princes' armies were placed under imperial command. Ferdinand's son, Ferdinand III, inherited the hostility of Sweden and France and the doubtful loyalty of the German princes.

Ferdinand III, Holy Roman Emperor

Ferdinand III, b. July 13, 1608, d. Apr. 2, 1657, was the Holy Roman emperor who ended the THIRTY YEARS' WAR in Germany. During the lifetime of his father, Ferdinand II, he succeeded to the thrones of Hungary (1625) and Bohemia (1627). He was an opponent of Albrecht von WALLENSTEIN, whom he succeeded as imperial commander in chief in 1634. In that year he won the battle of Nördlingen against the Swedes. As emperor (from 1637), Ferdinand took the lead in the negotiations that finally led to the Peace of Westphalia in 1648.

See also: WESTPHALIA, PEACE OF.

Ferdinand I, King of Naples

Ferdinand I, king of Naples, b. 1423, d. Jan. 25, 1494, was the illegitimate son of ALFONSO V of Aragon, who seized Naples in 1442. Succeeding to the Neapolitan throne in 1458, Ferdinand was faced with a baronial revolt in favor of the rival king, RENÉ OF ANJOU. This was suppressed in 1462, but Ferdinand's viciously authoritarian policies provoked another unsuccessful revolt (1485–87). In the tumultuous affairs of Italy as a whole, Ferdinand allied himself chiefly with Florence, with whose help he expelled (1481) the Turks from Otranto.

Ferdinand I, King of Portugal

Ferdinand I, b. Oct. 31, 1345, d. Oct. 22, 1383, succeeded his father, PETER I, to the Portuguese throne in 1367. Laying claim to the Castilian throne, Ferdinand fought two humiliating wars (1369–71, 1372–73) against Henry II of Castile and a third (1381–82) against Henry's successor, John I. English help from JOHN OF GAUNT in the last two wars was to little avail. By the final peace (1382), John I of Castile married Ferdinand's only legitimate child, Beatrice. This marriage would have given Portugal to Castile on Ferdinand's death but for the revolution led by Ferdinand's half brother, JOHN I.

Ferdinand, King of Romania

Ferdinand, b. Aug. 24, 1865, d. July 20, 1927, succeeded his uncle, CAROL I, as king of Romania in October 1914. Although a Hohenzollern, and thus related to the German royal family, he was induced to enter (August 1916) World War I on the Allied side by promises of territorial concessions. Romania was soon overrun by Austro-German forces, and Ferdinand had to conclude a separate peace in May 1918. He reentered the war, however, on Nov. 10, 1918 just before its conclusion and thus won the promised territories—Transylvania, and much of the Hungarian plain

—in the peace settlement. Ferdinand was crowned king of Greater Romania in 1922.

Ferdinand III, Spanish King of Castile

Ferdinand III, c.1200–1252, was king of the Spanish realm of Castile from 1217 to 1252. After inheriting the neighboring León in 1230, he permanently united the two kingdoms. By a series of sieges he captured Córdoba (1236), Jaén (1245), and Seville (1248) from the Moors; he also received the submission of the Moors of Murcia (1243). Ferdinand's cultural initiatives were brought to completion by his son, ALFONSO X. Ferdinand was canonized in 1671.

Ferdinand VI, King of Spain

Ferdinand VI, b. Sept. 23, 1713, d. Aug. 10, 1759, was king of Spain from 1746 to 1759. His reign was a time of reform, prosperity, and peace. In 1746 he succeeded his father, PHILIP V, on the throne. Ably assisted by his prime minister, the marqués de ENSENADA, he improved the tax and customs administrations, strengthened the armed forces, and developed the nation's economy. He pursued a foreign policy of neutrality between France and Britain. By the Concordat of 1754, he reduced the influence of the Roman Catholic church in the secular life of Spain. He founded (1752) the Academy of Fine Arts and encouraged culture and science. He was succeeded by his half brother, CHARLES III.

Ferdinand VII, King of Spain

Ferdinand VII, b. Oct. 14, 1784, d. Sept. 29, 1833, was king of Spain from 1808 to 1833. The son of CHARLES IV, he was an absolutist monarch whose reign was marked by discontent and rebellion. A riot in March 1808 frightened Charles IV into abdicating his crown to Ferdinand. Soon thereafter, Ferdi-

Ferdinand VII of Spain, portrayed here by Francisco Goya, assumed the throne by forcing his father's abdication in 1808. Imprisoned in France for six years, Ferdinand returned to Spain and suspended the constitution adopted in his absence. A rebellion in 1820 forced him to accept the constitution, but the French intervened to restore him to absolute power.

nand and Charles were lured to a meeting with NAPOLEON I at Bayonne. Napoleon forced Ferdinand to return the crown to Charles and forced Charles to surrender his rights to Napoleon. Thereupon Ferdinand was imprisoned in France until 1814, while French troops ravaged Spain.

When Ferdinand returned to Spain as king in 1814, he repudiated the revolutionary Constitution of 1812, reestablished the Inquisition, and embarked on a reign of terror against all suspected liberals. After an uprising by liberal officers in 1820, Ferdinand was captured and forced to respect the constitution. He restored his absolute power in 1823 and then persecuted his enemies so cruelly that even his supporters were horrified.

Ferdinand was an intriguer who abused those he dominated and groveled before those he feared. In his last years, old age and the influence of his fourth wife, María Cristina, led him to soften his policies. She persuaded him to revoke the Salic Law provision forbidding female rulers so that their daughter, the future ISABELLA II, might succeed Ferdinand. Isabella's succession, however, was contested by Ferdinand's brother, Carlos, and the CARLIST wars resulted.

Ferdinand I, King of the Two Sicilies   Ferdinand I, b. Jan. 12, 1751, d. Jan. 4, 1825, was a Spanish Bourbon who ruled (1816–25) as king of the Two Sicilies. When his father became king of Spain in 1759 as CHARLES III, Ferdinand inherited the thrones of Naples (as Ferdinand IV) and Sicily (as Ferdinand III). In 1768 he married the Austrian Maria Carolina, sister of MARIE ANTOINETTE of France. In 1799 the French revolutionary armies took Naples, and the couple fled briefly to Sicily; in 1806, NAPOLEON I again took Naples and again the couple fled to Sicily. The Congress of Vienna restored Naples to Ferdinand in 1815; he then combined Naples and Sicily to form the kingdom of the Two Sicilies and ruled as Ferdinand I. He was succeeded by his son Francis I.

Ferdinand II, King of the Two Sicilies   Ferdinand II, b. Jan. 12, 1810, d. May 22, 1859, king of the Two Sicilies from 1830, was the son and successor of Francis I. He began his reign with an amnesty for political prisoners and various reforms but gradually became more reactionary. Although forced to grant a constitution when revolution began in 1848, he subsequently rescinded it. The use of artillery to crush the rebellion won him the nickname "King Bomba."

Ferguson, James Edward [fur'-guh-suhn]   James Edward Ferguson, b. Bell County, Tex., Aug. 31, 1871, d. Sept. 21, 1944, was a governor of Texas who, after being impeached and removed from office, exercised power through his wife, Miriam A. Wallace Ferguson (1875–1961), who was twice governor (1925–27, 1933–35). "Pa" Ferguson was elected governor in 1914, but, accused of corruption, he was removed in 1917 and barred from public office. In 1924, "Ma" Ferguson ran and won; she was elected to a second term.

Fergusson, Francis   Francis Liesseline Fergusson, b. Albuquerque, N.Mex., Feb. 21, 1904, d. Dec. 19, 1986, was a noted American critic and scholar and the author of several influential works on literature and drama. The best known is *The Idea of a Theatre* (1949), an innovative work that continues to shape the ideas and practices of dramatic criticism. Other works include *Dante's Drama of the Mind* (1953), on the *Purgatorio*, and *Trope and Allegory: Themes Common to Dante and Shakespeare* (1977).

Fergusson, Robert   The Scottish poet Robert Fergusson, b. Sept. 5, 1750, d. Oct. 16, 1774, helped lead the 18th-century revival of poetry in the Scots dialect. His *Poems* (1773 and 1779) were an important influence on Robert Burns. His powerful and spirited satirical verse, first published in Ruddiman's *Weekly Magazine* and collected in 1773, includes "Auld Reekie."

Ferlinghetti, Lawrence [fur-lin-get'-ee]   Lawrence Ferlinghetti, b. Yonkers, N.Y., Mar. 24, 1919 or 1920, is an American poet who became associated with the beat movement of the 1950s. In 1953 he and Peter D. Martin founded City Lights, the first all-paperback bookstore in the United States. Located in San Francisco, it became a cultural center for young writers of the BEAT GENERATION. With profits from that enterprise, the two began to publish City Lights Books and the Pocket Poets Series. Their first publication was *Pictures of the Gone World* (1955), Ferlinghetti's first book of poems. His second and best-known work was *A Coney Island of the Mind* (1958). Later works include *Starting from San Francisco* (1961), *Tyrannus Nix?* (1969), and the prose journal *Back Roads to Far Places* (1971).

Fermanagh [fur-man'-uh]   Fermanagh (1988 est. pop., 50,000) is a district, formerly a county, in south central Northern Ireland. It has an area of 1,851 km^2 (715 mi^2). Enniskillen is the district town. The district is bisected from northwest to southeast by island-dotted Lough Erne. On both sides of the lake the land is hilly, rising to elevations of over 600 m (2,000 ft). Quarrying and stock farming are the principal occupations, and tourism is important. Settled during the prehistoric period, the district has numerous Celtic remains. During the early 17th century many English and Scottish immigrants settled there.

Fermat, Pierre de [fair-mah']   Pierre de Fermat, b. Aug. 17, 1601, d. Jan. 12, 1665, was a French mathematician who made important discoveries in ANALYTIC GEOMETRY and NUMBER THEORY and also worked on probability theory and optics. Mathematics was only a hobby for Fermat, who was a lawyer and government official in Toulouse for most of his life.

Pierre de Fermat, a French mathematician of the 17th century, made significant contributions to the development of differential calculus, number theory, optics, and probability theory.

In 1636, Fermat presented a system of analytic geometry similar to the one that René DESCARTES would propose a year later. Fermat's work, based upon an attempted reconstruction of the work of the Greek mathematician APOLLONIUS OF PERGA, made use of the algebra of François VIÈTE. A similar attempt to reconstruct an ancient work led to methods, similar to differentiation and integration, for finding the maxima and minima points of curves and the areas enclosed by curves.

Fermat's greatest work was in number theory. He was especially interested in the properties of PRIME NUMBERS and in the determination of families of solutions to sets of similar problems. His most famous theorem, known as Fermat's last theorem, states that the equation $x^n+y^n=z^n$, where x, y, and z are positive integers, has no solution if n is an integer greater than 2. Fermat wrote in the margin of his copy of the works of Apollonius: "I have discovered a truly remarkable proof [of this theorem] which this margin is too small to contain." The theorem has still not been proved, although current number-theory conjectures seem to imply its validity.

Fermat worked with Blaise PASCAL on the theory of probabilities. Together, they formulated the principles on which Christiaan HUYGENS founded the calculus of probabilities. Fermat published almost nothing during his lifetime: he usually announced his discoveries in letters to friends or simply noted results in the margins of his books. His work was largely forgotten until the mid-1800s.

fermentation   Fermentation is the chemical process by which living cells degrade sugar in the absence of air to yield part or all of the energy needed by an organism. Fermentation is also called anaerobic respiration, or anaerobic glycolysis. Certain microorganisms, such as YEAST and some bacteria, exist in the absence of oxygen and are called ANAEROBES; but most living things possess, in addition to anaerobic respiration, a subsequent chemical process called aerobic respiration, which re-quires molecular oxygen.

In fermentation the sugar molecules are converted to alcohol and lactic acid. Beer, wine, and cheese production and several other commercial processes require fermentation of certain kinds of yeast, bacteria, and molds.

The major chemical steps in fermentation involve the breakdown of a sugar, such as glucose, into pyruvic acid. This conversion involves the sequential action of at least a dozen specific enzymes. About 40 years of intensive research were devoted to discovering the details of this process. The METABOLISM of glucose to form pyruvic acid occurs in all cells, and chemical energy is extracted and stored in a compound called adenosine triphosphate for later use in metabolism (see ATP).

Fermentation yields relatively small amounts of energy, and for this reason large amounts of glucose must be degraded by aerobic organisms to maintain life under oxygen-poor conditions. The aerobic respiratory process uses the chemical products formed in fermentation and is called the tricarboxylic acid cycle, or the KREBS CYCLE. In this next stage of metabolism, namely, the breakdown of pyruvic acid in the presence of oxygen, much larger amounts of energy are liberated.

Fermi, Enrico   [fair'-mee, ayn-ree'-koh]   The Italian physicist Enrico Fermi, b. Sept. 29, 1901, d. Nov. 28, 1954, is best known as a central figure in the MANHATTAN PROJECT to build the first ATOMIC BOMB. Fermi's early work on the statistical distribution of FUNDAMENTAL PARTICLES led him to divide these atomic constituents into two groups, known as fermions and bosons, depending on their spin characteristics. This division is now accepted as standard. His subsequent work on radioactivity and atomic structure involved experiments on the production of artificial radioactivity by bombarding matter with neutrons, for which he received the 1938 Nobel Prize for physics (see NUCLEAR ENERGY). In collaboration with other eminent scientists, Fermi experimented with nuclear fission at Columbia University. This work culminated in the first sustained nuclear

Enrico Fermi conducted Nobel-prize-winning experiments in radioactivity before emigrating from Italy to the United States and commencing work on the atomic bomb. Fermi developed a statistical method for predicting the behavior of atomic particles and later led the group that achieved the first self-sustaining fission reaction.

reaction, on Dec. 2, 1942, at the University of Chicago. Further work at Los Alamos Scientific Laboratory led to the construction of the atomic bomb. After the war, Fermi accepted a post at the newly established Institute for Nuclear Studies at the University of Chicago and continued his work in the field of neutron physics.

▬

Fermi National Accelerator Laboratory   The Fermi National Accelerator Laboratory, or Fermilab, is a high-energy physics research center that was founded in 1967 near Chicago and named for Enrico Fermi. Fermilab is operated by Universities Research Association, and it is funded by the U.S. Department of Energy. The facility houses a 500 billion, or giga, electron-volt (500-GeV) proton synchrotron accelerator (see ACCELERATOR, PARTICLE). The addition to the accelerator in 1983 of a superconducting magnetic ring, the Tevatron, increased the potential to 1,000 GeV (1 TeV), and the later addition of an antiproton storage ring enabled researchers to achieve collision energies of about 1.8 TeV by 1987 (see DETECTOR, PARTICLE).

▬

fermion [fur'-mee-ahn]   A fermion is any FUNDAMENTAL PARTICLE that has half-odd-integral spin; that is, its angular momentum is an odd multiple of the quantity $h/2\pi$. Fermions, unlike bosons, obey the Pauli EXCLUSION PRINCIPLE. Light fermions, such as electrons, are called LEPTONS; heavy fermions, such as protons and neutrons, are called BARYONS.

▬

fermium [fur'-mee-uhm]   The chemical element fermium, named for Enrico Fermi, is a metal of the ACTINIDE SERIES in Group IIIB of the periodic table. Its symbol is Fm, its atomic number is 100, and the atomic weight of its stablest isotope is 257. Like other TRANSURANIUM ELEMENTS, fermium does not occur naturally. It and einsteinium were first produced in a thermonuclear explosion in the South Pacific in 1952 and identified by the American chemist Glenn Seaborg and his collaborators. All of its isotopes are radioactive, their half-lives ranging from a few milliseconds to about 100 days.

▬

fern   Ferns are vascular plants often placed in the class Filicineae in the five-kingdom system of classification. Their distinguishing features include conducting tissue, reproduction by spores, and leaves with a branching vein system. So-called fern allies (CLUB MOSSES, HORSETAILS, QUILLWORTS, and spike mosses) differ in having needlelike or scalelike leaves, each with but a single unbranched vein.

Ferns are found in all regions of the world except for the most severe deserts. They occur well above the Arctic Circle as well as in dry, rocky regions, high mountains, and lowland forests. Ferns are most richly developed in wet forests of tropical mountainous regions. In these regions the ferns are predominantly EPIPHYTES, which grow on the trunks and branches of trees and derive moisture and nutrients from mosses and humus accumulated on the trees.

Stout, erect stems and large fronds characterize many ferns of the genus Marattia, which includes 60 species found in the tropics and in New Zealand. These ferns bear their sporangia in clusters, known as synangia, which occur in pairs along each side of many leaf veins.

About 12,000 fern species are known. They are arranged in about 350 genera in 28 families. The precise numbers are debated by botanists and depend on opinions regarding the relative importance of certain characteristics.

Structure and Size. The most conspicuous part of the fern is its leaves, or fronds; the stem and roots are relatively inconspicuous. The stem is usually specialized as a rhizome, which creeps on or just beneath the soil level. The form of a fern varies considerably. Many have the typical dissected fronds associated with ferns, but other species have fronds that are undivided and straplike, grasslike, or star-shaped. One of the most distinctive fea-

Salvinia natans is a small, floating fern of Europe. Water ferns of the genus Salvinia bear three leaves at each node, or stem joint: two floating, or air, leaves (1) and one finely divided water leaf (2), which may function as a root.

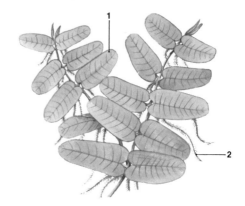

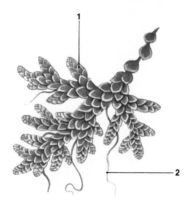

The mosquito fern is a North American water fern that has been introduced into Europe. It bears minute air leaves (1) and has roots (2) that hang freely in the water. The leaves of Azolla contain a symbiotic blue-green alga, Anabaena azollae, which apparently fixes atmospheric nitrogen for its host.

The royal fern grows in the wetlands, bogs, and meadows of North America and northwestern Europe. Under favorable conditions it may reach a height of more than 1.8 m (6 ft). Feathery, light-brown, spore-bearing leaflets (1) occur at the tips of fertile leaves; the sterile leaflets (2) are oblong and widely spaced.

tures of ferns is the way in which the leaves are developed during growth. In most other plant groups the leaves enlarge in all directions at once, but in ferns they mature progressively from the base to the tip, resulting in a coiled juvenile leaf, called a crosier or fiddlehead. As the frond matures at the base, it gradually unrolls.

Most ferns are between 10 and 91 cm (4 and 36 in) long. Tree ferns, however, have stems that are often 18-m-high (60-ft) trunks, crowned with fronds measuring 3 m (10 ft) long. At the other extreme are certain tropical-rainforest ferns with fronds only one cell thick. These "filmy ferns" may have fronds less than 13 mm (0.5 in) long.

The adder's-tongue fern (right) and moonwort (left) belong to the family of succulent ferns, Ophioglossaceae, which is not closely related to other fern groups. Adder's-tongue, common in fields and woodlands, bears a single green leaf and a fertile stalk that resembles a snake's tongue. Moonwort, found on dry meadows and hillsides, has leaflets shaped like half-moons and a stalk topped by long, spore-bearing clusters. Both species are small, usually less than 15 cm (6 in) tall, and produce fronds annually from underground stems.

Various ferns occupy aquatic habitats. The water clover, genus *Marsilea*, has rhizomes rooted in the mud with fronds like four-leaf clovers above the water. The mosquito fern, *Azolla*, and water spangles, *Salvinia*, float on the surface, with roots or rootlike appendages dangling beneath.

The Reproductive Cycle. A noteworthy feature of the fern's REPRODUCTION cycle is that two very different reproductive forms exist in every species, a phenomenon known as ALTERNATION OF GENERATIONS. The familiar form of the fern is the sporophyte generation. The other form, the gametophyte generation, exists as an inconspicuous plant, the prothallus.

A mature fern plant bears spore cases (sporangia) on its frond, usually on the lower surface. In most ferns the sporangia are found in clusters, called sori, of several to 100 sporangia or more. Each sporangium, consisting of a stalk and capsule, generally produces 64 spores. The spores are discharged from the sporangia and fall to the ground or float some distance in the air. Those falling in moist regions germinate, sending out a green filament of cells that broadens with further growth to form the heart-shaped prothallus, which obtains water and minerals from the soil by hairlike rhizoids. Antheridia, containing sperm, and archegonia, each containing an egg, are produced on the lower surface of the prothallus. The sperm require water, such as rain or dew, in which to swim to the egg. The fertilized egg divides many times to form the new fern, thus completing the life cycle.

Vegetative Reproduction. In addition to reproduction by spores, many ferns reproduce vegetatively. Some produce buds on the roots or the fronds. The members of the Boston fern genus, *Nephrolepis*, send out slender, hairlike stems (stolons) that produce new plants when they touch the soil. Many ferns multiply through rhizome branching. Some ferns are propagated commercially by tissue culture; this is done by removing a living stem tip and growing it on nutrient agar. With special sterile treatment it will grow and divide, creating hundreds of plants from a single stem tip.

Evolution. Ferns evolved in the Devonian Period, nearly 390–340 million years ago. During the Carboniferous Period (the Coal Age), ferns and seed ferns, which may have evolved from a common ancestral group, were a major part of the vegetation. The Cretaceous Period marks the appearance of modern ferns. The seed ferns, extinct today, probably gave rise to the flowering plants and to the cycads.

Fernández de Córdoba, Gonzalo [fair-nahn'-dayth day kohr'-doh-bah, gohn-thah'-loh] Gonzalo Fernández de Córdoba, b. Sept. 1, 1453, d. Dec. 1 or 2, 1515, was a Spanish general known as el Gran Capitán. He fought in the wars to drive the Muslims from Spain and helped negotiate the surrender (1492) of the Moorish kingdom of Granada. After France had invaded the Kingdom of Naples in the ITALIAN WARS, Fernández de Córdoba was sent (1495) to Italy with an army; he soon forced the French to withdraw. When the Treaty of Granada (1500), which divided Naples between France and Spain, proved unworkable, the war was resumed. Fernández de Córdoba's brilliant victories at Cerignola and at Garigliano in 1503 brought all of Naples under Spanish rule. He was viceroy of Naples from 1504 to 1507.

Fernández de Lizardi, José Joaquín [fair-nahn'-dayth day lee-thahr'-dee, hoh-say' hoh-ah-keen'] José Joaquín Fernández de Lizardi, b. Nov. 15, 1776, d. June 21, 1827, was a Mexican novelist, poet, dramatist, and avid supporter of Mexico's independence from Spain. His literary reputation is based on three novels, *The Itching Parrot* (1816; Eng. trans., 1942), *La Quijotita y su prima* (Miss Quixote and Her Cousin, 1819), and *Don Catrín de la Fachenda* (1832). *The Itching Parrot*, a scathing satire of Mexico's middle class, reflects both the influence of the 18th-century French *philosophes* and the form of the Spanish picaresque novel. It is considered the first Latin American novel.

Fernando Po see BIOKO

Ferrar, Nicholas [fair'-ur] Nicholas Ferrar, b. Feb. 22, 1592, d. Dec. 4, 1637, was an English religious figure who founded the community of Little Gidding. Giving up a brilliant political career, he settled (1625) at Little Gidding, Huntingdonshire, where he led his household, consisting of his mother and about 30 others, through a schedule of regulated prayer, work, and neighborhood assistance. His Anglican lay community incurred Puritan hostility and was broken up during the English Civil War. T. S. Eliot used the community as the setting for his poem *Little Gidding*, part of *Four Quartets*.

Ferrara [fer-rah'-rah] Ferrara (1988 est. pop., 143,046) is the capital city of Ferrara province in the Emilia-Romagna region in northern Italy, 45 km (28 mi) northeast of Bologna. Processed fruits and sugar, chemicals, plastics, and shoes are made there. Monuments include the medieval Este Castle (begun 14th century), the Cathedral of San Giorgio (begun 1135), and the Renaissance Schifanoia and Diamanti palaces.

First mentioned in 8th-century sources, Ferrara was, from the early 13th century, a principality of the ESTE family, with its great Renaissance court. The Council of Ferrara was held there in 1438. In 1598, Ferrara became part of the Papal States. The pope ceded it to the French in 1797 but regained it in 1815. In 1860, Ferrara became part of united Italy.

Ferrara-Florence, Council of The Council of Ferrara-Florence (1438–45), held successively at Ferrara, Florence, and Rome, was an ecumenical council of the Roman Catholic church convened for the primary purpose of ending the schism between that church and the Eastern ORTHODOX CHURCH. After much discussion of their theological differences, the two churches were formally reunited in 1439. The Orthodox leaders had difficulty, however, winning approval from the clergy at home, and all semblance of unity dissolved after the fall of the Byzantine Empire to the Ottoman Turks in 1453.

The council also negotiated reunion with several smaller eastern churches (see ARMENIAN CHURCH, NESTORIAN CHURCH, JACOBITE CHURCH, and EASTERN RITE CHURCHES) and challenged CONCILIARISM.

Ferraro, Geraldine Geraldine Anne Ferraro, b. Newburgh, N.Y., Aug. 26, 1935, was nominated as the first woman vice-presidential candidate of a major U.S. party in 1984. Ferraro, a lawyer, became an assistant district attorney in Queens, N.Y., in 1974. Four years later she won election to Congress as a Democrat. Twice reelected, she gained (1983) a seat on the House budget committee and in 1984 chaired the Democratic platform committee. Before the 1984 nominating convention, the almost-certain Democratic presidential candidate, Walter Mondale, chose Ferraro as his running mate; at the convention they both were nominated. Ferraro became a national figure as she campaigned across the country and debated her Republican opponent, Vice-President George Bush, on television. The Mondale-Ferraro ticket, however, was crushingly defeated by President Ronald Reagan and Bush in the November election.

ferret [fair'-et]   Ferrets are mammals belonging to the WEASEL family, Mustelidae, order Carnivora. The ferret of Europe is the domesticated form of the polecat *Mustela putorius*. Since ancient times the ferret has been used to kill rats and to drive rabbits from their burrows. The black-footed ferret of the western United States is *M. nigripes*, which is on the verge of extinction.

The endangered status of the black-footed ferret probably results from reduced populations of prairie dogs, its main prey. These ferrets may use prairie dog burrows for shelter.

ferrite [fair'-yt]   Ferrites are ceramiclike, magnetic materials consisting of magnetic oxides, often ferric oxide combined with one or more other metals such as magnesium, zinc, or nickel. Ferrites exhibit a permanent MAGNETISM known as ferrimagnetism. Because of their magnetic properties, ferrites are used extensively in electronics and in radio technology. Memory cores in computers, cores for high-frequency coils, transformers, and antenna rods for AM radios are made of ferrites.

Ferry, Jules François Camille [fair-ee']   The French statesman Jules Ferry, b. Apr. 5, 1832, d. Mar. 17, 1893, reformed France's public school system and laid the foundation of the French colonial system. He served (1870–71) as mayor of Paris during the Prussian siege of the city and while the COMMUNE OF PARIS was in control. During most of the period from 1879 to 1885, Ferry was a government minister, serving twice as premier (1880–81, 1883–85). He was responsible for the laws of 1882 that established free and compulsory primary education and outlawed clerical teachers. He also helped acquire Tunisia, Tonkin (now part of Vietnam), Madagascar, and part of the Congo as French colonial holdings. His government fell after a French setback in Tonkin. In 1893, Ferry became president of the senate, but in the same year he was assassinated by a religious fanatic.

Fertile Crescent   Coined by the orientalist James Breasted in 1916, the name *Fertile Crescent* is given to the area of the Middle East where the earliest known civilizations of the ancient world began. The region is situated between mountains to the north and desert to the south and extends like an arc from the Mediterranean Sea to the head of the Persian Gulf, passing through present-day Israel, Jordan, northern Syria, southern Turkey, northern Iraq, and western Iran. The Fertile Crescent includes the areas once occupied by the ancient kingdoms of Palestine, at its western end; Assyria, in the central portion; and Babylonia and Elam, in the eastern part. A cultivatable area known for its arid summers and rainy winters, the Fertile Crescent coincides with the region where farming originated in the Middle East in the 9th millennium BC.

fertility, human   In humans, *fertility* is a medical term used to indicate a woman's capacity to conceive or a man's capacity to induce conception, whereas the term *infertility* indicates a failure or lack of such capacity. When used in DEMOGRAPHY, the term *fertility* refers to the frequency of births, whereas the term *fecundity* means the capacity for REPRODUCTION.

Medically speaking, primary infertility, or sterility, is the failure of a woman to conceive after one or more years of sufficiently frequent, normal sexual intercourse. Secondary infertility is the inability to conceive during the year following a pregnancy. To learn why sterility occurs in a couple, they are given medical tests—including testing of a SEMEN sample and tests to establish whether ovulation is occurring regularly—to detect the presence of any illness or abnormality that may be preventing pregnancy. A primary cause of reversible sterility in men is varicocele, a varicose condition of veins in the scrotum. Other simple causes of a low SPERM count are stress, fatigue, and excessive use of alcohol or tobacco. A total lack of sperm, however, is considered untreatable.

In women, failure to ovulate may result from glandular or psychological disturbances that can be corrected. Obstructions of the fallopian tubes that prevent passage of the fertilized egg may be caused by infections and can also be treated, by surgery. Human PITUITARY GLAND extracts, rich in follicle-stimulating hormone (FSH), can sometimes stimulate ovulation. These extracts, however, given under the name Pergonal, have induced multiple births in a high percentage of the women receiving them (see MULTIPLE BIRTH). Another so-called fertility drug, clomiphene citrate, or Clomid—a synthetic antiestrogen—has induced a smaller percentage of such births but can also cause uncomfortable side effects. ARTIFICIAL INSEMINATION techniques may also be employed. Conversely, couples wishing to prevent conception may resort to a number of BIRTH CONTROL methods.

fertility rites   Fertility rites are ceremonies of a magic-religious nature performed to insure the continuity of life. From earliest time, humans have performed these rites in an attempt to control the environment. Expressed as invocations, incantations, prayers, hymns, processions, dances, and sacred dramas, these ritual activities were believed to be closely connected with the processes of nature. If the enactment of fertility rites could induce fertility in the animal and human worlds, the vegetable world would also be stimulated to reproduction, resulting in an abundant harvest. The basis for such rites was usually a belief in sympathetic MAGIC, based on the assumption that the principle of life and fertility was one and indivisible.

A persistent theme of primitive fertility rituals was the freeing of the waters and the subsequent regeneration of the earth. Many hymns of the *Rig-Veda* are supplications to Indra, in his role as god of weather and war, to slay the giant who had imprisoned the great rivers of India (see VEDAS). Such personification of natural phenomena was common. Another prevalent myth of pastoral societies, often enacted as sacred drama, was the search of the earth goddess for her lost lover, brother, or child who either has been killed or has disappeared from Earth. Symbolizing death and the return of vegetation and life, this myth was recorded as early as 3000 BC in the Babylonian cult of ISHTAR (Inanna) and Tammuz, and it is traceable through the Sabeans at Harran (present-day Yemen). Another example is the death and resurrection of the Phoenician-Greek deity ADONIS, beloved of Aphrodite. The Greek myth of Demeter and Persephone (Kore) represents the same theme, as does the Egyptian myth of Osiris and Isis.

Sacred marriages frequently have formed part of the fertility ritual; the effectiveness of this symbolic union at times depended on the chastity of the participants. Ritual prostitution, human and animal sacrifice, and displays of phallic symbols were also sometimes believed to stimulate fertility. In a number of preliterate societies, the role of the god was combined with that of the king, and the fertility of the land and people was linked with the king's state of perfection and purification.

Processions and dances also play a fundamental part in fertility rites: the sword dance of the Maruts in the *Rig-Veda*; of the Greek Kouretes, a band of youths of semidivine origin; and of the Corybantes, Bacchantes, and Maenads are all intimately linked with the worship of the vegetation spirit. In Britain, May Day celebrations and the Maypole dance originate in spring fertility festivals. Many similar rites are recalled in the folk traditions of various European nations.

---

fertilization   Fertilization is the stage of sexual REPRODUCTION in which a male reproductive cell, or sperm, fuses with a female reproductive cell, or egg, resulting in the mixing of the genetic information carried in the parent cells. Fertilization in plants or animals initiates the development of the embryo and begins the events in the development of the adult individual.

Two basic patterns of mating and fertilization occur among animals. In external fertilization in fish, frogs, and toads, for example, mating partners come close to each other and simultaneously spawn—that is, release sperm

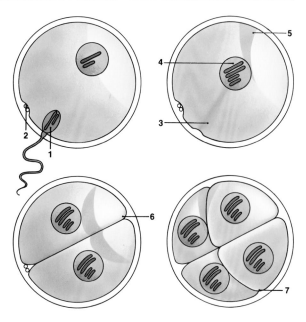

Fertilization of a frog's egg occurs in shallow water. When a sperm (1) from the male penetrates the egg, the second polar body (2) forms. The sperm leaves a trail (3) caused by the displacement of granules in a layer of pigment. The nuclei of the sperm and egg fuse, forming a zygote (4). Penetration by the sperm induces a shift in the pigment layer, resulting in the formation of a gray crescent (5) opposite the point of entry, which determines the first line of cleavage (6). Successive divisions (7) form a ball of cells.

and eggs directly into the water. Frequent chance collisions among the closely spaced reproductive cells, or gametes, then lead to many fertilizations. The second pattern is internal fertilization, which is characteristic of such land animals as mammals, birds, reptiles, insects, spiders, and many worms. Mating partners come into physical contact, and an orifice or copulating organ of the male ejects flagellated, or swimming, sperm into the female's reproductive system.

Fertilization in the higher plants occurs as the POLLEN grain contacts the stigma of a FLOWER of the same species. The pollen tube, after penetrating the tissues of the flower, produces two sperm cells; one sperm will fuse with an egg cell within the stigma to complete fertilization.

---

fertilizer   A fertilizer is any natural or manufactured material that is added to soil to increase plant growth. Plants require the primary nutritional elements, nitrogen, phosphorus, and potassium; the secondary elements, calcium, magnesium, and sulfur; and small amounts of boron, chlorine, cobalt, copper, iron, manganese, molybdenum, and zinc—called micronutrients or trace elements. Since plants obtain all these elements from the soil, they must be added to soils deficient in them. Manufactured fertilizers have become essential in modern agriculture. Their wide use has significantly improved the production and quality of food and feed crops.

History of Fertilizer Use

The value of animal MANURE for improving the productivity of land was recognized perhaps as early as the beginnings of agriculture (see AGRICULTURE, HISTORY OF). Greco-Roman agricultural writers enumerated the merits of using natural animal and plant fertilizer. The Elizabethan philosopher Sir Francis BACON was the first to describe scientific research on fertilizers made from COMPOSTS and manures.

The second John Winthrop (1606–76), a founder of the Connecticut colonies, established a stock company for manufacturing SALTPETER (potassium nitrate) from the excreta of farm animals. Most of the early fertilizer products, however, were made from agricultural and industrial residues. Peruvian GUANO was first imported for use as a fertilizer in 1849. The German chemist Justus von LIEBIG demonstrated the importance of mineral elements in the soil to the healthy growth of plants. The production of synthetic nitrate for fertilizer began in the years after World War I.

Composition and Grades of Fertilizers

The usefulness of a fertilizer for crop production depends on its chemical composition. Although the value of a fertilizer is dependent chiefly on its content of nitrogen (N), phosphate (P_2O_5), and potassium (K_2O), the presence or absence of other elements may be a factor in its choice for a particular crop. Fertilizers are numbered according to the proportion of nitrogen, phosphate, and potassium, respectively. Thus, a 10-20-20 fertilizer contains 10% nitrogen, 20% phosphate, and 20% potassium.

The term *simple* is normally used to denote a fertilizer containing a single plant nutrient. For example, ammonium sulfate is a simple nitrogen fertilizer. Some fertilizer compounds contain two of the primary plant nutrients and are called multiple nutrient materials.

The choice of fertilizers also involves the physical condition of the material. Phosphates and potassium compounds are usually applied in solid form, since they rarely present caking problems. Solid nitrogen fertilizers, on the other hand, frequently cake or absorb moisture. Large-scale applications of nitrogenous fertilizers are usually dispensed in the form of anhydrous AMMONIA, a pressurized, liquid ammonia.

Problems Associated with Fertilizer Use

The problems involved in the heavy use of fertilizers are related to pollution and the quality of crops.

Eutrophication. When a body of water is overly rich in plant nutrients, the growth of algae and other aquatic vegetation expands far beyond normal limits. If this process, called EUTROPHICATION, continues for a considerable length of time, the water may eventually silt up and the area will become bog. The important nutrients involved in this process are nitrogen and phosphorus.

Effects on Crop Quality. The extensive use of fertilizers may have a noticeable negative effect on both the growth and the quality of certain plants and crops, such as potatoes, tobacco, and forage grasses.

New Sources in the Future

Technologies are being developed that may soon make possible new fertilizer materials and methods for applying them.

Sewage Sludge. Liquid SLUDGE—the end product of sewage treatment—has great potential as a fertilizer, and some areas have experimented with sludge composting. New methods for treating sludge, to remove unwanted elements and to ensure that all infectious matter has been destroyed, are being tried.

Manures. Huge quantities of manure accumulate in regions where large numbers of cattle or poultry are found. Techniques are being developed for processing this manure, removing disease microorganisms by sterilization, and converting manure into a more transportable form.

▬

Fessenden, Reginald Aubrey [fes'-en-den]   The American physicist and electrical engineer Reginald Aubrey Fessenden, b. East Bolton, Quebec, Oct. 6, 1866, d. July 22, 1932, is known for his early work in wireless communication. He began his research at the University of Pittsburgh; after designing a high-frequency alternator, he broadcast (1906) the first program of speech and music ever transmitted by radio. That same year, he established two-way transatlantic wireless telegraph communication. Fessenden also invented the heterodyne system of radio reception, the sonic depth finder, the radio compass, submarine signaling devices, the smoke cloud (for tank warfare), and the turbo-electric drive (for battleships).

▬

Fessenden, William Pitt   William Pitt Fessenden, b. Boscawen, N.H., Oct. 16, 1806, d. Sept. 8, 1869, was a leading senator during the U.S. Civil War and Reconstruction period. Elected U.S. senator from Maine in 1854, Fessenden, who opposed extension of slavery into the western territories, was an organizer of the Republican party. A member of the Senate Finance Committee from 1857 and its chairman from 1861, he played a major role in the financial administration of the Civil War. In 1864–65 he was secretary of the treasury. Returning to the Senate in 1865, Fessenden chaired the Joint Congressional Committee on Reconstruction and wrote most of the report (1866) that asserted congressional control over RECONSTRUCTION. In 1868 he was one of seven Republican senators who voted for acquittal in the impeachment trial of President Andrew Johnson.

▬

fetal alcohol syndrome   Fetal alcohol syndrome (FAS) is a grouping of defects that may occur in infants born to women who drink alcohol during pregnancy. Signs of FAS include low birth weight and an abnormally small head; facial deformities such as small and narrow or very round eyes, flattened midface and widely spaced nose, very narrow upper lip, and oddly set ears; and mild to moderate mental retardation. As FAS children develop, they also often exhibit behavioral and cognitive problems. In some cases the defects are severe and are accompanied by other systemic abnormalities. When some but not all of these signs are observed, they are more generally known as fetal alcohol effects (FAE).

FAS has been observed worldwide. In the United States, perhaps one out of every 750 newborn infants displays the full range of FAS sysmptoms, indicating that 30 to 40 percent of mothers who drink heavily give birth to such children. No safe lower limits can be placed on drinking levels, however, because even women who drink as little as two drinks a week have given birth to children with FAE.

fetish [fet'-ish]   A fetish is an object believed to have magical powers; it may be either a natural object, such as a shell, or an artifact, such as a wood carving. The word is derived from the Portuguese *feitico*, meaning a charm, talisman, or AMULET. Portuguese sailors coined the term in the 15th century when they observed the veneration that West-Coast Africans had for such objects, which they wore on their persons.

The most important aspects of the fetish are that it is believed to embody the power of the sacred and that it is portable, making it always accessible to the bearer. Auguste Comte and Charles de Brosses interpreted the fetish as a basis for their theories concerning the origin of religion.

fetishism [fet'-ish-izm]   Fetishism is sexual interest focused on an object, symbol, or body part. Articles of clothing such as panties, bras, shoes, stockings, or handkerchiefs may be objects of intense sexual interest. Fetishists, usually male, also fixate upon body parts such as eyes, ears, hair, hands, or feet.

A minimal degree of fetishism can probably be found in most people. Fetishism as a psychosexual abnormality

The African fetish figure wears or bears magical objects believed to contain powerful spirits. The many objects on this Kongo fetish include small wood sculptures, bits of cloth, nails, and pieces of metal. This fetish is malevolent: its spirits, when released, do harm.

exists when individuals have strong preferences for a fetish, or believe they must have the fetish in order to achieve sexual gratification. The fetish may even be preferred to a sexual partner.

fetus   see EMBRYO; PREGNANCY AND BIRTH

Feuchtwanger, Lion [foysht'-vahng-ur, lee'-ohn]
Lion Feuchtwanger, b. July 7, 1884, d. Dec. 21, 1958, was a German historical novelist and playwright. To actualize themes for the present, he combined psychological insights with historical parallels to contemporary events. His most famous work, *Jud Süss* (1925; trans. as *Power*, 1926), depicts the rise of a ruthless 18th-century Jew who regains his humanity by resisting conversion to Christianity.

feud   A feud is an ongoing exchange of hostilities between two closely related groups of people. Antagonisms are fueled by intermittent acts ranging from insults to physical violence. Only rarely are all parties to the conflict involved in fighting, however, and strict rules of conduct usually exclude women and children from the hostilities. Actual fighting may be rare, but adult men must be prepared to offend and defend at all times lest their personal honor or that of their group or lineage be defamed. In long-standing feuds, every social issue may become a new source of disagreement.

Feuds have generally occurred between groups of people sharing the same occupations and religious and civil institutions but who retain a high degree of local autonomy. A well-known example is the 19th-century feud between the Hatfields and the McCoys of the Appalachian Mountain region of the eastern United States. Feuds were also common in the frontier areas of 19th-century America. Although feuding has been outlawed in most countries of the West, the hostile exchanges of the feud still occur in various non-Western societies and even among some neighboring urban groups in America today. Especially in the urban ghetto, acts of violence sometimes help to sustain strong social ties and to define social relationships among the young men of such groups as they pass from boyhood to manhood.

feudalism   Feudalism was a medieval contractual relationship among the European upper classes, by which a lord granted land to his man in return for military service. Feudalism was further characterized by the localization of political and economic power in the hands of lords and their vassals and by the exercise of that power from the base of castles, each of which dominated the district in which it was situated. The term *feudalism* thus encompasses a division of governmental power spreading over various castle-dominated districts. It does not, however, refer to the social and economic relationships between the peasants and their lords, which are defined as MANORIALISM.

This 14th-century manuscript shows King Philip VI of France, flanked by his vassals, hearing a case against Robert of Artois. In feudal society, lords were expected to take counsel from their vassals. (Bibliothèque Nationale, Paris.)

Origins and Early History. Feudalism was, in its nascence, a blend of Roman custom (for example, conditional tenure of land dependent upon the fulfilling of named obligations) and Germanic elements (for example, sworn fealty, or faithfulness). Because the military service of KNIGHTS was a central element of feudalism, some historians find the introduction of heavy cavalry during the 8th century a key factor in its development; others point to the introduction of the stirrup, which greatly increased the efficiency of fighting on horseback.

Systematic feudalism is generally thought to have emerged in the Frankish territories during the 9th and 10th centuries. Civil wars and the last wave of invasions of Europe by the Magyars and the Vikings accelerated the devolution of defense to the local level. During this period of breakdown of centralized royal control, the church came to govern its own holdings, and effective secular government contracted to the small units ruled by castles, in which lords and their men were bound together by service-and-protection contracts.

In theory, diagrammatic feudalism resembles a pyramid, with the lowest vassals at its base and the lines of authority flowing up to the peak of the structure, the king. In practice, however, this scheme varied from nation to nation. In the East Frankish (German) kingdom, which became the nucleus of the HOLY ROMAN EMPIRE, the pyramid ended at the level below king or emperor, that of the great princes. In other words, the German kings were never able to impose themselves at the top of a system that

had developed out of royal weakness. They were recognized as feudal suzerains but did not exercise sovereignty. In the West Frankish kingdom (France) the kings finally overcame the same handicap, using their positions as feudal suzerains to become feudal sovereigns. In England the kings were at the top of the pyramid, ruling by grace of their offices rather than by the grace of their feudal positions. The extent of feudalism must not be exaggerated, however. Many portions of Europe were never completely feudalized; feudalism as described here was largely confined to northern France, western Germany, England, the Norman kingdom of Sicily, the Crusader states, and northern Spain.

Institutions. Feudal institutions varied greatly from region to region, and few feudal contracts had all the features here described. Common to all, however, was the process by which one nobleman (the vassal) became the man of another (the lord) by swearing homage and fealty. This was originally done simply to establish a mutually protective relationship, but by the early 11th century vassalage brought with it a fief—land held in return for military service. With the vassal's holding of a fief went rights of governance and of jurisdiction over those who dwelt on it.

Lord and vassal were interlocked in a web of mutual rights and obligations, to the advantage of both. Whereas the lord owed his vassal protection, the vassal owed his lord a specified number of days annually in offensive military service and in garrisoning his castle. The lord was expected to provide a court for his vassals, who, in turn, were to provide the lord with counsel before he undertook any initiative of importance to the feudal community as a whole—for example, arranging his own or his children's marriages or planning a crusade.

Financial benefits accrued largely to the lord. A vassal owed his lord a fee known as relief when he succeeded to his fief, was expected to contribute to the lord's ransom were he captured and to his crusading expenses, and had to share the financial burden when the lord's eldest son was knighted and his eldest daughter married. In addition, a vassal had to seek his lord's permission to marry off his daughter (lest the land conveyed as dowry fall into the hands of an antagonist) and for himself to take a wife. Should the vassal die leaving a widow or minor children, they were provided for by the lord. Should the vassal die without heirs, his fief escheated, or reverted to the lord.

Decline. Feudalism had hardly begun before its first important sign of decline appeared. This was the inheritance of fiefs, replacing the previous original individual feudal contract; when a lord was no longer able to enter into an agreement with his vassal, freely accepted by both parties, then the personal nature of the feudal contract was seriously undermined. This transformation occurred before 1100, as did the beginning of the commutation of personal military service into money payments (called scutage in England), which further undermined the personal loyalty central to original feudalism. A late medieval outgrowth of this commutation was contract service in return for land or money, embodying loyalty to a lord in return for help (maintenance) and protection—what was known in England as bastard feudalism. This form of social bond enabled wealthy lords to field an army quickly when needed and gave them tangible and effective means to assert their own private influence in political and social life, to the detriment of orderly central government. Something else that appeared early in the history of feudalism was liege homage, by which a man who was the vassal of more than one lord chose one as his paramount lord, thus again subverting the original feudal idea of personal loyalty between lord and vassal.

The centralization of strong lordships, whether as kings (as in England and France) or territorial rulers (as in the Holy Roman Empire), obviously undercut the localization of government so essential to feudalism. So too did new forms of warfare during the 14th and 15th centuries, which made the limited service of the feudal army of knights anachronistic. Other reasons for feudalism's decline were familial and social. Family ties came to be seen as more important than particularistic territorial concerns; the economic and social gulf between greater and lesser nobles grew wider; and respect for historical ties of mutual relationships between lord and vassal steadily weakened. These circumstances, as well as the increasing division of inheritances, all combined to destroy feudalism, slowly and inexorably. The process was largely complete by the end of the 14th century.

Significance. The historical significance of feudalism defies brief statement. Feudalism afforded the structure by which most medieval European monarchies centralized. Constitutionally, the English-speaking world owes to feudalism the right of opposition to tyranny, representative institutions, resistance to taxation levied without consultation, and limited monarchy—since the king was bound by custom, by his own law, and by the necessity to practice self-restraint lest he be restrained by the community. Feudalism also contributed the contract theory of government—the idea that both the government and its citizens have reciprocal rights and obligations. Feudal legacies in cultural matters include CHIVALRY, from which many modern standards of a gentleman are derived; CASTLE architecture; and the epic, romance, and courtly literature.

Feuerbach, Anselm [foy'-ur-bahk, ahn'-selm]
Anselm Feuerbach, b. Sept. 12, 1829, d. Jan. 4, 1880, was a leading German academic painter, one of a group known as the "German-Romans" that included Arnold BÖCKLIN, Franz von Lenbach, and Hans von Marées. Much of Feuerbach's life was spent in Rome and Venice, where he was especially attracted to the art of Titian and Veronese.

Feuerbach's portraits, particularly those of his mistress and model Nanna Risi, are highly esteemed. Idealism and lofty, classical themes characterize his mythological paintings, such as *Medea* (1870; Staatsgemäldesammlungen, Vienna) and *Orpheus and Eurydice* (1869; Kunsthistorisches Museum, Vienna). After 17 years in Rome, Feuerbach was appointed professor of painting at the Vienna Academy in 1873. He remained there for three years, working on decorations for the assembly hall, but resigned after a nervous breakdown.

Feuerbach, Ludwig Ludwig Andreas Feuerbach, b. July 28, 1804, d. Sept. 13, 1872, was a German philosopher noted for his highly critical psychological analysis of religious belief and for his contribution to MATERIALISM. A theology student at Heidelberg and Berlin, he was drawn into philosophy through the influence of G. W. F. HEGEL. In 1836, Feuerbach moved to Bruckberg and collaborated with Arnold Ruge on the *Hallische Jahrbücher*, a review in which many of Feuerbach's writings were first published. During this period most of Feuerbach's significant books appeared: *The Essence of Christianity* (1841), *Principles of the Philosophy of the Future* (1843), and *The Essence of Religion* (1846). In his later years Feuerbach became a symbol for German liberals. His philosophical anthropology became a new point of departure for Hegelians such as Friedrich ENGELS and Karl MARX.

The German idealist Hegel believed in the primacy of an absolute reason that realized itself through nature and humanity; Feuerbach believed in the primacy of a person's own reason, which creates the only authentic reality he or she can know and the only selfhood he or she can use. Hegel had placed reality in abstract thought; Feuerbach placed reality in people.

This criticism of IDEALISM led Feuerbach to a critique of religion. God and an absolute reason, Feuerbach held, are merely projections of the human mind. When they are endowed with the best attributes, people are left with only the lesser ones. The resulting sense of sin and impotence impoverishes human life. Religion, Feuerbach conceded, had made a contribution to human evolution, but he held that religion was just another unconscious product of humankind's faculty for mythmaking. This faculty, Feuerbach said, could now become conscious through a knowledge of anthropology, psychology, and physiology. With such knowledge, humans could create true health and happiness here on Earth. Feuerbach concluded that theology and philosophy should properly be concerned only

Iphigenia, *painted by Anselm Feuerbach in 1862, is a monumental representation of his mistress and model, Nanna Risi. The subject, from Greek mythology, is the ill-fated daughter of Clytemnestra and Agamemnon. (Hessisches Landesmuseum, Darmstadt.)*

with the nature of human beings and with the humanization of God.

---

fever   Fever, or pyrexia, is a BODY TEMPERATURE that is elevated above the normal range: normal oral temperatures range from 98.6° F (37° C) in persons confined to bed to 99.0° F (37.4° C) in active persons; temperatures taken rectally usually register slightly higher. Body temperature is usually kept within the normal range by several mechanisms, which are controlled and integrated mainly in the hypothalamus region of the brain. Fever is not a disease itself but a symptom of disease. It is a sign of infectious disease, such as pneumonia, and may accompany certain kinds of cancers, a stroke or a heart attack, and various other disorders. Because many microorganisms cannot survive elevated temperatures, fever is generally considered a defense mechanism against infections. Temperatures above 112° F (44.5° C) are usually fatal because they cause irreversible damage to the nervous system. In most cases fever can be reduced by aspirin or other fever-reducing drugs.

---

feverfew   [fee'-vur-fue]   Feverfew, *Chrysanthemum parthenium*, is a bushy, hardy perennial plant in the family Compositae. Long a garden favorite, it is also found in the wild. Feverfews are erect and leafy, growing to a height of 90 cm (3 ft). The leaves are strongly aromatic and pinnate, with three to seven oval leaflets, each of which is further divided into lobed segments. Flower heads are numerous, barely 2 cm (0.8 in) in diameter, and button-like, with a yellow disk and white rays. The plant blooms during the summer and grows readily from seed.

Feverfew is a strongly scented, summer-flowering chrysanthemum. It has historically found many uses —as an herb, for relief of fever, as an insect repellent, and as a flavor in tea or wine.

Feydeau, Georges   [fay-doh']   Georges Feydeau, b. Dec. 8, 1862, d. June 5, 1921, was a French dramatist who wrote popular farces about extramarital intrigues and domestic strife. His intricate, well-constructed plots are filled with complex deceptions, farfetched schemes, misunderstandings, and cases of mistaken identity that he always resolved ingeniously. Feydeau used elaborate stage settings and props to give credence to his plots. His best-known play is *La Dame de chez Maxim* (The Lady from Maxim's, 1899); others include *Hotel Paradiso* (1894; Eng. trans., *c*.1957), *A Flea in Her Ear* (1907; Eng. trans., 1968), and *Occupe-toi d'Amélie* (Keep an Eye on Amélie, 1908).

Feynman, Richard Phillips   [fyn'-muhn]   The American physicist Richard Phillips Feynman, b. New York City, May 11, 1918, d. Feb. 15, 1988, contributed to the joining of relativity and quantum theory with electromagnetism to form QUANTUM ELECTRODYNAMICS. He is also known for his reformulation of QUANTUM MECHANICS and his research on liquid helium. In 1965 he shared the Nobel Prize for physics with Julian Schwinger and Sin Itiro Tomonago for their contributions to electrodynamics.

Feynman earned his Ph.D. from Princeton University in 1942, worked on the MANHATTAN PROJECT during World War II, and served on the faculty of Cornell University before going to the California Institute of Technology in 1950. In 1986 he was a member of the presidential commission that investigated the Space Shuttle *Challenger* disaster. A writer of scientific works such as *The Character of Physical Law* (1967) and *Statistical Mechanics* (1972), Feynman was also a popular lecturer and author of an informal memoir of his career as a physicist, *Surely You're Joking, Mr. Feynman!* (1985).

Fez   Fez (French: Fès; Arabic: Fas), the capital city of Fez province, north central Morocco, lies about 195 km (120 mi) southeast of Tangier; its population is 448,823 (1982). Fez is a sacred Islamic city and center of learning and was once the northern capital of Morocco. The main industry is tourism; local leatherwork and textiles are well known. The city consists of an old walled section and a new section to the south.

Founded as early as 790, Fez became the capital of Arab Morocco in 808 under Idris II. He built the famous Quarawiyin Mosque (859), which houses Al Quarawiyin University (859). The Marinids, who captured Fez in 1250, erected the Royal Palace complex and a series of elaborate tombs. The city was under French protection from 1912 to 1956.

Fianna Fáil   [fee'-uh-nuh foyl]   Fianna Fáil (Gaelic, "Warriors of Ireland") is one of the two major political parties in the Republic of Ireland, the other being FINE GAEL. Fianna Fáil, organized in 1926 by Eamon DE VALERA, advocates an independent and united Ireland. The party held power from 1932 until 1973, except for the years 1948–51 and 1954–57. It was again in office from 1977 to 1981, in 1982, and from 1987.

---

fiber, natural   Fibers obtained from a plant or an animal are classed as natural fibers (for other types, see

Jute (left), *flax* (center), *and cotton* (right) *yield important vegetable fibers. Jute and flax fibers are derived from the stems; cotton fibers are the seed hairs of the plant.*

SYNTHETIC FIBERS). The majority of these fibers are used in weaving textiles, although the coarser plant fibers are also used for rope and twine. Plant fibers come from the seed hairs, leaves, stems (bast fibers), and husks of plants. Animal fibers are provided, generally, by animal hair and, in the case of silk, by the secretion of the silkworm.

Plant Fibers. The most abundant and commonly used plant fiber is cotton, gathered from the cotton boll, or seedpod, when it is mature. The short, fluffy fibers must be "ginned" to separate fiber from seed. After the fibers have been combed to align them all in one direction, they can be spun into yarn. Spinning, an operation most natural fibers undergo, is accomplished by twisting the short fibers into strong, continuous strands of yarn or thread. Other seed-hair fibers include kapok, used for pillow stuffing.

Fibers taken from the plant leaf are called "hard," or cordage, fibers because they are used principally to make rope. The most important leaf fibers are those from the sisal, or agave, plant grown in Brazil and Africa and from a Mexican agave that produces a fiber called henequen. Both sisal and henequen fibers are stiff, strong, and rough textured. Abaca, or manila hemp, is a fiber from the leafstalk of a banana plant, *Musa textilis*, which grows in the Philippines. Abaca is the strongest of the leaf fibers and is used primarily for cordage. Most leaf fibers come from tropical areas. The palmetto, the only native U.S. leaf-fiber plant, grows in the Southeast; its fibers are used in brushes.

Stem, or bast, fibers include the important flax, hemp, and jute plants. Softer and more flexible than the leaf fibers, they are stripped from the plant stems after the stems have been softened in water. Hemp comes from the stems of the *Cannabis sativa* plant—the same plant that produces marijuana. Until it was replaced by abaca

Under magnification, goat hair (1) *is coarse and brittle. Sheep's wool* (2) *is fine, soft, and elastic. Camel's hair yarn* (3), *from the fine underhair of Asian camels, yields a fabric that is softer and warmer than wool. Angora rabbit hair* (4) *is lightweight and springy. Cashmere* (5), *from the undercoats of Kashmir goats, is prized for its softness and silky luster. Horsehair* (6) *is round, coarse, and bristly.*

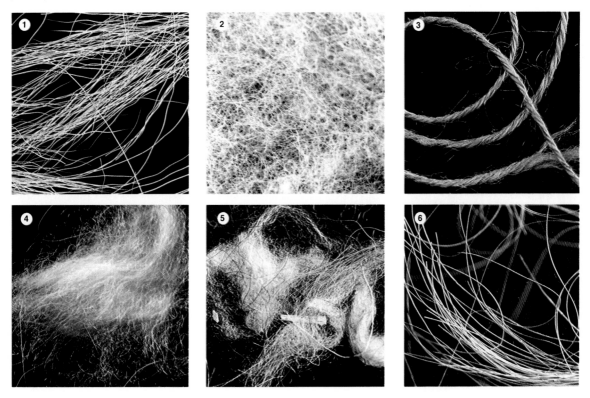

and sisal, hemp was the principal cordage fiber. It is used today for twine and for rough fabrics, such as burlap. Flax stems produce that fiber, which is woven into linen. Jute, a plant growing primarily in India and Bangladesh, provides fiber for twine, burlap, and sacking. Ramie, a relatively new textile fiber, is taken from the plant *Bohmeria nivea*, grown principally in the People's Republic of China. Kenaf, from a hibiscus grown mainly in India, is used for canvas and cordage.

Coir is the rough-textured fiber that comes from the husk of coconuts. It is used as a brush bristle or is spun into a thick twine for weaving into door mats and other floor coverings.

Animal Fibers. Wool, the long, fine hair of sheep, is the most important animal fiber. The fine underhair of the angora and cashmere goats, the angora rabbit, the camel, the alpaca, and the vicuña have a special softness and, often, high bulk (as in mohair, from the angora goat).

Silk is a protein extruded in long, continuous strands by the silkworm as it weaves its cocoon. The fine strands of several cocoons are unwound and twisted together to make silk thread, which produces fabrics of a unique softness and luster.

fiber optics   A relatively new technology, fiber optics is the channeled transmission of light through hair-thin glass fibers. The light is prevented from escaping the fiber by total internal reflection—a process that takes place when a light ray travels through a medium with an index of refraction higher than that of the medium surrounding it. In this case the fiber core has a higher refractive index than the material around the core, and light hitting that material is reflected back into the core, where it continues to travel down the fiber.

Fiber-optic technology has had its greatest impact in telecommunications, where optical fibers transmit audio, video, and data information as coded light pulses. In fact, fiber optics is rapidly becoming the preferred mode of transmitting communications of all kinds. Its advantages over older methods include vastly increased carrying capacity (due to the very high frequency of light), lower transmission losses, lower cost of basic materials, smaller cable size, and almost complete immunity from stray electrical fields (interference).

The feasibility of a light-wave communications system had to await the invention (1960) of the LASER and the subsequent development of reliable ways to generate, reamplify, and detect light pulses. Advances occurred in the 1970s, and by 1977 glass-purifying and fiber-drawing techniques had also reached the stage where interoffice light-wave communications were possible. With further technological development the first intercity communications route was opened in 1983.

A Long-Distance Fiber-Optics Communications System. AT&T's Northeast Corridor Network, which runs from Virginia to Massachusetts, utilizes fiber cables carrying upward of 50 fiber pairs. Using a semiconductor laser or a light-emitting DIODE as the light source, a transmitter codes the audio or visual input into a series of light puls-

es, called bits. These travel along a fiber at a bit-rate of 90 million bits per second. Pulses need reamplifying, or boosting, about every 10 km (6.2 mi) and finally reach a receiver, containing a semiconductor photodiode detector, which amplifies, decodes, and regenerates the original audio or visual information.

Light Propagation and Signal Loss. The glass fibers used in present-day fiber-optic systems are based on ultrapure fused silica. Fiber cannot be made from ordinary optical glass because the glass is so dirty that impurities reduce signal intensity excessively. These impurities must be removed—often to the parts-per-billion level—before useful long-haul fibers can be drawn. But even perfectly pure glass is not perfectly transparent. It attenuates, or weakens, light in two ways. One, occurring at shorter wavelengths, is a scattering caused by unavoidable density fluctuations within the fiber. The other is a longer wavelength absorption by atomic vibrations (phonons).

Light injected into a fiber can adopt several zigzag paths, or modes. When a large number of modes are present they may overlap, for each mode has a different velocity along the fiber (modal dispersion). Mode numbers decrease with decreasing fiber diameter and with a decreasing difference in refractive index between the fiber core and the surrounding region. Fibers are therefore made very thin, with a core region having an index value about one percent larger than that of the surrounding region. A single, or monomode, system is ideally possible. Present systems, however, are multimode and operate at wavelengths less than the ideal 1.5 μm. Prepared monomode transoceanic links, with 4,200 voice circuits per fiber pair, are planned for operation in the future.

Other Applications of Fiber Optics. Noncommunication advances in fiber optics have fallen into two main areas, flexible and rigid fibers. Sensors are a major flexible-fiber application, and uses include the measurement of pressure, temperature, rotation, fluid flow, and electric current. Fiber-optics sensitivity is excellent, and measurements are made without electrical connections. Other flexible-fiber applications concern high-intensity illumination in general, instrument illumination for automotive and avionic systems, power transmission for use with robotics, surgical and dental procedures, and image guiding. The last involves fiber bundles that are spatially aligned from end to end, and the technique is used for direct viewing of otherwise inaccessible areas, as in medical ENDOSCOPES. In rigid-fiber optics, fibers are fused into a solid block. These optic plates are used for image transfer from a cathode ray tube to a permanent photographic recording. Applications include facsimile systems, phototypesetting, recording oscilloscopes, and computer graphics.

fiberglass   Fiberglass consists of glass fibers drawn or blown directly from a GLASS melt. Blown fibers are usually 15–38 cm (6–15 in) long, whereas drawn fibers may be several kilometers long. Fiberglass is most commonly used in a composite with a plastic polymer. Such composites are resistant to moisture and rot and are used in automobile bodies, boats, and other structural applications requiring light weight, strength, and corrosion resistance. Fiberglass can also be used for thermal and electrical insulation.

Long glass fibers are made by melting glass "marbles" in an electric furnace, then drawing the fibers continuously through holes in a platinum bushing and winding them onto a revolving drum. The shorter blown fibers are made by air-steam or flame-blowing processes that pull streams of melted glass into fibers. Drawn fibers are typically 10–25 microns (0.0004–0.001 in) in diameter; blown fibers may be as little as about two-millionths of a centimeter in diameter.

A typical composition of fiberglass ("E" glass) is 54% silica, 15% alumina, 16% calcia, 5% magnesia, 9.5% boron oxide, and 0.5% sodium oxide by weight.

Fibonacci sequence [fee-boh-nah'-chee] A Fibonacci sequence is a SEQUENCE in which each term is the sum of the two terms immediately preceding it. It is named for its discoverer, Leonardo Fibonacci (also known as Leonardo Pisano). The Fibonacci sequence that has 1 as its first term is 1, 1, 2, 3, 5, 8, 13, 21, 34, 55,... . The numbers may also be referred to as Fibonacci numbers. The defining property can be given symbolically as $C_n = C_{n-1} + C_{n-2}$. This equation is a recursion relation, or recurrence relation, which relates different terms of a sequence or of a series. Fibonacci sequences have proved useful in NUMBER THEORY, GEOMETRY, the theory of continued fractions, and genetics. They also arise in many seemingly unrelated phenomena, for example, the GOLDEN SECTION, a shape valued in art and architecture because of its pleasing proportions, and the spiral arrangement of petals and branches on certain types of flowers and trees.

fibrillation   see PALPITATION

Fichte, Johann Gottlieb [fik'-te]   Johann Gottlieb Fichte, b. May 19, 1762, d. Jan. 27, 1814, was a German transcendental idealist philosopher. Fichte first became known for his *Essay towards a Critique of All Revelations* (1792), in which he developed Kant's justification of faith in the name of practical reason. His *Addresses to the German Nation* (1807–08) strongly influenced the development of German nationalism. Fichte taught at the University of Berlin from 1810 until his death.

Crucial to the metaphysics of Fichte is his concept of the creative ego. According to him, this ego is neither subjective nor personal but, instead, is the universal and absolute ego from which all objective reality is derived. The ego is not an object of experience, although it is responsible for experience and is known through its activity within the consciousness itself. Because the activity of the ego is ethical, its major manifestation is in human ethical activity. Ultimately, in Fichte's view, the moral order of reality is identified as God, which is neither personal nor providential. Some viewed the philosophy of Fichte as an expression of atheism, whereas others considered it a form of pantheism.

Fichte deduced the nature and function of the state, with its system of rights and duties, from the moral nature of reality. The rights of all people, and the growth of the state as the necessary condition of the fulfillment of these rights and their corresponding duties, are derived from individuals' freedom and moral consciousness. If all people were fully developed morally, a state would be unnecessary. Fichte considered the state as a necessary instrument of social and moral progress, required by the basic nature of the human condition.

Ficino, Marsilio [fee-chee'-noh, mahr-seel'-ee-oh]
The Italian philosopher and theologian Marsilio Ficino, b. Oct. 19, 1433, d. Oct. 1, 1499, was the most influential Christian Platonist of the Italian Renaissance. In 1462 he became the head of the Platonic Academy near Florence, where he spent most of his life translating the works of Plato from Greek into Latin and writing commentaries on them and the principal Neoplatonists (see NEOPLATONISM). Ficino believed that true philosophy and true religion are in harmony with each other. He stressed themes of good, love, man, and immortality.

fiddler crab   Fiddler crabs are any of a group of small beach-dwelling crabs of the genus *Uca*. They are so named because the males have one extremely large claw that may weigh as much as half the weight of the entire animal; the second claw is relatively diminutive. Widely distributed, especially in tropical regions, fiddler crabs live in mud or sand burrows. The varied courtship behavior of fiddler species includes ritualized waving of claws, display of vivid colors, production of sounds by rubbing parts of bodies together, and dancing movements.

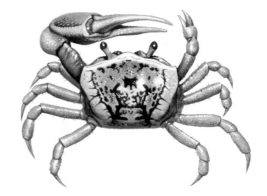

A male fiddler crab waves its enlarged "fiddle claw" as part of its courtship display; the movements vary from species to species.

Fiedler, Arthur [feed'-lur]   The conductor Arthur Fiedler, b. Boston, Dec. 17, 1894, d. July 10, 1979, celebrated a half century as leader of the BOSTON POPS ORCHESTRA in 1979. He attended (1911–15) the Royal Academy

The American conductor Arthur Fiedler led the Boston Pops Orchestra from 1930 to 1979, delighting audiences with his innovative repertoire of light classical music.

of Music in Berlin. Returning to the United States, he became a violist with the Boston Symphony. Fiedler organized the Boston Sinfonietta, a chamber orchestra, in 1925 and inaugurated the Esplanade Concerts, free summer concerts held on the shores of Boston's Charles River, in 1929. He became permanent conductor of the Boston Pops a year later. He was also guest conductor of the San Francisco Symphony, the New York Philharmonic, and the NBC Symphony. His deft handling of the light classic and popular repertoire endeared him to a large audience, and in 1977 he was awarded the Presidential Medal of Freedom.

Fiedler, Leslie A.   Leslie A. Fiedler, b. Newark, N.J., Mar. 8, 1917, is an American critic, fiction writer, poet, and teacher whose provocative analyses of literature and society advance the theory that literature is an expression of neurosis. His two major studies of American fiction, *An End to Innocence: Essays on Culture and Politics* (1955) and *Love and Death in the American Novel* (1960), assert that racism, repressed homosexual emotion, and misogyny are primary influences in American art and life. His original discussions range from his Jewish heritage to Shakespeare and American Indians. His literary study *Freaks* (1978) explains how grotesque deformity can become the norm and ideal in literature. *Fiedler on the Roof* (1987) is a collection of essays.

Field (family)   An American business family, the Fields have been associated since the 1880s with Chicago's leading department store, Marshall Field. The family's enterprises also include a large newspaper and publishing business.

Marshall Field I, b. Conway, Mass. Aug. 18, 1834, d. Jan. 16, 1906, was a clerk in a Pittsfield, Mass., dry-goods store before moving to Chicago in 1856. In 1865 he organized the firm of Field, Palmer and Leiter, which,

in 1881, became Marshall Field and Company. An innovator in merchandising methods, Field increased the store's annual business to $40 million by 1895. A noted philanthropist, Field founded what is now the Field Museum of Natural History in Chicago.

His grandson, **Marshall Field III**, b. Chicago, Sept. 28, 1893, d. Nov. 8, 1956, founded (1941) the *Chicago Sun*, which he later merged (1948) into the *Sun-Times*. His communications ventures were consolidated (1944) in Field Enterprises Inc. (later World Book–Childcraft International).

Marshall Field IV, b. New York City, June 15, 1916, d. Sept. 18, 1965, and **Marshall Field V**, b. Charlottesville, Va., May 13, 1941, expanded the family enterprises. A period of retrenchment began in the 1970s when the *Chicago Daily News*, bought in 1959, ceased (1978) publication. The *World Book Encyclopedia* was sold (1978), and the Marshall Field department store was bought (1982) by a British conglomerate, which in turn sold (1990) it.

Field, Cyrus W.   Cyrus West Field, b. Stockbridge, Mass., Nov. 30, 1819, d. July 12, 1892, was a promoter who laid the first transatlantic telegraph cable. He was a successful merchant who retired at the age of 33 to devote himself to his great dream. Field formed the New York, Newfoundland, and London Telegraph Company with charters from the British and American governments and with financial backing from Peter COOPER and others on both sides of the Atlantic. Three attempts in 1857 to lay a cable between Newfoundland and Ireland failed, but a fourth attempt in 1858 succeeded long enough to make Field a hero before the cable stopped functioning. In 1866 he tried again, chartering the world's largest steamship, the *Great Eastern.* His success this time brought him fame and a new fortune. During the 1870s he bought control of the New York Elevated Railroad Company and served as its president. In his later years he lost his wealth as a result of bad investments.

Cyrus Field posed for this photograph holding a length of the transatlantic telegraph cable that made him famous. After four attempts, Field's scheme to lay more than 2,980 km (1,852 mi) of submarine telegraph cable succeeded in 1866, a feat that provided near-instantaneous communications between Great Britain and the United States.

Field, David Dudley, Jr.   David Field, b. Haddam, Conn., Feb. 13, 1805, d. Apr. 13, 1894, was an American lawyer and legal reformer. After setting up practice in New York City, he began (1837) to work for reform of the New York State legal system. The result was the 1848 Code of Civil Procedure, adopted or used as a model by many other states and by foreign countries.

Field, Marshall   see FIELD (family)

Field, Stephen Johnson   Stephen Johnson Field, b. Haddam, Conn., Nov. 4, 1816, d. Apr. 9, 1899, was a justice of the U.S. Supreme Court. In 1849 he left New York City, where he had practiced law with his brother, David Dudley, and settled in California. He was elected to the California state legislature in 1850. In 1857 he was appointed to the state supreme court and in 1863 to the U.S. Supreme Court, remaining there until 1897. During his long tenure Field was noted for his dissents, many of which reflected a strict-conservative view of the law.

field hockey   Field hockey, a stick and ball game related to ICE HOCKEY and LACROSSE, originated in ancient Egypt, Persia, and Greece and assumed its present form after its spread to Europe. The English organized the game, which they called *hockie* and the French called *hoquet*, and instituted most of the modern rules. The first field hockey club, Blackheath, was formed sometime before 1861. Because of its extreme popularity in British colonies, particularly in India, Britain and its former possessions have dominated field hockey in the Olympics.

In the United States, the game is played primarily by women. One of America's greatest women players was Anne Townsend, who was selected for the All-America team from 1924 to 1939.

The field hockey playing field measures 100 yd (91.5 m) long and 60 yd (54.9 m) wide. The center of the field contains a circle 1 yd (92 cm) in diameter from which play starts at the game's onset and at the half. At each end of the field is a goal, consisting of two upright poles 7 ft (2.13 m) high, 4 yd (3.66 m) apart, and backed by a net attached to the poles and crossbar. A semicircular striking area extends 16 yd (14.64 m) around the goal. A point is scored by hitting the ball into the net from within the striking circle. A stick with a crook is used to maneuver the ball. The ball—white, usually leather covered—weighs between 5½ and 5¾ oz (155 and 163 g) and is between 2⅞ and 3⅜ in. (7.3–7.7 cm) in diameter. Teams consist of 11 players: five forwards, three halfbacks, two fullbacks, and a goalkeeper. A goalkeeper may stop a shot with his or her stick or body, while other players may use their sticks or hands.

Field Museum of Natural History   The Field Museum of Natural History, located in Chicago and known from 1943 to 1966 as the Chicago Natural History Museum, was founded in 1893 by the wealthy businessman Marshall Field. The museum's extensive collections originated with the World's Columbian Exposition held in Chicago in 1893 and have since been sustained by gifts from the Field family and other private and public benefactors. Divided into departments of anthropology, geology, botany, and zoology, the museum's 13 million objects include displays of artifacts from ancient civilizations, gems and jewels, fossils, meteorites, and animals from around the world in lifelike settings.

field spaniel   The field spaniel is a rare gundog. Only a few are registered each year in the United States and in Britain, its native land. The breed was created by crossing Sussex spaniels with cocker spaniels that were apparently a type called the Welsh cocker. Field spaniels are medium-sized dogs, standing about 45 cm (18 in) high at the shoulder and weighing 16–23 kg (35–50 lb). They have moderately long, pendant ears. The coat is flat or

Field hockey has been a women's team sport in the northeastern United States since its introduction in 1901.

The field spaniel, a hunting dog used to flush game, was developed in England in the late 1800s. Crosses with English springer spaniels in the early 1900s improved the breed, which had become so low and elongate that its field performance was hampered.

slightly wavy, never curly, and should be silky in texture and long enough to provide protection from the elements. The ears, chest, legs, and underbody are moderately feathered. Field spaniels are black, liver, golden liver, red, or roan, with or without tan markings over the eyes and on the cheeks, feet, and pasterns. Markings are discouraged.

Henry Fielding, an 18th-century English satirist, mocked contemporary morals in his comic novels Joseph Andrews *(1742) and* Tom Jones *(1749). Before turning to prose fiction, Fielding enjoyed popularity as a playwright.*

Fielding, Henry   Henry Fielding, b. Apr. 22, 1707, d. Oct. 8, 1754, one of the greatest English novelists of the 18th century, and an important playwright and essayist, was largely responsible for the emergence of the novel as a prominent literary form.

After attending Eton and Leyden University, Fielding earned his living as a dramatist. His first play, *Love in Several Masques,* was produced in 1728, when he was 21. Such farces as *Tom Thumb* (1730) made Fielding England's most successful playwright. His political satires, however, such as *Pasquin* (1736), about the corrupt administration of Sir Robert WALPOLE, led to the Licensing Act of 1737. He then turned to the study of law and to editing (1739–41) a vigorous essay-periodical, *The Champion.*

The success of the novel *Pamela: or Virtue Rewarded* (1740–41) by Samuel RICHARDSON provoked Fielding to write (1741) a satire, dubbed *Shamela,* on its bourgeois morality. A more thoughtful comic romance about Pamela's reputed brother, *Joseph Andrews,* followed in 1742. The novel's favorable reception may have inspired Fielding to publish a collection of essays, poems, plays, and prose fiction under the title *Miscellanies* (1743). The third and last volume of this work was the satiric *Jonathan Wild,* called "the finest example of sustained irony in English fiction."

For almost a decade after, Fielding devoted himself largely to political pamphlets and essays. His periodicals the *True Patriot* (1745–46) and *Jacobite's Journal* (1747–48) responded to the Jacobite threat posed by the exiled house of Stuart. The Jacobite Rebellion of "Bonnie Prince Charlie" in 1745 also served as historical background in Fielding's greatest fictional work, TOM JONES (1749). By writing about an "ordinary" person, however, Fielding made many of the conventions of myth and romance freshly accessible to the new bourgeois world of the novel.

Fielding's last essay-periodical, *The Covent-Garden Journal* (1752), includes some of his most humorous pieces; but the tone of his final novel, *Amelia* (1751), is equivocal. Its narrative of domestic problems created by another improvident (but now married) hero, Booth, and suffered by his level-headed wife, Amelia, does not always seem consistent with Fielding's "comic-epic" style and romance conventions.

Failing health resulting from his strenuous duties as a principal magistrate of London caused Fielding in 1754 to seek relief in Lisbon, where he died and was buried. His painful trip there is recorded with great good humor in his final work, *Journal of a Voyage to Lisbon* (1755).

Fielding's enduring reputation and influence in prose fiction have varied only with varying modes of critical taste. He has never lost his reading audience, and his two finest works have been popularized anew in the rollicking films *Tom Jones* (1963) and *Joseph Andrews* (1977).

Fielding, William Stevens   The Canadian political leader William Stevens Fielding, b. Nov. 24, 1848, d. June 23, 1929, began his career as a journalist in Halifax, Nova Scotia. A Liberal, he was elected (1882) to the Nova Scotia legislature and served (1884–96) as premier of that province. As federal minister of finance (1896–1911) under Sir Wilfrid Laurier, Fielding negotiated the reciprocity agreement with the United States that caused the fall of the Laurier government in 1911. In 1917 he broke with the Liberals over the issue of military conscription, which he supported. Reconciled with his party, he served (1921–25) again as finance minister under Mackenzie KING.

Fields, Lew   see WEBER, JOSEPH, AND FIELDS, LEW

Fields, W. C.   W. C. Fields, b. William Claude Dukenfield in Philadelphia on Jan. 29, 1879 or 1880, d. Dec.

W. C. Fields introduces himself to Mae West in this scene from their comedy classic, My Little Chickadee *(1940). Both on screen and in real life, Fields maintained the image of a cynical rogue mocking middle-class values.*

FIG   259

25, 1946, was known on stage, screen, and radio for the highly original, misanthropic cast of his humor. Whether in the role of unscrupulous con man or henpecked, hard-drinking husband, Fields would brag of his hatred for dogs, children, policemen, bankers, wives, and mothers-in-law. During the 1930s he switched from stage roles and silent films to radio and sound films, where his inimitable persona was captured in such favorites as *You Can't Cheat an Honest Man* (1939), *The Bank Dick* (1940), *My Little Chickadee* (1940), with Mae West, and *Never Give a Sucker an Even Break* (1941). He also portrayed Mr. Micawber in the 1935 film version of *David Copperfield*.

Fife   Fife is a former county, now an administrative region, in east central Scotland. Situated on the North Sea coast between the firths of Tay and Forth, it has an area of 1,308 km^2 (505 mi^2) and a population of 344,700 (1988 est.).

The land undulates upward from the low, fertile coastline to the Lomond and Ochil hills. Agriculture is highly developed along the coast and in the Eden River valley. In the south Fife's cities, including DUNFERMLINE, KIRKCALDY, and Burntisland, manufacture ships, linen, and electronics. The coastal towns have fishing fleets, and tourism is important in SAINT ANDREWS, the ancestral home of golf.

Fife was occupied by the Picts, the Romans, and the Danes before becoming part of the kingdom of Scotland in the 11th century. The county was reorganized as a region in 1975.

fife   The fife, a small FLUTE with six to eight holes on top, has been known since the time of the Crusades. It was introduced into the British military from Switzerland during the 16th century. Displaced by other instruments in the 17th century, the fife reappeared during the 18th century, when it was used to play military calls accompanied by drums. Because it can play only the diatonic scale, its use has been limited. George Frideric Handel and Giacomo Meyerbeer did, however, write operatic scores with parts for the fife.

15th Amendment   see CIVIL RIGHTS; CONSTITUTION OF THE UNITED STATES

5th Amendment   see BILL OF RIGHTS; CONSTITUTION OF THE UNITED STATES

fifth disease   Erythema infectiosum, or fifth disease, is a mild ailment of children, adolescents, and, rarely, adults. Its symptoms develop after an incubation period of five to ten days and include a low-grade fever, fatigue, and redness on the cheeks. Within two days a rash appears on the arms, legs, and trunk; it often fades and reappears during the normal five- to ten-day course of the disease. In some cases high fever, sore throat, vomiting, diarrhea, swollen lymph nodes, and joint pain may occur. Arthritis is another possible complication, mainly in adults.

Fifth disease is one of the few human diseases known to be caused by a PARVOVIRUS. No specific treatment is required.

Fifth Republic   see FRANCE, HISTORY OF

fig   Figs comprise a large genus, *Ficus*, of deciduous and evergreen tropical and subtropical trees, shrubs, and vines in the mulberry family, Moraceae. Commercially, the most important fig is *Ficus carica*, the tree that produces the edible fig fruit. Among the most ancient cultivated fruit trees, the fig is indigenous to the eastern Mediterranean and the southwest region of Asia, where its cultivation probably began. It is now grown in warm, semiarid areas throughout the world.

The fruit-bearing fig ranges from a bushlike 1 m (3 ft) to a moderately tall tree that may grow up to 12 m (39 ft) in height. It is characterized by its dark green, deeply lobed leaves. The fig bears no visible flowers; instead, its flowers are borne within a round, fleshy structure, the syconium, which matures into the edible fig. The common fig bears only female flowers but develops its fruits without pollination. Varieties of the Smyrna type also bear only female flowers, but in order to produce fruit they must be pollinated by a process known as caprification.

Caprifigs. The caprifig is a wild form of fig tree whose male flowers produce inedible fruits that are host to the fig wasp, *Blastophaga psenes*. Fig wasps lay their eggs in the caprifig flowers; the eggs hatch within the developing caprifig, and the mature female wasps seek new flowers in which to lay their eggs. When caprifigs are hung among the branches of a cultivated fig, the pollen-dusted wasps squeeze through the narrow openings at the ends of the syconia and pollinate the flowers inside. The wasps die within the syconia, and their bodies are absorbed into the developing fruit. Figs produced by caprification are usually larger than the common fig.

The common orchard fig, a bushlike tree with deeply lobed leaves, originated in the Middle East. Its fruit is a fleshy receptacle (cross section, center) *containing numerous small seeds.*

Fig Cultivation. Fig trees are propagated through rooted cuttings taken from the wood of older trees. They grow best in moderately dry areas that have no rain during the period of fruit maturation, when humidity might hinder the process of fruit drying. The partially dried fruit drops to the ground, where it is gathered and the drying process completed. Some fruit may be picked before it dries and eaten as fresh fruit. Figs are classified either as Smyrna type, Common type, or San Pedro type figs. Smyrna figs produce only a summer crop. Common and San Pedro figs may also produce a spring, or breba, crop that requires caprification.

Other Important Fig Species. The rubber plant, *F. elastica,* is a popular houseplant. Grown as a tree in tropical regions, it produces a latex sold as Assam rubber. The pipal, or bo tree, *F. religiosa*, is considered sacred by Buddhists. The gigantic BANYAN tree, *F. benghalensis*, often produces edible fruits.

---

fighting fish   Fighting fish, or bettas, are labyrinth fish of the genus *Betta*, so classified because of the labyrinthine chamber above the gills, which enables the fish to breathe air. Twelve species of bettas occur in swampy, lowland freshwaters of Southeast Asia. The Siamese fighting fish, *B. splendens*, has been cultured for many years.

---

figured bass   Figured bass, also known as thoroughbass or continuo from the Italian *basso continuo*, refers to a bass line in the music of the 17th and 18th centuries and also to the method of chordal accompaniment using that bass line as a basis for improvisation. The bass notes are often "figured"—marked with numerals or musical signs that indicate the harmonies intended by the composer, while allowing the performer considerable scope for invention. With few exceptions, most music of the baroque and early classical periods contained a figured bass. Usually either harpsichord or organ was used, although lute, guitar, harp, theorbo, and other instruments were possible. The figured bass was normally strengthened by a second performer playing the same bass notes.

A figured bass suggests only a general harmonic outline, but the harmonic support of the improvisation was essential to the sound of baroque and later-18th-century music because it supplied the tonal direction and structural organization of each composition. The figured bass was in use for more than 150 years, during which many treatises on the subject were written for students.

figurehead   see FOLK ART

---

figures of speech   In its broadest sense a figure of speech is any intentional departure from the ordinary form, use, or arrangement of words for the purpose of making expression more striking or effective. Ancient rhetoricians identified about 250 such figures of speech. These included such devices as *antithesis,* the expression of contrasting ideas in parallel form ("Better to reign in hell than serve in heaven"); *alliteration,* most often defined as the close repetition of initial consonant sounds in important words ("hell" and "heaven" in the preceding example); and *repetition,* the repeating of any element in an utterance, including sound (as in alliteration and RHYME), a word or phrase, a pattern of accents (as in meter), or an arrangement of lines (as in stanzas). Under a broad definition, even variant spellings of a word, as in contractions ("'tis," "o'er," "t'other"), qualify as figures of speech.

Under a narrower definition, a figure of speech, or *trope,* is an expression that means something else or something more than what it says; it is language that departs from its literal meaning. In this sense—the sense usually intended when we speak of figurative language—a figure of speech bypasses logic and appeals to the imagination. Thus, paradoxically, it makes possible the expression of meanings more forcefully and more fully than can be accomplished by using literal language.

A simple example is SIMILE, a stated comparison between things essentially unlike, as in "My love is like a red, red rose." This comparison sounds almost logical, but in fact it is not, for a woman could never be confused literally with a rose; the meaning, however, is more vividly and fully conveyed than in the literal paraphrase, "My beloved is beautiful." If the word *like* is removed from this simile, it becomes a METAPHOR, an unstated comparison between things essentially unlike and, in a literal sense, illogical. In metaphor, the things compared may be either named or implied. "Sheathe thy impatience" compares impatience to a sword. "Night's candles are burnt out" compares stars to candles. Emily Dickinson's poem, "I like to see it lap the miles," compares a railroad train to a horse, although neither is named.

Personification, the attribution of human characteristics to something nonhuman ("So when he calls me, Death shall find me ready"), is a subtype of metaphor, comparing the thing meant to a person. Closely related to personification, and often used with it, is *apostrophe,* in which someone absent or dead, or something nonhuman, is addressed as if the person or thing were human, present, alive, and could respond ("Ring out, wild bells, to the wild sky"; "Milton! thou shouldst be living at this hour").

Although classification is difficult and imperfect, the tropes mentioned above all rest, in some way, on comparison. Based on contiguity are *synecdoche,* the use of the part for the whole ("Everyone who wants a roof should have one"), or occasionally, of the whole for the part; and *metonymy,* substitution for the thing meant of something closely associated with it ("The palace should not scorn the cottage"). Metonymy and synecdoche are so nearly alike that the distinction between them is disappearing, and both are often referred to as metonymy.

Related to metonymy and metaphor is the *literary symbol*—an object, person, situation, or action that means more than what it is. Unlike the figurative term in a metaphor (candles in "Night's candles are burnt out"), a symbol means itself and something more, too. It has both literal and metaphorical meanings ("Two men look out through the same bars;/One sees the mud, and one the stars"). A peculiar value of symbol is that although it

AT A GLANCE

FIJI

Land: Area:18,274 km² (7,056 mi²). Capital and largest city: Suva (1986 est. pop., 69,665).

People: Population (1990 est.): 759,567. Density: 41.6 persons per km² (107.6 per mi²). Distribution (1988 est.): 37% urban, 63% rural. Official language: English. Major religions: Protestantism, Hinduism, Islam.

Government: Type: republic. Legislature: Parliament (suspended 1987). Political subdivisions: 4 provinces.

Economy: GDP (1989 est.): $1.32 billion; $1,750 per capita. Labor distribution (1986): agriculture and fishing—44%; government and public authorities—15%; trade—11%; commerce and services—9%; manufacturing—8%; construction—5%. Foreign trade (1988): imports—$454 million; exports—$312 million. Currency: 1 Fiji dollar = 100 cents.

Education and Health: Literacy (1987): 80% of adult population. Universities (1990): 1. Hospital beds (1987): 1,721. Physicians (1987): 271. Life expectancy (1990): women—70; men—66. Infant mortality (1990): 22 per 1,000 live births.

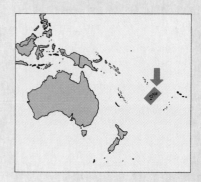

may have a single ulterior meaning, it often suggests a variety of other possible meanings. It is thus an especially rich figure of speech.

Opposed to the figures based on comparison or contiguity are those based on contrast. Two of these are *verbal irony*, which states the opposite of what is meant; and *paradox*, an apparent contradiction that is somehow true. A paradox is usually resolved by seeing that one (or both) of its contradictory terms is itself used figuratively or has a double meaning ("Believe him, he has known the world too long,/And seen the death of much immortal song"). The paradox of the immortal song that dies is resolved when it is recognized that the word *immortal* is used ironically. The aged reader has seen the death of many poems once falsely proclaimed by the critics as "immortal." A special kind of paradox is the *oxymoron,* a compact figure in which successive words apparently contradict each other ("Women! my strongest weakness"). Closely related to verbal irony are *hyperbole,* or overstatement, saying more than is actually meant ("At every word a reputation dies"); and *litotes,* or understatement, saying less than what is meant or saying it with less force than seems warranted, frequently using a negative assertion ("One could do worse than be a swinger of birches").

Figurative language serves to convey thoughts, feelings, and perceptions that cannot be adequately expressed in literal language. Indeed, language evolves largely through metaphor. The word *astonishment,* for example, is derived from roots meaning "struck by thunder." The invention of fresh metaphors today still makes possible the expression of emotions and concepts for which no names exist.

Fiji [fee'-jee]   Fiji is an independent nation in the South Pacific Ocean, about 2,100 km (1,300 mi) north of New Zealand. It is an archipelago of more than 800 islands spread over about 1,600,000 km² (1,000,000 mi²). A British colony for nearly a century, Fiji became independent in 1970.

Land and People

Only about 105 of Fiji's islands are inhabited. The larger islands are volcanic and mountainous except in the river valleys; the smaller islands are mostly coral. The largest island, Viti Levu, where almost 80% of the population live, covers 10,386 km² (4,010 mi²); Suva, the capital and largest city, is located on its southeast coast. The climate is tropical, with an annual mean temperature of 27° C (80° F); rainfall varies from 1,780 mm (70 in) in the west to more than 2,540 mm (100 in) in the east. Vegetation varies according to rainfall, with dense forests in the mountains, tropical savanna grasslands in the west, and dense vegetation in the east. Mount Tomaniivi (1,323 m/4,341 ft), on Viti Levu, is Fiji's highest point. Mangrove trees dominate coastal areas.

Native Fijians, who represent only 44% of the population, are mainly of Melanesian stock. Indians, who constitute about half of the population, are descended from field workers brought by the British. Although the Indians are forbidden land ownership, they operate most of the sugar plantations. Linguistic and religious differences exist between the two groups. Although English is the official language, Fijians speak their own language and are primarily Christian (85% Methodist). The Indian population, which is 70% Hindu and 25% Muslim, speak a dialect of Hindi. There are also small Chinese and white minorities. Fiji experiences tensions as a result of its diverse ethnic composition. Primary education is neither free nor compulsory, but the literacy rate is high. The University of the South Pacific (1968) is at Suva.

Economic Activity

Fiji's economy is primarily agricultural. Sugarcane, produced for export, constitutes about 70% of total agricultural output. Coconuts and ginger are also raised for export; cassava, sweet potatoes, and rice are grown for domestic consumption. Tourism has declined slightly but remains important; in 1987, 190,000 visitors came to Fiji. Gold is the leading mineral product. The underdeveloped industrial sector produces some consumer goods and food products. Fiji is attempting to reverse its foreign trade deficit by diversifying exports and increasing manufacturing, although the political situation has reduced foreign investment. Exploration for offshore oil is being conducted, and pine forests (for timber) are being planted. The fishing industry has grown rapidly.

History and Government

Fiji was probably settled by about 500 BC. The first European discovery was by the Dutch navigator Abel Tasman, in 1643. During the first half of the 19th century, shipwrecked sailors and missionaries settled in Fiji. Their in-

Suva, the capital and chief port of Fiji, is located near the mouth of the Rewa River on the southeastern coast of Viti Levu, the largest of the nation's islands. Suva is the largest city in the South Pacific.

fluence led first to conflicts and then warfare between Fiji's indigenous tribes. Finally, in 1874, Paramount Chief Cakobau invited Great Britain to assume sovereignty of the islands. Under British rule, sugarcane plantations were established.

Fiji gained independence on Oct. 10, 1970. In May 1987, after the ruling Fijian-dominated National Alliance party was defeated by an Indian-backed coalition, tensions between Fijians and Indians contributed to a military coup led by Lt. Col. (later Col.) Sitiveni Rabuka. Fiji's Supreme Court declared the coup illegal, and the governor-general assumed executive power. His plans to establish a caretaker government including all major groups prompted another coup by Rabuka. On Oct. 6, 1987, Rabuka declared Fiji a republic; he turned power over to a civilian government on December 5. In 1990 a new constitution guaranteeing Fijians a permanent legislative majority was approved.

filariasis [fil-uh-ry'-uh-sis]   Filariasis is a collective term for the parasitic diseases caused by the roundworms called filariids, which constitute the superfamily Filarioidea (see NEMATODE). The diseases are observed in all vertebrates except fish. Many infestations are mild, producing no symptoms, or minor dermatitis and inflammation. A few filarial diseases in humans can be serious, although rarely fatal; in dogs—and sometimes cats—the infestation known as heartworm, caused by *Dirofilaria immitis*, is often fatal (see DOG; DISEASES, ANIMAL).

Human filarial diseases are largely restricted to tropical and subtropical regions. They are transmitted from person to person by any of several genera of mosquitoes or biting flies, which introduce the larval stage of the worm into the bloodstream. The adult worms live in various body tissues; the elongated embryos, called microfilariae, circulate in the bloodstream, where they frequently show a diurnal or nocturnal periodicity in their numbers.

The disease most commonly known as filariasis occurs

in Africa, Asia, and the South Pacific region. It is caused by *Wuchereria bancrofti, Brugia malayi*, and a few other roundworm species, and is transmitted by mosquitoes. The adult worms live within the lymph ducts or glands, where they may eventually obstruct lymph circulation. This leads to edema, or the abnormal accumulation of tissue fluid. The extremities and scrotum are most often affected and may swell to enormous proportions, a condition commonly called elephantiasis; the skin over the swollen areas becomes dark, thick, and coarse. The original infestation is dealt with fairly successfully by drugs that attack the adult worms, microfilariae, or both, but treatments for elephantiasis are less effective. Eradication of the mosquito vectors of the disease is the key to control of filariasis, but this has often proved quite difficult or impossible.

Another filarial disease, onchocerciasis (RIVER BLINDNESS), can cause loss of vision if untreated; it occurs in Africa and Central and South America. African EYE WORM, *Loa loa*, by contrast, is rarely serious.

filbert

filbert [fil'-burt]   The filbert, or hazelnut, is the fruit of plants belonging to the genus *Corylus* of the birch family, Betulaceae. Of the 10 major species, the most widely grown are the European filbert, *C. avellana*; the American filbert, *C. americana*; the Turkish filbert, *C. colurna*; and the beaked filbert, *C. cornuta*. Filberts are deciduous shrubs or small trees (although some varieties may reach heights of 18 m/60 ft) native to the temperate zone. Native varieties grow wild throughout America but are cultivated only in areas that do not have late spring frosts, since the flowers, which open in mild winter and early spring weather, are vulnerable to frost-kill.

Most filberts require more than one variety for pollination. They grow in a wide range of soils and are propagated by seed, layering, or grafting.

The giant filbert tree, native to southeastern Europe, grows to 9 m (30 ft) in height and bears heart-shaped leaves. Leafy husks (bottom center) cover the large, edible nuts (bottom right).

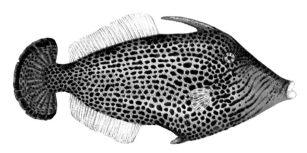

The fan-tailed filefish has a strikingly flat body and rough skin, hence the name.

filefish

filefish [fyl'-fish]   Filefish is the common name of about 85 species of plant-eating fish constituting the subfamily Monacanthinae in the TRIGGERFISH family, Balistidae. Common in warm ocean waters, filefish are named for the sandpaperlike skin of most of the species. The small-mouthed, flattened body generally reaches a length of 25 cm (10 in), but *Aluterus scriptus* grows to 1 m (3 ft) long.

filibuster

filibuster [fil'-uh-buhs-tur]   A filibuster, in politics, is an effort made by a minority of members in a representative assembly to prolong debate in order to delay a vote. Filibustering tactics are often used in the U.S. Senate, which until 1917 had no provision for limiting debate on an issue. In that year a rule was passed to permit closing of debate (CLOTURE) by a vote of two-thirds of the members present and voting. The rule was amended in 1949 and 1959; in 1975 it was changed again to require an affirmative vote by three-fifths of the total Senate membership. Filibustering senators from the South were able to block civil rights legislation on several occasions. They were defeated in 1964 when, after 75 days of delay, the Senate invoked cloture to pass the Civil Rights Act of 1964.

The term *filibuster* (from the Spanish *filibustero*, "freebooter") was originally applied during the 17th century to buccaneers who raided the Spanish colonies in the Americas. In the 19th century it was used for adventurers and soldiers of fortune who sought to create revolutions in Latin America.

Filipino language

Filipino language   see MALAYO-POLYNESIAN LANGUAGES

Fillmore, Millard

Fillmore, Millard [fil'-mohr, mil'-urd]   Millard Fillmore was the 13th president of the United States (1850–53), succeeding to that office on the death of Zachary TAYLOR.

Fillmore was born in Cayuga County, N.Y., on Jan. 7, 1800. An apprentice wool carder, he gained his first formal education in 1819, when a slow period at work enabled him to attend New Hope Academy for six months. He then purchased a release from his apprenticeship, worked in a law office, and passed the bar examination in 1823. His law practice flourished, first in East Aurora,

MILLARD FILLMORE
13th President of the United States (1850–53)

Nickname: "The American Louis Philippe"

Born: Jan. 7, 1800, Summerhill, N.Y.

Profession: Lawyer

Religious Affiliation: Unitarian

Marriage: Feb. 5, 1826, to Abigail Powers (1798–1853); Feb. 10, 1858, to Caroline Carmichael McIntosh (1813–81).

Children: Millard Powers Fillmore (1828–89); Mary Abigail Fillmore (1832–54)

Political Affiliation: Whig

Died: Mar. 8, 1874, Buffalo, N.Y.

Buried: Forest Lawn Cemetery, Buffalo, N.Y.

Vice-President: None

Millard Fillmore

N.Y., and then in Buffalo, N.Y., which in 1830 he made his permanent home.

Early Political Career. Fillmore began his political career in the mid-1820s, as one of the many young men swept up in the ANTI-MASONIC movement of western New York. Elected to the state assembly in 1828, Fillmore successfully sponsored a bill to end imprisonment for debt. In 1832 he was elected to the U.S. Congress as an Anti-Mason. In Congress, Fillmore joined the WHIG PARTY, the coalition opposed to Andrew Jackson. He served as a Whig congressman from Buffalo from 1837 to 1843 and became a strong advocate of internal improvements and of the protective tariff. As chairman of the House Ways and Means Committee, he led passage of the Whig Tariff Act of 1842.

During the 1840s, Fillmore became identified with the conservative wing of the Whig party in New York. The liberal faction, led by Thurlow WEED and William H. SEWARD, was sympathetic to the growing antislavery movement. Seward and Weed also sought to attract to the Whigs voters from the great numbers of immigrants who flooded into New York after 1842. Fillmore, although against slavery, opposed the abolitionists as disruptive of the Whig party and of the nation itself. He was similarly skeptical about the quick naturalization of foreigners, who voted in droves for the Democratic party. As the Whig nominee for governor of New York in 1844, Fillmore attributed his narrow defeat to the hostile votes of abolitionists and Irish Roman Catholics.

Vice-Presidency and Presidency. In 1848 the Whigs chose an outsider, Gen. Zachary Taylor, a Louisiana

slaveholder who had never voted and was not a Whig, as their presidential candidate. To reconcile the more traditional elements of the party, the convention named Fillmore as the Whig vice-presidential candidate. Despite rising animosity over the question of the expansion of slavery into territories won in the MEXICAN WAR, the narrow victory of Taylor and Fillmore held out hope of a conciliatory national solution to the problem. The hope proved false. Taylor was fiercely resistant to the proposals that emerged in 1850 to resolve the dispute over slavery, although the measures had the strong support of Whig founders Henry CLAY and Daniel WEBSTER.

At the height of the sectional crisis Taylor died unexpectedly, and on July 9, 1850, Fillmore became president. Dramatically and decisively, the new president committed himself to sectional compromise. Accepting the resignations of Taylor's cabinet, he appointed Daniel Webster, the major Northern advocate of compromise, as his secretary of state and also named Whigs favorable to compromise to the other cabinet posts. As fast as Congress could approve the bills making up the COMPROMISE OF 1850, Fillmore signed them into law. His administration strictly enforced the most controversial of the new measures, the FUGITIVE SLAVE LAW, which required Northerners to collaborate in the return of escaped slaves to their Southern owners. During the remainder of his term, Fillmore became the first president to approve federal aid for the building of railroads and the first to send a trade mission (led by Commodore Matthew C. PERRY) to Japan.

Because of his enforcement of the Fugitive Slave Law, Fillmore was the favorite of Southern delegates to the divided Whig presidential convention of 1852. His antagonists were Northern Whigs, led by his old New York rivals Seward and Weed, who favored the choice of an antislavery presidential candidate. After 53 ballots, the Northerners succeeded in pushing through an antislavery nominee, Gen. Winfield Scott. The divided Whigs were defeated by Democrat Franklin Pierce in the election, and the Whig party thereafter began to disintegrate.

Later Life. Fillmore again sought the presidency in 1856. He profited from the rapidly rising nativist movement, which opposed the deepening influence of Catholic immigrants in U.S. life and politics. The KNOW-NOTHING PARTY, founded on nativism, named Fillmore its presidential nominee in 1856. He also won the nomination of the remnant of the Whig party, now dominated by Southerners. Pitted against both Democrats and Republicans, Fillmore carried only Maryland in the election but won more than 40 percent of the vote in 10 other Southern states.

After retiring from politics, he became active in the civic life of Buffalo, and died there at age 74 on Mar. 8, 1874.

film   see ANIMATION; CINEMATOGRAPHY; DOCUMENTARY; FILM, HISTORY OF; FILM PRODUCTION

---

film, history of   Film is considered the youngest art form. The motion picture was developed in the 1890s from the union of still PHOTOGRAPHY, which records physical reality, with the persistence-of-vision toy, which made drawn figures appear to move. Four major film traditions have developed since then: fictional narrative film, which tells stories about people with whom an audience can identify because their world looks familiar; nonfictional documentary film, which focuses on the real world either to instruct or to reveal some sort of truth about it; animated film, which makes drawn or sculpted figures look as if they are moving and speaking; and experimental film, which exploits film's ability to create a purely abstract, nonrealistic world unlike any previously seen.

Because of his fame, his success at publicizing his activities, and his habit of patenting machines before actually inventing them, Thomas EDISON received most of the credit for having invented the motion picture; as early as 1887, he patented a motion picture camera, but this could not produce images. In reality, many inventors contributed to the development of moving pictures. Perhaps the first important contribution was the series of motion photographs made by Eadweard MUYBRIDGE between 1872 and 1877. Hired by the governor of California, Leland Stanford, to capture on film the movement of a racehorse, Muybridge tied a series of wires across the track and connected each one to the shutter of a still camera. The running horse tripped the wires and exposed a series of still photographs, which Muybridge then mounted on a stroboscopic disk and projected with a magic lantern to reproduce an image of the horse in motion. Muybridge shot hundreds of such studies and went on to lecture in Europe, where his work intrigued the French scientist E. J. MAREY. Marey devised a means of shooting motion photographs with what he called a photographic gun.

Edison became interested in the possibilities of motion photography after hearing Muybridge lecture in West Orange, N.J. Edison's motion picture experiments, under the direction of William Kennedy Laurie Dickson, began in 1888 with an attempt to record the photographs on wax cylinders similar to those used to make the original phonograph recordings. Dickson made a major breakthrough when he decided to use George EASTMAN's celluloid film instead. Between 1891 and 1895, Dickson shot many 15-second films using the Edison camera, or Kinetograph, but Edison decided against projecting the films for audiences, in part because the visual results were inadequate and in part because he felt that motion pictures would have little public appeal. Instead, Edison marketed an electrically driven peep-hole viewing machine (the Kinetoscope) that displayed the marvels recorded to one viewer at a time.

Edison thought so little of the Kinetoscope that he failed to extend his patent rights to England and Europe, an oversight that allowed two Frenchmen, Louis and Auguste LUMIÈRE, to manufacture a more portable camera and a functional projector, the Cinématographe, based on Edison's machine. The movie era might be said to have begun officially on Dec. 28, 1895, when the Lumières presented a program of brief motion pictures to a paying audience in the basement of a Paris café.

Edward Muybridge, an early pioneer of motion picture development, used a series of sequential cameras to photograph a running horse. This study, published in 1878 as The Horse in Motion, *influenced the development of both movie cameras and projectors.*

The kinetoscope, invented (1888) by William Dickson in Thomas Edison's laboratory, was an early peep-show machine.

The earliest films presented 15- to 60-second glimpses of real scenes recorded outdoors (workmen, trains, fire engines, boats, parades, soldiers) or of staged theatrical performances shot indoors. These two early tendencies—to record life as it is and to dramatize life for artistic effect—can be viewed as the two dominant paths of film history.

Georges MÉLIÈS was the most important of the early theatrical filmmakers. A magician by trade, Méliès, in such films as *A Trip to the Moon* (1902), made things seem to appear and disappear. Early English and French filmmakers such as Cecil Hepworth, James Williamson, and Ferdinand Zecca also discovered how rhythmic movement (the chase) and rhythmic editing could make cinema's treatment of time and space more exciting.

American Film in the Silent Era (1903–1928)

The Great Train Robbery (1903), directed by Edwin S. PORTER of the Edison Company, introduced much freer editing and camera work to tell its story, which included bandits, a holdup, a chase by a posse, and a final shootout. When other companies (Vitagraph, the American Mutoscope and Biograph Company, Lubin, and Kalem among them) began producing films that rivaled those of the Edison Company, Edison sued them for infringement of his patent rights. This so-called patents war lasted 10 years (1898–1908), ending only when nine leading film companies merged to form the Motion Picture Patents Company.

One reason for the settlement was the enormous profits to be derived from what had begun merely as a cheap novelty. Before 1905 motion pictures were usually shown in vaudeville houses as one act on the bill. After 1905 a growing number of small, storefront theaters called nickelodeons, accommodating fewer than 200 patrons, began to show motion pictures exclusively. By 1908 an estimated 10 million Americans were paying their nickels and dimes to see such films. Young speculators such as William Fox and Marcus Loew saw their theaters grow into enterprises worth $150,000 each within five years. The popularity of the moving picture led to the first attacks

against it by crusading moralists, police, and politicians. Local censorship boards were established to eliminate objectionable material from films. In 1909 the infant U.S. film industry waged a counterattack by creating the first of many self-censorship boards, the National Board of Censorship (after 1916 called the National Board of Review), whose purpose was to set moral standards for films and thereby save them from costly mutilation.

A nickelodeon program consisted of about six 10-minute films, usually including an adventure, a comedy, an informational film, a chase film, and a melodrama. The most accomplished maker of these films was Biograph's D. W. GRIFFITH, who almost singlehandedly transformed both the art and the business of the motion picture. Griffith made over 400 short films between 1908 and 1913, in this period discovering or developing almost every major technique by which film manipulates time and space: the use of alternating close-ups, medium shots, and distant panoramas; the subtle control of rhythmic editing; the effective use of traveling shots, atmospheric lighting, narrative commentary, poetic detail, and visual symbolism; and the advantages of understated acting, at which his acting company excelled. The culmination of Griffith's work was *The Birth of a Nation* (1915), a 3-hour epic of the Civil War and Reconstruction.

The decade between 1908 and 1918 was one of the most important in the history of American film. The full-length feature film replaced the program of short films; World War I destroyed or restricted the film industries of Europe, promoting greater technical innovation, growth, and commercial stability in America; the film industry was consolidated with the founding of the first major studios in Hollywood, Calif. (Fox, Paramount, and Universal); and the great American silent comedies were born. Mack SENNETT became the driving force behind the Keystone Company in 1912; Hal Roach founded his comedy company in 1914; and Charlie CHAPLIN probably had the best-known face in the world in 1916.

During this period the first movie stars rose to fame, replacing the anonymous players of the short films. In 1918, America's two favorite stars, Charlie Chaplin and

These early-20th-century projectionists are cranking the projector and rewinding the film-strip by hand. Manually operated camera-projectors, derived from Edison's kinetoscope and developed in France by the Lumière brothers, could be used anywhere.

Mary PICKFORD, each signed contracts for over $1 million. Other familiar stars of the decade included comedians Fatty Arbuckle and John Bunny, cowboys William S. HART and Bronco Billy Anderson, matinee idols Rudolph VALENTINO and John Gilbert, and the alluring femmes Theda BARA and the "It Girl," Clara BOW. FILM SERIALS became popular, particularly *The Perils of Pauline,* starring Pearl White. Along with the stars came the first movie fan magazines, beginning with *Photoplay* in 1912.

In the next decade, 1918 to 1928, film companies became monopolies in that they not only made films but distributed them to theaters and owned the theaters in which they were shown as well. This vertical integration provided the commercial foundation of the film industry for the next 30 years. Two new producing companies were Warner Brothers (1923), which would rise with its early conversion to synchronized sound, and Metro-Goldwyn (1924; later Metro-Goldwyn-Mayer), the producing arm of Loew's, under the direction of Louis B. MAYER and Irving Thalberg.

In 1921, after several nationally publicized sex and drug scandals, the industry headed off the threat of federal CENSORSHIP by creating the office of the Motion Picture Producers and Distributors of America (now the Motion Picture Association of America), under the direction of Will H. HAYS.

It was the great age of comedy. Chaplin retained a hold on his international following with full-length features such as *The Kid* (1920) and *The Gold Rush* (1925); Harold LLOYD climbed his way to success—and got the girl—no matter how great the obstacles, in *Grandma's Boy* (1922) and *The Freshman* (1925); Buster KEATON remained deadpan through a succession of wildly bizarre sight gags in *Sherlock Jr.* (1924) and *The General* (1926); Harry Langdon was ever the innocent elf cast adrift in a mean, tough world; and director Ernst LUBITSCH, fresh from Germany, brought his "touch" to understated comedies of manners, sex, and marriage.

The decade also saw the first great American war film (*The Big Parade,* 1925), Westerns (*The Covered Wagon,* 1923; *The Iron Horse,* 1924), and biblical epics (*The

The Great Train Robbery *(1903), directed by Edwin S. Porter, was the first film to contain two concurrent story lines.*

Ten Commandments,* 1923, and *King of Kings,* 1927, by Cecil B. DE MILLE). Other films of this era included Erich Von STROHEIM's sexual studies, Lon CHANEY's grotesque costume melodramas, and the first great documentary feature, Robert J. FLAHERTY's *Nanook of the North* (1922).

European Film in the 1920s

In the same decade, the European film industries recovered from the war to produce one of the richest artistic periods in film history. The German cinema, stimulated by EXPRESSIONISM in painting, poetry, and the theater and by the design theories of the BAUHAUS, created bizarrely expressionistic settings for such fantasies as Robert Wiene's *The Cabinet of Doctor Caligari* (1919), F. W. MURNAU's *Nosferatu* (1922), and Fritz LANG's *Metropolis* (1927). The Germans also brought their sense of decor, atmospheric lighting, and penchant for a frequently moving camera to such realistic political and psychological studies as Murnau's *The Last Laugh* (1924), G. W. PABST's *The Joyless Street* (1925), and E. A. Dupont's *Variety* (1925).

Innovation also came from the completely different

The Edison Company, although a major contributor to the development of motion pictures, declined in importance because of its insistence on single-reel films and its unsuccessful attempt to monopolize film production and distribution.

Charlie Chaplin's first sound film, City Lights *(1931), attracts a large crowd at the Broadway Theatre. Chaplin used music but no dialogue to underscore a highly successful mixture of comedy and pathos.*

approach in the USSR, where movies were intended not only to entertain but also to instruct the masses in the social and political goals of their new government. The Soviet cinema used montage, or complicated editing techniques that relied on visual metaphor, to create excitement and richness of texture and, ultimately, to shape ideological attitudes and to provide its semiliterate people with a history that offered a rationale for the revolution. The most influential Soviet theorist and filmmaker was Sergei M. EISENSTEIN, whose *Potemkin* (1925) had a worldwide impact. Other innovative Soviet filmmakers of the 1920s included V. I. PUDOVKIN, Lev Kuleshov, Abram Room, and Alexander DOVZHENKO.

The Swedish cinema of the 1920s relied heavily on the striking visual qualities of the northern landscape. Mauritz Stiller and Victor Sjöström mixed this natural imagery of mountains, sea, and ice with psychological drama and tales of supernatural quests. Under the influence of SURREALISM and Dadaism, filmmakers working in

France—Marcel DUCHAMP, René CLAIR, Fernand LÉGER, Jean RENOIR, and Luis BUÑUEL and Salvador DALI in *Un Chien andalou* (1928)—all made antirealist, antirational, noncommercial films that helped establish the avant-garde tradition in filmmaking.

The Arrival of Sound

The feasibility of sound film was widely publicized only after Warner Brothers purchased the Vitaphone from Western Electric in 1926. The original Vitaphone system synchronized the picture with a separate phonographic disk. For *The Jazz Singer* (1927), Warners added four synchronized musical sequences to a silent film. When Al JOLSON sang and then delivered several lines of dialogue, audiences were electrified. The first 100 percent sound film, *Lights of New York*, followed in 1928. The silent film was dead within a year.

The most effective early sound films were those which played most adventurously with the union of picture and

Stars and directors became synonymous with their genres. Valentino personified romance, Chaplin comedy, and De Mille the spectacle, in such films as The Sheik *(1921)* (left), City Lights *(1931)* (center), and The Ten Commandments *(1923)* (right).

The Public Enemy *(1931), featuring James Cagney* (right), *is a classic gangster film, a genre prevalent during the 1930s.*

sound track. Walt DISNEY'S cartoons, for example, carefully orchestrated animated motion with musical rhythm and inventive sound.

Hollywood's Golden Era

The 1930s was the golden era of the Hollywood studio film. It was the decade of the great movie stars—Greta GARBO, Marlene DIETRICH, Jean HARLOW, Mae WEST, Katharine HEPBURN, Bette DAVIS, Cary GRANT, Gary COOPER, Clark GABLE—and some of America's greatest directors. Josef von STERNBERG became legendary for his use of exotic decor and sexual symbolism; Howard HAWKS made driving adventures and fast-paced comedies; Frank CAPRA blended politics and morality in a series of comedy-dramas; and John FORD mythified the American West. The gangster film introduced Americans to the tough doings and tougher talk of big-city thugs, as played by James CAGNEY, Paul MUNI, and Edward G. ROBINSON. Musicals included the witty operettas of Ernst Lubitsch, the backstage musicals of Busby BERKELEY, with their dazzling kaleidoscopic dance numbers, and the smooth, more natural song-and-dance comedies of Fred ASTAIRE and Ginger ROGERS. Synchronized sound also produced screwball comedy, which explored the dizzy doings of fast-moving, fast-thinking, and, above all, fast-talking men and women.

Spurred by the depression and by the threat of economic boycott by the newly formed Catholic Legion of Decency, the motion picture industry adopted an official Production Code in 1934. Written in 1930 by Daniel Lord, S.J., and Martin Quigley, a Catholic layman who was publisher of *The Motion Picture Herald,* the code explicitly prohibited certain acts, themes, words, and implications. The result was the curtailment of explicit violence and sexual innuendo, as well as much of the flavor that had characterized films earlier in the decade.

Europe During the 1930s

With the coming of sound, the most stylish productions of the British film industry were the historical dramas of Sir Alexander KORDA and the mystery-adventures of Alfred HITCHCOCK. The major Korda stars, as well as Hitchcock himself, left Britain for Hollywood before the decade ended. More innovative were the government-funded documentaries and experimental films made by the General Post Office Film Unit under the direction of John Grierson.

Soviet filmmakers had problems with the early sound-film machines and with the application of montage theory (a totally visual conception) to sound filming. They were further plagued by restrictive Stalinist policies. The style of the German cinema was perfectly suited to sound filming, and German films of the period 1928–32 show some of the most creative uses of the medium. When the Nazis came to power in 1933, however, almost all the creative film talent left Germany. An exception was Leni RIEFENSTAHL, whose theatrical documentary *Triumph of the Will* (1934) represents a highly effective example of Nazi propaganda translated into cinematic terms.

French cinema, the most exciting alternative to Hollywood in the 1930s, produced many classic films. The decade found director Jean Renoir—in *Grand Illusion* (1937) and *Rules of the Game* (1939)—at the height of his powers; René Clair mastered both the musical fantasy and the sociopolitical satire (*À Nous la liberté,* 1931); Marcel PAGNOL brought to the screen his trilogy of Marseilles life, *Fanny;* the young Jean VIGO expressed youthful rebellion and mature love; and director Marcel CARNÉ; teamed with poet Jacques Prévert to produce haunting existential romances of lost love and inevitable death in *Quai des brumes* (1938) and *Le Jour se lève* (1939).

Hollywood and World War II

During World War II, many of the most accomplished Hollywood directors and producers went to work for the War Department. Frank Capra produced the "Why We Fight" series (1942–45); Walt Disney, fresh from his

Fred Astaire and Ginger Rogers, one of the most successful partnerships in film history, execute a dance sequence in the great Hollywood musical comedy Top Hat *(1935).*

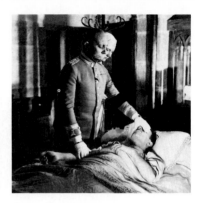

Complex cinematography was brilliantly exploited by Busby Berkeley in productions such as Dames *(1934)* (left), *by Orson Welles in his masterpiece,* Citizen Kane *(1941)* (center), *and by Jean Renoir in France's prewar classic,* Grand Illusion *(1937)* (right).

Snow White (1937) and *Fantasia* (1940) successes, made animated informational films; and John Ford, Garson KANIN, John HUSTON, and William WYLER all made documentaries about important battles. Among the new American directors to make narrative films were three former screenwriters, Preston STURGES, Billy WILDER, and John Huston. Orson WELLES, the boy genius of theater and radio fame, also came to Hollywood to shoot *Citizen Kane* (1941).

Postwar Decline

Between 1946 and 1953 the movie industry was attacked from many sides. As a result, the Hollywood studio system totally collapsed. First, the U.S. House of Representatives' Committee on Un-American Activities investigated alleged Communist infiltration of the motion picture industry in two separate sets of hearings. In 1948, The HOLLYWOOD TEN, 10 screenwriters and directors who refused to answer the questions of the committee, went to jail for contempt of Congress. Then, from 1951 to 1954, in mass hearings, Hollywood celebrities were forced either to name their associates as fellow Communists or to refuse to answer all questions on the grounds of 5th Amendment protection against self-incrimination.

In 1948 the United States Supreme Court, ruling in *United States* v. *Paramount* that the vertical integration of the movie industry was monopolistic, required the movie studios to divest themselves of the theaters that showed

their pictures. At the same time, movie attendance began a steady decline; the film industry's gross revenues fell every year from 1947 to 1963. The most obvious cause was the rise of television. In addition, European quotas against American films bit into Hollywood's foreign revenues.

While major American movies lost money, foreign art films were attracting a growing audience, and these foreign films created social as well as commercial difficulties for the industry. In 1951, *The Miracle,* a 40-minute film by Roberto ROSSELLINI, was attacked by the New York Catholic Diocese as sacrilegious and was banned by New York City's commissioner of licenses. The 1952 Supreme Court ruling in the *Miracle* case officially granted motion pictures the right to free speech as guaranteed in the Constitution, reversing a 1915 ruling by the Court that movies were not equivalent to speech.

Hollywood attempted to counter the effects of television with a series of technological gimmicks in the early 1950s: 3-D, Cinerama, and CinemaScope. The industry converted almost exclusively to color filming during the decade, aided by the cheapness and flexibility of the new Eastman color monopack, which came to challenge the monopoly of Technicolor. Hollywood searched for a new audience and a new style. There were more socially conscious films, such as Fred ZINNEMANN's *The Men* (1950) and Elia KAZAN's *On the Waterfront* (1954); more adaptations of popular novels and plays; more independent (as opposed to studio) production; and a greater concentration on FILM NOIR—grim detective stories in brutal urban settings. Older genres such as the Western flourished, and MGM brought the musical to a pinnacle in a series of films produced by Arthur Freed and directed by Vincente MINNELLI, Gene KELLY, and Stanley Donen.

European Film in the Postwar World

The defection of mass American audiences to television, their replacement by those willing to experience more unsettling film entertainment, the film festivals where international films competed for commercial distribution, and foreign governmental support of film production all contributed to the growth of non-American film industries in the postwar years.

The famous "fight scene" between Una Merkel (left) *and Marlene Dietrich* (right), *interrupted by James Stewart* (center), *in* Destry Rides Again *(1939) was considered daring in its time.*

Postwar foreign filmmakers, such as Rossellini, in The Miracle *(1948)* (left), *De Sica, in* Umberto D *(1952)* (center) *and Kurosawa, in* Rashomon *(1950)* (right)*, experimented with form, content, and technique while confronting social issues.*

Italy. The European film renaissance can be said to have started in Italy with such masters of NEOREALISM as Roberto Rossellini in *Open City* (1945), Vittorio DE SICA in *The Bicycle Thief* (1948) and *Umberto D* (1952), and Luchino VISCONTI in *La Terra Trema* (1948). Federico FELLINI broke with the tradition to make more poetic and personal films such as *I Vitelloni* (1953) and *La Strada* (1954), then shifted to a more flamboyant style in the 1960s with *La Dolce Vita* (1960), *8 1/2* (1963), and *Fellini-Satyricon* (1968). A new departure—both artistic and thematic—was evidenced by Michelangelo ANTONIONI in his subtle psychosocial trilogy of films that began with *L'Aventura* (1960). The vitality of Italian filmmaking continued with the political and sexual allegories of Pier-Paolo PASOLINI (*The Gospel According to St. Matthew*, 1964; *Teorema*, 1968; *Salo*, 1977); with Bernardo BERTOLUCCI's fusion of radical political consciousness and a stunning visual style (*The Conformist*, 1970; *Last Tango in Paris*, 1972; *The Last Emperor*, 1987); and with retrospective glimpses of Italian history and cinema by Paolo and Vittorio Taviani (*Padre Padrone*, 1977; *The Night of the Shooting Stars*, 1983) and Giuseppe Tornatore (*Cinema Paradiso*, 1989).

France. With the coming of NEW WAVE films in the late 1950s, the French cinema reasserted the artistic primacy it had enjoyed in the prewar period. New Wave directors included Claude CHABROL (*The Cousins*, 1959), François TRUFFAUT (*The 400 Blows*, 1959; *Jules and Jim*, 1961), Alain RESNAIS (*Hiroshima Mon Amour*, 1959), and Jean Luc GODARD, who, following the success of his offbeat *Breathless* (1960), became progressively more committed to a Marxist interpretation of society in *Two or Three Things I Know about Her* (1966), *Weekend* (1967), and *La Chinoise* (1967). While Truffaut became obsessively concerned with the value of cinema as art, education, and communication (*The Wild Child*, 1969; *Day for Night*, 1973; *The Last Metro*, 1980), Godard became obsessively concerned with the way cinema masks the covert operations of ideology in bourgeois society (*Tout va bien*, 1972; *Sauve qui peut*, 1980; *First Name: Carmen*, 1983). Louis MALLE explored such charged subjects as incest and collaborationism in *Murmur of the Heart*

(1971), *Lacombe Lucien* (1974), and *Au Revoir les enfants* (1988).

Sweden. From Sweden Ingmar BERGMAN emerged in the 1950s as the master of introspective, often death-obsessed studies of complex human relationships. Although capable of comedy, as in *Smiles of a Summer Night* (1955), Bergman was at his most impressive in more despairing, existentialist dramas such as *The Seventh Seal* (1957), *Wild Strawberries* (1957), *Persona* (1966), and *Cries and Whispers* (1972), aided by a first-rate acting ensemble and brilliant cinematography. In later films, such as *The Magic Flute* (1974) and *Fanny and Alexander* (1982), Bergman cast off his fatalistic obsessions to reaffirm the magic of theater and cinema.

Great Britain. The British cinema had been largely reduced to inexpensive comedies by the early 1950s, usually starring Alec GUINNESS. Over the next decade, however, Britain regained a healthy share of the world market with films such as Jack Clayton's *Room at the Top* (1958); Tony RICHARDSON's *Look Back in Anger* (1959), *The Entertainer* (1960), *A Taste of Honey* (1961), and *Tom Jones* (1963); Joseph Losey's *The Servant* (1963) and *Accident* (1967); and Ken Russell's *Women in Love* (1969). The popularity of the James Bond spy series, which began in 1962, gave the British film industry an added boost. In the 1980s elegant adaptations of classic British novelists were popular worldwide—notably E. M. Forster's *Passage to India* (1984) and *A Room with a View* (1985), and THE DEAD (1987), from James Joyce's *Dubliners*.

Eastern Europe and the Soviet Union. The postwar cinemas of Eastern Europe walked a tightrope between their rich artistic tradition and official Soviet policies of artistic suppression. The Polish cinema enjoyed two major periods of creative freedom—in the late 1950s and early 1960s, and in the late 1970s and early 1980s. Roman POLANSKI began with psychological studies of obsessed or neurotic characters (*Knife in the Water*, 1962; *Repulsion*, 1965), only to leave Poland for both American genre films and European literary adaptations (*Rosemary's Baby*, 1968; *Macbeth*, 1971; *Chinatown*, 1974; *Tess*, 1979). Andrej Wajda remained in Poland to direct films in both periods of expressive freedom (*Kanal*, 1957;

Werner Herzog's Nosferatu *(1979) retells the Dracula story, first filmed by F.W. Murnau in 1922. The many other versions include Tod Browning's classic* Dracula *(1931), with Bela Lugosi.*

Ashes and Diamonds, 1958; *Man of Marble*, 1977; *Man of Iron*, 1981).

With sketches of Czech life, films from tiny Czechoslovakia dominated the international festivals for much of the 1960s. The major directors either remained silently in Czechoslovakia after the 1968 Soviet invasion (Jiri Menzel, *Closely Watched Trains*, 1966) or emigrated to the West (Jan Kadar, *The Shop on Main Street*, 1965). Most successful of Czech émigrés has been Milos FORMAN (*Loves of a Blonde*, 1965; *The Firemen's Ball*, 1967), who found a home in Hollywood with his off-beat sketches of oddballs and loners (*One Flew over the Cuckoo's Nest*, 1975; *Amadeus*, 1984).

The first Soviet films to make an impact beyond the sphere of influence of the USSR were either sentimental recollections of the struggle against the Nazis (*The Cranes Are Flying*, 1959; *Ballad of a Soldier*, 1960) or the Boris Pasternak translations of Shakespeare classics, directed by Grigory KOZINTSEV (*Hamlet*, 1963; *King Lear*, 1971). Before *Glasnost* the most adventurous Soviet directors made films only with difficulty (Andrei Tarkovsky: *Andrei Rublev*, 1966; *Solaris*, 1971). New standards were evident in the sex and nudity in Vasily Pichul's *Little Vera* (1989).

Germany. The rise of a postwar generation of German filmmakers, nurtured almost exclusively on American films and actively supported by the German government, produced the most impressive new national cinema. Volker Schlondorf specialized in literary adaptations (*Young Torless*, 1966; *The Tin Drum*, 1981), while Wim Wenders made German echoes of the American genre films that shaped his own view of both film and the world (*Kings of the Road*, 1976; *The American Friend*, 1977; *Paris, Texas*, 1984; *Wings of Desire*, 1987). Werner HERZOG directed psychological studies of obsessed characters who try to dominate their landscapes (*Aguirre, the Wrath of God*, 1972; *Kaspar Hauser*, 1974; *Fitzcarraldo*, 1982). Rainer Werner FASSBINDER, the most eclectic of

the new German group, mixed a radical critique of bourgeois society, a sadomasochistic view of sexual power relationships, and references to the Hollywood cinema (*Ali: Fear Eats the Soul*, 1972; *Fox and His Friends*, 1974; *The Marriage of Maria Braun*, 1978; *Berlin Alexanderplatz* [made for television], 1980). Among more recent German films to attract international attention was Michael Verhoeven's *Nasty Girl* (1990), a different kind of exploration of the Nazi past.

Spain. The most distinguished Spanish filmmaker, Luis BUÑUEL, rarely worked in Spain; he broke new ground with ironic examinations of the internal contradictions of religious dogma (*Nazarin*, 1958; *Viridiana*, 1961; *The Milky Way*, 1969) and middle-class life (*The Discreet Charm of the Bourgeoisie*, 1972; *That Obscure Object of Desire*, 1977). A younger generation of Spanish filmmakers has now begun to emerge, greatly influenced by Buñuel and led by Carlos Saura (*Cria*, 1976; *Carmen*, 1983), and Pedro Almodovar (*Women on the Verge of a Nervous Breakdown*, 1988).

Nonwestern Film Production

In the postwar era, directors outside the Western tradition for the first time brought their regional perceptions and concerns to an international audience.

Japan. From Japan came Akira KUROSAWA, whose exploration of the elusive nature of truth in *Rashomon* (1950) opened the way for subsequent acceptance of his samurai dramas (*Seven Samurai*, 1954; *Yojimbo*, 1961) and literary adaptations (*Throne of Blood*, 1957; *Ran*, 1985). He was joined by Kenji MIZOGUCHI, known for his stately period films *Ugetsu* (1953) and *Sansho the Bailiff* (1955), and Yasujiro OZU, who studied modern domestic relations. Nagisa Oshima (*Death by Hanging*, 1968; *In the Realm of the Senses*, 1976), shares many of the political and stylistic concerns of Jean Luc Godard.

India. The Indian film industry produces more feature films than any other in the world for a vast population that has still largely been unable to afford television sets. While most of these films follow clear formulas, the problems of an India in transition have been vividly brought to life in the quiet, reflective films of Satyajit RAY, particularly in the trilogy *Pather Panchali* (1955), *Aparajito* (1956), and *The World of Apu* (1958).

Third World. Many other nations of Asia, Africa, and Latin America have begun to produce films, primarily for their own regions but occasionally in the international market. Cuba dominates the Latin American cinema, with a vast government-funded film school and studio, but the films of Tomas Gutierrez Alea (*Death of a Bureaucrat*, 1966; *Memories of Underdevelopment*, 1968) have resonances for audiences outside Cuba. With the loosening of political restrictions, the Brazilian cinema emerged in the 1980s with the films of Hector Babenco (*Pixote*, 1981; *Kiss of the Spider Woman*, 1985).

Films from the People's Republic of China have begun to circulate in the West. Other Far Eastern movies include those from Hong Kong, mostly of the kung fu variety.

Australia. Although essentially Western, the Australian cinema shares many thematic concerns with nations that see themselves as historically colonized and economically exploited by the West. After a series of stunning successes directed by Peter Weir (*The Last Wave*, 1977; *The Year of Living Dangerously*, 1982), Bruce Beresford (*Breaker Morant*, 1980), Gillian Armstrong (*My Brilliant Career*, 1979), Fred Schepisi (*The Chant of Jimmie Blacksmith*, 1978), and George Miller (the *Mad Max* series), many directors and stars have left Australia for Hollywood.

American Film of the 1960s and 1970s

Throughout the 1960s and '70s the American film industry accommodated itself to the competition of the world market, to a film audience that had shrunk from 80 million to 20 million weekly, to the tastes of an increasingly young and educated audience, and to the new social and sexual values. The Hollywood studios that survived in name (Paramount, Warners, Universal, MGM, Twentieth Century–Fox) became primarily offices for film distribution, often subsidiaries of huge conglomerates like Coca Cola or Gulf and Western.

American movies of the period, from the beginning of the Kennedy presidency to the era of Watergate, moved strongly into social criticism (*Doctor Strangelove*, 1963; *The Graduate*, 1967; *Bonnie and Clyde*, 1967; *2001: A Space Odyssey*, 1968; *The Wild Bunch*, 1969; *M*A*S*H*, 1970; *The Godfather*, 1972; *The Conversation*, 1974; *One Flew over the Cuckoo's Nest*, 1975). The 1930 Hollywood Production Code collapsed; its 1968 replacement, the Motion Picture Rating System (originally G, M, R, and X), indicated the level of audience maturity each film demanded.

The most successful directors of the period—Stanley KUBRICK, Robert ALTMAN, Francis Ford COPPOLA, Woody ALLEN, Arthur PENN—played most imaginatively with the tools of film communication itself. The new stars of the 1960s and 1970s (with the exceptions of Paul NEWMAN and Robert REDFORD), like the content of their films, were more offbeat and less glamorous than their predecessors—Robert DE NIRO, Woody Allen, Jane Fonda (see FONDA family), Dustin HOFFMAN, Jack NICHOLSON, Al PACINO, Barbra STREISAND, Diane KEATON, Meryl STREEP. The U.S. DOCUMENTARY was reborn in the work of Fred WISEMAN and the Maysles brothers.

American Film Today

Films since the late 1970s have reaffirmed some myths of American life and movies, and sought new ones. The epics of Steven SPIELBERG and George LUCAS (The *Star Wars* trilogy, 1977–83; *Close Encounters of the Third Kind*, 1977; the Indiana Jones trilogy, 1981—1989; *E.T.: The Extraterrestrial*, 1982) offered an escape from social reality aided by the often beautiful, sometimes awesome effects of visual technology (see CINEMATOGRAPHY; COMPUTER GRAPHICS). Darker myths of horror, terror, and irrational menace drove the *Halloween* and *Friday the 13th* series as well as *Alien* (1979), *Poltergeist* (1982), and their sequels and imitators. The American family was reconsidered in *Kramer vs. Kramer* (1979), *Ordinary People* (1980), *Terms of Endearment* (1983), and *Post-*

In Return of the Jedi *(1983), the third of George Lucas's popular* Star Wars *series of science fantasy films, good triumphs over evil amid amazing galactic special effects.*

cards from the Edge (1990). The *Dirty Harry* series of Clint EASTWOOD films, as well as the Rocky and Rambo films of Sylvester Stallone, affirmed the power of assertive individualism. The "Teen Pic" both acknowledged the age of the majority of the movie audience and adapted the classic *bildungsroman* (a novel, usually about the moral or intellectual maturing of youth) into optimistic teenage American terms (*Saturday Night Fever*, 1977; *Flashdance*, 1983; *Risky Business*, 1983; *The Breakfast Club*, 1985). *Who Framed Roger Rabbit* (1988) revived the animated film. The box office success of *Pretty Woman* and *Ghost* (both 1990) marked the return of romance.

The film and television industries of the 1990s are virtually indistinguishable. Not only do feature films use television technologies (videotape, video cameras, and

The forced evacuation (1975) of Cambodia's capital Phnom Penh by the Khmer Rouge is pictured in The Killing Fields *(1984), a vivid re-creation of a country in chaos.*

video monitors), but every feature film is composed for eventual viewing on television. The conversion of feature films to the VCR has almost totally eliminated Cinema-Scope and other striking technologies—reversing the visual tendency of four decades toward increasingly complex, contrapuntal compositions and the emphasis on stylistic values on which the cinema has depended.

See also: ANIMATION; FILM PRODUCTION.

—

film noir [film nwar]   The term *film noir* ("dark cinema") was first used by French critics to describe a genre of American suspense film of the 1940s and '50s whose urban, often nighttime settings and fatalistic themes suggested an unstable world full of danger and moral corruption. The oblique lighting and off-balance compositions typical of the visual style of such films heightened the effect of disillusionment and bitter realism. Famous examples of film noir include *Double Indemnity* (1944), *The Big Heat* (1953), and *Touch of Evil* (1958).

—

film production   As a general term, film production is all the work that goes into the making of a film, including its planning and realization. What is actually produced during this period is an approved, final negative. During the distribution phase that follows production, multiple prints are struck from the negative, and the movie is released, marketed, and exhibited.

As a more specific term, production is one phase of overall production activity, essentially the shooting phase. Every film goes through the following stages: development, when the project is conceived, written, and financed; pre-production, when the shooting is prepared for; production, when most of the script is staged, shot, and recorded; and post-production, when the picture and sound are edited and polished.

On location for The Big Chill *(1983), director Lawrence Kasdan checks the camera viewfinder. Mounted on a movable platform, the camera can be positioned high enough to get a long shot of the scene below.*

Terminology. A few definitions are necessary here. A *shot* is a continuously exposed piece of film, or the continuous view that is presented between one cut and another. A *take* is an attempt to photograph and/or record a particular shot. Most industry CINEMATOGRAPHY is done on 35-mm negative film. Takes approved by the director are printed, evaluated (in the form of *dailies* or *rushes*—that is, daily rolls of rush-produced picture and transferred synchronous sound—so that the director, cinematographer, and actors can see and hear the results of the previous day's shooting), and eventually cut by the editor into a *workprint* (a trial version of picture and sound, to which the original camera negative may be matched and cut). A particular shot is taken by one camera, equipped with one lens, from a particular vantage point—that is, from a particular camera *setup*.

In an edited film a *scene* will usually consist of more than one shot, and a full-fledged dramatic encounter in a given location may entail a variety of setups and as many shots as desired. A *sequence* is a consecutive series of shots and/or scenes, and it is not restricted to covering action in a single location.

Development. Development begins when someone gets an idea for a movie. Legally, development begins when the producer hires a writer. The writer may begin with a *treatment,* or scene-by-scene story outline, which is eventually expanded into a full-length screenplay. The writer's key contribution is the structuring of the narrative; he or she surrenders all control over the script when it is sold. The script is then *broken down*, or analyzed as to its production requirements: how much each scene is liable to cost, what props and costumes will be necessary, and how efficiently the scenes may be arranged into an economical shooting schedule.

Once the script has been written, legally researched for possible libel or other actionable qualities, approved, and broken down, and budgeting and financing has been secured, a start date is set—or the project is, for one reason or another, denied final approval and put in *turn-around* (offered to anyone who will reimburse the costs of development).

Pre-Production. Pre-production is the period of converting the screenplay into a blueprint for the production of specific scenes; finding locations, hiring the cast, fixing the final budget, and determining the shooting schedule; designing and constructing the sets, making or buying the costumes, designing the makeup; researching to determine the accuracy of details; and working out the mechanical special effects—those which can be staged before the camera, as opposed to optical special effects, which are done in the laboratory.

The essential collaboration during the development period is between the writer and the producer. During pre-production the creative collaborators are the director, the designer, and the cinematographer. The work of breaking down the script and drafting the shooting schedule is done by the production manager, who is the producer's representative on the set.

Production. Production is the period of principal photography—essentially the shooting and recording, by the first unit, of those scenes in the script which involve the principal actors, under the supervision of the director. A second or third unit, each with its own director and crew, may shoot scenes with crowds or stunt doubles, big action sequences, or landscape and aerial shots. An insert unit shoots close-ups that are cut in, such as inserts of maps, documents, and so forth.

The director is primarily responsible for the integration of camerawork, performance, and editing, and his or her creative control extends until the completion of the first edited version. The composition of a given shot may be chosen by the cinematographer or the director. In consultation with the director, the cinematographer determines how the shots will be lit. The actual work is executed by electricians under the supervision of the *gaffer* (the principal electrician). Most of the moving and hauling is done by *grips*, who are supervised by the key grip.

Live sound is recorded by the production sound team; in most cases one person is in charge of the microphones, another takes care of the tape recorder. Sound tracks may be recorded with or without camera synchronization.

The script supervisor keeps track of which scenes have been shot, as well as of *continuity*, the details within scenes that must match (or relate together logically) from one shot to another.

Post-Production. The fragments of picture and sound that have been so carefully planned and executed are assembled into a whole during post-production. The rolls of negative exposed by the production camera are printed (creating the positive daily rolls that are then cut up for the workprint) and then broken down—cut, rolled up, and stored—into labeled scenes. When the workprint has been edited, or cut to the film editor's, director's, and producer's satisfaction, the original negative footage that corresponds to the workprint footage (and bears the same numbers along its edge) is trimmed and assembled. The workprint may be spliced and respliced until each cut has been perfected. One never experiments with the negative, however, which is handled as little as possible and is spliced permanently with cement.

The daily sound rolls (reels of magnetic tape in sync with the camera rolls) are transferred to *mag film* (sprocketed film base of the same gauge as the picture, and coated with magnetic oxide), so that there is one *frame* of sound for each frame of picture. The sound may be cut and spliced just as easily as the picture. The dialogue track is cut along with the picture by the film editor.

Optical special effects are made by an independent unit, and titles are prepared by the art department. Visual devices like fades, dissolves, and wipes are created in the laboratory on an optical printer; and all of these shots are cut into the edited negative at virtually the last moment.

The soundtrack consists of dialogue, music, and effects. The typical soundtrack includes dialogue and other tracks that are created during post-production and synchronized with the picture. A good deal of dialogue is post-synchronized (particularly if the original has been marred by background noise), as are virtually all music and the majority of effects.

In most cases the composer begins to score a movie

Actor David Naughton is transformed into a werewolf in An American Werewolf in London *(1981). Here, Naughton is being inserted into his costume.*

only when it has reached the workprint stage. The composer works with the music editor, who prepares, times, and cuts the music track. The sound effects editor, who works with the greatest number of tracks, assembles all those sounds which are neither dialogue nor music. When all of the tracks have been edited and re-recorded, the final soundtrack is mixed, in sync with the workprint.

The cinematographer, the director, and the editor work closely with the laboratory until a final trial composite print, or *answer print*, meets their approval. The negative that produced that print becomes "*the* negative" from which, at the onset of the distribution phase, release prints will be struck.

film serials Film serials, the bulk of which were produced in Hollywood between 1913 and the late 1940s, were interrupted melodramas or mysteries ("cliffhangers") that typically consisted of 12 to 15 episodes varying in length from 18 to 30 minutes. Up to 1930, approximately 300 silent serials appeared—the first was *The Adventures of Kathlyn* (1913); the most popular was Pathé's *The Perils of Pauline* (1914), starring Pearl White. At least a part of their charm derived from carefully timed dramatic sequences that substituted for a lack of narrative depth. Among the best-known serials of the sound era, during which Westerns, space stories, and fantasy dominated, were *The Lone Ranger, Captain Video, Flash Gordon, Zorro, The Masked Marvel,* and *The Green Hornet.*

filter, electronic A filter is an electronic circuit that selectively passes or rejects electrical signals according to their frequency by means of a network of capacitors, resistors, and inductors. Filters are classified according to their function. A low-pass filter transmits signals that have a frequency below a specified level; a high-pass filter transmits only high-frequency signals. Band-pass filters pass a narrow range of frequencies while rejecting signals having higher or lower frequencies. Band-elimination filters transmit all but a narrow band of frequencies.

An important class of filter is the active filter. Whereas a conventional or passive filter attenuates some of the signal it is designed to transmit as well as much of the signal it is designed to reject, active filters use one or more operational AMPLIFIERS to restore the level of the desired signal to its original amplitude.

Filters are widely used in electronic circuits. They are used to reduce or eliminate electrical NOISE, enhance the quality of speech transmission systems, and eliminate fluctuations in the amplitude of an electrical current.

---

filtration   In ANALYTICAL CHEMISTRY filtration is a separation method used mostly to separate a precipitate from the solution in which it was formed. A solid-liquid mixture is transferred onto a porous material, such as paper, that allows passage of the liquid (filtrate) but retains the solid. Filtration is also used on a large scale for the separation of solids from liquids in industrial chemical processes.

Common analytical filtration media include different kinds of paper and filter crucibles of various types (sintered glass, porous porcelain or aluminum oxide, and Gooch), all of which are available with different porosities for retaining precipitates having different particle sizes and properties. Filter paper used for quantitative analyses must be of the "ashless" type; it is always destroyed by ignition and leaves less than 0.0001 g of ash. Filter paper is especially suitable for gelatinous precipitates and those which require high-temperature ignition before weighing.

Most filter crucibles have porous bottoms built in. A Gooch crucible, however, has a removable mat (usually asbestos) supported on a perforated bottom. Suction is applied to draw solution through the filter; consequently, filtration and washing require less time. Unless there is a special objection to its use, a filter crucible is preferred over filter paper for gravimetric analysis (see QUANTITATIVE CHEMICAL ANALYSIS).

finance, U.S. government   See BUDGET; INCOME, NATIONAL

---

finance, state and local   State and local finance is the science and practice of raising and expending public revenues by subnational units of government. In federal systems, sovereignty is shared between the central (that is, federal) government and a number of state (or provincial) governments. Local governments, in contrast, are not sovereign but are the creations of the state or provincial governments.

State Finance. In the United States the major objects of state-government expenditure are education, highways, public welfare, and health and hospitals. Although states differ, a substantial portion of some of these expenditures (especially education) is administered through grants to local governments. Individual and corporate INCOME TAXES, general SALES TAXES, and selective sales taxes (including motor-fuel taxes) are the major sources of internal revenue for state governments. About one-fourth of their revenue comes from the federal government. BOND financing also is available to many states, though often restricted by the state constitution.

Local Finance. Local governments in the United States include counties, townships, municipalities, school districts, and special districts. Special districts are formed for particular purposes, such as transportation, irrigation, sewer service, harbor facilities, and so on. School and special districts overlap other local governments. PROPERTY TAXES are the major source of internal revenue for local governments, although municipalities and special districts obtain significant amounts from local income taxes, local sales taxes, and user or service charges. Revenues from both state and federal governments are also important, and most local governments can sell bonds to finance construction of public facilities.

Problems. State and local governments, as the levels of government closest to the people, face an especially strong challenge to provide desired public services at least tax cost. Since World War II the revenue base for central cities has been eroded by migrations of industry and citizens to suburban areas, while INNER CITY service demands have increased. Severe financial crises have arisen for many cities.

Relations with the federal government also involve problems. Many public services (such as education and welfare) are a mixture of local and national interests, and the precise division of authority and responsibility is difficult to establish. In the 1960s and '70s federal grants-in-aid to states and localities expanded greatly both on a categorical (program-by-program) basis and as general REVENUE SHARING (sometimes called block grants; revenue sharing ended in 1986). Matching requirements committed state and local money to these programs. In the late 1970s state and local governments began significant cutbacks because of citizen demands for tax relief at the same time as pressure grew to balance the national budget through federal cutbacks.

---

finch   Finch is a general term popularly applied to more than 1,000 species of stout-billed, seed-eating birds that are classified in several different families and subfamilies. Among the weaverbirds, family Ploceidae, for instance, are many species called finches (see WEAVER FINCH). The WAXBILLS, Estrildidae, are also a type of finch. Charles Darwin based much of his theory of evolution on birds now known as DARWIN'S FINCHES (Geospizidae). In a more restricted sense, however, finches belong primarily to the subfamily Carduelinae of the great family Fringillidae, which also includes the cardinals, buntings, grosbeaks, towhees, sparrows, and many other birds. Other carduelines that are not specifically named finch include the siskins, redpolls, crossbills, and pine grosbeaks.

Most finches, regardless of their classification, are primarily seedeaters, with stout bills and a well-developed gizzard. But even the seedeaters usually feed their young, for a few days at least, on more easily digested insects. Exceptions occur among the GOLDFINCHES, redpolls, and

The purple finch is a sparrow-sized bird native to North America. The male (top left) *is purple red, particularly on the head, breast, and rump; the female* (lower left) *is flecked with brown. Similar in size, both the male* (top right) *and the female* (lower right) *gray-crowned rosy finch have brown-to-black plumage with red or grayish white areas.*

some other carduelines.

Many finches are brightly colored with red, yellow, or blue predominating. Most finches are very musical, with songs that vary from the soft twittering of goldfinches and canaries to the spirited warble of the purple finches in flight. Many authorities consider finches the highest and latest development on the avian evolutionary ladder.

Fine Gael [fin'-e gayl]

The Fine Gael, or United Ireland party, is one of the two major political parties of Ireland. Before 1935 it was called Cuman na nGaedheal (Society of the Gaels). Formed by those who supported the 1921 treaty creating the Irish Free State, it was the ruling party from 1923 to 1932, when the republican FI-ANNA FÁIL won power. Since then Fine Gael has formed five coalition governments (1948–51, 1954–57, 1973–77, 1981–82, 1982–87). Traditionally a more conservative party than Fianna Fáil, it draws much of its support from the middle class.

finfoot

The finfoots, or sun-grebes, are medium-sized, long-bodied birds of the family Heliornithidae. They use their large, lobed toes as paddles when diving and swimming in pursuit of fish and other aquatic life. They inhabit streams in the tropics of South America, Asia, and Africa.

Finger Lakes

The Finger Lakes are a series of long, narrow glacial lakes in west central New York State. From west to east the principal lakes are Conesus, Hemlock, Canadice, Honeoye, Canandaigua, Keuka, Seneca, Cayuga, Owasco, Skaneateles, and Otisco. The lakes vary in length from 18 to 64 km (11 to 40 mi) and are up to 6 km (3.7 mi) wide.

Formed by successive continental ice sheets expanding southward along the paths of preexisting stream valleys, the lakes occupy steep, narrow rock troughs. Seneca, which is 174 km² (67 mi²) in area and 188 m (617 ft) deep, is the largest. The Finger Lakes add much to the natural beauty of a region in which resorts and state parks

attract many vacationers. The region is the center of New York State's wine industry.

fingerprinting

Fingerprinting is the science of using the friction ridge patterns on the fingertips for identification purposes and is one of the earliest forms of scientific evidence to be recognized by courts of law. An individual's ten fingerprints form an indelible, unchangeable signature, and fingerprint records can be used for identification, despite changes in an individual's appearance or age.

The present system of fingerprint classification is derived from the system published in 1900 by Sir Edward

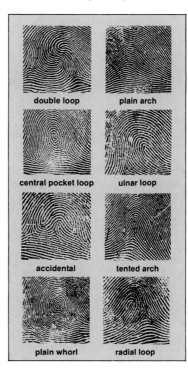

double loop   plain arch

central pocket loop   ulnar loop

accidental   tented arch

plain whorl   radial loop

The Henry system, one of several systems devised for classifying fingerprints, is used in most English-speaking countries. It was developed early in the 20th century by an Englishman, Sir Edward Henry, who classified fingerprints according to eight types, based on three fundamental ridge patterns of loops, arches, and whorls. Complete classification requires a knowledge of the type and number of ridges on all ten fingers.

Henry of Scotland Yard. It is based on the classification of three general patterns—arches, loops, and whorls—which are subdivided into types. This subdivision is extended by ridge counts. Fingerprint cards are filed according to classification type, and the cards can be retrieved by computer for comparison with new, unidentified fingerprints.

One of the most important uses of fingerprints is to prove a suspect's presence at a crime scene. Oil or perspiration on the friction ridges is often transferred to objects handled at a crime scene. These latent prints must be developed by dusting them with fine powder or, if they are on porous material, by treating them with chemicals. A new laser technique is being developed for recording latent fingerprints from surfaces that do not show prints when conventional methods are used. The laser technique can reveal prints that are up to 10 years old.

Fink, Mike

Mike Fink, c.1770–1823, an American frontier hero, was a keelboatman on the Ohio and Mississippi rivers whose physical prowess became legendary in oral and written folklore. A formidable brawler dubbed "king of the keelboatmen," he was also known for his skill in telling tall tales.

Finland

Finland (Finnish: Suomi) is the fifth largest country in Europe, excluding the USSR. Its population center is farther north than that of any other country, except Iceland; its capital, Helsinki, is, after Reykjavik, Iceland, the world's northernmost capital city. About one-third of the country lies north of the Arctic Circle. Finland is bordered on the north by Norway, on the east by the USSR, on the south by the Gulf of Finland, and on the west by the Gulf of Bothnia and Sweden. The country is one of the world's leading manufacturers and exporters of timber and paper products, and its economy depends heavily on the forestry industry.

Land and Resources

Most of Finland is lowland. The highest elevations are in the extreme northwest where Haltia (Lapp: Haldetšokka), the highest point on Finland, rises to 1,328 m (4,357 ft). An ancient granite bedrock shield underlies Finland and is crossed by numerous major fracture lines that appear as gorges, long, narrow lakes, or elongated bays at the coast.

Physical Regions. Finland has three main physical regions: the coastal lowlands, the lake district, and the northern uplands. The coastal lowlands, about 65–130 km (40–80 mi) wide, extend along the indented coastlines of the Gulf of Finland on the south and the Gulf of Bothnia on the west. Thousands of rocky islands lie off the coasts, the principal group being the Åland (Finnish: Ahvenanmaa) Islands. The lake district in southern central Finland is heavily forested and has numerous swamps and bogs. The northern upland, much of which lies north of the Arctic Circle, has poor soils and is the most sparsely populated region of Finland. In the far north, arctic forests give way to tundra, a frozen, forestless region.

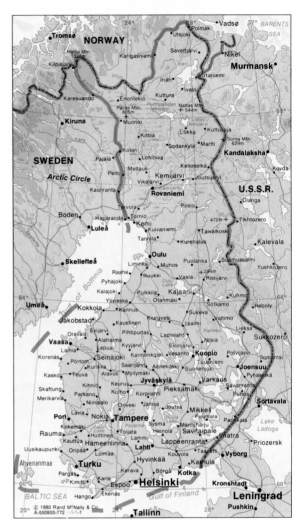

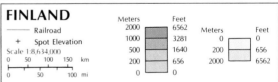

FINLAND

	Meters	Feet		Meters	Feet
——— Railroad	2000	6562		0	0
+ Spot Elevation	1000	3281		200	656
Scale 1:8,634,000	500	1640		2000	6562
0 50 100 150 km	200	656			
0 50 100 mi	0	0			

Soils. The most common soil is till—an unstratified mixture of clay, sand, and gravel—which covers the bedrock almost everywhere. Large areas of clay are found in south and southwest Finland. Peat covers more than 30% of the land area. The soil is usually 3–4 m (10–13 ft) thick but in some places is as thick as 110 m (360 ft). Clay is best suited for agriculture; till and rocky soil, for forestry.

Climate. Finland's climate exhibits both maritime and continental influences. Surrounding seas cool the climate on the coast in spring but warm it in fall. The climate be-

REPUBLIC OF FINLAND

Land: Area: 336,700 km² (130,000 mi²). Capital and largest city: Helsinki (1988 est. pop., 489,965).

People: Population (1990 est.): 4,977,325. Density: 14.8 persons per km² (38.3 per mi²). Distribution (1989 est.): 61.8% urban, 38.2% rural. Official languages: Finnish, Swedish. Major religions: Evangelical Lutheranism, Eastern Orthodoxy.

Government: Type: republic. Legislature: Eduskunta. Political subdivisions: 12 provinces.

Economy: GNP (1988): $92 billion; $14,670 per capita. Labor distribution (1987): agriculture, forestry, and fishing—10.1%; mining and manufacturing—21.9%; services—24.6%; trade—14.1%; other—29.3%; unemployed (1988)—4.5%. Foreign trade (1988): imports—$22 billion; exports—$22.2 billion. Currency 1 markaa = 100 penniä.

Education and Health: Literacy (1990): almost 100% of adult population. Universities (1986): 13. Hospital beds (1986): 60,448. Physicians (1987): 10,889. Life expectancy (1990): women—80; men—71. Infant mortality (1990): 6 per 1,000 live births.

comes more continental, that is, more extreme, toward the east and north. The extreme north is influenced by the Arctic Ocean. Rainfall decreases from 700 mm (28 in) in southern Finland to 400 mm (16 in) in northern Finland. The heaviest rainfall is from August to September, the lightest from February to April. The summer lasts two to four months, the growing season four to six.

Drainage. Finland is known as a land of lakes and islands. The 60,000-odd lakes average 7 m (23 ft) deep and usually have indented shorelines and islands. They are connected by rivers and canals to form long lake systems. Finland's largest lake, Saimaa, is actually a system of more than 100 interconnected smaller lakes. Finland's rivers are short and shallow.

The coast of Finland is more than 1,100 km (700 mi) long, but because it is heavily indented, the shoreline measures nearly 5,000 km (3,000 mi). Finland has about 30,000 coastal islands of which the southwest archipelago is unusual for its shape and beauty.

Vegetation and Animal Life. Forests cover about 60% of the total area. Pines constitute 55% of the forests; spruces, 30%; and birches, 14%. Flora includes 1,227 different species of herbaceous plants and shrubs, 800 species of moss, and more than 1,000 species of lichen. Fauna includes 67 species of mammals (including bear, elk, and wolf), 230 species of birds, and 77 species of fish (33 of which are economically valuable).

Resources. Forests are Finland's most important natural resource, and the country has 18.7 million ha (46.7

million acres) of productive forestland. Minor mineral deposits include copper, nickel, iron, zinc, chromium, lead, and iron pyrites, but they are mostly too small for mining. Limestone and granite are quarried for building materials, and one large mine in eastern Finland produces copper and zinc. Despite abundant water supplies, water must often be transported from long distances to the population centers.

People

Racially, the Finns are mixed, most being either of East-Baltic stock (living mainly in eastern Finland) or of Nordic stock (in the west and south, especially on the coast and in Ahvenanmaa). A small number of LAPPS live in northern Finland (see LAPLAND). Other ethnic groups include about 4,000 Gypsies, 1,500 Jews, and 1,000 Turks.

The Finnish language belongs to the Finno-Ugric family of the URAL-ALTAIC LANGUAGES; it is related to Hungarian. Finnish is spoken by 93.2% of the population, Swedish by 6.6%. Most of the Swedish-speaking people live in the southern coastal area, Ahvenanmaa, and on the coast of Ostrobothnia. About 2,300 persons speak Lapp, which is also of Finno-Ugric origin.

The constitution of Finland allows freedom of worship. Members of the Evangelical Lutheran church constitute 92% of the population; the Orthodox church, 1%; the Roman Catholic church, 1%; the other denominations, 1%; and those with no church affiliation, 5%. The Lutheran and Orthodox churches are recognized as official state churches.

Demography. Although Finland is about ten times the size of the Netherlands, its population is only about one-third as great. The most densely populated area is the southwest, with approximately 70 persons per km^2 (180 per mi^2); the least densely populated area is Lapland, with only 2–3 persons per km^2 (5–8 per mi^2).

Scattered settlements characterize the countryside. Rapid urbanization began after World War II, when 425,000 refugees from Soviet-occupied land were resettled. A majority of them moved to the cities. The largest cities—HELSINKI, TAMPERE, TURKU, and Lahti—are located in the south and southwest.

Education and Health. All children must attend the nine-year comprehensive school. The second stage of education comprises a three-year senior secondary school or a vocational school. At the end of senior secondary school all students take a matriculation examination, and those who pass it can apply to universities or other institutions of higher education.

The standard of national health care is high. The National Health Act of 1972 abolished physicians' fees and provided for the creation of municipal health-care centers throughout the country. The number of hospital beds in relation to population is one of the highest in the world. Heart and lung diseases are the most serious national health problems.

The Arts. The oldest Finnish literature is in the form of epic poetry, legends, stories, and proverbs. Elias Lönnrot (1802–84) collected folk literature and published *Kalevala*, the Finnish national epic. The most important writers of Finnish literature are Aleksis Kivi (1834–72), Frans Eemil SILLANPÄÄ; (who received the Nobel Prize for literature in 1939), and Mika Waltari. Perhaps the most famous poet is Eino Leino (1879–1926); the best-known contemporary poet is Paavo HAAVIKKO.

Finnish music has an excellent international reputation. The best-known Finnish composer outside of Finland is Jean SIBELIUS. Other important composers are Fredrik Pacius (1809–91), Oskar Merikanto (1868–1924), Aarre Merikanto (1893–1958), Leevi Madetoja (1887–1947), and Uuno Klami (1900–61). The folk-music tradition is strong, and the Kaustinen Folk Festival draws large crowds every summer. (See also SCANDINAVIAN MUSIC.)

The high standard of Finnish architecture can be seen even in old church buildings. Eero SAARINEN, Eliel SAARINEN, and Lars Sonck (1870–1956) pioneered the national romantic style, designing both private houses and monumental public buildings. Neoclassicism was introduced by J. S. Sirén (1889–1961), and functionalism by Alvar AALTO. Aalto is also an urban planner, interior designer, and industrial and furniture designer.

The oldest paintings are found in the murals of old churches. Albert Edelfelt (1854–1905) and Akseli Gallen-Kallela (1865–1931) are representatives of the golden era of Finnish painting; their ideas were derived from history and *Kalevala.* Hugo Simberg (1873–1917) was one of the first symbolic painters; Tvko Sallinen (1879–1955) was a well-known expressionist; and Vilho Lampi (1898–1936) represented primitivism.

Economic Activity

Finland's most important industry has traditionally been wood processing, including the production of pulp and paper, but today the metal and engineering industries are the largest source of industrial employment. The chemical industry is now also significant. Next in importance are the food, textile, and electrotechnical industries.

Power. In the mid-1970s, 70% of Finland's energy came from imported coal and petroleum. By the mid-1980s that figure had dropped to less than 50%, chiefly because of increased use of nuclear power. Finland has four nuclear power plants in operation. The other main domestic energy sources are wood, industrial waste, and peat. The use of wood has decreased, and the use of peat increased.

Agriculture. Cultivated land constitutes only about 10% of the total land area, but Finland is almost self-sufficient in agricultural production. The production of grain, dairy products, meat, and eggs exceeds domestic consumption. Wheat and rye are the most important bread grains; other important crops include hay, potato, oats, and barley. Finland's climate and small farms favor dairy and livestock production, which accounts for most of the farm income. Mechanization and fertilization have increased productivity.

Forestry. Forests cover about 60% of the total land area, or about 22.4 million ha (56 million acres), of

Helsinki, the nation's capital and largest city, is located on the Gulf of Finland. During the 9-month winter, icebreakers are necessary to keep the harbor open to navigation.

Finland's low-lying topography was shaped by the advance and retreat of glaciers during a succession of ice ages. The rivers, lakes, and streams formed by glaciation provide Finland with virtually inexhaustible potential for hydroelectric power.

which 18.6 million ha (46.5 million acres) are productive. Since the 1950s wide-scale swamp drainage, fertilizing, and reforestation have improved production. Private individuals control about two-thirds of the forest land; about one-quarter is state owned.

Transportation. Roads are the leading means of transportation in Finland; three-fourths of all households have at least one car. Railways connect the country with Sweden and the USSR, and a subway system began operating in Helsinki in 1982. Waterborne traffic is hampered by frozen rivers and harbors during the winter, but the use of icebreakers makes this a less-serious problem today than in former times.

Trade. Finland is dependent on foreign trade. Although exports are diverse, forest products and metal and engineering products account for nearly three-fourths of the total value of exported goods. The major imports are raw materials, fuel, and machinery. Finland is an associated member of the European Free Trade Association (EFTA), but trade with the European Community (EC) surpasses trade with the members of EFTA. Finland continues to have strong economic ties with the USSR, and in 1989 the two countries renewed their bilateral trade agreement.

Government

The constitution of Finland was adopted on July 17, 1919. Finland is a republic, headed by a president elected for a six-year term. The general electorate—all citizens over age 18—chooses a college of 301 electors, which in turn selects the president. Supreme executive power is vested in the president, who is responsible for the country's foreign relations. Legislative power is shared by the president and the one-chamber parliament of 200 members. The council of state (cabinet), which is headed by a prime minister, is responsible for the country's general administration. Judicial power is vested in independent courts of justice. The country is divided into 12 provinces, which are subdivided into municipalities. The unit of local government is the commune.

History

Lapp settlements existed in Finland as early as 7500 BC. Finns began to migrate to the country from the Baltic states during the 1st century AD. Permanent Finnish settlements had developed in southern Finland by 1000. Beginning in the 12th century, Sweden gradually con-

Timber, Finland's greatest single source of revenue, is floated along an extensive network of inland waterways to a collection depot near a mill, where it will be processed.

The open-pit copper mine near Outokumpu, in southeastern Finland, is the site of the nation's most extensive mineral deposits. Large amounts of copper, lead, and gold have been found.

quered Finland and introduced Christianity to the Finns. The Pähkinänsäari peace treaty in 1323 established the boundary between Sweden and Novgorod, the Russian power to the east. In the 16th century, as Sweden consolidated its authority in Finland, Lutheranism was proclaimed the official religion. The peace treaty of Stolbovo (1617) gave Sweden the eastern parts of Finland and Inkerinmaa (Ingria). These, however, were lost to Russia in the Uudenkaupunki peace treaty (Treaty of Nystad) in 1721. During the 18th century a growing separatist movement in Finland demanded independence.

As a result of the war of 1808–09, Sweden surrendered Finland to Russia, and it became an autonomous grand duchy with the tsar assuming the title grand duke of Finland. The duchy was allowed to retain its old constitution. It had its own parliament, government, administration, law and courts, postal services, army (until 1904), and currency. In 1906 the Finnish diet was replaced by the unicameral parliament, and simultaneously universal suffrage was adopted.

At times, strong attempts were made to Russianize Finland, provoking a growing desire for complete independence. After the Russian Revolution of November (N.S.) 1917, Finland declared its independence on Dec. 6, 1917. Civil war broke out in 1918, with Soviet-supported Communist troops fighting German-supported

non-Communists, the latter led by Carl Gustaf Emil MANNERHEIM. In 1920 peace was concluded with the USSR following a territorial war over KARELIA, but relations between the two countries remained cool. By the outbreak of World War II, Finland had adopted a policy of neutrality, and when the USSR demanded Finnish territory and military bases for defense against Germany, Finland refused. On Nov. 30, 1939, Soviet troops invaded Finland, beginning the RUSSO-FINNISH WAR. In March 1940, by the Treaty of Moscow, Finland ceded Karelian territories to the USSR. When Germany invaded the USSR in 1941, Finland reoccupied its former territories. In 1944, however, Soviet troops staged a counterinvasion and, by the armistice signed in September 1944, Finland was forced to cede the Karelian Isthmus and other eastern lands, the corridor in the extreme north to the Barents Sea, and to grant a 50-year lease to a military base at Porkkala. The USSR returned the military base in 1955 in exchange for the renewal of a friendship treaty signed in 1948. Since World War II, Finland has maintained a careful neutrality, often with special regard to the USSR, its powerful neighbor to the east. Finland's policy of neutrality was largely formulated by Urho K. KEKKONEN, who served as president from 1956 until 1982. It was reaffirmed by Mauno Koivisto on his election to the presidency in 1982, and confirmed by Mikhail Gorbachev in 1989.

The Lapps, a seminomadic people who inhabit northern Finland and much of subarctic Scandinavia, have traditionally herded the reindeer that inhabit the region.

Finland joined the United Nations and the Nordic Council in 1955 and signed an agreement with the European Community in 1973.

Finland, Gulf of

The Gulf of Finland is a shallow arm of the Baltic Sea that extends east-west for about 400 km (250 mi) between Finland and the USSR. The two largest cities on the gulf are Helsinki, the capital of Finland, and Leningrad, the second largest city of the USSR. At its eastern end the gulf is connected by the Saimaa Canal to several lakes, the largest of which, Ladoga, is in the USSR. The canal is used for shipping cargo.

Finn mac Cumhail

[fin muh-kool'] In Irish folklore, Finn mac Cumhail is the hero of a group of ballads and tales known as the Fenian cycle, set about the 3d century AD. The posthumous son of Cumhail, Finn was reared by peasants and entered the service of the seer Finn Eger. Finn mac Cumhail accidentally tasted the salmon of Lynn Feic, which was the source of all wisdom, when he burned his thumb while cooking the salmon and sucked on the thumb to soothe it. Thereafter, he obtained wisdom merely by chewing his thumb. The stories deal primarily with the struggle of Finn, his son Oisin, his grandson Oscar, and the Fianna warriors against the Fomors, giants representing the forces of darkness. (See also OSSIAN.)

Finnegans Wake

Massive in size, dauntingly obscure, and full of verbal extravagance, James JOYCE's novel *Finnegans Wake* (1939), centering on a Dublin family, proceeds by analogy and parallel to incorporate virtually all history and much of art, psychology, and mythology. For his structure, Joyce relies on Giambattista Vico's cyclical view of history, which posits four ages: the divine, the heroic, the human, and the age of confusion. The novel, accordingly, is divided into four parts, each corresponding to a particular age with its characteristic features and attributes. In this richly experimental work, begun in 1923, Joyce joins the local and the universal through his portrayal of the creative father of the Earwicker family, his quarreling sons, and his renovating wife.

Finney, Charles G.

Charles Grandison Finney, b. Warren, Conn., Aug. 29, 1792, d. Aug. 16, 1875, was an American lawyer, theologian, and revivalist. His revivals featured daring, new methods of evangelism—protracted meetings of nightly gatherings and the "anxious bench," where souls under conviction could pray for salvation. Finney encouraged people to exert themselves in becoming Christians and in overcoming social ills such as slavery. In 1835 he became professor of theology at Oberlin College, where he taught until 1875. He was president of the college from 1851 to 1866.

Finnish language   see URAL-ALTAIC LANGUAGES

Finnish literature   see FINLAND

Finnish-Russian War   see RUSSO-FINNISH WAR

Finno-Ugric language   see URAL-ALTAIC LANGUAGES

fir

Firs are cone-bearing evergreen trees belonging to the pine family, Pinaceae. There are about 40 species of true firs, genus *Abies*; all are native to the Northern Hemisphere. They grow in cool regions extending southward into the mountains of Guatemala, northern Africa, the Himalayas, and Taiwan.

Fir trees usually have bark with resinous blisters that produce furrows. Needles are flattened or sometimes four-angled, pointed, or notched, and are often arranged in two rows; they live for seven to ten years. Cones, which are egg-shaped or cylindrical, usually occur on topmost branches and mature in one season. The genus *Abies* is easily distinguishable from other CONIFERS by the disklike leaf scars and by the erect cones that break up as soon as the seeds are ripe.

The wood of fir is soft and easily worked. Because it is odorless, it is in demand for butter, lard, and grocery boxes. After treatment with a preservative it is sometimes used for telephone poles and for piles. Oleoresins are extracted from some firs and are known in the trade as Canada balsam, or Strasburg turpentine, and leaf oils.

Some firs have been introduced into the United States

The fir is a handsome North temperate evergreen tree grown for its wood and used in landscaping. Two species of fir are the grand fir (left), which grows to a height of 91 m (300 ft), and the white fir (right). Firs bear upright cones (center) and needles that are aromatic when crushed.

as landscape trees. The Spanish fir, *A. pinsapo*, is commonly grown in the Pacific Northwest. Another commonly grown ornamental is *A. nordmanniana*.

Firdawsi [fur-dow'-see] Firdawsi, *c*.935–*c*.1020, whose original name was Abolqasem Mansur, is considered one of the greatest Persian poets and is the author of the Iranian national epic, the *Shah Namah* (Book of Kings). Little is known about his life except that he lived and died in the eastern Iranian province of Khorasan. Most of what is written about him appears to be legend.

The *Shah Namah*, nearly 60,000 couplets long, traces the fortunes of Persia dynasty by dynasty, from the creation of man to the Arab conquest (*c*.637–51). It was based on earlier chronicles by other poets and legends passed down to Firdawsi. He began the work during the Samanid dynasty, worked on it continuously for 35 years, and completed it in 1010, after the conquest by Mahmud the Ghaznavid, who initially rejected it. The work had a profound effect on Persian literature and provided favorite themes for Persian painters.

fire Fire is a rapid, sustained chemical reaction that produces light and heat. Except in cases where special oxidants are used, fires are the result of a fuel rapidly combining with the oxygen in the air.

The ability of primitive societies to use fire was crucial to their development and success. Every human culture of the recent past is known to have had experience with fire; a site near Nice, France, has yielded evidence that hominids used fire even half a million years ago. Although the first sources of fire were assumed to be the results of natural effects (lightning or volcanism), the methods originally used for deliberate firemaking are not clearly

known. It is likely, though, that some means of generating heat by friction was first used; many variations of this principle have been employed. Fires can also be ignited by percussion methods, such as by striking the mineral

Primitive methods of igniting wood chips enabled Neolithic man to produce at will the essential tool of fire. The fire plow (1), used today among primitive peoples in Polynesia and parts of Africa, ignites tinder by friction generated when a wood cylinder is rubbed in a groove. The fire drill (2) and the bow drill (3) both generate heat when a stick is revolved rapidly in a wood socket. The fire piston (4), found in Indonesia, uses the heat of quickly compressed air to ignite tinder placed within a wood or bamboo tube.

pyrite to produce a slow-burning spark.

The three traditionally essential ingredients of fire are heat, fuel, and oxygen; a fire can be extinguished by removing or consuming any one of these. A closer understanding of the chemical reactions of the oxidation process shows that a fourth ingredient is involved: chemical FREE RADICALS. The fire is thus perpetuated by a free-radical CHAIN REACTION, and a recent approach to fire control uses chemically active inhibitors and suppression agents to terminate the chain. These may be used to directly extinguish fires, or they may be applied to materials to render them fire-resistant.

See also: COMBUSTION; FIRE EXTINGUISHER; FIRE PREVENTION AND CONTROL; FLAME; MATCH.

fire engine The world's first fire engines date from Alexandria in the 1st century BC. They were huge, water-filled syringes used to squirt a stream of water on the fire. By the time of the Great Fire of London (AD 1666), crude, hand-operated pumps had been developed; they were supplied with water by bucket brigades but were unable to generate enough water to cope with a large fire.

The first steam-powered fire engine was built in 1829 by George Braithwaite. Paul Rapsey Hodge, an English engineer, built America's first self-propelled steam fire engine in 1840. The first truly successful steam fire engine was built in 1852 by Moses Latta of Cincinnati, Ohio. Called the *Joe Ross*, it rode on two rear wheels, with one front wheel for steering. It weighed 9 metric tons (10 U.S. tons), and four horses were required to pull it. Although it was a ponderous machine, it signaled the end of man- and horse-drawn engines.

By the end of the 19th century, engineers were working on a steam-propelled vehicle that would be entirely independent of auxiliary power, but soon after, the internal-combustion engine displaced the steam engine.

Early motorized pumpers had two engines, one to propel the vehicle and one to drive the pump. The first pumper having a single engine that did both jobs was manufactured at the beginning of the 20th century, by the Waterous Fire Engine Works of Saint Paul, Minn.

Ladders on fire engines were introduced in the 18th century. They first were used only to help people escape from the upper floors of buildings on fire.

In about 1832, sectional ladders that could be joined together to make one long ladder were developed in London. The first successful aerial ladder truck was invented in 1868 by Daniel Hayes, a San Francisco fireman.

Modern aerial ladders are operated hydraulically and

The earliest fire-fighting devices included the hand-held syringe (left), used since ancient times, and the two-man tub pump (right), developed in Europe during the 17th century.

The first steam-pumped fire engine (left) was invented (1829) by George Braithwaite of London. A logical development of the steam engine used to pump water from mines, the steam fire engine was, however, slow to gain acceptance by traditional fire companies. Paul R. Hodge's "Exterminator" (right), the first self-propelled steam fire engine, was introduced in New York in 1841. Weighing eight tons, this inefficient vehicle often broke down.

(Above) *By the late 19th century, manufacturers began to produce lightweight, efficient steam pumps. Horse-drawn steam engines, such as this double vertical piston engine, were used until the advent of the internal combustion engine.*

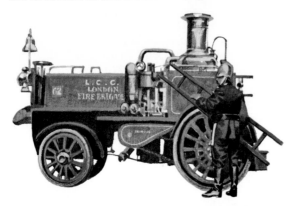

The self-propelled steam fire engine, developed during the late 19th century, was used primarily for large fires in urban areas. Called the "Fire King," this engine was built in 1899 by the firm of Merryweather and Sons.

can reach a height of nearly 50 m (164 ft). They are usually mounted on turntablelike disks, allowing great flexibility in fire-fighting and rescue operations. Today's fire fighters often use elevating platforms and aerial towers.

fire extinguisher   Portable fire extinguishers are devices used to extinguish fires in their early stages. A fire extinguisher consists of a container, an extinguishing agent, a pressure-producing device, and a mechanism, such as a hose and a nozzle, for discharging the contents.

An early type of extinguisher was the "squirt," a pumplike device consisting of a cylinder and a plunger for discharging water. "Fire annihilators" were large containers of water or other liquids that were designed to burst when thrown on a burning object.

The first modern portable extinguisher consisted of a metal cylinder filled with a solution of sodium bicarbon-

ate and water beneath a container of sulfuric acid. When the extinguisher was inverted, the acid mixed with the solution to form carbon dioxide gas, which expelled the liquid through a small, hand-held hose. These soda-acid extinguishers have gradually been replaced by a multipurpose, dry-chemical extinguisher that is effective on a wide range of fires.

To designate the suitability of a fire extinguisher for a particular fire, fires are classified according to the material that is on fire. Class A fires involve ordinary combustibles such as paper, wood, and cloth; Class B fires cover flammable and combustible liquids, greases, and similar materials; Class C fires are those involving electrical equipment; and Class D fires are limited to combustible metals such as magnesium.

See also: FIRE PREVENTION AND CONTROL.

fire prevention and control   In the United States more than 3 million fires occur each year, causing thousands of deaths (some 6,000 annually), hundreds of thousands of injuries, and billions of dollars in property damage. Despite a dramatic drop in recent years, the U.S. rate of fire-caused deaths is the highest of the industrialized nations.

The United States has the highest rate of ARSON (deliberate burning) in the world. The crime of arson causes almost 1,000 deaths yearly and contributes more than $1.5 billion to fire-related damage.

Fire Departments

Until the mid-18th century, city dwellers had only the fire watchman and the volunteer bucket brigade to protect them from fires. Benjamin Franklin organized the first permanent fire company in 1736 in Philadelphia. By the late 1800s, however, a series of devastating fires had claimed thousands of lives and destroyed whole sections of many U.S. cities. The principal causes for these conflagrations were poor building construction and shoddy materials, insufficient water supplies, and a fragmented system of fire fighting by volunteer fire departments.

By 1900, salaried fire departments, steam-propelled fire engines, telegraph fire-alarm systems, and fire hydrants were in use in the largest U.S. cities. Today nearly every city and town in the United States is served by an organized fire department. In larger cities, fire fighters are paid for full-time service. In small towns and villages, fire fighters are often volunteers who receive no pay or "call" fire fighters who are paid for each alarm they answer. The United States has some 30,000 fire departments; 28,000 are volunteer. About 1.5 million fire fighters provide fire prevention and fire-fighting services.

Fire fighting is an extremely hazardous occupation, with more than 100 fire-fighter deaths and more than 100,000 injuries every year.

Fire Fighting

The first essential in a fire-fighting system is a method of giving an alarm to the fire department. Modern fire-alarm systems may be simple pull-alarms in street boxes or sophisticated voice boxes with which the caller can talk directly to the fire department.

The basic fire-fighting vehicle is a self-propelled truck, the FIRE ENGINE, adapted for a variety of functions and carrying an extensive assortment of tools and equipment: pumps, hoses, water tanks, ladders, and portable tools and appliances. The type of engine equipment will vary with the intended service. Pumpers and ladder trucks are designed for different purposes.

Other fire-fighting equipment that may be brought to the scene of the fire includes portable FIRE EXTINGUISHERS, radios, electric lights and generators, and foam-making equipment.

Preventive Technology

Increased scientific knowledge about the nature of fires now permits accurate computer simulation of the progress of a fire. Computer simulation can also measure the effectiveness of such preventive devices as smoke detectors, sprinklers, and fire-resistant materials. The period before a fire within a room "flashes over"—that is, grows from a small fire into one where the entire room is ablaze—may be only a few minutes. A simulation can demonstrate the most efficient escape routes.

Well over three-quarters of all U.S. homes now have at least one SMOKE DETECTOR, and local fire ordinances usually require the installation of detectors in all new homes.

The most effective means of controlling fire in large buildings are automatic fire sprinkler systems. Water pipes are positioned behind the ceilings; at intervals, sprinkler heads protrude into the room. Sufficient heat destroys the seals in the sprinklers, releasing a steady stream of water.

Fire Suppressants. Water is still the most commonly used extinguishing agent. It cools the burning material and smothers the fire. For special situations, however, other extinguishing agents are more effective. Fire-fighting foam is used primarily to fight fires involving flammable liquids. Carbon dioxide suppresses fires involving gas, flammable liquids, electrical equipment, and ordinary combustible material such as paper and wood. Halon was a preferred extinguishing agent for fire suppression on airplanes and in installations of electronic equipment, because its dense vapor left little residue. Its use, however, is being phased out because of its destructive effect on the atmosphere's ozone layer.

Fire-Safety Codes and Standards. Major elements of fire-prevention technology are the codes and standards developed to prevent fires. The National Fire Protection Association (NFPA) publishes fire-safety standards for such diverse areas as nuclear plants, high-rise buildings, and hospitals.

Building Design. Three principal elements determine the degree of fire hazard in a building: its structure, its contents, and the interior finishes. The interior finishes, such as wood paneling, wallboard, acoustical tile, furniture, and carpeting fabrics, must all be evaluated for their flammability characteristics. In many cases, local codes give minimum fire-resistance standards for interior-finish materials; many materials carry flammability information.

Large fires often produce billows of smoke, fumes, and flame and are extremely difficult and dangerous to extinguish. Despite advances in fire-fighting equipment and techniques, fires claim 6,000 lives annually in the United States alone.

A building's contents may affect the severity of a fire. Local fire departments should be made aware of the storage of highly flammable materials, or of products that could produce toxic gases when they burn.

Forest Fires

The responsibility for forest-fire control in the United States is shared by the states and the U.S. Forest Service of the federal government. Because the majority of U.S. forest fires are believed to begin through human intent or carelessness, the most effective preventive technique is disseminating information on the dangers.

All forest fires begin on the floor of the forest, where the most easily flammable debris—leaves, twigs, and small growth—burns first. Forests may sometimes be cleared of this debris, often by carefully controlled burning. Where the danger of fire seems imminent, as in hot, dry seasons, firebreaks—clear channels that have been emptied of all flammable materials—are bulldozed through.

In heavily forested areas a firewatch system is usually maintained during dry periods. Consisting of a chain of

In Yellowstone National Park, a fire fighter shovels dirt to smother flaming underbrush during the great fire of the summer of 1988. Almost 180,000 ha (450,000 acres) were touched by the fire. Half of that area was completely burned. For many years, fire-management policy in the park had been to allow fires to burn themselves out. A combination of drought and high winds, however, increased the size and ferocity of the 1988 fire to almost unmanageable proportions. When flames threatened homes outside the park, fire fighters were called in. The fires were not completely extinguished until the rains came in November.

lookout towers often supplemented by small aircraft, the system is linked by radio to a central office that can dispatch fire-fighting crews as soon as a blaze is spotted.

Although fighting a large forest fire requires large crews, heavy equipment, and considerable knowledge of how fire behaves under the rapidly changing conditions within a forest, fire-fighting techniques are basic and simple. In order to stop the fire, it is necessary to remove the fire's fuel—by creating firebreaks, spreading chemicals that decrease the flammability of wood, pumping water, or spreading smothering materials such as dirt or sand.

Under difficult conditions—when the forest is unusually dry and winds are high—even the most well-organized firefighting crew may be unable to stop a forest fire.

See also: COMBUSTION; FIRE; FLAME.

firearms   A firearm is a weapon that uses the force of an explosive propellant to project a missile. Firearms, or small arms, are distinguished by caliber (the width of the barrel opening), and comprise weapons up to and including those of .60 caliber (0.6in/15.24-mm bore), and all gauges of SHOTGUN. (CANNON is the term for those weapons with calibers greater than 0.8 in, or 20 mm. Larger-caliber weapons are usually categorized as ARTILLERY.) Among small arms, the RIFLE and shotgun are both long-barreled weapons used for long-range shooting; the PISTOL has a shorter barrel and is accurate only at relatively short ranges. The REVOLVER, usually a pistol, has a revolving barrel that allows repeat firing. The MACHINE GUN is an automatic firearm, the first of a line of weapons including assault rifles and submachine guns.

Early Firearms. The precise origin of firearms is unknown, although they were certainly in use by the early 14th century and were fairly common in Europe by mid-century. These early guns were little more than large-caliber tubes of wrought iron or cast bronze, closed at one end and loaded by placing GUNPOWDER and projectile in the muzzle, or open end. They were fired by touching a burning wick, or match, to the powder at a "touch-hole" bored in the top of the barrel. To make certain that the powder would ignite, a recess was incised around the hole into which additional powder—the primer—was poured.

Firing Mechanisms. The first major improvement in small arms was the introduction of a mechanical firing mechanism, or lock, which lowered the match to the touch hole with a pull of the trigger. This matchlock improved accuracy by permitting the gunner to concentrate on aiming the weapon, rather than having to guide the match to the primer. In use by the early 15th century, matchlock guns were the first small arms to have a significant impact on the conduct of warfare. Matchlock mechanisms became increasingly sophisticated over the next two centuries, but all required a smoldering match to ignite the primer. The principle of self-ignition was introduced in the early 16th century with the invention of the wheel-lock, which fired the powder by mechanically generated sparks. Wheel-locks were the weapon of choice for cavalrymen of the time.

The problem of protecting the primer from rain while making it easy to fire was partially solved by the development of the flash pan, a small covered dish that held the primer. The invention of the flintlock improved on the flash-pan design. The flintlock was a spark-generating mechanism in which a flint, actuated by the trigger, struck the metal handle of the pan cover, at the same time pushing the cover back so that the powder was exposed to receive the sparks. The flintlock was the dominant ignition system from the early 1600s. The British "Brown Bess" MUSKET was introduced in the 1690s and remained in service without significant modification until the 1840s.

The evolution of military firearms is traced by studying selected historical weapons. The matchlock petronel (A), used during the late 16th century, was fired by touching a lighted match to the priming powder through the operation of the trigger; the curved stock helped absorb the recoil. The wheel-lock, as in this 17th-century English pistol (B), was favored by cavalrymen but was too fragile for use by the infantry. The smoldering match was discarded in favor of a spring-wound wheel that struck a piece of iron pyrite, directing sparks to the priming powder. The Kentucky rifle (C), a long-barreled, muzzle-loading weapon, was developed by the Pennsylvania Dutch and was produced first with flintlock and later with percussion firing mechanisms. The Spencer Model 1860 (D), widely used by Union cavalry during the U.S. Civil War, was the first successful repeating carbine. The first practical revolver, the Colt Patterson percussion pistol (E), was manufactured from 1836 to 1842. The lever-action repeating Winchester Model 73 (F) was the favored multipurpose weapon of settlers in the American West. The Maxim gun (G), developed by Hiram S. Maxim, was adopted by the German army in 1908. Firing 450 rounds per minute, it was the first successful automatic machine gun.

Rifling. Smoothbore muskets were notorious for their short range and poor accuracy. Seeking to improve performance, gun makers etched spiral grooves, or rifling, inside the musket barrel. The grooving imparted a spin to the projectile, thus stabilizing its trajectory. Rifles became popular with hunters in both Europe and America, but they were impractical for most military uses because they were difficult to load. In 1849 the French army captain Claude Minié invented the conical minié ball, which was easily dropped down the barrel of a rifled musket but expanded to engage the rifling when the weapon was fired. Rifles using expandable bullets had four times the range and accuracy of the smoothbore musket. Their introduction to the battlefield began a new and bloody era of warfare.

Metallic Cartridges. The percussion cap, invented in the early 19th century, provided for more reliability than had earlier ignition mechanisms. A small copper cup containing an explosive charge that ignited when it was struck by a small hammer (later, a firing pin), the percussion cap was soon attached directly to metallic cartridges containing gunpowder, thus joining the ignition system, propellant, and projectile in one easily loaded package (see AMMUNITION).

Because the metallic cartridge achieved a gas-tight seal with the barrel, all of the gases generated by the gunpowder explosion were channeled forward, to propel the cartridge, and none could escape to the rear and into the face of the shooter. Breech-loading using loose powder had been impractical, since the gases escaped back into the action. The invention of the cartridge led to the fabrication of the first practical breech-loading weapons. By the late 1860s the muzzle-loader had become obsolete. Ammunition magazines, which could hold many cartridges, and other quick-loading mechanisms were devised for breech-loaders in the last half of the 19th century, producing repeating rifles capable of rapid, accurate fire even at long range.

Assault Rifles. Machine guns had made their appearance in the 1860s. In World War I, though heavy and requiring more than one man to operate, they had a devastating effect and forced changes in military tactics and strategies. By World War II, light machine guns and automatic rifles were in common use. The lighter a weapon was made, however, the more difficult it was to control during automatic fire. In 1943 the Germans introduced the first true assault rifle, an automatic weapon that used mid-sized cartridges that attained ranges approaching those of standard rifle ammunition, but produced considerably less recoil. The Soviet Kalashnikov rifle (AK-47) and the U.S. M-16 are contemporary assault rifles. They are fully- and semi-automatic, and are capable of accurate rapid fire.

See also: SHOOTING.

firebrick   see REFRACTORY MATERIALS

firefly   Fireflies, also called lightning bugs, are members of the family Lampyridae, order Coleoptera. These beetles are 0.5 to 2 cm (0.2 to 0.8 in) long, with the head characteristically concealed from above by the pronotum, an extension of the thorax. Many species in this family possess luminous glands in one or more segments of the abdomen, which emit cold light that is used as a mating signal (see BIOLUMINESCENCE). Many species have wingless females, and these, along with the luminous larvae, are often called glowworms.

The firefly species P. pennsylvanica, *common to the eastern United States, is a long, slender beetle with luminescent abdominal segments. During evenings in June and July, meadows are transformed with the flashing lights of thousands of fireflies.*

fireproofing   see FIRE PREVENTION AND CONTROL

Firestone, Harvey S.   Harvey Samuel Firestone, b. Columbiana, Ohio, Dec. 20, 1868, d. Feb. 7, 1938, was a leader in the U.S. tire and rubber industry. He first became interested in tires while working as a salesman for his uncle's buggy company. In 1896 he formed a compa-

ny in Chicago to sell tires. He moved to Akron, Ohio, in 1900 and formed the Firestone Tire & Rubber Company, of which he was president until 1932.

In 1906 Firestone became the principal supplier of tires for the Ford Motor Company and subsequently developed a close friendship with Henry Ford. Firestone introduced detachable rims and, in 1923, the balloon tire. In the 1920s the company established huge rubber plantations in Liberia. By the late 1930s, Firestone was supplying a quarter of the tires used in the United States.

fireworks   Fireworks are devices that use explosive, flammable material to create spectacular displays of light, noise, and smoke. Although they are usually thought of today in connection with celebrations, one of their earliest uses was in warfare, which is a role they still play. Pyrotechnics is the art and technology of making and using fireworks.

The Chinese are often credited with the invention and early development of fireworks. The knowledge spread west, through Arabia to Europe. But as late as the 18th century, fireworks still lacked what is now considered an essential characteristic: color. By the early 19th century potassium chlorate was in use; with the addition of various metallic salts to it, brilliant colors could be produced. Various chemical compounds such as potassium chlorate, potassium nitrate, and potassium perchlorate contain the oxygen necessary for COMBUSTION of the pyrotechnic mixture. The salts of these metals produce the colors indicated: strontium produces a red color; copper produces blue; barium, green; and sodium, yellow. Magnesium and aluminum powder add extra sparkle and flash.

Nearly all types of fireworks have a body that is built up by rolling paper around a form until the desired thick-

A Roman candle consists of a sealed cardboard cylinder (1) *packed with several layers of fuses, metal salt pellets, and gunpowder. A burning taper is used to light a slow-burning fuse* (2), *which lies above a salt pellet and a gunpowder charge. When the burning fuse reaches the salt pellet* (3), *the pellet begins to burn, igniting the gunpowder. The gunpowder charge ejects the flaring pellet as a sparkling ball of color* (4) *and ignites a fuse below it. The entire cycle is then repeated* (5).

1   2   3   4   5

The colors, fiery flashes, and star-burst effects of fireworks displays are produced by using metal salts and metal powders in combination with an explosive. Sodium salts produce a yellow flash; barium, a bright green one; and magnesium, brilliant sparks.

ness is reached. The casing must be packed so that the pyrotechnic compound is thoroughly compressed, because any cavity left in the mixture can lead to malfunction at the time of ignition.

Civilian, decorative fireworks include rockets, fountains, and sparklers. Special displays are produced by attaching fireworks to a frame in a particular pattern. Military pyrotechnics are used for various purposes. Illumination devices, which normally have a magnesium mixture for the filler, can illuminate a battlefield for short periods. They can be activated by a trip wire, shot by artillery or mortars, or dropped by parachute. Pyrotechnics launched

by a small rifle or rocket are available in several colors for SIGNALING. Artillery simulators, which are actually large, smoke-emitting firecrackers, add realism to training maneuvers, and smoke devices are used to screen a unit's movement from the enemy.

---

first aid   First aid is the immediate, temporary care given to a sick or injured person before medical help is obtained. In cases such as heart attack, poisoning, or severe bleeding, immediate assistance may be lifesaving. Persons trained in first-aid techniques are able to assess

Unconsciousness may result from asphyxia, poisoning, epilepsy, heart attack, or other causes. Often the cause is unknown to the person administering first aid. The mouth is first cleared of foreign matter (A); then the victim is placed on his or her abdomen (B), with the head turned to the side to ease breathing. If the victim is not breathing, artificial respiration should be administered and medical help obtained.

A
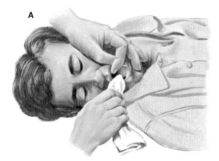

B

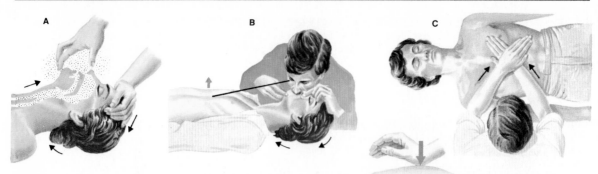

To administer mouth-to-mouth artificial respiration, the rescuer should turn the victim on his or her back; remove any foreign matter from the mouth; tilt the victim's head back and push the chin up (A) to open the airway; place the mouth tightly over the victim's mouth while pinching the victim's nostrils closed (B); blow air into the victim's mouth and lungs until the chest rises; then pause and watch the chest fall. This procedure should be repeated until the victim resumes breathing. If the heart is not beating, the person giving first aid should apply external cardiac compression (C) on the lower sternum (breastbone), alternating compression with mouth-to-mouth respiration.

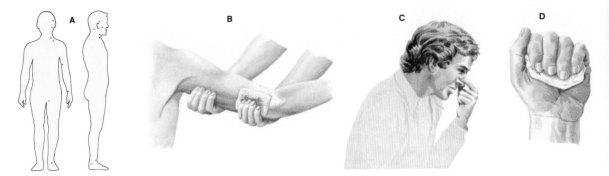

Severe bleeding is treated by applying direct pressure (B) to the wound and elevating the injured part of the body. If direct pressure fails to stop bleeding from an artery, pressure may also be applied to the supplying artery at a "pressure point" (A, indicated by dots). The victim of a nosebleed, usually a minor injury, should be placed in a sitting position (C), leaning forward, and with the nostrils pressed together. Bleeding from the palm of the hand can be controlled by the victim's forming a fist on a clean dressing (D).

(A) Superficial burns may be treated by placing the burned area under cool running water or by immersion in cool water. (B) Severe burns should be covered with loose, clean, dry dressings to prevent infection; the victim should be kept lying down and treated for shock if it occurs. (C) On encountering a person with burning clothing, the person giving first aid should smother the flames with a rug or blanket. (D) The head of a victim with burns on the mouth or throat should be positioned to help keep the air passage open.

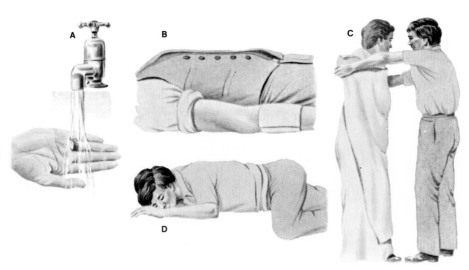

the nature and extent of an emergency and determine what procedures are appropriate. Although they will not be able to diagnose completely and precisely, as a physician would, first-aid training should enable them to make intelligent decisions about the best course of action to follow.

The need for training in first aid is evident, considering that millions of accidents occur in homes each year, with falls being the most common, followed by burns, suffocation, and poisoning, especially of children. More than 100,000 Americans are killed in such accidents each year.

Approximately half a million Americans die of heart attack annually, many of them before professional help can arrive or before the patient can be taken to a hospital. Studies indicate that many of these heart-attack victims would have survived the initial attack if they had been kept breathing by CARDIOPULMONARY RESUSCITATION (CPR) long enough to have received treatment in a hospital. This is only one of the many reasons why at least one member of each family should attend a course in first aid or CPR, and every household should have a first-aid kit and manual.

Persons administering first aid are protected from legal liability for negligence by Good Samaritan Laws in 14 states, as long as they used first aid to the best of their ability and knowledge. In the other states, there is an unwritten law to this effect, and the court system has never found anyone guilty of negligence as long as they used good common sense and there was no intent to do harm when they gave first aid.

1st Amendment The 1st Amendment to the CONSTITUTION OF THE UNITED STATES is the best-known provision of the BILL OF RIGHTS. It prohibits Congress from making any laws that abridge or restrict FREEDOM OF RELIGION, FREEDOM OF SPEECH, FREEDOM OF THE PRESS, or the right to assemble peaceably and to petition the government for redress of grievances. In *Gitlow* v. *New York* (1925)—and in other important cases (*Near* v. *Minnesota*, 1931; *DeJonge* v. *Oregon*, 1937; *Cantwell* v. *Connecticut*, 1940)—the Supreme Court held that the protection of these fundamental liberties applied also to the states under the DUE PROCESS clause of the 14TH AMENDMENT.

Differences and difficulties in interpretation have characterized much of the later history of the 1st Amendment. For example, the amendment prevents Congress from making any law regarding the "establishment of religion," but this clause has been interpreted either as barring the government from giving preferment to any particular religion or as requiring a complete and total separation of church and state. Moreover, in spite of the apparent absolute prohibition in the amendment's language "Congress shall make no law...," Congress has, in fact, many times passed laws "in the public interest" that restrict freedom of speech and press. Among the most famous of these acts are the ALIEN AND SEDITION ACTS (1798), the SMITH ACT (1940), and the MCCARRAN ACT (1950). In addition, federal agencies and prosecutors have initiated actions that, where allowed, have resulted in certain limitations on freedom of speech and press.

In ruling on the constitutionality of various restrictions on these CIVIL RIGHTS, the Supreme Court has at various times tended to support either the rights of the individual or the interest of society. Since the early 1950s, however, the Court has also followed a balancing approach whereby the private and public interests are weighed in each case.

See also: CENSORSHIP; CIVIL DISOBEDIENCE; PORNOGRAPHY; SCHENK V. UNITED STATES.

---

fiscal policy Fiscal policy is one course of action that a government follows to stabilize the national economy by adjusting levels of spending and TAXATION. (The other major type of stabilizing action is MONETARY POLICY.) In a modern industrial economy, government spending is one major component of the aggregate demand for goods and services that directly affects EMPLOYMENT AND UNEMPLOYMENT. Changes in tax rates influence private investment and consumption, the other two major components of aggregate demand. When the economy is operating at less than full employment—a situation of deficient aggregate demand—fiscal-policy theory indicates that government spending should be increased and taxes reduced to stimulate business investment and consumer spending. Government spending should be reduced and tax rates increased to diminish investment and consumption when aggregate demand is excessive and the economy experiences INFLATION. In conditions of both inflation and unemployment (STAGFLATION), fiscal-policy decisions become problematic.

Primarily as the result of the theoretical work of John Maynard KEYNES, discretionary fiscal policy—deliberate government action to change taxes and expenditures in order to correct for RECESSION or inflation—has been a much-used tool of government economists since the 1930s. In recent years, however, economists belonging to the supply-side school (see ECONOMICS) have argued that Keynesian fiscal policy cannot resolve the stagflation problem. Supply-siders believe that stagflation is caused primarily by growth of the government sector and by the dampening effects of high taxes. They argue in favor of tax cuts to stimulate production.

Fischer, Bobby Robert James Fischer, b. Mar. 9, 1943, Chicago, Ill., was world chess champion and one of the most talented players in the history of the game. Fischer became an international grandmaster by age 15 and left high school to devote himself to professional competition. He was United States champion (1957–61, 1963–67) and world champion (1972–75), becoming the first American to win the world title since its establishment in 1886. To attain it, Fischer defeated all opponents in a series of qualifying matches in 1971 and went on to snap the Russian monopoly of the title by defeating then-champion Boris SPASSKY. Fischer forfeited the title in 1975.

Fischer, Emil Hermann The German chemist Emil Hermann Fischer, b. Oct. 9, 1852, d. July 15, 1919, made important contributions to organic chemistry. As early as 1875 he had prepared phenylhydrazine, and in 1884 he demonstrated that it could be used as an agent for separating and identifying sugars that have the same empirical formula. His greatest success was the synthesis of glucose, mannose, and fructose in 1890 and the determination of their projection formulas (showing the spatial relation of atoms in molecules with the same structural formula).

In 1897, Fischer recognized that uric acid and xanthine are oxides of the base purine. From xanthine he synthesized theobromine and caffeine and determined their structures. For his work on carbohydrates and purines Fischer received the 1902 Nobel Prize in chemistry.

Fischer then turned to the study of proteins, and between 1899 and 1908 found effective ways of separating the amino acids derived from them. In 1914, Fischer prepared the first synthetic nucleotide, a component of the nucleic acids found in the proteins of cell nuclei.

During World War I, Fischer took an active part in the effort to develop a way of converting fatty acids to serve as food, the result of which was ester margarine. Despondent over the war and illness, Fischer committed suicide.

Fischer-Dieskau, Dietrich [fish'-ur dees'-kow, deet'-rik] The German baritone Dietrich Fischer-Dieskau, b. Berlin, May 28, 1925, is considered by many the greatest lieder singer of his generation. While he was a prisoner of war in Italy in 1945, the Americans recognized his talent and sent him on a singing tour of POW camps. After the war he resumed studies with Hermann Weissenborn and started his professional career. Thanks to his recordings of Bach cantatas and Schubert's song cycle *Die Winterreise*, his recital debut in 1947 was sold out. He made his operatic debut (1948) at the Berlin State Opera in Verdi's *Don Carlos*. He has appeared with the Munich and Vienna State Operas and, from 1951, at all the major European music festivals. He first toured the United States in 1954. He has recorded more than 450 Schubert songs and has written a book on Schubert and one on Wagner and Nietzche.

Fischer von Erlach, Johann Bernhard [fuhn air'-lahk] Johann Bernhard Fischer von Erlach, b. July 20, 1656, d. Apr. 5, 1723, was one of the most intellectual and influential Austrian architects of the baroque period (see BAROQUE ART AND ARCHITECTURE). His work encompassed a variety of European trends, but he assimilated them into a personal style, giving impetus to the Austrian baroque. The impact of ceiling painting was evidenced in his interior decorations for the mausoleum of Ferdinand II in Graz (1687). He tutored the crown prince (later Holy Roman Emperor Joseph I) in 1689 and established a position for himself in court architecture. Schloss Frain in Moravia (1690–94), with its dominating oval plan and

great hall, was his first major baroque building. In 1705 he became surveyor general of imperial buildings.

His Church of the Holy Trinity (1694–1702) in Salzburg reflects Francesco Borromini's Saint Agnese (1653–57) in Rome, but Fischer gave his church a sense of depth not possible at Saint Agnese. His crowning achievement was the Karlskirche in Vienna (begun 1716), completed by his son Joseph Emanuel (1693–1742). A unique structure, Karlskirche includes numerous decorative and iconographic motifs. The elliptical plan continues in the elevation, and Johann Michael Rottmayr's (1654–1730) ceiling fresco further enhances an upward movement, causing a unified spatial organization.

Among his secular architecture were SCHÖNBRUNN PALACE (c.1696), Palais Trautson (1700–12), and the Imperial Library of Vienna (1723–35). Completed by his son, the library exhibits an imposing interior of complex spatial units determined by differentiated vaulting zones.

Fish (family) The Fish family of New York has been prominent in public life since the Revolutionary War.

Nicholas Fish, b. Aug. 28, 1758, d. June 20, 1833, was an officer in the Revolutionary army. He was a New York City alderman from 1806 to 1817 and later served as state adjutant general, director of federal revenue, and as chairman of the board of trustees of Columbia University.

His son, **Hamilton Fish**, b. Aug. 3, 1808, d. Sept. 6, 1893, was elected to the U.S. House of Representatives as a Whig in 1842. He became governor of New York in 1849 and was a U.S. senator from 1851 to 1857. He joined the Republican party in 1856, after the Whigs disbanded. Fish was appointed secretary of state by President Ulysses S. Grant in 1869. He negotiated the Treaty of Washington (1871), which settled the Alabama Claims dispute with Britain.

Other prominent members of the Fish family include two sons of Hamilton: **Nicholas** (1848–1902), who served as minister to Belgium, and **Hamilton** (1849–1936), who was elected to the House of Representatives in 1909. The younger Hamilton's son, also named **Hamilton** (1888–1991), served as a Republican in Congress from 1920 to 1945. A vocal anti-Communist and isolationist, he was a leading opponent of the policies of President Franklin Roosevelt.

fish Fish are cold-blooded aquatic animals with backbones, gills, and fins. Most fishes are torpedo-shaped (fusiform) for efficient travel through water, but much variation in shape occurs, from flattened and rounded, as in flounders, to vertical and angular, as in sea horses. Fishes range in size from the pygmy goby, *Pandaka pygmaea*, of the Philippines, which reaches only 12 mm (0.5 in) in length and about 1.5 g (0.05 oz) in weight and is sexually mature at 6 mm (0.25 in), to the whale shark, *Rhincodon typus*, which grows to 18 m (60 ft) long and more than 20 U.S. tons in weight.

Fish were among the first animals systematically hunted by primitive humans. Even today, relatively primi-

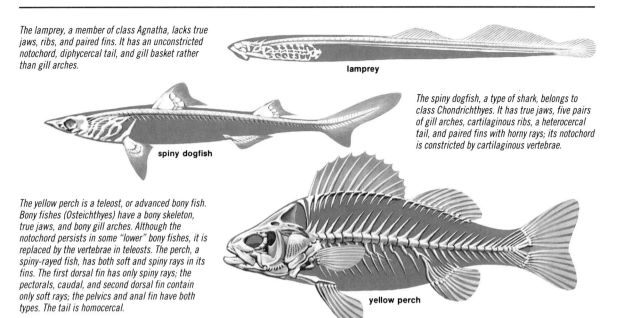

The lamprey, a member of class Agnatha, lacks true jaws, ribs, and paired fins. It has an unconstricted notochord, diphycercal tail, and gill basket rather than gill arches.

lamprey

The spiny dogfish, a type of shark, belongs to class Chondrichthyes. It has true jaws, five pairs of gill arches, cartilaginous ribs, a heterocercal tail, and paired fins with horny rays; its notochord is constricted by cartilaginous vertebrae.

spiny dogfish

The yellow perch is a teleost, or advanced bony fish. Bony fishes (Osteichthyes) have a bony skeleton, true jaws, and bony gill arches. Although the notochord persists in some "lower" bony fishes, it is replaced by the vertebrae in teleosts. The perch, a spiny-rayed fish, has both soft and spiny rays in its fins. The first dorsal fin has only spiny rays; the pectorals, caudal, and second dorsal fin contain only soft rays; the pelvics and anal fin have both types. The tail is homocercal.

yellow perch

tive societies in the South Pacific and South America depend largely on fish for food, while in many industrialized nations, fish still constitute a major part of the diet. Fishes are harvested for unprocessed human food, fish meal, animal feed, and oil. They also are pursued avidly by sport anglers. Currently, however, the increasing human population, overfishing to supply this population, and pollution of the world's waters are all cutting heavily into the world supply of fish and threatening the existence of a number of species. At the same time, regulations to curtail the taking of certain species or sizes are virtually unenforceable on an international level.

Distribution

Fish are found throughout the world, from altitudes of more than 3,800 m (2.3 mi), as in Lake Titicaca in the Andes, to depths of about 10 km (6 mi) in the Pacific Ocean. Some, such as certain killifishes, genus *Cyprinodon*, inhabit hot springs, where the water temperature may reach 45° C (113° F); others, such as the icefishes, *Chaenocephalus*, are found in Antarctic seas, where the water temperature may fall below 0° C (32° F). About 107 species are distributed worldwide in tropical and subtropical waters, but many species have limited ranges, among the smallest being that of the killifish *Cyprinodon diabolis*, confined to a single spring in Nevada.

About 70% of the Earth's surface is covered by oceans and seas, and about 3.5% of the land surface (1% of the Earth's total surface) is covered by fresh water. Inhabiting these waters are an estimated 20,000 or more fish species, equal to or exceeding the number of all other vertebrate species combined. About 60% of the fish species live in marine waters; the remaining 40% are found in fresh water.

Most of the world's fishes are continental in orientation, living either as part of the freshwater systems on land or as sea-dwellers staying near and influenced by the coastal environment. High densities of marine fish populations occur near coasts because the waters there are very rich in nutrients.

Anatomy

The living species of fish are usually divided into three classes: the Agnatha, the jawless fishes, comprising the hagfishes and lampreys; the Chondrichthyes, the cartilaginous-skeleton fishes, such as sharks and rays; and the Osteichthyes, the bony-skeleton fishes, comprising all other living fishes. The skeletons of these three groups vary in fundamental ways. In the hagfishes and lampreys the backbone is basically a notochord, a rodlike structure composed of unique notochordal tissue. In sharks and rays the notochord is surrounded and constricted by spaced rings of cartilage, the vertebrae, to form a backbone. The remainder of the skeleton is also cartilaginous, not bony, but in many forms the cartilage is partly calcified, and thereby hardened, by the addition of calcareous salts. In primitive bony fishes, such as the sturgeon, the vertebrae spaced along the notochord are still largely cartilaginous, but in most advanced bony fishes the vertebrae are bony and are united to form the backbone, and the notochord is no longer present.

Some fishes, such as lampreys, lack ribs; others have either a single or a double pair of ribs attached to each trunk vertebra. Among the higher bony fishes there also may be small, riblike intermuscular bones.

Body apppendages are of two kinds, cirrhi and fins. Cirrhi are flaps of flesh that may appear on any part of the body; they often serve as camouflage. Fins are either me-

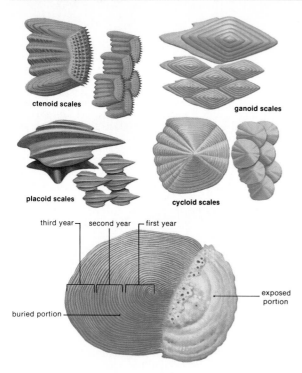

ctenoid scales

ganoid scales

placoid scales

cycloid scales

third year — second year — first year

exposed portion

buried portion

Drawings show scale types on the basis of shape: ctenoid, ganoid, placoid, and cycloid. Most often, scales form an overlapping pattern like shingles on a roof. The cycloid scale (enlarged) of a salmon shows concentric bony ridges, or circuli, which reflect the growth patterns of the individual; clusters of ridges, called annuli, mark each yearly growth cycle.

dian or paired. Median fins occur along the centerline of the body, at the top, the bottom, and the end. The top, or dorsal, fin may consist of one to several fins, one behind the other, and may include a fleshy fin, called the adipose fin, near the tail. The bottom, or anal, fin is located on the belly behind the vent, or anus. The end fin is called the tail, or caudal, fin.

The dorsal and anal fins may be supported by cartilaginous rods, as in the lampreys; by cartilaginous rods and horny rays, as in sharks; by horny rays, as in the spiny-finned fishes; or by bony rays (derived from scales), as in the soft-rayed fishes. The tail fin may be protocercal, the body continuing straight back as a middle support between the upper and lower lobes of the tail; heterocercal, with the end of the body turning up and continuing to the tip of the upper lobe; or homocercal, in which the last few vertebrae are fused and joined with other bony elements (hypurals) to support the tail-fin rays.

The paired fins correspond to the arms and legs of land vertebrates. The pectoral fins are situated at the front of the body behind the gill openings and generally function to provide maneuverability, but may be highly modified to fulfill other functions. The simplest internal support for the pectoral fins occurs in the sharks, where a U-shaped cartilaginous skeletal structure, called the pectoral girdle, joins and helps support the two pectoral fins.

In the higher bony fishes the pectoral girdle is composed of bone and is more complex in structure. The pelvic fins, also called the ventral fins, are located along the bottom of the body. They may be in the middle of the belly, as in salmon; below the pectorals, as in the largemouth bass; or in front of the pectorals, as in cods. Pelvic fins also serve as maneuvering structures and also may be modified to serve other uses. The supporting pelvic girdle is lacking in many bony fishes; in most fishes in which the pelvic girdle is present it is represented by a single skeletal element on each side of the body.

The scales of fish are colorless; a fish's coloring arises from structures beneath or closely associated with the scales. Not all species of fishes have scales, or the scales may be so small as to make the fish appear scaleless. Scales also may be present only on small areas of the body. The arrangement of scales may be imbricate (overlapping) or mosaic (fitting closely together or just minutely separated).

There are four basic scale types. Placoid scales, found on sharks and rays, are toothlike in structure. They do not increase in size as do the scales of bony fishes; new scales must be added as a shark grows. Cosmoid scales are found on the primitive coelacanth and, in a highly modified form, on lungfishes. Ganoid scales, as found on gars, are typically squarish. Leptoid scales, consisting of a single layer of bone, are found on the higher bony fishes and occur in two forms: cycloid (circular) and ctenoid (toothed).

Circulation

The blood of the fish serves, as does the blood of other vertebrates, to transport oxygen, nutrients, and wastes. The typical fish's circulation is a single circuit: heart-gills-body-heart. The heart is two-chambered, with an upper atrium and a lower ventricle. There are two accessory chambers: the thin-walled sinus venosus, which collects blood and leads into the atrium, and the conus arteriosus, an enlargement of the main artery leading out of the ventricle.

Respiration

To live, fish must extract oxygen from the water and transfer it to the blood. This is done by gills, lungs, specialized chambers, or skin, any of which must be richly supplied with blood vessels in order to act as a respiratory organ.

Gills are made efficient in a number of ways. (1) A large surface area for gaseous exchange means that more oxygen can enter the bloodstream over a given period of time. A single gill of a bony fish consists of a curved gill arch bearing a V-shaped double row of gill filaments. Each filament has many minute folds in its surface, giving it a sort of fuzzy appearance and increasing the amount of surface area along a given length of filament. Consequently, the surface area of the gills is commonly 10 to 60 times more than that of the whole body surface. (2) A short diffusion, or travel, distance for the oxygen increases the rate of oxygen entry into the blood. The blood traveling in the folds of the filaments is very close to the

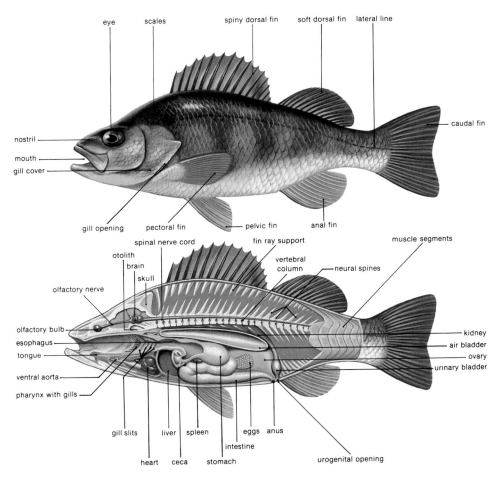

External and internal features of the yellow perch are illustrated. Most fishes are covered by scales; not all fishes have all the fins shown here. Muscles, needed for swimming, account for much of a fish's body weight. Sensory organs include lateral line system, nostrils, lidless eyes, and otoliths (ear stones) for equilibrium. The drawings also show gas exchange, digestive, excretory, and female reproductive organs.

oxygen-containing water, separated from it by a very thin membrane. (3) By using countercurrent circulation in the gill, the blood in the filament folds travels forward, in the opposite direction to the water flow, so that a constant imbalance is maintained between the lower amount of oxygen in the blood and the higher amount in the water, ensuring passage of oxygen to the blood. If the blood were to flow in the same direction as the water, oxygenated blood at the rear of the gills would be traveling with de-oxygenated water and not only could not extract oxygen from the water but would even lose oxygen to it. (4) Gills have little physiological dead space. The folds of the filaments are close enough together so that most of the water passing between them is involved in the gas-exchange process. (5) Water flows continuously in only one direction over the gills, as contrasted with the interrupted, two-way flow of air in and out of lungs of mammals.

A fish out of water usually dies because its gills collapse, reducing the area of the respiratory surface, and become dry, effectively stopping the diffusion of oxygen into the blood. Many fishes, however, have evolved methods of extracting oxygen from air. Such adaptations permit these fishes to live in oxygen-poor waters, where they

come to the surface to gulp air, or in waters subjected to drying; or they may enable a species to exploit environments, such as damp beaches, unavailable to other fishes. One method of air breathing is the development of gills that either secrete mucus or trap moisture that supports the gills and keeps them wet. Another method is to breathe through a damp skin, as do the freshwater eels. Very commonly, special chambers have been developed in the mouth, throat, or head in which inspired air is brought into contact with moist tissues richly supplied with blood vessels. Some fishes have thin-walled areas in the intestine where oxygen can be extracted from swallowed air. In still others, the swim bladder is modified into an air-breathing apparatus. Air breathing has become so important to some species that they will drown if not allowed access to air.

Body Temperature

Fish are described as cold-blooded, meaning that their body temperature varies with the external temperature. Fish produce metabolic heat, but much of it is lost to the outside at the gills; a fish's body temperature is usually within a degree or so of the water temperature. Tunas and

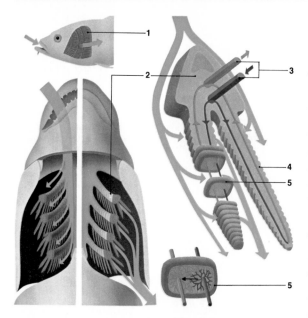

In most bony fishes oxygen and carbon dioxide are exchanged in the gills (1). Four bony gill arches (2) on either side of the head bear arteries (3), which run through V-shaped gill filaments (4). Each filament is formed into platelike sections (5) filled with capillaries that are near the gill surface, bringing the blood close to the oxygen-rich water. Water (blue green) taken in through the mouth flows over the filaments in only one direction. Blood circulating within the filaments flows in the opposite direction, ensuring that deoxygenated blood (blue) comes in contact with fully oxygenated water. This countercurrent circulation system facilitates the efficient intake of oxygen and the release of excess carbon dioxide into the water.

mackerel sharks, however, are warm-bodied fishes. Their countercurrent circulatory networks have paired ingoing and outgoing blood vessels. The heat of the warm blood

going to the gills is transferred to the cooled blood coming from the gills, keeping the heat within the fish's body. With such networks, yellowfin and skipjack tunas, for example, keep their body temperature from about 5° to almost 12° C (9° to 21° F) above the water temperature. One advantage of warm-bodiedness is an increase in muscle power. Muscles contract more rapidly when warm, without loss of force. This means more speed in pursuing prey, escaping enemies, and shortening the time required for long-distance migration.

Water Balance

The blood of freshwater fishes is typically saltier than the water in which they live. Osmotic pressure, the force that tends to equalize differences in salt concentrations, causes water to diffuse, or enter, into the fish's body, primarily through the gills, mouth membranes, and intestine. To eliminate this excess water, freshwater fishes produce a large amount of very dilute urine. As these fishes are gaining water, they are losing salts. Salts contained in their foods are insufficient to maintain the proper salt balance. Freshwater fishes have therefore developed the capacity to absorb salts from water by means of their gills.

Marine bony fishes, in contrast, have blood that is less salty than seawater, and consequently they lose water and absorb salts. To offset this loss of fluid, marine fishes drink seawater and produce very little urine. The drinking of seawater, however, adds to the concentration of salts. These salts are eliminated through the anus or the gills.

Swimming

Many fishes swim by contracting and relaxing a succession of muscle blocks, called myomeres, alternately on each side of the body, starting at the head and progressing down toward the tail. The alternate shortening and relaxing of successive muscle blocks, which bends part of the body first toward one side and then toward the other,

Tuna and related fishes swim by moving the tail fin from side to side with powerful strokes; only the tail stalk bends. At the other end of the spectrum of swimming motions, the eel moves with a series of distinct waves which travel down its body. Most fishes, as illustrated by the dogfish, exhibit intermediate characteristics: they swim with reduced body waves and amplified tail movements.

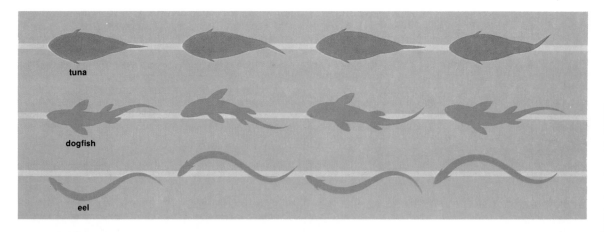

(Left) *A marine fish, such as the jack* (above), *loses water by osmosis through gills and skin; it drinks seawater* (green arrow) *to offset this loss. A freshwater fish, such as the Alaska blackfish* (below), *absorbs much water, and excretes the excess* (dark arrow) *as dilute urine.*

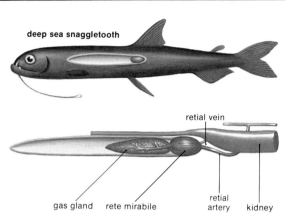

Drawing of a deep sea snaggletooth indicates the position of the gas bladder and rete mirabile. The gas bladder (detail below), which lies just below the kidney, regulates buoyancy. The rete mirabile, with its countercurrent system of capillaries, and gas gland, which secretes lactic acid, act to inflate the gas bladder.

results in a series of waves traveling down the fish's body. The rear part of each wave thrusts against the water and propels the fish forward. This type of movement is quite clearly seen in the freshwater eel. Because movement of the head back and forth exerts drag, which consumes additional energy and slows travel, a great many fishes have modified this snakelike motion by keeping the waves very small along most of the length of the body, in some cases showing no obvious movement at all, and then increasing them sharply in the tail region. It is the end of the traveling waves that moves the tail forcefully back and forth, providing the main propulsion for forward motion.

Some fishes, such as the blenny, which has been timed at 0.8 km/h (0.5 mph), swim very slowly. In contrast, the salmon may reach a sustained speed of 13 km/h (8 mph). Tunas may reach speeds of 80 km/h (50 mph), and swordfish, 97 km/h (60 mph).

Gas Bladder

Because a weightless, or buoyant, body requires a minimum of energy to keep it at a given depth, and because a weightless body requires less energy than a weighted body to move at a given speed, many fishes have evolved means of reducing their body weight, or density, relative to the density of water. A fish whose total body density

Arrows indicate the forces that water exerts on a swimming fish. As the tail moves from side to side, the water pushes against it (diagonal arrow). *The forward component of this force* (heavy arrow) *propels the fish forward. The lateral component* (broken vertical arrow), *which would turn the fish to the side, is offset by the force of the water that acts upon the fish's sides* (solid vertical arrows).

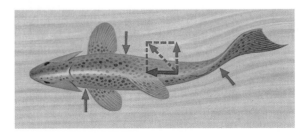

equaled that of water would be effectively weightless, neither rising nor sinking. Because fat is less dense than water, one method of reducing body density would be to increase the proportion of fat within the body. Theoretically, about one-third of a fish's body weight would have to be made up of fat in order to make the fish weightless in seawater. This condition is approached in some species of deep-sea sharks having very large livers that contain a great amount of squalene, a fatty substance that is significantly less dense than seawater.

Another method of reducing density is to include gases within the body. Many fishes have a gas-filled bladder that serves this function. The gases within the bladder are similar to those in air but are present in different and widely varying proportions. The degree of body volume that must be taken up by gas in order to achieve weightlessness depends mainly on whether the fish is freshwater or marine. Fresh water is less dense than seawater and consequently provides less buoyancy. Freshwater fishes, therefore, require a larger gas bladder than do marine fishes to keep them from sinking.

If the gas bladder contained an unchanging quantity of gas, the fish would be weightless at only one depth. The reason for this is that as pressure increases with depth, gas in the bladder is compressed, decreasing the bladder's volume and increasing the relative density of the fish. The quantity of gas within a fish's bladder must therefore be adjustable. If, as in the carp, the gas bladder is connected by a duct to the gullet, gas may be expelled through the mouth and gill cavities as the fish rises, and, in a similar manner, gas may be added to the bladder by swallowing air at the water surface. For most fishes, however, coming to the surface to gulp air prior to going deeper is impractical, and in many fishes the gas bladder has no connection to the outside. In these fishes adjusting the quantity of gas within the bladder is done by transferring gases from the gas bladder to adjoining blood vessels and back again.

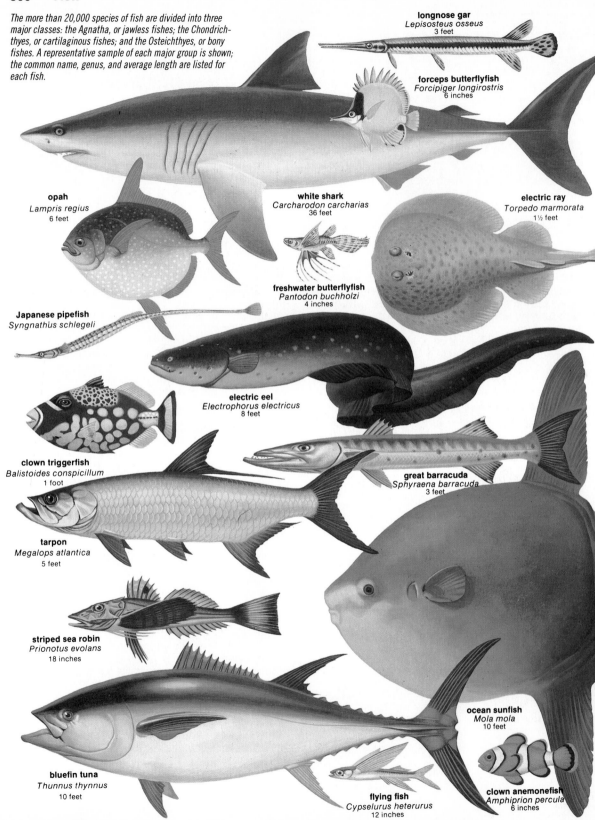

The more than 20,000 species of fish are divided into three major classes: the Agnatha, or jawless fishes; the Chondrichthyes, or cartilaginous fishes; and the Osteichthyes, or bony fishes. A representative sample of each major group is shown; the common name, genus, and average length are listed for each fish.

longnose gar
Lepisosteus osseus
3 feet

forceps butterflyfish
Forcipiger longirostris
6 inches

opah
Lampris regius
6 feet

white shark
Carcharodon carcharias
36 feet

electric ray
Torpedo marmorata
1½ feet

freshwater butterflyfish
Pantodon buchholzi
4 inches

Japanese pipefish
Syngnathus schlegeli

electric eel
Electrophorus electricus
8 feet

clown triggerfish
Balistoides conspicillum
1 foot

great barracuda
Sphyraena barracuda
3 feet

tarpon
Megalops atlantica
5 feet

striped sea robin
Prionotus evolans
18 inches

ocean sunfish
Mola mola
10 feet

bluefin tuna
Thunnus thynnus
10 feet

flying fish
Cypselurus heterurus
12 inches

clown anemonefish
Amphiprion percula
6 inches

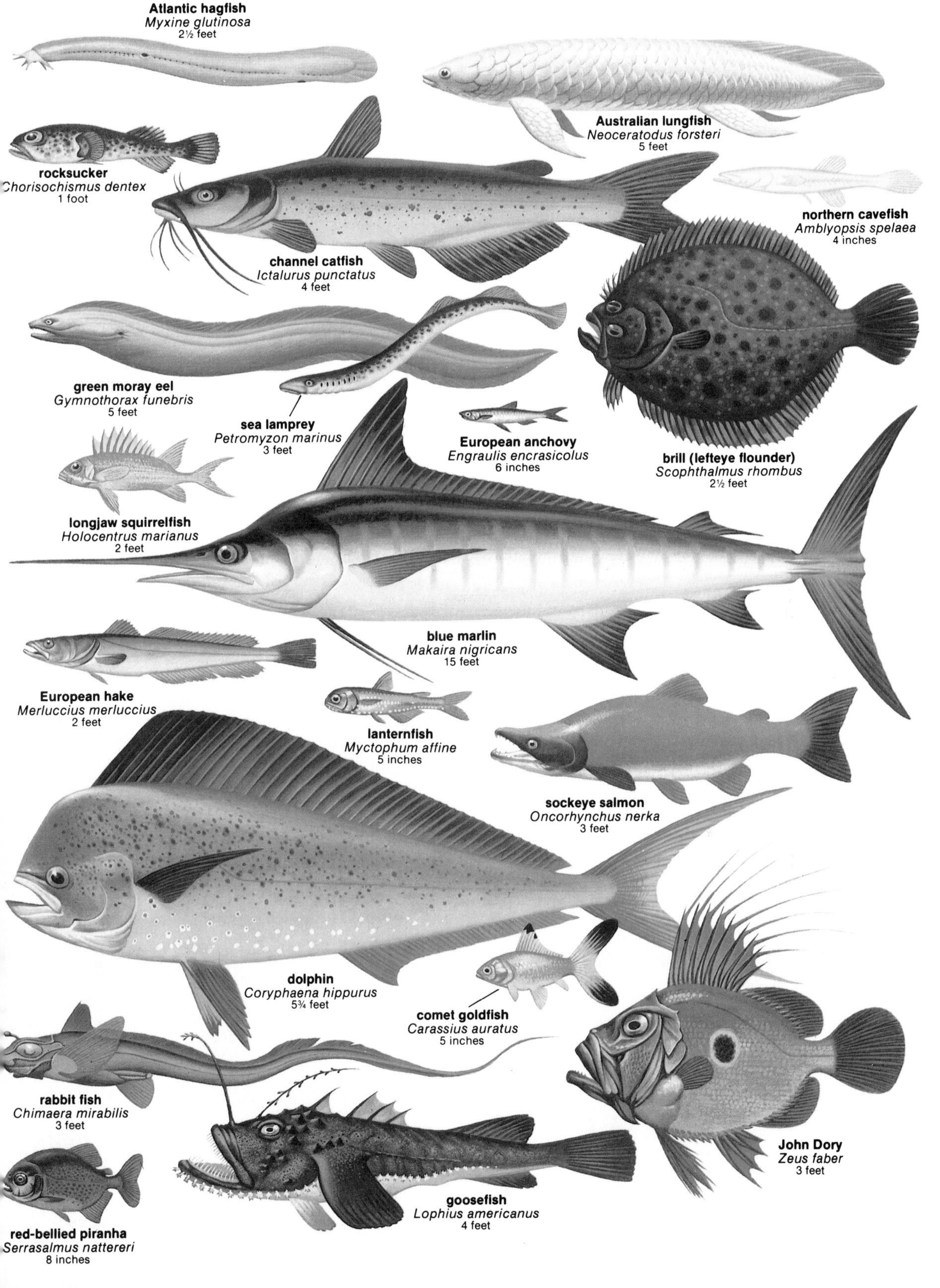

Atlantic hagfish
Myxine glutinosa
2½ feet

Australian lungfish
Neoceratodus forsteri
5 feet

rocksucker
Chorisochismus dentex
1 foot

northern cavefish
Amblyopsis spelaea
4 inches

channel catfish
Ictalurus punctatus
4 feet

green moray eel
Gymnothorax funebris
5 feet

sea lamprey
Petromyzon marinus
3 feet

European anchovy
Engraulis encrasicolus
6 inches

brill (lefteye flounder)
Scophthalmus rhombus
2½ feet

longjaw squirrelfish
Holocentrus marianus
2 feet

blue marlin
Makaira nigricans
15 feet

European hake
Merluccius merluccius
2 feet

lanternfish
Myctophum affine
5 inches

sockeye salmon
Oncorhynchus nerka
3 feet

dolphin
Coryphaena hippurus
5¾ feet

comet goldfish
Carassius auratus
5 inches

rabbit fish
Chimaera mirabilis
3 feet

John Dory
Zeus faber
3 feet

red-bellied piranha
Serrasalmus nattereri
8 inches

goosefish
Lophius americanus
4 feet

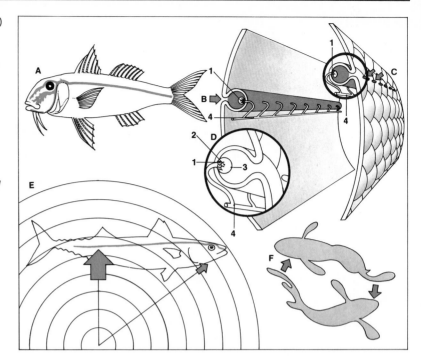

The lateral line system (red) *of a red mullet* (A) *is located in the head and along the sides of the body. It consists of fluid-filled canals* (B) *under the skin, which open through small pores* (C). *Within the canals* (D) *are groups of sensory cells* (1) *with projecting hairs* (2) *surrounded by a gelatinous cap* (3), *which send continuous trains of impulses along nerves* (4) *to the brain. Pressure waves in the water stimulate the sensory cells, changing the frequency of the nerve impulses and allowing the fish to detect objects and other fishes. By comparing the pressure waves reaching different parts of its body* (E), *a fish can locate an object. Fighting fish* (F) *respond to pressure waves, caused by body movements.*

Lateral Line System

The lateral line system, found in many fishes and in some aquatic amphibians, is sensitive to differences in water pressure. These differences may be due to changes in depth or to the currentlike waves caused by approaching objects. The basic sensory unit of the lateral line system is the neuromast, which is a bundle of sensory and supporting cells whose projecting hairs are encased in a gelatinous cap. The neuromasts continuously send out nerve impulses. When pressure waves cause the gelatinous caps to move, bending the enclosed hairs, the frequency of the nerve impulses is either increased or decreased, depending on the direction of bending.

Neuromasts may occur singly, in small groups called pit organs, or in rows within grooves, when they are referred to as the lateral line system. The lateral line system runs along the sides of the body onto the head, where it divides into three branches, two to the snout and one to the lower jaw.

A swimming fish sets up a pressure wave in the water that is detectable by the lateral line systems of other fishes. It also sets up a bow wave in front of itself, the pressure of which is higher than that of the wave flow along its sides. These near-field differences are registered by its own lateral line system. As the fish approaches an object, such as a rock or the glass wall of an aquarium, the pressure waves around its body are distorted, and these changes are quickly detected by the lateral line system, enabling the fish to swerve or to take other suitable action. Because sound waves are waves of pressure, the lateral line system is also able to detect very low-frequency sounds of 100 Hz or less.

An interesting adaptation of the pressure-sensitive systems is seen in the modified groups of neuromasts called the ampullae of Lorenzini, which are found in sharks and certain bony fishes. The ampullae of Lorenzini act as electroreceptors and are able to detect electrical charges, or fields, in the water. Most animals, including humans, emit a DC field when in seawater. This is presumably caused by electrical potential differences between body fluids and seawater and between different parts of the body. An AC field is also set up by muscular activity (contractions). A wound, even a scratch, can markedly alter these electrical fields. The cat shark, *Scyliorhinus*, is known to catch prey by using its ampullae of Lorenzini to detect the electrical field generated by flatfish (plaice) buried beneath the sand.

Reproduction

Most fishes are egg-layers, but many bear living young. Live-bearing fishes may be ovoviviparous, in which the eggs essentially simply hatch within the female, or viviparous, in which the unborn young are supplied nourishment through the mother's tissues. In some ovoviviparous fishes the embryo develops in the egg while the egg is still within its follicular covering within the ovary, and ovulation (or release of the egg) and birth occur at the same time. In other ovoviviparous forms the eggs are released from the protective follicles into the cavity of the hollow ovary, where development continues. In some viviparous fishes the walls of the egg follicle are in intimate contact with the embryo, supplying it with nourishment. In the viviparous sharks, a part of the oviduct, or egg channel, is developed into a uterus; the modified yolk sacs of the young are joined to pockets within the uterus.

In live-bearing fishes and in some egg-layers, fertilization occurs internally, and methods have been evolved for introducing the sperm into the female's body. In sharks the pelvic fins of the male are modified into intromittent organs called myxoptergia, and in the male topminnows the anal fin is modified into a similar-functioning intromittent organ called the gonopodium.

At least three modes of reproduction—heterosexual, hermaphroditic, and parthenogenetic—are found in fishes. In the most common form, heterosexual reproduction, there are separate male and female parents, but even here there is considerable variation. In some live-bearing fishes, the female is able to store sperm for up to 8 or even 10 months, and this sperm is used to fertilize new batches of eggs as they develop. In some cases, a female may carry sperm from several males at once.

In hermaphroditic reproduction, a single fish is both male and female, produces both eggs and sperm (either at the same time or at different times), and mates with other similar hermaphroditic fishes. External self-fertilization occurs in one hermaphroditic fish, which sheds egg and sperm simultaneously. In another, internal self-fertilization may occur. In certain fishes there is a time sequence of hermaphroditism, young fishes reversing their sex as they grow older.

In parthenogenetic reproduction, unfertilized eggs develop into embryos. This is known to exist in at least one fish species, *Poecilia formosa*, of the Amazon River; however, even though development proceeds without fertilization in some of these females, mating with a male is still required to stimulate egg development.

Parental care also shows great diversity. Some fishes, such as the Atlantic herring, form huge schools of males

Although some Osteichthyes, or bony fishes, are live bearers, the majority lay eggs that are fertilized externally. In typical egg-laying fish, such as perch, the female (A) produces many small eggs in the ovary; the eggs pass through the oviduct and the urogenital opening and are deposited in the water. Similarly, the male (B) produces sperm in the testis; the sperm then passes through the vas deferens and the urogenital opening into the water, where fertilization occurs.

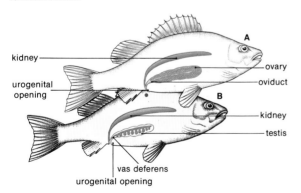

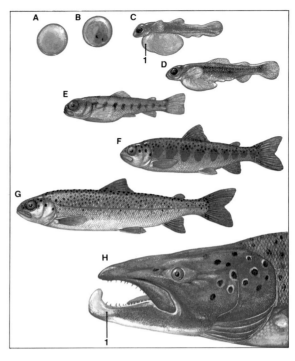

The Atlantic salmon (closely related to the trout) stays in fresh water for 1 to 5 years before migrating to the sea as an adult. It returns to fresh water only to spawn and die. Fertile eggs about 6 mm (0.24 in) in diameter are translucent (A), and infertile eggs are opaque white. The developing embryo has prominent eyes (B). Newly hatched larvae (C) depend on the yolk sac (1) for food. Larvae are about 24 mm (1 in) long when the yolk sac is almost consumed (D). Larvae 4 cm (1.6 in) long have fully formed mouths and feed on small aquatic organisms (E). A young fish, about 10 cm (4 in) long, is called a parr and is marked with about 10 mauve blotches (parr marks) along its flank (F). Parr marks are lost when the freshwater period is complete (G). At this stage the fish is called a smolt and measures some 20 cm (8 in) in length. Large, aged males (H) returning to fresh water to spawn have a crooked lower jaw, or kype (1).

and females and freely shed their eggs and sperm (milt), then abandon the eggs. Other fishes build nests and care for both the eggs and the newly hatched young. Others have evolved methods of carrying the eggs with them, commonly in their mouths but also in gill cavities or in special pouches on the body.

Evolution

The first fishes, and indeed the first vertebrates, were the ostracoderms, which appeared in the Cambrian Period, about 510 million years ago, and became extinct at the end of the Devonian, about 350 million years ago. Ostracoderms were jawless fishes found mainly in fresh water. They were covered with a bony armor or scales and were often less than 30 cm (1 ft) long. The ostracoderms are placed in the class Agnatha along with the living jawless fishes, the lampreys and hagfishes, which are believed to be descended from the ostracoderms.

Like other cichlids, male and female Jack Dempseys (top) *share parental duties, such as guarding and fanning their eggs. Newly hatched fry stay close to the parents. Mouth brooders, including Tilapia cichlids* (bottom)*, protect the fry in their mouths.*

The first fishes with jaws, the acanthodians, or spiny sharks, appeared in the late Silurian, about 410 million years ago, and became extinct before the end of the Permian, about 250 million years ago. Acanthodians were generally small sharklike fishes varying from toothless filter-feeders to toothed predators. They are often classified as an order of the class Placodermi, another group of primitive fishes, but recent authorities tend to place the acanthodians in a class by themselves (class Acanthodii) or even within the class of modern bony fishes, the Osteichthyes. It is commonly believed that the acanthodians and the modern bony fishes are related and that either the acanthodians gave rise to the modern bony fishes or that both groups share a common ancestor.

The placoderms, another group of jawed fishes, appeared at the beginning of the Devonian, about 395 million years ago, and became extinct at the end of the Devonian or the beginning of the Mississippian (Carboniferous), about 345 million years ago. Placoderms were typically small, flattened bottom-dwellers. The upper jaw was firmly fused to the skull, but there was a hinge joint between the skull and the bony plating of the trunk region.

The cartilaginous-skeleton sharks and rays, class Chondrichthyes, which appeared about 370 million years ago in the middle Devonian, are generally believed to be descended from the bony-skeleton placoderms. The cartilaginous skeletons are considered to be a later development.

The modern bony fishes, class Osteichthyes, appeared in the late Silurian or early Devonian, about 395 million years ago. The early forms were freshwater fishes, for no fossil remains of modern bony fishes have been found in marine deposits older than Triassic time, about 230 million years ago. The Osteichthyes may have arisen from the acanthodians. A subclass, Actinopterygii, the ray-finned fishes, became and have remained the dominant group of fishes throughout the world. It was not the ray-finned fishes, however, that led to the evolution of the land vertebrates.

The ancestors of the land vertebrates are found among another group of bony fishes called the Choanichthyes or Sarcopterygii. Choanate fishes are characterized by internal nostrils, fleshy fins called lobe fins, and cosmoid scales. The choanate fishes appeared in the late Silurian or early Devonian, more than 390 million years ago, and possibly arose from the acanthodians. The choanate fishes include a group known as the Crossopterygii, which has one living representative, the coelacanth *Latimeria.* During the Devonian Period some crossopterygian fishes of the order (or suborder) Rhipidistia evolved to become the first amphibians.

Living fishes are often divided into three different classes. Divisions within these classes, however—particularly within the bony fishes (Osteichthyes)—are much in dispute. Different names are applied to the same group, and any given group may be regarded as either a subclass, an order, or some other rank, depending on the authority consulted. The following general classification includes as many alternative definitions as space allows:

Class Agnatha or Cephalaspidomorphi, the jawless fishes
    Subclass (or order) Cyclostomata, the lampreys and hagfishes (*In certain classifications, the lampreys and hagfishes are each considered separate superclasses: Cephalaspidomorphi and Pteraspidomorphi, respectively.*)

Class Chondrichthyes, the cartilaginous-skeleton fishes
    Subclass Holocephali, the chimaeras, or ratfishes
    Subclass Elasmobranchii, the sharks, skates, and rays

Class Osteichthyes, the bony fishes
    Subclass (or order) Crossopterygii, the coelacanths
    Subclass (or order) Dipnoi or Dipneusti, the lungfishes
    (*In some classifications, the above two subclasses are treated as orders of a single subclass, the Choanichthyes or Sarcopterygii, the lobe-finned fishes.*)

Some deep-sea fishes have the ability to swallow fishes much larger than themselves. The black swallower reaches a maximum size of 15 cm (6 in), yet it can swallow fishes up to 25 cm (10 in) long. The swallower's jaw is loosely hinged, allowing it to open wide enough to swallow large prey, which is then passed into the expansible stomach (A, side; B, top).

A

B

Subclass Actinopterygii, the ray-finned fishes

Infraclass (or superorder) Chondrostei, the primitive ray-finned bony fishes: sturgeons, paddlefish, and bichirs (*In some classifications, the bichirs are placed in a subclass of their own, the Brachiopterygii.*)

Infraclass (or superorder) Holostei or Neopterygii, the intermediate ray-finned fishes: gars and the bowfin (*In certain classifications, the gars are treated as a separate superorder, the Ginglymodi. The term Ginglymodi also has been used to designate the gars as an order, but this term has been replaced at the ordinal level by the term* Lepisosteiformes; *orders are now indicated by the ending-*formes.)

Infraclass (or superorder) Teleostei or Neopterygii, the advanced bony fishes: herring, salmon, perch.

Fish, Hamilton   see FISH (family)

fish farming   Fish farming, or aquaculture, is the raising of food fishes and other aquatic life in protected enclosures or in controlled, natural environments. Although the cultivation of fishes for commercial harvesting is an ancient practice in some countries—the farming of carp provides a significant proportion of the protein supply in China, for example—in the United States and Europe it is still a relatively small industry. In the coming years, however, new technologies and methods may increase aquaculture yields, much as poultry production soared in the 1950s after the mechanization of that industry.

In the United States more than 10 percent of the fish harvest is produced by aquaculture. Almost all the commercially marketed U.S. catfish, crawfish, and rainbow trout, and about half the oysters, are aquaculture products.

Catfish is the largest crop, grown primarily in Mississippi, Arkansas, and Louisiana. Catfish cultivation is relatively simple because the fish are omnivorous feeders and reproduce easily. Crawfish—cultivated mainly in Louisiana—is the second largest fish crop and, like catfish, is relatively easy to grow, requiring no additional food beyond what the crawfish can forage in the ponds where they are stocked. Trout, the third most important crop, is produced almost exclusively in Idaho, where there is an abundant supply of fast-running river water. Pacific salmon are produced annually from hatcheries in the northwestern states. Young salmon smolts are released into the ocean and caught when they return to spawn; or they may be raised in pens and harvested after one year, when they weigh about 0.5 kg (1 lb).

The U.S. oyster crop has been decreasing for many years, in part because of water pollution, overfishing, and the loss of viable habitats. New methods of feeding and cultivation are being tried, but their success depends on conditions that are often beyond the control of the oyster farmer.

Culture systems for other aquatic species are also being developed, both in the United States and overseas. For example, abalone cultivation has begun in California

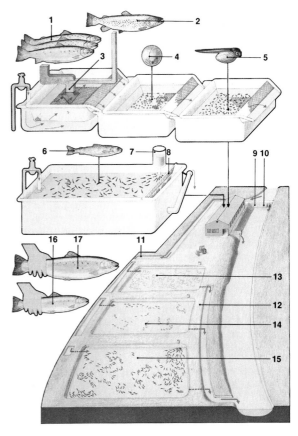

The process of raising brown trout begins when eggs and milt from adult female and male fish (1, 2) are mixed (3). The fertilized eggs are hatched (4) and reared through the larval stage (5) in temperature-controlled incubators. At about 3 weeks, the fry (6) are transferred to fry tanks, where automatic feeders (7) release controlled amounts of food; a fish screen (8) prevents their escape. At 12 weeks, the fry are moved to earth ponds situated on a river; a dam (9) diverts water for the ponds. A fish ladder (10) permits movement of the river fish, and inlet and outlet channels (11, 12) keep the pond water fresh. Ponds (13–15) hold fish at different growth stages. At 24 months (16), trout reach edible size. At 36 months (17), they are mature and can breed.

and freshwater shrimp are raised in Hawaii. The Japanese have established a small marine shrimp and fish industry and have attempted to raise lobsters and crabs. Israel and the Philippines both have large freshwater fish-farming programs.

See also: FISHING INDUSTRY.

fish hawk   see OSPREY

Fisher, Geoffrey Francis   Geoffrey Francis Fisher, b. May 5, 1887, d. Sept. 14, 1972, was archbishop of Canterbury from 1945 to 1961. Educated at Oxford, he was headmaster of Repton School (1914–32), bishop of Chester (1932–39), and bishop of London (1939–45). A keen ecumenist and able administrator, he was a president of the World Council of Churches from 1946 to 1954. He visited Pope John XXIII in 1960, the first meeting of an archbishop of Canterbury with a pope since the Reformation.

Fisher, Saint John

Saint John Fisher, b. 1469, d. June 22, 1535, was an English Roman Catholic prelate and humanist executed for treason during the Reformation. As bishop of Rochester (1504) Fisher was openly opposed to the dissolution of HENRY VIII's marriage to CATHERINE OF ARAGON. He also refused to recognize royal supremacy and the end of papal jurisdiction over the church in England. After he failed to take the oath required by the Act of Succession (1534), he was imprisoned in the Tower of London. When Pope Paul III showed his support for Fisher by naming him a cardinal on May 20, 1535, Fisher's fate was sealed; he was tried for treason and executed. He was canonized in 1935. Feast day: June 22.

Fisher of Kilverstone, John Arbuthnot Fisher, 1st Baron

The British admiral Lord Fisher, b. Jan. 25, 1841, d. July 10, 1920, entered the Royal Navy in 1854 and became admiral of the fleet in 1905. As first sea lord in the Admiralty (1904–10), Fisher improved the military preparedness of the navy, introducing, among other things, a new class of battleship, the Dreadnought (1906), and converting the fleet from coal to oil, a step that led the British to acquire oil interests in the Middle East. Fisher's policies enabled the Royal Navy to match the German naval buildup under Admiral von TIRPITZ and to neutralize the German fleet during World War I. Brought back as first sea lord under Winston CHURCHILL in 1914, Fisher opposed the disastrous Gallipoli campaign and resigned in May 1915.

fishing

The sport of fishing has been practiced widely throughout the world for countless years. In the United States alone, about 35 million fishing licenses are issued each year. That number does not include children or saltwater fishermen, neither of whom require licenses.

Types of Fish. Anglers fish for thousands of species. The larger species are found in salt water. A 1,208-kg (2,664-lb) white shark was caught by rod off Australia in 1959. The most popular freshwater fish is the white sturgeon; among saltwater fish, the flounder, bluefish, cod, striped bass, tuna, pompano, sea trout, porgies, red snapper, halibut, and haddock. The popular freshwater fish include black bass, various types of trout, sunfish, crappies, salmon, perch, pike, muskies, sturgeon, and shad. Some fish live in both fresh and salt water. Amphidromous species (milkfish, snook) move from fresh to salt water, but not for the purpose of spawning. Anadromous species (Atlantic salmon, alewife, shad) move from oceans to rivers in order to spawn. Catadromous fish (American eel) move from fresh to salt water in order to spawn.

These sport fishermen are in the Gulf of Mexico off Biloxi, Miss. In these warm Gulf Stream waters, game fishes include bonito, marlin, bluefish, sailfish, tuna, and several types of trout.

Methods of Fishing. There are three general methods of sport fishing—trolling, casting, and still fishing. To troll, the angler lets out line attached to a baited hook or lure, which is pulled along as the boat moves through the water. To cast, the angler flips a baited hook toward an area where the fish are likely to lurk, such as in a weed bed or under a fallen tree. For still fishing, the angler sits on shore or anchors the boat and sinks a weighted line with bait and hook into the water; often a bobber is attached to the line to indicate movement if the fish should nibble. Sometimes the boat anchor is not dropped, so that the boat can drift. Other less frequently practiced methods of fishing include harpooning and fishing with bow-and-arrow. In wintertime many anglers ice-fish by cutting holes

Artificial lures, such as spoons (1, 2) and spinners (3, 4), attract fish with their wobbling action and flashing colors. The streamer (5), a wet fly, is designed to sink swiftly; the dry fly (6), which resembles a larval insect, floats on the surface. Jointed plugs (7, 8) feature an erratic motion similar to that of an injured minnow.

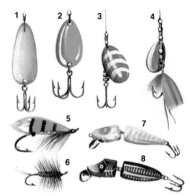

Fishing techniques differ according to the species of fish being sought. (Below) Carp, catfish, and panfish can be caught in still water by casting a baited hook to rest on the bottom. (Left) Many varieties of trout and salmon, which prefer fast-moving water, are caught with spinning lures and small artificial flies.

in the ice; they sometimes fish from inside a small enclosure called a fish shanty.

Bait. Fish are attracted to hooks by either natural or artificial baits. For freshwater fish, natural baits include worms, night crawlers, minnows, small baitfish (such as shiners and suckers), hellgramites, and crickets. The most popular saltwater baits are crayfish, clams, or small pieces of fish. Hundreds of artificial lures, shaped as small fish, worms, flies, or colorful objects, are also used.

Fishing Poles and Reels. Most fishing rods are made of tubular fiberglass, although some expensive fly rods are made of split bamboo. Fishing reels come in five general classifications: fly reel, bait-casting reel, spin-casting reel, opened-face reel, and larger reels for saltwater fish and more powerful freshwater fish such as sturgeon or muskies. The reels allow the angler to cast, or throw out the line, and retrieve it untangled. Sport fishing is one of the largest and most profitable recreation businesses in the United States.

fishing industry Commercial fishing is a worldwide enterprise that involves the capture of ocean and freshwater fish, shellfish, and marine mammals, and their processing for market. Fishing equipment ranges from small boats whose nets are cast and hauled in by hand to factory ships equipped with the most advanced technologies for finding, harvesting, and processing huge quantities of fish. These large catches are made at heavy expense, however, not only in the cost of the equipment and fuel, but also in the potential depletion of fishery resources.

The major portion of the total fish harvest consists of relatively few fish species, which are divided into two groups. Pelagic species—those which inhabit the near-surface layers of the oceans—include several species of herring, tuna, salmon, anchovies, pilchard, sardines, menhaden, and mackerel. Demersal species—fish that inhabit the near-bottom layers of the ocean—include cod,

sole, halibut, haddock, hake, and flounder. Large catches are also made of animals called SHELLFISH—shrimp, lobster, scallops, oysters, clams, crabs, mussels, and squid. The major marine mammal, the whale, has lost most of its former commercial importance (see WHALING).

Almost all large pelagic and demersal fish catches are made over the continental shelf, the underwater plateau surrounding the continents and large islands. In these waters temperatures, water depths, and the currents that influence the quantities of available food create an environment that is highly favorable to the existence of large

Of the hundreds of species of fish that inhabit the sea, the anchoveta (A), cod (B), herring (C), haddock (D), and sardine (E) are among the most important commercially for the fishing industry. The anchovies and sardines are smaller members of the herring family; all three are pelagic fish. Codfish and haddock are related and are usually caught near the bottom. The herring and codfish families combined account for 40 percent of the world's total annual catch of fish.

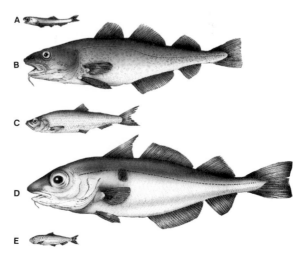

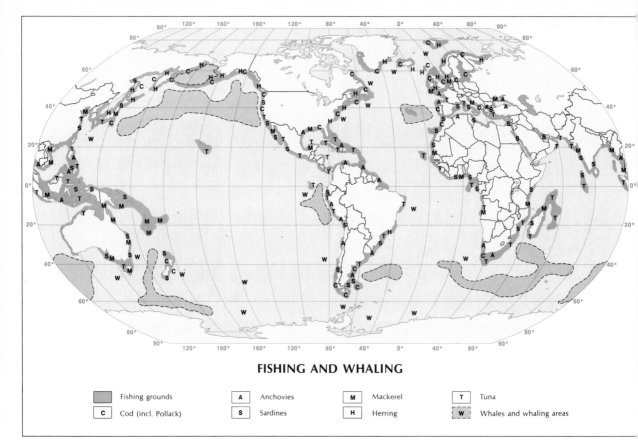

FISHING AND WHALING

▓ Fishing grounds	**M** Mackerel	**T** Tuna
C Cod (incl. Pollack)	**A** Anchovies	**H** Herring
S Sardines		**W** Whales and whaling areas

schools of fish. The animals living in and on the bottom of the continental shelf serve as additional food sources for demersal fish. Furthermore, most species spawn on continental shelves, and the main nursery grounds of many species are also in coastal regions.

After being beheaded and de-tailed, fresh-caught tuna are numbered and arranged in rows in a Tokyo wholesale fish market. The large yellowfin tuna is particularly prized for sushi, the Japanese raw fish cuisine.

The Development of the Fishing Industry

Prehistoric peoples were hunters and food collectors, and they found much of their food in lakes, rivers, and shallow coastal ocean waters. Shellfish were the most accessible food fish, and the large shell heaps found throughout the world bear witness to the first fishing technique, the use of bare hands.

During the Mesolithic Period (c.10,000–6000 BC) certain cultures that depended almost entirely on a diet of fish developed primitive fishing technologies, including stone-pointed fishing spears, fishing lines and nets, and bone harpoons. Improved equipment increased the size of catches. Drying, salting, and other techniques preserved the catch.

As larger fishing craft were built, vessels ventured farther into the oceans, and sea fishing developed into a well-defined vocation. Early ocean fisheries were confined to the coastal regions of settled areas and to the Mediterranean Sea. Gradually the rich fishing regions of the Atlantic Ocean and the North and Baltic seas began to be exploited.

The opening of the fishing areas around Nova Scotia and Newfoundland had a considerable effect on European history. First fished by the French in the early 1500s, by the beginning of the 17th century the North Atlantic

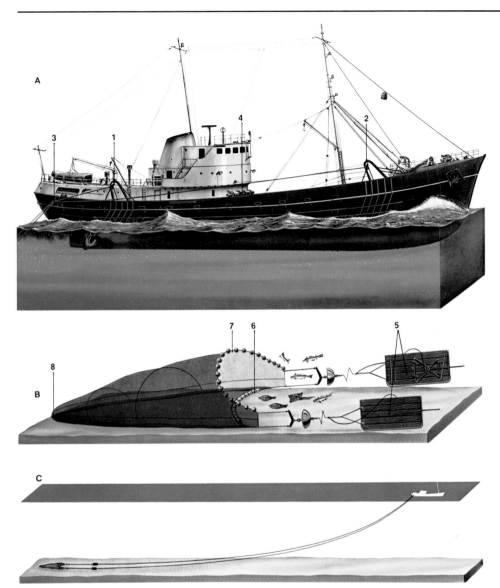

Otter trawling is an important form of commercial fishing. An otter trawl is a net that is towed along the ocean bottom by long cables called warps. On the side trawler (A), the warp cables pass through fore and aft gallows (1, 2) mounted on one side of the ship, then through a towing block (3). When full, the trawl is hauled to the surface by powerful winches (4). On the trawl itself (B), the towing cables are attached to otter boards (5), iron-shod wood panels that pull sideways as they are dragged forward, keeping the trawl mouth open horizontally; heavy rollers on the net's bottom lip (6), and floats along the top (7), keep the mouth open vertically. The trawl net tapers to a narrow end (the cod end) that is laced closed (8). When the trawl is hoisted on deck, the end-lacing is released and the catch is dropped into the ship. Otter trawling requires great lengths of cable (C).

fisheries had become the principal source of New World wealth for England.

Principal Fisheries

The most important world fisheries are located in waters less than 400 m (1,300 ft) in depth. The major fishing grounds are in the North Atlantic (including the GRAND BANKS and the Georges Banks off the New England coast), the North Sea, the waters over the continental shelves of Iceland and Norway, and the Barents Sea; in the North Pacific, particularly the Bering Sea, the Gulf of Alaska, and the coastal areas around Japan; and in the Pacific waters off the coasts of China and Malaysia. Other important fishing grounds are found off the Peruvian coast and off the coast of the southeastern United States.

Fishing is often restricted to the spawning periods of a particular species. Fortunately, different stocks of the same species often have different spawning times on different grounds, and this fact enables the fishery to be extended over longer periods. For example, the Norwegian "spring herring" gathers for spawning mainly in January and February; the "big herring" (stors-ild) spawns in September to December.

The local fisheries of the African coast, and many of those found elsewhere in the tropics, remain relatively undeveloped. The principal limiting factors are: first, the narrowness of the continental shelf, which limits the presence of demersal fish, and the existence of a straight coastline that offers few possibilities for good harbors; second, the high temperatures, which affect the keeping

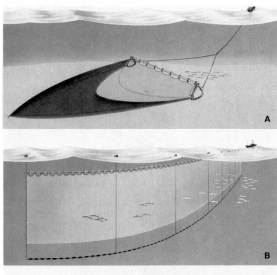

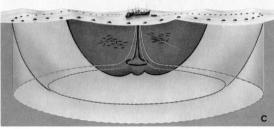

The beam trawl (A) is a net bag used to catch demersal fish and shrimp in relatively shallow water. The bag's mouth is held open by a beam, and the bag is dragged over the seabed on metal skids. The gill net (B) is a long, floating net attached to the end of a drifting boat. Pelagic fish are trapped by their gills as they try to pass through the net's mesh. The purse seine (C) is used to trap pelagic schools of fish. The long, float-suspended net is towed in a wide circle around a shoal until the two ends of the net meet. The net is then pursed, or closed, by drawing in a line that runs through loops on the lower edge, to form a huge bag that can be hauled aboard.

quality of the fish catch; and third, limited access to the interior, making marketing difficult.

Major Fishing Countries. Catches of fish and shellfish throughout the world rose during the 1980s, totaling more than 90 million metric tons (99 million U.S. tons) in 1986. Almost half the catch, 40.5 million metric tons (about 44.6 U.S. tons), is taken by Asian countries, principally Japan.

The total catch of marine fish and shellfish in the United States throughout the 1980s averaged about 3 million metric tons (3.3 million U.S. tons) annually. Tuna and shrimp are the most valuable catches. The haddock fishery off the New England coast is also important, although haddock landings have decreased sharply due to overfishing. The same fishery yields cod and flounder. Salmon and halibut are harvested in the Northeast Pacific, and the anchovy fishery off the California coast produces fish for processing and for live bait.

Fishing Technologies

In most modern fishing fleets the basic fishing vessel is the trawler, equipped with a diesel engine and outfitted with a variety of equipment for fish finding and capturing. Echo sounders and sonar devices detect the presence of fish in waters up to 400 fathoms deep (730 m/2,400 ft) and are also used to ascertain water depths and the roughness on the ocean bottom. Airplanes are used to scout scattered shoals of pelagic fish.

Fish Harvesting. The standard methods of catching fish involve either nets, hooked lines, or traps. Pelagic fish are most often harvested using purse seine nets, which are set in a wide circle around the school and then closed (or pursed) and drawn up. Straight drift or gill nets—whose mesh is just large enough to allow the heads of fish to pass through while trapping them at their gills—are used to catch salmon, tuna, cod, and other fish. Demersal fish may be netted in otter trawl nets, sock-shaped nets pulled along the ocean bottom, or with beam trawls that are used in shallower waters, primarily for shrimp. Hooked groundlines, called longlines, are used in halibut fishing. They may reach lengths of many miles, with baited hooks attached at intervals of 6 to 9 m (20 to 30 ft). Floating longlines are used primarily in tuna and salmon fishing, as are trolling lines, shorter lines that are towed behind a moving boat.

Fish Processing. Large fishing vessels on long voyages are equipped to keep their catch edible by refrigerating or quick-freezing it. A fully equipped factory ship—a huge vessel accompanied by a fleet of smaller catcher boats—also has machinery on board for fish filleting and freezing or canning. Some also have facilities for drying and grinding fish into fish meal.

Fisheries Management

As early as the 1890s it was acknowledged that fishery resources are limited and that they must be managed through international agreements. In 1902 the International Council for Exploration of the Sea (ICES) was formed by the major European fishing countries. The founding of ICES led to several conventions for the regulation of fisheries by mesh size of nets, and by quotas, in order to obtain "maximum sustainable yields"—the highest yields consistent with the maintenance of fish stocks. Although such conventions have been effective in the Northeast Atlantic, they have not operated as well in other regions. The extension of national jurisdictions over fisheries resources to a 200-naut-mi (370-km/230-mi) zone, beginning in the 1970s, has further limited the effectiveness of many international conventions.

In the United States the Fishery Conservation and Management Act of 1976 places all marine resources from the coast to 200 naut mi offshore under U.S. jurisdiction. Management is effected through regional fisheries councils, which also grant permits to foreign countries to harvest specified quantities of certain fish species in return for a fee. In addition, quotas on commercially important fish such as salmon have been set for the American fishing fleet, which is restricted in terms of both the

A bulging net of fish is thrown into a fish hatch of a stern-fishing trawler. In ships close to port the fish are stored in refrigerated brine or melting crushed ice. In ships far from port, the fish are cleaned and quick-frozen.

total catch of any particular species and the season when such fish may be harvested.

World Catches

In 1948 the total world fish catch was about 19 million metric tons (about 21 million U.S. tons). With advanced harvesting technologies, the total catch rose to more than 60 million metric tons (about 66 million U.S. tons) by 1970. Despite major fluctuations, the trend has since been upward: almost 77 million metric tons (almost 85 million U.S. tons) in 1982, 92 million metric tons (about 101 million U.S. tons) in 1986.

The causes for fluctuating—and, in some species groups, diminishing—catches are varied and include factors that are beyond human control: for example, the change in the ocean currents that caused the disappearance of the anchovy from the coastal waters off Peru (see EL NIÑO). Overfishing, which is the harvesting of a species to a point where it cannot reproduce itself in significant numbers, is partly responsible for the decline of California sardines. Species that are now in danger of being overfished include cod, haddock, halibut, salmon, and several species of tuna and whale.

Beginning in the early 1980s, Japanese, Taiwanese, and South Korean fishing fleets began to use a new fishing technique to make large-scale squid catches. Huge, 15-m-deep (50-ft) drift nets made of unbreakable nylon, each stretching 90 m (295 ft), are lowered off the boats each evening. Together, the nets from a single boat form a great wall just under the ocean's surface. They drift all night, entangling any sea creatures swimming into their meshes. In the early morning the boats return to pull in the nets with their catch: many squid, but also salmon, steelhead trout, seabirds, and ocean mammals as big as porpoises and seals. The large shortfalls in the numbers of salmon taken in Alaska in recent years and the disappearance of steelhead trout are, it is believed, directly tied to the use of drift nets.

Future Possibilities

Most present fishery resources are fished to their limits, at least for those species which have commercial importance. Other species, however—notably whiting, hake, squid, and pollack—offer great commercial possibilities if markets can be developed for them.

The improved cultivation of marine resources offers another possibility for increasing the number of food fish. Salmon, for example, are being raised in pens in Norway and along the North American coasts (see FISH FARMING).

See also: FISH; separate articles on individual fish species.

—

Fisk, James   James Fisk, b. Bennington, Vt., Apr. 1, 1834, d. Jan. 7, 1872, was a financier and stock speculator who became known as the "Barnum of Wall Street." He left school at an early age and worked at odd jobs before becoming a buyer for Jordan and Marsh, a Boston dry goods firm. After the Civil War he was an agent for the financier Daniel DREW, who helped him open a brokerage firm. With Drew and Jay GOULD, Fisk was a principal in the "Erie War," the struggle to prevent Cornelius Vanderbilt from gaining control of the Erie Railroad. In 1869, Fisk and Gould attempted to corner the gold market, an adventure that ended in the BLACK FRIDAY panic of September 24.

The business tactics and stock speculations of the American financier James Fisk secured him a vast fortune. Working closely with Jay Gould and Daniel Drew, Fisk manipulated the stock of the Erie Railroad for personal gain. The attempt of these men to corner the gold market resulted in the "Black Friday" panic of Sept. 24, 1869.

Fisk University   Established in 1867 as a college for blacks, and still having a large black enrollment, Fisk University is a private coeducational liberal arts school affiliated with the United Church of Christ. It is located in Nashville, Tenn.

fission, nuclear   Nuclear fission is a special type of nuclear reaction in which a heavy nucleus breaks up into two smaller nuclei or fragments. Fission may occur spontaneously or by the bombardment of a nucleus with a particle such as a neutron or a proton or with gamma radiation. Many different nuclei may undergo fission, but all have some common characteristics. Fission is a complex process, and it creates many different products. In addition to the two fragments, neutrons, beta particles, neutrinos, and gamma radiation are also emitted in a fission process.

The phenomenon of fission is a statistical process in the sense that there are about 50 different ways a nucleus may undergo fission, producing a different pair of primary fragments each time, and creating some one hundred different nuclei. Some modes of fission are more probable than others. One characteristic of the process is that the fissioning nucleus breaks into two unequal parts, creating a lighter fragment and a heavier fragment. These nuclei are formed with excess energy that they do not have in their normal, or ground, states, and they must de-

(A) *A thermal, or low-energy, neutron* (black) *may be absorbed by a uranium-235 (U-235) nucleus, containing 92 protons* (red) *and 143 neutrons, to form an unstable uranium-236 nucleus. The U-236 nucleus fissions, or splits, into two smaller nuclei, such as barium-141 (Ba-141) and krypton-92 (Kr-92), and 2 or 3 neutrons. (B) Neutrons from a fissioned nucleus* (1) *may strike another U-235 nucleus* (2) *and cause it to fragment and release more neutrons, producing a chain reaction if enough U-235 neutrons are present. Neutrons may also be absorbed by nonfissionable U-238 nuclei* (3) *or previously created fission products* (4). *A fission product such as tellurium-135* (5), *for example, decays to xenon-135* (6), *which absorbs neutrons without splitting.*

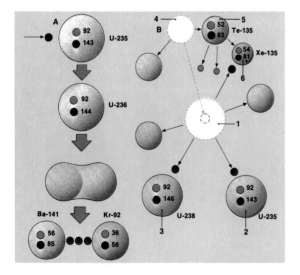

excite, or lose energy, usually by the emission of gamma radiation and sometimes by neutron emission. Each primary fragment formed is rich in neutrons and is radioactive. It undergoes successive BETA DECAY, each time creating a new element until a stable final nucleus is formed. The radioactive nuclei can be chemically separated and can be used in research, medicine, engineering, and agriculture.

Some nuclei, such as uranium-235, which contains 92 protons and 143 neutrons, are more apt than others to undergo fission when bombarded by low-energy neutrons. For this reason uranium-235 is used as the fissionable material in the construction of a nuclear reactor. Each fission process causes additional neutrons to be emitted. The excess neutrons thus produced can cause more fissions in the fissionable material, generating a CHAIN REACTION in the reactor.

Fitch, John   John Fitch, b. East Windsor, Conn., Jan. 21, 1743, d. July 2, 1798, is best known as the builder of the first practical STEAMBOAT. Following experiments with STEAM ENGINES, he navigated a paddle-powered steam craft on the Delaware River in 1787. That same year, he built a 13.7-m-long (45-ft) steamboat and again demonstrated it on the Delaware—20 years before Robert Fulton launched (1807) the commercially successful *Clermont*.

In 1790, with a larger boat, Fitch inaugurated the first regularly scheduled steamboat service in the world, between Philadelphia and Burlington, N.J. He was unable to obtain financial backing for other projects, and he died destitute and despondent after suffering from a prolonged illness.

FitzGerald, Edward   In translating the work of the Persian poet OMAR KHAYYAM, English writer and translator Edward FitzGerald, b. Mar. 31, 1809, d. June 14, 1883, created one of the best-loved and most memorable poems in the English language. A friend of Tennyson and Carlyle, FitzGerald devoted himself to Oriental studies after 1850, publishing his freely adapted RUBAIYAT OF OMAR KHAYYAM in 1859. This reflective poem, with its haunting stanzas on love, death, and the passage of time, did not become widely known until after the translator's death. FitzGerald also wrote aphorisms and translated Spanish and Greek playwrights.

Fitzgerald, Ella   The singer Ella Fitzgerald, b. Newport News, Va., Apr. 25, 1918, is second only to Billie Holiday in the influence she has had over several generations of pop-music singers. Her career began (1934–39) with Chick Webb's band, which she led for a year after his death. Since recording (1938) "A-tisket, A-tasket," she has had countless hits, has sung with Duke Ellington, Count Basie, and other major bands, and has appeared as a soloist with more than 40 symphony orchestras. A great scat singer and ballad interpreter, she has consistently lifted often trivial material to the level of high jazz art.

Fitzgerald, F. Scott

Francis Scott Key Fitzgerald, b. Saint Paul, Minn., Sept. 24, 1896, d. Dec. 21, 1940, was an American writer of fiction whose work spanned the years between World Wars I and II. A master of the short story and the novel of manners, Fitzgerald is recognized as one of the most important writers of his time, especially for helping to create the image of the Jazz Age. Both his life and his works also offer an acute commentary on the disillusion and depression of the 1930s.

Fitzgerald was of Irish ancestry on both sides and distantly related to Francis Scott Key, for whom he was named, and to Maryland aristocracy. His mother's father, Philip McQuillan, was a successful wholesale merchant, and the failure of Fitzgerald's father to hold a job left the family dependent on the McQuillan wealth. Because of his mother's ambitions, Fitzgerald was sent east to a Catholic prep school in 1911, but he always retained something of the wonder and defensiveness of the provincial coming into a more worldly society. He went on to Princeton University in 1913 but left in his junior year, partly because of ill health but chiefly because of low grades. Although he returned the next fall, he did not stay to receive a degree. Instead, he entered the army as a second lieutenant in 1917.

Fitzgerald's Princeton years were important nonetheless. They provided an outlet for his writing talent, introduced him to more and better literature than he had known before, and brought him together with other literary young men, notably Edmund Wilson. Princeton also furnished most of the material for *This Side of Paradise* (1920), the success of which launched his career.

Throughout the 1920s Fitzgerald's life and much of his fiction was preoccupied with Zelda Sayre, the Alabama girl he married immediately after the publication of his first novel (see FITZGERALD, ZELDA SAYRE). The central characters of *The Beautiful and Damned* (1922), his

F. Scott Fitzgerald, an American author, chronicled the social climate of the 1920s. Fitzgerald's works contain many autobiographical elements; his personal life was marred by the unsatisfying affluence and empty hedonism depicted in his novels.

second novel, are a couple like the Fitzgeralds, who lead a life of drinking, partying, and endless talk. Going to Europe, first in 1921, was an adventure and an escape. It was during their second period there, from 1924 to 1926, that Fitzgerald completed what many consider his best work, The GREAT GATSBY (1925). As the 1920s advanced, Fitzgerald's drinking became regarded as alcoholism, while Zelda's erratic behavior was diagnosed (1930) as schizophrenia. His difficulty in organizing his novel *Tender Is the Night* (1934) was largely from the strain of their conditions.

Fitzgerald's life reached a low point in 1935, when he suffered the nervous collapse that he later brilliantly described in three essays called *The Crack-Up* (1945). By that time Zelda's mental illness had begun to require hospitalization, and she was in and out of mental institutions for the rest of her life. The couple lived apart during much of the decade, their daughter, Scotty (1921–86), becoming increasingly Fitzgerald's charge. His work, off and on, as a movie scriptwriter marks his last years; at his death he was working on a novel about Hollywood, *The Last Tycoon* (1941).

FitzGerald, Garret

Garret FitzGerald, b. Feb. 9, 1926, was twice prime minister of Ireland (June 1981–February 1982 and December 1982–February 1987). FitzGerald served (1973–77) as foreign minister under Liam Cosgrave and became leader of the Fine Gael party in 1977. Governing as head of a Fine Gael-Labour coalition, he concluded (1985) an agreement with Britain establishing a common Anglo-Irish policy for Northern Ireland but failed to deal effectively with unemployment. FitzGerald's coalition fell when Labour withdrew its support in January 1987.

Fitzgerald, Robert

Translator, poet, critic, and Harvard professor Robert Stuart Fitzgerald, b. Geneva, N.Y., Oct. 12, 1910, d. Jan. 16, 1985, was best known for his expressive blank-verse translations of classical Greek authors. With Dudley Fitts, Fitzgerald produced notable English versions of Euripides' *Alcestis* (1936) and Sophocles' *Antigone* (1939) and *Oedipus Rex* (1949). His reputation, however, rests mostly on his translations of three epics: Homer's *Odyssey* (1961; Bollingen Prize) and *Iliad* (1974) and Vergil's *Aeneid* (1983). Fitzgerald also published four collections of his own poetry, as well as a book about literary criticism, *Enlarging the Change* (1984).

Fitzgerald, Zelda Sayre

Zelda Sayre Fitzgerald, b. Montgomery, Ala., July 24, 1900, d. Mar. 10, 1948, was a writer married to and overshadowed by the celebrated author F. Scott FITZGERALD. Although her life was marred by schizophrenia, her short stories, essays, and novel (*Save Me the Waltz,* 1932) indicate talent of a high order. Some of the material in her journals was used by Fitzgerald, particularly in his novel *Tender Is the Night* (1934).

Fitzgerald-Lorentz contraction The Fitzgerald-Lorentz contraction is an effect first postulated in 1892 by George F. Fitzgerald and amplified in 1895 by Hendrik A. Lorentz. It was proposed in an attempt to explain the null result of the Michelson-Morley experiment, performed in 1887, which measured the time taken for a light beam to travel a distance *d* and back when the direction of motion of the beam was parallel to the supposed direction of motion of the laboratory, or observer, through the "ether." The time was compared with that for the same trip when the laboratory moved perpendicular to the light's direction. In this case, the laboratory's motion was the Earth's motion through space. The ether was the medium through which light was presumed to travel with speed *c*.

According to classical theory, the time taken for both round trips should be different. The Michelson-Morley experiment, however, demonstrated no difference in travel times. Fitzgerald suggested that if the length of the parallel arm *d* were contracted to $d\sqrt{1 - v^2/c^2}$ (where *v* is the speed of the laboratory) while that of the perpendicular arm remained unchanged, the prediction would agree with the experiment.

Lorentz later proposed a model for matter that incorporated this effect. He stated that the atoms and molecules that compose matter would, under the effect of motion, be compressed along the direction of motion. It would be impossible to measure this deformation; a ruler placed alongside a speeding object would be similarly shortened.

Albert Einstein showed, in his theory of relativity, that the contraction was a fundamental consequence of the assumption that the speed of light is the same in all reference frames. The effect is only significant at speeds that are a sizable fraction of the speed of light.

Fitzpatrick, Sir Charles Sir Charles Fitzpatrick, b. Dec. 19, 1853, d. June 17, 1942, was a Canadian jurist who first won attention defending the insurgent Louis Riel in 1885. Elected (1896) to the Canadian House of Commons as a Liberal, he served as federal minister of justice from 1902 to 1906, when he was named chief justice of the Canadian Supreme Court. He was later lieutenant governor of Quebec (1918–23).

Fitzpatrick, Thomas The American fur trapper, guide, and Indian agent Thomas Fitzpatrick, b. 1799, d. Feb. 7, 1854, was one of the famous mountain men of the Rockies. Born in Ireland, he emigrated to the United States as a youth. He joined several trapping expeditions, and, during the 1830s, operated the Rocky Mountain Fur Company with James Bridger and others. In 1836, Fitzpatrick began to serve as a guide; he escorted the missionary parties of Marcus Whitman and Pierre Jean De Smet to the Northwest, guided (1841) the first wagon train of settlers to California, and accompanied John C. Frémont's 1843–44 expedition. After 1846, Fitzpatrick was Indian agent for the Upper Platte River region; he negotiated (1851) the Fort Laramie Treaty, which established boundaries for the Plains tribes and guaranteed the safety of whites traveling the Oregon Trail.

Fitzsimons, Thomas Thomas Fitzsimons, b. Ireland, 1741, d. Aug. 26, 1811, was a U.S. political and business leader who signed the Constitution. An active supporter of the American Revolution, Fitzsimons led a company of home guards during the war and became a member (1782–83) of the Continental Congress. After serving in the Pennsylvania state legislature (1786–87), he was a delegate to the 1787 Constitutional Convention. Fitzsimons was elected as a Federalist to the U.S. House of Representatives (1789–95), where he supported Alexander Hamilton's bank and tariff policies. For many years a member of the Philadelphia Chamber of Commerce, he founded the Bank of North America.

Fiume see Rijeka

Five, The see Russian music

Five Civilized Tribes The Five Civilized Tribes was a loose confederation, formed in 1859, of North American Indians in what was then Indian Territory (in present-day Oklahoma). The group comprised the Iroquoian-speaking Cherokee and the Muskogean-speaking Chickasaw, Choctaw, Creek, and Seminole. They were described as "civilized" because of their early adoption of many of the white man's ways. Under the Indian Removal Act of 1830, the Five Tribes were deported from their traditional homelands east of the Mississippi and forced to settle in Indian Territory. Each organized an autonomous state modeled after the U.S. federal government, established courts and a formalized code of laws, constructed schools and Christian churches, and developed a writing system patterned on the one earlier devised by the Cherokee.

Members of the Five Tribes absorbed many cultural features of their white neighbors, including plow agriculture and animal husbandry, European-style houses and dress, and even the ownership of black slaves. Some tribesmen joined the Confederate forces during the Civil War. Thereafter the United States instituted a policy of detribalization and gradually curtailed Indian control of tribal lands. The tribal nations remained independent until 1907, when statehood was granted to Oklahoma and the federal government opened Indian Territory to white settlement. Today, many descendants of the Five Tribes live on reservations in Oklahoma.

Before forced settlement in Indian Territory, the members of the Five Tribes shared many culture traits. All relied primarily on maize agriculture, with fishing, hunting, and foraging an important but subsidiary means of subsistence. Village life was highly developed. Households generally included small extended families, with kinship based on a matrilineal clan system. Independent communities were politically integrated into confederacies.

Temple architecture, ceremonial centers, and elaborate rituals such as the CORN DANCE, existed. Traditional crafts included coiled pottery, woven blankets, and articles of wrought copper.

Five Nations   see IROQUOIS LEAGUE

—

fjord [fee-ohrd'] Fjords are long, narrow, deep, and relatively straight arms of the ocean that may project many kilometers inland. Bordered by steep walls commonly thousands of meters high, and by truncated spurs, their beauty is enhanced by waterfalls that drop from great heights. In Alaska and Greenland, fjords terminate landward in tidewater GLACIERS from which icebergs calve; in Norway and New Zealand, fjords terminate in steep bedrock slopes. Found in high latitudes along mountainous coasts, they are glacially eroded valleys that became submerged when they were invaded by the ocean. The depth of the fjords, more than a thousand meters in some places, is due mainly to the depth of glacial erosion (see EROSION AND SEDIMENTATION) below sea level, not to a rise of sea level after the valleys were formed.

—

Flack, Audrey Audrey Flack, b. May 30, 1931, a noted American photorealist painter, was one of the first artists to openly acknowledge the use of photographs as the basis for her compositions in the early 1960s (see PHOTOREALISM). In 1969, Flack developed a technique of airbrushing paint over images that were projected from color slides onto a canvas, thus eliminating the need for preliminary drawing. Her cluttered still-life paintings engage the viewer with their exaggerated scale, minute detail, and trompe l'oeil spatial effects, as well as their kitsch subject matter. *Gambler's Cabinet* (1976; Collection Meisel Gallery, New York City) is typical of her work.

—

flag A flag is a piece of colored fabric that serves as a symbol or a signaling device. Basically, flags are messages from a person or a group of people. They express numerous kinds of messages—protection, victory, challenge, submission, pride, honor, threat, loyalty, and hope. Patriots express their love of country by hoisting flags; victorious armies humiliate their enemies by displaying captured flags; dictators use flags to help mold public opinion; and activists challenge the government by flaunting outlawed banners. Ships fly flags both for identification (by nation, shipping line, or both) and for SIGNALING.

As a form of political expression, flags are closely related to such other symbols as official seals, coats of arms, armbands, and emblems such as the American eagle, the hammer and sickle of Soviet Communism, and the swastika of Nazism.

Flags are normally of cloth or other flexible material and are made in such a way as to be displayed from a rigid staff. Today, flags are usually made of cotton, wool, or synthetic fabrics; however, they are sometimes metal, plastic, or paper. Formerly, flags were made of silk or lin-

en. The size of a flag depends on its intended use. For example, small ones are used as table decorations, and the largest flag in regular use, in Brazil, is 70 by 100 m (more than 200 by 300 ft).

The importance of a flag lies in its symbolism rather than in its material or size; its color and design are the basis for expressing that symbolism. Although all colors may be and have been used, most nonmilitary flags use one or more of six colors—red, yellow, blue, green, black, and white. Designs are of every imaginable form, from the solid red of revolution to intricate patterns incorporating hundreds of elements; but the majority of flags are simple. For ready identification, especially at sea or at a great distance, the following basic geometric patterns are popular: an emblem centered on a plain field, with or without a border; quartered or crosswise divisions; a plain field with a distinctive rectangular area in the upper hoist area (known as the canton); and vertical or horizontal stripes. Combinations of these patterns are also used.

A specialized vocabulary has developed to describe the parts and the uses of flags. The study of all aspects of flag design, history, symbolism, etiquette, terminology, and development is known as vexillology (from the Latin *vexillum*, meaning "flag").

Origin

The date of the earliest flag is not known, but archaeological records from the ancient Middle East, Egypt, China, and America suggest that the use of flags was nearly universal among early civilizations. These earliest flags frequently consisted of a carved emblem at the top of a pole, sometimes with ribbons attached below. Natural subjects, especially wild animals, were felt to be appropriate symbols and indeed are still found in modern heraldry—from the lions in the royal standard of Britain to the bison on the state flag of Wyoming.

The use of cloth flags attached along the side of a pole may have been a Chinese invention, since woven silk was developed very early in the Far East. The beginnings of modern flag design, that is, the combination of colors and forms on cloth to transmit certain ideas, may be seen in the development of HERALDRY during the 12th century in Europe and slightly later in Japan. Heraldry was the design of coats of arms to distinguish individuals, families, and institutions. Although not all flags are heraldic, many of the rules that developed in European heraldry furnish the basis for the most expressive flags.

One of the most important developments in flag history has been the proliferation of national flags, which began in the late 18th century and still continues. The American and French revolutions of 1775 and 1789, respectively, associated specific designs and colors with the concepts of liberty, independence, democracy, nationalism, and political mobilization of the masses.

Flag Symbolism

The UNION JACK of the United Kingdom combines the crosses of St. George, St. Andrew, and St. Patrick, the patron saints of England, Scotland, and Ireland, respectively. The five points of the star in the national flag of

FLAGS FROM WORLD HISTORY

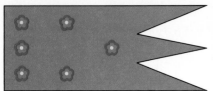

CHARLEMAGNE

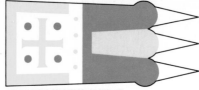

WILLIAM I (THE CONQUEROR) OF ENGLAND

GENGHIS KHAN

PEASANTS' WAR (16TH-CENTURY GERMANY)

PETER I (THE GREAT) OF RUSSIA

HUDSON'S BAY COMPANY

JOSÉ DE SAN MARTIN

CHINA UNDER THE CH'ING DYNASTY (19TH-CENTURY)

FLAG PROPOSED BY CECIL RHODES FOR BRITISH AFRICA

FLAGS FROM AMERICAN HISTORY

VIKINGS

CHRISTOPHER COLUMBUS

HENRY HUDSON

BRITISH EXPLORERS AND SETTLERS (FIRST UNION JACK)

FRENCH EXPLORERS AND SETTLERS (17TH AND 18TH CENTURIES)

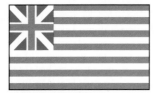

CONTINENTAL COLORS (1776)

FIRST STARS AND STRIPES (1777-95)

ESEK HOPKINS, FIRST COMMANDER IN CHIEF OF THE CONTINENTAL NAVY

FIRST STAR-SPANGLED BANNER (1795-1818)

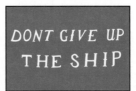

OLIVER HAZARD PERRY (WAR OF 1812)

TEXAS REPUBLIC (1836)

BEAR FLAG REPUBLIC (1846)

STARS AND BARS OF THE CONFEDERACY (1861-63)

FORT SUMTER FLAG (1861)

STARS AND STRIPES (OLD GLORY) IN 48-STAR VERSION (1912-59)

FLAGS OF AFRICA

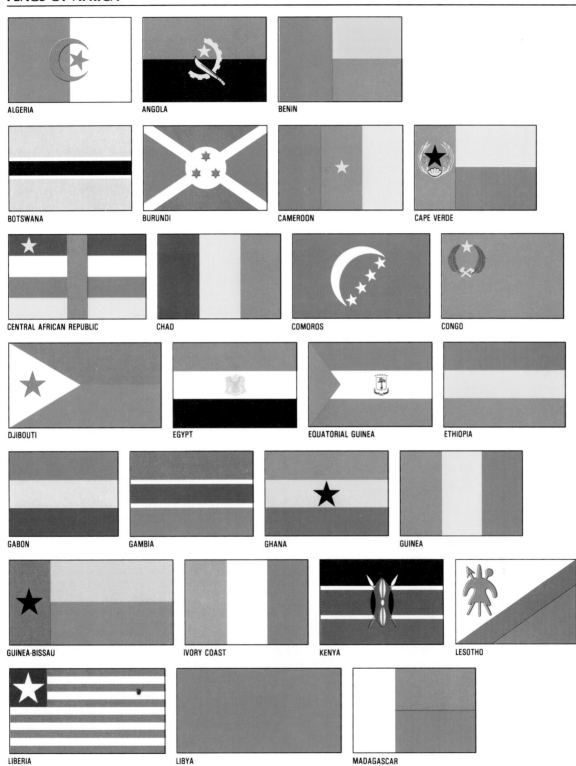

ALGERIA

ANGOLA

BENIN

BOTSWANA

BURUNDI

CAMEROON

CAPE VERDE

CENTRAL AFRICAN REPUBLIC

CHAD

COMOROS

CONGO

DJIBOUTI

EGYPT

EQUATORIAL GUINEA

ETHIOPIA

GABON

GAMBIA

GHANA

GUINEA

GUINEA-BISSAU

IVORY COAST

KENYA

LESOTHO

LIBERIA

LIBYA

MADAGASCAR

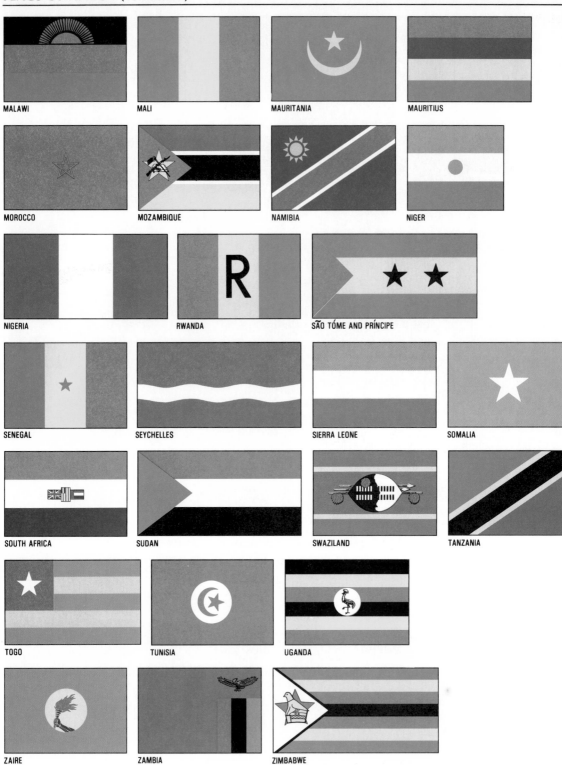

MALAWI

MALI

MAURITANIA

MAURITIUS

MOROCCO

MOZAMBIQUE

NAMIBIA

NIGER

NIGERIA

RWANDA

SÃO TÓME AND PRÍNCIPE

SENEGAL

SEYCHELLES

SIERRA LEONE

SOMALIA

SOUTH AFRICA

SUDAN

SWAZILAND

TANZANIA

TOGO

TUNISIA

UGANDA

ZAIRE

ZAMBIA

ZIMBABWE

FLAGS OF ASIA

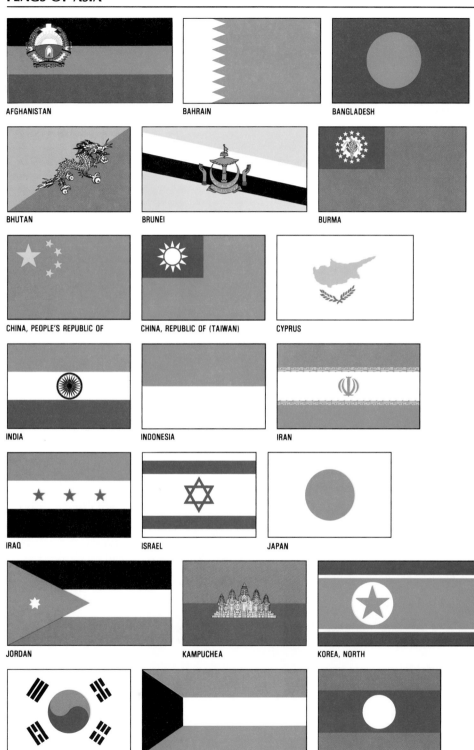

AFGHANISTAN

BAHRAIN

BANGLADESH

BHUTAN

BRUNEI

BURMA

CHINA, PEOPLE'S REPUBLIC OF

CHINA, REPUBLIC OF (TAIWAN)

CYPRUS

INDIA

INDONESIA

IRAN

IRAQ

ISRAEL

JAPAN

JORDAN

KAMPUCHEA

KOREA, NORTH

KOREA, SOUTH

KUWAIT

LAOS

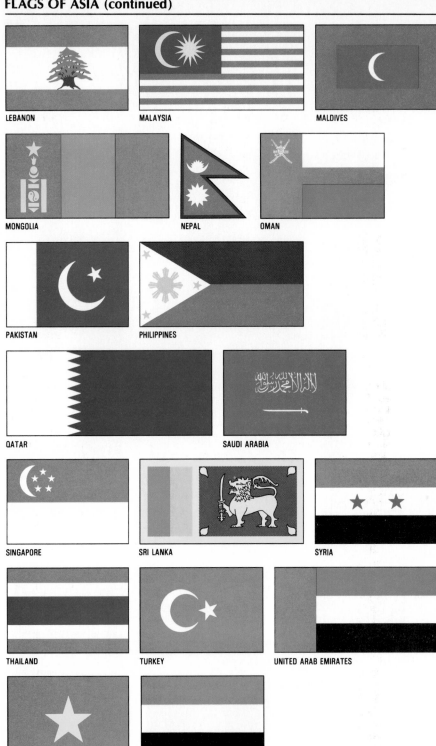

LEBANON

MALAYSIA

MALDIVES

MONGOLIA

NEPAL

OMAN

PAKISTAN

PHILIPPINES

QATAR

SAUDI ARABIA

SINGAPORE

SRI LANKA

SYRIA

THAILAND

TURKEY

UNITED ARAB EMIRATES

VIETNAM

YEMEN

FLAGS OF EUROPE

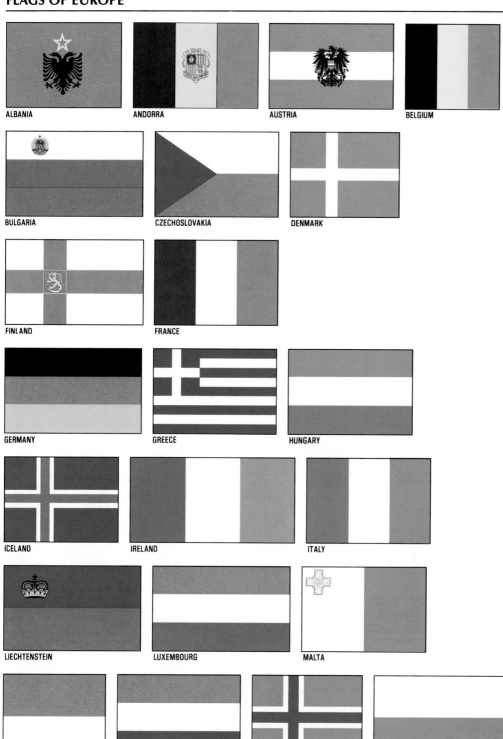

ALBANIA

ANDORRA

AUSTRIA

BELGIUM

BULGARIA

CZECHOSLOVAKIA

DENMARK

FINLAND

FRANCE

GERMANY

GREECE

HUNGARY

ICELAND

IRELAND

ITALY

LIECHTENSTEIN

LUXEMBOURG

MALTA

MONACO

NETHERLANDS

NORWAY

POLAND

FLAGS OF EUROPE (continued)

PORTUGAL

ROMANIA

SAN MARINO

SPAIN

SWEDEN

SWITZERLAND

UNION OF SOVIET SOCIALIST REPUBLICS

UNITED KINGDOM

VATICAN CITY

YUGOSLAVIA

FLAGS OF SOUTH AMERICA

ARGENTINA

BOLIVIA

BRAZIL

CHILE

COLOMBIA

ECUADOR

GUYANA

PARAGUAY

PERU

SURINAME

URUGUAY

VENEZUELA

FLAGS OF NORTH AMERICA

CANADA

MEXICO

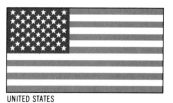

UNITED STATES

FLAGS OF THE CARIBBEAN

ANTIGUA AND BARBUDA

BAHAMAS

BARBADOS

CUBA

DOMINICA

DOMINICAN REPUBLIC

GRENADA

HAITI

JAMAICA

SAINT KITTS-NEVIS

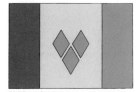

SAINT LUCIA

SAINT VINCENT AND THE GRENADINES

TRINIDAD AND TOBAGO

FLAGS OF CENTRAL AMERICA

BELIZE

COSTA RICA

EL SALVADOR

GUATEMALA

HONDURAS

NICARAGUA

PANAMA

FLAGS OF OCEANIA

AUSTRALIA

FIJI

KIRIBATI

NAURU

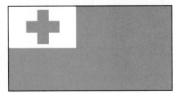

NEW ZEALAND

PAPUA NEW GUINEA

SOLOMON ISLANDS

TONGA

PAPUA NEW GUINEA

TUVALU

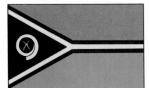

VANUATU

WESTERN SAMOA

FLAGS OF AUSTRALIA

NEW SOUTH WALES

NORFOLK ISLAND

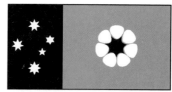

NORTHERN TERRITORY

QUEENSLAND

SOUTH AUSTRALIA

TASMANIA

VICTORIA

WESTERN AUSTRALIA

FLAGS OF CANADA

ALBERTA

BRITISH COLUMBIA

MANITOBA

NEW BRUNSWICK

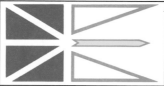

NEWFOUNDLAND

NORTHWEST TERRITORIES

NOVA SCOTIA

ONTARIO

PRINCE EDWARD ISLAND

QUEBEC

SASKATCHEWAN

YUKON TERRITORY

FLAGS OF INTERNATIONAL ORGANIZATIONS

UNITED NATIONS

RED CROSS

RED CRESCENT

RED MAGEN DAVID

OLYMPICS

NATO

ORG. OF AMERICAN STATES

COMECON

ORG. OF AFRICAN UNITY

ARAB LEAGUE

FLAGS OF UNITED STATES TERRITORIES

AMERICAN SAMOA

PALAU (BELAU)

GUAM

NORTHERN MARIANAS

MARSHALL ISLANDS

FEDERATED STATES OF MICRONESIA

PUERTO RICO

U.S. VIRGIN ISLANDS

FLAGS OF THE UNITED STATES

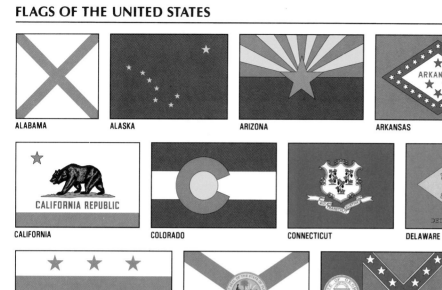

ALABAMA

ALASKA

ARIZONA

ARKANSAS

CALIFORNIA

COLORADO

CONNECTICUT

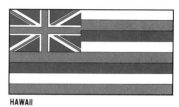

DELAWARE

DISTRICT OF COLUMBIA

FLORIDA

GEORGIA

HAWAII

IDAHO

ILLINOIS

INDIANA

IOWA

KANSAS

KENTUCKY

LOUISIANA

MAINE

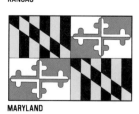

MARYLAND

MASSACHUSETTS

MICHIGAN

MINNESOTA

MISSISSIPPI

MISSOURI

MONTANA

NEBRASKA

FLAGS OF THE UNITED STATES (continued)

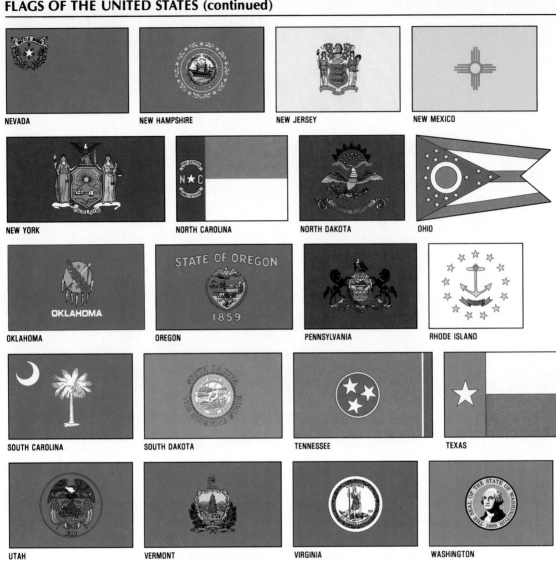

NEVADA

NEW HAMPSHIRE

NEW JERSEY

NEW MEXICO

NEW YORK

NORTH CAROLINA

NORTH DAKOTA

OHIO

OKLAHOMA

OREGON

PENNSYLVANIA

RHODE ISLAND

SOUTH CAROLINA

SOUTH DAKOTA

TENNESSEE

TEXAS

UTAH

VERMONT

VIRGINIA

WASHINGTON

WEST VIRGINIA

WISCONSIN

WYOMING

FLAGS OF THE U.S. GOVERNMENT

PRESIDENT

VICE-PRESIDENT

SECRETARY OF STATE

DEPT. OF THE TREASURY

SECRETARY OF DEFENSE

ATTORNEY GENERAL

DEPT. OF THE INTERIOR

DEPT. OF AGRICULTURE

SECRETARY OF COMMERCE

DEPT. OF LABOR

DEPT. OF TRANSPORTATION

DEPT. OF HEALTH AND
HUMAN SERVICES

DEPT. OF HOUSING AND
URBAN DEVELOPMENT

DEPT. OF ENERGY

DEPT. OF EDUCATION

U.S. ARMY

U.S. MARINE CORPS

U.S. NAVY

U.S. AIR FORCE

U.S. COAST GUARD

JACK OF U.S. WARSHIPS

Somalia represent a claim to the five territories in which the Somalis live. The red of revolution and communism serves as the background for the national flag of China, and its five gold stars reflect not only the old Chinese imperial color but the importance the Chinese have traditionally assigned to the symbolism of five. When Adolf Hitler came to power in Germany in the 1930s, he replaced the black-red-gold of German liberal democracy with the black-white-red "blood and iron" flag of the 19th-century German Empire. Later he substituted the swastika banner of his own Nazi party.

Flags of the United States

In the United States, cities, counties, states, military units, businesses, churches, scout organizations, labor groups, political parties, private yachtsmen, and many others have distinctive flags.

Surprisingly, the origins of the national flag, the Stars and Stripes, are somewhat obscure. The flag was officially adopted on June 14, 1777, when the Continental Congress resolved that "the Flag of the united states be 13 stripes alternate red and white, that the Union be 13 stars white in a blue field representing a new constellation." Its immediate predecessor, the Continental Colors, had consisted of 13 horizontal red and white stripes for the 13 colonies represented in the Continental Congress, with the British Union Jack as a canton to indicate that the rebels were demanding the historic rights of British citizens. Stars were uncommon in flags in that era, and how and why stars were chosen to replace the Union Jack is not known.

The colors red, white, and blue were clearly derived from British sources; many English flags had red and white stripes. Americans at the time of the national centennial in 1876 warmed to the popular though doubtful story about the young seamstress Betsy Ross, who supposedly sewed the first flag for George Washington. Although according to historical records she did indeed make flags, no evidence indicates that she was involved in making or designing the first Stars and Stripes.

After Vermont and Kentucky joined the Union, 2 stars and 2 stripes were added (1795) to the flag. Such a 15-star, 15-stripe flag inspired Francis Scott KEY to write "The Star-Spangled Banner." The design of the flag was changed again in 1818, when the decision was made to keep the 13 stripes permanently and add stars to indicate the current number of states in the Union.

Altogether the Stars and Stripes has been through 27 versions, the most recent introduced on July 4, 1960, when Hawaii was admitted to statehood. Until 1912 no official pattern existed for the arrangement of the stars. Flags of the 19th century varied greatly in their star patterns, in the number of points on the stars, in the shades of red and blue, in the width-to-length ratio of the flag, and in other details. Design and color were first standardized in the 20th century.

Etiquette of the Flag

Traditionally flags have been respected, and rules have governed their display. During the 20th century, however, flag etiquette has received particular attention. In the United States the anniversary of the flag's adoption (June 14) has been celebrated as Flag Day since 1916; it is a legal holiday in Pennsylvania.

In 1942 the U.S. Congress adopted a Flag Code, subsequently amended, setting forth uniform procedures for displaying the flag. The two most important guides are tradition and common sense. For example, the U.S. flag had traditionally been flown only during daytime, but since the activities of the nation go on 24 hours a day, in recent years it has become common to fly the flag at night. Courtesy and common sense suggest that a flag should be spotlighted at night. Likewise, because of improved manufacturing techniques, flags can now withstand moisture and need not be lowered in harsh weather.

In the United States when the U.S. flag is hoisted with other flags, it should take precedence; the way in which this status is achieved depends on the circumstances. For example, international custom dictates that the flag of one nation should not be displayed above that of another nation; nor should the flag of one nation be larger than that of another when they are raised together. When the flag of the United States is displayed with other national flags within the United States, therefore, its precedence is established by its being placed at the head of the line of flags or to its own extreme right. The Flag Code includes rules for displaying the flag at half staff to mourn the dead and for displaying the flag on special holidays, in parades, with the flag of the United Nations, and in other circumstances. The following is the official salute to the flag in its current form: "I pledge allegiance to the flag of the United States of America and to the Republic for which it stands, one Nation under God, indivisible, with liberty and justice for all."

A number of legal battles have been waged over the so-called desecration of the flag. For example, members of the Jehovah's Witness religious sect refuse on principle to salute the flag, and they have been prosecuted for it. Political protesters, like those opposed to the Vietnam War in the 1960s, have tried to dramatize their cause by burning the flag or otherwise defacing it. The courts have usually held that the flag is meant to symbolize freedom and therefore may be treated by citizens as they see fit, regardless of the outrage this may produce in others.

Their potential for expressing deep-felt emotions in a condensed but obvious form has made flags an important medium of political communication in the 20th century.

----

flagella [fluh-jel'-uh]   Motile, threadlike organelles that project from the surface of a cell are called flagella. They are usually at least as long as the cell body. Flagella function either in moving the cell or in moving fluids or small particles across the cell surface. They are commonly found on unicellular and small multicellular organisms and on the male reproductive cells of most animals and many plants. The number of flagella per flagellated cell varies in different species from one to many, but usually there are only a few. Flagella have two fundamentally different structures. Those of bacteria are simple polymers of one kind of protein (flagellin) attached at the cell surface to a much more complex basal structure. Those of Protozoa and all higher organisms are membrane-bounded bundles of fibers arranged in the same standard pattern as in cilia, which are shorter and more numerous than flagella.

flagellants [flaj'-uh-lents] During the Middle Ages the flagellants were groups of Christians who subjected themselves to ritualized whipping as atonement for sin. Individual flagellation had become a common form of ecclesiastical punishment as early as the 4th century, and monastic communities allowed voluntary group flagellation as a form of penance later in the medieval period. Organized bands of flagellants made their first known appearance in Europe in the mid-13th century. The major factors stimulating this phenomenon seem to have been famine and war, which were interpreted in the prophecies of Joachim of Fiore (c.1132–1202) as a sign of divine displeasure at the sinfulness of the world. The movement died down but revived spontaneously during the plague years of the Black Death (1348–50). Although condemned by Pope Clement IV in 1349 and by the Council of Constance (1414–17), manifestations of flagellant activity continued through the 15th century. Similar practices were found in antiquity among the Spartans and Romans; in Islam they are still found among SHIITES. Flagellation is also still a part of some North American Indian initiation rites.

Flaget, Benedict Joseph [flah-zhay'] Called the "bishop of the wilderness," Benedict Joseph Flaget, b. Nov. 7, 1763, d. Feb. 11, 1850, was a French-born Roman Catholic priest who fled the French Revolution and came to the United States in 1792. Appointed bishop of Bardstown, Ky., in 1810, he traveled hundreds of kilometers on horseback each month, supervising the frontier churches under his care and doing mission work among the Indians.

Flagstad, Kirsten [flahg'-staht, kirsh'-tuhn] Kirsten Flagstad, b. July 12, 1895, d. Dec. 7, 1962, a Norwegian singer, had one of the most beautiful voices of this century, a rich, dark soprano used with unfailing accuracy and musicianship. She studied in Oslo and made her debut there in 1913 in Eugen d'Albert's *Tiefland*. After having specialized in operetta, Flagstad made a successful Bayreuth debut (1934), but it was her sensational appearance (1935) in New York as Sieglinde that established her as one of the greatest Wagnerian sopranos. During World War II she chose to remain with her family in Norway and was later unjustly accused of collaborating with the Nazis. Retiring from the operatic stage in 1955, she continued to sing in Norway and to make recordings and was named director (1958–60) of the Norwegian Opera. Flagstad was also a gifted inter-

preter of solo songs.

Flagstaff Flagstaff, a city in north central Arizona, is the seat of Coconino County. It is located about 200 km (125 mi) northeast of Phoenix and has a population of 45,857 (1990). Flagstaff is a cultural and educational center: Lowell Observatory (from which the planet Pluto was first observed), Northern Arizona University (1899), and a National Aeronautics and Space Administration (NASA) laboratory and library are all located in or near the city. The economy is based on lumbering, cattle ranching, and tourism. Sunset Crater, Wupatki, and Walnut Canyon national monuments, Coconino National Forest, and the Navajo and Hopi Indian reservations are nearby. The city was settled in 1876.

Flaherty, Robert Joseph [flay'-urt-ee] Robert Joseph Flaherty, b. Iron Mountain, Mich., Feb. 16, 1884, d. July 23, 1951, was a filmmaker whose originality and poetic vision helped create a romantic tradition in documentary films. Before making *Nanook of the North* (1922), a depiction of Eskimo life and his first and most famous film, Flaherty explored Canada as a mapmaker. His interest in native cultures and the simple agrarian life is reflected in later films—*Moana* (1926), *Tabu* (1931), *Man of Aran* (1934), and *Louisiana Story* (1948).

Flamboyant Gothic style see GOTHIC ART AND ARCHITECTURE

flame A flame is the region in a gaseous medium where combustion takes place, accompanied by the evolution of heat and, usually, light. (Hydrogen, for example, burns with a nearly invisible flame.) Flames were initially used for heat and illumination but now are used chiefly for heat. The efficient recovery of heat requires its extraction from the hot gases by direct conduction, since very little is transferred by radiation (see HEAT AND HEAT TRANSFER). Fireplaces generally give warmth by radiation, which means that most of the heat from the flames is lost up the chimney; the heating efficiency of a fireplace is greatly improved by circulating air through the fireplace by means of ducts.

A distinction can be made between two types of flames: premixed and diffusion. In a premixed flame, a gaseous fuel is mixed with air or oxygen and fed to a flameholder such as a Bunsen burner or cooking stove. The efficiency of this method typically produces a clean, smokeless flame. Solid and liquid fuels burn in a diffusion flame. Wax, for example, the fuel for a candle, melts and is drawn up by the wick, where it vaporizes. The wax vapor emerges from the wick while air diffuses from the outside; a hollow flame results in the region where they meet. The yellow color is due to the presence of hot, incandescent carbon particles, which subsequently cool and become smoke.

See also: COMBUSTION; FIRE.

flamenco [fluh-meng′-koh]   Flamenco is a predominantly improvised expressive dance that is derived from old gypsy dances in southern Spain; some ethnologists believe it to be of Indian origin. The term *flamenco* actually represents three unified elements: dance, song, and music. Accompanying voice, guitar, and drums (never castanets) define the dance's rhythm (*compas*) and its emotional motivation (*duende*). Once these are established, the dancer develops the coordinating sinuous arm and hand gestures with intricate heelwork. Theatricalized flamenco routines bear no relation to the pure folk art, which is a spontaneous and personal exploration of emotion, whether sorrowful or gay and frivolous.

flamingo [fluh-ming′-goh]   Flamingos are large wading birds with very long legs and neck, an abruptly turned-down bill, and an unfeathered face. They are found in Africa, Asia, Europe, South America, and the Caribbean area. Wild flamingos are sometimes seen in Florida, but they do not naturally nest in the United States. Flamingos are white, pinkish white, or vermilion, with black flight feathers (remiges); they stand from 90 cm to 1.5 m (3 to 5 ft) tall. Flamingos feed on minute animal and vegetable matter, such as algae and diatoms, or on small mollusks or crustaceans. When feeding, the flamingo places its head and bill upside down below the surface of the water. Using its thick, fleshy tongue, the bird forces muddy water through the serrated edges of its bill, thus straining the water and trapping the edible material in it.

Flamingos, highly gregarious throughout the year, nest in colonies; in some species, such as the lesser flamingo,

The greater flamingo, a wading bird that lives in large colonies, strains mud bottoms of rivers and lakes for algae and small aquatic animals with its crooked beak. The flamingo constructs a cylindrical mud nest (left) for its egg, which both parents care for.

Phoeniconaias minor, these colonies may number as many as 2 million birds. The nest is a cone of mud up to about 45 cm (1.5 ft) high; one or two whitish eggs are laid in a depression at the top of the cone. Both sexes incubate the eggs. The young hatch after about a month and have a straight bill, which begins to develop a bend within a few weeks.

The 4 to 6 living species and 14 extinct species of flamingos constitute the family Phoenicopteridae, which is usually placed in an order of its own, Phoenicopteriformes.

Flamininus, Titus Quinctius [flam-i-ny′-nuhs, ty′-tuhs kwink′-shuhs]   Titus Quinctius Flamininus, c.229–174 BC, was a Roman statesman and general. Elected consul for 198 BC, he defeated PHILIP V of Macedonia at Cynoscephalae in 197 and the next year proclaimed freedom for Greece. He forced Nabis, king of Sparta, to surrender Argos and was honored as a liberator when in 194 he withdrew Roman troops from Greece. The Aetolian League's alliance with ANTIOCHUS III, however, brought back the Romans in 191. Flamininus attempted to preserve Greek local autonomy, but this policy was abandoned soon after his death.

Flamsteed, John [flam′-steed]   John Flamsteed, b. Aug. 19, 1646, d. Dec. 31, 1719, was the first director of the ROYAL GREENWICH OBSERVATORY in England. He distinguished himself especially through the compilation of star catalogs. An extremely frail and sickly man throughout his life, Flamsteed nevertheless obtained an M.A. from Cambridge after four years of nonresident enrollment. Upon his appointment as first astronomer royal in 1675, he applied himself with single-minded devotion to the task of determining accurate stellar and lunar positions as an aid to navigation. This program of astrometry was identical to that of Tycho Brahe and Johannes Hevelius, but Flamsteed's innovation was to employ a telescopic sight on his 7-ft (2-m) sextant to make the observations. This method resulted in an approximate 15-fold increase in accuracy, to about 10 seconds of arc, over Brahe's work. After a famous controversy in which Isaac Newton and Edmond HALLEY conspired (1712) to publish parts of Flamsteed's work without his permission, the complete *Historia Coelestis Britannica,* containing the positions of some 3,000 stars, appeared posthumously in 1725. It was followed by the *Atlas Coelestis* (1729).

Flanagan, Edward J.   Edward Joseph Flanagan, b. Ireland, July 13, 1886, d. May 15, 1948, was a Roman Catholic priest who worked first with derelict men and then with delinquent and homeless boys in the archdiocese of Omaha, Nebr. Believing that "there is no such thing as a bad boy," he created BOYS TOWN, a community in Douglas County, Nebr., run by the hundreds of boys who live in it. Father Flanagan, as he was known, captured public support for his project and became an authority on juvenile delinquency.

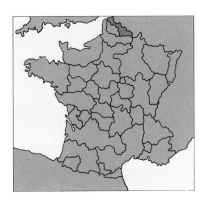

During the Middle Ages, Flanders, which occupied portions of present-day France, Belgium, and the Netherlands, became an important commercial center.

Flanders [flan'-durz]   Flanders, a region on the North Sea, was the heart of economic and political development in the Low Countries during the Middle Ages. At its most extensive, it included the present Belgian provinces of West and East Flanders and parts of modern France and the Netherlands. In the past foreigners often used the name for all of the Low Countries. Now it loosely refers to the Belgian regions in which Flemish, or Dutch, is spoken.

With its favorable location, Flanders became a wealthy trading center with numerous industrial towns, such as BRUGES and GHENT. The principal industry, woolen textiles, was heavily dependent on wool imports from England.

Established as a county in the 9th century, most of Flanders was a fief under the French crown until the early 16th century. For several centuries the counts of Flanders were virtually independent rulers. They played a leading role in the Crusades in the 12th century.

With the outbreak of urban rebellions in the 14th century, the counts and nobles turned for support to the French king, and the burghers, led by the Artevelde family of Ghent, repeatedly allied themselves with England during the HUNDRED YEARS' WAR. During this period of turmoil, democratic governments, the first in northern Europe, were introduced. By the end of the 14th century, however, Flanders had come under Burgundian rule and lost its independence.

Flanders declined under the HABSBURGS, who succeeded to the Burgundian inheritance in 1482. Their harsh rule provoked a revolt in the Low Countries in the mid-16th century (see DUTCH REVOLT). Flanders was soon pacified by the Spanish, but it suffered economically. The region was then the scene of repeated warfare between the Habsburgs and France, which conquered numerous areas in southern Flanders. By the 18th century Flanders was a predominantly agricultural region. In 1815 it became part of the kingdom of the Netherlands, and in 1830 it was incorporated in the new kingdom of Belgium.

flannel   Flannel is a soft, warm fabric with a slightly napped, or brushed, surface. Flannels are napped by brushing wires gently over the fabric surface to raise the fiber ends. The resultant pockets of interlocking fiber trap air, increase the bulk of the fabric, and make it warmer and more absorbent. Flannel, which may be made from wool, cotton, a blend of wool and cotton, or synthetic fibers, is used for clothing, infants' wear, and sheeting.

flash flood   SEE FLOODS AND FLOOD CONTROL

flash point   The flash point of a substance is the lowest temperature at which the vapor of the substance can form an explosive mixture with air. Flash point information is valuable in determining the potential fire hazard of chemicals; the lower the flash point, the more hazardous the chemical. The flash points of some common flammable materials are: butane, −104° C (−156° F); ethyl ether, −45° C (−49° F); and benzene, 10° to 12° C (50° to 54° F).

flashback   SEE NARRATIVE AND DRAMATIC DEVICES

flat-coated retriever   The flat-coated retriever's principal ancestor was the extinct North American breed known as the St. John's dog, from Newfoundland, yet the breed is almost exclusively English in development and popularity. Only a few flat-coats are registered each year with the American Kennel Club.

The breed was developed during the second half of the 19th century and was originally known as the wavy-coated retriever. It is a sturdy, medium-sized dog; it stands about 58 cm (23 in) at the shoulder and weighs 27–32 kg (60–70 lb). The breed is black or liver in color, and has a dense, flat coat of fine texture and quality.

The flat-coated retriever, an excellent hunting and retrieving dog, was bred in England about the middle of the 19th century. Like other retrievers, this medium-size dog has a keen sense of smell and is willing to pursue game into water.

flatbed cylinder press   SEE LETTERPRESS

flatfish   Flatfishes are marine bottom-dwelling fish that lie on their left or right sides rather than on their bellies. Their bottom sides are usually white or, if pigmented, much lighter than the upper sides. Both eyes are located on the upper side of their heads. Species of flatfishes inhabit oceans worldwide and are found in both cold and warm waters but are most abundant in temperate waters. Flatfishes are included in the order Pleuronectiformes. Six families in this order are psettodids (Psettodidae), citharids (Citharidae), left-eyed flounder (Bothidae), right-eyed flounder (Pleuronectidae), SOLES (Soleidae), and tonguefish (Cynoglossidae).

Flounder. In the waters of the western north Atlantic, FLOUNDER predominate in the flatfish fauna. Among the right-eyed flounder are Atlantic HALIBUT, *Hippoglossus hippoglossus*; American PLAICE, or dabs, *Hippoglossoides platessoides*; witch flounder, *Glyptocephalus cynoglossus*; yellowtail flounder, *Limanda ferruginea*; and winter flounder, *Pseudopleuronectes americanus*. The Atlantic halibut, found in the subarctic Atlantic, is reported to reach a length of more than 2.7 m (9 ft) and a weight of more than 320 kg (700 lb). This fish is a voracious feeder, preying mostly on fish but also on many invertebrates. The American plaice may reach a length of almost 1 m (3 ft) and a weight of 6.5 kg (14 lb). It, too, is a cold-water species and is found in shallow waters near shore. Its principal food seems to be invertebrates. The witch, yellowtail, and winter flounder reach a length of 60 cm (2 ft) and feed mainly on invertebrates.

Along the western Atlantic coast, a common species of left-eyed flounder is the summer flounder, *Paralichthys dentatus*. It is reported to grow to a length of almost 1 m (4 ft) and a weight of 12 kg (26 lb). The summer flounder moves inshore along beaches and into bays in summer and migrates to the continental shelf to depths of 45–150 m (150–500 ft) in winter. It is an active, predaceous species.

Sole. Flatfishes belonging to the sole family are less numerous than those belonging to the families of the right-eyed and left-eyed flounder. Because of the epicurean appeal of the European sole, *Solea solea,* and the association of the term *sole* with an excellent-tasting fish, however, many species of flounder have been given the name *sole.* Along the Atlantic coast of the United States, the witch flounder is marketed as gray sole and subspecies of winter flounder as lemon sole. Numerous species of flounder along the Pacific coast of the United States have been marketed as soles. Few species of true soles exist along the western Atlantic coast. A common species, the hogchoker, *Trinectes maculatus,* although recorded from Cape Cod to Virginia, is most abundant from Virginia southward. It reaches a length of about 20 cm (8 in).

Life Cycle. All species of flatfishes are bottom-dwellers. They are prolific spawners. A 90-kg (200-lb) Atlantic halibut has been estimated to produce more than 2,000,000 eggs, and the smaller American plaice has been reported to produce 60,000 eggs. Hatching time

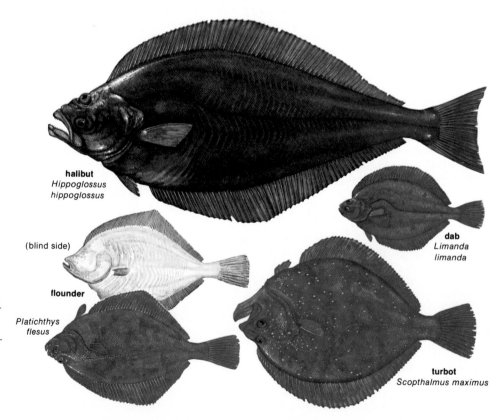

halibut
*Hippoglossus
hippoglossus*

(blind side)

flounder

*Platichthys
flesus*

dab
*Limanda
limanda*

turbot
Scopthalmus maximus

The flatfish is a bottom-dwelling marine fish that has both eyes on one side of its head. Many are photochromatic, or color sensitive; they camouflage themselves by spontaneously changing appearance to match that of their environment.

may vary from several days to weeks, depending on the water temperature. The larval fish floating in the water have a normal appearance, with a single eye on each side of the head. In later larval stages, one eye migrates to the opposite side of the head adjacent to the other eye. At the same time, the fish's coloration deepens. Pigment appears on the eyed side, and as the larva grows it gradually turns over on the noneyed side and settles to the bottom.

The flatfish's blind side frequently shows poorly developed side fins, a distorted mouth, and fewer and less-developed teeth. Flatfishes can change their color and markings to blend with the bottom, enabling them to hide from predators as well as from prey.

Flathead

The Flathead, a North American Indian people of the Salishan linguistic family, inhabited southwest Montana's Bitterroot River valley, at the easternmost extreme of the Plateau culture area, in the early 19th century. The Plains Indians came to call them Flatheads to distinguish them from more westerly Salishan-speaking groups who practiced ritual head deformation.

Like other Interior SALISH tribes, the Flathead fished during spring; in summer they depended on the women for root and berry foods and in late summer, on the men for deer and elk meat. In the fall they migrated eastward to hunt bison through the winter. Their typical Plateau culture was transformed by Plains traits related to horse riding and organized bison hunting. The Flathead originally lived in long A-frame lean-tos but later also used TEPEES. Horse raids and war honors stimulated the ranking of families by wealth and reputation. A semihereditary chief governed with the assistance of a tribal war leader, a council of lesser chiefs, and an informal police. Enemy tribes included the BANNOCK, BLACKFOOT, and SHOSHONI.

The Flathead began to trade their beaver and bison skins for guns, kettles, beads, needles, and cloth in the 1820s and '30s, and in 1841 a mission was established among them. The U.S. government began (1855) to consolidate the Flathead, KUTENAI, and Pend d'Oreille and did nothing to halt white settlement in their territory. After agreeing (1872) to migrate north from their aboriginal homeland, the Flathead again suffered substantial land reductions through allotment and sales beginning in 1904. The Flathead numbered between 600 and 1,000 in the early 19th century. In 1990 the tribal enrollment of the Flathead Reservation (including a group of Kutenai) was 6,652. Tribal government is by an elective council of 10.

Flatt and Scruggs

Guitarist and singer Lester Raymond Flatt, banjoist Earl Eugene Scruggs, and their band, the Foggy Mountain Boys, epitomized bluegrass music during the 1950s and '60s. Flatt, b. Overton County, Tenn., June 28, 1914, d. May 11, 1979, and Scruggs, b. Cleveland County, N.C., Jan. 6, 1924, met in the early 1940s as performers at the GRAND OLE OPRY. In 1948 they formed their own group and won national acclaim through such recordings as "The Ballad of Jed Clampett," theme music for the television show "The Beverly Hillbillies" (1962), and "Foggy Mountain Breakdown," which became the theme music for the film *Bonnie and Clyde* (1968). In 1969 the team broke up. Flatt continued to play unamplified, traditional bluegrass, while Scruggs turned to country rock.

flatworm

Flatworm is the common name for flat-bodied, wormlike animals belonging to the phylum Platyhelminthes and including the free-living flatworms (such as PLANARIA, class Turbellaria) and the parasitic FLUKES, class Trematoda, and TAPEWORMS, class Cestoda. Platyhelminths are considered the most primitive bilaterally symmetrical animals (the two lateral halves are mirror images) and the most primitive group of animals possessing a proper excretory system—tubes running down either side of the body and opening to the exterior through pores that link a series of "flame cells" containing cilia (hairs).

Flatworms possess neither a body cavity (coelom) nor a respiratory or circulatory system. The digestive system (absent in tapeworms) has a single opening serving as both mouth and anus. Turbellarians range in size from 0.5 cm (0.2 in) for the majority to 60 cm (2 ft) in length, are usually marine, and glide on a ciliated lower epidermis or swim by body undulation. They are carnivorous and have the ability to grow new parts (regeneration). Trematodes attach by hooks and suckers to their host; the most significant to humans is the genus *Schistosoma*, responsible for SCHISTOSOMIASIS (bilharziasis), a parasitic disease. Most tapeworms consist of a front segment (scolex) with suckers and hooks for attaching to the host's intestine; the rest of the animal is a series of separate segments, or proglottids, produced by budding from the front end.

Flaubert, Gustave

[floh-bair'] Gustave Flaubert, b. Dec. 12, 1821, d. May 8, 1880, the author of *Madame Bovary* (1857; Eng. trans., 1957), one of the most influential prose works of the 19th century, produced only five novels and a few shorter works in his lifetime; he devoted years to revising and polishing each. A master stylist whose novels have the studied perfection of poetry, Flaubert was, paradoxically, hailed as a realist, although his themes were romantic, and his plots and characters were largely secondary to his preoccupation with style.

Flaubert was raised in the hospital of Rouen, where his father was chief resident surgeon. Slow to develop and often compared unfavorably with his older brother, who distinguished himself in medicine, Gustave soon saw himself as others saw him—the idiot of the family. In 1843, having failed his law examinations at the University of Paris, he devoted himself to writing. A year later, afflicted with epilepsy, he was given an allowance by his father and settled at Croisset, near Rouen. Although he had not yet published anything, Flaubert proceeded to make friends in Parisian literary circles and to work on the preliminary versions of two novels that were not to appear for decades: *A Sentimental Education* and *The Temptation of St. Anthony.*

The 19th-century French author Gustave Flaubert crafted his writings with a strong sense of realism, precise objectivity, and technical perfection.

From 1849 to 1851, Flaubert traveled through the Near East and North Africa, returning to Croisset with notes and memories of exotica that were to be incorporated years later into *Salammbô*;. In 1856, after five years of labor, he completed *Madame Bovary*, but even before it reached the bookstores in Paris, it was impounded. This novel—the story of Emma Bovary's restless search for a life beyond the dull existence she shares with her doctor husband in a drab Norman farming town, her escape through adultery and finally suicide—caused Flaubert to be brought to trial for its supposedly immoral and irreligious ideas.

In 1855, Flaubert returned to *The Temptation of St. Anthony*, begun in the 1840s, and while completing his research on the ancient world, he decided to create an oriental extravaganza around a Carthaginian priestess who breaks her vows for a young warrior. The result, *Salammbô*; (1862; Eng. trans., 1886), is the novelist's most romantic work.

After decades of revising, Flaubert finally published *A Sentimental Education* (1869; Eng. trans., 1964) and *The Temptation of St. Anthony* (1874; Eng. trans., 1910); neither found favor. Flaubert was shattered by the failure of *St. Anthony*, a veritable prose poem that had been his life's work.

His animosity toward the bourgeoisie, which could inspire him to heights of lyricism, led him to begin a bitter comic novel, *Bouvard et Pécuchet* (1881; Eng. trans., 1954), about two aging bachelors who blunderingly rediscover the history of human progress through a series of ill-conceived experiments. He was forced to abandon the novel by the bankruptcy of his niece's husband, whom he saved by divesting himself of most of his property. As a distraction from his financial insecurity, as well as the deaths of his beloved friend George SAND and his former mistress Louise Colet, Flaubert turned to a shorter fictional form. In less than three years he produced as many splendid novellas: "St. Julian the Hospitaller," "Hérodias," and "A Simple Heart." Published as *Three Tales* (1877; Eng. trans., 1967), the book's immediate success did much to bolster his morale but little to ease his finan-

cial plight. He managed to complete *Bouvard et Pécuchet* just before his sudden death from apoplexy.

___

flavors and fragrances   Flavors and fragrances are substances that stimulate the senses of taste and smell. With the exception of the four primary taste sensations— sweet, bitter, salty, and sour—flavor characteristics are the result of our perception of odor; the difference between a flavor and a fragrance is in large part only a semantic distinction. Thus, a substance that provides an odor in PERFUMES may also be used to add flavoring to a food.

Most natural flavorings and fragrances are derived from plant substances—either from the aromatic, volatile vegetable oils known as ESSENTIAL OILS, or from the nonvolatile plant oils called RESINS. The natural aromatic substances are usually costly and limited in supply. Over the past century, success in reproducing some of these substances synthetically has created a new industry that today produces hundreds of flavors and fragrances for use in food, perfumes, and other products.

Some fragrant substances are relatively easy to synthesize. Vanillin, the aromatic ingredient in vanilla, can be readily reproduced by synthesis. Many flavors and fragrances, however, have scores, if not hundreds, of components that contribute to their aroma. Only recently has it become possible to determine their chemical structure. Once the chemical identity of the components is known, it is often possible to make them synthetically.

New products with unknown toxicology must be tested for safety, and, when used in foods, must be accepted as safe by the U.S. Food and Drug Administration. (See FOOD ADDITIVES.)

The availability of synthetic flavors and fragrances makes possible a large variety of products. An example is the chemical compound B–phenylethyl alcohol, a vital ingredient in any rose fragrance; it may be extracted from natural rose oil at a cost of thousands of dollars per kilogram, or an identical, synthetic substance can be made at one percent of this cost.

___

flax [flaks]   Flax, a genus, *Linum,* of annual and perennial plants, is grown primarily for its fiber, used in making LINEN, or for its seeds, the source of LINSEED OIL. Many types of ornamental flax are cultivated in gardens. Several varieties of one species, *L. usitatissimum,* produce flax fiber and seed.

Native to temperate and subtropical regions, flax is one of the oldest cultivated plants. Linen fabrics and bundles of flax fiber have been found among the remains of the Neolithic Swiss Lake Dwellers. Flax was cultivated by the ancient civilizations of the Middle East, by the Romans, and in medieval Europe. In the 19th century, cotton textiles largely supplanted linen; the 20th-century development of synthetic fibers reduced the need for flax still further.

Fiber flax grows best in a cool, moist climate; seed flax prefers a dry environment. Fiber varieties are planted close together to encourage taller stalks and minimal

Flax has been cultivated since prehistoric times for its stalk fiber (bottom right), *used to make linen, and for its seed* (top right), *which yields linseed oil.*

branching. For seed production, in which the fiber is not extracted, shorter, branching varieties of flax are used.

When the plant turns brown, flaxseed is harvested by machine. Fiber flax is harvested either by hand or by machine, the seeds are removed, and the stalks are bundled and soaked, or retted, to loosen the fibers. Retting may last up to six weeks, after which the stalks are dried, beaten, and scraped, or scutched, to remove the fibers. Finally, the long fibers are separated by combing, or hackling, and are spun. Flax produces a strong thread used for sewing, netting, twine, and toweling, as well as for weaving into linen.

Flaxman, John [flaks'-muhn]

John Flaxman, b. July 6, 1755, d. Dec. 7, 1826, was the most influential exponent of NEOCLASSICISM in British sculpture during the late 18th and early 19th centuries. The son of a maker of plaster casts, he was a child prodigy, first exhibiting at the Free Society of Artists in 1767. In 1775, Flaxman was employed as a modeler for Josiah WEDGWOOD'S pottery works, designing reliefs and medallions on classical themes. In addition to his work for Wedgwood, he began (1782) to undertake the first of his many funerary monuments. In 1787 he went to Rome, the center of neoclassical ideas; he undertook important sculpture commissions, including a reconstruction (1792) of the Belvedere Torso as *Hercules and Hebe* (destroyed). He also illustrated many classical texts in a refined linear drawing style, which were engraved and which won him international admiration.

Flaxman returned to London in 1794 and soon exerted an influence on British art similar to that which his con-

temporary, Jacques Louis David, exerted in France. His funeral monuments of this period adorn the crypts of many English cathedrals, including Saint Paul's Cathedral and Westminster Abbey. Among his most successful later works are *Satan Overcome by St. Michael* (1822; Petworth Collection, London) and his illustrations of *Hesiod* (1817), which combine his earlier classicism with a religious mysticism that indicates a sympathy for the emerging romantic spirit.

flea

The flea is any wingless, bloodsucking insect of the order Siphonaptera that parasitizes warm-blooded animals. Most are 0.1–0.4 cm (0.04–0.16 in) long and have enlarged, muscular hindlegs adapted for leaping.

The Oriental rat flea is the primary vector, or transmitter, of bubonic plague from rodents to humans. Plague was a major scourge of civilization in past centuries and today is still widespread among wild rodents of the western United States. Rodent fleas may also transmit murine typhus from rodents to humans.

Fleas exhibit complete metamorphosis, with a larval form that feeds on organic debris. In the wild, flea larvae subsist on the hair, skin, droppings, and food scraps that accumulate in nests and lairs of animals. They also live in the bedding of livestock and pets, as well as in dirty rugs. The larval stage lasts 15 to 200 days, and the adults may live almost a year.

A few species of fleas are inactive parasites and remain attached to their hosts for long periods. Among these are the chigoes, which infest feet and toes of persons who walk barefoot in tropical and subtropical regions. The site of attachment may swell painfully and become infected. Sticktights are inactive fleas that are serious pests of poultry. Chickens and turkeys may have hundreds of sticktights attached to their heads, causing irritation, loss of weight, and blindness.

An adult female Oriental rat flea (A) *feeds on the host's blood before laying eggs* (B) *in the dirt or in the host's nest. The eggs hatch into larvae* (C) *that feed on organic debris and eventually molt into pupae* (D), *emerge as adults, and seek new hosts.*

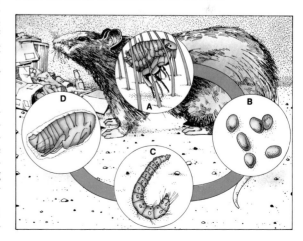

Sir Alexander Fleming, a British bacteriologist, discovered the antibiotic penicillin in 1928 while examining a bacteria culture contaminated with mold.

Fleming, Sir Alexander   The British bacteriologist Sir Alexander Fleming, b. Aug. 6, 1881, d. Mar. 11, 1955, discovered penicillin during his years of research on antibiotics. Born in Lochfield, Scotland, he received (1906) his medical degree from St. Mary's Hospital in London. During World War I he began searching for antibacterial substances and in 1921 discovered lysozyme, an antibiotic enzyme that attacks many types of bacteria. In 1928, Fleming found that a *Penicillium* mold had accidentally contaminated a staphylococcus culture and stopped the bacteria's growth. The mold's antibacterial substance, which he named PENICILLIN, was nontoxic and effective against many bacteria harmful to humans. Fleming shared the 1945 Nobel Prize for physiology or medicine with British scientists Ernst Boris Chain and Sir Howard Walter Florey, who were able to purify and obtain enough penicillin for human trials.

Fleming, Sir Ambrose   An electrical engineer who invented the thermionic valve (the first ELECTRON TUBE), Sir John Ambrose Fleming, b. Nov. 29, 1849, d. Apr. 18, 1945, also contributed to the science of photometry (see PHOTOMETER), the measurement of the intensity of light. His work with the thermionic valve in 1904 and 1905 was important to the development of RADIO. From 1885 to 1926, Fleming taught at the University of London. He was knighted in 1929.

Fleming, Ian   Ian Fleming, b. May 28, 1908, d. Aug. 12, 1964, at one time a journalist, stockbroker, and British naval intelligence officer, is best known as the creator of James Bond, fiction's most famous spy. The winning formula in each of 13 Bond novels mixed old-fashioned intrigue and jet-age exoticism with the idiosyncrasies of Agent 007 in his continuing battle against bizarre international conspiracies. *From Russia, with Love* (1957; film, 1963) gained authenticity from Fleming's experience in Moscow as a secret agent. Other Bond novels that enjoyed immense popularity when transferred to

the screen include *Dr. No* (1958; film 1963), *Goldfinger* (1959; film 1964), *You Only Live Twice* (1964; film 1967), *The Spy Who Loved Me* (1962, film 1977), and *Moonraker* (1955; film 1979).

Fleming, Peggy   Peggy Gale Fleming, b. San Jose, Calif., July 27, 1948, is an American figure skater who dominated the sport in the 1960s with her dazzling ballet-like moves on ice. A skater from the age of nine, she rose rapidly among the ranks of Americans after a plane crash eliminated the U.S. national team in 1961. She was sixth in the 1964 Olympics, won national championships five straight years, reigned as world champion for three years (1966–68), and culminated her competitive career with the 1968 Olympic singles title at Grenoble, France. She is one of the most famous in a long line of American skaters. She turned professional in 1968.

Flemish art and architecture   Flemish art and architecture refers to works produced in an area that roughly corresponds to present-day BELGIUM. The correct name of this area is Southern Netherlands, but it is commonly known as Flanders, for the largest of its provinces.

With few exceptions, Flemish artists achieved their most significant successes in painting rather than in sculpture or in architecture. The most creative and influential Flemish artistic activity occurred during the 15th century and the first decades of the 17th century. During the 15th century, Flanders, then ruled by the dukes of Burgundy, was politically and artistically affiliated with France. Artists worked for prosperous local patrons, especially in Ghent, Bruges, and Brussels, and for the Burgundian court. After the marriage (1477) of Mary of Burgundy to Maximilian of Austria, Flanders was part of the Habsburg empire (see HABSBURG dynasty) through the end of the 17th century.

Painting

From the 11th through the 14th century manuscript illumination (see ILLUMINATED MANUSCRIPTS) was the most common form of painting. The finest examples, such as the work of Jean Bondol (fl. 1368–c.1381), date from the second half of the 14th century. Like other Flemish painters who worked in France, Bondol combined the elegant stylization of French manuscripts with a less idealized depiction of landscape and secondary figures. The supreme achievement of this form was the *Trés Riches Heures de Jean duc de Berry*, painted by the LIMBOURG BROTHERS prior to 1416. This manuscript represents the highest development of the International Style in art and anticipates, in its detailed depictions of everyday life, the Flemish interest in GENRE PAINTING.

In the 15th century manuscript illumination was supplanted in importance by painting on wooden panels. The characteristics of these panel paintings can be summarized by contrasting the principal Flemish innovation of the 1420s—the medium of oil paint—with the contemporary Italian development of linear PERSPECTIVE. Flemish artists applied oil paint in superimposed translucent layers, attaining the unprecedentedly rich, glowing colors that are a hallmark of their painting. Jan van EYCK, in such works as the *Madonna with Chancellor Rolin* (c.1434; Louvre, Paris), was the first to realize the full potential of the new medium.

The symbolic mentality of the Middle Ages was accompanied by a keen interest in the secular, material world, and Flemish late-Gothic paintings, despite their religious subjects, often contained many carefully assembled mundane details. Even the most commonplace objects were treated as vehicles for religious symbolism. For example, in the *Mérode Altarpiece* (c.1425–27; The Cloisters, New York City), by the Master of Flémalle (see CAMPIN, ROBERT), the towel is both a functional household object and a symbol of the Virgin's purity.

Jan van Eyck was the first Flemish painter to sign his works. His paintings, dispassionate and calm, are exceptional in their handling of light and detail. Rogier van der WEYDEN was much more concerned with the rendering of human emotions. Hans MEMLING excelled in portraiture, depicting his contemporaries with unaffected simplicity and startling directness of observation. The melancholy, spiritual intensity of Hugo van der GOES anticipated the work of expressionists such as Vincent van Gogh.

With the advent of the 16th century and the spread of humanism in Flanders, Flemings began to emulate Italian Renaissance art. Jan GOSSAERT, known as Mabuse, introduced the Italian manner of depicting nude figures and

The 15th-century Flemish master Hans Memling painted most of his works for the Hospital of Saint John in Bruges. The Saint Ursula reliquary (1489) is in the form of a chapel with six painted panels narrating the martyrdom of Saint Ursula and her followers. This end panel typifies the balance and piety pervading Memling's devotional works.

The Flemish artists of the 15th century were innovators in their use of oil paints to achieve rich colors and shadings. Jan van Eyck's Madonna with Chancellor Rolin *(c.1434) exemplifies this technique. (Louvre, Paris.)*

was the first to bring the true mythological subjects to the Netherlands. Although Quentin MASSYS, the founder of the Antwerp school of painting, remained closely tied to northern tradition, he assimilated Leonardo da Vinci's technique of subtle shading of light and darker tones, as well as some of his compositional ideas. Under Italian influence late-Gothic Flemish art began to imitate the style of MANNERISM; the traditional Flemish fascination with the particular gave way to generalization and large-scale patterning.

While these developments were taking place, Flemings continued to be renowned for their talent as portraitists. Moreover, by the mid-16th century landscapes and scenes of everyday life had evolved into independent subjects, and still-life painting was moving in the same direction. Peter Bruegel the Elder (see BRUEGEL family) was the greatest painter to concentrate on traditionally northern subject matter. He too absorbed Italian influence, although on the level of pictorial organization rather than that of specific motifs. Unlike the Italians, Bruegel did not idealize human beings but depicted them in minutely detailed realistic settings.

The Northern and Southern Netherlands, politically separate from 1609, became artistically distinct. In both countries the 17th century marked a turning away from the abstraction and artificiality of Mannerism, and baroque art had a very different character in Flanders than in Holland (see DUTCH ART AND ARCHITECTURE). Catholicism was reinstated in Flanders, and church patronage of art continued. With all subjects, Flemish painters used rich colors and decorative compositions and frequently represented dramatic action.

Whereas in the Northern Netherlands several distinct local styles flourished, Flemish painting was dominated by a single genius, Peter Paul Rubens. Rubens was the first to synthesize Flemish and Italian traditions. He united the Flemish interest in finely detailed landscape, rich color, and intricate texture with the Italian tendency to generalize and compose in large-scale patterns, producing monumental scenes of great vitality.

Among those influenced by Rubens were Anthony Van Dyck, one of the most perceptive portraitists in the history of art, and Jacob Jordaens, who delighted in representing the bustle of the mundane world. The artistic authority of Rubens is also evident in the work of landscape and still-life painters, but his influence on those painters who worked on a small scale was less pervasive. Adriaen Brouwer combined a Flemish sense of lively movement with a Dutch emphasis on tonal values. Jan Bruegel the Elder maintained a delicate, miniaturist approach, which was quite distinct from the manner of Rubens.

With the death of Rubens the golden age of Flemish painting came to an end. During the 18th and 19th centuries most Flemish artists followed the trends in French art. Jacques Louis David was exiled to Brussels in 1815, and his form of Neoclassicism had a great impact upon Flemish painting. James Ensor was exceptional in his originality; his highly personal style, with its eerie colors and macabre, fantastic distortions, influenced the expressionist painters of the 20th century (see Expressionism).

The most renowned Belgian painters of the 20th century are the surrealists René Magritte and Paul Delvaux (see Surrealism, art).

Sculpture

During the Carolingian period (see Carolingian art and architecture), the valley of the Meuse River became a center for ivory carving and metalwork. Rénier de Huy and Nicholas of Verdun, the two greatest Flemish Romanesque sculptors (see Romanesque art and architecture), were both Mosan goldsmiths. Rénier de Huy's masterpiece is the cast-brass baptismal font (c.1107–18) for the Church of Saint Barthélémy at Liège. Nicholas of Verdun's highly influential works, such as the engraved and enameled altar frontal (finished 1181) for Kolsterneuburg, near Vienna, introduced a greater naturalism in the representation of human emotions and used the lines of drapery to suggest the motion of human forms.

During the Gothic period, the most accomplished sculptor at the Burgundian court was Claus Sluter, a Dutchman who spent part of his career in Brussels. Sluter's powerfully individualized figures mark a crucial step in the emanicipation of sculpture from its subordination to architecture.

During the 16th century, Italian works became very influential in the Flemish sculptural centers of Antwerp and Mechelen. The most talented Flemish-born sculptor of the period, Giovanni da Bologna, spent his highly successful career in Italy. The same was true of François Duquesnoy, the preeminent Flemish sculptor of the 17th century. Those sculptors who remained in Flanders and who worked, often anonymously, for local churches produced unusual and distinctive works. In the second half of the 17th century and throughout the 18th century, developments in the traditional art of decorating wooden

(Left) *Pieter Bruegel the Elder, considered the greatest Flemish painter of the 16th century, was known for his genre paintings of everyday life.* The Peasant Wedding *(1568) captures the action and movement of his subjects and is rich in symbolic detail. (Museum of Art History, Vienna.)* (Right) *Peter Paul Rubens fused the styles of the Italian and Flemish traditions to produce such masterpieces as* The Three Graces *(c.1639). (Prado, Madrid.)*

(Above) *The 17th-century sculptor Rombout Verhulst fashioned this terra-cotta bust of Maria van Reygersberg. (Rijksmuseum, Amsterdam.)* (Left) *The Town Hall of Antwerp (1561–66) was designed by the Flemish architect Cornelis Floris. Based on Mannerist design, the building is heavily ornamented with statuary.*

church furniture culminated in the treatment of confessionals and pulpits as settings for large, complicated figural ensembles, for example, the pulpit (1699) at Brussels Cathedral by Hendrik Verbruggen.

French-derived neoclassicism was the dominant style of the first half of the 19th century; the most noteworthy sculptor of the later period was Constantin MEUNIER, a realist who was influenced by the style of Auguste Rodin, as can be seen in his *Monument to Labor* (c.1893–1905; Brussels Museum). In the 20th century, sculpture remains a less important art than painting, as has always been the case in the Flemish tradition.

Architecture

Artistic and cultural activity during the Romanesque period centered on monasteries and the powerful bishoprics of Tournai and Liège. Saint Barthélémy at Liège (11th–12th century) is one of the few surviving pieces of architecture from this period. Because of local prosperity, Romanesque buildings were replaced throughout the 13th, 14th, and 15th centuries by new, Gothic structures. As Saints Michael and Gudule at Brussels (begun c.1226) illustrates, Flemish architects did not emphasize verticality to the same degree as did the French. The most innovative developments occurred with secular architecture, such as market halls, whose existence and size reflected the continuing increase in cloth manufacture and trade. Examples include the Cloth Hall at Ypres (c.1304–80) and the Town Hall at Bruges (begun 1376). Prominent belfries were a characteristic feature of these buildings.

Not until the 16th century did Flemish architects turn away from the Gothic style and begin to imitate Italian Renaissance and Mannerist buildings. The Town Hall in Antwerp (1561–66), designed by Cornelis Floris and others, combines local and imported forms. The tightly crowded and linear design indicates its Mannerist character. In contrast, the Jesuit Church of Saint Charles Borromeo at Antwerp (begun 1615), designed by Pieter Huyssens and others, displays the full, flowing forms and the richer play of light and shade that are characteristic of baroque architecture. The finest example of the Flemish baroque is the exuberant, triple-arched portico that Rubens designed for his own house in Antwerp.

Flemish architecture in the 18th, 19th and 20th centuries generally followed European trends. The work of Victor HORTA is an important exception: the buildings in Brussels that he designed during the 1890s are early examples of ART NOUVEAU. Henri Van de Velde was important for his early espousal of principles that later informed much 20th-century architecture. He stressed the necessity of discarding excessive architectural ornament, advocated functionalism, and recognized the beauty of mechanical forms.

Flemish language   see GERMANIC LANGUAGES

Flemish literature   see DUTCH AND FLEMISH LITERATURE

Fletcher, John   see BEAUMONT, FRANCIS, AND FLETCHER, JOHN

Fleury, André Hercule de [flur-ee', ahn-dray' air-kuel' duh]   André Hercule de Fleury, b. June 22, 1653, d. Jan. 29, 1743, was a French churchman who rose to royal favor as tutor of the young LOUIS XV and served as his chief advisor from 1726 to 1743. The son of a tax collector, Fleury became LOUIS XIV's almoner in 1683. After serving (1698–1715) as bishop at Fréjus, he returned to court as the dauphin's preceptor just before he ascended the throne as Louis XV (1715). Fleury became a member of the royal council in 1723 and its presiding minister and a cardinal in 1726.

Currency stabilization, government support of trade, extensive road building, and efficient local administration by intendants contributed to a long cycle of prosperity after 1730. At the same time, however, forced road labor (*corvée*), indirect-tax farming, mercantilist controls over industry, and forced royal compromises with the PARLEMENTS over JANSENISM were mixed blessings. After negotiating France's acquisition of Lorraine through involvement in the War of the POLISH SUCCESSION (1733–38), Fleury was forced into the costly War of the AUSTRIAN SUCCESSION (1742–48).

Flexner, Abraham [fleks'-nur]   Abraham Flexner, b. Louisville, Ky., Nov. 13, 1866, d. Sept. 21, 1959, was an influential critic and reformer of American educational methods. An admirer of the German system of higher education, Flexner in his first book, *The American College* (1908), criticized the American system of electives, lectures, and assistantships. In a later study, *Universities: American, English, German* (1930), he advocated the German-university ideal of scholarship rather than teaching, an ideal realized in the INSTITUTE FOR ADVANCED STUDY in Princeton, N.J., which Flexner was instrumental in founding and of which he was director (1930–39).

Flexner's most influential work was his *Medical Education in the United States and Canada* (1910), in which he rated 155 medical schools. His findings led to the closing of almost half the schools and to a major transformation of medical education in North America. While at the Rockefeller Foundation (1913–28), Flexner administered a large medical-education fund that provided endowments for teaching and research and created faculty positions for doctors at university-connected teaching hospitals.

His unorthodox ideas on secondary education, first put into practice at the school he opened (1891) in Louisville, Ky., were published in *A Modern School* (1916) and bore fruit with the Rockefeller Foundation's establishment of the Lincoln Experimental School (of Teachers College, Columbia University).

---

flicker   Flickers are any of six species of woodpeckers belonging to the genus *Colaptes* in the woodpecker family, Picidae. The common flicker, *C. auratus,* found in North America from Alaska to Mexico and in the West Indies, reaches slightly over 30 cm (12 in) in overall length. It has a brown back marked with dark spots and bars, white undersides spotted with black, and a black crescent on the breast. Males and young females have cheek stripes behind the bill. Variants of the common flicker include an eastern form, known as the yellow-shafted flicker or yellowhammer, and a western form, called the red-shafted flicker. The five other species of flickers inhabit Cuba and South America. Unlike other woodpeckers, flickers often feed on the ground, seeking insects, especially ants.

---

flight   Flight is the ability to move with direction through the air, an ability shared by many animals. Humans can fly only in the machines they have devised.

BATS, most BIRDS, and many INSECTS practice true natural flight: that is, the motions of their wings produce the air lift necessary to take off, fly, and land. A number of other kinds of animals can glide for brief distances through the air. They do so by means of stretchable body membranes, as with various small mammals and some lizards and snakes, or by means of enlarged fins, such as the FLYING FISH. A few species of fish actually flap their fins in the air like birds (see HATCHETFISH).

Many birds have the ability to soar: they can remain airborne by floating without wing movement, supported by a rising column of air. For such birds as the EAGLE and CONDOR, the little energy they expend in soaring may compensate for the very large amounts of energy needed for these birds to launch themselves into the air from a standing position.

The travel range of flying animals can be enormous. The monarch butterfly (see BUTTERFLIES AND MOTHS) can fly 1,000 km (620 mi) without stopping to feed. Bird flights of 650 km (400 mi) in 24 hours have often been recorded.

The machines that carry humans into the air are of two varieties. Lighter-than-air vehicles contain a gas that is more buoyant than air: hydrogen or helium in AIRSHIPS; heated air inside BALLOONS. Heavier-than-air flight is provided by HELICOPTERS, GLIDERS, and AIRCRAFT. The lifting force in an aircraft is generated by the wings; the propulsive force, an engine-driven PROPELLER or a JET PROPULSION engine, moves the vehicle through the air fast enough for the wings to produce sufficient lift. A rocket (see ROCKETS AND MISSILES) is a specialized flight vehicle that can also move beyond the atmosphere by the force of engine thrust alone.

See also: AERODYNAMICS; ASTRONAUTICS; BIOLOGICAL LOCOMOTION.

---

flight, human-powered   The concept of human-powered flight dates to ancient times. The societies of the ancient Near East were rife with legends of flying humans. The most enduring of these classic mythological tales is that of DAEDALUS and Icarus. The monk Eilmer of Malmesbury (AD *c.*1000) succeeded in making a short gliding flight from Malmesbury Abbey in Wiltshire. Many of these individuals envisioned complicated ornithopters (flying machines with flapping wings) of the same general type conceived by Leonardo da Vinci. Once Giovanni Borelli's work *De motu animalium* (On the Movement of Animals, 1685) demonstrated that the muscular structure of a human was inadequate for ornithopter flight, the primary effort in aeronautics was directed toward extending aerodynamic knowledge, deriving lightweight structures, and developing suitable engines.

A £50,000 prize that was established in 1959 by British industrialist Henry Kremer attracted many well-conceived projects designed for 1- and 2-person crews to pedal an aircraft over a specified 1-mi (1.6-km), figure-8

The Daedalus *resembles an exotic dragonfly. The sparest of aerodynamic designs, it consists of a 34-m (112-ft) wing, cabin pod, pedal-powered propeller, and tail assemblage—all mounted on an 8.8-m (29-ft) hollow rod.*

course. The prize was finally won on Aug. 23, 1977, by the *Gossamer Condor*, an ultralightweight vehicle, constructed of cardboard, piano wire, aluminum tubing, and Mylar clear plastic, with a 29-m (96-ft) wingspan. Bryan Allen, a competitive bicyclist and biologist, piloted the aircraft over the course.

Human-powered flight represents the coming together of the highest technical standards with great physical stamina and endurance of the pilot. Although physical requirements limit its applicability, the *Gossamer Condor* has inspired others since its prize-winning flight. A number of records have been set and broken by pilots flying and pedaling ultralightweight aircraft. In June 1979 a flight was made across the English Channel. In January 1987 a new distance record of 60 km (37.3 mi) was set for human-powered flight. That record was broken in April 1988 by a flight of 118 km (74 mi).

Flinders, Matthew The English seaman Matthew Flinders, b. Mar. 16, 1774, d. July 19, 1814, was one of the world's most accomplished navigators and hydrographers. After serving in the South Pacific with William BLIGH, he sailed (1795) for Australia, where, with naval surgeon George Bass, he circumnavigated Van Diemen's Land (Tasmania). Because of his brilliant hydrographic work he was sent (1801) to chart the Queensland coast. Although dogged by ill luck, he completed the first circumnavigation of Australia in June 1803. Shipwrecked while returning to England, Flinders sought assistance from French-held Mauritius. Because France was at war with Britain, however, he was held prisoner there for seven years (1803–10).

Flint Flint, a city in eastern Michigan, is a major automobile-manufacturing center and the seat of Genesee County. The population of the city is 140,761 (1990), and 430,459 persons reside in the metropolitan area. The city began as a fur-trading post that was built on the Flint River in 1819. Early settlers turned to lumbering, which in turn led to a prosperous carriage-making industry. Car manufacturing began in the early 20th century. The modern city has a diversified industrial base, but General Motors is the major employer.

flint see CHERT AND FLINT

flintlock see MUSKET

Flintshire [flint'-shir] Flintshire is a former county in northeastern Wales along the Irish Sea coast. From the coast the land gradually rises to the Clwydian Hills. In the fertile Clwyd and Dee river valleys, agriculture is the principal economic activity. Sheep and cattle are raised at higher elevations, and coal is mined in the mountains. Iron and steel, chemicals, textiles, and aircraft are manufactured in the vicinity of Flint, and tourism is important.

Neolithic and Bronze Age remains indicate the early inhabitation of Flintshire. It was subsequently occupied by the Celts, the Romans, the Saxons of Mercia, and the Normans. In 1284, Edward I made Flintshire a county; in 1974 it became part of the new county of CLWYD.

Flood see DELUGE

floodplain Along many rivers there occurs a flat, elongated strip of land called a floodplain. As the name suggests, this LANDFORM originates from the periodic flooding of the river, a process that results in widespread deposition of sediment. Floodplains that are inundated every one or two years are commonly referred to as active or living. The unconsolidated sediment, mostly suspended clay and silt, that settles out during flooding is derived from erosion of the surrounding land in the drainage basin (see EROSION AND SEDIMENTATION).

Although deposition of suspended sediment beyond the bank tends to build up the floodplain, raising it as much as 1 cm (0.4 in) a year, the dominant sedimentation process is the formation of wholly or partially submerged bars in the river channel. Point bars characteristically develop around the inner convex banks of MEANDER bends, whereas longitudinal and diagonal bars develop in streams whose channels are divided into interlacing networks. Point bars are commonly separated from the adjacent floodplain by a slight depression known as a swale.

The current around a meander bend erodes the bank, resulting in a lateral shift of the river course. For a river that has almost reached equilibrium, erosion on the outer (concave) bank is nearly balanced by deposition on inner (point bar) banks downstream. Therefore, as the river shifts course, the point bar and swale system—hence, the floodplain—grows laterally, a process known as lateral accretion. Alternating point bars and swales on a floodplain surface afford clear evidence of shifts in river course. Lateral shifts in a river channel tend to limit the upward growth of the floodplain caused by overbank deposition. In braided rivers, the stabilization of bars and islands by vegetation contributes to the growth of the floodplain.

Floodplain alluvium is composed mostly of stratified clay, silt, sand, and gravel, generally with some admixture of organic material of vegetal origin. The sand and gravel often display cross-bedding, and the entire alluvial sequence is characterized by a fining upwards in grain size. Because of channel migration and the variability of in-channel processes, alluvial fill displays lateral textural variations. Rapid deposition of overbank material in the vicinity of the channel leads to LEVEE formation, especially where vegetation is available to trap sediment.

Floodplains commonly have poor surface and subsurface drainage. They display a variety of morphologic features, including levees, flood basins, backswamps, OXBOW LAKES, and various types of bars and alluvial islands. Downcutting of the river into its floodplain may result in formation of river terraces. Finally, floodplains provide rich agricultural lands that in many parts of the world are highly populated. Their main disadvantage stems from the natural hazard of flooding, sometimes on a catastrophic scale (see FLOODS AND FLOOD CONTROL).

See also: RIVER AND STREAM.

——

floods and flood control   A flood is the inundation of normally dry land resulting from the rising and overflowing of a body of water. The effects of floods, both beneficial and destructive, have been recorded for at least 5,000 years.

A familiar flood story is that in the Book of Genesis. The event upon which this Old Testament tale is based may have occurred about 3000 BC, when the Euphrates River inundated a vast area, including Ur in Southern Mesopotamia. (See DELUGE.)

The benefits of *regular* flooding were appreciated in ancient Egypt, where the floodwaters of the Nile brought fertile silt and much-needed water to the fields each year. The Pharaohs, recognizing that flooding meant prosperity, levied higher taxes after floods.

Coastal Floods

Floods are classified in various ways for many special purposes. In the most useful general classifications, coastal flooding of lakes and oceans is distinguished from river flooding. Coastal flooding can be caused by high, wind-generated WATER WAVES, exceptionally high tides, SUBSIDENCE of coastal areas, and TSUNAMIS (seismic sea waves). Coastal flooding is of special concern because, in many countries, population is concentrated along coastlines.

Although exceptionally high tides rarely produce serious and widespread damage on their own, they may significantly increase the hazard of flooding in combination with even moderately severe storms. Hurricanes and major storms produce most coastal floods. In 1970 a major storm (cyclone) in the Bay of Bengal produced heavy seas that inundated coastal regions of East Pakistan (now Bangladesh), killing some 200,000 people. Wind-generated waves well over 30 m (100 ft) in height have been observed in the open ocean. Fortunately, these huge waves usually diminish in size before reaching coastlines. On the other hand, tsunamis, caused by EARTHQUAKES, landslides (see LANDSLIDE AND AVALANCHE), and volcanic

Torrential rain beginning on Apr. 12, 1979, caused Mississippi's Pearl River to overflow, leaving more than 17,000 people homeless in the city of Jackson. The river finally crested more than 7.6 m (25 ft) above flood level on April 17, claiming a total of eight lives and causing property damage estimated in excess of $500 million.

eruptions, are low (less than a meter high) in the open ocean. They travel at speeds up to 800 km/h (500 mph), however, and grow higher as they near land; tsunamis 18–30 m (60–100 ft) high are not uncommon.

River Floods

RIVER AND STREAM flooding results from a variety of causes. Natural causes include rain, snowmelt, and ice jams (see ICE, RIVER AND LAKE). Floods on rivers result from prolonged periods of precipitation over broad regions. This was the case in June 1972, when six days of rain from Hurricane Agnes battered the eastern United States.

Cloudburst floods are caused by extremely intense rainfall (23 cm/10 in or more an hour), but they are short-lived, rarely continuing for more than a few hours at a given location. These floods often occur rapidly and with little warning—hence the name flash floods.

Moderate amounts of warm rain falling on a snowpack, particularly if the ground beneath the snow is frozen and unable to absorb the moisture, can cause severe flooding. Such was the case in New England in March 1936, when snowmelt equivalent to 25–75 cm (10–30 in) of rain occurred.

Floods may result from the failure of artificial structures such as DAMS. Dams fail because of poor design or siting, geologic hazards such as earthquakes and landslides, or simply old age. One of the most devastating U.S. dam failures occurred in February 1972 at Buffalo Creek in Logan County, W.Va. A dam used to impound coal-mining wastes, as well as water, completely collapsed after three days of rain.

Flooding is also caused by the constriction of streams by engineering projects such as landfills; removal of vegetation, which accelerates the rate of rain runoff; and paving and construction, which reduce the land's capacity to absorb rainfall.

Warning Systems

Deaths caused by flooding in the United States have averaged about 200 annually since 1970, and property losses have reached more than $4 billion per year. Losses would be far higher were it not for the 50 state offices of the National Weather Service's River and Flood Forecasting Service, which issue flood forecasts and warnings.

The U.S. Coast and Geodetic Survey, with the cooperation of the armed forces and the Federal Aviation Agency, maintains the Seismic Sea Wave Warning System, a network of seismic- and tide-monitoring stations.

Flood frequency analyses are performed by hydrologists, engineers, and planners, using records of past streamflow to estimate the probability of occurrence of floods of various sizes. For example, if a flood of a particular size has a probability of one chance in one hundred of being equaled or exceeded each year, it is said to be a "100-year flood."

Flood Control

Coastal flooding is an almost insoluble problem. Even where major flooding is practically an annual occurrence, the need for land far outweighs the dangers of flood. For example, much of the agricultural area in Bangladesh is a vast, low-lying plain formed by the deltas of three great rivers. If the yearly MONSOON brings heavy rains, or a cyclone (see CYCLONE AND ANTICYCLONE) or hurricane raises water levels, the plain is inundated, settlements disappear, and inhabitants are swept away. In the Netherlands, after the catastrophic storm of 1953, which destroyed dikes and flooded polder lands, the Dutch devised the DELTA PLAN (completed in 1985) to provide COASTAL PROTECTION for the most vulnerable areas of the southern coast. A surge barrier has also been erected (1982) on the River THAMES just below London.

Two different and at times competing approaches are used in attempting to prevent or reduce damage due to river flooding: structural and nonstructural. The structural approach relies on dams and reservoirs, levees or dikes, modification of stream channels, flood-diversion systems, and treatment of watersheds. Flood-control dams impound water at times of flood to mitigate downstream hazard; then, after the threat subsides, water is slowly released. Artificial levees raise the height of streambanks,

SIGNIFICANT FLOODS WITHIN THE PAST CENTURY

Year	Location and Cause
1883	Java and Sumatra. Tsunami, following the explosion of Krakatoa. Some 36,000 lives lost.
1887	Henan, China. Huang He, swollen by rains, overflows levees, floods 150,000 km² (50,000 mi²). 900,000 lives lost.
1889	Johnstown, Pa. Dam failure. 2,200 lives lost.
1900	Galveston, Tex. Hurricane flooding. 6,000 lives lost.
1916	The Netherlands. North Sea storms flood lowlands. 10,000 lives lost.
1928	Florida. Hurricane causes Lake Okeechobee to flood. 2,400 lives lost.
1938	North China. Chinese forces blow up dikes on the Huang He, to impede Japanese advance. Estimated 1 million lives lost.
1960	Chile, Hawaii, Japan. Giant tsunami following a major Chilean earthquake inundates coastal areas in all three countries.
1963	North Italy. Landslide into the reservoir of the Vaiont Dam sends a huge wave into valley below. 2,000 lives lost.
1970	E. Pakistan (now Bangladesh). Cyclone-generated floods inundate coastal regions. 200,000 lives lost (official estimate).
1971	Orissa State, India. Cyclone and sea surge hit the coast. 10,000 lives lost.
1979	Morvi, India. Heavy monsoon rains cause collapse of river dam, 7,000 to 10,000 lives lost.
1982	Peru. Torrential rains cause lake to overflow into Chantay-acu River valley. 2,500 lives lost.
1985	Northeastern Brazil. Rain-caused floods leave 1 million homeless.
1988	Bangladesh. Monsoon flooding inundates 3/4 of country; 2,500 dead, 28 million homeless.
1988	Sudan. Torrential rains flood the Nile. 1.5 million homeless in Khartoum area; number of dead unknown.

thus reducing the likelihood of flooding. Straightening of channels to allow floodwaters to flow faster and therefore shallower is yet another method. In some places, floodwaters are diverted into previously prepared holding basins to reduce the flood crest downstream. Another approach is to diminish the amount of water entering streams by reforesting watersheds and by detaining runoff high in the headwaters of a river.

Critics of the structural approach note that the cost of flood-control structures often exceeds the value of the property being protected. In addition, the failure of an artificial levee can be extremely serious. Channel straightening is often temporary, since rivers often develop new bends.

Advocates of the nonstructural approach prefer using zoning, subdivision regulations, and public acquisition to prevent new building in FLOODPLAINS. They encourage using these lands for compatible purposes, such as for agriculture.

Critics of the nonstructural approach agree that avoidance of flood-prone areas is desirable. They point out, however, that many major cities were sited adjacent to bodies of water for purposes of transportation, power generation, and water supply, and that it is economically unfeasible to abandon these metropolitan areas.

Recent trends in flood control have been toward the use of both approaches. The National Flood Insurance Act, enacted (1968) by the U.S. Congress, provides affordable flood insurance to the owners of buildings in communities that participate in land-use programs to reduce flood damage risks.

Florence   Florence (Italian: Firenze) is the capital city of both Firenze province and the Tuscany region of central Italy; it lies on the Arno River at the foot of the Apennines. The population is 421,299 (1987 est.). A great outburst of artistic and architectural activity occurred in Flor-

ence from the 13th to the 15th century, and the city's cultural treasures have made tourism the economic mainstay. Since the late 19th century, large residential and manufacturing districts have sprung up around the old city core. Florence is famous for its gold and silver jewelry, leatherwork, high-fashion clothing, shoes, ornamental glass, and furniture. It is also an important rail center.

The Artistic Heritage of Florence. Many of Florence's best known architectural treasures are religious buildings, notably the Baptistry of San Giovanni (c.1000), considered the oldest building in the city, and San Miniato, another fine Romanesque church. The bronze-relief baptistry doors, designed by Lorenzo GHIBERTI, were constructed in the first half of the 15th century. The bell tower of the Gothic cathedral of Santa Maria del Fiore was designed by GIOTTO DI BONDONE. The cathedral, which contains MICHELANGELO's sculptural masterpiece the *Pietà*; (c.1546–50), was begun in 1294 and consecrated in 1436. The dome was designed (c.1420) by Filippo BRUNELLESCHI. Brunelleschi also designed the Ospedale degli Innocenti, whose wide arches are decorated with glazed terra-cottas by Luca della Robbia (see DELLA ROBBIA family).

Not far from the cathedral is the Medici parish church of San Lorenzo, which contains magnificent sculptures Michelangelo made for the tombs of Giuliano and Lorenzo. The 13th-century Franciscan church of Santa Croce— its interior decorated by Giotto, CIMABUE, DONATELLO, Brunelleschi, and others—has a MICHELOZZO-designed Medici chapel in which Michelangelo, Galileo, Machiavelli, and Rossini are buried.

The Piazza della Signoria contains the Palazzo Vecchio, built in the 14th century as the seat of Florentine government. The BARGELLO, which also dates from the 14th century, is now a state museum. The enormous PITTI PALACE (begun 1458) was the official home of the king when Florence was Italy's capital (1865–70).

Florence has about 40 art museums, which house the works of such masters as Masaccio, Fra Angelico, Botti-

(Left) *The Cathedral of Santa Maria del Fiore's famous dome, designed* (c.1420) *by Filippo Brunelleschi, dominates this view of Florence. The Campanile of the Gothic cathedral was designed by Giotto.* (Right) *The 14th-century Ponte Vecchio is the oldest bridge in Florence and the only one spared during the destruction of World War II. It is lined with goldsmith and silversmith shops dating from the 16th century, when Florence flourished as the financial and artistic center of Italy.*

celli, Leonardo da Vinci, Raphael, Donatello, Ghiberti, Luca della Robbia, Michelangelo, Titian, Tintoretto, Veronese, and Rubens. The Pitti and the UFFIZI hold two of the world's greatest collections of medieval and Renaissance art. The city's national library and state archives house incomparable manuscript collections.

History. Originally Etruscan, then Roman (until the 5th century), Gothic, Byzantine, and Lombard, Florence reached its peak of economic, political, and cultural splendor between the 13th and 16th centuries. Commercial power developed in earnest after Florence became a free commune in 1115. Ripped by civil strife until the late 13th century, Florence nevertheless flourished as a trade and industrial center. It was ruled by an oligarchy of merchants and bankers and gradually attained supremacy over the surrounding area. In 1348 more than 60% of the nearly 100,000 inhabitants were killed by the Black Death (BUBONIC PLAGUE), temporarily halting growth.

Three hundred years of domination by the MEDICI family began in 1434 with Cosimo (1389–1464). Medici control, largely the result of financial power and political skill, was interrupted by the revolution of 1494–98, led by the Dominican religious reformer Girolamo SAVONAROLA. In 1527, Emperor CHARLES V restored the Medici, and Alessandro (*c.*1510–1537) became the first duke of Tuscany. Cosimo I (1519–74), who was created the first grand duke in 1569, brought almost all of Tuscany under his rule. The grand duchy was ruled by the house of Habsburg-Lorraine after the Medici line died out in 1737. Tuscany was annexed to the new kingdom of Italy in 1861, and Florence was made the capital of the kingdom in 1865. After the capital was moved (1871) to Rome, the city declined.

Threatened for centuries by flooding from the Arno River, the city was devastated by a 1966 inundation.

Supported by contributions from all over the world, experts worked for years to salvage the city's art treasures.

Flores, Juan José [floh'-rays]   Juan José Flores, b. July 19, 1800, d. Oct. 1, 1864, served as a commander during Ecuador's wars of independence and was its first president. In 1830 he led Ecuador's secession from Simón Bolívar's Gran Colombia and became president of the new republic. A conservative, he was opposed by the liberals under Vicente Rocafuerte, with whom he agreed to alternate office after civil war in 1834. Flores stepped down then, but at the end of his second term (1839–43) refused to do so. In 1845 he was deposed and fled the country. From 1860 to 1864 he was commander of the army in the conservative regime of Gabriel García Moreno.

Florey, Sir Howard Walter   see PENICILLIN

floriculture [flohr'-i-kuhl-chur]   Floriculture is the branch of HORTICULTURE concerned with the commercial growing of plants for their FLOWERS and with the cultivation and sale of HOUSEPLANTS. The principal commercial flower crops grown in the United States are roses, carnations, chrysanthemums, snapdragons, gladioli, and orchids, although many other flower species are also cultivated. Crops are grown throughout the year in southern California and Florida, and greenhouse crops are raised in every state.

Greenhouse Floriculture. Successful greenhouse floriculture requires the maintenance of a totally managed environment. Such growth factors as soil, temperature, water, and types and amounts of nutrients must be meticulously controlled. Photoperiod, the precise length of

Workers tend this Dutch tulip field completely by hand. After the flowers are cut, the bulbs are harvested, cleaned, and prepared for sale. Daffodils, crocuses, and hyacinths are also grown in the colorful bulb fields.

Although some flowers have been cultivated for as long as 2,500 years, widespread interest in plant breeding began in Europe only about 400 years ago, when scientific expeditions began bringing back many new specimens from different parts of the world. Modern floriculturists have selectively bred plants for desired characteristics, such as color, size, and number of blooms, and length of flowering season; Flowers are grown both outdoors and in greenhouses. Popular cultivated flowers include daffodils (A), crocuses (B), hyacinths (C), lilacs (D), lilies (E), freesias (F), irises (G), carnations (H), anemones (I), dahlias (J), cyclamens (K), and chrysanthemums (L).

daylight that triggers flowering in each plant species, is lengthened by using artificial light or shortened by shutting out sunlight. Soluble fertilizers are added to the watering system according to carefully measured formulas, and the addition of small amounts of carbon dioxide to greenhouse air increases the rate at which flower crops grow. In large, sophisticated greenhouses most of these factors are controlled through automated systems.

Commercial Bulb Growing. In addition to the production of flowers and potted plants, a large industry flourishes, primarily in Holland, that is devoted to the raising of flower bulbs. Tulips, hyacinths, narcissus, crocuses, irises, and other flowering plants that produce underground bulbs, corms, or rhizomes are grown on dune sands and polders. After the flowers are cut, the bulbs are harvested and treated with heat and disinfectants to destroy bulb-infesting parasites. Bulbs are produced both for planting in gardens and for commercial flower production.

A Changing Industry. Flowers, among the most perishable of all crops, must be marketed within a short time after they are cut. Until air transport became a feasible shipping mode, most commercially grown flowers were raised in greenhouses near the cities that were their main markets. Greenhouse floriculture, however, is very costly. Although it continues to be important, flowers grown in the open air at a fraction of greenhouse costs are now cultivated in warm, sunny regions and shipped quickly to urban centers.

Florida

Florida Florida, a favorite destination of millions of tourists, is a fast-developing state of the southeastern United States. Mostly a peninsula, Florida is bordered by Alabama and Georgia on the north, the Atlantic Ocean on the east, the Straits of Florida on the south, and the Gulf of Mexico and Alabama on the west. The first European to visit the region was the Spanish explorer Juan PONCE DE LEÓN in 1513, who called it *Florida* ("feast of flowers"), either because he saw a profusion of flowers on its coast or because it was Easter week (*Pascua florida*). The first permanent European settlement in the continental United States was at SAINT AUGUSTINE in 1565.

Land and Resources

Florida is low-lying and level, with an average elevation of about 30 m (100 ft). The highest point, in Walton County in the northwest, is 105 m (345 ft) above sea level. Florida has 2,172 km (1,350 mi) of coastline, more than any other state except Alaska; 933 km (580 mi) of the coastline border the Atlantic, and 1,239 km (770 mi) border the Gulf of Mexico. The uneven coastline is indented with estuaries, bays, inlets, lagoons, rivers, and barrier islands. The FLORIDA KEYS, an arc of islands, lie off the state's southern tip.

Physiographic Regions. The land area of Florida and its continental shelf make up the Florida Plateau, which separates the Atlantic Ocean from the Gulf of Mexico. Volcanic mountains buried during the Paleozoic Era (600 to 225 million years ago) form the base of the Florida Plateau. Sands and other materials that were deposited on the base have formed sedimentary rocks more than 1,200 m (4,000 ft) thick. The plateau has shifted over the centuries, and it is now tilted from east to west, with the eastern part higher than the western part as evidenced by the gulf's broad continental shelf.

The Florida Plateau is divided into five land regions—the coastal lowlands, the EVERGLADES, the central highlands, the northwestern highlands, and the Marianna lowlands. The coastal lowlands include the Atlantic and Gulf zones and contain 70% of Florida's population. The Everglades were originally a sea bottom. As the area was raised, the Okeechobee Basin remained higher than the area to the south. Water from Lake OKEECHOBEE overflows to the south and southwest, creating a sea of water grasses, open water areas, cypress forests, and mangrove swamps. The central highlands are marked by sinkholes, lakes, and springs. A part of the OKEFENOKEE SWAMP is in the far north, astride the border with Georgia. West of the

FLORIDA

Land: Area: 151,939 km² (58,664 mi²); rank: 22d. Capital: Tallahassee (1990 pop., 124,773). Largest city: Jacksonville (1990 pop., 672,971). Counties: 67. Elevations: highest—105 m (345 ft), in Walton County; lowest—sea level, at Atlantic coast.

People: Population (1990): 13,003,362; rank: 4th; density: 85.6 persons per km² (221.7 per mi²). Distribution (1988): 90.8% metropolitan, 9.2% nonmetropolitan. Average annual change (1980–90): +3.3%.

Government (1990). Governor: Lawton Chiles, Democrat. U.S. Congress: Senate—1 Democrat, 1 Republican; House—9 Democrats, 10 Republicans. Electoral college votes: 21. State legislature: 40 senators, 120 representatives.

Economy: State personal income (1988): $204.8 billion; rank: 4th. Median family income (1979): $17,280; rank: 39th. Agriculture: income (1988)—$5.8 billion. Fishing: value (1988)—$169 million. Forestry: sawtimber volume (1987)—40.5 billion board feet. Mining: value, nonfuels only (1987)—$1.3 billion. Manufacturing: value added (1987)—$28 billion. Services: value (1987)—$55.4 billion.

Miscellany: Statehood: Mar. 3, 1845; the 27th state. Nickname: Sunshine State; tree: sabal palmetto palm; motto: In God We Trust; song: "Old Folks at Home" ("Swanee River").

Orange Blossom

Mockingbird

SUWANNEE RIVER are the northwestern highlands, with elevations rising above 91 m (300 ft). The Marianna lowlands bisect the northwestern highlands.

Soils. The coastal lowlands have poorly drained, sandy soils. In the Everglades the soil is primarily peat and muck. Well-drained sands, with small amounts of silt and clay, are found in the central highlands. The well-drained soils in the northwestern highlands and Marianna lowlands, with some clay content, are the best agricultural soils.

Rivers and Lakes. The state's longest river, the Saint Johns, flows north from Indian River County to the Atlantic Ocean, near Jacksonville. Other major waterways in the state include the Apalachicola, Kissimmee, Peace, Perdido, St. Marys, Suwannee, and Withlacoochee rivers.

Florida's groundwaters are primarily supplied by the Floridan aquifer, which extends across the entire state, except in the far west. Lake Okeechobee is the largest lake in the state and the fourth largest natural lake within the United States. Central Florida is the site of numerous sinkhole lakes.

Climate. Florida's climate is influenced by the state's location, its peninsular shape, and its numerous inland water bodies. No place in the state is more than 110 km (70 mi) from open water. Winds that blow over the GULF STREAM moderate the climate.

The Florida Keys have a tropical climate, with average temperatures ranging from 22° C (71° F) in January to 29° C (84° F) in July. Northern Florida has a subtropical to temperate climate; Tallahassee has average temperatures of 12° C (53° F) in January and 27° C (81° F) in July.

The southeastern coast and the northwestern panhandle receive an average of 1,626 mm (64 in) of precipitation each year. In north central Florida the average annual precipitation is approximately 1,321 mm (52 in). Thunderstorms occur frequently, especially in central Florida. Since 1900 more than 20 major hurricanes have hit Florida, mostly in the southern and panhandle areas of the state.

Vegetation and Animal Life. Slightly more than half of Florida's land area is covered with forests. Common hardwoods include ash, hickory, magnolia, mahogany, and oak. Mangrove and cypress flourish in the southern swamplands, such as Big Cypress Swamp and the Everglades. Pines predominate in the north. Palm trees grow throughout most of the state. The swamplands are noted for their epiphytes (air plants), such as Spanish moss, nonparasitic plants that typically hang from trees (espe-

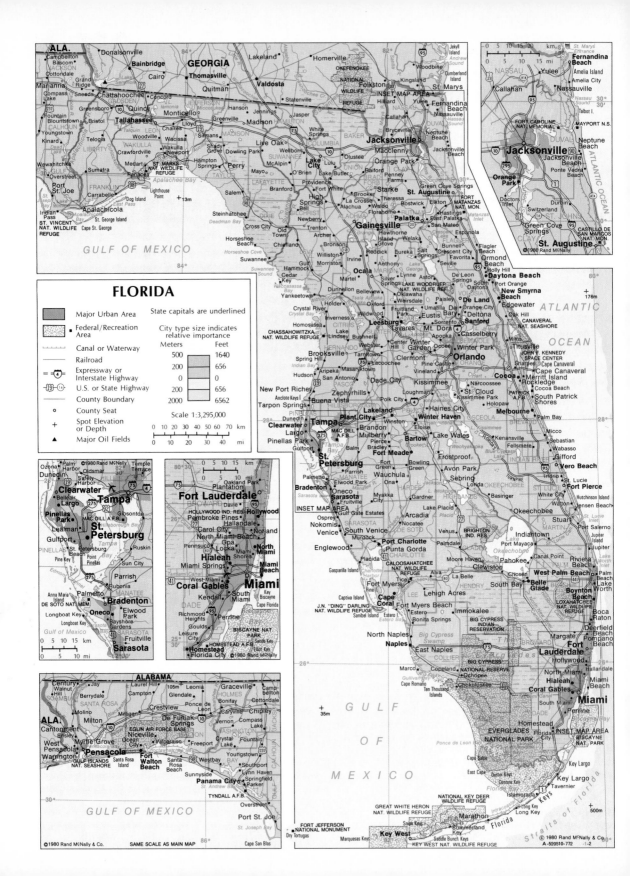

(Left) *Miami Beach, located on a barrier island between the Atlantic Ocean and Indian Creek, contains some of the most valuable property in the world. The beaches of this resort city cater to Florida's leading industry— tourism.*

(Below) *Cypress trees, often with Spanish moss hanging from their branches, are common in Florida, frequently growing in swamps. Florida has the most extensive subtropical wilderness areas in the United States.*

cially oak and cypress); tall saw grass is also common in these wet regions.

Florida has a great variety of wildlife. Large mammals include whitetail deer, black bears, bobcats, and a few cougars. Foxes, muskrats, otters, possums, rabbits, raccoons, and squirrels are abundant. Swamps provide a habitat for alligators. Game birds, such as wild turkeys and quail, and water birds, such as egrets, flamingos, gulls, herons, and pelicans, are found. Common freshwater fish species include black bass, bream, catfish, and trout; marine animals include barracuda, bonito, dolphins, mackerel, marlin, menhaden, black mullet, pompano, tarpon, crabs, shrimp, and large turtles.

Mineral Resources. Florida has extensive phosphate deposits, found mainly in the central part of the state, and limestone, located throughout the state. Kaolin and other clays, sand and gravel, ilmenite, monazite, and zirconium are also found. Relatively small petroleum deposits are in the southwest.

People

Florida's population is 13,003,362 (1990), an increase of 33.4% since 1980. The state's percentage increase from 1980 to 1990 was far higher than the national average of 10.2%, and in absolute numbers Florida's total gain of 3,257,038 inhabitants was surpassed only by California. Between 1970 and 1980, Florida's population grew by about 43.5%. Most of the population increase in the 1960s, '70s, and '80s was due to in-migration. Many new Floridians are retirees, whose presence accounts for the state's high proportion of persons aged 65 or more years—17.8% of the state's population, compared to the national average of 12.4%. Florida's population density is about 86 persons per km^2 (222 per mi^2), and more than 90% of the population are classified as urban (1988).

The chief cities are (in order of population) JACKSONVILLE, MIAMI, TAMPA, Saint Petersburg, HIALEAH, ORLANDO, FORT LAUDERDALE, TALLAHASSEE, Hollywood, Clearwater, Miami Beach, Gainesville, Coral Springs, Cape Coral, Pompano Beach, Lakeland, and WEST PALM BEACH. The great majority of Florida's inhabitants are white; blacks make up about 14% of the population. Significant numbers of Hispanics (about 12% of the population), especially Cubans who immigrated during the 1960s and in 1980, live primarily in the greater Miami area, as well as in Tampa. A Greek community lives in Tarpon Springs, on the west coast. About 36,335 American Indians live in the state. The SEMINOLE Indians live mostly in the Everglades. Roman Catholics form the largest single religious denomi-

(Right) *Extensive citrus groves cover the landscape near Winter Garden, in central Florida, west of Orlando. Florida leads all states by a considerable margin in the production of oranges, grapefruit, and tangerines.*

(Below) *The 22-story tower of Florida's capitol, which was completed in 1977, looms above the previous state capitol in Tallahassee.*

Orlando, Florida International University (1965) at Miami, the University of North Florida (1965) at Jacksonville, the University of South Florida (1956) at Tampa, and the University of West Florida (1964) at Pensacola.

Cultural Institutions. Notable museums include the John and Mabel Ringling Museum of Art, at Sarasota, with a major collection of European paintings; the Florida State Museum, at Gainesville, with notable displays on archaeology; the Dade County Art Museum, at Miami; the Cummer Gallery of Art, at Jacksonville; the Museum of Florida History, at Tallahassee; and Marineland of Florida, near Saint Augustine. Music and opera are performed by the Florida Symphony (Orlando) and the Florida State Opera (Tallahassee).

Historical Sites. Castillo de San Marcos National Monument contains a masonry fort, begun in 1672, built by the Spanish to protect Saint Augustine. De Soto National Memorial, near Bradenton, commemorates the landing (1539) of the Spanish explorer Hernando de Soto. Fort Jefferson National Monument, in the DRY TORTUGAS islands, is the site of an immense fortification that served as a Federal military prison during and after the U.S. Civil War.

Sports and Outdoor Recreation. Because of its climate and location, Florida offers extensive opportunities for outdoor sports. The state has numerous beach resorts, as well as ample facilities for marine and freshwater fishing, pleasure boating, waterskiing, and other water sports. Each year many major-league baseball teams conduct spring training in the state from February to early April. The Orange Bowl, played at Miami, is a noted annual postseason college football game.

Communications. Florida's first radio station (1920) and first television station (1949) began broadcasting from Miami. Numerous radio and television stations are

nation in Florida. Among Protestants, the Baptists and Methodists are particularly strong. Florida also has a sizable Jewish community.

Education and Cultural Activity

Education. The 1868 state constitution authorized a statewide system of public education. Public elementary and secondary schools in Florida enroll about 1,796,000 (1990) pupils. The University of Florida (1853) at Gainesville was the first institution in the state university system. Others include Florida State University (1857) at Tallahassee, Florida Technological University (1963) at

now in operation. The state's first newspaper was the *East Florida Gazette*, established in 1783 in Saint Augustine. Today the *Miami Herald* is considered Florida's most influential newspaper. A leading Spanish-language daily is *Diario Las Americas*.

Economic Activity

Florida has a diversified modern economy. Tourism and other service industries and government (including military installations) are the chief employers. The state's economy benefits from the many retired persons who live in Florida on pensions earned elsewhere.

Agriculture. Florida is a major agricultural state. Its most important products are citrus fruits—especially oranges. Other principal crops are vegetables (particularly tomatoes); sugarcane, the state's major field crop; tobacco; soybeans; nuts, especially peanuts and pecans; and noncitrus fruits, mainly watermelons, cantaloupes, and strawberries. Income is also derived from livestock and the production of dairy products and eggs. The raising of Thoroughbred horses is also a major endeavor in Florida, particularly on the horse farms in Marion County.

Forestry and Fishing. Lumbering is a relatively small but significant industry in Florida; softwoods are the chief trees cut. Florida's commercial fish catch is among the highest in value in the nation. Important species include shrimp, black mullet, and blue crab. Most fish are caught off the west coast.

Mining. Florida is a leading state in nonfuel mineral output. Its principal minerals are phosphate, of which Florida is the nation's leading producer; petroleum and natural gas; stone; clay; sand and gravel; limestone; ilmenite; and dolomite.

Manufacturing. Florida has a relatively small manufacturing sector. Chief manufactures are processed food, especially citrus products, such as frozen orange juice concentrate; transportation equipment; electrical equipment; chemicals; fabricated metals; paper and paper goods; printed materials; and cigars.

Tourism. The warm climate of southern Florida during the winter is a favorite attraction for vacationers from the northeastern United States and Canada. In addition to the many beach resorts on both coasts, points of interest include CAPE CANAVERAL, the site of the John F. KENNEDY SPACE CENTER; Walt Disney World, near Orlando (see DISNEYLAND AND WALT DISNEY WORLD); Cypress Gardens, near Winter Haven; Busch Gardens, in Tampa, containing a large zoo; and Everglades National Park.

Transportation. Florida has well-developed road and railway systems. Its busiest seaports are Tampa-Saint Petersburg, Jacksonville, Port Everglades (at Fort Lauderdale), and Miami. Important waterways include sections of both the Gulf Intracoastal Waterway and the Atlantic Intracoastal Waterway. Miami International Airport is one of the nation's busiest.

Energy. Petroleum is the source of about 60% of the energy produced in Florida. Other sources include natural gas and coal. Most electricity is produced in thermal plants, but the state also has nuclear power facilities and a few small hydroelectric installations.

Government and Politics

Government. Florida is governed under a constitution of 1885, as revised in 1968 and later amended. The chief executive is the governor, popularly elected to a 4-year term; a governor may not serve more than 10 consecutive years. As opposed to most other states, other statewide elected officials have considerable authority independent of the governor and appreciably limit the power of the chief executive. The Florida legislature is made up of a senate, whose 40 members are popularly elected to 4-year terms, and a house of representatives, whose 120 members are popularly elected to 2-year terms. The highest tribunal in the state is the supreme court, composed of 7 justices appointed by the governor to 6-year terms; one of the justices is elected by the court to serve for 2 years as chief justice. The large majority of the state's 67 counties are administered by 5 county commissioners.

Politics. Democrats have dominated Florida politics on the state and local levels since 1876, although in recent decades two Republican governors have been elected—in 1966 and 1986. By the mid-20th century, however, Republicans had made considerable gains in national presidential elections, and since 1952, Democratic presidential candidates have carried Florida only in 1964 and 1976.

History

Human settlement dates from about 8000 BC. At the time of the first European contact in the early 16th century,

Cape Canaveral, on Florida's east coast, is the site of the missile complex from which all manned U.S. spacecraft have been launched.

four major Indian groups lived in what is now Florida: the APALACHEE in the northwest; the Calusa in the southwest; the Tequesta along the southeastern coast; and the Timucua in the north central region.

European Rule. In 1513, Juan Ponce de Léon landed on the northeast Florida coast and claimed Florida for Spain. In 1521 he returned to found a colony, but was unsuccessful and was killed the same year. In 1528, Pánfilo de NARVÁEZ, another Spanish explorer, anchored in Tampa Bay and then traveled inland. In 1539, Hernando DE SOTO landed near Tampa Bay, exploring that area and then northern Florida. Another Spaniard, Tristán de Luna, failed in two attempts to establish a permanent colony on Pensacola Bay beginning in 1559.

In 1564 the French Huguenot René de LAUDONNIÉRE, built Fort Caroline, near present-day Jacksonville. PHILIP II of Spain sent a military expedition, led by Pedro MENÉNDEZ DE AVILÉS, to destroy the French settlement. Arriving in 1565, Menéndez established Saint Augustine and massacred the French; he captured Fort Caroline and founded another settlement there. The Spanish subsequently built forts and missions across northern Florida and around the southwestern coast. During the SEVEN YEARS' WAR (1756–63) between Britain and France, Spain sided with France and lost Cuba in 1762. Under the terms of the peace treaty (1763), Spain traded Florida to Britain in exchange for Cuba.

Under British rule, Florida was divided into two separate colonies, East Florida and West Florida. During the American Revolution, Floridians remained loyal to Britain; but by the Treaty of Paris (1783), English hegemony in Florida was ended and the region was returned to Spain.

U.S. Acquisition. During the WAR OF 1812, Britain used Pensacola as a naval base, but in 1814 it was captured by American troops. In 1819, Spain agreed to transfer Florida to the United States, which assumed control in 1821. The following year, Florida was organized as a territory; soon many settlers, including Indians, streamed into Florida from the North. Conflicts erupted with the Seminole Indians, who were defeated in the Second Seminole War (1835–42). Some of the Seminole were removed to Oklahoma, and a small band migrated south to the Everglades.

Statehood. Florida entered the Union as a slave state on Mar. 3, 1845. By 1860 the population was about 140,000, of whom 63,000 were black. Florida seceded from the Union on Jan. 10, 1861, and subsequently joined the Confederacy. Most of Florida's coastal towns were captured by Union forces early in the war, but Tallahassee remained under Confederate control throughout the war. The Battle of Olustee, which took place in Florida on Feb. 20, 1864, was one of the last Confederate victories.

In 1868, after a new constitution guaranteeing blacks the right to vote had been adopted, the state was readmitted to the Union. An era of rapid economic growth began in the 1880s—great deposits of phosphate were discovered, citrus groves were planted, southern swamplands were drained and converted to farmland, and railroads and tourist facilities were constructed.

The Modern Era. During the early 1920s, Florida experienced a great land boom. Real estate prices rose spectacularly until 1926, when a combination of factors led to a rapid and severe drop in values. Later in 1926, Miami, one of Florida's chief boom cities (its population had grown from 1,681 inhabitants in 1900 to 69,754 in 1925), was badly damaged by a hurricane. The state's economy had largely recovered by 1929, when the Great Depression began, resulting in a high unemployment rate.

From 1920 to 1930, Florida's population had grown by more than 50%, reaching about 1,468,000 inhabitants. Growth continued during the 1930s and accelerated in the 1940s, when war-related activities spurred additional development. By 1950, Florida had about 2,771,000 inhabitants, and during both the 1950s and '60s its population grew by about 2 million persons. In the postwar period the tourist and retirement industries grew rapidly, as did commercial farming. The aerospace industry developed in association with the Cape Canaveral missile and space-flight center. Floridians adhered gradually to the 1954 U.S. Supreme Court decision outlawing segregated schools, and by the early 1970s most public educational institutions in the state had integrated student bodies. During the 1960s and in 1980 thousands of refugees from the Castro regime in Cuba settled in Florida, especially in Miami, greatly taxing the resources of the state and of Miami. Rioting erupted in June 1980 in Miami's black community because of tensions resulting from the Cuban immigration and the acquittal of four white policemen accused of beating to death a black businessman. The state's phenomenal population growth continued, with Florida's population nearly doubling between 1970 and 1990.

Florida, Straits of   The Straits of Florida connect the Gulf of Mexico with the Atlantic Ocean. The passage (up to 145 km/90 mi wide) is bounded by the Florida Keys on the north and by Cuba and the Bahamas on the south. The Florida Current (part of the GULF STREAM) flows eastward through the straits.

Florida Keys   The Florida Keys are a chain of islands that extend for about 240 km (150 mi) from the tip of Florida into the Gulf of Mexico to Key West, the westernmost island. They are linked to the mainland by the Overseas Highway, whose longest bridge extends for 11 km (7 mi) over the Gulf. Key Largo is the largest island in the chain, whose primary industry is tourism.

---

flotsam, jetsam, and lagan   Under admiralty (maritime) law, the terms *flotsam, jetsam*, and *lagan* refer to goods that are cast away or otherwise lost at sea in a storm or similar emergency. Flotsam are any goods or parts of a ship found floating at sea. Jetsam (from *jetsason*) are goods voluntarily cast into the water in an attempt to keep a ship afloat by decreasing its weight. Goods that are thrown overboard and are attached to a cork or buoy to facilitate later recovery are called lagan or ligan. Goods washed ashore are classified as wrack. Admiralty law holds that rescuing people and property aboard helpless ships is a duty, and that anyone who does so is entitled to a reward, the amount of which is determined by a court.

flounder Flounder are species of chiefly marine, carnivorous FLATFISH belonging to the Bothidae and Pleuronectidae families, order Heterosomata. All have in common a remarkable adaptation: both eyes migrate to either the right or the left side of the head during the larval stage, shortly after hatching. As a result, flounder swim on one side with the eyes pointing up. All are predaceous. Flounder can readily change their coloration and can mimic both the color and pattern of the ocean bottom. Flounder are caught for sport, as well as for their commercial value as a food fish.

Adult flounders have both eyes located on one side of the head (top); the lower, colorless side is blind.

flour Flour is a food prepared by grinding and sieving WHEAT. Wheat flour is particularly suitable for use as an ingredient in the preparation of baked products. When it is mixed with liquid in the correct proportions, its major protein components (collectively known as gluten) form an elastic network that is capable of holding leavening gases and that will set to a rather firm, spongy structure when heated in an oven.

Wheat is divided into hard wheats, whose flours yield doughs that are elastic and have excellent gas-holding or expansion properties, and soft wheats, whose flours are used for cakes, cookies, pie crusts, and similar products where a high volume is not essential and a tender or crumbly texture is desired. All-purpose flour is usually made from a combination of hard and soft wheats.

The milling process by which flour is made separates the wheat endosperm (the starchy interior portion of the kernel) from the BRAN layers and the wheat germ, and then grinds the endosperm chunks to a fine powder. After each stage of the grinding process, stacks of screens with different mesh sizes separate the ground material into several streams. These streams may be further processed by grinding, or they may be drawn off for feedstuffs or combined to yield flours with different properties.

By combining properly selected streams, the miller can make flours of widely varying quality from the same wheat. Ordinarily, about 70 percent of the kernel emerges from the process as flour of some sort. Mill streams consisting of the bran and germ, together with the endosperm particles that cannot be separated from them, are usually mixed together and sold as ingredients for animal feed.

In whole wheat flour, the ground bran, germ, and endosperm are ultimately combined to produce a material similar in composition to the original grain. Whole wheat flour is darker, coarser, and stronger in flavor than white flour.

flowchart A flowchart is a pictorial description of a procedure to be followed in solving a given problem. Frequently used to outline computer programs and ALGORITHMS, flowcharts are made up of boxes connected by arrows. To perform the process described in a flowchart, one begins at Start and follows the arrows from box to box, performing the actions indicated. The shape of each box indicates what kind of step it represents, such as processing, decision making, and control.

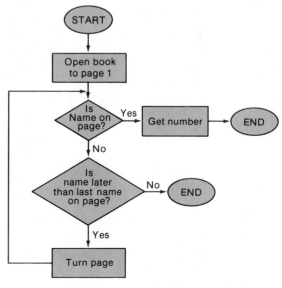

Flowcharts are useful in designing computer programs and for communicating program descriptions because they can suppress unnecessary details and have a precise meaning if carefully used. The standard flowchart forms are not convenient for all programming languages, and many variations are in use. Flowcharts may also be used to represent an overall view of manufacturing processes.

See also: COMPUTER PROGRAMMING.

---

flower The flower is the reproductive structure of AN-GIOSPERMS, or flowering plants. Compared to the reproductive structures of other plants, the flower is unique in several ways. It consists of four kinds of modified leaves, two of which (stamens and pistils) bear POLLEN and SEEDS. Several nonflowering plants also produce pollen and seeds on modified leaves, but in the angiosperms the modified leaf called the pistil forms an ovary that completely encloses the ovule, which becomes the seed. The term *angiosperm* is derived from the Greek and means "seed in a vessel."

According to the fossil record, flowering plants appeared only about 140 million years ago, during the early Cretaceous Period. They now dominate the world's vegetation. There may be more than 250,000 angiosperm species, compared to fewer than 1,000 species of GYM-NOSPERMS and fewer than about 40,000 other types of vascular plants (ferns and their relatives) and bryophytes (liverworts, mosses, and hornworts).

More than any other major plant group, the flowering plants are ecologically related to animals. Modern animals, including humans, could not exist as they do now without flowering plants, and flowering plants have flourished because of the animals with which they exist and have existed. Most flowering species depend on animals for reproduction. Insects commonly carry pollen from the stamens to the pistils; bats and birds participate in POLLI-NATION of some species. The dispersal and successful growth of the seeds are further ensured by other animals that are attracted to their colorful and aromatic flowers and tasty fruits. Many kinds of fruits and seeds (the exclusive products of angiosperms) are also collected and consumed by humans, and the seeds are planted in extensive systems of agriculture. In still another relationship between plants and animals, only the special growing cells at the base of a grass (angiosperm) leaf seem especially well adapted to animal grazing.

Structure of Flowers

Four kinds of modified leaves make up a complete flower: pistils and stamens (primary reproductive structures), and petals and sepals (secondary structures). The pistil is the female reproductive structure. It has a stigma, where the pollen becomes attached and germinates; a style, through which the pollen tube grows; and an ovary with one or more ovules. The egg cell that will unite with the sperm cell (delivered by the pollen tube) forms in the ovule. The stamen is the male structure; its filament supports an anther, in which the pollen is formed. The often brightly colored petals are important in attracting pollinators, and the often leaflike sepals enclose the bud before the flower opens. The many species of flowering plants are usually distinguished from each other by the manner in which these four basic flower parts are modified.

Some flowers have only one pistil, others have two or a few, and still others have many. The several pistils in the single flower may be separate or fused to each other; in the latter case, they may be joined only at the ovaries or along their entire length. The ovary may contain one to many ovules, and these may be arranged in various ways. Frequently the ovaries are attached to the receptacle (the end of the stem, or peduncle, that supports the flower parts) at the same level as the other flower parts, in which case the ovary is said to be superior (hypogynous). In some cases the other flower parts are attached above the ovary, which is then said to be inferior (epigynous). In the rose family, the stamens, petals, and sepals are attached around the ring of a cup with the ovaries at the bottom of the cup (perigynous).

Stamens also vary in several ways, although not as markedly as ovaries. Classification schemes often depend on the number of stamens in a given flower and whether they are attached oppositely or alternately with the petals.

The petals, taken together, form the corolla, which takes numerous and often beautiful forms. Besides the number of petals, two other variations occur, which are especially important. First, petals may be separately attached to the receptacle, or they may be united along their edges to form a tube. Second, the corolla may be radially symmetrical, with petals radiating out in all directions from the center of the flower (as in a buttercup, geranium, lily, or rose), or some petals may have shapes different from others, so that the flower has dorsiventral symmetry—one in which a vertical plane divides the flower into two equal, mirror-image halves (as in a snapdragon, honeysuckle, or orchid).

Many flower petals have patterns of pigments that absorb only in the ultraviolet part of the spectrum. Thus, insects, which have eyes that are sensitive to ultraviolet light, see patterns on the flower that are not visible to humans. These patterns frequently consist of radiating lines that lead the insect to the source of nectar. A few flowers (for example, clematis) have no true petals but do have colorful sepals.

If a flower is lacking any one of the four basic parts, it is said to be incomplete. If it is lacking one of the essential reproductive parts (stamens or pistils), it is said to be imperfect. This terminology can be somewhat confusing. For example, flowers that have both stamens and pistils but lack petals or sepals are described as perfect incomplete flowers. Imperfect flowers can be either male or female. If both male and female flowers occur on the same plant, the plant is said to be monoecious; if male and female flowers are on separate plants, the species is dioecious. Corn is a monoecious plant, with its tassels (stamens) at the top and its ears (pistils) on the stem below. Cottonwoods are dioecious—the male trees produce pollen, and the female trees produce seeds.

In most angiosperms, pollen is transferred by insects, but in some major groups, pollen is transferred by the

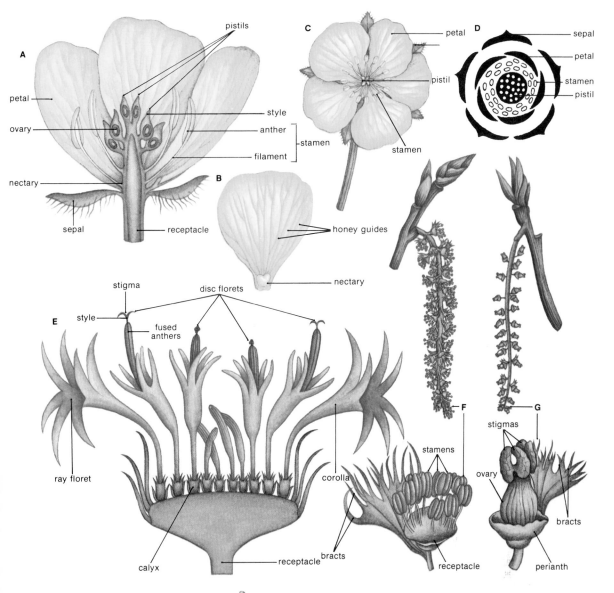

A

petal

pistils

ovary

style

anther

filament

stamen

nectary

sepal

receptacle

B

honey guides

nectary

C

petal

pistil

stamen

D

sepal

petal

stamen

pistil

E

stigma

style

disc florets

fused anthers

ray floret

corolla

calyx

receptacle

bracts

F

stamens

receptacle

G

stigmas

ovary

bracts

perianth

(Above) *Flowers contain the reproductive organs of angiosperms. Some plants have flowers with both male and female appendages and are known as perfect flowers. Others have separate, or imperfect, male and female flowers. As indicated in this cross section, buttercups (A) have perfect flowers. The pistil, or female reproductive structure, includes the stigma, style, and ovary. The stamen, or male structure, comprises the filament and anther. The sepals, collectively, form the calyx, and the petals form the corolla. Each petal (B) is marked by honey guides, radiating lines that lead insects to the nectary. The arrangement of the various floral parts is shown in a top view (C) and is represented by a floral diagram (D). Plants in the composite family, such as the cornflower (E), have flowers that consist of two types of florets. The outer ray florets are sterile; the disk flowers contain fertile reproductive organs. Other angiosperms, such as the black poplar, are dioecious; catkins of male (F) and female (G) flowers grow on separate trees. (Left) Various flowers are adapted to different types of pollination. Buttercups (A) are nonspecialized; they are pollinated by a number of insects. Gorse (B) is specialized for bee pollination. Flowers of this type have brightly colored petals, and their nectaries are accessible only to specialized organs. Hibiscus species (C) are adapted for bird pollination; hummingbirds are among the principal bird pollinators. Hazel (D), like most trees, is wind pollinated. Its flowers hang in long, thin catkins.*

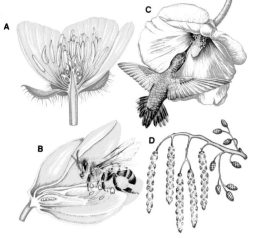

A

B

C

D

wind. Insect-pollinated flowers often have rather showy corollas. These are sometimes modified in ways that ensure the dusting of pollen onto the insects as they penetrate the flowers in search of nectar. The dusted insects transfer the pollen to the stigma of the next flower they enter. Flowers pollinated by moths, hummingbirds, or bats may have specialized corollas that match the appropriate organs of the animals seeking the nectar.

Some species of flowers that are pollinated by the wind are not at all showy. Often the anthers of these flowers are suspended on long filaments so that the pollen dusts freely into the wind, and the pollen grains may be winged, which allows them to be carried more easily on the breezes. Styles and stigmas may also extend some distance from the flower; these catch the blowing pollen. Sepals and petals may be either absent or quite small. Grasses are wind-pollinated, as are many trees—for example, maples, oaks, and walnuts.

Flower Arrangement on the Plant

A group of flowers on a plant is called an inflorescence. A great variety of inflorescences occur among the angiosperms. The simplest is a single, solitary flower at the end of a stem, with leaves at the base. It is rare for an entire plant to have a single flower, as is true of the tulip; but a solitary, terminal flower at the end of the main stem, with axillary flowers in the angles between leaves and stems, is common.

The common sunflower (A) *has an inflorescence consisting of many smaller flowers, or florets, that act as one large flower. This flower head, borne on a receptacle* (1), *includes outer ray florets* (2) *and inner disk florets* (3). *Pappus scales* (4), *or modified sepals, separate the florets. The disk florets consist of a fused corolla* (5) *enclosing fused male anthers* (6) *and a female stigma* (7), *which is connected by the style to the ovary. The structure of the ray florets is similar, but the corolla* (8) *is greatly expanded.*

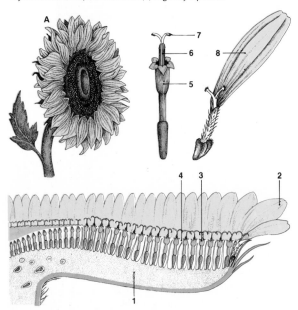

A number of flowers radiating along a single stem, sometimes with modified leaves (bracts) at the base of the peduncles, is a raceme. Most racemes are indeterminate, meaning that the youngest flowers are at the tip of the stem in the center of the raceme. A spike occurs when the flowers in the raceme are attached closely to the main stem. For example, a head of wheat is spiked, as are virtually all grass flowers. A compound raceme with several branching stems, each forming a raceme, is called a panicle. In a few species, the oldest flowers may occur near the stem tips of a raceme or panicle; this structure is a cyme. When all the peduncles of several flowers in an inflorescence radiate from the same point, they form a flat-topped, or sometimes rounded, umbel.

Flowers densely packed together on short peduncles and a short main axis form a head; clover is an example of this formation. The most common flower heads occur in the large sunflower, family Compositae. In a sunflower or daisy, two kinds of flowers occur in the head: ray or strap flowers, which consist of one long petal with an ovary and sometimes stamens; and disk flowers, which consist of five greatly reduced, radially symmetrical petals at the tips of a corolla tube, plus an ovary and usually stamens. The sepals in a composite flower head may have been modified to form filaments, such as the parachute on a dandelion seed. Two other special inflorescences are the catkins, rather loose, hanging spikes of flowers; and the spadices, which are spikes of male flowers above female flowers surrounded by large, sometimes colored leaves called spathes. Catkins occur on birch and other trees; spadices can be seen on calla lily and jack-in-the-pulpit.

The Seed and the Fruit

The products of the flower are the seed and the fruit. The seed is the mature ovule. It includes a minute embryonic plant and, almost always, stored food that will supply the seedling when it begins to grow after sprouting, or germination. In a restricted botanical sense, the fruit is the mature ovary wall, but often food is stored in accessory tissues besides the ovary wall (SEE FRUITS AND FRUIT CULTIVATION).

Flowering Time

Some plants, called annuals, germinate from seed and then flower and die within one year. Winter annuals may germinate in late autumn, live through the winter as slow-growing seedlings under the snow, and grow and flower in spring or early summer. Many cereals are winter annuals, but often a single species has winter-annual and spring-annual varieties, as is the case with barley, rye, and wheat. Biennials typically germinate in the spring, grow as a rosette—a circle of leaves close to the ground, as in beet or dandelion—during the first summer, and send up a flowering shoot during the second season. Perennials, which grow and flower for several seasons, are called polycarpic. Monocarpic plants are those which flower only once and then die. These include annuals and biennials but also a few species such as bamboo and the century plant, agave, that grow for several years, flower once, and then die.

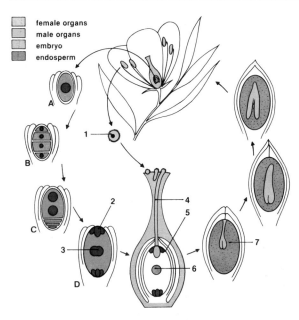

Pollen grains (1), the male sex cells, develop within the anther. Female sex cells develop within the ovule by a process of cell division (A–C) that produces an embryo sac (D) containing the egg (2) and a large cell with two polar nuclei (3). The pollen grain adheres to the stigma and sends a pollen tube (4) into the ovule. Two sperm nuclei pass through the tube; one fertilizes the egg (5), and the other fuses with the polar nuclei (6) to form the endosperm. The ovule becomes the seed. The endosperm supplies food for the embryo (7).

How Flowers Form

Although a vast body of descriptive data is available on plant development, many problems remain unsolved. It is apparent, however, that a precise schedule for development is followed, and the role of genetic material in determining this process is acknowledged.

A plant stem grows by the division of a group of cells near the tip of the stem. Regions of active cell division and growth in plants are called meristems. At some time during the life of the plant, the meristems at the stem tips or in the lateral buds stop producing stems and leaves and produce flowers instead. Frequently this occurs in response to environmental changes, especially in temperature and light conditions.

Temperature and Light. Winter annuals and biennials form flowers in response to the low temperatures of winter. Many species of plants are induced to flower by several days to weeks of temperatures close to or just above the freezing point of water. The flowering of summer vegetables is promoted by a brief exposure to lower temperatures; a few perennials also respond this way.

Light also variously affects flowering plants. A few species seem to flower in response to increased light intensity; others respond to lower intensities. Most species, however, respond not to the intensity of light but to its duration, or to the duration of the dark period, or to a combination of both.

In 1920 two U.S. scientists, W. W. Garner and H. A. Allard, reported that tobacco plants remained vegetative in the fields during the summer but flowered profusely in the winter greenhouse. They tested several different environmental factors, one of which was the length of day. When their test plants were placed in cabinets in midsummer at about 4:00 PM and removed at 8:00 AM the next morning, the plants flowered profusely, just as they had in the winter greenhouses.

Garner and Allard found that several species responded to short days (or, as later studies would suggest, long nights), and they called these short-day plants. Examples are cocklebur, chrysanthemum, poinsettia, and morning glory. Other species responded in an exactly opposite way: when the days got longer, they would begin to bloom. These were called long-day plants. Beet, dill, Darnel ryegrass, spinach, henbane, radish, a tobacco species, and various cereals are good examples. The flowering time of a few species such as tomato, cucumber, globe amaranth, sunflower, a tobacco species, and garden pea seems to be unaffected by day length, although the number or size of flowers or fruit set may be influenced strongly. Garner and Allard called this phenomenon, which demonstrates the effect of light on plants, photoperiodism.

Photoperiodism. In the 1930s, in the USSR, Mikhail Chailakhyan noted that the leaf was the part of the plant that responded to the length of day or night. If the leaf of a short-day plant is covered with a black bag, for example, the plant will flower, even though the stems and the buds (which will become flowers) remain under long-day conditions. Long-day plants will not flower when their leaves

Studies of photoperiodism indicate that plants respond to periods of darkness rather than light. A short-day plant, such as cocklebur, needs a minimum period of uninterrupted darkness to induce flowering; it will not bloom if the darkness is interrupted even briefly. A long-day plant, such as spinach, will not flower when given 16 hours of darkness, but will flower if this period is interrupted.

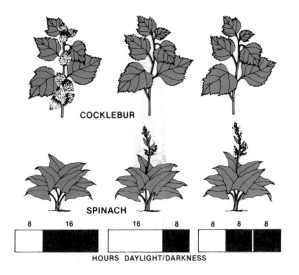

COCKLEBUR

SPINACH

HOURS DAYLIGHT/DARKNESS

are covered with a black covering long enough to give the leaf only short-day conditions. It appears that the leaf detects the day length and sends a signal to the bud where flowers actually form. It is conceivable that this signal is an electrical, or nervous, impulse, but it seems much more likely that it is a chemical substance, or hormone.

In 1938, Karl Hamner and James Bonner showed that interrupting a long dark period with light causes plants to respond as though they were experiencing long days instead of short days. The discovery of the night-interruption phenomenon led to further research, the results of which have allowed a greater understanding of the particulars of this phenomenon. For example, it was discovered that the intensity of light required to produce this effect varies from species to species.

Individual species also have specific requirements for a minimum light or dark period. For example, cocklebur, a short-day plant, requires a minimum of about 8.5 hours of darkness to induce flowering. When these plants are given 16 hours of darkness, a period of time that normally induces a high level of flowering, they are most strongly inhibited by a light interruption given at about 8.5 hours.

Orange-red wavelengths are the most effective in producing the night-interruption phenomenon. Furthermore, it was discovered in the early 1950s that the effects of a night interruption with orange-red light could be almost completely reversed if the exposure was followed by a second exposure to far-red wavelengths (wavelengths as long as the human eye can detect). Thus, if a cocklebur plant is given a 16-hour dark period that is interrupted after 8 hours with orange-red light, it remains vegetative. If the interruption with orange-red light is immediately followed by an exposure to far-red illumination, the plant flowers; effects of the red light are nullified by far-red light.

It was soon found that many plant responses follow part of the same pattern. For example, if lettuce seeds are allowed to absorb water and are then exposed to orange-red light, they germinate; if the exposure to orange-red is followed by an exposure to far-red light, they do not. Orange-red light also causes dark-grown stems to stop elongating, leaves to expand, hooks on seedlings to unfold, apple skins to turn red, and other phenomena to occur. In each of these cases, subsequent exposure to far-red light reverses the orange-red effect.

It was postulated that a plant pigment exists that is converted from one form to another by orange-red light and back to the original form by far-red light. This pigment was called phytochrome, and in 1959 it was first extracted from plant tissues. It proved to be a protein, one of the most important pigments in the plant kingdom. Phytochrome seems to be the means by which the plant "knows" whether it is in the light or the dark. Most light sources, including sunlight, act primarily as orange-red sources. Time measurement, however, consists of much more than phytochrome.

The Classification of Flowering Plants

Plant taxonomists classify angiosperms into two groups: the Monocotyledoneae and the Dicotyledoneae, usually called monocots and dicots. (See COTYLEDON.) Examples of the

Monocots, such as the autumn crocus (A), have only one cotyledon (1), or seed leaf, in the embryo; most monocots have parallel-veined leaves (2). Dicots, including the creeping buttercup (B), have two cotyledons (3); most dicots have net-veined leaves (4).

monocots are lilies, rushes, sedges, grasses, irises, orchids, and palm trees. Examples of dicots are honeysuckles, sunflowers, buttercups, roses, most deciduous broad-leaved trees (all but ginkgo), mustards, mallows, primroses, phloxes, snapdragons, mints, goosefoots, and geraniums.

Monocots are characterized especially by having only one cotyledon as part of the embryo in the seed; the dicots have two cotyledons. The veins in a monocot leaf are typically parallel; those in a dicot leaf typically form a network. Monocot flower parts usually occur in threes; dicot flower parts occur in twos, fours, or usually fives. Monocot stems have their vascular bundles (groups of transporting cells) enclosed in a sheath of cells and scattered in a pith tissue; dicot stems have vascular bundles arranged in a ring, and often there is a cambium that allows the stem to become thicker in diameter from year to year. Monocot stems, even palm trees, do not grow in thickness from year to year.

Taxonomists disagree as to whether the angiosperms should be considered a division, a class, or a subclass (see CLASSIFICATION, BIOLOGICAL). A few taxonomists consider the dicots and the monocots to represent classes (if the angiosperms form a division), but most taxonomists call the dicots and the monocots subclasses. All taxonomists agree, however, that the monocots and dicots form logical groups within the angiosperms. There is also general agreement about the arrangement of monocot orders.

The question of how to arrange dicot orders is not entirely resolved. Two systems exist. One of these assumes that petal structure is especially important. Those plants having united petals would form one major group within the dicots; plants with separate petals would form another group. The second system assumes that ovary position is the most important criterion. Those dicots having superior ovaries would form one evolutionary sequence, while those orders with inferior ovaries would form another line.

See also: ALTERATION OF GENERATIONS; BOTANY; EVOLUTION; HOUSEPLANTS; PLANT PROPAGATION.

Flowers of Evil, The   see BAUDELAIRE, CHARLES

Floyd, Carlisle   Carlisle Floyd, b. Latta, S.C., June 12, 1926, is a composer best known for his operas, particularly *Susannah*. He studied composition with Ernst Bacon at Syracuse University and taught at Florida State University from 1947 to 1977. *Susannah*, based on a libretto by Floyd, won the New York Music Critics Circle citation as the best new opera produced in New York in 1956. Among Floyd's other operas are *Wuthering Heights* (1958), based on the novel by Emily Brontë, *Of Mice and Men* (1970), after the novel by John Steinbeck, and *Willie Stark* (1983), from Robert Penn Warren's novel *All the King's Men*.

Floyd, John Buchanan   John Buchanan Floyd, b. Montgomery County, Va., June 1, 1806, d. Aug. 26, 1863, was President James Buchanan's secretary of war (1857–60) on the eve of the U.S. Civil War. He was accused of transferring funds and weapons to the South, but the charges were never proved. He resigned when Buchanan refused to evacuate federal troops from Fort Sumter, which Floyd said had been occupied on Dec. 26, 1860, against War Department orders. Floyd served as a Confederate brigadier general at Fort Donelson and fled (February 1862) just before the fort fell to Ulysses S. Grant.

Floyd, Pretty Boy   The American gangster Charles Arthur "Pretty Boy" Floyd, b. Akins, Okla., 1901, d. Oct. 22, 1934, robbed many midwestern banks and allegedly killed ten people. The ruggedly handsome Floyd, branded "Public Enemy No. 1," was killed by FBI agents. A folk hero in Oklahoma, he was mentioned sympathetically in John Steinbeck's *Grapes of Wrath*.

flu   see INFLUENZA

---

flügelhorn   [flue'-gul-hohrn]   The flügelhorn is a member of the BUGLE family of wind instruments that in-

The flügelhorn, a brass wind instrument, was first made in Austria between 1820 and 1830. The three-valved B-flat soprano flügelhorn is the most popular.

cludes the baritone, euphonium, and bass TUBA. It is comparable to the CORNET in size and pitch, but it has a larger bore and bell and a mellower tone. The flügelhorn is not often used in American BANDS, but it is regularly used in England and continental Europe. Ottorino Respighi wrote for it in *The Pines of Rome* to simulate the sound of ancient Roman instruments.

---

fluid mechanics   Fluid mechanics, or hydrodynamics, is the study of the effect of forces on fluids (liquids or gases) at rest or in motion. Although the basic laws of conservation of mass, momentum, and energy hold for fluids just as they do for solids, they exhibit a different mathematical form. The study of fluid mechanics is therefore considered a separate field from that of solid mechanics or the mechanics of particles and rigid bodies. The field of fluid mechanics can be further divided into hydrostatics (fluids at rest), hydraulics (liquids in motion in channels and pipes; see HYDRAULIC SYSTEMS), AERODYNAMICS (the flow of gases), gas dynamics (flow of gases when compressibility is significant), and MAGNETOHYDRODYNAMICS (flow of ionized gases).

Development of Fluid Mechanics

Rational fluid mechanics is thought to have begun with ARCHIMEDES, who in the 3d century BC stated his law of buoyancy. Nothing further was accomplished in the field until 1605, when Simon STEVIN published his *Hydrostatics*. In 1644, Evangelista TORRICELLI stated his law of efflux, and in 1663, Blaise Pascal rediscovered Stevin's laws. Twenty-five years later, Sir Isaac NEWTON summed up all of fluid mechanics as it was known at that time in book 2 of his *Principia* and added some original ideas, including his hypothesis of viscosity.

The basic laws of ideal, frictionless fluids were finally given mathematical form by Leonhard EULER in 1755. Euler based his work in part on earlier work by Daniel and Jacques BERNOULLI. In 1827, Claude Navier derived the equations of viscous flow, which were published by Sir George Gabriel Stokes in 1845. Today solutions of the Euler equations, with corrections developed early in the 20th century by Ludwig Prandtl and Theodore von KÁRMÁN, are used to describe the flight of aircraft and spacecraft; to calculate flow past ships, trains, automobiles, and such stationary structures as buildings and bridges; and to describe the flow in pumps, turbines, and chemical-processing plants. They are also used to describe the motion of the atmosphere and the oceans, the flow in channels and pipes and over dams, and the flow of ionized gases (plasmas).

Properties of Fluids

The distinguishing feature of a fluid, in contrast to a solid, is the ease with which the fluid may be deformed. If a shearing force, however small, is applied to a fluid, the fluid will move and continue to move as long as the shear acts on it. For example, the force of gravity causes water poured from a pitcher to flow; it will continue to flow as long as the pitcher is tilted. If the pitcher is turned back up the flow ceases because the gravitational force is then exactly balanced by the pressure force of the pitcher wall.

Unlike liquids, gases cannot be poured from one open container into another, but they, too, deform under shear stress. Because shear stresses result from relative motion, they are equivalent whether the fluid flows past a stationary object or the object moves through the fluid.

Even though a fluid can deform easily under an applied force, the fluid's viscosity creates resistance to this force. The VISCOSITY of gases, which is much less than that of liquids, increases slightly as the temperature increases, whereas that of liquids decreases when the temperature increases. Highly viscous liquids are more properly the subject of the study of rheology; fluid mechanics is primarily concerned with Newtonian fluids, or those in which stress, viscosity, and rate of strain are linearly related.

Hydrostatics—Fluids at Rest

When a fluid is at rest or in equilibrium with the forces acting on it, motion does not have to be considered. Hydrostatics is a special case of how fluids at rest are affected by pressure exerted by external forces, such as the atmosphere or a piston and the body force due to gravity. The gravity force exhibits its effect in the increase in pressure with depth due to the weight of the fluid above the point of observation. Thus the increase in pressure p with depth h below the free surface is equal to the specific weight w times h or $\Delta p = p - p_0 = wh$, where p_0 is the pressure at the surface. PASCAL'S LAW states that in a fluid at rest the pressure on a surface is independent of the orientation of the surface.

Fluid Flow—Real Fluids

The equations governing the flow of real fluids are complex; in the case of turbulent flow, they are not completely known. Laminar flow is described by the Navier-Stokes equations, for which solutions can be obtained only in simple cases that nevertheless are of great importance in understanding fluid flow. Approximate solutions in more complex situations can be obtained by using large digital computers.

If the velocity of the flow increases, the flow becomes unstable, and transition from laminar to turbulent flow takes place. The fluid particles begin to flow in highly irregular paths. Eddies form and transfer momentum over distances varying from a few millimeters, as in controlled laboratory experiments, to several meters, as in a large room, around the exterior of buildings or other structures, and in the oceans or the atmosphere. Accordingly, the equations of turbulent flow are more complex; for any solution they require empirical relations obtained from carefully controlled experiments.

The key physical process in the flow of real fluids is the conversion of mechanical energy into heat that is the result of viscosity in laminar or turbulent flow. Many practical problems in flow through pipes and channels have been solved by using simple empirical laws that embody a friction factor and that account for energy loss.

fluidized bed combustion   Fluidized bed combustion (FBC) is a technique for efficiently producing heat from such low-grade fuels as high-sulfur coal and coal waste or agricultural and municipal wastes. Air is blown into a bed of fine sand (causing the sand to churn almost like a boiling fluid), the bed is heated red hot by the injection and ignition of a start-up gas, and the chopped or ground fuel is slowly fed in. The emission of the gaseous pollutants produced by conventional fuel burning is eliminated in FBC installations. When limestone is mixed with the coal, sulfur dioxide is removed in the form of calcium sulfate solids; and because FBC furnaces operate at lower temperatures than other types, they emit far less nitrogen oxide. Although FBC technology is not yet at the commercial stage, small-scale projects have been successful.

fluke   A fluke is a parasitic flatworm of the class Trematoda. The one-piece body is shaped like a simple leaf, usually with the mouth at the anterior end. One or more suckers enable the fluke to hold to its host, and a muscular pharynx is used to suck in tissues or body fluids. Eggs are deposited in the host's organ or in tissues where the mature worms reside; they reach the outside by way of the feces.

Some flukes attack only one kind of fish, amphibian, or reptile and live externally or in its mouth cavity or urinary bladder. Most flukes are internal parasites, living in the lungs, digestive tract, or blood vessels of some vertebrate animal, but have developmental stages in one or more invertebrate animals such as snails or crustaceans. The vertebrate host becomes infected either by eating the invertebrate host or by direct invasion by immature flukes. Sexual reproduction of the parasite occurs in the vertebrate host, and asexual reproduction may take place in the invertebrate host.

fluorescence   [flohr'-es-ens]   Fluorescence is a phenomenon in which certain substances emit light when stimulated by other radiation, notably ultraviolet light. The atoms or molecules of the fluorescent substance are raised to an excited state by the absorption of the incident radiation and then return to their original state by reemitting light. The process is characterized by relatively prompt emission, occurring within about 10^{-8} seconds after excitation. If the atoms or molecules remain in the excited state for longer periods, the phenomenon is called PHOSPHORESCENCE.

Fluorescent emission is of a longer wavelength than the excitation radiation in those instances in which single-quantum photoabsorption is the rule. Laser technology has made multiple-quantum photoabsorption processes practical, however, and this can result in fluorescent emission at shorter wavelengths than the incident laser source.

Fluorescence can be exhibited by substances in solid, liquid, or gaseous states. Many minerals display vivid colors when irradiated with ultraviolet light. For gases, fluorescent emission occurs with high efficiency only when the incident light is at or near the resonant wavelength for the absorption transition. Ultraviolet light is not the only common source of excitation radiation. Electron bombardment serves as such a source in cathode-ray tubes, which include television screens. Scintillation counters use phosphors that emit light as a result of α, β, or γ radiation.

A recent application of fluorescent emission in the laser field involves certain organic dyes, such as rhodamine. These dyes are efficient sources of tunable laser oscillation when excited by other lasers operating at fixed wavelengths.

---

fluorescent light A fluorescent light is a highly efficient light source that uses a mercury arc and a fluorescent phosphor coating inside its tube. It is most widely used in factories, offices, stores, and schools. The principles of the fluorescent lamp have been known since the 1860s. The French physicist A. H. BECQUEREL made a primitive fluorescent lamp in 1867, and many other inventors, including Thomas Edison, experimented with fluorescence. The fluorescent lamp did not become practical, however, until about 1939.

The mercury arc in a fluorescent lamp operates between two heated coils called cathodes. Much of the arc's energy is emitted in the invisible ultraviolet range, but the phosphor coating in the tube converts it to visible wavelengths. Different phosphors can produce a range of colors varying from cool to warm.

Fluorescent lamps lack the flexibility of incandescent lamps in that wattage cannot be changed simply by removing one lamp and putting in another. Since the resistance of a mercury arc decreases as current increases, the current would destroy the lamp if not controlled. Therefore a ballast must be used to limit the current and—for most sizes—to increase the voltage for reliable starting and stable operation. Each lamp size requires a different ballast.

The great advantages of a fluorescent light are its high light output per watt and its long life. A 40-watt fluorescent lamp produces more than 70 lumens per watt and lasts 15,000–20,000 hours. By contrast, a 40-watt incandescent lamp produces only 12 lumens per watt and has a rated average life of 1,500 hours. Recently developed tubes are compact (as small as 6 in. in length) and can be used with rapid-start ballasts, which allow quick lamp starting.

See also: LIGHTING DEVICES.

---

fluoridation Fluoridation is the process of adding fluoride to water supplies as a preventive measure against tooth decay (see TEETH). Fluorides—that is, ions of the element fluorine—occur naturally in many waters, often to the extent of 0.1 to 0.2 parts per million (ppm) but sometimes in excess of 4 ppm. U.S. Public Health Service (PHS) studies in the 1930s and 1940s indicated a

correlation between higher fluoride concentrations and lower rates of tooth decay. Experimental programs involving artificial fluoridation at selected sites were devised to test this possibility, but before completion of the programs the PHS officially endorsed fluoridation in 1950. Since then, water supplies for about 50% of the U.S. population have come to be fluoridated, with similar or even higher percentages in Canada, Ireland, Australia, and New Zealand. Great Britain and the Soviet Union fluoridate water supplies for less than 20% of their populations, however, and most countries of Western Europe no longer fluoridate their water at all.

Fluoridation continues to be endorsed by the PHS, but it has long been a source of controversy. Scientists who question the practice do so on the basis that insufficient research has been done on the possible adverse effects of fluoride on some segments of the population. They also suggest that statistical support for fluoridation needs careful reexamination.

---

fluorine Fluorine is a pale yellow, poisonous, highly corrosive gas. It is the lightest member of the HALOGENS, Group VIIA of the periodic table, and the most reactive of all elements. Its symbol is F, its atomic weight is 18.99840, and its atomic number is 9. The name *fluorine* is derived from the mineral fluorspar, CaF_2, which, in turn, is derived from the Latin *fluo* ("flow"), because until AD 1500 it was used as a flux in metallurgy.

Discovery

By 1670 the German scientist Heinrich Schwanhard had discovered that glass can be etched by fluorspar treated with a strong acid. This treatment generates hydrofluoric acid, HF, a highly corrosive acid still used for etching glass. Although Carl S. Scheele of Sweden is often credited with the discovery of hydrofluoric acid, it seems apparent that he and most of his contemporaries believed that the acid is an integral part of the fluorspar, not realizing the significance of adding a strong acid when activating the mineral. The true nature of the acid did not begin to emerge until early in the 19th century. Unsuccessful attempts to separate and characterize the unknown element by the electrolysis of fluorspar were made by Edmond Frémy in France and George Gore in England, among others. Success came in 1886 when Henri Moissan, a student of Frémy, used a solution of potassium acid fluoride, KHF_2, in anhydrous hydrofluoric acid as the electrolyte.

Natural Occurrence

On the Earth, fluorine is widely distributed among natural compounds, but its extreme reactivity precludes its presence in elemental form. Although constituting only 0.065 percent of the Earth's crust, fluorine is found in oceans, lakes, rivers, and all other forms of natural water; in the bones, teeth, and blood of all mammals; and in all plants and plant parts. In spite of its ubiquity, as yet no universally acceptable evidence exists that fluorine is a necessary ingredient of living beings. Fluorine is found most abundantly in nature as the minerals fluorspar (FLUORITE, CaF_2), CRYOLITE (Na_3AlF_6), and fluorapatite ($CaF_2 \cdot 3Ca_3[PO_4]_2$).

Properties

Fluorine exists as a diatomic gas, F_2. Highly toxic, it has a characteristic pungent odor that can be detected before hazardous concentrations build up. Fluorine boils at $-188°$ C, and its melting point is $-219°$ C.

Only one stable isotope of fluorine occurs, ^{19}F. The fluorine atom has seven electrons in its outer shell and requires an additional electron for maximum stability. This electron is strongly attracted by the positively charged nucleus because of the small size of the fluorine atom, accounting for the extreme electronegativity of the element. As a result, fluorine has a valence of -1 and forms compounds with all elements except the noble gases helium, neon, and argon. Fluorine salts are called fluorides.

Fluorine is manufactured by electrolyzing a mixture of potassium fluoride and hydrogen fluoride. It is stored and shipped in containers lined with TEFLON or made of a special steel. The latter becomes coated with iron fluoride, thus retarding further reaction.

The Fluorine Industry

The earliest large-scale commercial use of fluorine-containing compounds was probably the result of the work of General Motors Corporation chemists Thomas Midgley and Albert Henne, who, in the 1920s, set out to develop a refrigerant that did not have the drawbacks of those used at the time. The result was a chlorofluorocarbon, dichlorodifluoromethane, CCl_2F_2, now called FREON-12. It is nonflammable, noncorrosive, and nontoxic; it liquefies easily and boils at a low temperature ($-29.8°$ C). The use of chlorofluorocarbons was rapidly expanded into the field of AEROSOL propellants. Their use declined after 1977, however, when it was found that they deplete the ozone in the upper atmosphere, and several nations have proposed banning their use as propellants and refrigerants by the end of the 20th century (see OZONE LAYER).

The fluorochemical industry actually began in the United States about 1940, when the Du Pont Company developed a polymer of a tetrafluoroethylene, Teflon. The introduction of this product resulted in a dramatic increase in fluorine requirements (see PLASTICS). Use of gaseous diffusion of uranium hexafluoride to concentrate uranium isotopes for the manufacture of nuclear weapons further increased the demand for fluorine.

Uses and Compounds

In addition to its use in uranium processing, refrigerants, and aerosol propellants, fluorine is used in dentifrices, as a catalyst in producing the dodecylbenzene used to make detergents, and in polyfluorohydrocarbons such as Teflon, noted for their nonstick properties and resistance to corrosion.

Sodium fluoride, NaF, is used as a sterilant, an insecticide, and a water-treatment agent in fluoridating municipal supplies. It is also a paint preservative, it renders

enamels opaque, and it is used in dyes and in the primary-metal and ceramics industries. Boron trifluoride is a catalyst in the alkylation of benzene for detergent production and in the manufacture of polymers and copolymers for adhesives.

Other chemically important compounds of fluorine are antimony trifluoride (SbF_3), an organic chemistry catalyst; and sulfur hexafluoride (SF_6), a gaseous insulator. Fluorine compounds are of interest whenever incombustibility or oil and water resistance are important.

---

fluorite [flohr'-yt]　Fluorite, calcium fluoride, CaF_2, is a major industrial mineral used as a flux in steel making as well as in the preparation of hydrofluoric acid and, in the ceramics industry, in glasses and enamels. Fluorite's vitreous, cubic crystals (isometric system) and cleavable, granular masses have a wide color range (often green, blue, or purple) and may fluoresce under ULTRAVIOLET LIGHT. Hardness is 4, specific gravity 3.0–3.3. Fluorite forms under a wide variety of conditions: as a VEIN DEPOSIT produced by hydrothermal alteration, as beds and GEODES in sedimentary rocks, in HOT SPRING deposits, and in PEGMATITES.

See also: FLUORESCENCE.

Fluorite is a widely distributed, brittle, transparent-to-translucent calcium fluoride mineral of great industrial importance. Impurities cause fluorite, colorless or white when pure, to vary widely in color.

---

fluorocarbon [flohr'-oh-kahr-buhn]　A fluorocarbon is an organic chemical that has one or more fluorine atoms. More than 100 fluorocarbons have been classified, and because a hydrogen atom in any hydrocarbon may be substituted by a FLUORINE atom, the list of potential fluorocarbons is virtually endless. Fully substituted fluorocarbons are called perfluorocarbons and are chemically inert, nontoxic, odorless, and nonflammable.

The FREON group of fluorocarbons includes Freon-11 (CCl_3F), used as an aerosol propellant, and Freon-12 (CCl_2F_2), a commonly used refrigerant. Freon is now thought to contribute to atmospheric OZONE LAYER depletion, which causes the Earth's surface to be exposed to excessive ultraviolet radiation. Although this has not been fully proven yet, the use of fluorocarbons as aerosol propellants has been in decline since the mid-1970s. In 1988 the Du Pont Company and the Dow Chemical Company, major producers of fluorocarbons, agreed to phase out fluorocarbon production.

Tetrafluoroethylene ($CF_2{=}CF_2$) can be polymerized by a free-radical agent to form Teflon, and Fluothane ($CF_3CHCIBr$) is used as an anesthetic.

fluoroscope The fluoroscope is an instrument designed to allow observation of the internal structure of an opaque body by using X RAYS. In industry it is used to detect flaws in materials and devices. In medicine it is used to view the internal organs of the human body. A fluoroscope consists of an X-ray source and a fluorescent screen. The patient is placed between the source and the screen so that the X rays pass through the patient's body. When they strike the fluorescent screen, they produce visible light by the process of FLUORESCENCE. The intensity of the light produced depends on the nature of the tissue through which the X rays must travel. For example, bone effectively blocks X rays and produces a dark shadow on the screen. An advantage of the fluoroscope is that it allows a physician to view organs in motion, instead of "frozen," as they are in an ordinary X-ray photograph. The photograph, however, gives better clarity. A problem in fluoroscopy is that it requires a large dose of X rays, which may be hazardous to both the patient and the operator. By the use of image intensifiers it is possible to reduce this dosage. Such a procedure has almost completely replaced the standard fluoroscope.

See also: RADIOGRAPHY; RADIOLOGY.

flute The flute is a woodwind instrument that dates from ancient times. Sound is produced from a flute by blowing onto a sharp edge, causing air enclosed in a tube to vibrate. In tropical regions and in the Orient flutes are commonly made from bamboo tubes. End-blown flutes may be simple tubes with a sharp edge or notch, or they may have an inserted block, as in RECORDERS and whistles. The widespread side-blown or transverse flute is now common in the West.

About 1670 the transverse flute began to be made in three sections—the cylindrical head joint, the middle joint, and the foot joint with inverse conical bore—and had six finger holes plus one closed key. It was usually constructed of boxwood, the joints and ends strengthened by decorative ivory rings. The instrument's lovely, mellow tone inspired a large solo literature. Chromatic notes (sharped and flatted tones) were nevertheless difficult to play in tune in tonalities other than D Major and those closely related. The addition of more keys solved some of these problems.

Theobald Böhm experimented with the flute from 1832 to 1847, desiring to give it a bigger tone. He finally produced a modern flute with a parabolic (bowl-shaped)

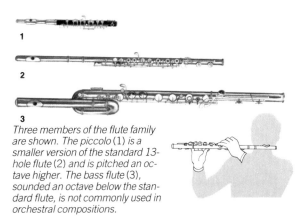

Three members of the flute family are shown. The piccolo (1) is a smaller version of the standard 13-hole flute (2) and is pitched an octave higher. The bass flute (3), sounded an octave below the standard flute, is not commonly used in orchestral compositions.

head joint attached to a cylindrical body with open-standing keys and finger pads to cover large finger holes. The modern flute has a range from middle B^b upward for about three octaves. The basic instrument (without B^b key) is approximately 66 cm (26 in) long. In Europe flutes are often constructed of wood; silver is commonly used in the United States.

Other orchestral flutes are the PICCOLO, a brilliant instrument pitched an octave higher than the standard flute, and the alto flute, pitched a fourth lower than the standard instrument. The rare bass flute, pitched an octave below the standard instrument, is not a regular member of the orchestra.

fly Fly is the common name for insects of the order Diptera, or true flies, which includes the small HOUSEFLY, FRUIT FLY, MOSQUITO, gnat, midge, blowfly, and botfly, and the nearly 2.5-cm-long (1-in) DEERFLY, HORSEFLY, and crane fly.

The term *fly* is applied to such non-Diptera as the butterfly, dragonfly, mayfly, and stone fly. Unlike these and other insects, true flies have a single pair of membranous fore-wings, with knob-shaped vestigial wings instead of hind wings. The vestigial wings, called halteres, are used as balancing organs.

The mouthparts are specialized for lapping or sucking in some flies and for piercing and sucking in others. Almost all species have antennae and large compound eyes. A network of thick veins strengthens the wings; the pattern of these venations is used for identification and classification. One theory is that the veins evolved from tracheae, a system of tubes common in insects that supplies oxygen to the tissues.

All flies develop through metamorphosis in four stages: egg, larva, pupa, and adult. The larvae, called maggots, lack eyes, legs, wings, antennae, and distinct mouthparts and body regions. The pupa is defenseless but generally escapes predators because it is dark brown and buried in soil or heaps of waste.

Flies and Disease. Some of the most serious diseases among humans—DENGUE FEVER, viral ENCEPHALITIS, FILARIASIS, MALARIA, and YELLOW FEVER—are transmitted by mos-

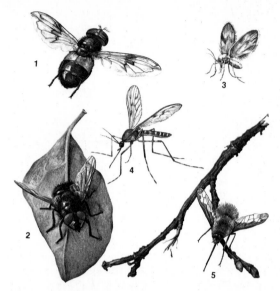

Dipterans, or true flies, belong to the fourth largest order of insects. They possess one pair of functional wings and one pair of modified, knoblike wings that maintain equilibrium during flight. Common flies include the hover fly (1), family Syrphidae; the blowfly (2), family Calliphoridae; the moth fly (3), family Psychodidae; the mosquito (4), family Culicidae; and the bee fly (5), family Bombylidae.

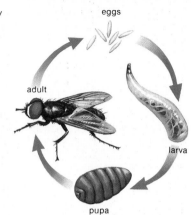

The life cycle of a housefly is typical of all true flies and consists of four stages: egg, larva, pupa, and adult. An adult female lays 100 to 160 eggs at a time, usually in decaying organic matter. Each egg, 1 mm (0.04 in) long, hatches into a larva in 12 to 24 hours. After several days the larva changes into a pupa, which is encased in a tough shell. In 3 to 5 days a full-sized adult fly emerges. During warm weather, it will live about 1 month.

quitoes. Many hundreds of thousands of people living along Africa's rivers are permanently blinded by small roundworms introduced by the bite of the blackfly.

In much of the world today, poor sanitation, domestic flies, and intestinal diseases are constant and related problems. In Latin America, Africa, and India, blowflies and houseflies are especially abundant; they shuttle between feces and human food, carrying the agents of CHOLERA, DYSENTERY, diarrheal disease, and gastroenteritis. Some species prefer the eye and transfer the microbes of

pinkeye, CONJUNCTIVITIS, and TRACHOMA from diseased to healthy eyes; others spread yaws, a skin disease, when they feed on cuts and sores.

Some adult flies are harmless but deposit their eggs in wounds or body openings of livestock and humans. The larval flies, or maggots, consume living tissue, and the wound enlarges as more females are attracted to the site for oviposition. Such maggot infestations are called myiasis. Agricultural crops, such as wheat and onions, are also attacked.

Beneficial Roles. Beneficial activities of flies include pollination, the reduction and recycling of plant and animal wastes, and the unique contribution of the fruit fly, *Drosophila*, to genetics and our understanding of heredity. In the 1930s, before the advent of antibiotics and sulfa drugs, doctors cured stubborn cases of osteomyelitis with sterile blowfly maggots. The maggots ate only the dead and decaying tissue, cleaning out the wound, suppressing harmful bacteria with their secretions, and encouraging growth of healthy tissues.

Common Types and Life Cycle. The Nematocera, so called because they have long antennae, are primitive flies that include crane flies, mosquitoes, and midges. The Brachycera have short antennae and include the more evolved horseflies and blackflies. Both the Nematocera and the Brachycera emerge as adults through straight breaks in the puparial case.

The most advanced types, such as common domestic flies, emerge from a circular opening at the end of the puparial case. The newly emerged adult has crumpled wings, a soft body, and spindly legs. After the fly exerts blood pressure on different parts of its body, the wings and abdomen soon expand. Within an hour or two the exoskeleton becomes hardened and darkened, and the insect is ready to fly.

Control of Flies. When the insecticide DDT was introduced after 1945, it was hailed as a panacea, until flies became resistant to it and its destructive environmental effects were discovered and carcinogenic effects suspected. Other insecticides followed, and flies developed resistance to one after another. Today it is recognized that good sanitation is the best method of fly control. Other

Most adult flies are anatomically similar to the housefly. Ranging from 1 mm (0.04 in) to more than 5.5 cm (2 in) in size, they usually have soft bodies, suctorial mouths, compound eyes, antennae, and a network of veins strengthening the wings.

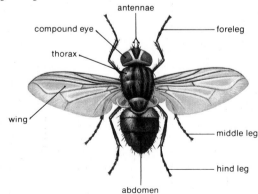

methods have also proved effective. *Bacillus thuringiensis*, a bacterial pathogen of maggots that is harmless to domestic animals and humans, is sprayed in barnyards to control flies. The destructive primary screwworm fly has been controlled by continual release of irradiated sterile males, which mate with wild females who then produce no offspring.

flycatcher (bird)   Flycatcher is the common name for insectivorous songbirds of the Old World family Muscicapidiae and the New World family Tyrannidae. The tyrannids are mainly tropical, but about 30 species occur regularly in North America north of Mexico, and several species have reached Alaska. Most of them return to tropical or subtropical regions for the winter. Among the best-known North American flycatchers are the kingbirds, phoebes, and wood pewees.

Flycatchers feed by darting after insects from their perches. North American forms are characterized by wide, flat bills equipped at the base with bristles for snaring insects. Some flycatchers, especially those in the tropics, build elaborate nests. The nests may be long and sleevelike or large and bulky. North American flycatchers

Flycatchers snap up insects in midflight and harass larger birds. (Bottom) The great crested flycatcher decorates its nest with snake skins, bits of cellophane, and other unusual material. (Center) The scissor-tailed flycatcher, common to Texas, used its long tail feathers to maneuver during aerial acrobatics. (Top) The willow flycatcher is often seen along wooded lake shores in North America.

usually lay from four to six eggs, sometimes more; tropical species may lay only two. The eggs are white and usually marked with brownish blotches. Incubation periods vary from 13 to 16 or more days.

flycatcher (plant)   see CARNIVOROUS PLANTS

flying buttress   see BUTTRESS

flying fish   Flying fish are surface-dwelling fishes of the open oceans and belong to the family Exocoetidae. They are easily recognized by their enlarged pectoral fins and the elongation of the lower portion of their tail fin, and by their characteristic leaps and glides over the ocean surface. One species, the Atlantic flying fish, *Cypselurus heterurus*, is found in warm waters on both sides of the Atlantic. It reaches 38 cm (15 in) in length. Flying fish do not fly by flapping their pectoral fins; instead, they leap into the air, hold the fins rigidly outspread, and glide like flying squirrels.

A typical flying fish uses its enlarged pectoral fins to produce its gliding flight above the ocean's surface. It is found throughout the open waters of the Pacific.

Flying fish glide through the air rather than fly. To become airborne, the fish swims at high speed (32 km/h; 20 mph) just beneath the surface. It rises on its tail fin and gains speed by vigorous sculling (50 beats each second). Taking off at 56 km/h (35 mph), it produces lift by stretching its enlarged fins. Glides of 200 m (660 ft) are recorded.

flying lemur   see COLUGO

flying saucer   see UNIDENTIFIED FLYING OBJECT

flying squirrel   A flying squirrel is a rodent that glides, rather than flies, by means of a thin, furry skin, or membrane, that extends out from the sides of the body and connects the front and hind legs. In North America, Europe, and Asia, these rodents are members of the squirrel family, Sciuridae. They include 35 species and constitute the squirrel subfamily Petauristinae. In Africa, another rodent family, the Anomaluridae, with 12 species, contains squirrellike animals with gliding membranes. These are known as African scaly-tailed flying squirrels. Glides of 450 m (1,500 ft) by the giant flying squirrel *Petaurista* have been recorded.

Flying Tigers   see P-40

Flynn, Elizabeth Gurley   Elizabeth Gurley Flynn, b. Concord, N.H., Aug. 7, 1890, d. Sept. 5, 1964, was an American radical leader and the first woman to lead the U.S. Communist party. She became a labor organizer for the Industrial Workers of the World in 1906 and led important textile strikes in Lawrence, Mass. (1912), and Patterson, N.J. (1913). In 1920, Flynn helped found the American Civil Liberties Union, and during the 1920s she worked on behalf of Sacco and Vanzetti. Flynn joined the Communist party in 1937 and was a member of its national committee during World War II. Arrested (1951) for violating the Smith Act, she was imprisoned from January 1955 to May 1957. As chairman of its national committee, she led the Communist party from 1961 until her death.

Flynn, Errol   Errol Flynn, the stage name of Leslie Thomas Flynn, b. Hobart, Tasmania, June 20, 1909, d. Oct. 14, 1959, was a film star known principally for his roles as a swashbuckling romantic hero. His adventure films include *Captain Blood* (1935) and *The Sea Hawk* (1940). In *Too Much, Too Soon* (1958), he played his friend John Barrymore (see BARRYMORE family).

flywheel   A flywheel is a heavy wheel that is rigidly attached to a shaft. Because of its rotary inertia, the flywheel resists changes in the speed of rotation of the shaft; it also can be used to store and deliver mechanical energy on demand.

In a piston engine (see INTERNAL-COMBUSTION ENGINE), a flywheel is used to moderate fluctuations in the speed of rotation of the crankshaft; these fluctuations result from the fact that the impulses transmitted from the pistons to the crankshaft through the connecting rods are intermittent. On machines for punching or forming sheet metal, the large forces that are periodically required are delivered by a flywheel, whose kinetic (rotary) energy is built up by a comparatively low-powered motor while the machine is idling.

Current concern for dwindling sources of energy has stimulated renewed interest in applications of flywheels. A promising recent application is a regenerative braking system in automobiles. When a car is braked by an ordinary braking system, its kinetic energy (energy of motion) must be dissipated as heat in the BRAKES. To accelerate the car again, the engine must supply additional energy. In regenerative braking, most of the energy is stored in a flywheel, instead of being dissipated as heat in the brakes. This flywheel energy is then used to assist the engine in accelerating the car. Flywheels for energy-storage systems must be capable of high speeds because the energy stored increases as the square of the rotational

speed. Hence, there is a continuing search of improved materials for such applications.

FM   see FREQUENCY MODULATION

FM radio   FM radio broadcasting relies on the FREQUENCY MODULATION transmission system developed in 1933 by Edwin Howard ARMSTRONG and is a principal alternative to AM radio broadcasting. FM stations were originally developed in the late 1940s and the 1950s to counter the commercial formats of AM stations, which depended heavily upon saturation advertising and repetitive playlists of popular songs. They catered to a more diversified audience and focused on in-depth news analysis and classical or semiclassical music.

With the proliferation of inexpensive AM-FM radios, the decline of network radio, and the increase in the number of local FM stations, however, the differences in programming between AM and FM stations since the 1960s have become less pronounced. Although some FM stations preserve the programming concepts of early FM, many have altered format and adopted AM's more commercial approach.

Because FM radio is transmitted in a very high frequency range (88–108 MHz in the United States), the transmission area is limited. The fidelity of the sound is, however, superior to that of the AM signal. Television sound is commonly transmitted on FM bands, and the broadcasting industry has recently introduced radio and TV simulcasts, in which the sound portion of a TV program is broadcast simultaneously on FM radio, allowing the listener to take advantage of STEREOPHONIC SOUND reproduction.

See also: AMPLITUDE MODULATION; RADIO AND TELEVISION BROADCASTING; TELEVISION.

focal point   see LENS

Foch, Ferdinand   [fawsh]   Ferdinand Foch, b. Oct. 2, 1851, d. Mar. 20, 1929, was commander in chief of the Allied armies in France in the final stages of WORLD WAR I

Marshal of France Ferdinand Foch assumed supreme command of the Allied forces on the western front in April 1918. After halting the German advance at the Marne in July, Foch launched the Allied counteroffensive that ended World War I in November.

and helped to bring about the Allied victory. A fervent Roman Catholic with Jesuit training, he joined the army in 1871 and studied at the École Supérieure de Guerre (war college), where he later taught tactics. From 1908 to 1911 he was the school's director.

In 1914, at the outbreak of World War I, Foch commanded the French Ninth Army in the first Battle of the Marne (see MARNE, BATTLES OF THE). He also commanded an army group in the Battle of the Somme (1916), but was then forced into retirement until he became chief of the French general staff in 1917. In April 1918, Foch was given unified command of all the Allied troops in France. Halting the German advance in the Second Battle of the Marne (July 1918), Foch mounted the counteroffensive that turned the tide of the war. He was made a marshal, and three months later he accepted the German surrender (November 1918).

fog   Fog consists of water drops formed in air near the Earth's surface as the air cools to its dew point. When, during the evening, the relative humidity is high, the wind is light, and the night is long, the cooling of air by radiation to the dew point at first produces DEW. Later in the evening, however, water begins to condense as fog. Initially, fog tends to be patchy and shallow. If a light breeze stirs the air, the fog may attain a depth of up to 100 m (300 ft). Ice fog may also occur.

Over flat country, fog becomes a solid deck. Radiation fog is most prevalent in autumn and early winter, when nights are longer but the air is still moist from summer. A fog deck will break during morning, but on overcast days and during winters at high latitude, it may break up at about noon; sometimes, in mountain valleys and Arctic areas, it does not dissolve for weeks. As stagnant, foggy air is filled with particulate material, it gives rise to the disagreeable condition known as smog (smoke plus fog).

During the winter and particularly over snow, warm, moist, tropical air driven, or advected, by wind to high latitudes is cooled from below. This can produce a fog deck, or advection fog, that is several kilometers thick. When such fog forms over the sea, it is called tropical air fog. Prevalent in areas where persistent summer winds blow for days and weeks at a time, this type of fog carries tropical air toward the cooler water that is always present in high latitudes.

Fog, when in the form of a cloud on the ground, develops when air from low plains moves gradually upward toward mountains and lower pressures. The rising air will often cool sufficiently from expansion to cause the temperature of the air to fall to the point at which upslope fog forms.

Foix   [fwah]   Foix (1982 pop., 9,212), a town in southwestern France, is located at the junction of the Arget and Ariège rivers in the foothills of the Pyrenees. It is a commercial center for the surrounding agricultural region. Textile manufacturing is the principal industry. Foix's 12th-century castle, which overlooks the city, is the major tourist attraction. From the 11th to the 13th century, Foix was the capital of the powerful counts of Foix. It resisted attack during the crusade against the ALBIGENSES but was captured by King Philip III in 1272.

Fokine, Mikhail   [foh-keen']   Mikhail Fokine, b. Saint Petersburg, Russia, Apr. 25 (N.S.), 1880, d. Aug. 22, 1942, is best known for his ballets *Les Sylphides, Firebird*, and *Petrouchka*, and ranks as one of the most important and influential choreographers of the 20th century. Fokine studied at the Imperial Ballet School and became a notable soloist in the Maryinsky Ballet (now Kirov). He left the Maryinsky company in 1909 to become chief choreographer for Serge DIAGHILEV's troupe of Russian dancers, which was to emerge as the BALLETS RUSSES and change the course of Western ballet history.

From his early days as a student, Fokine had rejected the artificiality of conventional ballets. In 1904 he had conveyed to the authorities of the Maryinsky troupe his desire for greater naturalism of movement and more integration of story, music, choreography, and scenic design. It was in these areas that he was later to serve Diaghilev's similar artistic vision, creating a total of 60 ballets in his lifetime. *Firebird* (1910) and *Petrouchka* (1911), both with scores by Igor Stravinsky, are characteristic of Fokine's innovative work. Both gave him ample scope to portray the artistic essence of the characters in the dancing; and both—departing from the traditional form of a balletic frame used to set off the ballerina in virtuoso technical displays—provided rich parts for the male dancer, who had been relegated to a minor role by the end of the 19th century. Fokine worked with most of the great companies in the first half of the 20th century. He died in New York City.

Fokker, Anthony Hermann Gerard   [fah'-kur]   Anthony Hermann Gerard Fokker, b. Apr. 6, 1890, d. Dec. 23, 1939, was an aircraft designer and manufacturer. He produced more than 40 types of airplanes for the German armed forces during World War I and devised the synchronizing gear system that enabled the pilot to fire a machine gun through the propeller without hitting the blades. After the war, Fokker—who had been born in Java of Dutch parents—became a naturalized citizen of the United States and devoted himself to developing commercial aircraft.

fold   A fold is any bent or curved domain in one layer or several stacked layers of rock. In a folded geological surface the region of greatest curvature is called its hinge; the less-deformed adjacent flanks are called its limbs. A fold may include any number of stacked parallel layers. The surface formed by joining the hinge lines of all the stacked folded surfaces is called the axial surface, hinge surface, or axial plane.

Descriptively, folds are classified as SYNCLINES AND ANTICLINES. Folds are upright when the axial plane is near vertical, inclined when it dips between 10° and 80°, and recumbent when it averages a dip lower than 10°. In iso-clinal folds, the two limbs are parallel to each other. Folds become overturned when the stratigraphic succession in one limb is reversed. In symmetrical folds (not necessarily upright) the axial plane is a plane of symmetry. Folds are also classified according to the mutual relationship of successive folded surfaces. They are parallel when successive folded surfaces remain mutually parallel to each other and similar when successive folded surfaces are ideally congruent. Most naturally occurring folds are, to various degrees, combinations of these two ideal types. Folds may serve as structural controls or as traps for mineral and fossil-fuel deposits.

Folding reflects the ductile behavior of rocks. A thin, flat layer or slab that is stressed can become curved in two basic modes. In bending, compression is at right angles to the slab; in buckling, it is parallel to the slab. Most folds are initiated by buckling through two mechanisms. In flexural-slip folding, the layers may slip past each other in much the same way that the pages of a book slip past one another when several are bent together. In passive folding, the layer boundaries may be completely passive, little more than patterns in a homogeneous packet of rock. Flexural-slip folding normally results in parallel folds, whereas passive folding tends to form similar folds. In most naturally occuring examples the two mechanisms act in combination to varying degrees. Ideally, passive folding may involve flow of rock across parallel bedding planes, such that some parts of the folded layers thin out and others thicken. The two limbs of the fold may not approach each other, and lateral shortening may not be necessary; folding is then entirely in simple shear. Generally, however, some lateral shortening occurs, along with a pure shear component of deformation. In diapir folds, active upward movement of cores of anticlines may result in piercing of the outer layers (see SALT DOME).

Strata can be laterally compressed to produce folds in various ways. They may buckle between more rigid basement blocks, or they may become folded as they glide under the direct or indirect influence of gravity. In most cases, folding is related to deformation in orogenic belts (see MOUNTAIN).

Foley, Thomas S. Thomas Stephen Foley, b. Spokane, Wash., Mar. 6, 1929, a Democratic congressman from Washington, became Speaker of the House in June 1989 after Jim WRIGHT resigned. First elected to congress in 1964, Foley gained a reputation as a liberal and conciliator. He was chairman of the agriculture committee (1975–81), majority whip (1981–87), and majority leader (1987–88) before becoming speaker.

Folger Shakespeare Library [fohl'-jur] The Folger Shakespeare Library, Washington, D.C., possesses the world's largest collection of Shakespeareana and is a major archival source for 16th- and 17th-century British history. Based on the collection of Henry Clay Folger and his wife, Emily, whose bequest established the institution, the li-

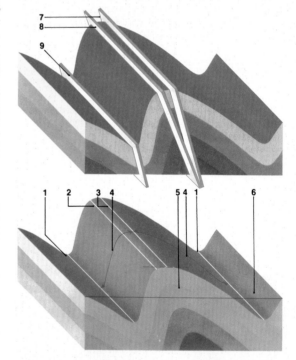

(Right) *The terminology used to describe the various features of a fold include a trough, or lowest surface* (1); *a hinge, or region of greatest curvature* (2); *a crest, or highest surface* (3); *limbs, or less-deformed adjacent flanks* (4); *an anticline, or upward archlike fold* (5); *a syncline, or inverted anticline* (6); *a crest plane* (7), *an axial, or hinge, plane* (8), *and a trough plane* (9). (Below) *In many places layered rocks, such as sedimentary strata, have been bent or buckled into more or less regular wavelike folds as a result of compressional forces. In a fold, the degree of compression determines the type of folding, or wrinkling, produced in the Earth's crust. When compression begins, a simple, symmetrical anticline, or arched-up fold* (A), *will probably form. As compression continues, the folding may become asymmetric in shape, developing into an inclined anticline* (B) *and then into a recumbent fold* (C), *in which the anticline lies over a syncline, or downfold. If the compressional forces are great, the rocks may fracture and move over the syncline to form an overthrust fold* (D). *A nappe* (E) *forms when the movement of the overlying mass of rock continues for more than 1 km (0.6 mi).*

brary now owns over 200,000 volumes and 50,000 manuscripts. Housed in a building completed in 1932, it is administered by the trustees of Amherst College.

---

foliation   Foliation is the planar arrangement of MINERALS or textural features in certain kinds of ROCK. Primary foliation develops when a rock is formed; secondary, afterward. In METAMORPHIC ROCKS, foliation is secondary. It forms as minerals under pressure or subjected to movement recrystallize and reorient themselves. In folded rocks, foliation may be parallel to the axial plane of the folds, as in SLATE, or it may be parallel to the original bedding.

Folies-Bergère   [foh-lee' bair-zhair'] The Folies-Bergère theater, which opened in Paris on May 1, 1869, was the birthplace of the modern musical revue. Still performing, the revue has typically featured comedy acts, partially nude women, lavishly colorful and spectacular productions, and singing stars.

---

folk art   Folk art is the art of the common people—typically peasants, fishers, and rural artisans—as contrasted with *fine art* produced by professionally trained artists. The term *folk art* originated during the 19th century and is related to the concepts of FOLKLORE, folk literature, and folk music. Created within a developed culture, folk art is distinct from so-called PRIMITIVE ART produced by the peoples of preliterate, preurban societies. A traditional, rural form, it differs from commercial decorative art.

Most of it is utilitarian in character and is not conceived of as art by those who have made it. Peasant houses, decorated furniture, costumes, pottery, woodwork, metal objects, toys, and painted signs are characteristic examples of folk art. Although some of these objects may be of high artistic quality, revealing the superior skill and inspiration of the individual artisan, folk art is highly traditional, using clearly defined conventions handed down from generation to generation, often over many centuries.

Although folk art still exists in some parts of Eastern Europe, Asia. and Africa, the spread of industrialization is rapidly undermining folk traditions even in those areas. Collections of traditional crafts and museums dedicated to their preservation are being formed in all countries to keep this precious heritage alive.

Western Traditions

Europe. A rich and varied folk art existed throughout Europe prior to the Industrial Revolution. Most of the surviving works date from the 18th or 19th century, although some objects may be older and all can be traced to more ancient traditions, some of which have existed for many centuries.

Among the European folk-art traditions, perhaps the most oustanding from an artistic point of view are those

Brightly painted hearts and flowers highlight the ornate surface decoration of this 19th-century Swedish corner cupboard from the province of Skåne. Folk furniture in Sweden, as in most European countries, shows distinct regional variations. (Nordiska Museum, Stockholm.)

of Scandinavia, Germany, Holland, and Switzerland. In Sweden the wooden peasant houses with their finely carved furnishings are particularly notable, as are the painted or woven wall hangings. Denmark excels in brightly painted peasant furniture displaying ornamental designs of birds and flowers. Much of the folk art of Iceland is distinguished by abstract band-and-scroll patterns that can be traced to the Nordic art of early Germanic times.

Distinctive regional folk-art traditions developed in Germany. The peasant houses of northern Germany, for example, with their brick construction and steep thatched roofs, are entirely different from those of the Bavarian Alps, with their wood construction, flatter roofs, and colorful painted decorations. In Holland, peasant embroidery and Delft pottery wares are characteristic but many other types of folk art are also found. Considering its small size and relatively homogeneous population, Switzerland has produced one of the most remarkable European traditions of folk art in terms of breadth and variety. In addition to gaily decorated houses (including the alpine chalet), garments, and carved wooden and pottery utensils of all types, Swiss tradition is notable for the fascinating painted masks that are still made in the Lötschenthal region of the Valais canton.

In southern Europe, Italy, Spain, and Portugal are the countries best known for their folk arts, some of which continue to flourish. Examples of local art still made by common people for their own use include the colorful Sicilian donkey carts along with small-scale versions made as toys. The brightly painted pottery of Spain and Portugal is still produced in various places, notably Toledo and Valencia.

France, too, possess a rich and varied tradition of folk objects of all types. Best known is the lacework of Brittany,

Sicilian folk artists cover their donkey carts with colorful painted designs. In this 19th-century example from Palermo, scenes of the legendary rape of the Sabines are portrayed on the side panels. (Lüden Collection, Wyk, Germany.)

the pottery of Normandy, and peasant furniture, especially that of the Alsace region. By contrast, little survives of the various lively folk traditions that existed during the 18th and early 19th centuries in Britain. Particularly outstanding in England were the sturdy salt-glaze wares and decorated pottery, for which Staffordshire was famous.

Much of the folk art of Eastern Europe reflects the influence of ancient Byzantine artistic tradition and the long years of Turkish rule under the Ottomans. Most remarkable, especially in the Slavic countries, are the textiles, particularly the embroidered peasant blouses, which are among the loveliest in Europe. Also distinctively Slavic are the flat-woven rugs and tapestries known as kilims, which are often based on Turkish prototypes. Similar decorative motifs may also be seen in the folk pottery of Hungary, Czechoslovakia, and Poland. Because Eastern Europe was industrialized later than other parts of the continent, the folk-art tradition lasted longer, extending into the 20th century and even to the present in some areas.

North America. The diverse folk-art traditions of North America stem from a variety of cultural traditions imported by the European settlers. The popular art of Massachusetts, Rhode Island, and Connecticut derived from English sources; the so-called PENNSYLVANIA DUTCH art was based on German models. New England is noted for its simple wooden farmhouses, its beautifully designed furniture, and its embroidered samplers. The folk artists of rural Pennsylvania are well known for colorful chests and painted ceramics as well as fraktur documents in decorative calligraphy and charming drawings. Especially renowned are the boldly patterned Amish quilts, considered one of the finest and most distinctively American folk

creations. Other characteristic productions of northeastern American artisans are the furniture of the Shakers, with its severe lines, the stone houses of the Huguenot settlers in the Hudson valley, and the salt-glaze ceramic vessels made in New York and New Jersey. Beautiful pottery was also produced in the mountain states of the South, notably in Virginia, Tennessee, and Kentucky.

In the folk art of the Southwest, Mexican influences are clearly evident and in some instances elements from the artistic heritage of the native Indian culture are incorporated. The Spanish influence is obvious in the 19th-century *santos*—small carved and painted figures representing Christ, Mary, and various Roman Catholic saints—intended to adorn niches in the walls of churches and to be carried in religious processions. These highly spiritualized images are considered masterpieces of popular religious carving.

Folk paintings and folk sculptures, often referred to by the terms *naive art* or, especially in describing paintings, *primitivist art*, form another major category of American folk art. Unlike the artisans who produced utilitarian objects, a number of the folk artists who made these works are known by name, and some of them, including Edward HICKS and Ammi Phillips from the 19th century, are well known today. The painters known as LIMNERS specialized in portraits of local people. Others painted the homesteads and landscapes of the region in which they worked.

Among folk sculptures, ship figureheads, often depicting enchanting ladies, are the most delightful, but a great variety of carvings of all types were executed. Sailors engraved designs on whale teeth, whalebone, and walrus ivory; this art is called SCRIMSHAW. Others carved toys and whirligigs, wooden figures of ducks and geese to be used as decoys, and the so-called cigar-store Indians, which were placed outside tobacconists' shops. Of metal sculptures, the weather vanes are often outstanding in both de-

Eastern Europe is noted for its folk costumes. This embroidered sheepskin vest was crafted in Transylvania (in present-day Romania) in the 1880s. Such garments were worn by both men and women. (Lüden Collection, Wyk, Germany.)

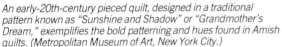
An early-20th-century pieced quilt, designed in a traditional pattern known as "Sunshine and Shadow" or "Grandmother's Dream," exemplifies the bold patterning and hues found in Amish quilts. (Metropolitan Museum of Art, New York City.)

Girl in a Garden (c.1830), by an anonymous American artist, illustrates the two-dimensional, exaggerated representations often characteristic of portraits by limners. (Abby Aldrich Rockefeller Folk Art Center, Williamsburg, Va.)

Wood carving, an early form of American folk art, found full expression in the creation of ships' figureheads. This carved wooden figurehead, Lady with a Rose (c.1800–10), is from Essex, Conn. (Mariners Museum, Newport News, Va.)

sign and imagery. The carved TOMBSTONES of the 17th to early 19th centuries found throughout the eastern United States often display elaborate graphic design as well.

Non-Western Traditions

The Far East. Folk-art traditions have flourished throughout Asia for centuries. In the Far East, the traditional folk art of China is noted for crudely executed but often charming folk wood-block prints, hand colored in bright hues; intricately formed paper cutouts; and a variety of folk potteries made at provincial kilns.

In Japan, folk art, or *mingei*, historically has played a vital role in the cultural expression of the nation as a whole. Still found all over Japan are austerely beautiful peasant houses with overhanging thatched roofs and simple interiors, testifying to the refined aesthetic taste of the rural population. Wood or stone folk sculptures representing popular deities were made in many sections of the country; the best known are the Jizo images produced on the island of Sado. Of folk paintings, the most characteristic are the votive pictures called *ema* and the popular pictures made for travelers passing through the village of Otsu on Lake Biwa.

The bulk of Japenese *mingei* consists of regionally distinct crafts of every kind produced in huge quantities throughout Japan. The best examples date from the Edo period (1615–1868), before Japan embarked on its in-dustrial development, but in isolated rural areas fine folk crafts are still being made. The finely decorated Seto oil plates used to catch the dripping oil in lanterns are among the most beautiful Japanese folk ceramics and today are highly esteemed by collectors. Also from Seto are the handsome stoneware plates, or *ishizara*, traditionally used in peasant kitchens. Woven or dyed garments from Okinawa are famous for the beauty of their colors and design. Other folk textiles include cotton or silk hangings, called *noren*, and bedspreads, or *futon*. Characteristically Japanese are the ingenious uses of vegetable fibers to form rain capes, snow boots, toy horses, brooms, and baskets of every description.

Closely related to the folk art of Japan is that of Korea, where traditions of excellent craftsmanship have existed

Lively folk renderings on wooden plaques, called ema, were presented as votive offerings at Buddhist temples in Japan. This 19th-century ema from a temple in Nara depicts an animal of the zodiac. (Japan Folk Crafts Museum, Tokyo.)

for many centuries. Outstanding examples include the splendid wooden chests, much sought after by modern collectors; the folk lacquers and ceramic wares; and the primitive, strong folk paintings.

Southeast Asia and India. In Southeast Asia, the folk pottery of Vietnam consists largely of rough porcelains decorated in blue and white in imitation of Chinese Ming ware, yet possessing a vigor and simplicity all its own. Indonesian BATIK folk textiles are in demand throughout the world for their artisanship and their designs. On the island of Bali, the paper or leather *wayang* puppets made for the shadow plays are unique folk-art objects. Also impressive are the brilliantly painted peasant houses with steeply gabled roofs and elaborate carvings.

In southern Asia, India possesses the oldest and richest tradition of folk art. Much of it is connected with religious ceremonies: folk sculptures made of bronze, wood, and clay represent the gods and goddesses of the Hindu

Among the most expressive forms of Balinese folk art are the painted-leather puppets associated with the wayang shadow play. Used to enact scenes from the Hindu epics, these highly stylized, cutout images are manipulated so as to cast shadows on a canvas backdrop.

pantheon. The most interesting of the bronzes come from the south of India and Bengal; the best known of the brightly painted wooden statues are those from Puri in Orissa, representing Vishnu in his incarnation as the Jaggannath (Lord of the Universe). Giant clay horses, sometimes 7 m (22 ft) high, come from Sirunathur in Madras. Embroidered materials with insets of mirror glass are from Kutch in western India.

Central and Western Asia. In central and western Asia, areas deeply influenced by Islam, there exists a rich folk tradition of textile, ceramic, and metal work. Throughout this area, carpets are central to the folk-art tradition, and those made in Turkey, the Caucasus, Iran, and Turkestan are rightly looked upon as masterpieces of this genre. Among the folk pottery of western Asia, particularly fine are the Turkish wares from Isnik, with their tulip designs and brilliant blue glazes, and the Iranian ceramics from Arak. Beautiful ceramic tiles are used in construction throughout this region. Etched or pierced metal is employed extensively for brass bottles and vessels of all types.

See also: ANTIQUE COLLECTING.

folk dance   Folk dance is not only the oldest form of dance, it is also the basis of all other dance forms, including ballet, modern dance, ballroom, disco, and jazz dance. A distinguishing feature of folk dance is that it is not a performing art, but a participatory activity. It is a type of traditional, communal dancing, passed down from generation to generation and done in a recreational atmosphere. The use of traditional costumes and accessories also aids in preserving a culture's link with its past.

The types of folk dances include war dances, contest dances, wedding dances, courtship dances, and dances for the fun of movement alone. The Philippine rice-planting dance and the Japanese coal miner's dance are types of work dances. Almost every country has a shoemaker's and a sailor's dance. Sailors brought the music and dance of their native countries to many foreign lands; therefore, tunes like the "Soldier's Joy," used for hornpipes and sailor's dances, are found throughout the world. The Mexican *El Bolonchon*, which honors the Virgin Mary, is one of the many religious dances. The Italian TARANTELLA is a furious dance that was traditionally thought to work off the effects of a tarantula's bite.

Circle Dances. The oldest form for folk dance is the circle dance, in which dancers follow one another around a ring. The American Indian hunting, rain, and war dances are circle dances, as are many of the African and Japanese dances. Hands can be held in a variety of ways to close up the circle, as in the HORA of Israel and Romania, the *kolo* of Yugoslavia, and the *syrtos* of Greece. Sometimes the circle changes into a long chain dance, with a leader weaving the dancers in patterns around a village or a city street as in the French *bourrée*, which is done in long lines, and the Norwegian *song-dance*. The Ukrainian *arkan* dance—which dates back to pre-Christian times and is danced only by men—honors the sun-god and ends dramatically with the dancers leaping over a roaring fire.

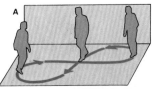

Two forms of the reel, a country dance originating in Great Britain and Ireland, are shown. A Scottish reel of three (A) is a pattern executed within a set, a group of three to four couples. The lead dancer weaves around two other dancers in a figure-8 pattern, alternately passing right and left shoulders. Another country dance is the traveling dance performed by four couples in parallel lines, exemplified here by the "Trip to Helsinki." A running step (B), in which the two lines of dancers skip forward and back twice, commences the dance. The men bow and the women curtsy (C) before beginning the "trip" (D), in which all dancers, placing their hands on the shoulders of the person to their left, cast off to the bottom of the set and circle back to their original positions. When "threading the needle" (E) the lead dancer leads the line under an arch formed by the second and third dancers, then under the arch formed by the third and fourth dancers. When performing the "waves" (F) the first and third couples form an arch under which the second and fourth couples pass. The configuration is repeated until each couple returns to their original position.

Circle dances were prevalent in the early history of the United States. Because of the Puritan influence, many people thought that dancing and music were sinful, and they tried to suppress both, but the people sang as they danced and termed the dances *play-party-games*. The most popular and continuing dances of this type include *Skip to My Lou, Shoo Fly, Jenny Crack Corn*, and *Pig in the Parlor*. Many of these vigorous play-party-game dances were originally courtship dances calling for frequent changing of partners.

Square Dances. The SQUARE DANCE is usually associated with the United States, but this type of dancing is common to many countries: the Danish *Hatter*, the Irish *Sweets of May*, the German *Man in the Hay*, the English *Newcastle*, and the Scottish *eightsome reel* are examples. A square dance called the *beseda* was put together in Czechoslovakia about 1900 as a means of unifying the country through dance; it consists of a potpourri of little dances from many provinces. American square dances developed primarily from dances of England, Scotland, and Ireland.

Contra Dances. Folk dances in which two long lines are formed with dancers facing each other are sometimes called longway, string, or line dances, but they are usually known as contra dances. Contra dances were brought to the United States mainly from the British Isles and have been best preserved in the New England states. The old English contra called *Childgrove* dates from 1701 and is still done in America and England. The most famous contra dance is known in the United States as the *Virginia reel*; it originated in England, where it was known as *Sir Roger de Coverley*.

Couple Dances. A much later development in folk dance, couple dances are still scarce in many parts of the world. Because they were isolated from the rest of Europe by both mountains and historical events, the Balkan countries were not influenced by other European dances. They have retained the circle dance form and do very few couple dances.

Folk Dance Steps. Many different steps are used in folk dancing, including walking, running, hopping, jumping, skipping, leaping, sliding, and stamping. The way these steps are done depends on the traditional style of the country in which the dance originated, as well as the musical accompaniment, the rhythm of the dance, the costume, the climate, the geography, the people, and the history of the country. In addition to the basic steps, there are special steps such as the polka, waltz, mazurka, schottische, galop, grapevine, and buzz. Steps that are used only in one country or one part of the world include the Swedish *hambo*, the Yogoslav *kolo*, the Yemenite step of Israel and Yemen, the Strathspey step of Scotland, the *jarabe* of Mexico, and the special squat step for Slavic men, called a *prysiadka*.

The use and positioning of the hands are as important as the feet in folk dancing and are often helpful in identifying the nationality of a dance. The hands are held rigidly at the sides of the body in an Irish jig, for example, but they are almost always placed on the hips, in a variety of holds, in Scandinavian dances and in those of Austria, Germany, and Switzerland. In circle dances hands are often placed on shoulders or in a back or front basket hold. Balkan dancers hold each other by the belt, often hanging onto little loops woven into the belts to strengthen their

Dancers at the annual Highland Games at Antigonish, Nova Scotia, perform the complicated steps of a Scottish sword dance above the crossed blades. Sword dances are found throughout the world in various forms.

hold. In Hungary men tuck their thumbs into their trouser pockets or belts, and German men tuck their thumbs under their colorful suspenders. Mexican men often dance with their hands behind their backs to keep their serapes (blankets) in place. The Ukrainian woman places her hands on her bosom to prevent her beads from crashing into her chin, and the Austrian or German woman holds one hand on her bodice to prevent the many heavy coins of her costume from bumping up and down. In some folk dances, such as the HULA of Hawaii, the hands are the most important part of the dance because their movements are used to relate a story.

Costume. The style of a folk dance is often determined by the costume the dancers wear: in countries where men wear spurs on their boots, there is much heel clicking to emphasize the spurs' sounds; where women have narrow skirts, there are no high kicks. Hungarian dances feature many spins and twirls to show off the many layers of full petticoats and the ribbons worn by the female dancers. Shoes with heels have to be worn by Spanish FLAMENCO and Mexican *zapateado* dancers to stamp out the rhythms that are featured in these dances. The Slavic squatting step can be done more easily by men wearing very baggy trousers. The short leather pants, or *lederhosen*, which are worn by German and Austrian men, make the *Schuhplattler* thigh-slapping sounds resound. Skirts are worn by men in some countries, such as the kilt worn by the Scottish and the Irish. In Greece men wear a short, white pleated skirt called a *fustanella*. Long embroidered aprons, which influence the movements of their dances, are worn by some Hungarian men.

Folk Dance Accessories. Many different accessories are used in folk dancing. In the Philippines the dancers use coconut shells, long bamboo poles, hats, fans, and kerchiefs. In Hawaii slashed bamboo sticks, called *puili* sticks, are used for striking the floor and the arms and shoulders of the dancers, who are dancing in a squatting

position. Almost every country has some sort of sword dance. In addition to castanets, finger cymbals and stones are used to produce the rhythm. Large poles and sticks are used in many men's dances. Masks are frequently used, as in the Mexican *Los Viejitos* ("Old Man's Dance"). In some dances bottles are carried on the head, or lighted candles are held throughout the dance. Ribbons, hoops, garlands or trays of flowers, whips, and bells tied around the ankles or wrists are some other accessories.

The handkerchief is the most common accessory used in folk dancing. Its most exciting use is in English Morris dancing, in which six men execute intricate steps while they twirl and fling kerchiefs into the air. The leader of Balkan dances has to be quite expert in keeping his or her steps in time while constantly twirling a handkerchief to set the pace of a dance. In Mexico, a man uses his sombrero in the national dance *jarabe tapatío*, or the Mexican hat dance. The man tosses the hat on the floor in front of a woman, and, if she accepts him, she dances on its wide brim. Folk dancers frequently accompany their movements with yells, rhymes, yodels, and other sounds.

There are many international folk festivals and folk dance camps and clubs in which people share and learn dances. In the United States there are monthly folk dance publications and newsletters. Many dances would probably have been lost if they had not been perpetuated by folk dance societies.

folk medicine   Folk medicine encompasses traditional healing beliefs and methods used in past and contemporary cultures mostly by people who are not licensed medical practitioners. As an integral part of a culture's knowledge and values, folk medicine is a system based on traditional modes of conduct for coping with sickness. Often sanctioned by empirical claims or magico-religious beliefs, these popular practices are used to alleviate the distress of diseases and to restore harmony in people who are emotionally or physically ill, or both. Folk medicine's lore is widely known among members of a culture and is usually handed down from generation to generation by word of mouth. In general, the system is flexible, allowing the introduction of new ideas about sickness and healing practices, many of them borrowed from classical and modern medicine.

Healers

To implement the various folk curing practices, most social groups have established a hierarchy of healers—beginning with the individuals affected, their immediate families and friends, knowledgeable herbalists, members of the clergy, faith healers, and SHAMANS, or medicine men. Many are consulted because of their empirical knowledge of roots and herbs possessing medicinal properties. Others are considered endowed with healing gifts because of station or accidents of birth. The belief that posthumous children have such talents is widely known in the United States. In the European folk-medicine tradition, seventh sons and daughters are said to possess unusual curing powers; the same applies to twins. Often spouses and children of known healers are automatically considered to have similar gifts. As in primitive medicine, many people affected by ailments that are considered minor and natural treat themselves, with the help of family members. Easily available herbal preparations known to most members of the culture are used to effect a cure. More difficult cases suspected to be of a magico-religious nature are referred to local healers endowed with special powers.

American Folk Medicine

Navajos. Native American folk medicine is popular in the less acculturated Indian tribes. A notable example is the Navajos still living in their homeland. Disease is considered a disruption of harmony caused either by external agents such as lightning and winds, powerful animals and ghosts, and witchcraft, or by the breaking of taboos. Three categories of folk healers are usually consulted: first the herbalists, for symptomatic relief of minor ailments; if no improvement is observed, then the hand trembler, or diviner, is called; finally, the singer, or medicine man, will carry out specific healing ceremonies suggested by the hand trembler's diagnosis. Ritual sweatbaths, drinking of herbs, and elaborate sandpainting ceremonies characterize Navajo folk healing.

Hot-Cold Theory. The hot-cold theory proposes that a healthy human body displays a balanced blending of hot and cold qualities. Sickness ensues if an excess of hot or cold food is eaten. The basic scheme, introduced into Latin America by the Spanish and reinforced by native cultural values, became firmly embedded in popular Latin healing traditions. The hot-cold scheme is applied to foods, diseases, and remedies. The terms *hot* and *cold* do not necessarily refer to the temperature of foods or remedies. Qualities are assigned on the basis of origin, color, nutritional value, and physiological effects of the food or remedy, as well as therapeutical action. Among New York Puerto Ricans, for example, bananas, coconuts, and sugar cane are considered cold, whereas chocolate, garlic, alcoholic beverages, and corn meal are hot. Cold-classified illnesses such as arthritis, colds, and gastric complaints must be treated with hot foods and remedies. Their hot counterparts—constipation, diarrhea, and intestinal cramps—require treatment with cold substances.

Black Americans. The medical folklore of black Americans contains elements derived from popular European and African beliefs, blended with religious elements belonging to Christian Fundamentalism and West Indian voodoo. Sickness is broadly divided into "natural" and "unnatural." The former comprises bodily conditions caused by evil influences and witchcraft after the loss of divine protection; the magical intrusion of "animals" into the body and the placement of a certain hex play prominent roles in the causation of disease.

Mexican-Americans. Folk medicine among Mexican-Americans, especially in West Texas, is based on pre-Columbian indigenous lore. Five types of folk illness are most prominent: *mal de ojo* (evil eye), *empacho* (gastrointestinal blockage due to excessive food intake), *susto* (magically induced fright), *caida de la mollera* (fallen fontanel, or opening in or between bones), and *mal*

puesto (sorcery). Prominent among Mexican-American folk healers is the *curandero*, a type of shaman who uses white magic and herbs to effect cures.

Folk Medicine Today

A number of folk remedies used in the past are now manufactured as pharmaceutical preparations prescribed by physicians. For examle, rauwolfia is an extract of the snakeroot plant, which was used for centuries in the Far East for its calming effect. It is now prescribed by physicians to lower blood pressure. Reserpine, a derivative of rauwolfia, has been used by psychiatrists in treating severe mental disorders.

---

folk music Folk music, narrowly defined, is music that lives in oral tradition and is learned "by ear," without the use of written music, primarily in rural cultures. Because folk music is relatively simple in a technical sense, it is known to and performed by most members of society. Usually, it is not performed by professional musicians or disseminated through institutions such as schools and churches but instead lives in the traditions of families and closely knit social groups such as villages. It is frequently associated with the activities that it accompanies, such as ritual, dance, and work. The term *folk music* normally applies to the music of the lower educational and socioeconomic strata in those societies that also have classical music traditions under the patronage of elite institutions such as courts, government-sponsored schools, and religious centers. In contrast to folk music, a classical music culture is maintained by highly trained professionals with access to written musical theory.

The concept of folk music in most of the Western world today has generally been expanded to include other phenomena, such as songs of rural origin performed by popular entertainers; the HYMNS of rural churches sung in distinctive folk styles; songs cast in the form of folk music but composed for political and social purposes by popular musicians such as Bob DYLAN, Pete SEEGER, and Janis JOPLIN and consumed through radio and records by urban audiences; authentic folk music forgotten in the villages but preserved by specially trained singers under government auspices, a practice common in eastern Europe; and the establishment of orchestras of folk instruments that perform in formal concerts, a custom widespread in the USSR. In this article, however, the more restricted definition of folk music is used.

The Folk Tradition. To exist for any length of time, a folk song must be accepted by a community—nation, village, family—and must be known to more than an elite. Another distinguishing feature of the folk song is its tendency to change as it passes from one person to another. Folk songs are composed by individuals, but once taught they are changed and often simplified. Each person who sings the song may develop his or her own version. In the course of this process, called "communal recreation," a tune may be fitted with a completely new set of words, or a text (such as "Barbara Allen") may be sung to a group

The American singer Joan Baez became prominent during the early 1960s for her moving interpretations of traditional folk songs. With contemporaries such as Pete Seeger and Bob Dylan, Baez played a major role in the development of the modern urban folk song as a vehicle for social protest.

of completely different tunes. A group of related tunes that seem to have descended from a single parent tune are called a tune family. A tune family tends to remain within a nation or language group, such as France or the English-speaking world. Researchers have speculated that the vast majority of Anglo-American folk songs belong to about 40—and most of those songs to only 7—dominant tune families. Some tunes that seem to have spread throughout Europe centuries ago have developed nationally distinctive variants in many countries. Tunes sometimes cross national boundaries, especially where there are mixed populations. Text types such as ballad stories are more internationally distributed than tunes. The folk ballad "Lady Isabel and the Elf Knight," for example, has been collected in most European nations but is sung to tunes that are not internationally related.

Changes are part of the folk process and result from the dependence on oral tradition. The function of a song in society may determine how much change is tolerated. Ritual songs are usually permitted less change than are songs sung mainly for entertainment, such as ballads. Folk music is frequently said to be functional because it is an integral part of other activities. Calendric songs, accompanying various seasonal changes, agricultural activities, and key stages in the life cycle, are particularly old. In a traditional folk society, music is essential in rituals and festivals. The words of a folk song may serve as chronicle or newspaper or may provide a way for young people to learn about their culture. In modern industrial nations, folk music is perpetuated by ethnic, occupational, and religious minorities, promoting their self-esteem and social solidarity. Isolated culture enclaves, such as Germans who lived in Yugoslavia before 1945 or Slovak-

Americans who live in Cleveland, often preserve particularly old forms of folk music.

Musical Style. All Western nations have ballads (songs that tell stories), dance songs, and work songs dealing with labor or agriculture. The most common structure of such songs is strophic: a tune, frequently consisting of four separate musical lines, is repeated several times, each time with a different stanza of the text. In contrast, much instrumental folk music consists of a series of short lines, each repeated once.

RHYTHM in folk music is often related to the rhythmic patterns of speech. For example, in English and German—languages that usually begin sentences with unstressed syllables or articles such as "the"—songs usually begin with an unstressed musical beat. Czech—a language in which all words begin with accented syllables—typically has songs beginning on the stressed musical beat. In most western-European styles, texts and tunes are organized by a stable number of metric feet (such as iambs or anapests); in eastern Europe the number of syllables per text line is usually the organizing principle.

Most cultures have many songs using pentatonic (five-tone) SCALES, with the five TONES usually arranged so that they can be played on the black keys of the piano. Seven-tone scales such as the common major and minor are also widespread, as are the Dorian and Mixolydian MODES, also found in the Gregorian chant of the Roman Catholic church. Most cultures also have an archaic layer of short, repetitive songs using only two or three PITCHES; this style is mainly found in children's songs, games, and vestiges of pre-Christian rituals.

Polyphonic music (see POLYPHONY), in which two or more tunes are sung at one time by small groups of singers or choirs, played by instrumental ensembles, or even played on a single instrument such as the Yugoslav double flute, is most common in eastern and southern Europe. Variations range from the accompaniment of a single sustained tone (drone) to the very sophisticated choral songs of Russia and isolated parts of the Balkans and Italy. Parallel singing is another prevalent form. Parallel thirds—singing the same tune at the interval of a third—is found in Spain, Germany, and Italy; parallel fourths and fifths are used in various Slavic countries, and parallel seconds, in Yugoslavia.

Singing style is one of the most characteristic features of folk music. The handling of rhythm differentiates two styles identified by Béla BARTÓK. In *parlando-rubato* singing, which is probably the older style, the singer stresses the words, embellishes tones, and departs frequently from the basic rhythmic structure. *Tempo giusto* singing follows metric patterns and maintains an even tempo. Both styles are found throughout Europe. Alan Lomax (see LOMAX family), using different criteria, found three main singing styles. The Eurasian, mainly in southern Europe and parts of Great Britain and North America—areas where solo singing is prevalent—is tense, ornamented, and rhythmically uneven. The Old European style, found in central and eastern Europe, where group singing is developed, is more relaxed and is sung with full voice in even rhythm, the voices blending well in the choruses. The modern European style, found in more recent music in western Europe, combines elements of the other two.

Instruments. Most folk music is sung, but much of it is also performed on a variety of instruments, which may be classed by origin. The simplest, which are shared by many tribal societies in the world, include rattles, bone whistles, and long wooden trumpets such as the Swiss ALPHORN. These were diffused throughout the world many centuries ago and are used in the West mainly as children's toys, for signaling, and to accompany remnants of pre-Christian rituals. A number of other instruments were adapted from Asian or African cultures; these include BAG-PIPES, BANJOS, XYLOPHONES, and the *gusle*, a Yugoslav one-string fiddle. Some instruments—simple and complex—originated and were developed in the folk cultures in which they are used. The *Dolle*, a fiddle made from a wooden shoe and common in western Germany, is a simple example. The more sophisticated bowed LYRE, once widespread in northern Europe, is now restricted to Finland. A final group includes instruments taken over by folk cultures from city, church, or court and often maintained long after they had been discarded and replaced in their place of origin. Examples are the HURDY-GURDY and the Norwegian Hardanger fiddle, a violin with sympathetic strings.

The Modern World. In the 20th century, especially since 1945, folk music has declined in its rural habitat as a result of the spread of industrialization, the fact that villagers now live much like city dwellers, and the ready accessibility of all kinds of music through the mass media. Folk music has also assumed new roles, including the reinforcement of ethnic identity among urban minorities, the advocacy of social change (as in the U.S. civil rights movement), and the building of national consciousness in heterogeneous nations. Folk music continues to be a vital force in the world's musical life.

folk song   SEE FOLK MUSIC

folklore   The term *folklore*, literally "folk learning," is generally limited to knowledge that is transmitted from one generation to another by word of mouth or imitation. In societies without writing, all traditional knowledge can be considered folklore; but in literate societies such as our own, folklore refers only to a fraction of the total CULTURE and consists principally of FOLK MUSIC, FOLK ART, FOLKWAYS, and FOLK MEDICINE as well as FOLKTALES, legends, myths, and proverbs. These latter forms of folklore, which are also known as folk literature, have been the primary focus of studies by folklorists. Since the 19th century, scholars have systematically recorded in writing (and more recently phonograph records and tape) folk tales, myths, legends, and other forms of folk literature in different parts of the world. They have charted the geographic distribution of many plots and motifs and analyzed the role of folktales, myths, proverbs, and other forms in various cultures. Many folktales, such as those recorded in Germany in the 19th century by the Grimm brothers and published as *Grimm's Fairy Tales*, have become part of children's written literature.

folktale   A folktale is a traditional oral prose narrative. Like other kinds of FOLKLORE, the folktale circulates by word of mouth in a consistent yet shifting form. No precise terminology exists to label the folktale and its subcategories. The term *folktale* itself is customarily used in a restricted way to signify oral fictions in which supernatural and magic-making beings, royal and aristocratic characters, and talking animals have the main roles. In popular usage this kind of story is called a FAIRY TALE. Fairy tales do not deal with fairies, however; the purportedly truthful accounts Irish storytellers tell of the sightings and powers of these diminutive creatures are more properly called legends, since they are not intended as fictions. A distinction needs to be made between folk legends in oral circulation and popular and literary legends that circulate through print and other media. Stories about Paul Bunyan, for example, appear chiefly in books and newspapers and are very rarely collected in the field by folklorists; they should be called popular legends rather than folk legends.

The length, subject matter, and form of folktales vary enormously. A one-minute joke and an adventure-laden romance requiring several nights to narrate can both qualify if they exist in oral variants. Folktales may be set in a mythical past, in historic times, or in the present. Since storytelling is a basic human need, folktales are told even in the midst of technological cultures saturated with electronic media. Modern Americans specialize in snappy jokes with a punch line and urban horror legends that are told as true.

These categories apply primarily to storytelling in the Western world. The folktales produced by tribal societies often include animal tales, in which beasts and birds behave like humans; dilemma tales, popular throughout black Africa, in which an unresolved ending is left for the audience to decide; and creation myths, which explain the origin of the Earth in ethnocentric terms. Frequently the primitive storyteller draws no clear distinction between fiction and reality. Every society known to humankind tells folktales, which take an endless variety of forms. What unites all these forms is the artistry of a teller and the responsiveness of an audience.

folkways   Folkways are the routine habits, customs, or patterns of social intercourse shared by members of a social group. Examples include such traditional customs as table manners and waiting one's turn in line. When such more or less automatically performed behaviors become well-established by conscious common agreement so that they are proper and indispensable to society, they become mores (Latin for "customs"). Neither folkways nor mores are laws, although they may be incorporated into laws. The term *folkways* was first used by the American sociologist William Graham SUMNER (1840–1910). He considered them obstacles to social progress.

follicle stimulating hormone   SEE HORMONE, ANIMAL; PITUITARY GLAND

Folsom culture [fohl'-suhm]   Folsom culture is the name of a prehistoric North American stone-tool complex characterized by distinctive fluted projectile points. The artifacts were initially discovered (1926) in association with the remains of extinct giant bison at a site near Folsom, in east central New Mexico. Evidence of Folsom culture has subsequently been found at other sites in the western and southwestern United States and in Canada. The Folsom points, which are about 5 cm (2 in) long, with a concave base and a lengthwise groove, or flute, date from c.9000–8000 BC. Other flint implements in the Folsom cultural complex include end scrapers with steep working edges, small perforators and gravers, side scrapers made from flakes, and chisels and knives. At the Lindenmeier site in northeast Colorado bone awls and a needle were also found.

Fonda (family) [fahn'-duh]   Henry, Jane, and Peter Fonda represent one of the few family acting dynasties in American film. **Henry Fonda**, b. Grand Island, Nebr., May 16, 1905, d. Aug. 12, 1982, was a versatile actor who began his career as a stage actor. Known for his slow, midwestern drawl and easy mannerisms, Fonda distinguished himself in a wide variety of Hollywood films: social drama (*The Grapes of Wrath*, 1940), light comedy (*The Lady Eve*, 1941), historical drama (*Young Mr. Lincoln*, 1939), Westerns (*My Darling Clementine*, 1946), war comedy-drama (*Mr. Roberts*, 1955), and political drama (*The Best Man*, 1964). Fonda, who appeared in 87 films (and 21 plays), won his first Academy Award for best actor for his performance in *On Golden Pond* (1981). His daughter, actress **Jane Fonda**, b. New York City, Dec. 21, 1937, once famous for her outspoken stands on political issues, has since been hugely successful as the author of a number of keep-fit books and videotapes. Her best performances have been in *Cat Ballou* (1965), *They Shoot Horses, Don't They?* (1969), *Klute* (1971; Academy Award

Henry Fonda, flanked by his children, Jane and Peter, accepts the American Film Institute's Life Achievement Award at a testimonial dinner held (March 1978) in his honor.

for best actress); and *Coming Home* (1978; Academy Award for best actress). She has also appeared in *Nine to Five* (1980) and *The Morning After* (1986). Her brother, **Peter Fonda**, b. New York City, Feb. 23, 1940, scored an unexpected success with *Easy Rider* (1967), a film that he produced independently. His later films, however, have been less successful.

Fonseca, Manuel Deodoro da [fun-sek'-uh, mahn-wel' dee-u-dohr'-u dah]   Manuel Deodoro da Fonseca, b. Aug. 5, 1827, d. Aug. 23, 1892, was the first president of the Republic of Brazil. An army officer, he helped depose Emperor PEDRO II in 1889, led the provisional government, and was elected president of the formally established republic in 1891. In November 1891 he was forced out of office and replaced by his vice-president, Floriano PEIXOTO.

Fontaine, Jean de La   see LA FONTAINE, JEAN DE

Fontainebleau [fohn-ten-bloh']   Fontainebleau (1982 pop., 15,679) is a municipality in northern France in Seine-et-Marne department. It is 64 km (40 mi) from Paris on the left bank of the Seine. Located in the Forest of Fontainebleau, it is a military center with a military college and an engineering school. By 1169, Fontainebleau was a residence of the French kings who were attracted by the forest's good hunting. The château, southeast of the town, was begun in 1528 by Francis I and served as the royal residence until construction of Versailles. Napoleon I held Pope Pius VII prisoner in the château from 1812 to 1814. It now serves as the summer residence of the president of France.

Fontainebleau, Château de   The Château de Fontainebleau, situated 64 km (40 mi) southeast of Paris in the forest of Fontainebleau, is one of the largest and most magnificent of the royal residences of France. The original building, of which very little remains, was a medieval hunting lodge. The present structure, comprising five separate groups of buildings, was begun in 1528 during the reign of Francis I. Francis gathered a large number of French, Italian, and Flemish architects, painters, and craftspersons to work on the château, thus introducing the styles of the Italian Renaissance into France and forming what has become known as the school of Fontainebleau. Later sovereigns, including Henry II, Francis II, Catherine de Médicis, and Henry IV, enlarged and embellished the building, which was provided with new furnishings by Napoleon I after the French Revolution. The spacious gardens were planned by André de Nôtre, a celebrated 17th-century landscape gardener, during the reign of Louis XIV.

Fontainebleau, school of   The term *school of Fontainebleau* designates two distinct schools of painting

The elaborate decoration of the Gallery of Francis I at Fontaine-bleau (c.1533–44), designed by Rosso Fiorentino and Francesco Primaticcio, illustrates the style favored by artists of the Fontainebleau school.

and architectural decoration. The first, and more important, school consisted of artists brought to France from Italy and the Netherlands by Francis I during the first half of the 16th century to work on the interior decoration of the newly constructed Château de Fontainebleau. Eminent painters and craftsmen who imported the style of the Italian Renaissance to France included Benvenuto CELLINI, Francesco PRIMATICCIO, and Rosso Fiorentino. Their collaboration with French and Flemish artists resulted in the international Mannerist style (see MANNERISM), which is characterized by its self-consciously elegant treatment of natural forms.

A second group of painters who inherited the Mannerist style but implemented it rather less forcefully were employed at the château during the reign of Henry IV, at the close of the 16th century. These included Ambroise Dubois, Toussaint Dubreuil, and Martin Fréminet. Though competent, they did not equal the achievements of their predecessors.

Fontana, Domenico The Italian architect Domenico Fontana, 1543–1607, traveled to Rome from his native Lugano in 1563, accompanied by his older brother Giovanni, who later became a celebrated engineer. Fontana was commissioned in 1585 by Cardinal Felice Peretti to design a chapel in the Basilica of Santa Maria Maggiore, and when the cardinal was elected Pope Sixtus V in the same year, Fontana became the architect to the papacy. During the 5-year reign of Sixtus, the city of Rome was extensively rebuilt under Fontana's direction; it took on the baroque form that survives to this day. Fontana's part in this large project included the designs of the Vatican, Lateran, and Quirinal palaces, the Vatican library, and completion of the dome of SAINT PETER'S BASILICA, all of which were executed between 1585 and 1590. In 1586, Fontana removed an ancient Egyptian obelisk from the side of the Vatican to its present position in front of Saint Peter's, where it distracts from the effect of Giovanni Lorenzo BERNINI'S colonnades. For this, as for

almost all his other work, Fontana has been denigrated by modern architectural historians, who have characterized his talent as uninspired and mediocre. Fontana was deprived of his post by Pope Clement VIII in 1592. He was obliged to move to Naples, were he built the Palazzo Reale (1600–02).

Fontane, Theodor [fohn-tah'-ne]   Theodor Fontane, b. Dec. 30, 1819, d. Sept. 20, 1898, was a German poet and travel writer and an important novelist. He worked as an apothecary before turning to journalism in 1850. He first became known for the patriotic ballads in *Gedichte* (Poems, 1851) and *Balladen* (Ballads, 1861). His *Wanderungen durch die Mark Brandenburg* (Travels through Brandenburg Province, 4 vols., 1862–82) is a historical travelogue. Fontane wrote his first novel, the historical *Vor dem Sturm* (Before the Storm, 1878), when he was nearly 60. He is now best known for his social novels set in or near late-19th-century Berlin. *Irrungen, Wirrungen* (1887; trans. as *Trials and Tribulations*, 1917), *Frau Jenny Treibel* (1892), *Effi Briest* (1895; Eng. trans., 1967; film, 1974), and *Der Stechlin* (Lake Stechlin, 1898) are among the best 19th-century German novels.

The 19th-century German author Theodor Fontane is best known for his realistic social novels. Set in a contemporary framework, the novels explore the rise of the middle class and their problems of redefining values.

Fontanne, Lynn   see LUNT, ALFRED, AND FONTANNE, LYNN

Fonteyn, Dame Margot [fahn-tayn']   Margot Fonteyn, b. Reigate, Surrey, May 18, 1919, d. Feb. 21, 1991, is an English ballet dancer whose career as a prima ballerina spanned several decades. Born Margaret Hookham, she traveled with her parents as a child to North America and China. Returning to London, she attended the Sadler's Wells Ballet School and made her debut as a snowflake in Tchaikovsky's *Nutcracker* at Sadler's Wells in 1934. Ninette de Valois picked her out to

Dame Margot Fonteyn appears with Rudolf Nureyev in a production of Prokofiev's Romeo and Juliet. *Fonteyn's exquisite style and characterization have made her one of the world's most admired dancers. In 1956, Fonteyn was created a Dame of the Order of the British Empire.*

succeed Alicia MARKOVA as the company's ballerina, and within five years she had danced *Giselle, Swan Lake*, and *The Sleeping Beauty*. Moreover, she became the chosen interpreter of the ballets of Frederick ASHTON, who joined the Vic-Wells Ballet (later Royal Ballet) in 1935 and began by creating *La Baiser de la Fée* for her. This first was followed by such ballets as *Apparitions, Nocturne, Horoscope*, and after World War II, *Symphonic Variations, Scènes de ballet, Cinderella, Daphnis and Chloé, Sylvia*, and *Ondine*, among others. Fonteyn was always notable for exquisite line, infallible musicality, and lyricism rather than virtuosity in elevation and pirouettes. Over the years she became a magisterial interpreter of such classic ballets as Marius PETIPA's *Sleeping Beauty, La Bayadère*, and *Raymonda*.

Fonteyn's partnership with Rudolf NUREYEV, beginning with *Giselle* in 1962, gave her a new lease on her career at an age when most dancers are contemplating retirement; Ashton set the seal on this partnership the following year with his *Marguerite and Armand*. Although she returned from time to time to her parent company, Fonteyn became a jet-age version of the peripatetic ballerinas of earlier times (such as Fanny Elssler and Anna Pavlova), appearing with many partners and companies all over the Western world. In 1979, on her 60th birthday, she was named *prima ballerina assolutta*, a title officially given only three times in the history of the Imperial Russian Ballet and its Soviet successors.

Foochow   see FUZHOU

food   see AGRICULTURE AND THE FOOD SUPPLY; COOKING; DIET, HUMAN; FOOD ADDITIVES; FOOD INDUSTRY; FOOD PRESERVATION; HEALTH FOODS; NUTRITION, HUMAN; articles on individual foods

---

food additives   A food additive is a nonfood substance added to food during its processing to preserve it or to improve its color, texture, flavor, or value. (By legal definition, the class also includes substances that may

become components of food indirectly, as a result of the manufacturing and packaging process. A chemical used to make cereal packaging paper, for instance, is considered a food additive if the packaged cereal absorbs it, even in minute quantities.) Some additives are intended as nutritional supplements. Iron, minerals, and vitamins are regularly introduced into foods to compensate for losses during processing or to provide additional nutrients. Flavoring agents make up the largest single class of additives and include salts, spices, essential oils, and natural and synthetic flavors (see FLAVORS AND FRAGRANCES). Additives that improve texture include emulsifiers, stabilizers, and thickeners. PECTIN and GELATIN thicken jams and jellies. LECITHIN acts as an emulsifier in dressings and chocolates.

The additives used to preserve food are primarily chemical microbial agents, such as the benzoates, propionates, and sorbates that retard spoilage by bacteria, yeasts, and molds. Antioxidants are used to keep fats and oils from spoiling and to prevent discoloration of smoked or canned meats. Ascorbic acid helps to prevent the discoloration of canned fruits.

Throughout culinary history, spices and salts have been added to food to preserve and flavor it. The wide use of synthetic additives, however, is a 20th-century phenomenon associated with the growth of the food industry. Some of the additives used today are, in the terminology of the U.S. Food and Drug Administration (FDA), Generally Recognized As Safe (GRAS). These were used in food prior to 1958 (when amendments to the Food, Drug, and Cosmetic Act required that new food additives be tested for safety) and had no recorded evidence of harmful effects. Since 1970, however, the FDA has been reviewing many of the substances on the GRAS list, and a few, such as the artificial sweetener cyclamate, have been banned. Others, such as the sweetener saccharin, have been removed from the list but may still be used; foods containing them, however, must carry warning labels. Health questions have also been raised about the new artificial sweetener, aspartame, which was approved in 1983 as an additive in foods and soft drinks. Synthetic food colors have also come under FDA scrutiny, and some dyes are now prohibited as food additives. The meat preservatives known as NITRITES came under similar scrutiny in the 1970s for possible carcinogenic effects, but by the mid-1980s the problem was determined to be limited to bacon. In 1986 the FDA banned the use of SULFITES as color preservatives in fresh fruits and vegetables; it had already required labeling of sulfite contents in other foods. More indirectly, the FDA banned the use of diethylstilbestrol (see DES) in 1979, because harmful residues showed up in food products.

Food and Agriculture Organization   The Food and Agriculture Organization (FAO), a specialized agency of the United Nations (UN), was established in 1945 as a research and coordinating organization to develop programs in the field of world food supply. Almost every UN member nation and several non-UN nations participate in the FAO, which is headquartered in Rome. The projects it initiates, primarily in the developing nations, are designed to improve efficiency in the production and distribution of agricultural products and to better the living conditions and nutrition levels of rural populations.

To achieve these aims, the FAO promotes the development of the basic soil and water resources of various countries. It encourages the global exchange of new agricultural techniques and improved plant types; combats epidemics of animal diseases; provides technical assistance; and promotes the development and utilization of the resources of the sea.

On an international level, the FAO works to establish a stable international market for agricultural commodities and plans projects in conjunction with other UN agencies, such as the World Health Organization and the International Bank for Reconstruction and Development (World Bank).

Food and Drug Administration The Food and Drug Administration (FDA) is the agency of the U.S. Department of Health and Human Services that oversees the safety of foods, drugs, cosmetics, and medical devices and operates the National Center for Toxicological Research. In 1906, in response to complaints about untested chemical additives in food, Congress passed the Pure Food and Drug Act (see PURE FOOD AND DRUG LAWS), which established the agency. Although initially the FDA could act only on FOOD ADDITIVES and drugs already in use and proven harmful, a series of subsequent laws expanded its jurisdiction. The Food, Drug, and Cosmetic Act of 1938 required manufacturers to test their products on both animals and humans before marketing them. In 1957 testing was required for new food additives, while the Delaney Clause (1958) prohibited the use of substances in food if they caused cancer in laboratory animals. In 1962 the FDA ruled that new drugs must be proven effective as well as safe and began a 20-year review to determine the effectiveness of prescription drugs already in use.

In 1962, having averted disaster by delaying approval of THALIDOMIDE, the FDA issued new regulations that made the drug review process far more stringent, and FDA approval for many new drugs now required up to three years of testing. "Fast-track" procedures have since been instituted for drugs with unique potential, but the weakness—as some see it—of many new testing requirements has aroused apprehensions about possible new drug hazards. Other issues of major significance remain unresolved, among them the use of antibiotics in animal feed and the nutrition labeling of foods. In addition, the efficacy of the Delaney Clause, which has structured both testing procedures and FDA decisions based on test results, is under question within the agency.

food industry The food industry comprises all business operations that are involved in producing a raw food material, processing it, and distributing it to sales outlets. The entire complex of the industry includes: farms and ranches; producers of raw materials, such as phosphates, for agricultural use; water-supply systems; food-processing plants; manufacturers of packaging materials and food-processing and transportation equipment; transportation systems; and retail stores and food-service operations such as restaurants, institutional feeding commissaries, and vending-machine servicers.

History of the Industry

The organized trading and transport of salt, spices, grain, olive oil, fermented beverages, and other foods have probably been practiced almost since the time of the first agricultural surpluses. Inventories of livestock and foodstuffs are among the first written records. Until modern preservation methods were developed, however, the kinds of foods that could be traded were limited to those which did not spoil quickly.

Most food-processing operations seem to have begun as extensions of kitchen preparation techniques, scaled up to furnish enough surplus product to be bartered or sold outside the household. Enlargement of a business entailed simply building more or larger processing equipment. Gradual improvements in design were made to increase yields or to improve quality. This was the general pattern until the Industrial Revolution, when major qualitative changes began to be made. Factories were greatly enlarged, and much of the manual labor was replaced by machinery. Also, entirely new principles of processing, such as canning and spray-drying, were invented. Channels of distribution became much more complex and extended, and special techniques for retaining quality were used, such as shipping by means of refrigerated railroad cars.

Distribution Patterns

Farmers, ranchers, other producers of agricultrual raw materials, and feedlot operators usually sell their output to collection points, such as grain terminals or stockyards. The terminal or stockyard supplies the processing companies, which select needed raw materials from the available stock and process them either into finished foodstuffs, for example, cuts of meat, or into food ingredients, such as flour.

From the processor, finished food products are sent to warehouses, which can assemble full truckloads of products originating from many different suppliers for shipment to one large retailer or to a number of smaller outlets in a given region, allowing a great reduction in unit transportation costs as compared to shipping a small quantity of one item directly from the producer to the retailer.

Processors of perishable foods (dairies, ice cream manufacturers, wholesale bread bakeries, and meat packers) usually maintain their own fleets of trucks for carrying fresh products directly to their retailer customers.

Restaurants purchase staples and nonperishable foods from the warehouses of specialized distributors. They also receive direct shipment from dairies, bakeries, and meat packers.

Food Processing

The food-processing industry is one of the biggest busi-

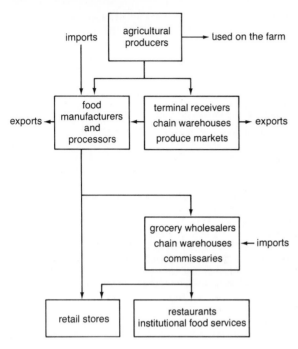

Flow of goods in the food industry

Testing is performed in accordance with standardized procedures. Tests may be based on physical properties such as dimensions, viscosity, chemical properties (such as vitamin content or pH), sensory attributes (such as appearance, taste, odor, texture), functionality (such as response to consumer cooking procedures), legal requirements, or public health considerations such as the presence of certain microorganisms. Objective chemical, physical, and microbiological analyses are preferred, but subjective testing for sensory properties by expert taste panels is also needed, since many of the quality characteristics important to consumers cannot be adequately measured by any existing objective procedure.

Evolution of Food Retailing

Prior to World War I most food was sold through small neighborhood groceries. The first successful food-store chain was the Great Atlantic and Pacific Tea Company (A&P), which was founded in 1859 but began its great expansion after World War I. Because chains could pool the purchases of many stores, coordinate distribution, and standardize management practices, marketing costs were reduced; a chain could undersell the independent store owner while maintaining adequate profit margins. To meet this challenge, independent store owners developed two different approaches: they joined voluntary cooperatives, which, for a licensing fee, provided many of the mass-purchasing and distribution efficiencies of chains; or they affiliated with a wholesaler-distributor network, which gave them some of the same advantages in return for semiexclusive dealing.

In the late 1980s some 60% of U.S. food sales originated in grocery stores (40% was consumed in restaurants and in other food-service establishments). Of this total, more than half was bought at supermarkets, stores whose annual volume exceeds $2 million. The number of "convenience" stores—small establishments, usually owned by chains, that sell a limited assortment of foods and achieve their largest volume on sales of milk and

nesses in the United States. In 1980 it employed about 1,700,000 people. Capital expenditures were almost $6 billion.

Nearly all food-processing companies, as well as many food-service chains, have a quality-control or quality-assurance department that evaluates raw materials, processes, and finished products. Most quality-control personnel are highly trained in chemistry, food technology, home economics, or microbiology.

The sale of "natural" foods was once confined to small specialty shops (left). Growing consumer interest in unprocessed foods, however, opened a new market for the giant food retailers. Today, packages of whole grains, raw nuts, and dried fruits produced without chemical preservatives can be found on the shelves of most supermarkets (right).

COST FACTORS CONTRIBUTING TO RETAIL PRICES OF CERTAIN FOODS IN GROCERY STORES

	Fresh Orange	Canned Tomato Juice	Chocolate Candy Bar	Loaf of Bread
Price to the consumer*	100.0	100.0	100.0	100.0
Price to the retailer, less discounts	64.2	78.5	75.0	81.5
Price to the wholesaler	—	72.4	71.2	—
Processor's costs and profits				
Ingredients and raw materials	20.1	10.9	38.5	18.0
Packaging materials	5.7	26.0	7.6	3.7
Labor and overhead (including utilities)	11.4	18.5	9.5	19.6
Transportation and storage	14.3	2.1	3.0	**
Selling expenses, including advertising and promotion	2.8	6.2	8.0	33.2
Profit before taxes	2.8	2.0	3.1	3.6
Scrap, spoiled, defective, trim, and returns	7.1	6.7	1.5	3.5

*These costs, in cents, are based on the price to the consumer of enough product to equal one dollar, before sales taxes. They are intended to be typical, but not necessarily averages, of data from any group of manufacturers.
**Included in selling expenses.

bread—multiplied, while small, owner-operated stores had difficulty competing with the larger units.

Computerization

Computers are increasingly used as tools to control inventories, cut operating costs, and assess changing consumer demands. Electronic scanning of Universal Product Code (UPC) symbols is designed to improve efficiency at the checkout counter, reduce errors, and assist inventory control. The UPC symbol is printed on each prepriced item, and it is "read" when passed over a scanner. The product identification is relayed by the scanning unit to a computer, which selects the appropriate price and description from its memory bank and causes this information to be printed on the cash register tape. The computer simultaneously deducts the item from a continuous inventory carried in its memory.

Industry Price Structure

A grocery product costing the wholesaler $1.00 reaches the supermarket customer at about $1.20. The gross margin of a chain retailer usually varies from 16% to 20%, which is expected to cover both wholesale and retail functions. An independent store operator who buys from cooperative purchasing operations or from an affiliated wholesaler can usually match chain prices and margins. In the latter case, the wholesaler would have a margin of about 4% to 5%, and the retailer, about 12% to 13%. Expenses of handling produce, frozen foods, health and beauty aids, and meats are greater, and the margins are correspondingly higher.

Food prices have increased almost continually in recent years, mainly because of rises in marketing costs—

the prices and quantities of labor, capital, and other factors employed in processing, wholesaling, and retailing food through food stores and public eating places. Costs per unit of food marketed have increased as a result of increases in consumption of prepackaged, ready-to-eat foods; a continuing trend toward away-from-home eating; service operations—delicatessens, bakeries, and so on—in food stores; rising wages and salaries; and higher costs for materials.

Government Regulations

The government's influence in the operations of the food industry is all-pervasive. Although the laws relating directly to food—the Pure Food, Drug, and Cosmetic Act and the Fair Packaging and Labeling Act (see PURE FOOD AND DRUG LAWS)—are quite comprehensive, the number in recent years of other statutes affecting the food industry has increased. Among these are the Consumer Product Safety Act; the Occupational Safety and Health Act; the Water Pollution Control Act; the Clean Air Act; the Federal Insecticide, Fungicide, and Rodenticide Act; and the Clean Water Act. Additionally, regulations or other actions of the Environmental Protection Agency, the Council on Environmental Quality, the Federal Energy Administration, the Energy Research and Development Administration, and the Department of Agriculture frequently affect food-industry operations.

See also: AGRIBUSINESS; FARMS AND FARMING.

---

food poisoning and infection   Food poisoning, or intoxication, is a group of disorders generally characterized by the symptoms of nausea, vomiting, and loss of appetite (anorexia); fever and abdominal pain or discomfort (gastroenteritis); and diarrhea, in varying degrees. It may result from poisons, or toxins, produced by microorganisms in food; ingestion of heavy metals such as copper and mercury; or ingestion of natural poisons such as those found in certain mushrooms and seafood.

Microorganisms. There are three ways in which disease results from contamination of food by microorganisms. The first is by direct infection of the gastrointestinal tract, usually by a *Staphylococcus* species. *Salmonella typhimurium* accounts for nearly 70 percent of food infection and is commonly found in meats, eggs, and milk. Allowing food to stand after exposure to *Staphylococcus* may permit the growth of a large number of organisms and the production of a potent toxin. Food handlers with *Staphylococcus* pustules on the hands or face are a major carrier. Gastrointestinal infection by these microbes usually causes gastroenteritis. Deaths are rare.

Second, if food contaminated by the bacterium *Clostridium botulinum* is improperly canned or bottled, the bacteria, under the anaerobic conditions of the container, are able to produce a toxin. The toxin, in turn, can produce the disease BOTULISM, despite the complete absence of bacterial multiplication. The botulin toxin resists intestinal enzymes; absorbed, it acts by paralyzing certain nerves that regulate muscle function. The most dangerous effect is weakness of the respiratory muscles, with resultant anoxia. The mortality rate can be as high as 65 percent, with most fatalities occurring between the second and ninth day after ingestion of the toxin. Potent antitoxins, prepared from the plasma of horses, are most effective before the patient shows symptoms.

Third, the syndrome of diarrhea and vomiting may result from infection by the protozoan *Entamoeba histolytica*, acquired by ingesting uncooked vegetables or drinking water (amoebic dysentery). Ulcerative lesions are produced in the intestine by the microorganism, which enters tissue by amoeboid motion and often erodes blood vessels. When mesenteric vessels are eroded, the parasite is carried to the liver, where abscess develops. The loss of fluids resulting from diarrhea and vomiting can lead to dehydration, which can threaten life in young or elderly patients. Treatment includes bed rest, fluids, and blood or plasma expanders if shock is impending. Good agents now exist for treating this parasite.

Metals. Ingestion of heavy metals can cause severe nausea, vomiting, and diarrhea. The severity of symptoms depends on the irritant and the dose, as well as on the resistance of the patient. Treatment consists of bed rest, fluids, and blood or plasma expanders in severe cases where shock is anticipated. Normally a chelating agent such as EDTA is used to form a complex with these metals, which are then eliminated naturally from the body.

Natural Poisons. Naturally occurring poisons in certain mushrooms, can cause sweating, cramps, diarrhea, confusion, and sometimes convulsions. Patients usually recover within 24 hours. If the infecting mushroom is *Amanito phalloides*, however, liver damage is common, leading to jaundice, and the mortality rate is about 60 percent or higher.

Fish poisoning can result from types such as sea bass, cavallas, mackerel, and puffers. Symptoms include numbness of the limbs, joint aches, chills, and fever. Muscle weakness and paralysis can also occur, and death may result within 24 hours. Mussels and clams may ingest a dinoflagellate (RED TIDE), which produces a toxin that is not destroyed by cooking. Symptoms include nausea, vomiting, and abdominal cramps; death may occur as a result of respiratory failure.

food preservation   The preservation of food is accomplished by controlling and, where possible, destroying the agents of food spoilage. These agents are present in abundance, not only within the food but also in the environments where foods are grown, harvested, processed, stored, and consumed. They include bacteria, molds, yeasts, insects, rodents, enzymes, and a wide variety of other chemical, biochemical, or physical factors.

Heat Processing. Most preservation processes are aimed at affecting bacteria, molds, and yeasts, and a number of methods are available for controlling or destroying these microorganisms. The food to be preserved can be subjected to temperatures that are high enough to kill most microorganisms. CANNING, the principal form of thermal, or heat, processing, has long been a major method of preservation. Foods sterilized in airtight, heat-resistant retort pouches (laminations of plastic and aluminum film) can be preserved indefinitely. Developed for the U.S. space program, these flexible pouches are now widely used in commercial food preservation.

Acids have a preservative effect, and acidic foods—tomatoes, for example—can be sterilized at a lower temperature than can bland foods. The organism that causes the deadly food-poisoning disease BOTULISM cannot grow in oxygen-free foods with a pH value below 4.5, a fairly high acidity.

Dehydration. DEHYDRATION of food is an effective weapon against microbial attack, since the free water in food is essential for the proliferation of bacteria. The preservation of food by drying is an ancient practice, but advances in food science and technology have created wholly new forms, such as compressed, freeze-dried foods that resume their original shape on rehydration.

Chemical Additives. Although a number of chemicals will destroy microorganisms, their use is restricted by the Food Additive Amendment of 1958. At low levels, and only in specified foods, ethyl formate, sodium benzoate, sodium and calcium propionate, sodium nitrite or nitrate, sorbic acid, and sulfur dioxide are permitted. Salt and sugar are effective preservatives; their action binds the water in a food so that it cannot be used by microorganisms. Smoke has some chemical preservation properties, since it contains guaiacol (2-methoxyphenol), which has limited bacteriocidal and antioxidant action. An antioxidant inhibits oxygen reactions, such as the chemical changes that cause food to become rancid or the bacteriological activity that can take place only in the presence of oxygen. The mild smoke treatment usually given meat or fish, however, is insufficient for lengthy preservation, and heat or cold is required to assure keeping quality. The principal purpose of smoking today is to give foods an appealing flavor. Some spices have value as antioxidants, but their primary function is flavor enhancement, as is the use of the additive MONOSODIUM GLUTAMATE.

Refrigeration and Freezing. Preserving food by refrigeration or by frozen storage is a widely used food-processing method. Low temperatures do not sterilize foods, but they slow down the growth of microorganisms and decrease the rate of the chemical reactions that deteriorate foods. Quick-frozen foods retain their nutrients almost intact, and the characteristics of their flavor remain virtually undiminished.

Preservation in Packaging. The plastic-aluminum retort pouch mentioned above is only one of a number of innovative ways to preserve food in packages. Fruits and vegetables are wrapped in plastic film, which is then shrunk tightly around the product to keep its freshness longer. Frozen vegetables need never be removed from the plastic bags in which they are packaged until after they are cooked.

Preservation by Radiation. Ionizing radiation, obtained from radioactive isotopes such as cobalt 60, can reduce or eliminate the microorganisms, insects, and parasites that live on food. Low levels of radiation kill some types of infestations. Very high levels can literally sterilize foods.

Some 20 countries, including the United States, have approved radiation for use on a limited group of foods: fresh fish, shellfish, and spices in Holland; potatoes in almost every country; and tropical fruits in South Africa. U.S. consumers, however, are wary of the process, and fresh-food sellers have discovered that irradiation changes textures, flavors, and colors in meats, seafoods, and some fresh produce.

Food Stamp Program   The U.S. Food Stamp Program, established in 1964, is designed to enable low-income households to buy quantities and kinds of food that would ordinarily be beyond their budgets. The program is administered by the Food and Nutrition Service of the U.S. Department of Agriculture, principally through welfare and public assistance agencies. Participants are given stamps that they can use to purchase food. A household is eligible to join the program if it has an income below a specified level and meets certain other qualifications. The stamps cannot be used to buy imported food or nonfood items, including household goods, cigarettes, tobacco, or alcoholic beverages. The federal government reimburses retailers for the difference between the food-stamp price and the regular price of items purchased. In 1977 the requirement that recipients pay for food stamps was abolished.

fool   Fools, or professional jesters, were employed by the wealthy and powerful from ancient Egyptian times until the 18th century. Often an insane or deformed person whose antics were a source of amusement, the fool may also have served as a scapegoat, or bearer of ill fortune. The long and complex tradition of fools in Western literature includes Sebastian Brant's satire *The Ship of Fools* (1494), translated into many languages and popular throughout Europe. Brant's perspective is shared by Desiderius Erasmus's ironic treatise *The Praise of Folly* (1509; Eng. trans., 1549), and finds its most powerful expression in the plays of William Shakespeare, where the fool's madness or innocence, real or feigned, gives him license to mock the pretensions and self-deceptions of his patrons. The motley clothing of the fool on the Elizabethan stage parodies the customs of sane society. Modern satiric comedy also relies upon the tradition of the fool. A notable example is the half-humorous, half-sinister figure of Harpo Marx.

Fools, Feast of   The Feast of Fools was a mock religious festival held in England and France between the 5th and 16th centuries during the week after Christmas. A self-styled bishop of fools would lead a group of lower clergy in parodying the customs and rituals of the church. Other actors disguised themselves in costume and engaged in obscene dances and songs. The feast was finally suppressed during the Reformation.

fool's gold   see PYRITE

Foot, Michael   Michael Mackintosh Foot, b. July 23, 1913, was leader of the British Labour party from 1980 to 1983. Foot entered Parliament in 1945 and for 9 years (1948–52, 1955–60) was editor of the left-wing journal *Tribune.* In the Labour government of the 1970s he served as secretary for employment (1974–76) and lord president of the council and leader of the house of Commons (1976–79). He resigned after leading the Labourites to defeat in the general election of June 1983.

foot-and-mouth disease   Foot-and-mouth is a highly contagious viral disease that can affect all cloven-hoofed animals. Although it is not prevalent in North America, it is constantly guarded against because it could easily be introduced through the import of live animals, fresh or frozen beef, or even animal bones used as fertilizer. Symptoms of the disease include fever, watery blisters in the mouth, excessive drooling, blistering between the hoof claws, and lameness. Occasionally, the disease will devastate a herd; more often, it does not kill but causes enormous economic losses through weight loss, quarantine, and poor performance of infected cattle. The protection afforded by vaccination is not permanent.

foot-binding   Foot-binding was a traditional Chinese custom whereby the feet of young girls were tightly bound with strips of linen in order to prevent further growth. The large toe was bent backward over the top of the foot, and the remaining toes were folded underneath. Girls between the ages of 5 and 12 were selected to undergo foot-binding, especially if they gave promise of future beauty. The process could not be reversed.

The origin of foot-binding, which is no longer performed, is obscure. At the beginning of the Song dynasty (AD 960–1279), the practice was confined to court dancers. Later the custom spread throughout all social classes in China. From a mark of beauty and gentility, it came to be a requirement for a bride. The upper classes, in particular, favored foot-binding because it showed that they could support women incapable of physical labor. In 1912 the Chinese government officially banned the custom.

foot disorders   The human foot, a complex structure that must bear the weight of the entire body, is prone to a number of disorders and injuries. Unlike other primate feet, it is adapted solely for use in locomotion. It consists of 26 bones plus muscles, tendons, blood vessels, nerves, skin, and nails. The two largest bones are in the ankle, or tarsal, region: the heel bone, or calcaneus; and the talus, a compact bone between the lower leg and the calcaneus, completing the body's weight-bearing axis. The midfoot contains five metatarsals, each forming a movable joint with one of the toes, or phalanges (see HUMAN BODY). Foot disorders are of three main types: those unique to the foot, those found elsewhere in the body but that are distinctly different in the foot, and those occurring similarly throughout the body.

Unique Conditions. Clubfoot is a disorder in which the foot is twisted inward and downward through shortening of ligaments and tendons. In some cases the condition is inherited; in others it appears to be caused by diseases or other factors. Mild cases may be treated with a progressive series of casts, but more severe ones require surgery.

Flatfoot and a narrow, rigid foot with a high arch are painful conditions usually treatable with arch supports. One form of flatfoot, pronation, is seen in infants and children and is usually not painful at that age. Ligament laxity allows the heels to roll outward, causing walking deformities and possible pain in later life unless corrected.

Bunions most commonly affect the joint between the big toe and its metatarsal bone. The bursa, a fluid-filled sac in the joint, becomes inflamed and swells (see BURSITIS), causing pain and often twisting the big toe toward the second toe. Disabling bunions require surgery. Corns are simply skin thickenings that become painful as they taper into the skin and cause pressure on nerve endings.

Distinctive Conditions. Plantar wart (also called a verruca) is caused by the same virus as that of the common WART elsewhere. On the sole of the foot, however, the firm wart acts like a pebble in a shoe, pushing against deeper skin layers that give way before it and causing great pain. Plantar warts may be treated by such techniques as freezing.

Ingrown toenail occurs on the rim of the nail of the big toe, when shoe pressure causes the skin to be forced over the nail. This carries bacteria beneath the skin surface, and infection results. Surgical removal of part of the nail may be required in severe cases. A variety of FUNGUS DISEASE called athlete's foot is caused by *Trichophyton nentagrophytes, T. rubrum*, and other fungus species. Most commonly, it occurs when the moist warmth of socks acts as an incubator for fungi picked up from the environment.

General Disorders. Joints of the foot may be affected by the various forms of ARTHRITIS found elsewhere in the body. These include rheumatoid arthritis, OSTEOARTHRITIS, and GOUT. Treatment of arthritis in the foot is substantially the same as in other parts of the body. Arthritic spurs on the big-toe joint cause rigidity that may make normal walking impossible in severe cases. Sometimes special shoes may be sufficient to alleviate the problem, but in some cases replacement of the joint with a synthetic one is required. Arthritic spurs are most common either on the top of the foot at the joint between the metatarsal and one of the ankle bones, or on the heel bone. Such spurs may require surgical removal.

Inflammations of the back part of the foot are common. The one most frequently seen is TENDONITIS of the Achilles tendon, the large tendon of the back of the heel. The inflammation may be a symptom of gout but is more commonly the result of stress. The posterior tibial tendon, which runs along the inner side of the foot, is a similar cause of pain in persons with flatfoot. The plantar fascia, a thick sheet of fibrous tissue running from the heel bone forward to the joints between the metatarsals and the toes, is a major support of the long arch of the foot, and

when it becomes inflamed it can cause great disability. Pain is usually relieved by firm arch supports.

Arterial diseases not uncommonly affect the foot, particularly ATHEROSCLEROSIS. Diseases of the arteries anywhere in the leg are likely to be observed first in the foot and especially in the toes, and they may produce extensive GANGRENE, or tissue death. Persons with DIABETES may develop this condition, sometimes necessitating amputation of part or all of the lower extremity.

Injuries. Twisting of the foot relative to the lower leg results in fractures about the ankle. Toes and metatarsal bones may be crushed by falling objects. Jolts caused by jumping can fracture the heel bone. Hairline fractures of the second metatarsal are now frequently seen in joggers.

——

football Football, in its American version, is a physically tough team sport that rivals baseball as the most popular athletic event for spectators in the United States. Millions watch football games on the interscholastic, intercollegiate, and professional levels. Games are often accompanied by halftime shows, with marching bands, and alumni or fan-club gatherings; fierce loyalties develop on the part of some spectators. Much illicit wagering takes place on games, even those at the secondary-school level. On the intercollegiate and professional levels, crowds of 50,000 to 100,000 at games are common, and millions more watch games on television.

Football is basically an autumn sport, with teams playing from 8 to 16 games, usually on successive weekends. The best of the teams then enter postseason playoffs. Many states have championships at the interscholastic (high school) level. The best of the college teams play in several bowl games—the most popular being the Rose Bowl, the Sugar Bowl, the Orange Bowl, and the Cotton Bowl. Although there is no one official college championship team, the unofficial intercollegiate champion is selected by a vote. (Coaches, sportswriters, and broadcasters cast ballots.) The professional teams of the National Football League (NFL) culminate their season with the Super Bowl game, between the winners of the American and National conference play-offs.

Despite its tremendous popularity in the United States, football has remained basically an American sport. Except for Canadians, who play the game with slightly altered rules (for example, 12 players to a side instead of 11 as in the U.S. game), football essentially has failed to take hold elsewhere. This fact has added to the mystique of the sport's popularity in the United States.

Rules of American Football

The rules of football have evolved over a long time, partly because American football can be directly traced to rugby and the modifications that Americans made to that sport to develop their own version. The rules are constantly changed to maintain a balance between offense and defense and to lessen the sport's violent nature. A set of football rules is long and sometimes almost unwieldy; high schools, colleges, and professionals play by three different sets of rules, which vary widely. The rules are enforced by a number of

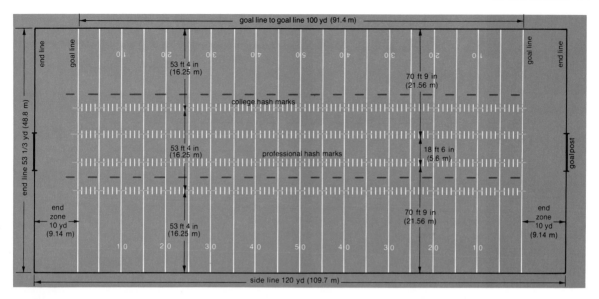

The diagram of a modern football field indicates the standard dimensions and the difference between hash marks observed in collegiate and professional play. Rule changes adopted (1912) by college officials established the 100-yard field of play.

officials on the field—ranging from four in high school games to seven in professional football.

A common denominator of all three levels of American football is the size of the field. It is 100 yd (91.4 m) long with two additional 10-yd (9.14-m) areas called end zones. The field is 53⅓ yd (48.8 m) wide. On the field, teams of 11 players line up in offensive and defensive positions. Teams advance the ball by running with it, passing (throwing) it, and kicking it. The lines at each end of the 100 yd are called goal lines, and the object of the game is for a player to cross the other team's goal line with the ball and thus score points.

Scoring. When a player carries the ball over the opponent's goal line or passes the ball to a teammate, who either catches the ball in the end zone or catches it within the playing area and carries it over the goal line, the team is credited with a touchdown, worth six points. A team can also score three points instead of trying for a touchdown by kicking the ball (a field goal) through the uprights and above the crossbar (the goalpost) of the end zone that the opponent is defending. The goalposts are stationed on the two end lines in all levels of football. Points can also be scored by stopping an opponent with the ball behind that opponent's own goal line (a safety, worth two points) and on a conversion play following a touchdown. In a conversion attempt, the team that has scored the touchdown is given an opportunity to kick the ball through the uprights or advance it across the goal line again from the opponent's 2-yd line (the 3-yd line in college football). In the National Football League, both types of conversion plays are worth one point; in college play, kicking is worth one point, but advancing over the goal line by a run or a pass is worth two points.

Operation of Play. College and professional games are 60 minutes long; high school games are 48 minutes. Play is divided into two halves, and the halves are divided equally so that in a complete game there are four quarters. The games actually last much longer, however, because the clock is stopped after scores and for penalties, measurements, injuries, out-of-bounds plays, and incomplete passes. Teams are allowed to take a limited number of timeouts; they also leave the field to take a rest break at halftime, at which time they can readjust their strategies.

Play begins with a kickoff, in which a member of one team kicks the ball off the ground (from its own 35-yd line in NFL games; from the 40-yd line in college and high school play). A coin flip just before the start of the game determines which team will perform the kickoff. Subsequent plays are begun with the center hiking the ball (passing it backward through the legs or handing it underneath the legs to a quarterback stationed directly behind) from the point—called the scrimmage line—where the center's team has advanced the ball. A play ends when the ballcarrier—a rusher (runner) or a pass-receiver—is tackled by an opponent; falls to the ground (in professional football, he must be tackled to the ground); or runs out-of-bounds; or when a forward pass is not completed (caught by a teammate).

The offensive team (the team in possession of the ball) lines up in different formations, dictated by strategy, and is allowed four plays, called downs, to advance the ball 10 yd. Each time the team does so, it is credited with a first down and is given four more downs to make 10 yd again. If the offensive team fails to advance 10 yd in any series of four plays, the opposition takes possession of the ball and goes on offense. Often a team that is stopped deep in its own territory with little chance of making the 10 yd will kick, or punt, the ball in order to put the oppo-

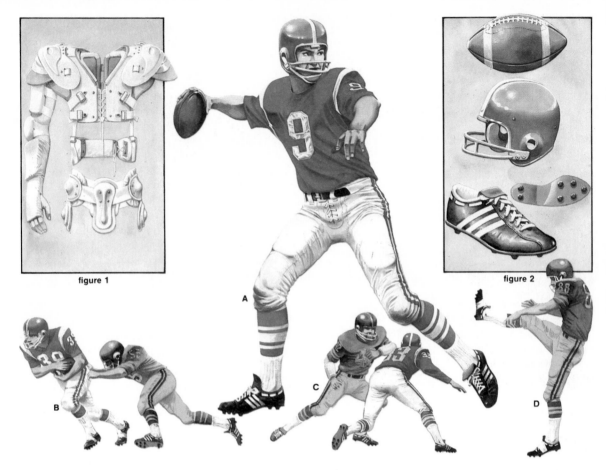

Some fundamental playing situations are demonstrated by the quarterback (A) attempting a pass, a running back (B) eluding a tackle, a lineman (C) blocking a defender, and a kicker (D) just having punted the ball to the opposing team. The contact involved in football requires that players wear padding (Fig. 1) to protect the ribs, hips, and upper torso. The basic gear (Fig. 2) includes: the ball, an inflated, leather-sheathed rubber bladder; a helmet with a protective face guard; and shoes equipped with cleated soles for traction.

nent farther back in its own territory. At any point in the game, however, the defense can get the ball by intercepting a pass or recovering a fumble (dropped ball). Generally, football teams have specialists for both offense and defense, and the same players do not participate in both phases of the game, although they are allowed to.

Equipment. The basic equipment for playing the game is a ball in the shape of an oblate spheroid 11–11¼ in (28–28.6 cm) long and 21¼–21½ in (54–54.6 cm) around its longest axis; the ball weighs 14–15 oz (396.9–425.25 g). The goalposts vary in different levels of play. In addition, players are heavily burdened with different types of protective equipment so that they resemble modern-day gladiators.

History of Football

Any number of theories exist about the evolution of American football, but most historians agree that it is a modification of the English game of RUGBY and of soccer. American football evolved slowly in the 19th century.

19th-Century Development. Football made its first appearance at the intercollegiate level. As a prelude to what would become an American game, collegians played rugby, but the sport was so grueling that it was barred at Harvard in 1860. Nine years later, on Nov. 6, 1869, two New Jersey universities, Rutgers and Princeton, played what is considered the first intercollegiate game in the United States—although it hardly resembled modern-day football, or even the football that was played at the turn of the century. There were 25 players on each side, and the scoring was decided by goals, not touchdowns, conversions, and field goals. Rutgers won that first game, and Princeton won a rematch a week later. Before long, other universities began taking up the game—Columbia in 1870, followed by Yale two years later.

This early football game pitting Yale against longtime rival Princeton was played in 1909, 40 years after the first intercollegiate game was contested. Yale, with a 10–0–0 record, was selected as national collegiate champion in 1909.

(Left) Jim Thorpe, an outstanding football player of the early 20th century, became a collegiate star at Carlisle (Pa.) Indian School, where he won All-American honors. As a professional, Thorpe stimulated the growth of the sport.

Harvard continued to play a game more similar to rugby; in 1875, however, when it played Yale, Harvard persuaded its opponent to play under new rules, which brought the game into a new era. Touchdowns counted only one point, compared to four for a successful conversion kick. A field goal was worth five points.

Walter CAMP, a freshman at Yale in 1876, became the organizational genius that the college game badly needed to unify and organize the rules. Under his influence the teams were decreased in size from 15 to 11. The field varied from 140 yd (128 m) by 70 yd (64m) to 110 by 53⅓ yd (100.5 by 48.8 m), and the ball was put in play by having the offensive team's center get the ball from his line of scrimmage to the quarterback. In 1889, another innovation Camp shared in was the selection of the first All-American team, which started the trend toward glamorizing individual stars.

The first significant rules convention was held in 1880. The participants neglected, however, to provide incentives for advancing the line of scrimmage, thus sustaining the dull, 90-minute game. In 1882, Camp successfully campaigned for the rule that made the offensive team give up possession if it moved the ball less than 5 yd forward in three downs.

Camp also standardized the scoring system in 1883, showing a strong prejudice toward the kicking influence of rugby and soccer. Touchdowns scored only two points, whereas the conversion kick scored four and field goals five.

20th-Century Innovations. Because of the violent, physical way in which football games were conducted in the 19th century, many deaths and maiming injuries occurred. As a result of 18 deaths and 159 serious injuries in 1905, President Theodore Roosevelt insisted that the colleges make their game safer or he might ban it. Repre-

In modern football, each play begins from the line of scrimmage, an imaginary plane spanning the width of the field, passing through the portion of the ball nearest to the defensive team. A minimum of seven offensive players must position themselves within a yard of the line of scrimmage.

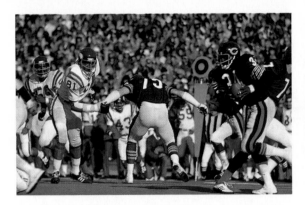

Running back Walter Payton of the Chicago Bears gains yardage on the ground during an NFL game. In 1984, Payton became the NFL's all-time leading rusher. He ended his career in 1987 with a total of 16, 726 yards.

Quarterback Joe Montana of the San Francisco 49ers prepares to release a forward pass, one means by which the offense may advance the ball. A legal pass must be thrown from behind the line of scrimmage.

sentatives of 62 colleges met in New York City after the 1905 season, and in early 1906 rules were suggested and approved that would eliminate the negative aspects. The emphasis was shifted from brawn to speed and strategy. The legalization of the forward pass made much of this possible. The game was also shortened from 70 to 60 minutes, and the required yardage for a first down was reset at 10 yd. A neutral zone was set up between teams at the scrimmage line, and the offense had to have a least six men on the line of scrimmage, thus eliminating the dangerous plays in which blockers took running starts before the snap of the ball. A seventh blocker on the line of scrimmage was mandated in 1910 to make the game even safer.

Football rules were changed constantly, however, to maintain the delicate offense-defense balance. After 1912, however, when the number of chances to make a first down was increased to four, the changes were less drastic.

The Passing Game. Modern football differs most from the turn-of-the-century game because of the skills of

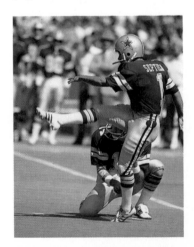

Rafael Septien of the Dallas Cowboys attempts to kick a field goal. The field goal, worth three points, is scored by placekicking the ball between the uprights of the goalpost.

passers. When the passing rule was instituted in 1906, few took advantage of it. Actually, some rules limited its advancement, including the one that said that no pass could travel more than 20 yd beyond the line of scrimmage and the one that stated that an incomplete pass resulted in a 15-yd loss.

The passing combination of quarterback Gus Dorais and Knute ROCKNE at Notre Dame in 1913 popularized the pass. This aspect of the game brought fame to Notre Dame and its future coach Rockne, who became a legend. Notre Dame defeated a powerful West Point team that year, with Dorais passing for 243 yd.

The ball was gradually made smaller as passing became more important. It was instrumental in increasing interest in professional football, which lagged well behind college football until the 1950s. The passing skills of such players as Sammy BAUGH, Otto GRAHAM, and Johnny UNITAS helped the professional sport achieve a rapid growth in popularity.

Professional Football. The game was first played with paid players in 1895, when a team from Latrobe, Pa., hosted a game with a team from nearby Jeannette. Except for barnstorming (touring) teams, however, there was little professional football of any significance until 1919, when the founders of what would become the National Football League met in Canton, Ohio, to organize the sport. Jim THORPE was named president of the league to capitalize on his reputation.

Professional football grew slowly, however. There were times of increased interest, such as the period during the 1920s when Red GRANGE signed to play professionally and drew crowds of 36,000 in Chicago and 68,000 in New York City. The college teams, including the Ivy League schools, still captured the attention of the sports public.

A second professional league, the All-America Football Conference, was founded in 1946 to compete with the NFL, but that league was absorbed by its competitor in 1950. The coming of the television age and America's unending thirst for more sports after World War II helped

NATIONAL FOOTBALL LEAGUE CHAMPIONS*

Year	Winner	Runner-up	Year	Winner	Runner-up
1933	Chicago Bears 23	New York Giants 21	1952	Detroit Lions 17	Cleveland Browns 7
1934	New York Giants 30	Chicago Bears 13	1953	Detroit Lions 17	Cleveland Browns 16
1935	Detroit Lions 26	New York Giants 7	1954	Cleveland Browns 56	Detroit Lions 10
1936	Green Bay Packers 21	Boston Redskins 6	1955	Cleveland Browns 38	Los Angeles Rams 14
1937	Washington Redskins 28	Chicago Bears 21	1956	New York Giants 47	Chicago Bears 7
1938	New York Giants 23	Green Bay Packers 17	1957	Detroit Lions 59	Cleveland Browns 14
1939	Green Bay Packers 27	New York Giants 0	1958	Baltimore Colts 23	New York Giants 17
1940	Chicago Bears 73	Washington Redskins 0	1959	Baltimore Colts 31	New York Giants 16
1941	Chicago Bears 37	New York Giants 9	1960	Philadelphia Eagles 17	Green Bay Packers 13
1942	Washington Redskins 14	Chicago Bears 6	1961	Green Bay Packers 37	New York Giants 0
1943	Chicago Bears 41	Washington Redskins 21	1962	Green Bay Packers 16	New York Giants 7
1944	Green Bay Packers 14	New York Giants 7	1963	Chicago Bears 14	New York Giants 10
1945	Cleveland Rams 15	Washington Redskins 14	1964	Cleveland Browns 27	Baltimore Colts 0
1946	Chicago Bears 24	New York Giants 14	1965	Green Bay Packers 23	Cleveland Browns 12
1947	Chicago Cardinals 28	Philadelphia Eagles 21	1966	Green Bay Packers 34	Dallas Cowboys 27
1948	Philadelphia Eagles 7	Chicago Cardinals 0	1967	Green Bay Packers 21	Dallas Cowboys 17
1949	Philadelphia Eagles 14	Los Angeles Rams 0	1968	Baltimore Colts 34	Cleveland Browns 0
1950	Cleveland Browns 30	Los Angeles Rams 28	1969	Minnesota Vikings 27	Cleveland Browns 7
1951	Los Angeles Rams 24	Cleveland Browns 17			

*League merged with the American Football League before the 1970 season, forming two conferences, the American and the National. Winners of the respective conference championships (listed separately) meet in the Super Bowl to decide the NFL championship.

AMERICAN CONFERENCE (NFL) CHAMPIONS

Year	Winner	Runner-up
1970	Baltimore Colts 27	Oakland Raiders 17
1971	Miami Dolphins 21	Baltimore Colts 0
1972	Miami Dolphins 21	Pittsburgh Steelers 17
1973	Miami Dolphins 27	Oakland Raiders 10
1974	Pittsburgh Steelers 24	Oakland Raiders 13
1975	Pittsburgh Steelers 16	Oakland Raiders 10
1976	Oakland Raiders 24	Pittsburgh Steelers 7
1977	Denver Broncos 20	Oakland Raiders 17
1978	Pittsburgh Steelers 34	Houston Oilers 5
1979	Pittsburgh Steelers 27	Houston Oilers 13
1980	Oakland Raiders 34	San Diego Chargers 27
1981	Cincinnati Bengals 27	San Diego Chargers 7
1982	Miami Dolphins 14	New York Jets 0
1983	Oakland Raiders 30	Seattle Seahawks 14
1984	Miami Dolphins 45	Pittsburgh Steelers 28
1985	New England Patriots 31	Miami Dolphins 14
1986	Denver Broncos 23	Cleveland Browns 20
1987	Denver Broncos 38	Cleveland Browns 33
1988	Cincinnati Bengals 21	Buffalo Bills 10
1989	Denver Broncos 37	Cleveland Browns 21
1990	Buffalo Bills 51	Los Angeles Raiders 3

NATIONAL CONFERENCE (NFL) CHAMPIONS

Year	Winner	Runner-up
1970	Dallas Cowboys 17	San Francisco 49ers 10
1971	Dallas Cowboys 14	San Francisco 49ers 3
1972	Washington Redskins 26	Dallas Cowboys 3
1973	Minnesota Vikings 27	Dallas Cowboys 10
1974	Minnesota Vikings 14	Los Angeles Rams 10
1975	Dallas Cowboys 37	Los Angeles Rams 7
1976	Minnesota Vikings 24	Los Angeles Rams 13
1977	Dallas Cowboys 23	Minnesota Vikings 6
1978	Dallas Cowboys 28	Los Angeles Rams 0
1979	Los Angeles Rams 9	Tampa Bay Buccaneers 0
1980	Philadelphia Eagles 20	Dallas Cowboys 7
1981	San Francisco 49ers 28	Dallas Cowboys 27
1982	Washington Redskins 31	Dallas Cowboys 17
1983	Washington Redskins 24	San Francisco 49ers 21
1984	San Francisco 49ers 23	Chicago Bears 0
1985	Chicago Bears 24	Los Angeles Rams 0
1986	New York Giants 17	Washington Redskins 0
1987	Washington Redskins 17	Minnesota Vikings 10
1988	San Francisco 49ers 28	Chicago Bears 3
1989	San Francisco 49ers 30	Los Angeles Rams 3
1990	New York Giants 15	San Francisco 49ers 13

the NFL grow. By the late 1950s the televising of football games, which was held to a minimum by the colleges, was utilized by the professional teams to promote their game. Rising attendance prompted the founding (1960) of a new circuit, the American Football League. The NFL and AFL competed to sign new players and wisely loosened their rules to allow more scoring. Before long they were competing on an equal level with the colleges for the football fan. The AFL was absorbed by the NFL in 1970 as a result of a merger agreement in 1966. From this

agreement came a plan for a postseason championship game, which became known as the Super Bowl, consistently the most popular televised sports event. The short-lived World Football League (1974–75) and United States Football League (1983–85) were other challengers to the NFL's supremacy.

Canadian Football. Like U.S. football, Canadian football developed from rugby and soccer during the late 19th century. In 1909, Lord Grey, governor-general of Canada, donated a trophy—subsequently called the Grey

SUPER BOWL*

Year	Teams and Scores		Place
1966–67	Green Bay Packers 35	Kansas City Chiefs 10	Los Angeles
1967–68	Green Bay Packers 33	Oakland Raiders 14	Miami
1968–69	New York Jets 16	Baltimore Colts 7	Miami
1969–70	Kansas City Chiefs 23	Minnesota Vikings 7	New Orleans
1970–71	Baltimore Colts 16	Dallas Cowboys 13	Miami
1971–72	Dallas Cowboys 24	Miami Dolphins 3	New Orleans
1972–73	Miami Dolphins 14	Wash. Redskins 7	Los Angeles
1973–74	Miami Dolphins 24	Minnesota Vikings 7	Houston
1974–75	Pittsburgh Steelers 16	Minnesota Vikings 6	New Orleans
1975–76	Pittsburgh Steelers 21	Dallas Cowboys 17	Miami
1976–77	Oakland Raiders 32	Minnesota Vikings 14	Pasadena
1977–78	Dallas Cowboys 27	Denver Broncos 10	New Orleans
1978–79	Pittsburgh Steelers 35	Dallas Cowboys 31	Miami
1979–80	Pittsburgh Steelers 31	Los Angeles Rams 19	Pasadena
1980–81	Oakland Raiders 27	Philadelphia Eagles 10	New Orleans
1981–82	San Francisco 49ers 26	Cincinnati Bengals 21	Pontiac
1982–83	Wash. Redskins 27	Miami Dolphins 17	Pasadena
1983–84	Oakland Raiders 38	Wash. Redskins 9	Tampa
1984–85	San Francisco 49ers 38	Miami Dolphins 16	Palo Alto
1985–86	Chicago Bears 46	New England Patriots 10	New Orleans
1986–87	New York Giants 39	Denver Broncos 20	Pasadena
1987–88	Wash. Redskins 42	Denver Broncos 10	San Diego
1988–89	San Francisco 49ers 20	Cincinnati Bengals 16	Miami
1989–90	San Francisco 49ers 55	Denver Broncos 10	New Orleans
1990–91	New York Giants 20	Buffalo Bills 19	Tampa

*AFL-NFL interleague championship 1966–70; NFL championship since 1970–71.

AMERICAN FOOTBALL LEAGUE CHAMPIONS*

1960	Houston Oilers 24	Los Angeles Chargers 16	
1961	Houston Oilers 10	San Diego Chargers 3	
1962	Dallas Texans 20	Houston Oilers 17	
1963	San Diego Chargers 51	Boston Patriots 10	
1964	Buffalo Bills 20	San Diego Chargers 7	
1965	Buffalo Bills 23	San Diego Chargers 0	
1966	Kansas City Chiefs 31	Buffalo Bills 7	
1967	Oakland Raiders 40	Houston Oilers 7	
1968	New York Jets 27	Oakland Raiders 23	
1969	Kansas City Chiefs 17	Oakland Raiders 7	

*League merged with NFL in 1970 and became the American Conference.

Cup—to be awarded annually to Canada's best football team. Although Grey Cup play became predominantly professional during the 1930s, amateur teams were not banned until 1956, when the current structure of the organization that would become (1960) the Canadian Football League (CFL) was solidified. Canadian football differs from its U.S. professional counterpart in several ways: the field is 110 yd (100.6 m) long and 65 yd (59.4 m) wide, with 25-yd-deep (22.9-m) end zones; there are 12 players per team on the field; the offensive team has 3 downs to gain 10 yd; an untouched punt or unsuccessful field-goal attempt may be recovered by the kicking team; after a touchdown, a team may try for 2 points; a team can score a rouge (1 point) if their opponents fail to run a kick out of their own end zone.

Foote, Andrew Hull [fut]   Andrew Hull Foote, b. New Haven, Conn., Sept. 12, 1806, d. June 26, 1863, was a U.S. naval officer. After engaging in suppression of the slave trade along the African coast (1849–51), he commanded (1856–58) the *Portsmouth* off China and led (1856) a raid to capture four barrier forts south of Guangzhou (Canton) that had fired on his ship. During the U.S. Civil War, Foote was in charge of Union naval operations on the upper Mississippi. In 1862 his gunboats assisted in the capture of FORT HENRY AND FORT DONELSON and Island No. 10. A temperance advocate, Foote brought about abolition (1862) of alcohol on naval ships.

Foote, Horton   The playwright and scriptwriter Horton Foote, b. Wharton, Tex., Mar. 14, 1916, has had remarkable success in mining the history of his family for his many dramas. An actor and theater manager, Foote began writing plays, most of them based in small-town Texas, in the early 1940s. His many screenplays include his adaptation of *To Kill a Mockingbird* (1962) and *The Trip to Bountiful* (1985), taken from his own 1953 play and TV script. Both screenplays won academy awards. From 1947 most of his work has appeared on television. Foote's daughter, Hallie, played her own grandmother in the three-play miniseries *Story of a Marriage* (1987).

foraminifera [fohr-am-i-nif'-ur-uh]   Foraminifera, often called forams, constitute an order, Foraminifera, of amoeboid marine PROTOZOA with calcareous shells. Pseudopods protrude through holes in the shells—hence the name Foraminifera, which means "hole bearers." Foraminifera shells may accumulate in tracts of ocean floor in such numbers that they form the predominant SEDIMENTS in such regions. Such sedimentary deposits may become transformed into CHALK and, if uplifted geologically, exposed at the Earth's surface.

Growth and Reproduction. The single cell of the living foraminiferal animal may have one or more nuclei. As the animal grows, it adds chambers to its shell, or test. The body substance (protoplasm) fills all these chambers, which are connected by openings called foramina. Pseudopods (long, fine extensions of the protoplasm) project through numerous small pores in the test. The pseudopods gather food and construct the new chambers.

Foraminifera reproduce by alternating asexual and sexual generations. Asexually produced organisms originate from the division of a single parental individual. At maturity, asexual individuals produce gametes (reproductive cells). Gametes from two different parents form a new individual, which reproduces asexually to complete the reproductive cycle.

Distribution. Nearly all foraminifera are marine, and the great majority of these are benthic (dwellers on the sea floor). Species of benthic forams that are restricted to particular types of sediment, temperatures, or salinity conditions may be good indicators of environmental factors. Particular species of planktonic (floating) forams,

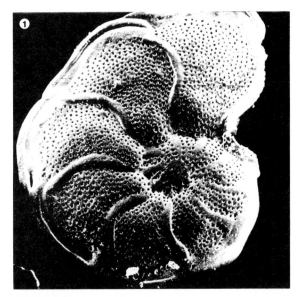

The foraminiferan Almaena taurica *(1), photographed with an electron diffraction microscope, is known from Upper Eocene deposits in the USSR.* Globigerinoides fistulosus *(2), known from the Middle Pliocene to recent epochs, has spherical chambers except for the last one or two, which form finger-shaped extensions.* Globigerina nepenthes *(3), with spherical to ovate chambers, occurs in Miocene and Pliocene strata. Elongation of the last two chambers characterizes* Globigerina digitata digitata *(4), found in the Quaternary Period. Shells of the species shown measure about 1 mm (0.04 in) in diameter.*

however, are often characteristic of cold-water or warm-water oceanic regions. Shifts in the geographic distribution of planktonic species in Pleistocene deposits are used to map the changing course of OCEAN CURRENTS of the last ICE AGE.

Importance. Foraminifera are important components of some well-known rock formations. They are abundant and useful for correlation in Cretaceous chalks like those which form the White Cliffs of Dover, on the southeastern coast of England. Large, coin-shaped forams (up to 20 mm in diameter), called nummulitids, are found in the limestone blocks of some of the pyramids of Egypt. In the 1920s, paleontologists demonstrated the value of fossil forams in stratigraphic correlation (determining the age of sedimentary formations; see FOSSIL RECORD). Foraminifera are found in sedimentary rocks of all geologic periods from the Cambrian onward, but they are most useful for correlation of Cenozoic, Late Paleozoic, and Mesozoic strata (see GEOLOGIC TIME).

Forams are so small (generally less than 1 mm in diameter) that they come up intact in small chips of rock obtained from wells drilled for oil. Thus they have played an important role in the development of the PETROLEUM INDUSTRY. Rapid evolutionary changes in the form of foraminiferal tests make forams good index fossils—indicators of the age of the strata in which they occur and thus the likelihood that the rock contains oil.

Forbes, John   John Forbes, b. Sept. 5, 1707, d. Mar. 11, 1759, was the British general who captured Fort Duquesne (Pittsburgh, Pa.) during the FRENCH AND INDIAN WAR (1754–63). In 1758 he marched from Philadelphia across the Alleghenies with several thousand Americans and British regulars, cutting a road that later became a major emigration route. When his agent Christian Frederick Post was able to secure the defection of the Indians on whom the French depended, Forbes took Fort Duquesne on Nov. 25, 1758, without a struggle. British control of the Ohio Valley was thus assured.

Forbidden City   The Forbidden City usually refers to the group of imperial buildings found within the Inner City of BEIJING (Peking), China. Walls up to 11 m (35 ft) high enclose the Forbidden City, whose buildings consist of palaces, shrines, and halls used by Chinese emperors between 1421 and 1911. Taiho Tian (T'ai-ho Tien), the Hall of Supreme Harmony, stands in the center of the compound and was used as the emperor's throne room. The white marble terraces, yellow-tiled roofs, and formal gardens attract many tourists to the Forbidden City, which has been open to the public as a museum since 1949.

LHASA, Tibet, is also referred to as the Forbidden City because of its isolation from the rest of the world and because of traditional Tibetan hostility toward visitors.

force   In physics, force is an influence that pushes or pulls matter and in so doing tends to induce motion. Force, which is intimately involved in all natural processes, ranges in magnitude from tiny subatomic forces to the great gravitational forces of planets and stars.

A force is a vector quantity, that is, it is composed of both a magnitude and a specific direction. If either component changes, the force itself is said to change. The analysis of force problems is facilitated by a special branch of mathematics known as VECTOR ANALYSIS, with which forces and their interactions may be framed in mathematical terms.

The study of the interaction of forces, objects, and motion, known as mechanics, is the oldest branch of physical science. Mechanics includes force systems in equilibrium (STATICS), the mathematics of motion (KINEMATICS), and the relationship of force and motion (DYNAMICS).

The effect of force on matter was described three centuries ago by Sir Isaac Newton in what are known today as Newton's LAWS OF MOTION. Using these natural laws, it was established that acceleration is caused by an unbalanced force; that force, mass, and acceleration are simply related; and that all forces in nature occur in opposing pairs. Newton also discovered the universal law of GRAVITATION, which relates the gravitational attraction of two bodies to their masses and to their separation distance. Other natural principles peculiar to specific areas of physics serve to relate the various parameters responsible for electrical, magnetic, frictional, aerodynamic, and other forces.

It is important to distinguish between mass, an inherent characteristic of matter, and the force experienced by that mass in a gravitational field. Specifically, a person's weight is not the same as the person's mass; it is merely the force exerted on the mass by gravity.

Ford (family)   The Ford family has had a major impact on the development of the U.S. AUTOMOTIVE INDUSTRY. **Henry Ford**, b. July 30, 1863, d. Apr. 7, 1947, was the son of William Ford, who had emigrated from Ireland in 1847 and settled on a farm in Dearborn, Mich. Henry disliked farm life and had a natural aptitude for machinery; when he was 15 he went to Detroit and trained as a machinist. In 1888 he married Clara Bryant. They had one child, a son, **Edsel**, b. Nov. 6, 1893, d. May 26, 1943.

Henry Ford began to experiment with a horseless carriage about 1890 and completed his first car, the quadricycle, in 1896. It was the sixth American-built gasoline-powered car. During the following years he tried unsuccessfully to get it into production. During this period he built racing cars and became a well-known racing driver. In 1903 he launched the Ford Motor Company with a capital of $100,000, of which $28,000 was in cash. By this time he had formulated his ideal of production: "The way to make automobiles is to make one automobile like another automobile, to make them all alike...."

He achieved spectacular success with the MODEL T Ford, introduced in 1908 and eventually produced (1913) on a moving ASSEMBLY LINE. His production methods were intensively studied. He resisted (1911) the holders of the Selden patent, which purported to be a basic patent on the gasoline automobile.

Ford became a figure of legend, the native genius who could work miracles. He had considerable mechanical ability, but his conclusions were reached intuitively rather than logically. He was basically uneducated, and given to naive ideas about the world. Eventually he was considered for public office. He ran as a Democratic candidate for the U.S. Senate in 1918 and was narrowly defeated. A few years later he was touted as a presidential candidate but, after some hesitation, withdrew on the advice of his close friends. In 1936 he and his son Edsel established the FORD FOUNDATION, to which they bequeathed much of the company's stock.

Henry Ford became a victim of his own success in that he clung to the Model T too long, refusing to see that its popularity was fading, and consequently lost first place in the industry to General Motors in 1926. He had turned the presidency of the Ford Motor Company over to Edsel in 1919, but never gave Edsel effective authority. The elder Ford remained firmly in control. He showed occasional flashes of his mechanical brilliance, producing the Model A (1928) and the V-8 engine (1932), but he was an aging autocrat who resisted change. Edsel died in 1943, and his father resumed the presidency.

By that time Henry Ford had had two strokes and was incapable of managing the company. **Henry Ford II**, b. Sept. 4, 1917, d. Sept. 29, 1987, Edsel's oldest son, was released from the navy and made executive vice-president. He became president in 1945. Unlike his father, who had not been allowed to go to college, Henry II attended Yale University. When he assumed control of the company at the age of 28, management was in chaos, labor relations were poor, and the financial situation was shaky. He recruited talent from outside the company and effected a sweeping reorganization. The company secured firm control of second place in the American automobile industry. Henry II retired from his top company posts in 1979 and 1980.

Ford, Ford Madox   Ford Madox Ford, originally named Ford Herman Hueffer, b. Dec. 17, 1873, d. June 26, 1939, was an English writer and editor best known for his advocacy of experimental fiction and for his intricate and subtle novel *The Good Soldier* (1915).

Ford was the son of a German émigré and the grandson of the Pre-Raphaelite painter Ford Madox Brown. He began writing at an early age, collaborated with Joseph Conrad on *The Inheritors* (1901) and *Romance* (1903), and in 1908–09 founded and edited the *English Review*. In this short-lived journal he published the works of such young writers as D. H. Lawrence and Ezra Pound. After service in World War I, Ford edited (1923–24) the *Transatlantic Review* in Paris, publishing such writers as James Joyce and Ernest Hemingway.

Although Ford published about 70 different works, he is best remembered today for five of his novels, beginning with *The Good Soldier*. This ironic work was a masterful exploration of life's illusions and realities. His distinguished tetralogy *Parade's End*, consisting of *Some Do Not* (1924), *No More Parades* (1925), *A Man Could Stand Up* (1926), and *The Last Post* (1928), deals with

The American inventor and industrialist Henry Ford poses in his quadricycle, an automobile powered by a 2-cylinder gasoline engine. Ford introduced modern mass-production techniques to the automotive industry with his amazingly successful Model T.

AT A GLANCE

GERALD RUDOLPH FORD
38th President of the United States (1974–77)

Nickname: "Jerry"

Born: July 14, 1913, Omaha, Nebr.

Education: University of Michigan (graduated 1935);
Yale University Law School (LLB 1941)

Profession: Lawyer, Public Official

Religious Affiliation: Episcopalian

Marriage: Oct. 15, 1948, to Elizabeth Bloomer Warren
(1918–)

Children: Michael Gerald Ford (1950–); John Gardner
Ford (1952–); Steven Meigs Ford (1956–);
Susan Elizabeth Ford (1957–)

Political Affiliation: Republican

Writings: *Portrait of the Assassin* (1965), with John R.
Stiles; *A Time to Heal: An Autobiography* (1979)

Vice-President: Nelson A. Rockefeller

Gerald R. Ford

an Englishman, Christopher Tietjens, whose certain and ordered world is shattered by the events leading to World War I. Ford also wrote a number of amusing, inaccurate memoirs, including *Thus to Revisit* (1921), *Return to Yesterday* (1931), and *It Was the Nightingale* (1933).

Ford, Gerald R.   Gerald Rudolph Ford, Jr., became the 38th president of the United States on Aug. 9, 1974, after Richard M. NIXON resigned to avoid probable impeachment as a result of the WATERGATE affair. For 25 years a Republican member of Congress without national ambitions, Ford had been appointed vice-president in 1973 by President Nixon to replace Spiro T. AGNEW, who resigned after being accused of bribery and of violations of the income tax laws.

Early Life. The only child of Leslie and Dorothy Gardner King, Ford was born on July 14, 1913, in Omaha, Nebr., and was originally named Leslie Lynch King, Jr. His parents were divorced when he was two years old, and his mother moved to Grand Rapids, Mich., where she met and married a businessman named Gerald R. Ford, who formally adopted the young boy and gave him his name.

In school, young Ford was a good student and an excellent athlete. He became a star center on the University of Michigan football team and graduated from the university in 1935 with a B average. After graduation, he took a job as a football and boxing coach at Yale University. He was soon admitted to the Yale Law School, finishing in the top third of his class. With the outbreak of World War II, his fledgling law practice in Grand Rapids was interrupted. He entered the navy, served aboard an aircraft carrier in the Pacific, and was discharged at the end of the war with the rank of lieutenant commander.

Ford returned to Grand Rapids and resumed his law practice. In 1948 he married Elizabeth ("Betty") Bloomer Warren, a fashion coordinator and former dance student whose first marriage had ended a year earlier in divorce. In the same year he entered the Republican primary in Michigan, upset the incumbent representative from the state's Fifth District, and easily won election to the House of Representatives in November. He won reelection every two years thereafter, until he resigned in 1973 to become vice-president.

In the House, Ford gained a reputation as a moderately conservative, hardworking, and loyally partisan member of the Republican party, who made up for his lack of legislative brilliance by providing effective personal service to his Michigan constituents. In 1965 he was chosen as House Republican leader. Had the Republicans gained a majority of the seats while he was party leader, he would certainly have been named Speaker of the House. After Spiro Agnew resigned on Oct. 10, 1973, however, Nixon nominated Ford as vice-president under the provisions of the 25th Amendment to the U.S. Constitution, the first time that the procedures outlined in the amendment were utilized. Following congressional approval of his appointment, Ford was sworn in as vice-president on Dec. 6, 1973.

Presidency. A little more than eight months later, Nixon resigned after the House Judiciary Committee voted to recommend his impeachment. Ford automatically succeeded him and thus became the first president in American history who had not been chosen in a national election either as president or as vice-president. Nevertheless, Ford's unaffected personal style and his attempts to bring the presidency closer to the public were well received by the American people.

His political problems began four weeks after he took office, when he issued a full pardon to Nixon for any crimes he might have committed as president. In addition, the Ford administration was faced with a major economic slump, in which inflation was uniquely combined with recession to produce stagflation. Ford engaged, moreover, in a running battle with the Democratic Congress. During his two and half years as president, he vetoed 61 bills that had been passed by Congress. Only 12 of the vetoes were overridden. The resultant popular impression that the government in Washington was deadlocked probably hurt Ford's reelection chances.

In foreign relations he generally followed his predecessor's policies. Major events during Ford's administration included the collapse of South Vietnam in 1975 and, in the same year, the overthrow of the Lon Nol regime in CAMBODIA by Communist forces. The latter led to the Mayagüez incident in which a small force of U.S. Marines were sent to recapture the U.S. freighter *Mayagüez* and its crew, which had been seized by Cambodian forces. Ford received the Republican nomination for the presidency in 1976, despite a serious challenge in state presidential primary election by former California governor Ronald REAGAN. At the beginning of the fall campaign, he trailed the Democratic nominee, Jimmy CARTER of Georgia, by ten points in the Gallup Poll; but after a vigorous campaign in the final weeks, Ford lost to Carter by only 2.1 percent of the popular vote. Although he was disappointed at the election results, he retired from public office with characteristic good grace.

Ford, Henry   see FORD (family)

Ford, John (film director)   John Ford was the name adopted by Sean Aloysius O'Feeny, b. Cape Elizabeth, Maine, Feb. 1, 1895, d. Aug. 31, 1973, an American film director whose works are noted for their sustained creativity, breadth of vision, and pictorial beauty. Ford began directing Westerns in 1917, but his first great success was not until *The Iron Horse* (1924), followed by another, *Three Bad Men* (1926). Thirteen more years passed, however, before Ford, whose name became associated with the Western film, would make another, *Stagecoach* (1939), still regarded as a classic of the genre. In the intervening years he directed such varied works as *Judge Priest* (1934), *The Informer* (1935), *Steamboat Round the Bend* (1935), and *The Hurricane* (1937).

Stagecoach was followed by an outpouring of major works—*Young Mr. Lincoln* (1939), *Drums Along the Mohawk* (1939), *The Grapes of Wrath* (1940), *The Long*

John Ford was an American filmmaker whose name is most closely associated with Western films. His direction in other movie genres, however, was equally adept.

Voyage Home (1940), and *How Green Was My Valley* (1941). These films celebrated community life and were imbued with an elegiacal sense of the past.

The war years resulted in the first American war documentary, *The Battle of Midway* (1942), and another of Ford's enduring works, *They Were Expendable* (1945). After the war, Ford returned to the Western with the lyrical *My Darling Clementine* (1946); a loose trilogy of cavalry life: *Fort Apache* (1948), *She Wore a Yellow Ribbon* (1949), and *Rio Grande* (1950); and an innovative blending of song and story in *Wagonmaster* (1950).

During the six years before Ford's next Western, he directed *The Quiet Man* (1952)—a touching and humorous story of an Irish-American's return to his homeland—and several other films. Returning to the Western with *The Searchers* (1956), Ford revealed a new ambiguity in his vision of the American past. Increasingly, in such later works as *The Man Who Shot Liberty Valance* (1962) and *Cheyenne Autumn* (1964), the exaltation of the civilizing of the West that was seen in his earlier films was darkened by a regret over the loss of freedom brought by civilization. During his career, Ford established and repeatedly used a stock company of actors, including Henry Fonda, James Stewart, John Wayne, Ward Bond, and Victor McLaglen.

Ford, John (playwright)   John Ford, b. Apr. 17, 1586, d. *c.*1639, English playwright, is generally considered among the best of the early Stuart dramatists. After writing several nondramatic pieces, Ford collaborated with Thomas Dekker on *The Witch of Edmonton* (1621). Among his own seven intense, pessimistic tragedies are *The Lovers's Melancholy* (1628), *The Broken Heart* (1633), *'Tis Pity She's a Whore* (1633), and *Perkin Warbeck* (1634). Influenced by Robert Burton and contemporary Neoplatonism, Ford's drama deals with a variety of love relationships. Though at times prurient, the plays in general are carefully balanced presentations of questionable moral stances.

Ford, Whitey   Hall of Fame member Edward Charles "Whitey" Ford, b. New York City, Oct. 21, 1928, pitched in more World Series (11) and won (10) and lost (8) more series games than any player in baseball history. Ford spent his entire career (1950, 1953–67) with the American League's New York Yankees, amassing 236 wins against 106 losses for a winning percentage of .690, a major-league record for pitchers with 200 or more career decisions. In 1961, Ford was 25-4 and won the Cy Young award as baseball's best pitcher. Another series record he holds is that for consecutive scoreless innings pitched—33.

Ford Foundation   The Ford Foundation is a private foundation established in 1936 by the FORD family, with a broad mandate to serve the general welfare. Later it received large bequests from Henry and Edsel Ford. The Ford Foundation's huge assets put it first among U.S. philanthropies.

Until 1950 the foundation's activities were directed to charitable and educational institutions in Michigan. Today policies are set by a board of trustees, with grant evaluation and program development administered at foundation headquarters in New York City.

Foundation bequests have been used to create the National Merit Scholarship Program; to help raise college faculty salaries; to provide challenge grants to universities and colleges; to create programs to limit population growth; to help establish American noncommercial television; and to provide grants to the arts. The foundation was headed by McGeorge BUNDY (1966–79), then by Franklin A. Thomas.

See also: FOUNDATIONS AND ENDOWMENTS.

Ford Trimotor   Known universally as the *Tin Goose*, the Ford Trimotor represented one of the most significant advances in air-transport design. A total of 200 of these planes were constructed in seven basic models. The aircraft, a sturdy, high-wing monoplane of all-metal construction, was equipped with three radial engines (hence the name). Its development, stimulated when the Ford Motor Company purchased (1925) the Stout Metal Air-

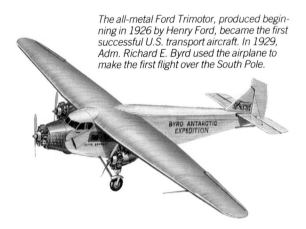

The all-metal Ford Trimotor, produced beginning in 1926 by Henry Ford, became the first successful U.S. transport aircraft. In 1929, Adm. Richard E. Byrd used the airplane to make the first flight over the South Pole.

plane Company, led to the Model 4-AT (1926) and the refined Model 5-AT (1928). The 4-AT had a 22.5-m (74-ft) wingspan and 15.2-m (50-ft) length. Variants were also produced for the military. The Trimotor remained an important transport plane through the early 1930s.

Fordham University   [fohrd'-uhm]   Established in 1841 and conducted by the Jesuits, Fordham University has its main campus in the Bronx, N.Y., with a branch at Lincoln Center in New York City. In 1974, Thomas More College (1964), an undergraduate school for women, merged with Fordham University. Fordham has schools of arts and sciences, law, business, social service, and education and a graduate school of religion.

foreclosure   see MORTGAGE

foreign aid   Foreign aid is assistance in the form of capital, goods, or services given by one country to another. The donor is usually a government or international organization, although assistance provided by private charitable groups is sometimes considered foreign aid as well. Foreign aid may take the form of direct grants or loans whose terms are less stringent than those usually set by commercial banks.

U.S. Aid Programs.   The United States began extending foreign aid in large amounts during World War II when it helped its military allies with shipments of war supplies under the LEND-LEASE program. Altogether, it extended assistance totaling $47.9 billion to 38 countries.

Between 1946 and 1987 the U.S. government disbursed over $330 billion in foreign aid; more than $236 billion of this was in the form of grants, and the rest was loans. About 63% of U.S. aid during this period was designed to facilitate the economic recovery of war-torn industrialized countries, to alleviate the immediate aftereffects of natural disasters, or to stimulate economic growth in less-developed countries. The other 37% was military aid to U.S. allies and other non-Communist countries.

Since World War II, foreign aid has been an important element of U.S. foreign policy. In 1947, President Harry S. TRUMAN proposed a $400 million aid program to help Greece and Turkey resist communism. This program, which became known as the Truman Doctrine, was the first U.S. aid policy aimed at containing communism. Later in the same year, Secretary of State George MARSHALL invited European nations to draw up a plan for postwar economic reconstruction to be financed by the United States. The MARSHALL PLAN, formally known as the European Recovery Program, disbursed more than $13 billion in economic aid in 1948–52, at least 90% of it in the form of grants. The Marshall Plan had two basic goals: to stimulate the economic recovery of Europe as a trading partner for the United States and to check the advance of communism in Europe by eliminating economic conditions that could be exploited by the Communists.

In his 1949 inaugural address, Truman called for "a bold new program for making the benefits of our scientific advances and industrial progress available for the improvement and growth of underdeveloped areas." This proposal, the fourth of a series in the address, resulted in the POINT FOUR PROGRAM of aid to less-developed countries. During the 1950s the United States placed increasing emphasis on such countries in its aid program.

Another important element of U.S. aid was the Food for Peace program, which made surplus agricultural commodities available to foreign countries on easy terms or as a gift.

The emphasis of U.S. aid programs has been redirected from Europe to Asia, including the Middle East. Europe received about 15% of the U.S. aid disbursed in 1945–87, but most of this was given in the years immediately following World War II. South Asia and the Middle East received more than 36% of U.S. aid in this period, Latin America received approximately 9%, and Africa received approximately 7%. Since the end of the Marshall Plan, South Vietnam, Israel, South Korea, India, Egypt, Turkey, Pakistan, and Taiwan have received the largest amounts of U.S. aid.

Aid by Other Countries. Foreign economic aid is provided by many countries other than the United States. Since 1960, Canada, Japan, and the Western European nations have emerged as increasingly significant sources of economic aid for the poor areas of the world, providing many billions of dollars for development. The United States regularly provided more economic aid than any other country until 1989, when Japan became the world's largest donor and lender of foreign aid. Several countries allocate larger percentages of their gross national product (GNP) for aid than does the United States. In 1987, Norway provided 1.09%; the Netherlands, 0.98%; Denmark and Sweden, 0.88%; France, 0.74%; and the United States, 0.20%.

Military aid is usually given directly by one country to another, but economic aid is often given indirectly through international organizations. The WORLD BANK Group—which includes the International Bank for Reconstruction and Development, the INTERNATIONAL DEVELOPMENT ASSOCIATION, and the INTERNATIONAL FINANCE CORPORATION—disburses the bulk of such multilateral aid. From 1946 to 1988 the World Bank Group distributed more than $184 billion in loans, most of which went to the less-developed areas of the world. India, Mexico, and Brazil were the major recipients of loans from the World Bank Group.

Communist countries have disbursed most of their aid directly rather than through international organizations. China's relatively small economic aid program disbursed more than $7 billion between 1954 and 1985. The USSR is the largest Communist aid donor; it disbursed about $14 billion to developing nations from 1954 to 1984, during which period Soviet military aid totaled about $75 billion. Soviet aid usually takes the form of loans and tends to be concentrated in a few countries, which have included Cuba, Poland, and Vietnam.

Foreign-aid programs, especially those aimed at promoting economic development, are continually being reappraised because they seldom yield spectacular results in the short run. The process of promoting economic development is slow and frustrating, and it often causes both donors and recipients to wonder whether it is worthwhile. Reappraisals of aid programs consider questions such as the following: To what extent could or should the developing countries rely on private capital to finance their development? To what extent should rich countries use trade preferences as disguised aid to poor ones? Can developing countries continue to repay past loans without retarding their economic development? (The Third World debt dilemma that rose in the 1980s underscored this question.) How can donors make sure that aid serves the long-term needs of the recipient? And how can a country accept foreign aid without incurring unacceptable political intervention in its affairs by the donor?

foreign exchange   See EXCHANGE RATE

foreign legion   see FRENCH FOREIGN LEGION

---

foreign policy   Foreign policy is the set of principles by which a country regulates its intercourse with other countries and the measures by which it implements these principles. Foreign policy is applied in a sphere in which no central authority is recognized; no truly enforceable INTERNATIONAL LAW or effective world government exists. As a result, the threat of a breakdown in cooperation and, ultimately, of resort to force is almost always present in foreign policy and gives it a quality of impermanence.

Foreign Alliances. To strengthen themselves, countries often form alliances. The major present-day alliance is the NORTH ATLANTIC TREATY ORGANIZATION, which consists of the United States, Canada, and a number of West European countries. Another major alliance, the WARSAW TREATY ORGANIZATION, which consists of the USSR and many countries of Eastern Europe, ceased to function by 1991, as Soviet power in the region collapsed. In addition to formal alliances, countries may pursue other forms of cooperation with friendly nations, including economic or military FOREIGN AID programs. In 19th-century Europe, two groups of countries were of approximately equal strength, and Great Britain was able to pursue a BALANCE OF POWER policy by leaning first toward one group and then toward the other. However, countries have to change their foreign policies when their relative power changes. For example, in 1939, Britain and France ranked among the greatest world powers. A few years later they had become second-rank powers, and the destiny of the world was being settled in Washington and Moscow.

Economic Interests. The increasing role of governments in regulating and implementing domestic economic goals complicates the task of conducting foreign policy, since almost all important domestic policy goals of modern industrial states have international implications. Japan's export-trade dominance in the 1970s and '80s created domestic problems for other nations, and threats to Japan's future prosperity. Intergovernmental arrangements for orderly marketing of such exports as steel, automobiles, and high-technology electronics equipment became important in the foreign policies of Japan, the United

States, and Western European countries.

The interconnection between domestic policy and foreign policy has led to the formation of international organizations such as the EUROPEAN COMMUNITY, the EUROPEAN FREE TRADE ASSOCIATION, the ORGANIZATION FOR ECONOMIC COOPERATION AND DEVELOPMENT, the ORGANIZATION OF PETROLEUM EXPORTING COUNTRIES, and the various bodies of the UNITED NATIONS. Most modern industrial states try to preserve as much domestic autonomy as possible, but at the same time seek to maximize the benefits of participation in INTERNATIONAL TRADE.

Spheres of Interest. Economic goals have always been important in the formation of foreign policy. Countries have engaged in economic ventures ranging from mere plunder to the establishment of colonies and empires based on the quest for wealth or the need for raw materials. In recent decades, as traditional political empires have declined, they have often been supplanted by business arrangements. In one way or another, foreigners still exercise decisive influence over the economies of many less-developed countries. France, for instance, still has strong economic and military influence in many of its former African colonies.

In countries with market economies, such as the United States, the decisions and actions of private companies often neutralize those of governments, and they limit governments' ability to conduct effective foreign policy. Communist governments, on the other hand, have traditionally exercised virtually complete control over economic relations abroad, since they permit no large-scale private enterprise. During the 1980s, however, China, and the Soviet Union (after the ascent to power in 1985 of Mikhail Gorbachev), began to adopt some aspects of western-style market economies.

The Role of Military Force. The Soviet-U.S. competition for power and influence has been the single most important influence in international relations since the end of World War II. Their relationship was for some years so hostile that it was called a COLD WAR. In other eras such a rivalry would almost certainly have led to a hot war, but the destructive power of nuclear weapons has caused the two superpowers to avoid direct military confrontations and to attempt to limit deployment of nuclear weapons through the Strategic Arms Limitation Talks and the Strategic Arms Reduction Talks (see ARMS CONTROL; DEFENSE, NATIONAL; NUCLEAR STRATEGY; STRATEGIC DEFENSE INITIATIVE). Each, however, has used military force against weaker countries, and smaller powers have fought bloody wars on the assumption that mutual deterrence would prevent either of the two giants from intervening. After Gorbachev sought to bring about fundamental societal changes, it seemed possible that the two superpowers might be able to realign their foreign policies to emphasize cooperation.

Civil and International Wars. The use of force across recognized international boundaries is no longer generally accepted behavior. Border wars are still fought, but contemporary warfare more often takes the form of civil wars, usually between separate, identifiable groups based in different regions of a single state. When these groups choose to fight, in contravention of the state's central authority, they in effect begin to make their own foreign policy. Civil wars rarely involve only a single country, however. The contending parties often seek help from other nations with which they share a common language, religion, or ideology, or which have an interest in protecting or undermining the current regime.

Whether or not to intervene in a foreign conflict is often a difficult decision for large, powerful countries. Intervention may range from covert assistance, such as camouflaged financial subsidies or weapons supplied through secret channels, to the sending of military "advisors" and the actual dispatch of combat troops. Economic SANCTIONS, such as those imposed by several nations against South Africa in 1985, are a common instrument of coercion.

Intervention by Great Powers. Since World War II both the United States and the USSR have intervened in many conflicts, both civil and international, sometimes with their own military forces. The USSR has intervened in three states on its own borders—Hungary (1956; see HUNGARIAN REVOLUTION), Czechoslovakia (1968), and Afghanistan (1979–89)—to restore to power or, in the case of Afghanistan, in an ultimately unsuccessful effort to retain in power political factions loyal to Moscow. The United States has fought protracted major wars far from its own shores: the KOREAN WAR (1950–53) and the VIETNAM WAR (1963–73). The second intervention was probably the most controversial foreign-policy episode in U.S. history.

Both the United States and the USSR have on occasion intervened by using troops from other countries. In 1961 the United States armed Cuban exiles and helped them launch an unsuccessful invasion of Cuba at the BAY OF PIGS. The USSR made a less direct use of Cuban troops in Africa in the late 1970s, when the Communist government of Cuba intervened at the invitation of several pro-Soviet African governments. In 1968 the USSR intervened in Czechoslovakia with its own forces and those of other Warsaw Pact countries. In the 1980s the contra rebels in Nicaragua were widely seen as U.S. surrogates.

The Influence of Public Opinion. The open nature of the American political system and the independent nature of Congress make the conduct of foreign policy more cumbersome in the United States than it is in other countries, even the more democratic ones. No other leader of a great power has ever suffered the fate of President Woodrow Wilson, who negotiated a treaty at the Paris Peace Conference in 1919 that the Senate refused to ratify. In the early 1970s the administration of Richard M. Nixon attained a relatively free hand in foreign policy, but by the late 1970s almost every foreign-policy initiative had become the subject of widespread and rather confusing debate. This contrasted sharply with policy-making in such centrally directed, authoritarian countries as the USSR.

The deep popular hostility in the United States to the use of U.S. military forces abroad, engendered by the long, costly, and unsuccessful intervention in Indochina, was evident in the widespread criticism of U.S. support of the Nicaraguan contras in the 1980s. This support, by sometimes covert means, became entangled with another covert operation—selling arms to Iran to secure the release of hostages—in the so-called IRAN-CONTRA AFFAIR. This foreign-policy scandal gravely weakened President Ronald Reagan, who ironically had been elected in 1980 during the prolonged IRANIAN HOSTAGE CRISIS on a platform of restoring American strength and pride. In 1987 the administration embroiled itself in further controversy by undertaking to protect Kuwaiti oil tankers in the Persian Gulf, thus throwing U.S. weight to the Iraqi side in the IRAN-IRAQ WAR. In the GULF WAR of 1990–91, however, the American public strongly supported President George Bush in his decision to send U.S. troops to the Persian Gulf to force Iraqi withdrawal from Kuwait; support for the president's foreign policy increased further after the overwhelming U.S. military victory.

See also: COMMUNISM; TARIFF; WAR.

foreign service   A foreign service is an organization of trained career officials who help implement the foreign policy of their government by representing their country in its relations with other countries or with international organizations. A foreign service is typically part of a foreign ministry (the Department of STATE in the United States). Most major foreign services maintain an embassy, consulates, and trade and cultural centers in each country with which they have diplomatic relations.

An embassy is headed by an AMBASSADOR, assisted by a staff of diplomats and attachés who have various functions. The political and economic sections report on developments in the host country. The consular section assists its nationals living or traveling in the host country with commercial and legal matters and issues visas to local residents who wish to travel to its country (see CONSUL, modern government official). The cultural section promotes the culture of its own country.

Diplomacy began to assume its modern form in the 12th and 13th centuries. Rules were developed by the Italian city-states to govern the appointment and conduct of ambassadors, and in 1455, the duchy of Milan established the first permanent embassy in Genoa. In the 16th century other European states followed the Italian example and appointed permanent ambassadors. Under the influence of 16th- and 17th-century writers, such as Hugo GROTIUS, the privileges of diplomats were more precisely defined and incorporated in international law. The Congress of Vienna in 1815 and the Vienna Convention on Diplomatic Relations in 1961 defined and redefined classes of diplomatic representatives. In the 20th century, consular and diplomatic services, formerly separate, have been merged in many countries, including the United States (1924).

Diplomats stationed in a foreign country enjoy privileges known as diplomatic immunity: they are not subject to local civil and criminal laws; they are free to communicate with their governments; and the embassy buildings and grounds are treated as the territory of their state. A country can expel a foreign diplomat whom it considers undesirable by declaring the diplomat persona non grata.

The period since World War II has seen new developments in international diplomacy. Heads of state now confer directly with each other, and foreign ministers engage in shuttle diplomacy—flying between capitals in continual negotiations. These developments have somewhat reduced the importance of foreign-service representatives in direct policy-making.

Foreman, George   George Foreman, b. Marshall, Tex., Jan. 22, 1948, is an American boxer and former world heavyweight champion with enormous punching power. Foreman won the 1968 Olympic heavyweight gold medal, then rose quickly professionally. He took the world heavyweight title from Joe FRAZIER with a 2d-round knockout on Jan. 22, 1973, but lost it in a stunning upset to Muhammad ALI on Oct. 30, 1974. After an even more surprising loss to Jimmy Young in 1977, Foreman retired, only to return to the ring 10 years later in an attempt to reestablish his reputation at an advanced age. After the Young fight, Foreman's record was 45-2, with 42 knockouts.

forensic science   Forensic science is the application of science to criminal investigation in order to provide evidence that can be used in the solution of criminal cases. Forensic scientists also play a vital role in criminal trials, where they may testify as expert witnesses. The many fields of knowledge that constitute modern forensic-science practices include pathology, toxicology, anthropology, odontology, psychology, and criminalistics. The forensic pathologist is concerned with determining the cause of sudden or unexpected death and will usually perform an AUTOPSY on the victim to detect any signs of injury or disease that may have contributed to the death (see also PATHOLOGY). The forensic toxicologist provides the pathologist with data relating to the presence of poisons or drugs found in a victim's body. The identification of bones and skeletal remains is the responsibility of the specialty called forensic anthropology, which is derived from the anthropological study of comparative body and bone measurements and morphology. Forensic odontology, or dentistry, utilizes dental evidence to identify human remains and is employed in the characterization of bitemark impressions. Forensic psychiatrists analyze human behavior and personality in connection with issues pertaining to a criminal act or to criminal conduct. Psychiatric examinations may serve to determine whether the state of mind of the accused at the time of the offense conforms to the definition of insanity in the jurisdiction where the crime occurred and whether the accused is competent to stand trial (see INSANITY, LEGAL).

The term *criminalistics* encompasses those areas of the physical and natural sciences applicable to the analysis of physical evidence—the objects retrieved from the scene of a crime that can aid investigators in determining whether a crime was committed or that can provide a link between a crime and its victims or perpetrators. Such evidence includes a great variety of materials—drugs, hair, fibers, soil, blood, paint chips, firearms, fingerprints (see FINGERPRINTING), documents—which must be analyzed to determine content, type, authenticity, and so on. A new technique, DNA "fingerprinting," can be used to identify the source of semen or blood stains.

Criminalistic services are provided by forensic chemists and biologists employed in crime laboratories. These facilities, first established in the United States in the early 1930s, operate at the federal, state, county, or municipal level of government. Most crime laboratories function as elements of police departments or under the direction of a prosecutor's or district attorney's office. The largest crime laboratory in the world is operated by the U.S. Federal Bureau of Investigation.

Forester, C. S. [fohr'-es-tur] Cecil Scott Forester, b. Aug. 27, 1899, d. Apr. 2, 1966, was a prolific English writer of novels, histories, biographies, and travel literature. Educated at Dulwich College, Forester won a wide international audience through his series of 11 historical novels depicting the career of Capt. Horatio Hornblower, a fictional British navy officer during the Napoleonic Wars. The first of these, *A Ship of the Line*, won the James Tait Black Memorial Prize for Literature in 1938. He described the series in *The Hornblower Companion* (1964). His other successful novels include *Payment Deferred* (1926), *The Gun* (1933; film, 1957), and *The African Queen* (1935; film, 1952).

forests and forestry A forest is a community of trees, shrubs, herbs, microorganisms, and animals, with trees the most obvious living structures. Trees can survive under a wide range of climatic conditions, but forests generally occupy the moister, less frigid parts of the terrestrial BIOSPHERE. They take part in natural processes of nutrient cycling and water purification and otherwise help maintain a clean environment. Forests are important sources of many products. Forestry is the science, art, and technology of managing these forest resources.

Forests

The large size and slow growth of trees make forests appear stable and permanent, but in fact they are dynamic sites of ongoing processes such as TREE growth and death and SOIL formation. The tree species in a particular area are also constantly changing as species migrate and new trees invade disturbed areas. Climates themselves change, but this generally occurs so slowly—over tens or hundreds of years—that a given forest area appears to contain a constant group of species.

Ecology. The inhabitants of forest communities interact in complex ways. Trees compete with each other for sunlight, moisture, and mineral nutrients. These materials are necessary for PHOTOSYNTHESIS, the process by which green plants produce organic compounds for energy to live and grow. As trees photosynthesize, they absorb carbon dioxide from the air and extract moisture from the soil. Trees help to retain water; heavy rains do not run rapidly off forest land. Natural or human activities that destroy forests result in increased runoff and in higher atmospheric levels of carbon dioxide.

Trees also serve as temporary repositories for mineral nutrients in ecosystems; these nutrients accumulate in tree roots and thus are not easily washed away. Natural or human destruction of forests alters the NUTRIENT CYCLES, especially in the case of the NITROGEN CYCLE, where plants play a substantial role. Regrowth of young forests may increase the nitrogen added to the ecosystem.

The process of soil development, aided by SOIL ORGANISMS, occurs in all forests. Microorganisms break down minerals in the soil and create passages for air and water movement, decomposing the remains of plants and animals and extracting and releasing nutrients. Depending on the climate, decomposition occurs at different rates. In cool or dry climates, organic matter will decompose slowly and a thick layer will develop, whereas in warm, moist climates, organic matter will decompose rapidly, releasing minerals that are quickly absorbed by plant roots. Little organic matter will accumulate.

After a forest is destroyed (all or in part) by a disturbance, such as fire or wind or avalanche, trees and other plants reinvade the area, halting erosion and nutrient loss and maintaining water quality. This series of changes in vegetation, known as ecological succession, makes the forest more suitable for some animals and plants and less suitable for others.

Types of Forests. Depending on environmental conditions, different tree species will be dominant at different successional stages. The characteristic group of tree species in a given area is referred to as a forest type. Within each type, certain species may be found most commonly under specific soil and climate conditions and at certain times after a disturbance; these species are best evolved physiologically to compete under these conditions. In areas of recurrent fire, for example, fire-resistant trees will likely predominate.

Forest communities with different genetic backgrounds that grow under similar soil and climate conditions in different parts of the world have many of the same structural characteristics. Thus, forests can be classified as major parts of many BIOMES. Taiga and boreal forests are coniferous forests with few species in areas of cool climates. Temperate deciduous forests are predominantly broad-leaved forests in areas of moderate temperature and rainfall with cold winters. Subtropical evergreen forests are a combination of broad-leaved and conifer forests in areas of sufficient rainfall and mild winters. Tropical rain forests are lush forests of complex structure with many species in warm, moist regions (see JUNGLE AND RAIN FOREST). CHAPARRAL or sclerophyllous forests are thicketlike forests of shrubs and small trees in areas with mild winters and warm, dry summers. Savannas are grasslands with scattered trees that occur in warm regions with seasonal drought.

Forestry

Forestry involves the use and management of forest resources. Forest uses can be divided into two categories: nonconsumptive and consumptive. Nonconsumptive uses, which remove little from the forest, include water-

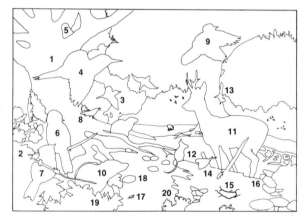

New Forest, located in southern England, typifies the temperate-climate woodland. The most common tree is the English oak (1); other trees are the hawthorn (2), and the hazel (3). Birds include the great spotted woodpecker (4), which drums by pecking a tree trunk with its beak. The tawny owl (5), common throughout Britain, roosts by day and hunts for small animals at night. A male European robin (6) sings to warn other robins away. A blue tit (7) now is commonly seen in gardens. A song thrush (8) has a complex song, which is warbled more than once before changing the melody. The Eurasian jay (9) collects and buries acorns. The badger (10), the roe deer (11), and the wood mouse (12) are mammals that inhabit the New Forest. The gray squirrel (13), native to North America, was introduced into Britain and spread rapidly. A mottled umber moth (14) and a wood louse (15) rest on an old log eaten away by a fungus, genus Polystictus (16). A ground beetle (17) walks along the forest floor, which is carpeted with mushrooms (18), primroses (19), and wood anemones (20).

shed protection, wildlife and fish habitat, recreation, and aesthetic uses. Consumptive uses involve the extraction of products; this often requires the harvesting of trees. Forest resources are renewable, since new trees can grow after the old ones are cut.

Products. The use of forests to obtain WOOD, chemicals, and other products is consumptive. About half of the wood harvested in the world is used directly for fuel. Wood is the primary fuel source in developing countries. Wood has been used for LUMBER for construction purposes for thousands of years. PAPER was first made from wood about 150 years ago, and it is still made primarily

from wood. The cellulose fibers in wood can also be used to make RAYON, photographic film, artificial sponges, synthetic lacquers, and other plastics.

Various chemicals are made from by-products of pulp and paper manufacture and from the independent distillation of wood; these include charcoal, acetic acid, methanol, various oils, and medicinal chemicals. Turpentine and tar may be obtained from destructive distillation or by scarring and scraping the wound of living pine trees. Maple sugar is obtained by taking the sap from the interior of living maple trees.

Management. Forests are managed for a variety of objectives, ranging from carefully tended plantations to relatively natural areas of no cutting and minimal protection from disturbance. The intensity of management depends on the growth potential of the forest and various economic and political objectives.

The ultimate unit of forest management is the "stand." A stand is a group of trees of uniform age, species, structure, and growth conditions. Stands vary in size from 0.4 to more than 40 ha (1 to 100 acres). The technology of manipulating stands is known as silviculture. Many silvicultural techniques mimic disturbances of some kind, often to remove existing trees or other vegetation in order to allow desired trees to become established and grow. Four methods are used to remove trees from forest stands: clear-cutting, or the cutting of all the trees at one time, creating an even-age stand by planting or natural regeneration; seed tree cutting, or the cutting of all the trees except for a few trees for reseeding, creating an even-age stand (except for the seed trees); shelterwood cutting, or the removal of an old stand of trees in a series of cuttings extended over several years, creating an even-age stand; and selection cutting, or the removal of a few mature trees, usually repeatedly, over relatively short intervals, creating an uneven-age stand. Each system has its advantages and disadvantages; the proper method must be chosen on the basis of management goals and conditions at the stand in question.

Silvicultural techniques constantly change with technological advances. They involve the use of fire, machinery, and chemicals for preparing stands for regeneration and for removing competing plants; nurseries for growing seedlings; genetic improvements resulting in more efficiently growing trees; fertilizers for increasing growth; and remote-control machines for pruning unwanted limbs.

It might seem odd to mention fire as one means of forest management, because the enormous destructive-

The work of a forester includes taking core samples from trees. Analysis of such a cross section helps trace a tree's life history.

ness of great forest fires is well known. Controlled fires, however, are useful in preparing ground for planting and in clearing the ground of weeds or fungal diseases that would harm seedlings. Controlled fires may also be used in attempting to block the course of great disaster fires. The majority of forest fires are caused by human carelessness, although many of the largest that sweep vast remote areas are produced by lightning. However damaging such natural fires are to human interests, they play a contributing role in forest evolution.

Selection cutting (1), which leaves small openings in the forest canopy, is used for such shade-tolerant trees as spruce. Clearcutting (2) removes all trees within a given area; such shade-intolerant species as black cherry and southern pine are planted, or regenerate naturally, in the large clearing. Seed tree cutting (3) leaves a few scattered seed-bearing trees to reforest the area. Shelterwood cutting (4) harvests trees in stages and is used for white pine and other species that require shade to develop.

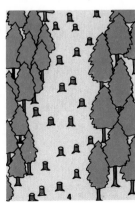

Conservation. Forests provide each of the uses described earlier, but only under certain conditions. Forests have changed and will continue to change as trees grow and die, species migrate, and climates change. Often a forest is stressed by these changes, and the trees can become weakened and infected by insects or diseases, resulting in their death. Air pollution and water pollution created by human or natural activity can further damage trees.

One objective of CONSERVATION is to prevent unintentional destruction of forests by disease, insects, and other agents. The other objective is to determine management goals for each area of forest. Once the objectives of each stand are determined, the actual management requires understanding of the natural sciences, long-term processes and history, and modern technologies. Deciding what values to conserve is a scientific, technological, and political subject.

The objectives of conservation have changed along with changes in such related areas as the understanding of forest process, human values themselves, demands on the forest, availabilities of various resources, and technologies. Early forest conservation in North America was aimed at protecting forested areas from clearing for agricultural lands. In the late 1800s and early 1900s forests were protected from fire, overharvesting, and overgrazing

by the establishment of fire-control practices, harvesting regulations, and grazing laws. Aesthetically unique areas and high-quality watersheds were set aside as national parks and forests. In the mid-20th century unproductive farmland was converted to forests through the subsidizing of reforestation, thus halting erosion and providing for future forests.

In recent decades there has been growing interest in conserving forests for nonconsumptive purposes. In the United States, management objectives for national forests have shifted from timber production to multiple uses. More areas of public lands are mandated for nonconsumptive uses such as watershed and wildlife management and recreation.

In tropical regions forest harvesting is occurring at a rapid rate. In parts of Africa, where the soils are easily eroded and the climate is unpredictable, forests and woodlands are being diminished. Agricultural practices may lead to deforestation under pressures of increasing population. Three solutions to the deforestation problem have met with some success: the first involves the use of local people in forest management; the second involves "agroforestry," or the planting of trees in croplands and pastures; and the third involves the use of the financial resources of developed countries.

----

forge   A forge is an establishment where metal is shaped, usually by heating and hammering. Both ferrous and nonferrous metals can be forged, including low-carbon steel, copper, and titanium. A forge may be distin-

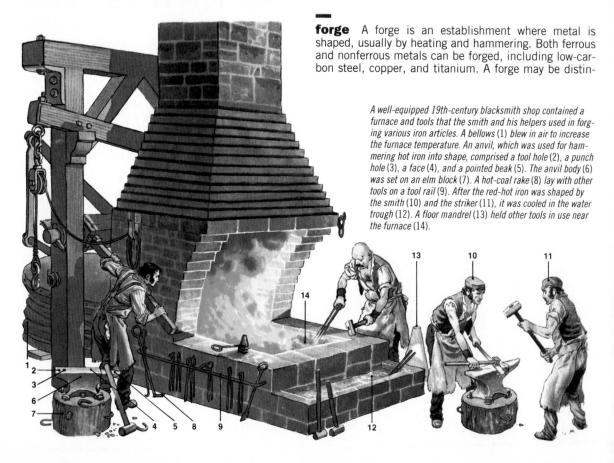

A well-equipped 19th-century blacksmith shop contained a furnace and tools that the smith and his helpers used in forging various iron articles. A bellows (1) blew in air to increase the furnace temperature. An anvil, which was used for hammering hot iron into shape, comprised a tool hole (2), a punch hole (3), a face (4), and a pointed beak (5). The anvil body (6) was set on an elm block (7). A hot-coal rake (8) lay with other tools on a tool rail (9). After the red-hot iron was shaped by the smith (10) and the striker (11), it was cooled in the water trough (12). A floor mandrel (13) held other tools in use near the furnace (14).

guished from a foundry, where metal is melted by furnaces and cast from molds. WROUGHT IRON may also be produced in a forge (see METALLURGY).

Forging is accomplished by the use of hammers, dies, and mechanical presses, and by the method known as roll forging. All of these methods work by applying pressure to a properly selected size of metal block, known as a billet, which is heated to the proper temperature. Hammering has evolved from the hammer and anvil of the BLACKSMITH to large drop hammers. The blocks of metal may also be shaped by the progressive use of dies, tools with cavities and contours previously cut into them (see TOOL AND DIE-MAKING). The method of pressing uses a motor-driven ram or hydraulic pumps to apply pressure to the metal.

Roll forging is used to shape metal into long, thin sections. The rolls are semicylindrical and have several grooves machined into them through which the unshaped billets pass from one size groove to the next. The metal is forced to conform to the size and shape of the grooves.

Forging is widely used because it is a mass production technique that can quickly make similar parts.

The art forger Alceo Dossena, who created the "Renaissance" Madonna and Child, worked only in the style of a particular artist or period and copied no specific work. Dossena's works were acclaimed as period masterpieces, and many were purchased by well-known collectors.

forgery Forgery is the fraudulent alteration of a written document with the intent to defraud, or the falsification of any instrument (such as a deed, bond, or stock certificate) for the purpose of deception or FRAUD. A person who signs another's name on a check is guilty of a forgery. When the forger presents the check to the bank and the bank cashes it he or she commits the companion crime called uttering a forged document. In some states, the two crimes of forgery and uttering have been combined into the crime of forgery. The forgery of government obligations, such as money or bonds, is called COUNTERFEITING.

forgery in art Forgery in art, the fabrication of an art object with intent to deceive a purchaser as to its true origin, is as ancient as the practice of collecting. Every kind of art has inspired spurious reproductions, and the history of forgery reflects changes in taste, since the forger supplies a demand for coveted objects and follows the preferences of the time. The techniques of the forger include direct copying of famous works, imitating the style of a particular painter or period, piecing together old fragments to simulate antiquity, and the false attribution of minor works to major artists.

An array of modern techniques including microscopic and chemical analysis, radio-carbon dating, and X-ray, infrared, and ultraviolet photography can now be used to detect forgeries. The most effective safeguard against deception, however, remains the judgment of a trained observer whose intuition can reject the false after long acquaintance with the values of genuine works.

forget-me-not Forget-me-nots, *Myosotis*, are a genus of annual, biennial, or perennial herbaceous plants belonging to the borage family, Boraginaceae. They produce blue, white, or pink flowers and thrive in cool, partially shaded, and moist locations. Dwarf varieties make excellent edging plants; one of the most attractive spring-bloom-

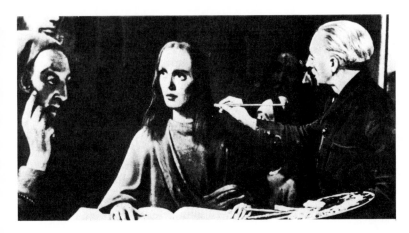

Hans van Meegeren, one of the most notorious forgers of the 20th century, sold paintings in the style of Vermeer to Nazi officials during World War II. Accused after the war of selling Dutch national treasures, he proved his innocence by painting another "Vermeer" in his prison cell (left).

The forget-me-not M. sylvatica bears tiny, delicate blossoms on thin stalks. It grows abundantly along shady streams and is cultivated as a border plant and under trees in gardens.

ing species is *M. dissitiflora*, the flowers of which are a delicate shade of blue. The forget-me-not blooms from April until well into June. It is the state flower of Alaska.

forgetting see MEMORY

Forlì [fohr-lee'] Forlì (1988 est. pop., 110,334), a city in northern Italy, is situated on the Montane River about 30 km (20 mi) from the Adriatic Sea. Forlì is the commercial and industrial center for the surrounding agricultural region. Its varied manufactures include textiles, furniture, light machinery, chemicals, and shoes.

Called Forum Livii by the Romans, it was a market town on the Via Aemilia. In the 11th century, Forlì became independent. It was ruled by the Ordelaffi family from 1315 to 1500, and it joined the Papal States in 1504. In 1860, Forlì became part of unified Italy.

formaldehyde [fohr-mal'-duh-hyd] Formaldehyde, HCHO, is the simplest member of the class of organic compounds known as ALDEHYDES. At room temperature formaldehyde is an extremely reactive colorless gas with a suffocating odor. It is commonly sold as an aqueous solution (formalin) or in solid polymeric forms (paraformaldehyde and trioxane). Formaldehyde is used in the manufacture of dyes, in the production of synthetic resins, and as a preservative for biological specimens.

Forman, Milos The Czech-born film director Milos Forman, b. Feb. 18, 1932, is noted for his ironic humor. His Czech films include *Peter and Pavla* (1964), *Loves of a Blonde* (1965), and *The Firemen's Ball* (1967). Among the movies he made after coming to the United States are *Taking Off* (1971); *One Flew Over the Cuckoo's Nest* (1975), for which he won an Academy Award for direction; *Hair* (1979); *Ragtime* (1981); *Amadeus* (1984), for which he received a second Academy Award; and *Valmont* (1989).

formic acid Formic acid, HCOOH, the simplest CARBOXYLIC ACID, is a strong reducing agent that exists as a colorless liquid. It is contained in the poison of stinging ants (Latin *formica*, "ant"), stinging caterpillars, and stinging nettles. Formic acid forms salts with alkali metals, and it forms esters with alcohols. It is widely used in electroplating, dyeing, tanning, and the manufacture of chemicals and medicines.

Formosa see TAIWAN

Forrest, Edwin Edwin Forrest, b. Philadelphia, Mar. 9, 1806, d. Dec. 12, 1872, was the most popular and perhaps the greatest American tragedian of the 19th century. He made his debut at the age of 14 and acted in many Shakespearean roles, particularly Othello. Forrest also had parts created for him by offering prizes to encourage American playwriting. His booming voice and fierce looks, coupled with his arrogance and short temper, suited contemporary histrionic fashion. His feud with the English actor William Charles MACREADY caused the 1849 ASTOR PLACE RIOT.

Forrest, John, 1st Baron Forrest John Forrest, b. Aug. 22, 1847, d. Sept. 3, 1918, was Western Australia's most notable explorer and political leader. He journeyed overland from Perth to Adelaide by the south coast (1870) and from Champion Bay to the telegraph post near modern Oodnadatta in central Australia (1874). The first premier of Western Australia (1890 to 1901), Forrest was elected to the Federal Parliament in 1901. There he promoted a railroad from Port Augusta to Kalgoorlie. He held several federal cabinet posts between 1901 and 1918, when he was created Baron Forrest of Bunbury. He was the first Australian to become a British peer.

Forrest, Nathan Bedford Nathan Bedford Forrest, b. Chapel Hill, Tenn., July 13, 1821, d. Oct. 29, 1877, was a Confederate general in the U.S. Civil War. A wealthy businessman in his native Tennessee, he entered the Confederate Army in 1861 and was made commander of a cavalry battalion raised and equipped at his own expense. Although he frequently served with a large army, Forrest performed best in independent mounted raids. He has been accused of condoning the massacre of African-American Union soldiers at Fort Pillow, Tenn., on Apr. 12, 1864. After the war he engaged in farming and railroading and was the leader of the Ku Klux Klan.

Forrestal, James V. [fohr-'es-tul] James Vincent Forrestal, b. Beacon, N.Y., Feb. 15, 1892, d. May 22, 1949, was an American investment banker and public official who served as the first U.S. secretary of defense. A successful Wall Street financier, Forrestal became an administrative assistant to President Franklin D. Roosevelt in 1940. He was undersecretary of the navy from 1940 to 1944 and secretary of the navy from 1944 to 1947. When the War Department and Navy Department were unified in 1947, President Harry S. Truman named Forrestal to be secretary of defense. He served until March 1949, when policy differences with Truman led to his resignation. Hospitalized for acute depression, he committed suicide.

Forster, E. M. [fohrs'-tur]   Edward Morgan Forster, b. Jan. 1, 1879, d. June 7, 1970, was a prominent English novelist, essayist, and short-story writer. Educated at Cambridge, and an important member of the BLOOMSBURY GROUP, he began his literary career in 1903 as a writer for *The Independent Review*, a periodical of liberal, anti-imperialist sympathies. *Where Angels Fear to Tread* (1905), his first novel, was followed by *The Longest Journey* (1907), *A Room with a View* (1908), and *Howard's End* (1910). After publication of his volume of short stories, *The Celestial Omnibus* (1911), he visited India, where he closely observed British colonial attitudes. During World War I he worked for the International Red Cross in Egypt, returning to London at war's end to pursue a career in literary journalism. In 1922 he made a second visit to India; he channeled his observations on both visits into his most enduring novel, *A Passage to India* (1924). He was made an honorary fellow of Kings College, Cambridge, where he delivered the Clark Lectures in literature, later published as *Aspects of the Novel* (1927). His work in later life included short stories, essays, and biography. An early novel, *Maurice*, completed in 1914, was not published until 1971, partly because of its frank portrayal of homosexuality.

Forster's finest achievements were his novels, in which character and the clash of ideas overshadow plot. His narrative point of view was normally that of an outsider, and his novels, especially *A Passage to India* and *Howard's End*, are sad examinations of the social codes and barriers that thwart communication and frustrate human feeling.

E. M. Forster, a major 20th-century British writer, infused his fiction with humanitarian ideals. His last novel, A Passage to India *(1924), examines the cultural difficulties brought about by British colonialism in India.*

Forsyte Saga, The   see GALSWORTHY, JOHN

Forsyth, John [fohr'-syth]   John Forsyth, b. Fredericksburg, Va., Oct. 22, 1780, d. Oct. 21, 1841, was a Georgia senator and supporter of President Andrew Jackson. He was a U.S. congressman (1813–18), ambassador to Spain (1819–23), and again a congressman (1823–27) before his term in the Senate (1829–34). In the NULLIFICATION crisis of 1832, he was largely responsible for preventing Georgia from following South Carolina's example in defying the federal government. In return for his loyalty, Jackson appointed (1834) him secretary of state, a post he held until 1841.

forsythia [fohr-sith'-ee-uh]   Forsythia, genus *Forsythia*, is any of several species of hardy, deciduous shrubs belonging to the olive family, Oleaceae. Forsythias are among the showiest of spring-flowering shrubs, producing brilliant yellow flowers in early spring before the leaves unfold. They are very adaptable plants and can grow in a variety of soils. The principal species are *F. suspensa*, which reaches heights of 2.4 m (8 ft) or more; *F. intermedia*, which has several varieties, including *spectabilis*, showy-border forsythia; *F. viridissima*, with bright-green stems; and *F. ovata*, a Korean species that is the hardiest and earliest to bloom.

Forsythia intermedia, a forsythia species, is a flowering deciduous shrub with arching branches that grow as high as 3 m (10 ft). Among the first shrubs to bloom in cool climates, forsythia produces bright yellow flowers in early spring.

Fort Benning   Fort Benning, site of the U.S. Army Infantry Center, is a 765-km^2 (295-mi^2) base located 14 km (9 mi) south of Columbus, Ga., on the Chattahoochee River. The number of personnel assigned there as of 1987 was 26,500. Besides infantry classes, airborne and ranger training courses are offered. Fort Benning contributes greatly to the economy of the Columbus area. Founded as Camp Benning in 1918, the base was named in honor of the Confederate army officer Henry L. Benning.

Fort Bragg   Fort Bragg is a 932-km^2 (360-mi^2) U.S. Army base located 16 km (10 mi) northwest of Fayetteville, N.C. The Special Warfare Center trains troops in psychological and guerrilla warfare. Since World War II the 82d Airborne Division has been housed there. The base was established in 1918 and named for Gen. Braxton Bragg of the Confederate Army.

Fort-de-France   [fohr-duh-frahns]   Fort-de-France (1982 pop., 97,814) is the capital of Martinique, a French overseas department in the Lesser Antilles. Located on the west coast, it is the largest city in the French West Indies. A commercial and shipping center on Fort-de-France Bay, the city exports sugarcane, rum, and bananas. The French fleet in the Caribbean is stationed there. Its climate is tropical, with a hurricane season lasting from July to November. Founded in 1672, the city was made the capital in 1680. It was severely damaged by an earthquake in 1839 and by fire in 1890. After the destruction of Saint-Pierre by the eruption of Mount Pelée in 1902, Fort-de-France became the island's commercial center.

Fort Dearborn   Fort Dearborn was a frontier military post established in 1803 on the site of present-day Chicago and named for the then secretary of war, Henry Dearborn. Its garrison was massacred by Indians in 1812, but the fort was reoccupied in 1816 and continued to be used until 1836.

Fort Dix   Fort Dix is a U.S. Army infantry training center located 27 km (17 mi) southeast of Trenton, N.J. It covers 130 km^2 (50 mi^2). It was founded in 1917 and named for John A. Dix, a Civil War major general. During World War II, five corps, ten divisions, and an air force were trained for overseas duty there, and more than 1,250,000 soldiers were discharged from Fort Dix after the war. McGuire Air Force Base borders the fort. A 1979 decision to close Fort Dix was later reversed, but plans for substantial cutbacks were announced in 1990.

Fort Donelson   see FORT HENRY AND FORT DONELSON

Fort Duquesne   [due-kayn']   Fort Duquesne, a wilderness fortification at the confluence of the Allegheny and Monongahela rivers on the site of present-day Pittsburgh, Pa., was a key position in the French line of defense against the British in the FRENCH AND INDIAN WAR (1754-63). Construction began in 1754, after which the fort served as a base for French and Indian raiding activity against the Virginia frontier. Although the French man-

aged to rout Gen. Edward BRADDOCK's advancing army in July 1755, the approach of Gen. John FORBES's army in November 1758 caused them to abandon Fort Duquesne.

Fort Henry and Fort Donelson   Fort Henry, on the Tennessee River, and Fort Donelson, on the Cumberland River, were strategic Confederate fortifications in the U.S. Civil War. Built by Confederate authorities in mid-summer 1861, they were designed to repel invasion of Tennessee and the Deep South. They were not well sited, but their very existence brought Union attention. A coordinated land and water offensive led by Gen. Ulysses GRANT and Flag Officer Andrew FOOTE captured first Henry (Feb. 6, 1862) and then Donelson (Feb. 16, 1862). The Donelson fight was fierce and might have gone either way, save for incompetence in the Confederate high command. The loss of these two strategic forts turned the flank of Confederate defenses at Columbus, Ky., and forced Gen. Albert S. JOHNSTON's withdrawal to the middle South. Confederate losses, including prisoners, at the two forts were more than 12,000 men, and these, combined with the psychological effect of twin defeats, cast gloom over the Confederacy.

Fort Hood   Fort Hood is a U.S. Army base covering 874 km^2 (338 mi^2), located 3 km (2 mi) west of Killeen, Tex. It houses armored and mechanized units. Founded in 1942 as Camp Hood, it was named for Confederate general John B. Hood; in 1950 it became Fort Hood.

Fort Knox   Fort Knox is a U.S. Army military post located approximately 50 km (30 mi) southwest of Louisville in Hardin and Meade counties, Ky. Established in 1917 as a training camp, it became a permanent military base in 1932. Since 1936, Fort Knox has been the site of the U.S. Gold Bullion Depository. The gold is stored in concrete and steel vaults inside a bombproof building (exterior dimensions: 37×32 m/121×105 ft), protected by guards armed with machine guns. The vaults are guarded by electronic devices, and the interiors are constantly visible to security personnel.

Fort-Lamy   see N'DJAMENA

Fort Lauderdale   Fort Lauderdale, Fla., located 40 km (25 mi) north of Miami, has a population of 149,377 (1990) and is the seat of heavily urbanized Broward County, which has 1,255,488 residents. Fort Lauderdale is best known as a vacation and retirement center. The city has a large boat basin, and about 10% of its 78-km^2 (30-mi^2) area is composed of a network of inland waterways that create small islands. The famous beach is one of the largest public beaches in the state. Electronics and concrete are produced, and dairy and citrus farming takes place in the surrounding area. Port Everglades is a major deepwater facility. A military post was established on the site in 1837. A settlement grew up around the fort and experienced its most rapid growth during the Florida land boom of the 1920s and again after World War II.

Fort McHenry   Fort McHenry was an American military installation built on an island in Baltimore harbor in 1799. During the War of 1812 it was bombarded (Sept. 13–14, 1814) by a British fleet, an attack that inspired Francis Scott KEY, a prisoner aboard a British ship, to write the STAR-SPANGLED BANNER. Later used as a storage depot and military prison, Fort McHenry was designated a National Monument in 1939.

Fort Moultrie   Fort Moultrie was a fortification on Sullivan Island at the entrance to the harbor of Charleston, S.C. A garrison of American troops under Col. William Moultrie (1730–1805) held this fort against a 10-ship British attack on June 28, 1776, in the American Revolution. It later became the Confederate headquarters for the bombardment of FORT SUMTER in April 1861, at the beginning of the U.S. Civil War. Fort Moultrie contains the tomb of the Seminole chief OSCEOLA, who was imprisoned there during the Seminole Wars.

Fort Niagara   Fort Niagara, a post on the Niagara River at Lake Ontario, guarded the passageway to the rich western fur-trapping lands. In the 1670s the French erected a stockade on the site, and in 1726 they completed a stone fort. The British captured the fort in 1759 during the French and Indian War, and they used it to launch frontier raids during the American Revolution. Fort Niagara was relinquished to American troops in 1796 as provided by Jay's Treaty (1794), but the British seized it again during the War of 1812. Returned to the United States in 1815, the fort served as a military post until 1946; it then became part of a New York state park.

Fort Smith   Fort Smith is one of the two seats of Sebastian County, in western Arkansas. It is located on the Arkansas River, near the Oklahoma border. It has a population of 72,798 (1990). The city grew up around a U.S. Army fort established in 1817. The California gold rush of 1848 transformed Fort Smith into a busy supply depot for westward-bound prospectors. Today its economy is based on the deposits of coal and natural gas, timber, and the fertile farmlands of the surrounding region. Its industries manufacture furniture, automobiles, electrical appliances, and metal, glass, paper, and plastic products. The Fort Smith National Historic Site is located there.

Fort Sumter   Fort Sumter, construction of which was begun in 1829 at the entrance to the harbor of Charleston, S.C., was the site of the CIVIL WAR's first shot on Apr. 12, 1861. Unimportant militarily, the fort became a vital symbol to both North and South.

Confederate troops open fire on Fort Sumter. The Federal garrison in Charleston harbor was forced to capitulate after two days of shelling (Apr. 12–13, 1861).

Confederate authorities sought throughout March 1861 to negotiate the peaceful evacuation of the Union garrison at Fort Sumter under Maj. Robert Anderson. Once convinced that Abraham Lincoln's administration would not give up the fort, President Jefferson Davis faced a crisis in diplomacy. If Sumter were not taken, the Confederate States could not boast independence; if action against it were delayed, South Carolina threatened unilateral seizure; and any action might trigger war with the United States. Davis and his cabinet, fearing Union reinforcement of the garrison, decided that domestic politics and international posture demanded Sumter's capture and ordered Gen. P. G. T. BEAUREGARD to take it. He opened fire at 4:30 AM on April 12. Anderson surrendered the next day, and his forces left the fort on April 14. War was on, and the U.S. flag was not raised again over the fort until Feb. 18, 1865.

Fort Ticonderoga   see TICONDEROGA

Fort Wayne   Located in northeastern Indiana where the Saint Joseph and Saint Marys rivers meet to form the Maumee, Fort Wayne is the seat of Allen County and the state's second largest city, with a population of 173,072 persons within the city and 363,811 in the metropolitan area (1990). It is a commercial and transportation center with diversified industries, including electronics and automotive parts. Within the city is the gravesite of Johnny Appleseed (John Chapman).

Fort Wayne was the chief village of the Miami Indians before the French established Fort Miami as a trading post there in the early 1680s. The British captured the fort in 1760 but were driven out by Indians during Pontiac's Rebellion in 1763. The present city traces its origin to a fort built by Gen. Anthony Wayne in 1794.

___

Fort Worth   Fort Worth, a city in north central Texas, lies 48 km (30 mi) west of DALLAS near the headwaters of the Trinity River. It is the seat of Tarrant County and has a population of 447,619 (1990), with 3,885,415 persons in the Dallas–Fort Worth metropolitan area. First a frontier outpost maintained (1849–53) by the U.S. Army, Fort Worth flourished in the early 1870s as a watering place on the Chisholm Trail. The arrival of the Texas and Pacific Railway in 1876 turned it into a cattle-shipping and meat-packing center and an important point for grain milling and distribution. The discovery of oil in 1917 only 145 km (90 mi) west transformed the city again into a booming center of refining operations. Today many other industries spur its economy, particularly the aerospace industry. The huge Dallas–Fort Worth Airport and Carswell Air Force Base are nearby. The city's cultural institutions include the Amon Carter Museum of Western Art, Fort Worth Art Center, and the Fort Worth Museum of Science and History. Texas Wesleyan College, Texas Christian University, and Southwestern Baptist Theological Seminary are located there.

___

Fortaleza [fohrt-uhl-ay'-zuh]   Fortaleza is located on the Paejú River along the northeast coast of Brazil. It is the capital of the state of Ceará, and the population is 1,582,414 (1987 est.) The city is a regional commercial center, fishing port, and beach resort. Textiles, soap, and refined sugar are its major products, and it ships raw materials such as carnauba wax and hides. Fortaleza is the site of the Federal University of Ceará (1955). Founded by the Portuguese in 1609, Fortaleza is today the focus of a large Brazilian regional development plan.

___

Fortas, Abe [fohrt'-uhs]   Abe Fortas, b. Memphis, Tenn., June 19, 1910, d. Apr. 5, 1982, was a prominent Washington, D.C., attorney and presidential advisor when President Lyndon B. Johnson appointed him to the U.S. Supreme Court in 1965. Johnson's subsequent nomination of Fortas as chief justice was blocked by Senate foes of his activist stand on civil liberties. In 1969, following charges of conflict of interest, Fortas resigned from the Court. His arguments in *Gideon* v. *Wainwright* (1962) established the right of the poor to legal counsel.

___

Forth, River   The River Forth originates in the highlands of south central Scotland. Flowing eastward, it widens to an estuary, the Firth of Forth, at Alloa, near Stirling. The combined length of the river and firth is 187 km (116 mi); the firth, which extends 89 km (55 mi) to the North Sea, is 31 km (19 mi) across at its widest point. Edinburgh's port, Leith, and Grangemouth are the principal ports. A naval base is located at Rosyth. The firth is

spanned by three bridges, including the Forth Railway Bridge, one of the first cantilever bridges ever built (1890), and the Forth Road Bridge (1964; 1,006 m/3,300 ft), one of the longest suspension bridges in Europe.

___

fortification   Fortification is the military science of strengthening terrain to protect armed defenders. Fortifications may be categorized according to intended duration of occupation. Temporary field fortifications—foxholes, trenches, breastworks, and fire bases—secure battlefield positions and are relatively simple. Permanent fixed fortifications, including citadels, castles, walls, and casemates, dominate key locations of lasting military value and are much more elaborate, usually consisting of stone or concrete constructions. Geographic extent offers a second way to distinguish defensive works. Fortresses protect a single point, such as a city. Lines shield an entire region. Fortifications often feature combinations of these basic types. Whatever the category, these military engineering projects are designed by combat engineers, built by available military and civilian labor, and defended by a garrison. Combat engineers also use their knowledge of fortification to direct siege operations aimed at the capture of enemy defensive systems.

Early Fortifications.   Since prehistoric times, outnumbered settled peoples have created defenses to hold mobile nomadic marauders at bay. Ancient and classical civilizations recognized the military utility and manpower economy inherent in prepared defenses. Excellent examples of all four major types of fortifications abounded in ancient times. The Roman legions' stout nightly camps set the standards for field works. Important fixed positions included the long walls that connected Athens to its port, Piraeus; these walls allowed Athenians to resist a lengthy Spartan siege during the Peloponnesian War (431–404 BC). Jerusalem, Tyre, and Loyang, China, were particularly formidable fortress cities.

Defensive lines, from the relatively modest 121-km-long (75-mi) HADRIAN'S WALL in Roman Britain to the massive 3,200-km (2,000-mi) GREAT WALL OF CHINA, separated barbarians from the civilized peoples of the ancient world. After the fall of the Roman Empire in the 5th century AD, fortifications in the West became more rudimentary. In their lengthy struggle with invaders such as the Vikings and the Magyars, settled peoples in western Europe developed a feudal military system of local defense. In each area, a few knights defended a large mass of serfs, who farmed for their overlords. In return for surrendering their freedom, in times of danger, the serfs could seek refuge in a central hilltop tower known as a keep. By AD 1000, keeps had begun to evolve into the familiar medieval CASTLE. Behind and atop the multiple concentric rings of tall stone walls bolstered by corner towers and fronted by a wide moat, knights could draw on stored food to hold out against besieging enemies.

The Early Modern Period.   Assailed by the consistent bombardment allowed by the development of GUNPOWDER, and undermined by the persistent burrowing of Renais-

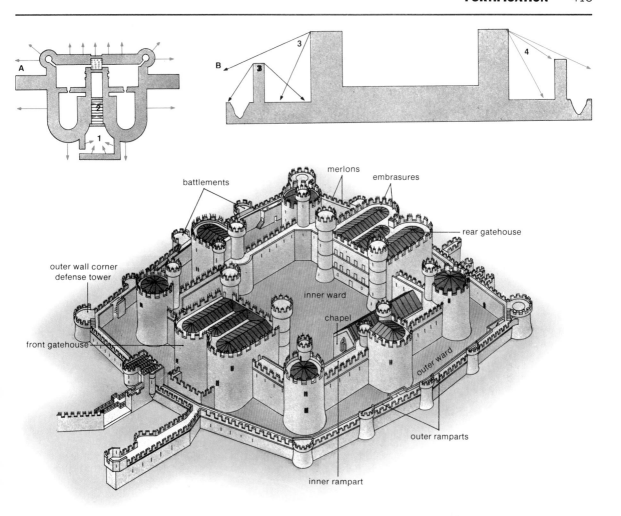

The concentric castle of the 13th century, protected by two (occasionally three) turreted outer walls and a complex system of inner defenses, was designed as an impregnable fortress. Shown in the detail (A) is the high gatehouse overlooking the gateway in the outer wall. Attackers who breached the first wall (1) faced a narrow passage into the gatehouse (2), where they were exposed to arrows from bowmen stationed above them. A cross section of the walls (B) shows the defensive firing lines (3, 4).

sance engineers, the high walls of medieval castles gave way. Enthusiasm for fortifications waned. The same mathematics that allowed precision gunlaying, however, permitted engineers to create new varieties of prepared defenses. King Louis XIV of France employed Sebastien Le Prestre de VAUBAN (1633–1707) to design a series of low-lying, angular stone works called star forts because of their shape when viewed from above. Throughout the wars of the 18th century and the Napoleonic period that followed, complicated army maneuvers often pivoted on such seemingly impregnable fortress complexes as Metz, Berlin, Vienna, and Verdun.

The 19th Century. The introduction of rifled weapons in the 19th century altered the situation that had prevailed since Vauban's time. The perfection of rifled artillery in the U.S. Civil War (1861–65) restored potency to the siege. This pattern prevailed in the siege of Paris during the Franco-Prussian War (1870–71), the struggle for Plevna during the Russo–Turkish War of 1877–78, and in the battle for Port Arthur during the Russo-Japanese War (1904–05). With the help of relatively rudimentary preparations, any competent rifle-armed defender could bludgeon an attacker to a bloody standoff. Unfortunately for most soldiers in Europe, these lessons were largely lost upon conservative generals still steeped in the Napoleonic traditions of few fortresses and wide maneuvers.

Contemporary Fortifications. Trends first seen in the U.S. Civil War reached their fruition in World War I. Continuous, opposing lines of field fortifications spanned both western and, to a lesser extent, eastern Europe. Layers of trenches, rimmed with sharp barbed wire and guarded by chattering machine guns and quick-firing ri-

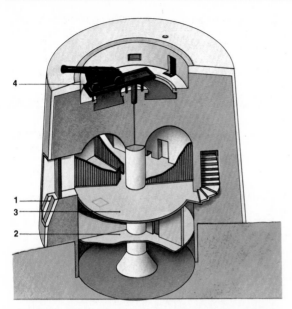

The Martello Tower was a peculiar kind of fortification used by the British in the early 19th century, when 74 of them were built on the south coast of England to protect it from an expected invasion by Napoleon. The towers were cylindrical in shape and constructed with thick stone walls. The only doorway (1) was placed 6 m (20 ft) above ground to make it difficult for attackers to gain entrance. A slide was extended through the door when supplies had to be brought in. Munitions and other supplies were stored in the cellar (2) and ground floor (3). A single long gun (4) was mounted on a pivoted platform on the roof for defense against attacking ships.

fled artillery, gave the entire war the characteristics of a ghastly, endless siege. Massed infantry assaults into the "no man's land" between the trenches invariably miscarried with horrific losses. Poison gas, flamethrowers, air bombardment, and even experimental use of tanks failed to break the deadlock. Only the German adoption of infantry infiltration tactics in 1918 restored fluidity to the battlefield. Elite stormtroopers snaked through enemy weak spots. Once through the crust of trenches, the stormtroops ravaged the enemy's unprotected rear-area supplies and headquarters. While they did break the trench stalemate, the German infiltrators took terrible casualties after the more numerous British, French, and U.S. forces reestablished solid defenses. By the war's end, the absolutely dominant value of defensive works seemed to be the chief military lesson.

Fearful of a German resurgence, the wary French took this presumed lesson to heart. Despite the fearful financial burden, France constructed the MAGINOT LINE, a nearly 322-km (200-mi) steel and concrete trench system along their border with Germany. Although it bristled with gun turrets and extended many stories underground, it did not shield the section of France bordering Belgium; such an extension was judged to be too expensive. The French hoped that their mobile field armies could use the incomplete Maginot Line as a pivot, much as Napoleon had done with earlier fortresses. The Germans did not

oblige, however. By 1940 the German military had wedded tanks and aircraft to their World War I infiltration tactics to create *blitzkrieg*—lightning war. In 1940, German mechanized units, striking through Belgium, speedily outflanked the French line, thereby turning the pivot point against its owners.

Throughout World War II, all combatants employed both fixed and field fortifications in both point and linear configurations, although advances in mobility ruled out a repetition of the continuous entrenched fronts of World War I. Significant fortification efforts included the British fixed defenses around Singapore, the U.S. fortress island of Corregidor, Russian antitank webs around Kursk, the German Atlantic Wall pillboxes and minefields in Normandy, and deep Japanese cave bunkers on Iwo Jima. Defenders might exact heavy tolls, but skilled attackers could seize these fortifications by concentrated use of artillery, airpower, and close cooperation among tanks, infantry, and engineers armed with flamethrowers and demolition charges.

Since World War II, all sorts of fortifications remain in use. Field fortifications predominated on conventional battlefields. Lines of traditional fieldworks, such as the U.S. Kansas Line in 1951 Korea, and temporary fortresses, such as the U.S. Khe Sanh Combat Base in 1967–68 Vietnam, continued to serve a purpose in limited conflicts worldwide. Fixed fortifications enjoy a small but potentially critical role in nuclear defenses. The United States, Soviet Union, People's Republic of China, and France all employ hardened concrete and steel missile silos and deeply buried command bunkers. Not surprisingly, nuclear "besiegers" have recently experimented with earth penetrators, larger explosive yields, and neutron radiation enhancement to cope with the latest defensive techniques. Thus far, the efficacy of nuclear fortifications and potential countermeasures remain untested by combat.

FORTRAN   see COMPUTER LANGUAGES

Fortuna [fohr-toon'-uh]   Fortuna, the Roman goddess of luck, fortune, and chance, had the power to lift up lowly mortals and cast down the mighty. She was worshiped under a number of forms; in Rome, altars were raised to Good Fortune, Public Fortune, and Private Fortune. Like her Greek counterpart Tyche, Fortuna's symbols in art were a ship's rudder and a cornucopia.

---

fortune-telling   Fortune-telling is the predicting of a person's destiny. Innumerable kinds of fortune-telling, or DIVINATION, were practiced by the people of ancient civilizations who believed that the future was determined by the gods and revealed to humans through omens, portents, and signs.

Most methods of fortune-telling involve the interpretative observation of objects, and they take their respective names from the specific objects that are "read." These objects can be those which naturally exist without human intervention, such as the stars (ASTROLOGY), the

A fortune-teller predicts the future by reading and interpreting the symbolic pictures on tarot cards. Pictures on the cards represent both the forces of nature and human vices and virtues.

lines of the palm (palmistry), and the leaves of plants (botomancy); or they can be man-made objects, such as TAROT or playing cards (cartomancy) and crystal balls (crystallomancy). Fortune-telling can also be performed by manipulating objects such as books (particularly the Bible).

Many fortune-telling techniques have long histories in both Eastern and Western cultures. Astrology was practiced in ancient Egypt, Greece, India, China, and Islam. The I Ching has been used by the Chinese for fortune-telling since the 2d millennium BC. Onomancy is the interpretation of the letters of one's name. It derives from the mystic belief found in the history of many world religions that the act of naming is the act of creation itself, and that a name contains all that an object or person is (see KABBALAH; GNOSTICISM.). Numerology, which may be considered a correlate of onomancy, assigns numbers to the letters of names; it also assigns numerological significance to every other aspect of a person's life. Like onomancy, it is found in many ancient cultures. Oneiromancy, the interpretation of dreams, predates the Greeks who gave it its name.

Fortune 500

The fortnightly U.S. business magazine *Fortune* is particularly noted for its annual compilation of the "Fortune 500" list of the 500 largest publicly held industrial corporations in the United States in terms of sales. *Fortune* was founded in 1930 by Henry Robinson LUCE, the publisher of Time, Inc. Besides compiling the "Fortune 500" list of U.S. companies, *Fortune* ranks the 500 largest companies outside the United States and the second 500 largest U.S. companies. *Fortune* also ranks the 50 largest U.S. banks; utilities; and retail, transportation, and diversified financial companies. All the lists include information on each company's assets, number of employees, net income, earnings per share of stock, and return on investment.

forty-niners   SEE GOLD RUSH

forum

The word *forum*, a Latin word meaning "open space" or "market place," refers generically to the open space in any Roman town or city where business, judicial, and municipal affairs and even, at times, religious activities were conducted. In many ways a forum was like the Greek AGORA, except that in a forum the space was more clearly defined, with buildings set closely together, often aligned on predetermined axes. In the later imperial forums in Rome open spaces were enclosed by parallel colonnades and dominated by temples often dedicated to Jupiter or Mars.

A typical forum was surrounded by market buildings, temples, and basilicas (spacious, roofed structures for conducting business or legal proceedings). Often, in planned towns that had begun as military camps, the forum lay at the meeting of the principal north-south street, the *cardo*, and the principal east-west street, the *decumanus*. The Roman architect Vitruvius (active 46–30 BC) suggested that a forum should be large enough to contain a crowd but not so large as to dwarf it, and that its proportions be 3:2 (length to width).

In ancient Rome, *Forum* was virtually a proper name for the ancient forum east of the Capitoline Hill and west of the Palatine Hill; it was the administrative and corporate heart of Rome. Large, imposing forums were built in Rome by successive emperors, among them Augustus, Nerva, Vespasian, and Trajan, who built the largest.

Ancient Rome's forum contains: Temple of Trajan (1); Trajan's Basilica Ulpia (2); Forum of Trajan (3); Forum of Augustus (4); Forum of Caesar (5); Curia (6); Temple of Juno Moneta (7); Temple of Jupiter (8); Temple of Concord (9); Forum Romanum (10); Basilica Julia (11); Forum of Nerva (12); Basilica Aemilia (13); Temple of Divus Julius (14); Arch of Augustus (15); Temple of Castor and Pollux (16); Temple of Minerva (17); Forum of Vespasian (18); Temple of Antoninus and Faustina (19); Regia (20); House of the Vestal Virgins (21); Temple of Sacrae Urbis (22); Temple of Romulus (23); Porticus Neronis (24); Basilica of Constantine (25); Temple of Venus and Rome (26); Vicus Jugularius (27); Via Sacra (28).

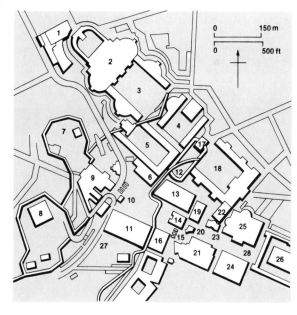

ILLUSTRATION CREDITS

3 The Bettmann Archive
4 Scala, Florence
5 The Bettmann Archive
7 National Portrait Gallery, London
8 Wide World Photos; Camera Press London/Globe Photos/Albert Watson
9 The Bettmann Archive
10 National Portrait Gallery, London
11 A. F. Kersting
13 Nico van der Stam
16 The Bettmann Archive
19 Lennart Nilsson
20 Photo Researchers/Russ Kinne
21 Brown Brothers
23 Photographie Giraudon
26 Scala, Florence
29 H. Roger Viollet; The Mansell Collection
37 © Hank Morgan
40 The Bettmann Archive
42 Picturepoint, London
43 Lothar Roth & Associates
44 Picturepoint, London; Magnum Photos/Rodger
47 Scala, Florence
49 A. F. Kersting; National Gallery, London
51 Photographie Giraudon
52 Het Spectrum
57 National Portrait Gallery, London; The Bettmann Archive; The Bettmann Archive
58 National Portrait Gallery, London; The Bettmann Archive; National Portrait Gallery, London
59 National Portrait Gallery, London; National Portrait Gallery, London; BBC–Hulton Picture Library
60 All pictures—National Portrait Gallery, London
61 National Portrait Gallery, London; National Portrait Gallery, London; The Bettmann Archive
62 The Bettmann Archive; The Bettmann Archive; National Portrait Gallery, London
63 The Bettmann Archive; The Bettmann Archive; National Portrait Gallery, London
64 All pictures—National Portrait Gallery, London
65 National Portrait Gallery, London; The Bettmann Archive; The Bettmann Archive
66 BBC–Hulton Picture Library; The Bettmann Archive; BBC–Hulton Picture Library

67 The Bettmann Archive
68 The Bettmann Archive
70 Courtesy Museum of Fine Arts, Boston
75 Photo Researchers/Art Twomey
82 Scala, Florence
88 Rand McNally & Company
90 Photographie Giraudon
104 Bavaria Verlag Bildagentur/Lüthy; Georg Gerster
105 Tom Prescott
108 The Bettmann Archive
112 Metropolitan Museum of Art, gift of Henry Walters, 1917
117 Rand McNally & Company
118 Photo Researchers/George Holton
122 Scala, Florence
125 Scala, Florence
128 The Bettmann Archive
130–131 Rand McNally & Company
131 Bruce Coleman Inc./Joachim Messerschmidt
132 Jan Rijsterborgh; Paul C. Pet; Paul C. Pet
133 Sem Presser; Paul C. Pet; Paolo Koch
137 Photo Researchers/Gordon Gahan
138 Bruce Coleman Inc./Joachim Messerschmidt
139 Photo Researchers/Paolo Koch; Magnum Photos/Burt Glinn; Magnum Photos/Eric Lessing; Photo Researchers/George Holton; Photo Researchers/Earl Dibble; Magnum Photos/Manos
141 Inter Nationes
142 Novosti Press
148 Het Spectrum
149 Holle Bildarchiv
152 Ashmolean Museum, Oxford
155 Photo Researchers/Van Bucher
156 Duomo/Adam J. Stoltman
158 The Bettmann Archive; The Bettmann Archive; The Bettmann Archive
169 Photo Michael Busselle/Aldus Books
184 C.T.I.O. Photograph, Courtesy P. Seitser
185 Hale Observatories
186 Hale Observatories
188 Scala, Florence
195 Het Spectrum
198 Kunsthaus, Zurich
199 Het Spectrum
202 UPI/Bettmann Newsphotos
204 The Sunday Times, London
205 The Bettmann Archive
204 Ewing Galloway
209 National Portrait Gallery, London
211 The Bettmann Archive

212 Grant Heilman Photography/John Colwell
215 Photo Researchers/Jack Fields
216 The Bettmann Archive
218 The Bettmann Archive; Service Photographique
219 Harper's Bazaar; Cooper-Hewitt Museum, The Smithsonian Institution's National Museum of Design; Fashion Institute of Technology (from Davidow Collection of Library Media Services)
220 Fashion Institute of Technology (from Davidow Collection of Library Media Services)
223 United States Information Service
226 Photographie Giraudon
231 The Bettmann Archive
232 Scala, Florence
233 Photo Researchers/A. Wamble; Photo Researchers/George Whitely
234 Photo Researchers/Russ Kinne
235 J. Lampert Promotions, Inc.
239 Mas Ampliaciones y Reproducciones
240 The Bettmann Archive
242 H. Roger Viollet; H. Roger Viollet
249 © Lee Boltin
250 Bibliothèque Nationale, Paris
253 All pictures—Het Spectrum
256 UPI/Bettmann Newsphotos; The Bettmann Archive
257 Focus on Sports/Bernard Suess
258 BBC–Hulton Picture Library; Brown Brothers
262 Superstock/Shostal; Rand McNally & Company
264 Corcoran Gallery of Art
265 International Museum of Photography at George Eastman House
266 Ralph Stein; The Science Museum, London
267 Culver Pictures; Museum of Modern Art, New York, Film Stills Archive
268 Culver Pictures; The Bettmann Archive; John E. Allen Collection; Museum of Modern Art, New York, Film Stills Archive
269 Museum of Modern Art, New York, Film Stills Archive; Culver Pictures
270 John E. Allen Collection; Culver Pictures; Rose Collection; Professional Picture Services
271 Museum of Modern Art, New York, Film Stills Archive; John E. Allen Collection; John E. Allen Collection
272 The Memory Shop
273 © Lucasfilm, Ltd.; Sygma
274 Archive Photos/Fotos International
275 Sygma/Bob Willoughby
277 Federal Bureau of Investigation
278 Rand McNally & Company
280 Werner Södeström Osakeyhtiö
281 Werner Södeström Osakeyhtiö
282 Comet; Explorer
283 Comet
287 Photo Researchers/C. Ray
288 Gamma-Liaison/Brad Markel

291 Sem Presser
306 Photo Researchers/Franke Keating
307 Focus on Sports/Brian Payne; Paul C. Pet
308 Photo Researchers/Helen Marcus
311 Bavaria–Verlag Bildagentur/G. Binanzer; The Bettmann Archive
313 Brown Brothers
336 Photographie Giraudon
338 The Bettmann Archive
339 Photographie Giraudon
340 Prado, Madrid
341 Het Spectrum; Stichting Bevordering Belangen Rijksmuseum Amsterdam
343 Sipa Press/Argyropoulos
344 Black Star/Herman Kokojan
346 Photo Researchers/Bernard Pierre Wolff; Spectrum Colour Library
347 Paul C. Pet
350 Rand McNally & Company
351 Photo Researchers/Van Bucher; Courtesy Florida Department of Commerce
352 Courtesy Florida Development Commission; Florida News Bureau
353 Courtesy Florida Department of Commerce
364 Photo Researchers/George Whitely
368 The Bettmann Archive
371 Nordiska Museum, Stockholm
372 Lüden Collection, Wyk, Germany; Lüden Collection, Wyk, Germany
373 Metropolitan Museum of Art, New York City; Abby Aldrich Rockefeller Folk Art Center, Williamsburg, Va.; Mariners Museum, Newport News, Va.
374 Japan Folk Crafts Museum, Tokyo; Foto-Archief Spaarnestad
376 Superstock/Shostal/Glen Baer
378 Magnum Photos/Landy
380 UPI/Bettmann Newsphotos
381 Scala, Florence; Popperfoto/Paul Popper
382 UPI/Bettmann Newsphotos
384 © Jonathan Levine; © Jonathan Levine
391 Yale University Library: Courtesy of the Western Americana Collection; Brown Brothers; Focus on Sports/Mickey Palmer
392 Focus on Sports/Mickey Palmer; Focus on Sports/Bernard Suess; Focus on Sports/Bernard Suess
395 Geocom BV
396 Courtesy Ford Company
397 White House Historical Society
398 Black Star/Francis C. Fuerst
405 Superstock/Shostal/D'Arazien
407 Ullstein GmbH, Berlin; Victoria and Albert Museum
409 National Portrait Gallery, London
411 The Bettmann Archive
415 Mary Evans Picture Library